# The World of Writing

## A Guide

**Kate Mangelsdorf**
*University of Texas at El Paso*

**Evelyn Posey**
*University of Texas at El Paso*

**Longman**

Boston   Columbus   Indianapolis   New York   San Francisco   Upper Saddle River
Amsterdam   Cape Town   Dubai   London   Madrid   Milan   Munich   Paris   Montreal   Toronto
Delhi   Mexico City   Sao Paulo   Sydney   Hong Kong   Seoul   Singapore   Taipei   Tokyo

**Executive Editor:** Suzanne Phelps Chambers
**Director of Development:** Mary Ellen Curley
**Editorial Assistant:** Laney Whitt
**Senior Development Editors:** Meg Botteon and David B. Kear
**Senior Supplements Editor:** Donna Campion
**Senior Media Producer:** Stefanie Liebman
**Senior Marketing Manager:** Sandra McGuire
**Production Manager:** Savoula Amanatidis
**Project Coordination, Text Design, and Electronic Page Makeup:** Electronic Publishing Services, Inc., NYC
**Cover Design Manager:** Nancy Danahy
**Cover Designer:** Nancy Sacks
**Cover Images:** (Clockwise from upper left) Group of college students of varying ages © moodboard/Corbis; Tree Plantation Program In Leh, © Mail Today/Getty Images; Ethiopian girl during Timkat Ceremony, © Buena Vista Images/Getty Images; Three college students looking at magazines © Neil A. Meyerhoff, Inc./Panoramic Images; Greenpeace activists © AFP/Getty Images; Chinatown, San Francisco, California, USA © Andrew Gunner/Photodisc, Getty Images; Group of College Students © Laurence Mouton/PhotoAlto/Corbis
**Photo Researcher:** Poyee Oster
**Senior Manufacturing Buyer:** Roy L. Pickering, Jr.
**Printer and Binder:** Quad Graphics–Taunton
**Cover Printer:** Lehigh-Phoenix Color Corporation–Hagerstown

For permission to use copyrighted material, grateful acknowledgment is made to the copyright holders on pp. C-1–C-2, which are hereby made part of this copyright page.

**Library of Congress Cataloging-in-Publication Data**
Mangelsdorf, Kate.
  The world of writing: a guide / Kate Mangelsdorf, Evelyn Posey.
      p. cm.
  Includes index.
  ISBN-13: 978-0-205-72399-7
  ISBN-10: 0-205-72399-3
  1. English language—Rhetoric—Problems, exercises etc. 2. Report writing—Problems, exercises etc.
  I. Posey, Evelyn Riggs.  II. Title.
  PE1408.M369 2010
  808'.042076—dc22                                            2010043814

1 2 3 4 5 6 7 8 9 10—QGT—13 12 11 10

**Longman**
is an imprint of

www.pearsonhighered.com

ISBN-13: 978-0-205-72399-7
ISBN-10:    0-205-72399-3

# Detailed Contents

## PART I Expanding Literacies   1

### Chapter 1 Words and the World   2

# Chapter 7  Explaining a Concept    166

# Chapter 8  Investigating a Cause    214

## Chapter 11   Solving a Problem   346

## Chapter 12   Advocating for Change   388

## PART V Handbook   H-1

# Thematic Contents

# Worldview

# Education

# Electronic Spaces

# Preface

The *World of Writing* prepares students for an increasingly globalized world in the twenty-first century. As composition instructors for twenty years and textbook authors for ten, we have used many excellent first-year composition textbooks, but none that adequately addressed the following twenty-first century realities of U.S. college students:

- the increased number of students who read and write in more than one language
- the importance of cultural identity
- the globalization of the U.S. workplace
- the widespread use of communication technology

Our belief is that twenty-first century students should develop multiple literacies to participate globally, collaborate productively, and read and write with more sensitivity across cultures. This textbook is based on that belief and, as a result, encourages students to draw on their language and cultural backgrounds and to bring their digital media experiences into the writing classroom.

*The World of Writing* is not just for bilingual or multilingual speakers, though. It is for all first-year composition students, including monolingual students. It is likely that they have studied a foreign language and/or know others who speak a language in addition to English. This textbook expands their ability to work in a multilingual world. Students who are not familiar with electronic literacies receive plenty of support that enables them to feel more confident about their abilities to analyze and compose multimedia texts.

## HOW THIS BOOK IS ORGANIZED

### Part I: Expanding Literacies (Chapters 1–4)

- A chapter on language that focuses on language learning, attitudes, and uses, and the differences between spoken and written language. Students write a literacy narrative about their own language uses.
- A chapter on analyzing rhetorical situations, including topic, audience, purpose, genre, visual design, exigence, and constraints. Students create different rhetorical situations.
- A chapter on developing a writing process. Students learn one process to use when writing but are also encouraged to develop their own.
- A chapter on strategies for reading print and multimedia texts, with particular attention to vocabulary development. Students annotate and summarize a text.

## Part II: Expanding Influence (Chapters 5–12)

- Eight chapters that cover a range of writing purposes: exploring events, making observations, explaining concepts, investigating causes, evaluating experiences, solving problems, arguing positions, and advocating change.
- Readings in each chapter that demonstrate how to write traditional essays, as well other types of writing (editorials, brochures, proposals, speeches, photo essays). Topics are on issues relevant to students' lives, including cultural identity, language acquisition, environment, careers and workplace, education, and electronic spaces.
- Writing assignments that ask students to analyze their rhetorical situation, including topic, audience, purpose, genre, visual design, exigence, and constraints.
- Samples of student writing at different stages of the writing process in each chapter.

## Part III: Expanding Writing Strategies (Chapters 13–17)

- Chapters on writing patterns, visual design, workplace writing, essay exams, and portfolios that prepare students for courses in other disciplines and for the workplace.
- Samples of student writing used as models.

## Part IV: Expanding Research (Chapters 18–20)

- Three research chapters on conducting field research, using sources, and documentation styles. MLA and APA documentation styles are covered.
- Plagiarism instruction that includes explanations of how various cultures view the ownership of texts.

## Part V: Handbook

- Instruction in spelling, punctuation, and grammar, with second language writing issues (such as articles, modals, and verb tense) integrated into the material.
- Emphasis on how language is used in academic writing. For example, instead of simply reading the dictionary definition of a preposition, students learn how a preposition is used in word combinations.
- Attention to strategies for increasing vocabulary.

## An Emphasis on Language for Today's Diverse Students

The number of multilingual writers in U.S. colleges and universities is increasing rapidly. In this textbook, support for multilingual writers is integrated into the text in a way that is transparent and non-intrusive. Issues such as language acquisition, cultural writing patterns, and writing with an accent are presented in ways that benefit both multilingual and monolingual writing students. Concepts such as the emotional filter and writing monitor, adapted from second language research, are made useful for all students. Vocabulary acquisition—necessary for almost every composition student—is also stressed. We provide additional support through:

*A chapter on language that focuses on language learning, attitudes, and uses, and the differences between spoken and written language.*

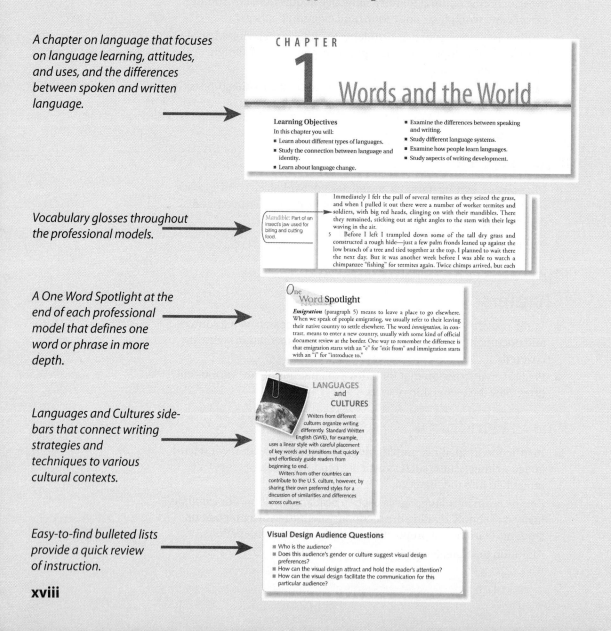

CHAPTER

# 1 Words and the World

**Learning Objectives**

In this chapter you will:

- Learn about different types of languages.
- Study the connection between language and identity.
- Learn about language change.
- Examine the differences between speaking and writing.
- Study different language systems.
- Examine how people learn languages.
- Study aspects of writing development.

*Vocabulary glosses throughout the professional models.*

**Mandible:** Part of an insect's jaw used for biting and cutting food.

Immediately I felt the pull of several termites as they seized the grass, and when I pulled it out there were a number of worker termites and soldiers, with big red heads, clinging on with their mandibles. There they remained, sticking out at right angles to the stem with their legs waving in the air.

5   Before I left I trampled down some of the tall dry grass and constructed a rough hide—just a few palm fronds leaned up against the low branch of a tree and tied together at the top. I planned to wait there the next day. But it was another week before I was able to watch a chimpanzee "fishing" for termites again. Twice chimps arrived, but each

*A One Word Spotlight at the end of each professional model that defines one word or phrase in more depth.*

**One Word Spotlight**

**Emigration** (paragraph 5) means to leave a place to go elsewhere. When we speak of people emigrating, we usually refer to their leaving their native country to settle elsewhere. The word *immigration*, in contrast, means to enter a new country, usually with some kind of official document review at the border. One way to remember the difference is that emigration starts with an "e" for "exit from" and immigration starts with an "i" for "introduce to."

*Languages and Cultures side-bars that connect writing strategies and techniques to various cultural contexts.*

**LANGUAGES and CULTURES**

Writers from different cultures organize writing differently. Standard Written English (SWE), for example, uses a linear style with careful placement of key words and transitions that quickly and effortlessly guide readers from beginning to end.

Writers from other countries can contribute to the U.S. culture, however, by sharing their own preferred styles for a discussion of similarities and differences across cultures.

*Easy-to-find bulleted lists provide a quick review of instruction.*

**Visual Design Audience Questions**

- Who is the audience?
- Does this audience's gender or culture suggest visual design preferences?
- How can the visual design attract and hold the reader's attention?
- How can the visual design facilitate the communication for this particular audience?

# Workplace, Community, and Globalization

Many of the readings (including digital texts such as websites and blogs) focus on issues related to globalization, such as cultural identity, language acquisition, environment, careers and workplace, and education. This emphasis on globalization, combined with information on multilingualism, prepares students for the twenty-first century workplace, where an increasing number of employees at all levels interact with people from around the globe. This interaction requires knowledge, tolerance, and understanding on the part of U.S. native English speakers when they interact with non-native speakers.

### Africa Through the African Eye

*Omotayo Olabumuyi*

Never have I been so aware of my identity as I was in my Individuals and Societies class when a presenter discussed the issue of AIDS in Tanzania, East Africa. I am one of the two Africans in the class, also the only one who has lived in Africa and not just toured it for a short while. The presenter asked if there were any people who had visited Africa. I looked round—less than one percent had our hands raised. Later on she asked for their general thoughts of what Africa was like. The responses were unbelievable; it then dawned on me that my identity was going to make the class a miserable one for me.

## Changing Names in a Changing World

### David Mould

Language is closely connected with national power, and as nations change, so do their names. In the following article, David Mould, a professor at Ohio University, shows that countries change their names as a part of claiming their nationalist identities.

South Africa's capital, Pretoria, is now officially Tshwane. Bangalore, India's IT capital, will become Bengaluru this year. New names are coming fast as regimes change and countries shake off (often belatedly) symbolic trappings of a colonial past.

In a globalized economy, it is not enough to memorize all those American state capitals. Now we need to know where Kinshasa is, book a flight to Ouagadougou, the vowel-rich capital of Burkina Faso,

*Specific themes covered in the readings include*
- *The pleasures and frustrations of learning new languages*
- *Who benefits (and who doesn't benefit) from a globalized workforce*
- *The development of cultural identities*
- *The role of Facebook and other electronic spaces in globalization*
- *The importance of education*
- *The "greening" of the U.S. workforce*
- *The declining job market for college graduates in China*
- *U.S. college students' perceptions of people from other countries*
- *The role of U.S. immigrants in the post-recession economy*

*Chapters on workplace writing, writing essay exams, and creating portfolios prepare students for courses in other disciplines and for writing in the workplace.*

**One Student's Memo.** Student writer Emily Conry was required to submit a memo to her instructor and classmates describing the rhetorical situation for a persuasive letter she planned to write.

| Title | Memorandum |
|---|---|

Heading

To:   Workplace Writing Class 3355

From:  Emily Conry

Date:  September 27, 2010

Re:   Persuasive Letter Proposal

Purpose

Please accept this memo as my description of the rhetorical situation for my persuasive letter.

Discussion with headings to signal new direction

**Topic**

My topic is new safety guidelines for exiting and entering my workplace at night. I believe that new safety procedures

# Communication Technology

In the twenty-first century, it's not enough to understand the printed word. Student must also know how visuals work to influence their understanding. In this text, they analyze visuals in each professional reading and for each Part II writing assignment, they consider visual design as part of their rhetorical analysis. Once they have chosen a genre, they consider the fonts, white space, color, borders, and images that they might use to communicate their message more effectively.

Students also learn the principles of good visual design for creating PowerPoint presentations, blogs, and websites. Chapter 14 expands on the advice given in earlier chapters and provides more instruction on analyzing visuals, designing documents, and creating online presentations.

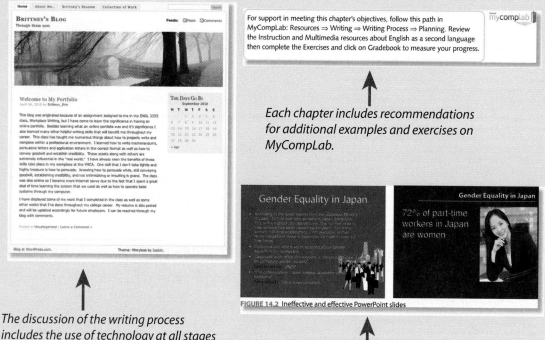

For support in meeting this chapter's objectives, follow this path in MyCompLab: Resources ⇒ Writing ⇒ Writing Process ⇒ Planning. Review the Instruction and Multimedia resources about English as a second language then complete the Exercises and click on Gradebook to measure your progress.

*Each chapter includes recommendations for additional examples and exercises on MyCompLab.*

FIGURE 14.2 Ineffective and effective PowerPoint slides

*The discussion of the writing process includes the use of technology at all stages of the process, and samples of writing like this blog.*

*The principles of analyzing and using visual design and visual elements are incorporated in all the chapters as part of the writing process, then given special attention in Chapter 14.*

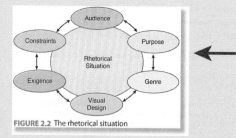

FIGURE 2.2 The rhetorical situation

*The discussion of the rhetorical situation, for instance, links visual design to audience, purpose, and genre.*

# Critical Reading, Writing, and Collaboration

The World of Writing helps students develop their own writing process and writing style. While the writing process covered in Parts 1 and 2 gives students the skills they need, the book also focuses on developing their own unique application of these skills. The Writing Assignments guide students through crafting their own writing, and a number of features help them think about the process, the selections, and their own writing from their own perspective. In today's world, working with others is an important skill. The World of Writing helps students build these self-reflection and collaborative skills with features like these:

*Activities ask students to consider their own experiences and how they relate to the topics and activities.*

**Develop Your Understanding**

**Activity 4.1** Write about all of the reading that you have done this past week. What were your main purposes for reading? What media did you use for reading (hard copy, Internet, cell phone, and so on). What language(s) did you use? What does this reveal about you as a reader? Compare your responses with your classmates'.

### Consider Your Viewpoint

1. If you are an immigrant or descended from immigrants, in which of the five immigration time periods described by the author do you or your ancestors belong?
2. What are some factors that make people hostile to immigrants?
3. The author does not mention illegal immigration in this essay. Why do you think this is so?
4. African-American slaves were the victims of forced immigration because they were brought to the United States against their will. How did this enslavement affect their descendants?
5. In the future, do you predict there will be more, less, or the same restrictions on immigrants coming to the Unite...

*Questions encourage students to use their unique cultural perspectives to reflect on the readings. At least one question asks them to analyze visual design elements of the genre or accompanying photograph.*

### Peer Review
#### Making an Observation

1. What is this observation's greatest strength?
2. What is being observed? Is this a topic that you would lik... more about? Why or why not?
3. Where might I add details to better support the main poi... sections or sentences would you like me to clarify? How v... ideas flow? Where do you suggest I add transitions to he... from one idea to another?
4. If I used research or interviews to support my observation... was this research used? How well did I avoid simply cutti... pasting information into the piece? How well are quotatio... paraphrases used? How well did I indicate the sources of... in the text of the piece and at the end?
5. What more would you like to know about this topic?
6. Underline any words or sentences that you think I should... because they do not communicate to you.
7. Place a checkmark in the margin next to any punctuation errors that you discover while reading this essay.

### Self-Evaluation Sheet
#### Investigating a Cause

1. Have I followed all instructions for this investigation of causes assignment? (Reread the assignment sheet and class notes.)
2. Have I identified a fact, event, or occurrence to investigate?
3. Are my thoughts about the causes of this well-ordered?
4. Is my paper written clearly and concisely? (Reread your paper out loud.)
5. Is each paragraph developed and does each contribute to the overall organization?
6. Do I introduce my investigative topic in such a way that the reader is engaged?
7. Do I conclude in such a way that there is a sense of closure?
8. Is the paper written in my own words?
9. Are my sentences well-written and varied? (Read each sentence beginning with the last one, working backward to the beginning of the paper.)
10. Is my word choice appropriate for the audience and purpose?
11. Have I checked for grammar, punctuation, and spelling errors? (Use a grammar handbook and the computer spell-checker.)
12. If I used other sources of information in this investigation, did I give credit both in the text and on a Works Cited or References page?

### Samples of Class Writing

Your portfolio should include only your best writing, so choose four or five pieces from your classes as examples. How do you know which pieces to include? Your best writing is probably those pieces you most enjoyed writing and that your peers and instructor told you that they enjoyed reading, too. To demonstrate your range of writing abilities, select pieces that showcase a variety of audiences, purposes, and genres. Then, select pieces that include:

- an effective introduction and thesis statement
- well-developed paragraphs
- good supporting details
- effective transitions
- an effective conclusion
- few or no errors in spelling, punctuation, or grammar

**One Student's Class Writing.** Student writer Maria Cervantes, a sociology major, decided to include this memorandum that she submitted to her English professor as a proposal for the topic she would write about during the semester.

*A dedicated chapter on Creating Portfolios prepares students for courses in other disciplines and in the workplace.*

*For each Writing Assignment, students collaborate with their classmates and learn the value of giving and receiving feedback on their writing by working through a Peer Review process. Students are then guided through the process of critically assessing their own work with a Self-Evaluation Sheet.*

**Connect With Others**

**Activity 6.3** Divide into groups with each group taking one of the model readings at the beginning of this chapter. For each reading, create a reverse outline of the organization of the piece. Then underline the key words and transitions. Discuss what you have found with your classmates.
Once you improve the organization of your piece, review what you have written in light of your original plans for the rhetorical situation.

*Each chapter includes activities designed to have students work in groups on such activities as developing topics.*

# Focus on Development of an Individual Writing Process

*Each chapter in Part 2 begins with three professional selections, to demonstrate the key elements and strategies of the writing. The selections include topics that are relevant for the student and focus on global and multicultural experiences.*

*The chapters guide the students through how the rhetorical situation relates to the writing. Each Writing Assignment explores how to use the writing process and provides guided instruction in developing a topic, and considering audience, purpose, genre, visual design, exigence and constraints.*

## The Rules of the Sport
### Adam Gopnik

Adam Gopnik writes for the *New Yorker*, a major U.S. magazine with a mostly college-educated readership that is best known for publishing essays in which writers record their observations of current life. Gopnik, who writes on topics ranging from baseball to art history, lived in Paris from 1995 to 2000 with his wife Martha and their young son; during that time he wrote essays about his experiences with Paris life that were published in *Paris to the Moon* in 2000. The following is an excerpt from that book.

Last year the French government assembled a committee to choose a name for the vast new stadium that's being built in a Paris suburb. The committee included an actor, an "artiste," some functionaries, and even a few athletes. It took a long time deliberating over its choice. Names were submitted: Some people liked the idea of naming the stadium after Verlaine or Saint-Exupéry, and lots of others liked the idea of calling it Le Stade Platini, after Michel Platini, the great French soccer player. At last, in December, the committee announced that it had come to a decision, and the government decided to broadcast the verdict on television. The scene was a little like the end of the Simpson trial: the worried-looking jurors filing to their seats, the pause as the envelope was handed to the minister of youth and sports, the minister clearing his throat to read the decision to the nation. The stadium that would represent France to the world, he announced, would be called (long, dramatic pause) Le Stade de France. The French Stadium. "Banal and beautiful at the same time," one journalist wrote. "Obvious and seductive. Timeless and unalterable."

It wasn't hard to detect, beneath the sturdy, patriotic surface of the new name, an undercurrent of ironic, derisory minimalism. The French are prepared to be formally enthusiastic about American-style stadiums and American-style sports, but they are not going to get carried away by it all. This realization first came home to me when I joined a pioneer health club on the Left Bank and spent four months unsuccessfully trying to get some exercise there.

"An American gym?" Parisians asked when I said that I was looking for someplace to work out, and at first I didn't know what to say. What would a French gym be like? Someone suggested that my wife and I join the Health Club at the Ritz; that was about as French as a gym could get. This sounded like a nice, glamorous thing to do, so we went for a trial

*Left Bank: An area in Paris on the southern bank of the river Seine.*

### Reflect on the Reading

1. Why does Gopnik begin this piece by describing the search for a name of a new French sports stadium?
2. According to Gopnik, what are some differences between the way that the French view athletics and the way that New Yorkers (and, by implication, Americans) view athletics?
3. Select six words from this piece that best depict the ways that the French view athletics, according to Gopnik.
4. Describe Gopnik's tone throughout the piece. What is his attitude toward the topic?
5. How does the title—"The Rules of the Sport"—relate to Gopnik's message?

## WRITING ASSIGNMENT

For this writing assignment, you will explore an event that was important to you. The event can be something you witnessed, something that happened to you, or something that you did. By writing about this event, you'll increase your understanding, create a written record, and communicate something important about yourself to others.

### Choosing a Topic

The event you decide to write about should interest you, spark some ideas, and potentially appeal to your readers. Because you'll share your writing with others, avoid selecting a very personal topic. The obvious choices for this assignment are rites of passage, or rituals that signal a new stage of life, and momentous events that are life altering. However, less obvious topics can sometimes lend themselves to more nuanced writing.

> *There are no mistakes, no coincidences. All events are blessings given to us to learn from.*
> —Elisabeth Kubler-Ross

### Analyzing the Rhetorical Situation

By analyzing your rhetorical situation, you can respond effectively to the context of this assignment. Your goal is to shape your writing so that your readers understand your message.

**Considering Audience and Purpose.** When you write about an event, you want your audience to understand your ideas and to find your writing memorable. The more you know about your audience, the greater the chances of this happening.

#### Audience Questions for Exploring an Event

- Who would be interested in reading about this topic?
- What does your audience already know about the topic? What do they need to know?
- What is their attitude toward the topic?
- Will their cultural background or gender affect the way they respond to the topic?
- Will their age or educational level affect their response?

*Students then develop their own writing, applying the skills they developed in Part 1, with careful attention to the rhetorical situation. The Peer Review worksheet and Self-Evaluation worksheet for each Writing Assignment help the students revise their work.*

*The chapter concludes with an annotated student sample to show how one student responded to the Writing Assignment.*

## Using the Writing Process

Now that you've analyzed your rhetorical situation, you can begin to write. To ensure the success of your piece, be sure to discover ideas, draft to explore ideas, revise to improve content, and edit to eliminate errors. Keep in mind that the writing process isn't usually as linear as these stages, so you might need to go back to an earlier stage as needed.

STAGE 1: Discovering Ideas
In Part I of this textbook, you learned a variety of ways to discover ideas. One way that is especially appropriate for an exploration of an event is to list ideas, also known as brainstorming.

## Peer Review
### Exploring An Event

1. What is the greatest strength of this piece?

2. What event is being described? To what extent does this topic interest you? What did you already know about this topic? What did you learn?

3. Based on your reading, what do you think is the significance of this piece? How easy or hard was it to understand the significance?

4. Where might I add description or dialogue to make my main point clearer? How can I improve my focus?

5. What parts of the piece could be omitted? Why do they need to be omitted?

6. How well does my topic flow? Where do the ideas seem choppy or jumpy?

7. Underline any words or sentences that you think I should revise because they do not communicate to you.

8. Place a checkmark in the margin next to any punctuation or spelling errors that you discovered while reading this draft.

## Self-Evaluation Sheet
### Exploring An Event

1. Have I followed all instructions for this assignment? (Reread the assignment sheet and class notes.)

2. How clear is the significance of the event?

3. How well have I used description and dialogue to help the readers picture what is happening?

4. How well-focused is my writing? Are there any unnecessary or distracting parts that can be omitted?

5. Does each paragraph contribute to developing the main point?

6. Does my opening paragraph make my audience want to continue reading?

## ONE STUDENT'S EXPLORATION OF AN EVENT

In Stage 1 of the writing process, we introduced you to Omotayo Olabumuyi, a student who was writing about an event that happened in one of his university classes. Here is the final version of his essay.

### Africa Through the African Eye
#### Omotayo Olabumuyi

Never have I been so aware of my identity as I was in my Individuals and Societies class when a presenter discussed the issue of AIDS in Tanzania, East Africa. I am one of the two Africans in the class, also the only one who has lived in Africa and not just toured it for a short while. The presenter asked if there were any people who had visited Africa. I looked round—less than one percent had our hands raised. Later on she asked for their general thoughts of what Africa was like. The responses were unbelievable; it then dawned on me that my identity was going to make the class a miserable one for me.

The first response was a loud shout from behind. "Primitive!" he yelled; next was "Native!" and then "Uncivilized!" It got worse when I heard a very silent hum sounding like "Animals!" Being an African, I was a little biased and my heart was torn apart until he made it clear that he wasn't calling the people animals. He better qualified himself by saying "Wildlife and the safari." Anyway, this was the sad beginning of the class that was going to disturb my state of mind for hours to come.

The presenter started off by correcting the erroneous responses, stating clearly that there are skyscrapers in the cities, the latest automobiles, cell phones, hotels, and most of the things that are enjoyed in the developed world. Then she proceeded to the crux of the issue but with a twist, knowing that she was speaking to an American audience. She spent most of the time speaking about wildlife and showing pictures of the lions, hippopotamus, all the beautiful animals that make Africa so close to nature. She only spent a little time speaking about the diseases and poverty.

From my understanding, she did this to give the audience a better perception of Africa. She did this so that they may see that Africa has a lot more than we see on TV. But it looked to me like she failed in changing the perceptions of the people. I was riveted in my seat, speechless as my mind raced through the rich culture of the African society made unappealing because of the poor economy. I was motionless as I empathized with the ill fate of the diseased Tanzanian people. But I was alone in this state of melancholy.

I managed to keep tears back as I looked around and saw the happy faces who could only imagine the excitement of what it would be like driving so close to a lion in the safari, or having to see a lion tear up a gazelle. The veil that prevented them from showing any sympathy grew thicker as she spoke of her experience while climbing Mount Kilimanjaro. The whole class was blown away, well distracted, and she tried relentlessly to bring the class back to the main health topic of the day. Dolefully, that was now more or less inconsequential.

Eventually, it was a very obnoxious question that captivated them and made them listen to what Africa is, aside from being a land where you visit to see animals in their natural habitat. The question was utterly disheartening. A boy asked the presenter what the WORST thing she had seen in Africa. It seemed to me that the boy could not imagine Africa as a land from which anything good can come out. He was hell bent on seeing more, more gory pictures of hunger and starvation, more stories of the different cultures that he perceived as crude, more disease, more to adorn his superiority. The presenter talked about a woman she had met who had killed herself because her whole family had died of AIDS and her own death was only a matter of months. I looked at the boy's face after the response, and it was initially emotionless—he wasn't impressed, nor was he moved. But then, seconds later, a smile surfaced on his face as he settled in his seat, satisfied, his ego appeased.

*Olabumuyi catches his readers' attention by describing how he feels in class.*

# Supplements

*The World of Writing* Instructor's Manual provides a wealth of material for both new instructors and veterans. The first part of the Instructor's Manual contains sections that will help instructors plan for and present an effective engaging course for a diversity of students.

- **Multilingual writers**—this unique chapter provides extensive teaching suggestions for working with multilingual writers, including the second language acquisition process, cultural and rhetorical considerations, creating writing assignments for multilingual writers, and evaluating multilingual writers' essays.

- **Understanding Student Learning Styles and Challenges**—to help instructors tailor their course to their students' various learning styles, this section includes suggestions for determining and then tailoring a course to various learning styles. A section on recognizing and working with disabled students provides suggestions on improving their reading and writing skills.

- **Creating and Assessing Writing Assignments**—this section includes suggestions for how to respond to student writing and conferencing with students. It covers establishing grading criteria for student writing, and includes sample standards for grading and other assessment worksheets. It also includes suggestions for how to evaluate student writing portfolios.

- **Teaching with Technology**—this section covers teaching with technology, including helpful website links, and publishing with technology. It also discussed the various formats for publication, and how to present them to students.

- **Teaching Reading Strategies**—this section provides suggestions for teaching the various critical reading strategies to improve student reading skills, including building vocabulary through reading.

- **Teaching Style and Revision**—to support the book's emphasis on self-reflection and peer evaluation, this section offers suggestions on how to teach revision and sample guidelines for peer review, and on how to teach the editing process to students.

- **Teaching Structure**—each of the rhetorical patterns are covered in this section, with suggestions for how to teach the structure of the patterns.

- **Preparing to teach the course**—this overview provides information about the course and the Instructor's Manual. It includes teaching suggestions for finding out about students, and the campus resources that can help instructors work with their students. A section on service learning provides suggestions for instructors who include service learning in their classes. Sample syllabi are included for both aims-based and genre-based

courses, and additional information is provided to help instructors build or modify their syllabus.

- **Planning the first day, the first week**—this chapter discussed how to introduce the course and the text to students, and how to administer a writing sample (including sample Diagnostic Writing Sample assignments). Icebreaker activities and a sample Student Information sheet provide opportunities for instructors to learn more about their students.

- **Planning class time**—this section includes suggestions for planning and running a class, including creating effective lesson plans, creating classroom order, and lecturing in a classroom. It also provides suggestions for establishing groups, including facilitating group work and classroom discussion, and managing and evaluating groups.

Provided by Carol Koris of Johnson and Wales University, the second part of the Instructor's Manual is a chapter-by-chapter guide that includes additional in-class and computer activities, writing activities, and suggestions for additional readings. WPA outcomes are correlated to the chapter content, and suggestions for MyCompLab resources direct instructors and students to additional resources.

**MyCompLab.** The only online application that integrates a writing environment with proven resources for grammar, writing, and research, MyCompLab gives students help at their fingertips as they draft and revise. Instructors have access to a variety of assessment tools including commenting capabilities, diagnostics and study plans, and an e-portfolio. Created after years of extensive research and in partnership with faculty and students across the country, MyCompLab offers a seamless and flexible teaching and learning environment built specifically for writers.

**Interactive Pearson eText.** An eBook version of *The World of Writing* is also available in MyCompLab. This dynamic, online version of the text is integrated throughout MyCompLab to create an enriched, interactive learning experience for writing students.

**CourseSmart.** Students can subscribe to *The World of Writing* as a CourseSmart eText (at CourseSmart.com). The site includes all of the book's content in a format that enables students to search the text, bookmark passages, save their own notes, and print reading assignments that incorporate lecture notes.

**Social Networking.** Join us to create an online community around your course. For additional teaching tips about this book and other resources and announcements visit Pearson's Facebook fan page for this book http://www.facebook.com/MangelsdorfPosey.

# Acknowledgments

We are deeply grateful to the many people who believed in this project and supported us throughout the development process. Suzanne Phelps Chambers understood what we wanted to do from the beginning: her dedication, expertise, and insights led to a book that can make a difference in students' lives. Meg Botteon's creativity, humor, and organizational savvy pushed us to think of alternatives, kept us firmly on track, and helped us persevere. David Kear skillfully guided this sometimes unwieldy manuscript through production. Laney Whitt's quick responses and helpful ideas were very much appreciated. Liz Mangelsdorf's outstanding photographs made this book visually dynamic and appealing. We also thank Tammie Bob and John Ross for sharing their students' essays and Keith Edwards for taking photos of his students and to Gerardo Robles for allowing us to use his photo as a chapter opener. We are also grateful to students Judith Almodovar, Nawja Al-Tabaa, Randi Bossie, Theresa Cast, Maria del Carmen Cervantez, Emily Conry, Susana Cruz, Angela D'Onofrio, Priscilla Duran, Lisa Estala, Matthew Guay, Barton Henderson, Kebba Khan, Charles Lujan, Brittney McBride, Laura Mendez, Christopher Morris, Christina Munoz, Rosa Orozco, Laura Parra, Tia Palsole, Stella Owens, Gilbert Serna, Shepherd Smith, Erik Vasquez, and Leola Young-Dozier for allowing us to publish their work, and Todd Ruecker for giving us permission to include some of his research. We also thank our first-year composition students who used and reviewed a draft of this manuscript. Most important, we thank our husbands Robert Rowley and Bruce King for their patience and support and Bob for his article and Bruce for his photos.

Finally, we are grateful to the following reviewers for their insights and comments:

Kathlyne Adams, *San Joaquin Delta College*
Susan Aguila, *Palm Beach State College*
Lauryn Angel-Cann, *Collin College*
Evelyn Beck, *Harrisburg Area Community College*
Tammie Bob, *College of DuPage*
Colin Charlton, *University of Texas-Pan American*
Avon Crismore, *Indiana Purdue Fort Wayne*
Marie Eckstsrom, *Rio Hondo College*
Patrice Fleck, *Northern Virginia Community College*
Melissa Freitag, *University of Wisconsin*
Michael Hainzinger, *Joliet Junior College*
Kimberly Harrison, *Florida International University*
Gina Hochhalter, *Clovis Community College*
Philip Hutcheon, *San Joaquin Delta College*
Karen Jackson, *North Carolina Central University*
Maria Jerskey, *LaGuardia Community College*
Peggy Jolly, *University of Alabama-Birmingham*
Dipo Kalejaiye, *Prince George's Community College*
Sara Kaplan, *Del Mar College*

Jessica Kidd, *University of Alabama-Birmingham*
Carol Koris, *Johnson & Wales University*
Lindsay Lewan, *Arapahoe Community College*
Rosemary Mack, *Baton Rouge Community College*
Anna Maheshwari, *Schoolcraft College*
Ilona Missakian, *Hondo College*
Anna Modzelewski, *Edmonds Community College*
Kate Mohler, *Mesa Community College*
Dawn Penich-Thacker, *Arizona State University*
Mauricio Rodriguez, *El Paso Community College*
DaRelle Rollins, *Hampton University*
John Ross, *Fort Hays State University*
Amy Shank, *Wenatchee Valley College*
Anne Twite, *Eastern New Mexico University-Ruidoso*
Chris Verschage, *Oklahoma City Community College*
William Zhang, *Des Moines Area Community College*

# About the Authors

## Kate Mangelsdorf

Kate Mangelsdorf is a Professor of Rhetoric and Writing Studies and Director of University Writing Programs at the University of Texas at El Paso (UTEP). Her research interests include critical literacies and second language writing. She has published many journal articles and book chapters and is a frequent presenter at professional conferences. With Evelyn Posey, she previously published *Choices: A Basic Writing Text with Readings* (4th ed.) and *Discoveries*. Her current scholarly focus is on standard language ideologies and language demarcations. She was the Principal Investigator on a grant from the Texas Higher Education Coordinating Board that supported a major redesign of UTEP's second-semester composition course. She also serves on the Executive Committee of CCCC.

She has held many administrative positions at UTEP, including Associate Dean of University College, Director of Developmental English, and Director of First-Year Composition. She is also the former Director of the Rhetoric and Writing Studies program and the PhD program in Rhetoric and Composition.

She received her PhD from the University of Arizona and has taught at UTEP since 1990.

## Evelyn Posey

Evelyn Posey is a Professor of Rhetoric and Writing Studies at the University of Texas at El Paso (UTEP). She has been active in the computers and writing community, writing articles and presenting papers on using technology in the composition classroom and serving on the CCCC Computer Committee. With Mangelsdorf, she previously authored two developmental composition textbooks: *Choices: A Basic Writing Guide with Readings,* 4th edition, and *Discoveries: A Step-by-Step Guide to Writing Paragraphs and Essays.*

She received a $3.4 million National Science Foundation grant for the advancement of women in science and engineering academic disciplines and now serves as a consultant to universities who wish to improve the recruitment and retention of women faculty.

A specialist in Composition and Rhetoric, she has served the university as Chair of the Department of English, Associate Dean of Liberal Arts, and Associate Vice President for Academic Affairs. For five years, she served as Director of English Education and Director of the West Texas Writing Project, a site of the National Writing Project.

She received her PhD from New Mexico State University and has been a member of the UTEP English faculty since 1990.

# PART 1 Expanding Literacies

# CHAPTER

# 1 Words and the World

## Learning Objectives

In this chapter you will:

- Learn about different types of languages.
- Study the connection between language and identity.
- Learn about language change.
- Examine the differences between speaking and writing.
- Study different language systems.
- Examine how people learn languages.
- Study aspects of writing development.

*Language is the bridge that connects people together.*

I magine everything that you might read in a single day: words on cereal boxes, computer screens, billboards, t-shirts, store receipts, and cell phones. Think of the writing that you do every day: text messages, notes, tweets, exams. You can write on a printed page, on your computer and phone screens, on a white board, on a brick wall. And the languages that you use can vary. You abbreviate words when you text-message. You use slang with your friends and formal language with your boss. In addition to English, you might speak Mandarin or Spanish or Arabic or Hindi.

These ways of reading and writing comprise your literacies. In the past twenty years, technology has greatly expanded the forms of literacies available to many people. Broadband transmissions have enabled electronic and digital communications. Immigration and economic globalization have spread languages and cultures. As a student in the twenty-first century, you can communicate in languages and formats unavailable to many people several decades ago.

**Activity 1.1** With your classmates, list the different languages that are spoken by students in your writing class. Include slang and dialects. Then list the different ways you all write, such as texting. Discuss with your classmates the diversity of languages and media that you use.

**Connect With Others**

## WORDS AND THE WORLD

Since you speak English, you might wonder why you need to think about other languages. English is considered a global language because it is used in business transactions throughout the world. Millions of school-children around the world are taught English as a foreign language from a young age. If a person from Argentina and a person from Germany meet at a business conference in Japan, the language they might have in common is English. So why think about language if most everyone speaks English?

In actuality, people from various parts of the world speak English differently. Native English speakers from Dublin, London, New York, and Sydney sometimes have trouble understanding each other because of their accents. And most people in the world who speak English are nonnative speakers—they learned it in school, from U.S. television, from friends. So the person from Argentina and the person from Germany at the business conference in Japan who speak English with each other will have different accents and different levels of language proficiency. They still communicate, but at times they struggle to find the right words, ask for phrases to be repeated, and use hand gestures to get a point across.

The world is growing flat, as the *New York Times* columnist Thomas Friedman has noted. Almost all U.S. businesses, large and small, have some contact with the international business world. If you're a doctor, you're using medical techniques developed by experts in India or Sweden. If you're a teacher, your students are from Nicaragua and Nigeria. No matter what your profession, at some point in your career you'll be working with people who learned English as a second or third language (as you might have). Their accents will be different from yours, they might make grammatical errors that you don't make, and they might have expectations about the communication process that surprise you. The more you know about language—such as how long it takes to learn another language and the stages that people go through as they learn— the more prepared you will be for working and thriving in the multilingual, multicultural marketplace.

## WHAT IS A LANGUAGE?

A language consists of symbols that are put together in speech or writing in certain ways to communicate with others. People from the same community, country, or culture will usually share the same language. A language can be English or Urdu or American Sign Language (ASL). It can also be

- body language, such as crossing your arms over your chest when you feel threatened.
- animal language, such as birdsong, purring, or growling.
- computer language, such as HTML.

Language is a universal way of communicating emotions and ideas. Through language we socialize with others, keep historical records, express religious or spiritual feelings, and conduct business. Our language is closely connected to our sense of who we are—in other words, our identity.

### Standard Languages

Defining a language can be more political than scientific, and language and nationalism are often connected. The United States does not have a national language policy, though many states have made English their official language. In contrast, other countries have used language policy to maintain national power. In the middle of the twentieth century, Chinese leaders decided that the version of Chinese spoken in the capital city of Beijing should be used throughout the country. Thus, the language that had been referred to (by English speakers) as North Mandarin became the standard language of China. If the country's leaders decided that North Mandarin was, essentially, *the* Chinese language, then other languages spoken in China (such as Cantonese in the south and Hsiang in the south central parts of the country) were to be considered varieties of Chinese, although speakers of these different dialects usually couldn't understand one another. This Chinese language policy has helped Chinese leaders maintain control over a vast territory of diverse peoples and cultures.

A standard language is considered the prestige language of a group of people. When you're taught to write in school, you're taught the standard language. In the United States, most people agree that standard English usage is necessary for success in the professional workplace.

## Dialects

A dialect is a variety of a standard language. Ordinarily, a standard language and its dialects are similar enough that speakers can understand each other. Most speakers of the same dialect live in the same geographical areas. Speakers of one of the southern U.S. dialects, for example, typically grew up in the southern United States. African-American Vernacular English (AAVE), also considered a dialect of English, is similar to southern dialects because many African-Americans originally came from the South. The combination of Spanish and English called Spanglish is usually found in regions of the United States where many Spanish-speaking people live, such as New York, Florida, Texas, and California. Typically, dialects are considered less prestigious than standard languages, although a standard language is really just the prestige dialect of a group of people. What makes a language "good" is simply the extent to which it can be used by people to communicate with others.

## Slang

Informal language used in everyday face-to-face or electronic communication, *slang* consists of made-up words, nonstandard usage, and figures of speech. Typically, young people create new slang vocabulary, and using slang is a sign that you are a group insider. Often words that originally began as slang are adopted into the standard language vocabulary.

**LANGUAGES and CULTURES**

**U.S. military jargon**

Squad: 10–11 soldiers

Platoon: 4 squads

Company: 2 or more platoons

Battalion: Several companies, about 400 soldiers

*"A language is a dialect with an army and navy"*

— *Max Weinreich*

*Piano,* for example, was at one time considered slang because the complete word was *pianoforte.* Particular groups (for example, hip-hop artists, surfers, baseball players) create their own slang. Some slang (*groovy, gee whiz*) is quickly outdated, while other slang (*wired, cool, glitch, freebie*) has a longer shelf life. Another form of slang consists of abbreviated writing used in texting, such as *b4, lol, qt,* and *gtyl.*

## Jargon

Specialized language in the workplace is called *jargon.* The medical field is especially known for its jargon, but workplaces ranging from accounting firms, fast-food restaurants, movie studios, and construction companies use their own language that outsiders find hard to understand.

**Connect With Others**

**Activity 1.2**   Taking into consideration standard languages, dialects, slang, and jargon, decide how many types of languages and dialects you speak. For slang and jargon, list a few words that you use. Keep in mind that you may speak slang and jargon in more than one language. With your classmates, list all of the different languages and dialects spoken in your classroom.

## LANGUAGE AND IDENTITY

A language is more than just words and grammar. It's also a way of viewing the world, maintaining a culture, and expressing your connections to others. Because your language is so closely tied to who you are, changing your language is like shifting your identity. Here's an example:

Robert is a twenty-year-old college student who lives at home with his mother, grandmother, and brother, who is five years younger than he is. His mother and grandmother came from Russia, and he and his brother were born in the United States. In the mornings Robert speaks only Russian with his grandmother. With his mother he speaks a combination of Russian and English, and with his brother he speaks English slang. At school, he speaks standard English in his classes and between classes he texts his friends. After school he goes to work as a server at a Mexican restaurant, where he speaks a little Spanish with the customers and uses the jargon of the restaurant business. After work he and several friends go to a nightclub to check out a new hip-hop singer, and they evaluate the singer using hip-hop slang.

By changing languages throughout his day, Robert is showing how he connects with different people and situations. At home with his mother and grandmother he speaks Russian in order to show his closeness to his family and his pride in his Russian heritage. He and his brother speak English together because they identify with and plan to stay in their birth country. He speaks standard English in college to demonstrate his respect for his professors and to get their respect. When he texts his friends, he's being a typical U.S. college student. At the restaurant he speaks the jargon to show that he knows the job and he speaks Spanish to get better tips. By using hip-hop slang at the nightclub he is demonstrating to his friends that he knows hip-hop music.

## LANGUAGES and CULTURES

Robert is typical of many bilinguals, or people who speak two languages, because he's stronger in one language (English) than another (Russian). He can speak conversational Russian, and he can read some Russian without much difficulty. However, he has trouble following a complicated or very fast Russian conversation, and he hasn't written in Russian since he was a small boy. In contrast, he can speak, read, and write English well.

## LANGUAGE CHANGE

With so many types of language being spoken, it is no wonder that language is in a constant state of change. Even a standard language—the language found in grammar handbooks, for example—changes. For instance, the word *ain't* is a contraction of *am not,* as in "I ain't going to the store." In standard English, *ain't* lacks acceptability. However, several hundred years ago in England *ain't* was considered correct standard English; in fact, it was used by the British aristocracy. The opposite can happen, too: Words that were once considered slang eventually are accepted into the standard language, as in the word *kid,* meaning *child.*

Other reasons that languages are always changing:

■ Human interaction. When people who speak different languages come into contact with each other, languages change. In the United States, immigrants speaking

*Important public documents such as drivers' handbooks that used to be printed only in English are now available in many different languages.*

languages other than English have added new vocabulary to English. One example: *klutz,* which refers to a clumsy person, is a Yiddish word spoken by Jewish immigrants to the United States in the early part of the twentieth century.

■ Globalization. English has become widely spoken by millions of people around the world, and the majority of English speakers worldwide learned it as a second or third language. As a result, varieties of the English language (called World Englishes) have appeared, so that the English spoken and written in India, China, Latin America, and so on are different, though people will still be able to understand each other. A similar type of language change has happened with other languages used worldwide, such as Spanish and Chinese.

■ Technological innovations. Not too long ago the verb *to google* didn't exist, a hacker was someone who couldn't play golf very well, and identity theft meant forging someone's signature.

■ Cultural changes. When new concepts enter a culture, new words will follow. The words *shopaholic, carjacking, detox, mcjob,* and *going postal* are fairly recent additions to English.

# Changing Names in a Changing World

## David Mould

Language is closely connected with national power, and as nations change, so do their names. In the following article, David Mould, a professor at Ohio University, shows that countries change their names as a part of claiming their nationalist identities.

South Africa's capital, Pretoria, is now officially Tshwane. Bangalore, India's IT capital, will become Bengaluru this year. New names are coming fast as regimes change and countries shake off (often belatedly) symbolic trappings of a colonial past.

In a globalized economy, it is not enough to memorize all those American state capitals. Now we need to know where Kinshasa is, book a flight to Ouagadougou, the vowel-rich capital of Burkina Faso (formerly Upper Volta), and make sure we spell Llubiljana correctly on that overnight package.

The name-changing process began slowly in the quarter century after World War II, as European colonies in Africa and Asia gained independence. The idyllically named Gold Coast became Ghana, the possessively named Dutch East Indies became Indonesia, and North and South Rhodesia—named for the British administrator Cecil Rhodes—became, respectively, Zambia and Zimbabwe, making up for a lack of countries whose names stared with "Z."

5    At first, these changes were easily absorbed by cartographers, travelers and social studies teachers. But the disintegration of the Soviet Union accelerated the trend: in less than a year, all the former Soviet republics became independent countries.

Georgia was an easy one for Americans to remember. But Turkmenistan's name was close enough to Turkey's to cause confusion. After several trips to Kyrgyzstan, I found colleagues claiming I had been in Kurdistan, which (depending on how things turn out in Iraq) may still show up on the map. Or they lumped Central Asian countries together into an amorphous "stan-land."

The changes are all about nation-building and asserting ethnic identity. All newly-independent nations try to recast history. They tear down statues of colonial administrators or Soviet leaders, rewrite school textbooks, open museums dedicated to long-forgotten national heroes, teach native languages, launch national airlines and, most symbolically, change the names of countries, cities and streets.

But name-changing can be divisive. In the 1830s, the Afrikaners (settlers of Dutch descent) left the British-dominated Cape in ox wagons on the Great Trek to the interior, settling in northern South Africa. Their leader was Andries Pretorius, for whom Pretoria was named.

When the city council voted to name the capital for the African king Tshwane, Afrikaners protested that the change undermined their history and traditions. The last apartheid-era president, F.W. de Klerk, said Pretoria was "a symbol of the anti-colonial war that Afrikaners fought against the British, which was one of Africa's earliest liberation struggles." The mayor said Tshwane, which also means "we are the same," would underscore South Africa's break with apartheid, and the name change was approved. This is the most high-profile of several battles over name changes. Now a government agency, the South African Geographical Names Council, is charged with reviewing proposals, and has approved over 200 name changes since 2002. But 57,000 more are under review.

10    Not all new names translate as nicely as Tshwane. When Kazakhstan's president, Nursultan Nazarbayev, decided to move the capital from cosmopolitan Almaty in the southeast to a more central location, he selected Aqmola, an agricultural center. In Kazakh, the name means "white tomb." This seemed to confirm the worst fears of government officials that they were being shipped off to perish on the wind-blown steppe.

Nazarbayev tackled the image problem by changing Aqmola to Astana, which means "capital." He also reportedly improved the weather. Journalists claim that in the winter before the move, TV weather forecasts regularly reported that Astana was a few degrees warmer than it actually was.

India has been slower to remove reminders of its colonial past. Over a half century since independence, it has changed the names of only four major cities—Mumbai (Bombay), Chennai (Madras), Kolkata (Calcutta) and Thiruvananthapram (Trivandrum). The change from Bangalore to Bengaluru—the abbreviated name in the local Kannada language—will mark the city's 500th anniversary this year. The name is said to have been given by a chieftain and his warriors who were offered a meal of boiled beans by a local woman. Tourism officials may decide that "the city of boiled beans" is not exactly the image they want to promote, but most think the similar-sounding name will be adopted quickly.

New names are not just good for business for branding experts, signmakers and cartographers—or material for geography bees. They symbolize broader political, social and cultural changes, and a struggle to control a country's past and future. It is less important for us to remember all the names than to understand why they change. As global citizens, it is a geographical challenge we must undertake.

# One Word Spotlight

*Cartographer* (par. 3) is someone who makes maps. The process of mapmaking is complex, involving aspects of science, design, and politics.

**Connect With Others**

**Activity 1.3**    After you read this article, discuss with your classmates why the name of a country or city is connected to political power. Why, for instance, is the United States called the "United States of America"?

# MULTILINGUALISM

Although determining what constitutes a language (as opposed to a dialect or language variety) is difficult, many experts believe that about 6000 languages exist today. It's not surprising, then, that most people in the world are *multilingual,* which means that they know two or more languages. In no country in the world is only one language spoken. While some people are *monolingual* (speak only one language), they most likely overhear or read at least one other language in their everyday lives. Even the names of car manufacturers—Toyota, Volvo, Saab, Hyundai—remind us of our global, multilingual planet. Sometimes the greatest variety of languages is spoken in the smallest countries. In Nepal, a small country between China and India, anywhere from 95 to 126 languages are spoken, depending on who is doing the counting.

**Activity 1.4**   How many languages have you encountered today? Take into consideration the languages you speak, the languages you've overhead, and the languages you've seen in writing. Consider signs, billboards, product names, advertisements, websites—the entire environment around you.

**Develop Your Understanding**

# SPEAKING AND WRITING

When you speak or write, you use language to communicate with others. Speaking and writing, however, can be very different.

The following is from a transcript of a press conference held by President Barack Obama in February 2009. President Obama is responding to a question about the challenges of bipartisanship, where Democrats and Republicans would work together to pass legislation:

> *President Obama*: Oh, I don't think—I don't think I underestimated it. I don't think the—the American people underestimated it. They understand that there have been a lot of bad habits built up here in Washington and it's going to take time to break down some of those bad habits.

This oral response to the question illustrates some of the differences between speaking and writing. When you speak, you are thinking on your feet. You might unnecessarily repeat yourself ("I don't think—I don't think"). You might hesitate between words ("the—the"). The meaning of a word might not be immediately clear (the *it* at the end of the second sentence refers to bipartisanship). However, your listeners don't care about unnecessary repetition or vague references as long as they understand your overall meaning.

*Conversational interactions cross cultural, language, and age boundaries.*

Now read a passage on bipartisanship from *The Audacity of Hope,* the book Barack Obama published in 2006:

> It is such partisanship that has turned Americans off. What is needed is a broad majority who are re-engaged and who see their own self-interest as inextricably linked to the interest of others.

This passage conveys a more complex understanding of bipartisanship than the President conveyed in his press conference—more than just getting people to work together, bipartisanship is getting people to understand that working together will benefit them as well as others. When writing his book, Obama most likely chose his words carefully, and he no doubt showed his drafts to others to see if they understood his points. However, like all writers, he could not know how his readers would respond because his readers were not in front of him.

What are some differences between speaking and writing?

- When you speak, you can use gestures and facial expressions to help you make your point. Your listeners can ask questions if they don't understand, and you can read their body language. In most situations listeners don't care if you repeat yourself or pause to search for words.
- However, in speech you might say something that you later regret. You can't take the words back.
- When you write you can erase words and revise your thoughts before you show it to anyone.
- Because you need to anticipate what your readers will think, writing is often more challenging and time-consuming than speaking.
- In many cultures, writing is the form of communication used in legal situations, as in contracts and licenses.
- Writing is often more formal than speaking, and depending on the situation, people are more likely to expect writers to use standard language.

These differences between speaking and writing don't mean that they're always kept separate. Many digital texts combine speaking and writing. The official White House website, for instance, includes videos of the president's press conferences and the text of his major speeches. In a sense, speaking and writing are also combined when people text each other. Texting resembles conversations because the communication is immediate and reciprocal, though it is actually a form of writing because it depends on symbols for communication.

# WRITING SYSTEMS

Human beings began to write thousands of years ago in places as different as China, Iraq, Egypt, India, and Central America. As a result of this geographic range, different systems of writing have evolved. A writing system consists of a series of symbols that are considered meaningful to a group of people speaking the same language. The writing system in Chinese and to a lesser degree Japanese, Korean, Vietnamese and other East Asian languages is logographic, meaning that one symbol (or character) represents one word. To be able to write in Chinese, you need to know at least 2000 different characters. Here is the word *write* in Chinese:

In contrast, most modern languages are alphabetic: One letter represents one or more sounds. Alphabets, which usually contain 20–30 letters, vary significantly around the world. The alphabet used in English is derived from the classical Roman alphabet. Here is how the word *write* is written in eight different languages:

Greek: γράφω
Spanish: escribir
Russian: писать
Arabic: يكْتُب
Polish: pisać
Indonesian: menulis
Turkish: yazı yazmak
Icelandic: skrifa

Languages also vary according to the direction in which they are written. Many languages are like English, when you write from the left to the right of the page. Traditional Chinese words were written from the top to the bottom of the page, from the right to the left. Arabic, Hebrew, and other Middle Eastern and Indian languages can be written left to right.

# CULTURAL PATTERNS OF WRITING

As writing systems differ throughout the world, so do patterns of writing. A writing pattern relates to how writing is organized in a text. In the United States, readers prefer writing that is organized in a straightforward way. In a standard U.S. academic essay, for instance, the writer announces the main point of the essay at the beginning in the introduction, develops several ideas directly related to the main point, and refers to the main point at the end. Unnecessary words are eliminated to help the reader understand the message as quickly as possible. In other cultures, however, such directness sometimes is seen as faulty. In countries where Spanish is the dominant language, writers often use figurative, poetic expressions that make the texts more aesthetically pleasing to the reader. In one type of a traditional Chinese essay, the writer deliberately strays from the main point of the piece in order to show a deeper, more sophisticated angle on the topic. In the Indian writing tradition, writers focus on helping readers come to the best understanding of a topic rather than simply announcing how the topic should be viewed.

## OWNERSHIP OF WRITTEN LANGUAGE

Another important cultural difference concerns the ownership of written language. In the United States, writers essentially own the words and ideas that they publish. Copyright laws prevent people from using another writer's words or ideas without giving credit through documentation, which includes giving the author's name and the source's page number in the paper and a "Works Cited" or "References" section at the end of the paper. Without such documentation, you can be accused of plagiarism. However, many other cultures traditionally view words and ideas as belonging to the people rather than to the individual. A writer might include the words of a well-respected person in a text without quotation marks or an endnote because those words are not "owned" by the original writer. In fact, the writer probably has memorized these words because they are highly valued by the culture. As a result, in these cultures it is permissible to use another person's words or ideas in a text without any documentation. It's important to remember, however, that in U.S. classrooms, documentation of information taken from other sources is required.

## LEARNING TO WRITE A SECOND LANGUAGE

Why learn a second language? Some people just want to be able to travel to another country, so they learn enough vocabulary to make everyday conversation. For many people, though, learning a second language is essential to meeting their professional and personal goals. They want to enter a profession that requires the knowledge of a certain language, or they immigrate to another country and want to learn the language of their new home. In order to succeed, they need to not just speak the language—they need to learn to read and write it. Learning to write a second language is a challenging, long-term, and rewarding process. You need to learn not just the grammar of the language but how to express complex ideas in a variety of forms that might range from a thank-you note to a lengthy research report.

To become proficient in writing another language so that you can succeed in school and the workplace, you need time, plenty of exposure to the language, practice, and motivation. Your experiences writing in your first language also play an important role.

## Time

While children can learn to converse in a new language quickly, to really learn a new language—to be able to speak, understand, read, and write complex ideas—takes around six or seven years of instruction and exposure to the language. While this might seem like a long time, it's only a few years more than it took to acquire your first language when you were a child.

*A boy in Guatemala learning to write in his first language.*

## Language Exposure

The more you are surrounded by written language, the easier it will be to use it. So in addition to taking writing classes, you should also try to read as much as you can in the language that you're learning. Reading for pleasure can help you learn more vocabulary, absorb the rhythm of the language, and get a sense for what sounds right. Read books, newspapers, magazines, and websites on topics that interest you.

## Practice

Even though you haven't fully mastered the language, you need to use it! In addition to writing for your class or workplace, try writing for yourself and those close to you. Write poems and short stories for fun. Compose letters and emails. Keep a journal for notes for yourself, word lists, or quotations that appeal to you. Don't be afraid to make mistakes in this informal writing.

## Motivation

Because learning to write in a second language takes time and work, you have to be motivated.

### LANGUAGES and CULTURES

Learning to write in your first language takes time, exposure to the written language, practice, and motivation.

- As you progress in college, you'll notice that your writing will improve
- The more you read, the greater your vocabulary and awareness of different sentence structures
- Try to write substantial texts every semester you're in college to maintain your skills
- Keep motivated by writing on topics that interest you

Even though one part of you wants to learn the language, another part of you might not. You might have conflicted feelings about the culture that the language represents, you might be worried about losing your first language, or you might not be that interested in entering a profession that requires the use of the second language. It's important to acknowledge these feelings and to know that even people who are very fluent and successful in their second language can still feel torn between the languages and cultures of their lives.

## Previous Writing Experiences

It's easy to think that when you learn a second language, your first language will get in the way. While you're trying to think of how to say something in English, for instance, you might only think of the word in another language. Overall, though, your fluency in one language helps you acquire a second language. In particular, the better you read and write in your first language, the easier you'll learn how to read and write in another language. This holds true even if your first language uses a writing system (such as Chinese or an East Asian language) that is very different from English.

### LANGUAGES and CULTURES

Another problem with trying to write and speak like a native speaker of English is—which English? U.S. English? British English? Australian English? Indian English?

## ACCENTED WRITING

When you learn another language, you will most likely have an accent. Very few people can speak another language without an accent. Similarly, even very fluent writers in another language have some kind of accent that tells people that they aren't writing in their first language. This accent can consist of a preposition (such as *at* or *in*) that isn't correct, or a word that doesn't have exactly the right meaning. When learning another language, don't feel frustrated if you can't sound or write just like a native speaker. You can still be a very good writer and have an accent.

## WHAT AFFECTS YOUR WRITING DEVELOPMENT?

In this book we'll be referring to two key concepts that will help you understand and improve your writing development. These concepts apply no matter what language you're writing in—your first, second, or third.

## Your Emotional Filter

As you know, a filter is a device through which material is passed. Water is filtered to get rid of impurities, coffee goes through a filter when it's brewed, and websites are filtered by computer software. Whenever you write, you're affected by an emotional filter. Some of these emotions are beneficial to learning, while others can be harmful.

- Emotions that can help you learn: pride, confidence, pleasure, and interest.
- Emotions that can hinder learning: anxiety, boredom, apathy, and fear.

Your previous writing experiences greatly affect your emotional filter. If in the past you've been criticized for how you write, received consistently low grades, and have written only in response to writing assignments or exams, then the emotions that you filter when you write might be negative. As a result, you might put off writing as long as possible, get writer's block, or rush through a writing assignment to get it over with. On the other hand, if in the past you've been praised for your writing, received good grades, and like to write for your own pleasure, your emotions might be positive. Most people filter a combination of positive and negative emotions as they write. In this book you will learn strategies to help you control the emotions that you filter as you write.

 Emotional Filter: The emotions that you experience when you write.

## Your Writing Monitor

When you monitor something, you keep track of how something is behaving or performing. For instance, parents monitor their children's eating habits to make sure they are getting enough vegetables. Whenever you write, you have a mental monitor that tells you when and how to apply writing rules and guidelines. Because of your monitor, you pause while you figure out how to spell a word, reread a paragraph to make sure your meaning is clear, or refer to a handbook to find out how to write a "Works Cited" page. Your monitor can range from low to high.

- A low monitor means that you aren't consciously applying rules as you write.
- A high monitor means that you are very aware of applying rules as you write.

Writing Monitor: Your awareness of writing rules as you compose.

When you apply your monitor depends on your writing situation and process. If you're jotting down a shopping list for a family member, your monitor will be low because he or she probably doesn't care how you spell "broccoli." On the other hand, if you're writing a resume for a job, your monitor will be high because even one error can eliminate you from the applicant pool. Similarly, if you're early in the writing process—freewriting or brainstorming, for instance—your monitor is low because you just want to get ideas down on paper. Later in the writing process your monitor will be high because you're correcting errors.

Depending on the circumstances, your monitor can impede or help your writing.

- If you're preparing a final draft and your monitor is too low, you might write too carelessly.
- If you're gathering ideas or drafting and your monitor is too high, you might be unable to put ideas down on paper because you're too concerned about correctness.

In this book you'll learn ways to appropriately use your monitor as you write.

# WRITING ASSIGNMENT

Reading and writing are shaped by where they occur. The way that you read and write for a school assignment is different from the way you read and write on Facebook. For school, most reading and writing is formal and will be evaluated. On Facebook, you read and write informally, in short bursts, and often use abbreviations, emoticons :), photos, videos, and music.

For this assignment, break your life up into different areas. Some examples are your family, friends, work, school, church, service organizations, hobbies, and clubs. Select three or four of these areas and list on a chart the different kinds of reading and writing that you do in each area. Here's an example of a chart that lists two different areas:

| | |
|---|---|
| Workplace | I write employee work schedules, monthly evaluation forms, notes to employees. I read memos from headquarters, reports from safety inspectors. |
| Friends | I read and write text messages, Facebook entries, blogs. |

After completing the chart, analyze the reading and writing that you do in each area, taking into consideration the questions *who, what, where, when, how,* and *why.* Compare and contrast the way you read and write in these different areas. Here's an example:

> There's not much reading to do at work, but I do spend a lot of time creating the work schedules and writing up monthly employee evaluations. I use a spreadsheet for the schedules. I don't enjoy any of this because I always get complaints—"you aren't giving me enough hours," or "don't mark me as late because I couldn't help it." With my friends I do a lot of texting, pretty much all the time that I'm awake. We abbreviate everything and I use Spanish with some of my friends. We do this to stay in touch and we have a lot of fun. My mother has started texting, but I'm more careful when I text her.

Finally, write about the meaningfulness of these types of reading and writing—which ones would you avoid if you could, and which ones do you enjoy, and why?

---

For support in meeting this chapter's objectives, follow this path in MyCompLab: Resources ⇒ Writing ⇒ Writing Process ⇒ Planning. Review the Instruction and Multimedia resources about English as a second language then complete the Exercises and click on Gradebook to measure your progress.

# 2 Rhetorical Situations

## Learning Objectives

In this chapter you will:

- Learn the definition of the word rhetoric.
- Learn to analyze a rhetorical situation.
- Understand how writing customs vary.

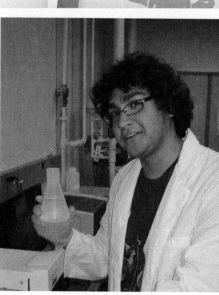

*How does this student's use of visuals make you want to hear what he has to say?*

I n the chapter opening photo, a chemistry student compares two copper complexes during his undergraduate thesis presentation. To give this presentation, he uses rhetoric to inform his audience and visuals to enhance the presentation. You may be familiar with the word rhetoric but think of it as a negative word. For example, you may think of rhetoric as the way a politician uses exaggerated promises to convince you to vote for him or her, or you may think of rhetoric as the way an advertiser uses glossy photos to entice you to buy a product you can't afford. However, the word *rhetoric* is neither negative nor positive. It simply refers to using language effectively, no matter what the purpose.

**Rhetoric:** The way you use language to entertain, inform, or persuade.

In addition to using rhetoric in face-to-face environments, college students sometimes use videoconferencing and blogs to communicate with students in classes across the globe. In the photo, students in a cross-cultural rhetoric project connect with students living in countries across three continents: Egypt, Sweden, and the United States. Students discuss how they live, share information about their education, and explore different cultural values.

Divided into cross-cultural groups, these students complete writing projects such as photo essays and brochures, all while exploring the differences in their communication styles. This cross-cultural communication requires students to pay close attention to how they speak and write to ensure that they are getting their point across to all audiences, whether on their own campus or across the world.

*Students participate in a cross-cultural rhetoric class.*

## RHETORICAL SITUATIONS

Rhetoric must include three related elements to be effective. As shown in Figure 2.1, there must be an author, a message to share, and an audience to receive the message.

Think of recent communications you have had. For example, when you arrived on campus, a friend may have wished you a good day. Your friend

Message

Author

Audience

**FIGURE 2.1** The rhetorical triangle

LANGUAGES
and
CULTURES

Aristotle defined a fourth element, *doxa*, for the rhetorical triangle to describe the common beliefs and values within a culture that affect the way the audience receives a particular message. Today, we use the word *orthodox* to describe someone who conforms to a particular societal, political, or religious doctrine. Throughout this textbook, sidebars such as this one will introduce you to how culture plays a role in communication.

was the author, the wish for the day was the message, and you were the audience. Once on campus, you may have turned in a history report. You were the author, the information provided in the report was the message, and your history professor was the audience. Before you left campus, you wrote yourself a note to do your math homework for tomorrow. You were both the author and the audience, and the message was "Get that homework done!"

In this textbook, you will examine a variety of ways to communicate, including essays, memoirs, blogs, reports, newspaper articles and editorials, reviews, brochures, and photo essays. You will learn to recognize and create effective communication in which the author and the audience reach a mutual understanding of the message. To communicate effectively, you begin by selecting and narrowing your topic and then analyzing the rhetorical situation. The rhetorical situation includes the topic, audience, purpose, genre, visual design, exigence, and constraints.

## Topic

In some situations, the topic of your writing is chosen for you. Your sociology instructor, for instance, requires that you write a paper describing your own cultural background, or your supervisor at work asks you to write a memo to your coworkers about a new way for scheduling work hours. Often, though, you will be able to select your own topic. When choosing a topic, pick one that interests you, that you already know something about or that you are willing to learn more about, and that will interest your readers. The readings in this and other textbooks are good places to start looking for topic ideas. If you have a general idea for a topic, you can also use web search engines such as *Google* and *Google Directory* to help you find a specific topic or *Google Scholar* to help you find scholarly articles on your topic.

### Topic Questions

- Is this an assigned topic, or do I have free choice?
- If assigned, what are the requirements?
- If free choice, what are some possible topics?
- Which of these interests me?
- Can I find enough reliable information about this topic to complete the assignment?

# Audience

You're writing to communicate something of interest, so you want to be sure that your readers, also known as your audience, understand your point. The more you know about your audience, the easier it will be for you to write. After all, it wouldn't make sense to write on advanced salsa moves to novice dancers or on the difference between football and rugby to champion rugby players. By answering questions about your audience before you begin to write, you will be able to choose details and present them in a way to appeal to this particular audience. You may need to do some research to learn about the people who will read your writing. If you are writing an essay for your fellow classmates, for instance, you might begin by reviewing your college website to learn more about the types of students who attend classes on your campus.

 Audience: The people who will read your writing.

While using this textbook, you will write for English-speaking readers, but they will come from a variety of language and cultural backgrounds. With the globalization of the U.S. workplace and the widespread use of communication technology, you can expect your readers to bring diverse experiences and understanding to their reading of your writing.

If your audience is from another culture, consider the types of information and organizational patterns that will appeal to them. If it's possible, you might also ask someone from the intended audience to help you answer the audience questions.

*You cannot teach a man anything; you can only help him find it within himself.*

—Galileo Galilei

---

## Audience Questions

- What is the average age of your readers?
- What is their gender, culture, standard language, and educational level?
- What is their attitude toward the topic?
- How much will they be interested in reading your writing?
- How much does this audience already know about the topic? How much do they need to know?

---

**Activity 2.1**  With your classmates, compare your college website to the website of another school. Describe the characteristics of the students who might attend each of these schools. How does each website appeal to its unique audience through its choice of words, graphics, and photographs? Through this comparison, what have you learned about the students on your campus that will help you to write for them as your audience?

**Connect
With Others**

## LANGUAGES and CULTURES

When writing for an expressive purpose, some multilingual writers choose to write in the language that reminds them of their families or homeland. Marjorie Agosin, a Chilean writer living in the United States, writes that "by writing in Spanish I could recover fragrances, spoken rhythms, and the passion of my own identity." Other writers, however, have a more complicated relationship with the language of their birth. Monileak Ourng, who was born in Cambodia but grew up in France, writes in an expressive essay about being considered a foreigner in Cambodia because she grew up in the West: "In the country where I was born, there was no way I could pass unnoticed: people there simply knew that I did not belong in that country." To her, it felt better to write in French or English, rather than the language of her birth.

# Purpose

Three common purposes for communication are (1) to express, (2) to inform, and (3) to persuade.

- When you write for an expressive purpose, you share your personal thoughts and feelings about a topic. When writing expressively you often use the pronoun "I."

- When you write for an informative purpose, you provide information you have gathered from other sources. Much of the writing that you do for college classes is informative.

- When you write for a persuasive purpose, you try to change your reader's mind or urge the reader to take action. Persuasive writing is considered more difficult than expressive or informative writing because it can be difficult to convince people to change their minds.

Often you'll have more than one purpose for writing, but generally one purpose will dominate. For example, if you keep a blog while spending the summer in Australia, your primary purpose would be expressive as you share your experiences. The blog could also be informative, though, if you provide factual information on the country and persuasive if you try to convince readers to visit Australia to see it for themselves.

 Purpose: What you hope to accomplish by putting something in writing.

### Purpose Questions

- Am I writing to share my personal history, thoughts, or feelings?
- Am I writing to explain something that I have learned?
- Am I writing to convince my readers to change their minds?
- Which of these is my primary purpose for writing?

 Genre: A specific format for writing, often determined by audience and purpose.

# Genre

Genre is an artistic, musical, or written composition presented in a specific format. When you write, you choose the genre or format that best fits your message and your audience's expectations. If you are applying for graduate school or employment, for example, you write a résumé and application letter. If you are writing to complain about service you received at a local restaurant, you write a persuasive letter. In college classes, you often write reports and essay exams. A genre often dictates the content and style of your message.

Examples of genres by purpose:

- expressive: journal entries, personal letters to friends and family, memoirs, and blogs in which you share information about your own background experiences or your personal thoughts and feelings
- informative: video documentaries, newspaper articles, business letters, and office memos
- persuasive: essays, pamphlets, editorials, speeches, and political comic strips

Some writing genres, such as memos and research reports, have similar features, while others can be noticeably different. For instance, blogs can vary dramatically in appearance, organization, and language. A famous singer's blog might contain photos, song snippets, and brief entries about the singer's concert schedule. In contrast, a blog written by a political analyst can feature lengthy essays and links to informative websites.

## Genre Questions

- Is there a genre that my audience expects me to use, or can I select a genre on my own?
- What do I know about the format of this genre?
- What do I need to learn about this format?

**Activity 2.2**   Divide into small groups, with each group assigned to find examples of writing in various genres. For example, one group might bring in magazines, another a local newspaper, and another college recruiting brochures. Discuss how the style and format changes from one genre to another.

**Connect With Others**

## Visual Design

Visual design—how something looks—helps you convey your message to your audience. Visual design includes the text fonts, white space, color, borders, and images such as illustrations and photos that we use to help communicate. Examine the "No Skateboarding" sign:

The message here is simple—skateboarding is not allowed in this particular area. A sign like this has to communicate quickly to any passerby. Therefore, the international symbol for "no," the circle with the diagonal

NO SKATEBOARDING

line, is presented in bold red over a simple drawing of a figure on a skateboard. To emphasize the message, "no skateboarding" appears below the symbol, with the word *no* in large letters. The simplicity and boldness of this visual design ensures that almost anybody will understand it.

Now, examine the "Danger" sign. Although the message is also simple, it uses a skull and cross bones, an international symbol for danger. As in the skateboard sign, red is used to attract attention. To emphasize the importance of this message, words are added in three languages. The boldness of this visual design and the use of the word "danger" ensures that most readers of the sign will stay out of this area.

In addition to improving communication, visual design can enhance your image with your audience. If you write a business letter on company stationery, you're telling the reader that you are authorized to write on the behalf of the company. A well-designed résumé helps you stand out to a potential employer. By following the conventions of a particular documentation style, such as using endnotes and a "Works Cited" page, you show that you understand how an academic field communicates. Visual design also can allow you to express your creativity, as when you design a website on which you post your work.

> ## Visual Design Questions
>
> ■ Is there a certain visual design that my audience expects?
> ■ How can I design my text so that it makes communication with my audience easier?
> ■ To what extent will my audience's culture and languages affect the way I design my document?

Exigence: A situation or circumstance that makes you want to communicate something to someone.

# Exigence

The word *exigency* refers to something that requires immediate action. In rhetoric, *exigence* is something that causes you to want to communicate with someone else. Sometimes you create the exigence yourself, such as when you want to write the owner of a local restaurant to complain about the poor service you received. Other times, the exigence is created for you, such as when your professor requires that you turn in a written assignment by a certain date.

The exigence can be something simple. For instance, you need to stay late at the library one night; because you don't want your family to worry, you leave a note on the kitchen counter explaining where you will be. An exigence can also be complicated and affect many people. As a result of the U.S. stock market downturn in October 2008, for instance, hundreds of analysts, public officials, and commentators explained this downturn to the public. An exigence can also be something that *doesn't* happen. A refund check, for instance, doesn't come on time, so you write a letter to the manufacturer requesting that it be sent immediately. When you consider exigence, the primary question you are answering is "Why am I putting this in writing?"

---

### Exigence Questions

- Why do I feel a need to communicate?
- Who do I want to communicate to, and for what reason?
- What do I hope to happen as a result of my communication?

---

## Constraints

Constraints include anything that might interfere with your ability to convey your message to your audience. When you take an essay exam, your constraints include a time limit and the need to respond to only the questions on the exam. In some parts of the world people can be constrained by the lack of available writing tools, books, and research materials.

   In essence, constraints are problems to be solved. If, for example, you're concerned that you might not have enough time to finish an essay exam, take measures to ensure that you keep track of the time, such as putting your watch on top of the desk. Sometimes constraints can work to your advantage. For example, some people feel that they write best when they're under a deadline.

 Constraints: The limitations of a writing situation.

## WRITING CUSTOMS

As writing systems differ throughout the world, so do ways of writing. One example is how writing is organized in a text. In the United States, readers prefer writing that is organized in a straightforward way. In a standard U.S. academic essay, for example, the writer announces the main point of the essay at the beginning in the introduction, develops several ideas directly related to the main point, and refers to the main point at the end. Unnecessary words are eliminated to help readers understand the message as quickly as possible. In other cultures, however, such directness can be seen as ineffective. The degree of directness in a text is determined by what readers expect, and these expectations are influenced by cultural norms. In one research study, for example, Finnish writers put their main points much later in their text than English-language writers. Differences in textual organization have been noted in countries ranging from Poland to India to China.

## Rhetorical Situations

After spending 27 years in prison, Nelson Mandela, recognized as the leader of South Africa's anti-apartheid movement, delivered this speech upon his release from prison in February 1990. Mandela prepared the speech in advance, but the actual delivery was subdued. He read the speech word for word from his notes. Because apartheid was just ending, Mandela realized that the political situation was volatile. He effectively used rhetoric to get his message across to his audience, while not inciting a civil war.

## Speech on Release from Prison, 1990

### Nelson Mandela

Comrades and fellow South Africans, I greet you all in the name of peace, democracy and freedom for all. I stand here before you not as a prophet but as a humble servant of you, the people. Your tireless and heroic sacrifices have made it possible for me to be here today. I therefore place the remaining years of my life in your hands.

*Nelson Mandela, with his wife Winnie at his side, leaves prison.*

On this day of my release, I extend my sincere and warmest gratitude to the millions of my compatriots and those in every corner of the globe who have campaigned tirelessly for my release. I extend special greetings to the people of Cape Town, the city which has been my home for three decades. Your mass marches and other forms of struggle have served as a constant source of strength to all political prisoners.

I salute the African National Congress. It has fulfilled our every expectation in its role as leader of the great march to freedom.

I salute our president, Comrade Oliver Tambo, for leading the ANC even under the most difficult circumstances.

5    I salute the rank-and-file members of the ANC: You have sacrificed life and limb in the pursuit of the noble cause of our struggle.

I salute combatants of Umkhonto We Sizwe (the ANC's military wing) who paid the ultimate price for the freedom of all South Africans.

I salute the South African Communist Party for its sterling contribution to the struggle for democracy: You have survived 40 years of unrelenting persecution. The memory of great Communists like Bram Fisher and Moses Mabhida will be cherished for generations to come.

I salute General Secretary Joe Slovo, one of our finest patriots. We are heartened by the fact that the alliance between ourselves and the party remains as strong as it always was.

I salute the United Democratic Front, the National Education Crisis Committee, the South African Youth Congress, the Transvaal and Natal Indian Congresses, and COSATU, and the many other formations of the mass democratic movement.

10    I also salute the Black Sash and the National Union of South African Students. We note with pride that you have endured as the conscience of white South Africans, even during the darkest days of the history of our struggle. You held the flag of liberty high. The large-scale mass mobilization of the past few years is one of the key factors which led to the opening of the final chapter of our struggle.

I extend my greetings to the working class of our country. Your organized strength is the pride of our movement: You remain the most dependable force in the struggle to end exploitation and oppression.

I pay tribute to the many religious communities who carried the campaign for justice forward when the organizations of our people were silenced.

I greet the traditional leaders of our country: Many among you continue to walk in the footsteps of great heroes.

I pay tribute for the endless heroism of youth: You, the young lions, have energized our entire struggle.

15    I pay tribute to the mothers and wives and sisters of our nation: You are the rock-hard foundation of our struggle. Apartheid has inflicted more pain on you than on anyone else.

On this occasion, we thank the world, we thank the world community for their great contribution to the anti-apartheid struggle. Without your support, our struggle could not have reached this advanced stage.

The sacrifice of the front-line states will be remembered by South Africans forever.

My celebrations will be incomplete without expressing my deep appreciation for the strength that has been given to me during my long and gloomy years in prison by my beloved wife and family. I am convinced that your pain and suffering was far greater than my own.

Before I go any further, I wish to make the point that I intend making only a few preliminary comments at this stage. I will make a more

> **Apartheid:**  A South African policy of segregation and discrimination against non-Europeans.

complete statement only after I have had the opportunity to consult with my comrades.

20      Today, the majority of South Africans, black and white, recognize that apartheid has no future. It has to be ended by our own decisive mass action in order to build peace and security.

The mass campaigns of defiance and other actions of our organizations and people can only culminate in the establishment of democracy.

The apartheid's destruction on our subcontinent is incalculable. The fabric of family life of millions of my people has been shattered. Millions are homeless and unemployed. Our economy lies in ruins and our people are embroiled in political strife.

Our resort to the armed struggle in 1960 with the formation of the military wing of the ANC (Umkhoto We Sizwe) was a purely defensive action against the violence of apartheid. The factors which necessitated the armed struggle still exist today. We have no option but to continue. We express the hope that a climate conducive to a negotiated settlement would be created soon, so that there may no longer be the need for the armed struggle.

I am a loyal and disciplined member of the African National Congress. I am therefore in full agreement with all of its objectives strategies and tactics.

25      The need to unite the people of our country is as important a task now as it always has been. No individual leader is able to take all this enormous task on his own. It is our task as leaders to place our views before our organization and to allow the democratic structures to decide on the way forward.

On the question of democratic practice, I feel duty-bound to make the point that a leader of the movement is a person who has been democratically elected at a national congress. This is a principle which must be upheld without any exception.

Today, I wish to report to you that my talks with the government have been aimed at normalizing the political situation in the country. We have not yet begun discussing the basic demands of the struggle. I wish to stress that I myself have at no time entered negotiations about the future of our country, except to insist on a meeting between the ANC and the government.

Mr. de Klerk has gone further than any other nationalist president in taking real steps to normalize the situation. However, there are further steps, as outlined in the Harare declaration, that have to be met before negotiations on the basic demands of our people can begin.

I reiterate our call for, inter-alia, the immediate ending of the state of emergency and the freeing of all—and not only some—political prisoners.

30      Only such a normalized situation, which allows for free political activity, can allow us to consult our people in order to obtain a mandate.

The people need to be consulted on who will negotiate and on the content of such negotiations.

Negotiations cannot take their place above the heads or behind the backs of our people.

It Is our belief that the future of our country can only be determined by a body which is democratically elected on a non-racial basis.

Negotiations on the dismantling of apartheid will have to address the overwhelming demands of our people for a democratic, non-racial and unitary South Africa.

35    There must be an end to white monopoly on political power and a fundamental restructuring of our political and economic systems to ensure that the inequalities of apartheid are addressed, and our society thoroughly democratized.

It must be added that Mr. de Klerk himself is a man of integrity who is acutely aware of the dangers of a public figure not honoring his undertaking.

But as an organization, we base our policy and our strategy on the harsh reality we are faced with, and this reality is that we are still suffering under the policies of the nationalist government.

Our struggle has reached a decisive moment: We call on our people to seize this moment, so that the process toward democracy is rapid and uninterrupted.

We have waited too long for our freedom. We can no longer wait. Now is the time to intensify the struggle on all fronts. To relax our efforts now would be a mistake which generations to come will not be able to forgive.

40    The sight of freedom looming on the horizon should encourage us to redouble our efforts. It is only through disciplined mass action that our victory can be assured.

We call on our white compatriots to join us in the shaping of a new South Africa. The freedom movement is a political home for you, too.

We call on the international community to continue the campaign to isolate the apartheid regime. To lift sanctions now would run the risk of aborting the process toward the complete eradication of apartheid.

Our march toward freedom is irreversible. We must not allow fear to stand in our way.

Universal suffrage on a common voters roll in a united, democratic and non-racial South Africa is the only way to peace and racial harmony.

45    In conclusion, I wish to go to my own words during my trial in 1964—they are as true today as they were then:

I have fought against white domination, and I have fought against black domination. I have cherished the ideal of a democratic and free society in which all persons live together in harmony and with equal opportunity. It is an ideal which I hope to live for and to achieve. But, if need be, it is an ideal for which I am prepared to die.

An analysis of the rhetorical situation for this speech would look like this:

**Topic.** In this speech on apartheid, Mandela declares that the anti-apartheid movement must continue until "the ideal of a democratic and free society" is accomplished.

**Audience.** Although 500,000 people attended Mandela's speech in Cape Town, South Africa, his actual audience was much larger because the speech was broadcast live by the world press. Indeed, Mandela counted on the support of people around the world to help him achieve his purpose.

**Purpose.** The purpose of Mandela's speech was to persuade. In addition to thanking those who supported him while he was in prison, Mandela wanted to gain international attention for his movement and encourage his supporters to continue the struggle to end apartheid.

**Genre.** The genre of a speech is common in political situations in which people are gathering to support a cause. A speech may resemble an essay on paper, but a speech usually contains shorter sentences, plenty of repetition, and what is known as the "rule of three." To help listeners remember what is being said, speakers tend to group thoughts into threes to make them easier to keep in mind. An example of the "rule of three" in Mandela's speech is "I greet you all in the name of peace, democracy and freedom for all."

**Visual Design.** We usually think of visual design in relation to a text, but visual design also relates to public displays. In this case, Mandela was speaking on the steps of the Cape Town City Hall, which added political legitimacy to his speech.

**Exigence.** As the best-known leader of the anti-apartheid movement at that time, Mandela spoke to draw international attention to the cause. He wanted to attract more support and also encourage people who had been working in the movement for years, at great sacrifice, to continue the struggle.

**Constraints.** The half a million people in Mandela's immediate audience waited for hours for him to arrive and so many were restless, with a few beginning to clash with riot police. Once on stage, Mandela had to focus his audience's attention on what he had to say.

The rhetorical situation of Mandela's speech illustrates how the different parts of the rhetorical situation—audience, purpose, genre, visual design, exigence, and constraints—blend to have an impact on the audience. Each part connects to another

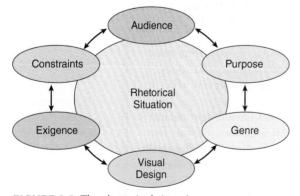

**FIGURE 2.2** The rhetorical situation

<br><br><br>

part and affects the rhetorical situation as a whole. Effective communication occurs within this web of connections.

In contrast, here is a review of the 2009 movie *Invictus* about Nelson Mandela's life. Notice how the rhetorical situation differs from Mandela's speech.

# Final Score: Future 1, Past 0

## A. O. Scott

Published:
December 11, 2009

It may not seem obvious at first, but Clint Eastwood's "Invictus," a rousing true story of athletic triumph, is also that director's latest exploration of revenge, the defining theme of his career. It is hard to think of an actor or a filmmaker who so clearly embodies a single human impulse in the way that Mr. Eastwood—from "Pale Rider" to "Mystic River," from Dirty Harry to "Gran Torino"—personifies the urge to get even.

He has also, of course, taken a critical view of the drive for vengeance, investigating its tragic roots and terrible consequences. A movie like "Unforgiven," most famously, suggests that violent revenge is regrettable. But rarely, in the world of Mr. Eastwood's films, is it avoidable.

"Invictus" is to some degree an exception, a movie about reconciliation and forgiveness—about the opposite of revenge—that gains moral authority precisely because the possibility of bloodshed casts its shadow everywhere. The film, based on John Carlin's book "Playing the Enemy," takes place in South Africa in the mid-1990s, just after Nelson Mandela's election as the country's first black president. Many of the whites in the film—most of them Afrikaner nationalists still attached to a system that kept their black compatriots poor, disenfranchised and oppressed—brace themselves for payback as Mandela assumes power. Quite a few of the president's black supporters expect it, too, as their due after decades of brutality and humiliation under apartheid.

But Mandela, played with gravity, grace and a crucial spark of mischief by Morgan Freeman, knows that score-settling would be a disastrous course for a new and fragile democracy. Passing by a newsstand on the morning after his victory, he spots a headline in Afrikaans. He has shown that he can win an election, it says, but will he show that he can govern? His bodyguards bristle at a pre-emptive low blow from a hostile press, but Mandela shrugs. "It's a fair question," he says.

5    And a perennially urgent one in any democracy. Mr. Eastwood and the screenwriter, Anthony Peckham, are too absorbed in the details of the story at hand to suggest historical analogies, but "Invictus" has implications beyond its immediate time and place that are hard to miss. It's an exciting sports movie, an inspiring tale of prejudice overcome and, above all, a fascinating study of political leadership.

But much of the ingenuity in Mr. Freeman's performance lies in the way he conveys that idealism and the shrewd manipulation of symbols and emotions are not incompatible, but complementary. Taking power a few years after being released from 27 years of incarceration, Mandela is already a larger-than-life figure, an idol in South Africa and around the world. His celebrity is something of a burden, and also an asset he must learn to use; his moral prestige is a political weapon.

But he is preoccupied, to the dismay of loyalists in his movement, with finding some kind of concord—not friendship, necessarily, but at least a state of non-enmity—with the people who hate and fear him: the whites who see him as a terrorist, a usurper and a threat to their traditions and values. Mandela's overtures to the Afrikaners—starting with his refusal to dismiss white members of the presidential staff and security detail—arise partly out of Gandhian principle, and partly out of political calculation. They are a powerful force in the army, the police and the South African economy.

Mandela's aides—in particular Brenda Mazibuko (Adjoa Andoh)—are baffled when he takes up the cause of the South African rugby team, a symbol of stiff-necked Afrikaner pride despised by most blacks. The team's Springbok mascot, named for a kind of gazelle, and its green-and-gold uniforms are nearly as loathsome as the apartheid flag, and when Mandela insists that the colors be retained, it seems almost like a betrayal of his life's cause. South Africa, a pariah in the world of international sports for a long time ("the skunk of the world," as Mandela puts it), is preparing to host the Rugby World Cup, and Mandela decides that if the nation is to find unity and self-respect the underachieving Springboks must win the championship.

And so an alliance develops between the president and François Pienaar, the Springbok captain, played with crisp, disciplined understatement (and utter mastery of a devilishly tricky accent) by Matt Damon. Pienaar's struggle to keep control of his team, and also to persuade them to accept some perplexing new social realities, is a microcosm of Mandela's larger project. And he quietly accepts Mandela, who shares with Pienaar the Victorian poem that gives the movie its title, as a mentor.

10    Beyond the politician, Mr. Freeman and Mr. Eastwood allow us glimpses of a complicated and somewhat melancholy man, carrying the loneliness of his long imprisonment with him and estranged from much

of his family. He is gracious and charming in small groups, a stiff but compelling public speaker and a boss whose authority is buttressed by a phalanx of devoted, sometimes skeptical aides.

But if "Invictus" is predominantly an absorbing character study of one of the most extraordinary characters of our time, it is also fleshed out with well-sketched minor players and subplots that illuminate the progress of racial rapprochement in its comic human dimension. The black bodyguards and their white colleagues proceed from hostility to wary tolerance to guarded warmth in a way that is pointed without being overstated. And that, for the most part, characterizes Mr. Eastwood's direction, which is always unassuming, unhurried and efficient. In this film he tells a big story through a series of small, well-observed moments, and tells it in his usual blunt, matter-of-fact way, letting the nuances take care of themselves.

And once again, as in "Letters From Iwo Jima"—a tragic rather than heroic inquiry into the nature of leadership—they do. "Invictus" is more sprawling than that film, and more willing to risk hokiness. That is a chance Mr. Eastwood is often happy to take, and no genre is more susceptible to it (or earns it more honestly) than the victorious-underdog team-sports movie. That the sport is as alien to most Americans as it is to black South Africans presents its challenges, but by the end you might care about rugby more than you thought you would, even if it remains harder to understand than politics.

The convergence of the two provides an occasion for some potent, intelligent filmmaking—a movie that hits you squarely with its visceral impact and stays in your mind for a long time after.

An analysis of the rhetorical situation for this movie review would look like this:

**Audience.** Scott's review is available online through the *New York Times* website. As a result, Scott potentially has an even broader audience for his review of the movie *Invictus* than Mandela had for his actual speech.

**Purpose.** The purpose of Scott's review is to persuade. Unlike Mandela who wanted to inspire the people of an entire nation to act, Scott simply wants to encourage his readers to see the movie.

**Genre.** The format of the movie review usually has longer, more developed paragraphs than a speech format. Because this is a newspaper article, though, the paragraphs are often still shorter than those in an essay.

**Visual Design.** Because this movie review is in print, the visual design follows the conventions of the *New York Times* review columns.

**Exigence.** A. O. Scott is a film reviewer for the *New York Times* and so regularly reviews films for his employer. He loves movies, but it's his job that keeps him writing about them.

**Constraints.** Readers of newspapers tend to scan articles quickly, so Scott must write an interesting review to keep his readers' attention.

# WRITING ASSIGNMENT

Find one speech, essay, newspaper article, movie review, brochure, or short video and write a one- to two-page essay in which you analyze the rhetorical situation. You may choose a favorite piece from a class you have already taken, a newspaper that you read daily, or you may go to the library or Internet to select one. Find a piece that interests you and that you would like to spend some time thinking about. It isn't necessary to summarize the piece; instead, respond to these questions:

1. What is the topic and main point?
2. Who is the intended audience?
3. What is the author's primary purpose: to express, inform, or persuade?
4. From the list at the beginning of this assignment, which genre did you choose? Why did you choose this particular piece to analyze?
5. Does the piece use special text fonts, color, borders, and images such as illustrations and photos? Why do you think the author used these in the piece?
6. Why did the author write on this topic? Does the author explain this in the piece? If not, can you hypothesize why?
7. What constraints, if any, does the author state interfered with writing this piece?
8. How effective is this piece to you as a reader? What do you like about it? What could still be improved?

mycomplab

For support in meeting this chapter's objectives, follow this path in MyCompLab: Resources ⇒ Writing ⇒ Writing Process ⇒ Planning. Review the Instruction and Multimedia resources about topic and thesis, then complete the Exercises and click on Gradebook to measure your progress.

# CHAPTER

# 3 Writing Process

**Learning Objectives**

In this chapter you will:

- Learn a widely used writing process.
- See how a student has used the process to write a paper.
- Consider how you might use this writing process.

*This student begins to write her paper. How does this compare to the way you would begin to write?*

I t's easy to think of writing as simply writing on a yellow tablet or entering text into a word processor. In reality, though, it isn't that simple, especially if you want a well-written document. To write effectively, you must write in stages. Each of these stages represents the critical thinking that you do to ensure that your writing communicates to your audience. With experience and practice, you will learn the process that works best for you. This chapter will introduce you to a widely used writing process that includes these stages:

- discovering ideas
- drafting to explore ideas
- revising to improve content
- editing for correctness

Whether you pass through every stage of this process depends partly on your audience and purpose. If you're jotting down a message to a friend, for example, you might write "Singapore Cafe" knowing that she will understand that you want her to make a reservation at your favorite restaurant. Your purpose is to convey simple information to someone who will easily understand it, so there is no need to go through a complete writing process.

However, imagine yourself writing an email letter to your manager to request a raise. First, you gather ideas for why you deserve a raise, write a draft of your letter, and read it to a colleague or friend who suggests how you might improve it. Then you rewrite the letter, perhaps several times, taking out unnecessary details and more forcefully restating why you deserve a raise. You proofread the letter for correct spelling, punctuation, and grammar. Finally, you do one last check of the entire process to ensure that you have done your very best writing. This could take several days, but you will have a well-written letter to present to your manager.

*The beautiful part of writing is that you don't have to get it right the first time—unlike, say, brain surgery.*

*—Robert Cormier*

The first two stages are the "creative" part of the writing process, when you discover what you know about a topic and put it into writing. The second two stages are the "critical" part, when you review what you have written to improve the content and eliminate any spelling, punctuation, and grammar errors. While you're in the creative stages, resist the urge to be too critical. What's most important is to get your ideas down. There will be time later to revise and edit your writing.

**Activity 3.1**   Draw a picture of yourself. Depending on your skill, you might draw a stick figure, a cartoon, or a detailed life drawing. Here is an example of a drawing done by one student.

Compare your drawing to the drawings done by your classmates and answer the following questions:

1. Why is there such a range of drawing abilities in this class?
2. If you wanted to improve your drawing ability, what would you need to do?
3. Describe the role that motivation, instruction, and practice play in developing your ability to draw.
4. How does improving your ability to draw compare with improving your ability to write?

**Connect With Others**

# DISCOVERING IDEAS

In Chapter 2, you learned how to choose a topic, narrow it, and analyze the rhetorical situation. Now that you have selected a topic, you may find that you need help finding and organizing ideas for it. Imagine, for example, that you must write an essay for your composition class, but you're not quite sure where to begin. There are a number of ways to help you discover ideas, including mapping, charting, listing, freewriting, questioning, using key words, and outlining. Student writer Shepherd Smith used several of these methods to discover ideas for an essay on American Sign Language. (Not all writers use all of these strategies to discover ideas. With practice, you'll discover which strategies work best for you.) A friend of his who was studying to be an ASL interpreter took him to a meeting of the local Deaf community. Shepherd was fascinated and so decided to learn more about this topic for his composition essay.

**LANGUAGES and CULTURES**
People who self-identify as belonging to the Deaf community or Deaf culture capitalize the word *Deaf* when they refer to themselves or others in their community. The Deaf community has identified American Sign Language (ASL) as their preferred way of communicating.

## Mapping

Mapping is a strategy that involves developing a visual representation of your topic. In addition to helping you visualize your ideas and details, it helps you to begin to organize your material. To map, write down your topic in the middle of a page or computer screen and place a circle around it. Write down specific ideas about that topic, circle them, and draw lines to connect them to the larger circle. Here is how a map of the topic "American Sign Language" might begin:

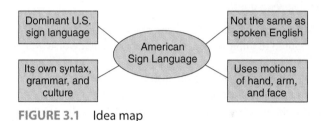

**FIGURE 3.1**   Idea map

## Charting

Similar to mapping, a chart is also a visual representation, but it shows how ideas relate to each other from beginning to end. Most often used when describing a process, you develop a chart by describing the steps involved. Here is how Shepherd might start a chart on how to learn American Sign Language:

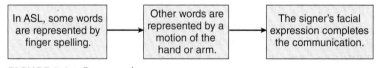

**FIGURE 3.2**   Process chart

## Listing

If you're not sure how you want to organize your thoughts, but just want to get them on paper, try listing. Also known as brainstorming, simply list in words or phrases what you already know about your topic. Shepherd used listing to record his observations at the local Deaf community meeting he attended:

- Proper nouns are communicated by finger spelling.
- Each letter of the English alphabet has a sign representation.
- People in Deaf circles are given a Deaf name by their friends.
- Deaf names are made up of the sign for the first letter of the name combined with a motion that describes the person.

# Freewriting

Freewriting helps you start putting your thoughts on paper in preparation for writing a complete draft. Write on your topic in complete sentences without stopping for a certain period of time or until you have reached a certain word limit. After discussing his observations of the Deaf community meeting with his friend, Shepherd used freewriting to connect more deeply with his topic:

> Getting immersed in signing was pretty intense! I walked in not even knowing my name in ASL, and by the end of the night I knew the alphabet, and about 40 other common words like dog, father, busy, etc. I learned how to spell my name pretty quickly, but apparently in the community there are "Deaf names" that have to be given to you by someone in the community. It's just the fingerspelling for the first letter of your name with a motion to go along with it. The name of one of the guys there started with an S, and his was the S on his chest, like superman! It was pretty cool. Apparently they meet pretty frequently, and are all pretty involved with each other. It looked like everyone was having a blast.

> You can tell that they have been signing for a while, because they sign so fast! It's hard even for one of my more experienced friends to keep up sometimes. Also, there isn't just one way to say something like in English. You can combine different signs with different expressions to mean totally different things. Much like people use certain words to be clever or funny, a certain sign can make or break a joke. Most of it was totally over my head, but I got some explained to me. I didn't even know that there were different kinds of sign language, but it varies from country to country, and even region to region in the U.S. I think ASL is the most popular though.

# Questioning

You might recognize this discovery strategy from journalism or even criminal justice procedures. With this strategy, you ask yourself a series of questions about the topic, such as Who? What? When? Where? Why? How? Here are examples of questions that Shepherd used to follow up on his preliminary inquiries:

1. Who uses ASL? Do all Deaf people use it?
2. What are the characteristics of ASL?
3. When do people learn to use it?
4. Where can I learn more about ASL?
5. Why is it important for others to know about ASL?
6. How does ASL help Deaf people communicate?

Key words:
The most
important
words that
describe your
topic.

# Using Key Words and Phrases

Learning to describe your topic with key words and phrases is especially useful if you plan to use library databases or conduct online research. For help finding information on using a key word search, Shepherd asked the reference librarian at his campus library for advice on his topic. The librarian suggested that Shepherd start with these key words and phrases:

- American Sign Language
- sign language
- deafness
- demography
- population

# Outlining

If you already have a good idea of what you want to say, you may want to organize your ideas into a traditional outline. Here is an early draft of Shepherd's outline:

I. History of ASL
   A. Historical beginnings
   B. Progression to current day
II. English/ASL Comparison
   A. Syntax
   B. Signs and delivery vs. vocal tone and inflection
   C. Fingerspelling
III. ASL as Culture
   A. Deaf names
   B. Different types of signs
   C. Deaf community
IV. Conclusion

You don't have to use every method of discovering ideas every time you write. Try the methods that you think will work best for you. For example, you might begin by listing all that you know about the topic or creating a map to begin organizing your thoughts. Questioning authorities on the topic can help you fill in the gaps. Use as many of these methods as you need to get ideas for your topic.

# DRAFTING TO EXPLORE IDEAS

 Draft: Writing the first version.

Now that you have discovered ideas, begin to draft your paper, focusing on gathering more ideas if needed and organizing them without too much concern about sentence structure, word choice, spelling, punctuation, or grammar. This is especially important if English is not your first or only language. For this first draft, use the language that you feel most comfortable with, and don't let your fear of making a spelling or grammatical error keep you from expressing your ideas. Drafting styles vary widely. Some writers draft quickly and spend considerable time revising, while others draft slowly and write fewer drafts. While using this textbook, you will experiment to see which method of drafting works best for you.

**Activity 3.2** In discussion with your classmates, share what you know about your own writing process. Where and when do you write best? Do you observe any rituals such as using a favorite chair or having a thesaurus handy? Do you draft quickly or slowly? Do you prefer drafting on a yellow pad or do you sit down at your computer right away? How will this process affect the way you write in this class?

As you draft, refer to the rhetorical analysis you did in Chapter 2. Pay close attention to the genre and visual design you chose and use that format to help shape your draft. For example, if you're writing an essay, you will use this format, including this heading on the first page:

## Connect With Others

[1" margins all around]

Your Name

Instructor's Name

Class Information

Date

Title (Centered)

Introduction (includes thesis statement)

Body Paragraphs (includes topic sentences)

Conclusion

**Introduction.**   The introduction to your essay serves two purposes. First, it gets your readers' attention. Second, your introduction usually announces your thesis statement, the sentence or sentences that state the topic of your essay. By presenting your thesis statement as part of your introduction, your readers know what to expect from your essay.

---

### Introduce Your Essay

- Begin with an interesting anecdote.
- State a startling fact or statistic.
- Use an effective quotation.
- Ask a question.

---

**Thesis Statement.**   Your thesis statement forecasts what your essay will be about, enabling your readers to focus attention on the main idea.

---

### Write a Thesis Statement

- State the topic of your essay.
- Indicate why the topic is important.
- Forecast the focus and main points of your essay.

---

**Body Paragraphs.**   Each body paragraph includes a topic sentence that serves as the main point of the paragraph, followed by information, including details, facts, and examples that support the topic sentence. Typically, each paragraph describes one of your essay's main points in detail. You decide how many body paragraphs you need based on how many main points are required to support your thesis statement.

---

### Draft Body Paragraphs

- Include a topic sentence in each paragraph.
- Use each paragraph to provide specific detail to support the topic sentence.
- Conclude each paragraph with a transitional sentence to the next paragraph.

---

**Conclusion.** In the conclusion, you write an effective closure for your essay so that your readers know that you are coming to the end. When writing a conclusion, don't make the mistake of introducing new material or ending too abruptly. Instead, wrap up what you have already said.

---

### Conclude Your Essay

- Restate the thesis statement.
- Provide a summary.
- Make a recommendation.
- Include a call for action.

---

## Your Emotional Filter

As you learned in Chapter 1, your past writing experience will have an impact on your writing now. As you begin to draft, ask yourself if there are emotions such as anxiety or a lack of concern about the assignment that might hinder your drafting of this piece. If you find that your emotional filter is preventing you from drafting, review the ways to control your emotional filter.

---

### Control Your Emotional Filter

- Go back and gather more ideas so that you feel adequately prepared and less worried.
- Plan to work in stages, knowing that effective writers seldom plan to finish a piece of writing in one session.
- Don't wait for inspiration. Force yourself to begin drafting.
- Pretend that you're writing to a friend who won't judge you and who will be interested in everything you write.

---

## Your Writing Monitor

Almost every writer knows what it's like to be at a loss for words: when you can't think of what to say, you don't know the right words, or you can't slow down your thoughts enough to focus on one idea. It's as if you drove your car into a ditch and the wheels just kept on turning without touching the ground. When you feel stuck, you can use several techniques to get yourself *un*stuck. To begin, you need to understand why you're stuck in the first place.

Sometimes writers are too conscious of their monitor. Your monitor is your awareness of what someone will think of your writing. If you sit down to write and immediately worry about what grade you will receive or if your boss will approve your request for a raise, your monitor is too active. This worrying can keep you from focusing on your message.

Sometimes writers get stuck because they can't think of how to express an idea in standard English. Your thoughts come quickly in a slang language or in another language altogether, but trying to transform them into standard English blocks the flow of your thoughts. If this happens to you, go ahead and write in the language that is easiest to use. This way, you have a record of your ideas without feeling pressured to produce the right words or correct grammar. Suppose you're writing about the need to improve computer efficiency on your campus. If you are computer savvy, you might use computer slang to get your ideas on paper. Later you can revise to choose words that more readers would understand. Here is an example of computer slang:

> The admin has really messed up this computer lab! With peeps in here 24/7, we need work stations that won't barf as soon as someone starts to use them. We can bang out the problems on the front end, but we'll need a real expert to fix the back end. The software is too bleeding edge for most students anyway. Let's face it, we could use some real chipheads in here.

You can also alternate languages. For instance, suppose you're writing about the need to increase recycling in your neighborhood but you can't think of the English word for "bin" as in "recycle bin." Simply write the word in the language that you know. Later you can find the correct word in English. Here is an example of this strategy:

> I think plastic bags in la marqueta pollute the planet and we should outlaw them. I don't know the numbers off the top of my head pero I know a lot of bags are blown all over and they probably don't disintegrate much. I see them all over the place. Even high in the trees. Why not bring back the brown paper bags? Who could pass leyas about plastic bags. City, state, Washington? I need to do mas research, pero this topic might be OK.

Finally, you might get stuck while you write because you have too many ideas in your head, making you feel frustrated and overwhelmed. As a result, you freeze up and can't write anything. When this happens, try to slow down your mind by taking deep breaths or listening to calming music. If this doesn't work, do something physical for a while—wash the dishes, take a walk—and then return to your writing. The physical activity reduces your anxiety and gives you a better focus. Once you have your emotional filter and monitor under control, you are ready to resume drafting.

## Control Your Monitor

- Try to stay in touch with your ideas rather than worry about how you are expressing yourself.
- Skip the introduction for now. You can come back to it when you're finished.
- Expect to have writing blocks, but develop ways to get around them.
- Remind yourself that you have plenty of time to revise and edit your writing before you give it to your readers.

# One Student's Work

Here is the first draft of Shepherd Smith's essay on American Sign Language. You will notice that many of his discovery ideas have found their way into this draft. You may also notice errors in spelling, punctuation, or grammar. Shepherd will correct these when he edits his paper later.

### ASL

Sign language is "a formal language employing a system of hand gestures for communication (as by the deaf)" (Merriam Webster). American Sign Language, commonly abbreviated ASL, is the dominant sign language in Deaf communities in the United States. ASL is not the same as spoken English, and has its own syntax, grammar, and culture.

Almost all words in ASL are represented by a motion mainly using the body and face. Unlike spoken English, a sentence in ASL does not involve communicating every single word. The meaning of the sign relies on the signer's facial expression and the execution of the motion. For example, the sign Guess is very similar to the sign Miss. They both look like someone trying to catch a ball, and missing. Which meaning is taken from the motion depends on the context, and facial expression. In English, someone would say, "Do you guys have any butter?" In ASL, the motion for butter (scraping the middle and index finger of the dominant hand on the opposing palm) would be used with a questioning expression, roughly translating to "Butter, no?" The syntax is quite different than English. The sentence structure of ASL is Subject-Verb-Object ("ASL University"). People who use signing will still understand regardless of the order, but some will insist that you do it the right way. It is similar to people who have not grown up with English mixing up the order of the words, or substituting in the wrong tenses or subjects.

Not every word has a single sign to go along with it. Proper nouns are communicated by fingerspelling. Each letter of the English alphabet has a sign representation. For names, cities, or any word that is unclear fingerspelling is used to physically spell out the word letter by letter. Sometimes even if a word has a sign associated with it, it is spelled out anyway for added emphasis. It is common for people within Deaf circles to be given a Deaf name. It takes too long to fingerspell out a person's name every time they are referenced, so instead the name is replaced with the sign for the first letter of the name combined with a motion that is specific to the person. For example, my friend Melissa's Deaf name is the letter M combined with the motion of bringing the letter up to the side of her mouth, because she smiles and talks a lot. You cannot give yourself a Deaf name; it has to be given to you by someone in the Deaf community.

Despite the differences between ASL and English most people pick up a few words here and there. The Deaf community is for the most part very welcoming of other people who are learning to speak their language. ASL is easy to pick up, but it takes a long time to master. Unless someone is directly involved in a Deaf community, they usually have to go to school to really get a grasp of the language. There are many different kinds of signs, and most of them are not very easy to interpret. Some are obvious, and could be understood even by those who do not know ASL, but most are not intuitive.

Even though most people don't know the difference between ASL and the other types of sign language it is still very prominently used in the United States. It's a great and effective way for those who are deaf to communicate, and it has even become a culture that binds them together.

# REVISING TO IMPROVE CONTENT

When you revise, you improve the development, organization, sentence structure, and word choice to ensure that your writing communicates effectively for the audience you have chosen.

## Review the Rhetorical Situation

To help you revise, set aside your writing for a day or two, reread, and then rewrite it. As you reread, review the rhetorical situation to help you improve your draft.

## Rhetorical Situation Review

- Topic: Have you selected a topic that interests you and that will be of interest to your readers?
- Audience: Reread your introduction, thesis statement, conclusion, and the first sentence of each paragraph. Do they meet the needs of your audience? Have you narrowed the topic sufficiently to appeal to your readers? Have you taken your readers' culture into account while writing?
- Purpose: Have you included enough detail to express, inform, and/or persuade? Develop those paragraphs that need additional detail.
- Genre: Check the format and consider improving the appearance of the document by adding visuals.
- Exigence: Why is it important for you to communicate on this topic? Why should you put it in writing?
- Constraints: What has prevented you from communicating effectively on this topic? Develop a plan for overcoming these remaining constraints.

Asking others for help, a strategy known as peer review, can be more effective than simply rereading your own draft over and over. Ask friends, family, and fellow students to read your writing and answer questions about your draft.

Peer review: To read someone else's work and make suggestions for revision.

Following is an example of a peer review sheet that you might use:

## Peer Review

1. What is this piece's greatest strength?

2. Is the piece adequately developed? Is it interesting to read? Where might the author add details to improve it?

3. Has the author expressed ideas logically and clearly? Which sections or sentences would you like the author to clarify?

4. Where might the author add transitions to help you move from one idea to another?

5. Do you feel that you know more about this topic after reading this piece? What more would you like to know about it?

6. Underline any words or sentences that the author should revise because they do not communicate effectively to you.

7. Place a checkmark in the margin next to any spelling or punctuation errors that you discover while reading this essay. (Please do not correct errors for the writer.)

## LANGUAGES and CULTURES

What happens when native and nonnative speakers of English are in the same peer review group? Researcher Wei Zhu conducted a study on this topic published in the *Journal of Second Language Writing* in 2001. She found that nonnative speakers tended to speak less, both in terms of the number of times and the length of time that they spoke. They also tended to volunteer feedback less often than the native English speakers. On the other hand, the feedback they gave was as good and useful as the feedback given by the native English speakers. This was a small study, so we can't assume that this happens in all peer review groups. However, this study suggests that both native and nonnative speakers of English can give equally helpful feedback to their classmates in peer review groups. No matter what your language background, it's important to speak up and listen carefully to what others have to say.

Your instructor may also ask you to read other classmates' writing and provide suggestions for improvement. When reviewing others' writing, it's important to provide meaningful feedback that focuses on the communication and how well the message is matched to the audience needs. Starting with a positive comment will put the author in the proper frame of mind to receive the constructive criticism to follow. This is particularly important if English is not the author's first language since the author's monitor is probably already high. Resist the urge to correct spelling, punctuation, and grammar errors. Also, keep the intended audience, purpose, and genre in mind as you review. Often you will have the opportunity to review your classmates' papers online where you can answer peer review questions and submit them to a course website or email them to the author.

Once peer review is complete, you will also be able to read other reviewers' comments of your paper and begin revising your draft, considering the following areas for improvement: development, organization, coherence, and vocabulary.

## Improving Development

As you revise, look at your draft to see if you need to add more information so that your readers will find it interesting and informative. During peer review, for example, one or more of your readers may have asked for clarification of something you wrote. This is an indication that you should develop this section.

Development: Greater detail on a topic.

### Ways to Develop an Essay

- Narration: relate a series of events: chronological, flashback, dialogue.
- Description: create an image by using the five senses.
- Examples: provide an illustration, facts, statistics.
- Process: describe how it works.
- Definition: tell what it means.
- Comparison and contrast: show similarities/differences.
- Classification: categorize into types.
- Cause and effect: explain why something happened.

# Improving Organization

When drafting, you must put your ideas in some order. In the United States, the expectation is that the organization will move your readers quickly and logically from your first paragraph to the last to make it easier for your readers to understand your message. As you revise, look again at the overall organization to ensure that each paragraph supports the thesis statement. Also consider how each paragraph is organized. Following are examples of three paragraph patterns.

**Directional Order.** Describe something from left to right or top to bottom:

> Using the drop-down boxes, you can customize who gets to see your info: "Only Friends," "Friends of Friends," or "My Network of Friends." To lock down your profile to friends only, you could set all these to "only friends." But since you have now created specialized lists, you'll want to use these instead. To do so, click the fourth option from the drop-down box: "Customize." From here, you can add lists of people who should NOT be able to see this part of your profile. For example, if you wanted to block a list of work colleagues or those in your family from seeing your status updates, you could do so here—just type the name of your list in the box "Except these people" and save your changes.
>
> —*Sarah Perez, "How to Friend Mom, Dad, and the Boss on Facebook . . . Safely"*

**Chronological Order.** State the events in the order that they actually happened:

> Even during the 1950s, when U.S. industry was a powerhouse, progressive policies were what spurred the expansion of the middle class—through the GI Bill, commitment to homeownership and the passage of the minimum wage. Those same initiatives created a more just society, which in turn helped foster the civil-rights movement, the women's movement and the environmental movement. America's future vibrancy depends on renewing those commitments for Latinos.
>
> —*Henry Cisneros, "A Fence Can't Stop the Future"*

**Order of Importance.** Arrange sentences within the paragraph from most to least important:

> Getting students to redirect their energy inward and to lower their ambitions is a sensible strategy, and if the government keeps up its job-creation efforts, it just might manage to keep the Chinese Dream alive, albeit in dog-eared form. Leaders are taking numerous steps in the right direction; besides the stimulus package, local governments are enhancing their student job fairs and organizing internships, for instance. But China's heady get-rich-quick days are

probably over. Future graduates will be joining a sophisticated white-collar job market in a far more cyclical economy. In all likelihood, they'll still achieve a better living standard than their parents and be able to take care of them in their old age. Yet the fat years are over, and Chinese leaders need to help college grads adjust their expectations accordingly.

*—Mary Hinnock, "To Save the Chinese Dream"*

Which have you used? How can you improve your writing by considering these paragraph patterns?

Another way to improve organization is to add transitions. Transitional words and phrases help your readers move from idea to idea smoothly. As you revise, read your draft from your readers' viewpoint. Where might transitional words and phrases help your readers more fully understand your message?

---

### Transitional Words and Phrases

- To add one idea to another: in addition, moreover, besides, also
- To compare ideas: similarly, in the same way, likewise
- To contrast ideas: however, nevertheless, although, in contrast, on the other hand
- To show result: as a result, since, therefore, consequently, accordingly
- To show an example: for example, for instance, to illustrate, specifically
- To summarize: therefore, in conclusion, consequently, accordingly, in other words

---

## Improving Coherence

Coherent: Easy to read and understand.

Your writing is coherent if your audience is able to see the relationship between your thesis statement and the ideas in the following paragraphs. Coherence also means that each paragraph is unified, with the sentences within a paragraph supporting the topic sentence of that paragraph. Review your writing from the readers' perspective. Can your readers move from idea to idea effortlessly? Which is the thesis statement? Which sentence in each paragraph is the topic sentence? Does every other sentence in the paragraph support the topic sentence, and do the topic sentences support the thesis statement? If not, revise or remove the sentences that do not. To check the coherence of your draft, create a map or an outline of it. Does the map or outline reveal a clear thought pattern?

As you revise your essay for coherence, also look more closely at your sentence length to determine whether you have written them in an interesting way. You are more likely to keep your readers' attention if you vary your sentence length and use a variety of sentence patterns.

# Word Choice

During revision, review your choice of words to determine how effectively they communicate to your audience.

## Word Choice

- Tell your readers something they don't already know.
- Choose an appropriate tone for your purpose and audience.
- Use common words: "face" instead of "visage," "read" instead of "peruse."
- Review any jargon or slang expressions such as "LOL," "24/7," or "heads up" to ensure that your intended audience will know what they mean.
- Avoid clichés, overused expressions.
- Eliminate wordiness.
- Use bias-free language.

**Activity 3.3**   Select an article from a newspaper website and analyze it for coherence and word choice. How could the author improve these to improve the communication?

**Develop Your Understanding**

# EDITING FOR CORRECTNESS

You edit to check for correctness by looking for errors in spelling, punctuation, and grammar. Since you have worked so hard to express your ideas, don't spoil the effect with distracting errors. Too many errors will cause your readers to pay attention to the errors instead of what you have to say.

## How to Edit

- Use a dictionary or computer spell check.
- Refer to the handbook section of this book or a grammar handbook and follow standard grammatical rules.
- Ask another student or writing tutor to read your writing for errors.
- As you edit, keep a section in your class notebook where you record the errors that you made on past assignments. Make a point of not repeating these errors.

Once you complete these writing process stages, look over what you have done one more time to determine if there is anything more you can do to improve the writing before you turn it over to the audience. When evaluating your own writing, it might be helpful to know what others, such as your instructors, are looking for when they read. Use this checklist to help you evaluate your writing.

## Writer's Checklist

**Rhetorical analysis and development**

☐ Followed instructions for the assignment.

☐ Selected and analyzed an appropriate audience.

☐ Determined your primary and secondary purposes for writing.

☐ Selected the appropriate genre.

☐ Made the important points you wish to communicate.

**Organization**

☐ Introduced your topic in a way that engages the readers.

☐ Used clear topic sentences.

☐ Organized your ideas logically.

☐ Wrote cohesive paragraphs.

☐ Included summary sentences at the end of paragraphs.

☐ Wrote a conclusion that provides a sense of closure.

☐ Used transitional words and phrases to guide your readers.

**Correctness**

☐ Wrote in clear, concise sentences.

☐ Used standard English.

☐ Used appropriate tone for your audience.

☐ Eliminated errors in spelling, punctuation, and grammar.

If you're proud of what you have written, you will be eager to share it with your intended audience. Your instructor may ask you to share your writing in a more public way by reading it aloud in class or sending it to your school or area newspaper. You might also publish your work by emailing it to interested readers or making it available on a blog or other website.

As you use this writing process, you will discover additional ways to discover ideas, draft, revise, and edit your writing. You will probably find that your process does not always follow these stages exactly. Instead, you will move back and forth among them until you achieve a finished piece of writing that effectively matches your message to the audience for which it is intended.

# ONE STUDENT'S WORK

Here is the final version of Shepherd Smith's essay on American Sign Language. You'll notice that he has developed, revised, and edited for correctness.

Smith 1

Shepherd Smith

Professor Tammie Bob

English 1101 Composition

2 November 2009

American Sign Language

The Deaf culture has come a long way since the Middle Ages when "people born deaf could not have faith, could not be saved and were barred from churches" ("Deaf"). The deaf couldn't even buy a home or get married until the 18th century. Around that time, signing emerged not only as a distinct language but also as a subculture, with its own customs and patterns. Contrary to popular belief, there is not one universal sign language. Sign language is "a formal language employing a system of hand gestures for communication (as by the deaf)" ("Merriam-Webster"). American Sign Language, commonly abbreviated ASL, is the dominant sign language in Deaf communities in the United States. ASL is not the same as spoken English, and has its own syntax, grammar, and culture.

Almost all words in ASL are represented by a motion mainly using the hands, arms, and face. Unlike spoken English, a sentence in ASL does not involve communicating every single word. The meaning of the sign relies heavily on the signer's facial expression and how they execute the motion. For example, the sign *guess* is very similar to the sign *miss*. They both look like someone trying to catch a ball, and missing. Which meaning is understood from the motion depends on both context and facial expression. Signs usually encompass more than one "word."

Essay double-spaced throughout.

Title centered.

Introduction gets readers' attention.

Thesis statement forecasts what the essay will be about.

Smith 2

It takes much longer for one sign to be completed than for one word to be spoken. However, because several meanings can be expressed by the facial expression, sign used, and other factors like which direction the sign is pointing, ASL and English take about the same amount of time to complete a sentence. In English, someone would say, "Do you guys have any butter?" In ASL, the motion for butter (scraping the middle and index finger of the dominant hand on the opposing palm) would be used with a questioning expression, roughly translating to "Butter, no?" The syntax is quite different than English. The sentence structure of ASL is Subject-Verb-Object ("ASL Linguistics"). People who use signing will still understand regardless of the order, but some will insist that you do it the right way. It is similar to people who have not grown up with English mixing up the order of the words, or substituting in the wrong tenses or subjects.

Not every word has a single sign to go along with it. Proper nouns are communicated by finger spelling. As illustrated in Fig. 1, each letter of the English alphabet has a sign representation.

Fig. 1 The American Manual Alphabet in Photos.

Source:   Cwterp. Wikipedia Commons,

http://en.wikipedia.org/wiki/File:ABC_pict.png.

*Body paragraphs include more detail than first draft.*

*Transitional sentence moves readers to new idea.*

*Graphic adds interest and information.*

Smith 3

For names, cities, or any word that is unclear, finger spelling is used to physically spell out the word letter by letter. Sometimes even if a word has a sign associated with it, it is spelled out anyway for added emphasis. It is common for people within Deaf circles to be given a Deaf name. It takes too long to fingerspell out a person's name every time they are referenced, so instead th name is replaced with the sign for the first letter of the name combined with a motion that is specific to the person. For example, my friend Melissa's Deaf name is the letter M combined with the motion of bringing the letter up to the side of her mouth, because she smiles and talks a lot. You cannot give yourself a Deaf name; it has to be given to you by someone in the Deaf community.

Within ASL, signs can be divided into three different categories: transparent, translucent, or opaque (Hinders). The meanings of transparent signs are easily guessed by non-signers. An example of a transparent sign would be the first person subject "I" where the signer simply points to himself, or the question "What time is it?" where the signer taps his finger on his wrist where a watch would be. The next group of signs, translucent, can make sense to non-signers, but only after they are explained. An example of a translucent sign would be "awake," where the signer puts both clenched hands next to his eyes, and points up with his index finger as he open his eyes, or "duck," where the signer makes a beak with his fingers and thumbs and opens it several times. Finally, the meanings of opaque signs are not guessable. An example of an opaque sign would be "basket," where the signer hits the wrist and then the elbow with an open palm, or "translate," where the signer taps together two fists, and then twists them and points in opposite directions. The majority of signs are opaque (Hinders).

Clear topic sentence forecasts what paragraph will be about.

Smith 4

Despite the differences between ASL and English most hearing people can pick up a few words of ASL here and there. The Deaf community is for the most part welcoming of other people who are learning to speak their language. ASL is easy to pick up, but it takes a long time to master. Unless someone is directly involved in a Deaf community, a person usually has to go to school to get a strong grasp of the language.

ASL is a vital part of the American Deaf community. It gives people with a disability the chance to fully function in a world that up until the last couple hundred years required the ability to hear. It is more than just a sign language; it is a unique culture that binds together Deaf communities all over the United States.

Conclusion sums up significance of ASL.

Smith 5

Works Cited

"ASL Linguistics: Syntax." *ASL University*. Lifeprint.com, n.d. Web.
    28 Oct. 2009.

"Deaf Time Line." *ASLinfo*. ASLInfo.com, n.d. Web. 28 Oct. 2009.

Hinders, Dana. "What Is American Sign Language?" wiseGEEK.
    Conjecture, n.d. Web. 28 Oct. 2009.

*Merriam-Webster Online*. Merriam-webster.com, n.d. Web. 28 Oct. 2009.

# WRITING ASSIGNMENT

Select a piece of writing that you have done for another class or in the work-place and by answering these questions, reflect on your own writing process:

1. What was the topic and who was the audience? Did you complete a rhetorical analysis before writing the piece? How well did you do in meeting your purpose for writing this piece?
2. What methods did you use to discover ideas for the topic? Did you gather enough information before you began to draft?
3. How did you draft the piece? What genre did you use? Did you add visuals?
4. Did you revise the piece before giving it to your readers? If yes, how did you go about revising? Did you ask anyone else to read your work before you revised it?
5. Did you edit it for correctness? What did you learn about the kinds of errors you make in your writing?
6. Based on this analysis of your writing process, what would you like to do to improve your writing in the future?

mycomplab

For support in meeting this chapter's objectives, follow this path in MyCompLab: Resources ⇒ Writing ⇒ Writing Process. Review the Instruction and Multimedia resources about the writing process, then complete the Exercises and click on Gradebook to measure your progress.

# 4 Reading

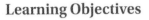

## Learning Objectives

In this chapter you will:

- Learn the purposes for reading.
- Practice critical reading strategies.
- Use reading to improve writing.
- Practice summarizing a text.
- Learn ways to improve your vocabulary.

*What are the advantages and disadvantages of using wireless reading devices?*

Just a decade or so ago, reading materials consisted of hard copies of books, magazines, or newspapers. Since then, new reading technologies have drastically altered people's reading processes. In 2008 the *New York Times* published "Literacy Debate: Online, R U Really Reading?" which examined how the different reading technologies are changing the ways that people read. Older readers tend to rely on print sources such as books, magazines, and newspapers, while younger readers use web-based sources. Some people claim that the proliferation of web-based material has decreased readers' attention spans and resulted in a more shallow reading experience. Others, however, say that because of electronic media more people are reading than ever before, which improves overall literacy rates. So which is better—traditional print reading or digital reading? Guess what: There is no right answer. What matters more than the medium you're using is *why* you're reading in the first place.

## LANGUAGES and CULTURES

For the most part, print and online texts in industrialized countries are plentiful. Public libraries ensure that reading materials are available to people from all economic backgrounds. In other parts of the world, however, access to texts in locally known languages can be severely limited. Because of this lack of access, people have fewer chances to learn to read at a level sufficient for educational advancement. The lack of books and other reading materials affects everyday life in many ways. For example, reading the directions on a bottle of medicine is impossible if you've never had enough reading materials to learn how to read.

# PURPOSES FOR READING

We read for many different (and often overlapping) reasons.

## Reading for Entertainment

Reading can be fun. A thriller, romance, or science fiction book lets you forget about your everyday existence by putting you in a different world. Additional benefits from reading for entertainment are that it can increase your reading speed, broaden your vocabulary, and increase your knowledge of sentence and paragraph structures. When you read for entertainment, you can choose how fast or slow you want to progress through the text.

## Reading to Interact with Others

When you read to interact, you check out what people have written to you on your phone or on the web, or in cards and letters. This type of reading helps to build relationships with others through exchanging information that can range from the very personal to the very mundane. Usually this type of reading is very fast—messages are short and easy to process.

## Reading for Facts

Sometimes you just need a single piece of information: what's on a menu, how to fill out an application, when you'll begin your next work shift. Typically this kind of reading involves scanning text quickly to pick out the facts that you want.

## Reading for Reflection

One of the most common reasons for reading is for spiritual or philosophical reflection. You might regularly read an important religious text (such as the Bible or the Koran) for inspiration or instruction, or you might enjoy reading quotations with uplifting messages that help you through hard times or simply a bad day. You might read your favorite philosopher for insight into complex issues, or even read a comic strip that satirically comments on daily life.

## Reading to Make Decisions

Should you vote for the Democrat or Republican candidate? You consult the candidates' websites to learn their views on the issues. Should you ask for a raise this month or wait until the first of the year? You read your company's financial reports and monitor recent economic analyses. Your purpose for reading is to help make a decision and take some kind of action. Generally when you read this way you proceed slowly so you can thoroughly understand the material.

## Reading for Academic Purposes

When you read for academic purposes, you progress slowly through the text, often rereading important passages or stopping to write down significant ideas. This kind of reading involves some facts, but for the most part you're focusing on ideas or concepts. In a history course, for example, you might be expected to know the dates of the U.S. Civil War, but that's only the start—you need to also understand why the Civil War occurred and what happened to the United States as a result.

   In general, reading for academic purposes is challenging and more time-consuming than other forms of reading. In a study on the reading habits of 4500 undergraduate college students, researchers Kouider Mokhtari, Carla A. Reichard, and Anne Gardner found that students preferred to use the Internet, watch television, and read for recreational

> *The more you read, the more things you will know. The more you learn, the more places you'll go.*
>
> —Dr. Seuss

purposes more than they liked to read for academic purposes.[1] The authors note, however, that students seemed to read academic texts "fairly diligently," perhaps an indication of the importance of academic reading for college success.

In the rest of this chapter you'll read more about reading for academic purposes.

## Develop Your Understanding

**Activity 4.1**   Write about all of the reading that you have done this past week. What were your main purposes for reading? What media did you use for reading (hard copy, Internet, cell phone, and so on). What language(s) did you use? What does this reveal about you as a reader? Compare your responses with your classmates'.

*Despite the rapid growth of electronic reading material, traditional books like the ones above will likely remain on shelves for a long time to come.*

## THE CONTEXT OF READING

When you read, you do more than decode letters on a page. You bring to the process of reading your experiences, attitudes, and assumptions about both the topic of the reading and the act of reading itself.

- Your experiences with the topic affect your understanding and engagement with the material. If you're reading about the U.S.–Vietnam war and have relatives who lived through or fought in that war, you likely will have some knowledge and interest that you'll bring to the topic.

---

[1]Mokhtari, Kouider, Carla A. Reichard, and Anne Gardner. "The Impact of Internet and Television Use on the Reading Habits and Practices of College Students." *Journal of Adolescent & Adult Literacy* 52.7 (2009): 609–619. Print.

- Social interactions have an impact on the process of reading. If you're a part of a book club, for instance, reading a selected book helps reinforce your connections with the other members of the book club.
- The language used in the text can influence your process. If the text is written in a language that you feel comfortable with, reading it will be easier—and perhaps more pleasurable—than reading a text in a language you're still learning.
- Previous reading experiences can affect how well and how much you read. If in the past you have been praised for your reading skill, you'll be more likely to seek out opportunities to read.

**LANGUAGES and CULTURES**

People with dyslexia include the boxer Muhammad Ali; businesspeople Ted Turner, Charles Schwab, and Richard Branson; entertainers Cher, Tom Cruise, Jay Leno, and Whoopi Goldberg; and designer Tommy Hilfiger. It is believed that Leonardo da Vinci, Thomas Edison, Pablo Picasso, and Albert Einstein also were dyslexic.

Dyslexia or other learning challenges can make the process of reading difficult and fatiguing. However, some psychologists have noted that people with dyslexia have been shown to be better problem solvers, more creative, and more visually oriented than the general population.

## CRITICAL READING

As you know, college students have to do a lot of reading. Instructors of general education courses such as history, psychology, and sociology often test students on a hundred pages or more of textbook material at a time. Depending on your major, you may be required to read several books per class every semester. Rather than expect you to memorize facts and dates, your instructors are more likely to expect you to read critically, which goes beyond a basic understanding of what the text says. Critical reading consists of

- understanding an author's purpose
- drawing inferences from the text
- evaluating the evidence and logic of an author's assertions
- extending ideas beyond the text
- examining an author's bias
- connecting ideas in one text to ideas in another text

In essence, critical reading involves constant questioning: What is the author's point? Why is the author saying this? How well does the author support this point? What can I add to the author's point? Is there any bias in this text? How does this idea compare with another idea?

# STRATEGIES FOR CRITICAL READING

If you're like most college students, you want to complete reading assignments both efficiently and effectively.

## Connect the Reading to the Class

In an ideal world you'd have all the time you need to read 120 pages of your psychology textbook. But it's more likely that you'll be reading it on the bus, or over lunch, or while you're waiting for the clothes to finishing drying. Therefore, you need to make the most of your time by focusing on the ideas in the reading that your instructor thinks are important.

**Take Good Class Notes.** If you have 120 pages to read on the topic of abnormal psych, you know that some ideas are more important than others. Most instructors indicate in class—directly or indirectly—the ideas they want you to learn. Concentrate on these ideas as you read. To do this, take good class notes.

Use a laptop or PDA to improve note-taking in class.

- Focus on recording ideas that your instructor repeats, writes on the board, and refers to in slides.
- Write down (or type up) any term that your instructor defines.
- Use your cell phone to take pictures of what was written on the board or presented on a slide, if possible.
- Attend any review sessions your instructor offers.
- Read your instructor's lecture outlines and slides if they're posted on the web.
- Discuss your notes with fellow students.
- Review your notes before and while you read to make sure you're concentrating on what your instructor might ask on a test or require in a paper.

If you're taking an online class, cut and paste or use electronic sticky notes to take notes on your instructor's lectures. A rapidly expanding array of digital tools, such as tablet PCs and phone apps, is making taking notes in a face-to-face or online class easier.

**Activity 4.2**   Compare the notes that you have taken for a course with the notes taken by a classmate. Do you both agree on the important concepts that the instructor is emphasizing? How can you improve on your class notes?

**Connect With Others**

## Preview, Read, Review

You might think that the reading process is simple—just start to read the text from beginning to end. However, educational research has shown that students who preview the reading and then review what they have read do better on tests than students who simply read the text word for word without previewing it or reflecting on it. By previewing, reading, and reviewing a text, you'll increase your critical reading skills.

**Preview the Material.**  To preview, you skim for key ideas before reading word for word, focusing on headings and subheadings, forecasting statements, glosses, and visuals. Previewing reading material prepares the brain to process information.

Preview the Text: Get a general idea what it's about before you begin to read it.

- Headings and subheadings consist of key ideas presented in phrases before a block of text. They're often in boldface type or are underlined.
- Forecasting statements tell you the main ideas in the next passage. A thesis tells the main point of the entire text, while a topic sentence gives the main idea of a paragraph. Forecasting statements usually appear in the beginning of the text and in the first or last sentences of subsequent paragraphs.

  *Forecasting statement:* A group of words (such as a thesis or topic sentence) that tells the reader the main idea of what will next be read.

- Glosses consist of explanations or definitions of important words or ideas. Usually glosses appear in the margins. A glossary, or definitions of important terms, might appear at the end of the book.
- Visuals include graphs, charts, diagrams, drawings, and photographs that are intended to help you grasp important points.

**Read and Annotate the Text.**  To read critically, take notes that increase your engagement with the text. Many students use a highlighter to mark important passages. In addition to highlighting, annotating the text increases your comprehension and ability to recall the important points.

The word *annotate* includes the word *note*. When you annotate, you write brief notes in the margins of the text. You can

- define important terms
- write important words to remember
- ask questions about confusing ideas
- jot down brief summaries
- evaluate the author's evidence and logic
- examine the text for possible bias
- make connections to ideas in other texts
- relate the author's points to your own life

Annotate the text: Write brief notes in the margins as you read the material. The noun form of the word is *annotation*.

Annotations can also make it easier for you to review the reading material before a test or an essay assignment.

Here's an example of an annotated paragraph from *Brown v. Board of Education* by James T. Patterson. The title alludes to the 1954 U.S. Supreme Court decision that made racial segregation in U.S. high schools illegal. This paragraph discusses the effects of the decision in the 1960s. Important words are highlighted, and annotations appear in the margins.

Law that gave voting rights to everyone.

Shake violently.

Bubbles are minor things. In what ways were these minor?

As it happened, however, many large expectations of the mid-1960s turned out to be too grand to achieve. The civil rights movement quickly lost force after 1965. Only five days after President Lyndon Johnson signed the Voting Rights Act in August 1965, race riots broke out in the Watts section of Los Angeles. Other, bloodier riots—notably in Newark and Detroit in 1967—convulsed cities in the next few years. At the same time, the civil rights movement split along racial lines, with some young militants demanding "black power." Many Americans were frightened and appalled by the riots. Others feared the rise of black power. Still others resisted the froth in the late 1960s of affirmative action and "forced busing" aimed at promoting "racial balance."

How would it split along racial lines? A White/Black split?

White Americans?

Summary: After 1965 violence about race frightened Americans.

Review the material: Quickly write about and study the text after you finish reading it.

**Review the Material.** By returning to the text after you have read it, you solidify your understanding of the material. Research has shown that one of the most effective ways to remember main ideas is to put the reading aside right after you have read it and then write down as fast as you can what you remember about it. This technique stimulates your memory and improves your comprehension. Another technique for reviewing the text is to go through the pages to study your annotations. Look up important words you didn't understand and reread sections that confused you. Get together with classmates to share ideas about the reading.

## Using Writing to Improve Reading

If the reading is important for your success in a class, take the time to write about the reading by keeping a reading log or visually depicting main ideas through mapping.

**Reading Log.** Keep a notebook or a document file so that you can write down your thoughts about the reading. An especially effective study strategy is to divide a piece of paper or your computer screen in half vertically. On the left side record important ideas in the reading—what the author was actually saying—and on the right side keep track of your reflections, questions, and other responses.

Reading log: A place to write and think about the reading material.

**Example of Reading Log for Paterson's Brown v. Board of Education:**

| | |
|---|---|
| Civil rights lost force after 1965 | What role did economic class play in White |
| Race riots | Americans' fear? |
| Black Power movement | Unlike King's nonviolent protests |
| White Americans' fear | School busing movement a failure—Blacks |
| Forced school busing | and Whites didn't like it |
| Affirmative action | Affirmative action still debated |

**Outlining and Mapping.** Techniques that help you create a mental representation of a text deepen your understanding of it. Two techniques are outlining and mapping. Outlining works well for people who like linear representations, while mapping is best for more visual learners. Here's an outline of this part of the chapter:

Outlining: A linear representation of a text.

Mapping: A representation of a text in diagram form.

I. Strategies for Reading to Learn
   a. Connect the Reading to the Class
      i. Take Good Class Notes
   b. Preview, Read, Review
      i. Preview the Material
      ii. Read and Annotate the Text
      iii. Review the Material

Here's a map of the same material:

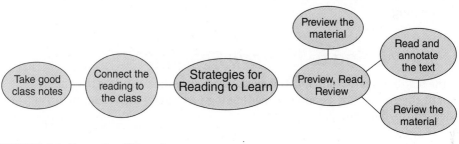

FIGURE 4.1  Example of Mapping

Both outlining and mapping help you distinguish between main and supporting ideas. Mapping also clarifies the logical connections between groups of ideas.

# WRITING SUMMARIES

In a summary you present the main ideas of a text. Summaries are one of the most common types of writing in the university and the workplace.

- A business report usually contains a summary, called an abstract or an executive summary, at the beginning. If short for time, readers can go to the abstract to find out the main points of the report.

- Summaries of articles are a common college assignment in a variety of classes. Instructors require summaries to help students understand important texts in the field.

- Research papers often contain brief summaries of important research findings.

- Annotated bibliographies consist of short summaries of research sources (such as books and articles) on a certain topic.

Summary: A shortened version of a text written in your own words.

Summaries are also written for multimedia texts. Magazines that list the ten best blogs of the year, for instance, will include short summaries of the winning blogs. Summaries are also included in reviews of movies, TV shows, CDs, and other digital entertainment forms.

The length of a summary depends on its audience and purpose, not on the length of the text. A book, for instance, can be summarized in one or two sentences. However, most summaries required in college are a paragraph or two long.

To write a good summary:

- Understand the material that you're summarizing. Use effective reading strategies to make sure that you know which ideas are most important and what they signify.
- Begin the summary with a sentence that includes the author and the title, as in this example: "In *Outliers: The Story of Success,* Malcolm Gladwell explains why some people are remarkably successful while others fail to reach their full potential."
- Give the main points in the text.
- Avoid using the author's own words even if you use quotation marks. Instead, express the ideas in your own language.
- If required, give a citation at the end of the summary that includes the author, title, and publishing information.

# Reading in a Foreign Language

## Scott Esposito

In writer Scott Esposito's blog, *Conversational Reading,* authors, readers, and publishers write about their reading experiences. In a piece from this blog called "Reading in a Foreign Language," Esposito, a native English speaker, describes his experiences reading his first book in a language other than English.

I recently finished the first book I have ever read entirely in a language other than English. It was *Las batallas en el desierto* by Jose Emilio Pacheco. It's a classic of Mexican literature, originally published in Spanish 1981 and translated into English as *Battles in the Desert and Other Stories* by New Directions in 1987.

As you might imagine for someone reading outside of his native language for the first time, this is a slight work: 68 pages total, and the chapters average from five to six pages each. It took me a while to get through it. I read it on and off over the course of a month with a Spanish-to-English dictionary in hand, proceeding at a rate of perhaps 3 pages per hour. I'm happy to report that my Spanish improved while I read *Las batallas*, and I was inspired to start in on Juan Rulfo's *Pedro Páramo*, a book that is a little more challenging than *Las batallas*.

I could tell my Spanish was better because the grammar became more intuitive and I could define more and more words from context (looking things up in the dictionary is a real speed-killer). This all made me wonder about how often I define words from context when I'm reading in English, and I think the answer is "surprisingly often." Picking one page at random from *Life: A User's Manual* (the book I'm currently reading in English), I find the following unknown words:

carotid artery; macintosh; *a fortiori*; rolling stock inspector

I didn't need to look up any of these, though, because I was able to reason that I didn't need a precise definition of any of them in order to understand what was going on. For instance, I don't know exactly what the carotid artery is, but I know enough to know that if an assassin's bullet hits it, that's bad. Likewise, I don't know what a rolling stock inspector is (maybe someone who checks the condition of livestock being delivered between destinations?), but I could tell that it wasn't really important information, so I didn't look it up.

5     It's different in Spanish because I have a much worse sense of knowing which unknown words I need to look up and which ones I don't. Many times while reading *Las batallas* I'd have a general sense of what was going on, but there would be a lot of details I was uncertain of. Which of these were crucial for my understanding of the book, and which of them were not? I couldn't tell, so I just looked up everything.

Other times, I would know all the words, but meaning would still elude me. What would be perfect grammar to a native Spanish speaker was to me a sort of koan; I had to sit there and puzzle over it until the translation into English suddenly struck me. For instance:

Estamos por salir.—Literally: We are for to leave.

Something like this doesn't seem quite right, but, after sitting there squinting at it, it eventually it occurs to me that it really is "We are ready to leave." There are lots of instances like this, and unless my dictionary lists this particular expression or something similar, then I just have to go on context and wait until the meaning strikes me. It's strange when these things would strike me. Oftentimes I'd be unable to translate something like this and just settle for a more-or-less correct understanding, and then, maybe a day later when I was in the shower, the expression would suddenly pop in my head with the attendant translation. It was as though my brain had been kicking it around the entire time, which may not be that far from reality. They say that as you learn a new language your brain literally rewires itself, and I could feel it happening; grammatical structures that seemed completely alien the first time through eventually became so familiar that I found myself almost using them in English.

Of course, there's also lots of idiomatic language that seems stranger still, like "*Te da el avión*,"—"He's giving you the airplane," which makes no sense at all unless I'm a pilot. It actually turns out that this is a figure of speech somewhat akin to "He's pulling your leg." Once you know it, you can kind of see it (but why a plane? Why not a ship, or a roomful of gold?), but good luck figuring that out on your own.

I was helped in all this by the very large number of cognates that English shares with Spanish. There's actually quite a lot, and it was fun trying to guess if the word went from English to Spanish or vice versa. It's not too hard to see that *postgraduado* started out in English, but I wonder if *finalmente* was in English first or Spanish. I had to watch out for false friends, however, of which *embarazada* is probably the best known. If I told any Spanish speakers that I was embarazada, they'd wonder how such a state was physically possible for a man.

10      Related were words that could be cognates with just a bit of imagination. Timbre in English is a kind of sound, but in Spanish you ring the *timbre* at someone's front door. These were kind of fun, because in unlocking the meaning I just to cross a slight synaptic (or is it syntactic?) gap, kind of like when you solve a riddle.

The act of reading itself felt contaminated by a number of different sensations that I don't usually encounter while immersed in a book. Most common was that little snap of pleasure you get when the solution to a riddle suddenly pops into your head. I suppose that if I had to compare it to reading in English, I'd say that it is somewhat analogous to the feeling you get when you spot an emerging theme in a novel, or suddenly concoct a theory as to how what you're reading in chapter 9 connects to what happened in chapter 2. There was also the constant weighing of speed versus accuracy. Do I read for the precise meaning sentence-by-sentence, or do I read an entire paragraph for the general idea, and then go back for specifics? Or do I just get the gist of this page and move on? Reading the book felt like a balancing act between just getting through it and reading deeply for things like voice, aesthetics, key phrases, subtext. Strangely, although I'll read pretty slow at times in English to enjoy the language or ponder what's going on, speed is never really a consideration.

Then there was the fatigue. In English I can basically read indefinitely; I don't stop because I get tired, but because there's other parts of life that need my attention. In Spanish, though, after about an hour or so my brain felt like it could use a break. It felt like a much more active kind of reading, which isn't to say that my brain is passive when reading in English, but just that whatever action takes place no longer feels like work. Whenever I finished a chapter of *Las batallas*, I felt a kind of satisfaction that I used to feel back when I regarded reading literature as work.

Reading in Spanish, I got a much better appreciation of what it is people do when they translate books into English. My brain seemed most comfortable turning the Spanish into English (as opposed to just directly linking up the Spanish word with the signs in my head), so I was effectively translating the book as I read it. (With *Pedro Páramo* I'm trying to avoid this, partly to encourage my development as a Spanish reader, and partly so I can get a better sense of the rhythm and cadence of Rulfo's prose, which, since Spanish is a romance language and English is not, should be considerably different than what I've experienced.) I began to see how much ambiguity is bound up in any translation. Of course this isn't necessarily news to anyone, the old debate about staying true to the literal meaning of the words versus trying to capture the feel of the language with a more imaginative translation, but actually experiencing it was different. Because of the differences in grammar, even a very "literal" translation required considerable leaps on my part, and, given my lack of fluency in Spanish, much of the time I was really just guessing that this was how a Spanish speaker would hear the words.

Overall, reading this translation gave me an inkling of the variety of aesthetic experiences that are out there in other languages. Up to this point, it's either been sheer faith or the assurances of author/linguists that have convinced me that more languages is better. I've taken it as axiomatic, as akin to the life and death of species. But now that I've actually seen literature in another language face to face, I feel like I've actually experienced some evidence of why it is better to have literature in more languages. This truly was different than reading in English, and perhaps as my Spanish improves I'll be able to see more and more of that.

## One Word Spotlight

***Koan*** (par. 6) is a word used in the practice of Zen Buddhism meaning paradox or mystery; the process of figuring out the meaning of the koan is similar to the process of reaching enlightenment. "Koan" is a Japanese word that originated in China around the sixth through tenth centuries.

**About the Reading**

**Activity 4.3** Summarize Esposito's description of his reading process and the conclusion he reaches.

# IMPROVING VOCABULARY

The better your vocabulary, the more you'll understand even the most complex texts. In general, the people who read the most understand the greatest number of words. However, even if you don't read a great deal you can learn enough words to understand the textbooks for your courses. In addition to learning the definitions of words, examine how words are used. Here are some strategies for improving your word knowledge.

## Focus on Important Words

Even the most experienced readers encounter words they don't understand. When reading a textbook, focus first on learning the words that convey important ideas. You can find these words in headings, subheadings, and boldface type. Significant words also appear in forecasting statements and are often repeated throughout the text.

## Make Educated Guesses about Word Meanings

Before consulting a dictionary for the meaning of a word, see if you can make an educated guess about what it means based on what is written before and after it. When you do this, you're making a hypothesis about a word's meaning. Then, as you continue to read, test your hypothesis to see if you're right. (This is the process that Scott Esposito used when he was reading his first book in Spanish.) By making educated guesses about the meaning of a word, you can save yourself the time of looking it up in a dictionary. For words that express key concepts, be on the safe side and consult a dictionary.

## Note Common Word Groups

In addition to individual words, concentrate on groups of words that are commonly found together. These include the following:

- word pairs such as "junk mail," "middle management," "nuclear family," "toxic asset"
- idioms such as "jump the gun," "elbow grease," "nose to the grindstone," "think outside the box"
- phrases common in academic writing such as "scholars agree that . . ." and "it is commonly believed that . . ."
- phrases belonging to an academic discipline that you're studying, such as "account analysis," "audit trail," and "managed earnings" from accounting

# Use Print and Online Reference Resources

Dictionaries will give you definitions of words, indicate how they are pronounced, and usually give examples of how the word is used. Consider the type of dictionary that is best for you.

**General Monolingual Dictionary.**  The most common kind of dictionary, a general monolingual dictionary gives many meanings of the same word, not just the most common meaning. All words are explained or defined in the same language, often with examples. The most commonly used definitions are presented first. For instance, the Random House Dictionary gives nine definitions of the word *genius*:

1. an exceptional natural capacity of intellect, especially as shown in creative and original work in science, art, music, etc.: *the genius of Mozart.*
2. a person having such capacity.
3. a person having an extraordinarily high intelligence rating on a psychological test, as an IQ above 140.
4. natural ability or capacity; strong inclination: *a special genius for leadership.*
5. distinctive character or spirit, as of a nation, period, or language.
6. the guardian spirit of a place, institution, etc.
7. either of two mutually opposed spirits, one good and the other evil, supposed to attend a person throughout life.
8. a person who strongly influences for good or ill the character, conduct, or destiny of a person, place, or thing: *Rasputin, the evil genius of Russian politics.*
9. GENIE (defs. 1, 3).

As you can see, the most commonly used definition of "genius" is the first one: "an exceptional natural capacity of intellect."

**Language Learner's Dictionary.**  This is a monolingual dictionary written for people learning a language. It is useful for even fluent or native speakers because it focuses on only the most common meanings of words and gives multiple examples of how the words are used in sentences. It will also note words that are frequently paired together. This is how the *Merriam-Webster's Learner's Dictionary* defines *genius*. Note the number of sentences that demonstrate different ways to use the word.

1. [*count*] **a :** a very smart or talented person : a person who has a level of talent or intelligence that is very rare or remarkable • Albert Einstein and Isaac Newton were great scientific *geniuses.* • a musical/artistic/creative *genius* • You don't have to be a *genius* to see that this plan will never work. **b :** a person who is very good at doing something • He was a *genius* at handling the press.
2. **a** [*noncount*] **:** great natural ability : remarkable talent or intelligence • She's now widely recognized as an artist of *genius.* • He's admired for his

comic/artistic/scientific *genius.* **b** [*singular*] **:** a great or unusual talent or ability—usually + *for* • She has a *genius for* knowing what will sell. • He had a *genius for* getting into trouble. [=he often got into trouble]

3. [*singular*] **a :** a very clever or smart quality • The (sheer) *genius* of his theory was not immediately recognized. **b :** a part of something that makes it unusually good or valuable • My plan is simple—that's the *genius* of it. • The *genius* of these new computers is their portability.

**a stroke of genius:** a brilliant and successful idea or decision • Deciding to relocate the company was *a stroke of genius.*

Learner's dictionaries also contain idioms ("stroke of genius" is an idiom). Some learner's dictionaries have an academic focus and feature words used in textbooks and college classrooms.

**Bilingual Dictionary.** In this type of dictionary, the words of one language are defined or explained in another language. Travelers, students, and business people often use a bilingual dictionary for quick reference. However, keep in mind that many words have no direct translation into another language, so be sure to use a bilingual dictionary that explains the meaning of a word if there is no synonym in the other language.

**Online Word Lists.** The Academic Word List (AWL), a free Internet resource originally published in 2000, contains 570 words that frequently appear in English-language academic texts. Online exercises using the AWL focus on using these words in typical academic passages.

**Online Translation Tools.** With websites such as Babel Fish and Google Translate, you can translate individual words, phrases, or paragraphs into a variety of languages. However, these tools have limitations because they can't decipher word nuances or help you understand grammatical constructions.

# Keep a Vocabulary Notebook

Vocabulary Notebook: A convenient place to define and give examples of words and their usage.

A vocabulary notebook contains lists and definitions of words, phrases, or idioms that are new to you. To be able to remember the new words, you need to review them repeatedly, so be sure the notebook is convenient. You can use a small notebook that fits into a pocket or purse, a larger one for your backpack, or an electronic notebook such as a document file or the "notes" section of your email or cell phone. Review the words whenever you have a few minutes to spare, such as when you're sitting in a doctor's office or waiting for a friend to arrive.

> **GENIUS**
>
> Very smart person.           Span: genio
> Person with a lot of talent.
> A part of something that's really good.
>
> Albert Einstein was a genius.
> A genius has an IQ over 140.
> She's a genius at getting people to do stuff (very good at).
> Stroke of genius (great idea).
> Work of genius.

**FIGURE 4.2** Sample notecard

In addition to recording the definition of a word in your notebook, give examples of how a word is used. When you see the word used in a new way, record that. Give the definition or a synonym in a language other than English if that will be helpful. The more you use the word in writing, the better you'll remember it.

## Fun Ways to Learn Vocabulary

- Several free websites feature a "word of the day," in which a word is defined and several examples of its use are given. By signing up for a "word of the day," you can be sure that your vocabulary will increase. Usually you can hear how the word is pronounced as well.
- Games and puzzles such as hangman, Scrabble, and crossword puzzles all foster vocabulary development and can be played electronically for free.
- Video games such as My Word Coach have been devised to help build vocabulary.

**Develop Your Understanding**

**Activity 4.4** Spend a week keeping a vocabulary notebook. Periodically during the week, review the words. Would you recommend this strategy for learning new words to others? Why or why not?

# WRITING ASSIGNMENT

Preview, read, and review the following reading selection from *A Narrative of the Life of Frederick Douglass*. Answer the questions that follow the reading. Then, using your annotations on the reading as well as your responses to the questions, write a brief essay examining the following main ideas:

- the significance to Douglass of learning to read
- the effect of the institution of slavery on both Whites and Blacks
- why learning to read threatened the institution of slavery in general and the authority of his master and mistress in particular

# From *Narrative of the Life of Frederick Douglass, An American Slave*

## Frederick Douglass

Frederick Douglass was a nineteenth-century African American who advocated for the rights of African Americans, women, Native Americans, and immigrants. Born into slavery in 1819, he escaped to his freedom in 1838 and spent the rest of his life as a writer and advocate. In 1845 he published his autobiography, *Narrative of the Life of Frederick Douglass, An American Slave.*

I lived in Master Hugh's family about seven years. During this time, I succeeded in learning to read and write. In accomplishing this, I was compelled to resort to various stratagems. I had no regular teacher. My mistress, who had kindly commenced to instruct me, had, in compliance with the advice and direction of her husband, not only ceased to instruct, but had set her face against my being instructed by any one else. It is due, however, to my mistress to say of her, that she did not adopt this course of treatment immediately. She at first lacked the depravity indispensable to shutting me up in mental darkness. It was at least necessary for her to have some training in the exercise of irresponsible power, to make her equal to the task of treating me as though I were a brute.

My mistress was, as I have said, a kind and tender-hearted woman; and in the simplicity of her soul she commenced, when I first went to live with her, to treat me as she supposed one human being ought to treat another. In entering upon the duties of a slaveholder, she did not seem to perceive that I sustained to her the relation of a mere chattel, and that for her to treat me as a human being was not only wrong, but dangerously so. Slavery proved as injurious to her as it did to me. When I went there, she was a pious, warm, and tender-hearted woman. There was no sorrow or suffering for which she had not a tear. She had bread for the hungry, clothes for the naked, and comfort for every mourner that came within her reach. Slavery soon proved its ability to divest her of these heavenly qualities. Under its influence, the tender heart became stone, and the lamblike disposition gave way to one of tiger-like fierceness. The first step in her downward course was in her ceasing to instruct me. She now commenced to practise her husband's precepts. She finally became even more violent in her opposition than her husband himself. She was not satisfied with simply doing as well as he had commanded; she seemed anxious to do better. Nothing seemed to make her more angry than to see me with a newspaper. She seemed to think that here lay the danger. I have had her rush at me with a face made all up of fury, and snatch from me a newspaper, in a manner that fully revealed her apprehension. She was an apt woman; and a little experience soon demonstrated, to her satisfaction, that education and slavery were incompatible with each other.

From this time I was most narrowly watched. If I was in a separate room any considerable length of time, I was sure to be suspected of having a book, and was at once called to give an account of myself. All this, however, was too late. The first step had been taken. Mistress, in teaching me the alphabet, had given me the *inch*, and no precaution could prevent me from taking the *ell*.

The plan which I adopted, and the one by which I was most successful, was that of making friends of all the little white boys whom I met in the street. As many of these as I could, I converted into teachers. With their kindly aid, obtained at different times and in different places, I finally succeeded in learning to read. When I was sent of errands, I always took my book with me, and by going one part of my errand quickly, I found time to get a lesson before my return. I used also to carry bread with me, enough of which was always in the house, and to which I was always welcome; for I was much better off in this regard than many of the poor white children in our neighborhood. This bread I used to bestow upon the hungry little urchins, who, in return, would give me that more valuable bread of knowledge. I am strongly tempted to give the names of two or three of those little boys, as a testimonial of the gratitude and affection I bear them; but prudence forbids;—not that it would injure me, but it might embarrass them; for it is almost an unpardonable offence to teach slaves to read in this Christian country. It is enough to say of the dear little fellows, that they lived on Philpot Street, very near Durgin and Bailey's ship-yard. I used to talk this matter of slavery over with them. I would sometimes say to them, I wished I could be as free as they would be when they got to be men. "You will be free as soon as you are twenty-one, *but I am a slave for life*! Have not I as good a right to be free as you have?" These words used to trouble them; they would express for me the liveliest sympathy, and console me with the hope that something would occur by which I might be free.

# One Word Spotlight

". . . had given me the *inch,* and no precaution could prevent me from taking the *ell*" (par. 3). The proverb "give the inch and they'll take the ell" came from the textile trade in Europe; an "ell" was approximately the length of a man's arm. The proverb in contemporary English is "give them an inch and they'll take a mile," which means if you give people a little, they'll end up taking advantage of you.

## Reflect on the Reading

1. Describe the way that Douglass's mistress changed her treatment toward him.
2. Explain this sentence: "She was an apt woman; and a little experience soon demonstrated, to her satisfaction, that education and slavery were incompatible with each other" (par. 2).
3. Why does Douglass express gratitude toward the white boys in the neighborhood?

## Consider Your Viewpoint

1. In what way does slavery seem to hurt Douglass's mistress?
2. Why was literacy—the ability to read and write—denied to slaves?
3. Douglass's autobiography was published in 1845. What might have been his motivation in writing this text?

For support in meeting this chapter's objectives, follow this path in MyCompLab: Resources ⇒ Writing ⇒ Writing Process ⇒ Planning. Review the Instruction and Multimedia resources about becoming a critical reader. Also follow this path: Resources ⇒ Research ⇒ The Research Assignment ⇒ Understanding the Research Assignment. Review the Instruction and Multimedia resources about creating effective notes. Complete the Exercises and click on Gradebook to measure your progress.

mycomplab

# PART 2 Expanding Influence

# CHAPTER

# 5 Exploring an Event

## Learning Objectives

In this chapter you will:

- Write about an event.
- Discover ideas through listing.

- Use effective description and dialogue.
- Clarify your main point.
- Improve the focus of your writing.

*Major events often bring people closer together. How is this family coping with the loss of their home?*

**M**ost events in your life are routine: driving to work, cooking dinner, studying for class. But then something happens or you do something that *isn't* routine. You start college. You're laid off from your job. You move to another country. In the photo on the chapter opening page, people are consoling each other after their house burned down. However, it isn't necessarily *what* happens that is momentous—it's what happens *as a result* of the event. What did you learn? How did you change? In this chapter you'll have the opportunity to explore an event in your life. Perhaps the event gave you insight into the type of person you want to be. It might have enlightened you intellectually, or it might have made you stronger. Some events change us immediately, while others affect us more gradually.

> *There is nothing so stable as change.*
>
> —*Bob Dylan*

## WRITING TO EXPLORE AN EVENT

Writing to explore an event is a type of expressive writing in which your purpose is to share your thoughts and feelings with others. To write about an event, you'll first gather ideas to find an appropriate topic for this assignment, one that interests you, is sufficiently narrow, and can appeal to your readers. After selecting the event to write about, you'll analyze your rhetorical situation, considering your topic, audience, purpose, genre, visual design, exigence, and constraints. You'll then follow a writing process that will allow you ample time to explore what this event meant to you and how to best communicate that meaning.

### Questions for Exploring Events

- What event do I want to explore?
- What would my readers want to know about the event?
- Which genre and visual design is best for communicating my ideas about this event?
- Why is it important to me to share this exploration of an event?
- What constraints might keep me from effectively writing about this event?

## MODEL EXPLORATIONS OF EVENTS

Writers explore their lives by writing about events that are important to them or that have had a profound effect on them. Such pieces are found in journals, letters, blogs, essays, and articles. While reading the following pieces, notice how these authors share a part of their personal lives with their readers.

# The Rules of the Sport
## Adam Gopnik

Adam Gopnik writes for the *New Yorker,* a major U.S. magazine with a mostly college-educated readership that is best known for publishing essays in which writers record their observations of current life. Gopnik, who writes on topics ranging from baseball to art history, lived in Paris from 1995 to 2000 with his wife Martha and their young son; during that time he wrote essays about his experiences with Paris life that were published in *Paris to the Moon* in 2000. The following is an excerpt from that book.

L ast year the French government assembled a committee to choose a name for the vast new stadium that's being built in a Paris suburb. The committee included an actor, an "artiste," some functionaries, and even a few athletes. It took a long time deliberating over its choice. Names were submitted: Some people liked the idea of naming the stadium after Verlaine or Saint-Exupéry, and lots of others liked the idea of calling it Le Stade Platini, after Michel Platini, the great French soccer player. At last, in December, the committee announced that it had come to a decision, and the government decided to broadcast the verdict on television. The scene was a little like the end of the Simpson trial: the worried-looking jurors filing to their seats, the pause as the envelope was handed to the minister of youth and sports, the minister clearing his throat to read the decision to the nation. The stadium that would represent France to the world, he announced, would be called (long, dramatic pause) Le Stade de France. The French Stadium. "Banal and beautiful at the same time," one journalist wrote. "Obvious and seductive. Timeless and unalterable."

It wasn't hard to detect, beneath the sturdy, patriotic surface of the new name, an undercurrent of ironic, derisory minimalism. The French are prepared to be formally enthusiastic about American-style stadiums and American-style sports, but they are not going to get carried away by it all. This realization first came home to me when I joined a pioneer health club on the Left Bank and spent four months unsuccessfully trying to get some exercise there.

"An American gym?" Parisians asked when I said that I was looking for someplace to work out, and at first I didn't know what to say. What would a French gym be like? Someone suggested that my wife and I join the Health Club at the Ritz; that was about as French as a gym could get. This sounded like a nice, glamorous thing to do, so we went for a trial

> **Left Bank:** An area in Paris on the southern bank of the river Seine.

visit. I ran out of the locker room and dived into the pool. White legs were dangling all around me—crowded to the edges, as though their owners were clinging to the sides of the pool in fear—and only after I rose to the surface did I see that the owners were all hanging from the edge of the pool, eating tea sandwiches off silver platters. Finally, after we'd done a lot of asking around, someone suggested a newly opening "New York-style" gym, which I'll call the Régiment Rouge. One afternoon Martha and I walked over to see what it was like and found it down at the end of a long, winding street. The gym was wedged into the bottom two floors of an institutional-looking Haussmann-era building. We went in and found ourselves surrounded by the virtuous sounds of Activity—sawing and hammering and other plaster dust-producing noises. The bruit seemed to be rising from a cavernlike area in the basement. At the top of a grand opera-style staircase that led to the basement were three or four fabulously chic young women in red tracksuits—the Régiment Rouge!—that still managed to be fairly form-clinging. The women all had ravishing long hair and lightly applied makeup. When we told them that we wanted to *abonner*—subscribe—one of them whisked us off to her office and gave us the full spiel on the Régiment Rouge. It was going to bring the rigorous, uncompromising spirit of the New York health club to Paris: its discipline, its toughness, its *regimental* quality. They were just in the middle of having the work done—one could hear this downstairs—and it would all be finished by the end of the month. The locker rooms, the *appareils Nautilus,* the stationary bicycles with electronic displays, the steam baths, the massage tables—everything would be not just *a l'américane* but *très New Yorkais.* Best of all, she went on, they had organized a special "high-intensity" program in which, for the annual sum of about two thousand francs (four hundred dollars), you could make an inexorable New-York style commitment to your physique and visit the gym as often as once a week.

It was obvious that the once-a-week deal was the winner—the closer, in Mamet language—and that though she had a million arguments ready for people who thought that when it came to *forme,* once a week might be going overboard, she had nothing at all ready for people who thought once a week might not be *forme* enough. We asked her if we could possibly come more often than that, and she cautiously asked us what we meant by "often." Well, three, perhaps four times a week, we said. It was not unknown, we added quickly, apologetically, for New Yorkers to visit a gym on an impulse, almost daily. Some New Yorkers, for that matter, arranged to go to their health club every morning before work. She echoed this cautiously too: They rise from their beds and exercise vigorously before breakfast? Yes, we said weakly. That must be a wearing regimen, she commented politely.

5      She paused and then she said, wonderingly, "Ah, you mean you wish to *abonner* for an infinite number of visits?" After much fooling around

**Haussmann-era:** Dating from the time of Baron Haussmann, the principle civic planner of Paris in the mid-nineteenth century.

**Bruit:** (French) noise, din.

**Mamet language:** David Mamet, U.S. playwright, whose characters use cutthroat sales tactics.

with numbers and hurried, hushed conferences with other members of the regiment, she arrived at a price for an infinity of *forme*. The difference between once a week and infinity, by the way, turned out to be surprisingly small, improvised prices being one of the unpredictable pleasures of Paris life. She opened dossiers for both of us; you can't do anything in France without having a dossier opened on your behalf. . . .

A few days after my oral interview I went back to the Régiment Rouge, and this time I actually got on one of the stationary bicycles and rode it for twenty-four minutes. I was in full New York regalia (sweatpants, headband, Walkman) and did it in good New York form (Stones blasting in my headphones, crying out, "One minute!" when there was a minute left to go). By now there were other people at the gym, though the man on the bicycle next to me was going at a speed barely fast enough to sustain life, while the woman beside him, who was on a treadmill, was walking at the right speed for window-shopping on the boulevard Saint-Germain on an especially sunny day when your heart is filled with love and your pockets are filled with money; it was as though she had set the machine at "Saunter."

I got down from my bike perspiring right through my T-shirt—the first person on the Left Bank, I thought proudly, to break a sweat at a gym. I walked back to the desk. "A towel, please," I panted (in French, of course). The girl in the red tracksuit at the desk gave me a long, steady, opaque look. I thought that maybe I had got the word for towel wrong (I hadn't, though), and after I asked again and got the same look in return, I thought it wise to try to describe its function. My description sounded like a definition from Dr. Johnson's dictionary: that thing which is used in the process of removing water from the surfaces of your body in the moments after its immersion. "Ah," she said. "Of course. A towel. We have none yet." She looked off into the middle distance. "This," she said at last, "is envisaged." I looked at her dumbly, pleadingly, the reality dawning on me. Then I walked all the way home, moist as a chocolate mousse.

A couple of days later I went for what I thought would be my last visit to the Préfecture de Police to get my *carte de sejour,* a process that had involved a four-ministry workout stretching over three months. The functionary seemed ready to give it to me—she was actually holding it out across the desk—but then she suddenly took one last look at the dossier the prefecture had on me and noticed something that she had somehow missed before. "*Alors, monsieur,*" she said, "you have not yet had a physical examination to make sure that you are in sufficiently good health to remain in France."

I didn't know what to say. "I belong to a gym," I said at last, and I showed her my card from the regiment.

10  "Well," she said, "this will be useful for your dossier." I couldn't argue with that.

*Carte de sejour*: (French) French residency document.

# One Word Spotlight

**Dossier** (paragraph 5) is a French word that refers to a file of documents on the same topic or the same person. It literally means *a bundle of documents labeled on the back* (*dos* comes from the Latin word for back or spine, *dorsum*). It originated in the latter half of the nineteenth century, when France and other countries were becoming increasing bureaucratic in government, law, and business. In the United States, *dossier* is commonly used to refer to documents, such as a résumé and letters of recommendation, which job seekers send to potential employers.

## Reflect on the Reading

1. Why does Gopnik begin this piece by describing the search for a name of a new French sports stadium?

2. According to Gopnik, what are some differences between the way that the French view athletics and the way that New Yorkers (and, by implication, Americans) view athletics?

3. Select six words from this piece that best depict the ways that the French view athletics, according to Gopnik.

4. Describe Gopnik's tone throughout the piece. What is his attitude toward the topic?

5. How does the title—"The Rules of the Sport"—relate to Gopnik's message?

## Consider Your Viewpoint

1. To what extent is Gopnik simply repeating cultural stereotypes, and to what extent is he providing new insights?

2. How do you think French people might respond to this piece?

3. How seriously do you think Gopnik wants us to take this piece?

4. Gopnik is describing French attitudes toward athletics from the perspective of an American—specifically, a New Yorker. How might a person from another culture view the same topic?

5. Some contemporary critics worry that one effect of globalization is the influence of U.S. culture throughout the world—a global McDonaldization. Based on "The Rules of the Sport," how likely is this, at least in France?

## Road Trip

### Sandeep Jauhar

In the following selection from the memoir *Intern: A Doctor's Initiation*, published in 2008, Dr. Sandeep Jauhar recollects one of his experiences as an apprentice doctor—an intern—in a New York hospital. Interns are assisted by more advanced medical students called residents; in this selection, Steve is the resident who is helping the author cope with his first hospital experiences. As this selection demonstrates, a memoir is an account of a time in one's life told in the form of a story. Dr. Jauhar survived his experiences as an intern and is now director of the Heart Failure Program at Long Island Jewish Medical Center.

*A hospital corridor.*

Mrs. Williams needed a CAT scan. She was on a stretcher, in a tangle of wires and tubes, a woman of about seventy with thinning gray hair and a churchgoing face. A nurse was giving me instructions for the road trip. "Just keep the monitor on her at all times," she barked, like a quarterback calling out a play. She picked up a section of clear plastic tubing. "This is your arterial line. And this here is your central venous pressure. I'm going to disconnect it; you don't need it. This is the heparin. This is the nitroglycerin." She pointed to the bulky yellow monitor at the foot of the bed. "The yellow line is your oxygen saturation. That's your heartbeat and that's your blood pressure." She reached underneath the stretcher, where a green metal canister was lying on its side. "That's your oxygen. It should last about thirty minutes."

She paused to take a deep breath. "This is your code box," she said, holding up a sealed gray box that looked like a mechanic's tool kit. Inside it were drugs—epinephrine, atropine, lidocaine—that I had never used. "Just break it open if you need it. Of course, if she arrests, you're going to use the paddles." I nodded; I had never used defibrillator paddles before. "You charge it like this, see." She turned the knob back and forth quickly. "One hundred joules, two hundred joules, three hundred joules, see." My face must have betrayed terror because the nurse offered an almost sympathetic smile. "Don't worry," she said. "If you need to, you can always call a code."

*Call a code:* Call for help in an emergency.

The middle-of-the-night road trip is an intern rite of passage. Steve and the other residents had done it, and there was no reason to think that I couldn't do it, too.

A young black man in dreadlocks and lime green scrubs showed up. He was my escort. Without a word, he grabbed hold of the back of the stretcher with one hand and a metal IV pole with the other and maneuvered it to the double doors. Then he punched a plate on the wall, the doors flung open, and we were off.

5      Coming out of the CCU, with me holding on to a side rail, we tried turning left, but the stretcher went crashing into the far wall. "Oh my!" Mrs. Williams exclaimed. She had few teeth, hollow cheeks, and kind of gummed her words when she spoke. I didn't know much about her, except that she had been admitted to the CCU with chest pains. That was pretty much all Amanda had signed out.

> CCU: Cardiac Care Unit

We rolled the stretcher down the checkerboard-tile floor, toward the freight elevator. Even at this late hour, I could see white-coated men sitting on stools in the satellite pharmacy, sorting pills. Their presence was both creepy and oddly reassuring. More banging, but we managed to steer the stretcher onto the corrugated metal floor of the freight elevator. With each bump I checked to make sure the IVs were still connected. An EKG sticker had come off her chest, dangling uselessly on a wire, making the heartbeat tracing temporarily go flatline before I pressed it back on. We rode up the sixth floor in silence, except for the reassuring *blip-blip-blip* from the monitor.

Coming out of the elevator, we made a left and rolled up a ramp and down a hallway, past the pediatric oncology wing. Suddenly we were in an old part of the hospital. The corridors were lined with beat-up chairs and rusting file cabinets below peeling paint. We stopped at an intersection. I looked up from the monitor nervously. "I hope you know where you're going, because I don't." My escort's flat, somber expression did not change. "I've only been here two weeks," I tried to explain.

Without a word, he turned left. A couple of turns later, we entered a darkened hallway. It had a faintly chemical smell, like that of a darkroom. "This is it," he mumbled, disappearing into a room. From the corridor I could see a doughnut-shaped CT scanner sitting on a metal gantry that looked like it could use a good scrubbing. After a couple of minutes, the escort came out and started walking back in the direction of the main hospital. "Hey!" I called out. "Where are you going?"

"Call me when you're done," he said without turning around.

10      "What's your number?" I shouted, but he was already gone.

A burly technician with tattooed arms came out of the room. "Okay, Doc, bring her in," he said.

I rolled the stretcher up to the radiology table. Mrs. Williams was now even more tangled up in wires and tubes. Her rumpled gown was slipping off her shoulders, exposing her breasts. The pulse oximeter had long since come off her finger. One of her IV lines had somehow made its way between the side rails. I disconnected it, looped it back over the railing, and quickly reattached it before any of the medicated fluid dripped onto the floor. The technician pumped on a pedal below the stretcher, raising it to the same level as the scanner. Then I pulled on a latch and lowered the side rail. "Give me your hand, Mrs. Williams," I said, reaching across the gantry.

"Hold on, Doc," the tech said. "We've got to give this line some slack or her IV is going to come right out." He pulled the metal pole in closer, but it didn't look like the tubing was going to be long enough. He stared at it for a few seconds. "Can we stop the drip?" he asked.

"Sure," I replied automatically. Which drug couldn't be stopped for just a few minutes?

15 I disconnected the line and reached again for Mrs. William's hand. "Doc, she's going to need some help." He went and got a white sheet. "Okay, pull her onto her side." As her face pressed up between the rails, he quickly tucked the sheet under her body and rolled her onto her back. Then we grabbed the sheet on each side and slid her over onto the scanner table.

"This is only going to take five minutes," I said, patting her on the hand. The tech and I went into the tiny control room. "Don't you want to be able to see the monitor?" he asked me, taking a seat at the console. "Yes, of course," I said. I ran in and turned it around.

Digital images of my patient's head soon appeared on a computer screen. "What is the scan for?" the tech inquired, adjusting a knob. After a pause, I said, "I'm not sure." In all the excitement, I had forgotten to ask.

The first images looked okay. Now it was time for higher-resolution cuts.

"She's got to lie real still for this next scan," the tech said.

20 I peeked into the room. Mrs. Williams's head was still in the scanner. "Try not to move, ma'am. We're almost done."

She groaned loudly. "I don't feels so good. Oh Lordy, I don't feels good."

"What's the matter?" I asked.

"My chest is hurtin'," she said.

Just my luck. Only one more pass through the scanner and now she was having chest pain? "That's okay," I said. "Just try to keep still."

25 She shifted her weight uncomfortably. "But I'm getting these pains in my heart."

"We'll take care of it once the scan is finished. You don't want to have to come back here, do you?"

She didn't answer.

"So please just lie still for a couple of minutes so we can finish up." I was focused on completing the scan, whatever the indication for it was.

"Let's do it," I said, returning to the control room.

30    "You sure, Doc?" the tech replied skeptically.

"Yes, I'm sure," I snapped. The tracings were fine; her heartbeat was regular. Tasks were piling up back in the CCU. I did not want to have to bring her back.

Midway through the final scan, she started moaning. "Oh Lord, oh my!" "Thirty seconds," the tech said, his eyes peeled to the screen. The mumbling got louder and her feet started shifting from side to side. "Oh Jesus, help me!" she groaned. "All right, Doc," he said, punching off a lit button. "I think we got what we needed."

We pulled Mrs. Williams back onto the stretcher. "Oh Lord, oh Jesus, get me out of here!" she wailed. I clenched my teeth to keep from laughing. For a moment the whole situation seemed rather comical. What was I doing here in the middle of the night, in this abandoned corner of the hospital, with this tattooed technician and this helpless old lady? The whole road trip had been so nerve-racking. I was just glad that it was over.

I quickly reconnected the IV line and turned the machine back on. *Beep . . . beep . . . beep.* I turned the machine off and tried again. More beeps and a red light started to flash. I tried silencing the alarm but it kept ringing. The rotors started whirring in my head. The IV had been delivering nitroglycerin. *Nitroglycerin is used to treat angina.* I turned the machine off and tried again. *Angina means decreased blood flow to the heart.* I punched the buttons on the front panel. *Decreased blood flow can cause chest pain.* I squeezed the bag, trying to get the drip restarted, but all I got were more flashing lights. Then it hit me square in the gut: *My patient was having a heart attack!*

35    Her moans and the alarms mixed into a dissonant instrumental. I spun toward the tech. "Do you have any nitroglycerin?" He looked at me like I was a lunatic. I flipped open the code box the nurse had given me. There were vials of lidocaine, epinephrine, atropine, saline. Not nitroglycerin. *Dammit,* I screamed in my head. Steve had told me to carry a bottle with me at all times, but I had ignored the advice.

Now I was in a full-blown panic. "I have to get her back to the unit," I cried. "Can you call Transport?"

"I already did," the tech replied, nonplussed. "But he said it would take a few minutes."

"I can't wait. Can you help me bring her back?"

He looked at me helplessly. "I can't leave, Doc. I'm the only one here and there's another patient on the way."

40    I grabbed the IV pole and the back of the stretcher and started racing toward the elevator. "Tell Transport to catch up with me," I shouted. I

swerved, barreling into a chair, backed up, and tried again. *If she dies, this is going to be your fault!* I screamed in my head. *You'll be fired. Risk management will have to get involved. How did you get yourself into this mess? Why did you insist on finishing the goddamn scan?*

"You're going to be okay, Mrs. Williams," I said, trying to mollify her as she started to shriek. "The nurses are going to give you some medicine and you're going to be just fine."

We got to an intersection. Which way? Earlier we had turned left, so now I had to turn . . . right. Simple calculations were eluding me. For a moment I thought about stopping to call a code. But where was I? It was the middle of the night and I was in the middle of a vacant corridor. How were you supposed to call a code anyway? Who were you supposed to ring? Where were the phones? *God,* I prayed, *if you get me through this, I'll be a better doctor. I'll take things more seriously. Please, just let me get through this night.*

Back at the freight elevator, I struck the button furiously and the doors opened. On the ride down, her cries were deafening. When the doors opened, I saw the escort. He appeared to be waiting for me. "Oh, thank God," I cried. "Help me get her back!" Without a word, he took the back of the stretcher and we raced it back to the CCU. On the way there, I tried to explain what had happened. "I stopped the nitroglycerin drip, and she started having chest pain, but then I couldn't get it restarted." He didn't appear to be listening. This was my mess, and he seemed to want no part in it.

When we rolled into the CCU, three nurses materialized immediately. Evidently the tech had called ahead to tell them I was on the way. "We couldn't get her into the scanner," I said breathlessly. "I stopped her nitroglycerin. I couldn't get it restarted. Maybe there's air in the line. It's her nitroglycerin. She's having chest pain."

45     "We'll take care of it," the nurse who had sent me out forty-five minutes earlier said calmly. I wasn't prepared for her sympathetic tone, and almost instantaneously tears filled my eyes. I felt guilty, undeserving of her empathy. "I stopped the nitro and she started having angina," I said again. "I didn't know what to do, so I brought her back."

"You did the right thing," the nurse said. "We'll take care of her."

I was so on edge that I felt numb. I hovered as the nurses whisked Mrs. Williams back to her room. As they got her into bed, I continued trying to explain my actions from the door. "We finished the scan. I probably shouldn't have disconnected the IV."

"It's okay," the nurse said. She smiled broadly. "Congratulations. You just made your first road trip."

When the nurses restarted the nitroglycerin drip, Mrs. William's angina subsided. Before long she was lying in bed comfortably. I was right, there had been a small air bubble in the line, making the machine turn off automatically. For a while I lingered outside the room, peeking through the curtain to check on her. Finally I slipped away. She was in good hands now, much better than mine.

50      I wanted to run away but there was nowhere to go. Back at the workstation I tried checking labs but I couldn't concentrate. There were still a slew of tasks to complete. Soon Steve was going to start walking around the unit to make sure everything was done, and after that I was going to have to print up flow sheets and start prerounding. I stared at my reflection in a glass door. The veins were popping out on my glistening temples. The image ricocheted off the glass door behind me, trailing off to infinity.

In semiconductor physics, there is a concept of an electron-hole pair. A hole is the absence of an electron. It is not a real particle, though it behaves like one. It is a shadow particle, a phantom, behaving exactly opposite to an electron. Gazing at my reflection, I was struck that in some fundamental way I had become a hole, a shadow of my former self, behaving antithetical to my true nature. I was a thinker, not a doer. This was too much doing for me. I was beginning to appreciate what it was going to take to make me into a doctor—into a man.

# One Word Spotlight

*Nitroglycerin* (paragraph 1), sometimes called *nitro*, is a chemical compound first devised in the mid-nineteenth century for its explosive power. The primary ingredient in dynamite, it was used as a blasting agent in the construction of railroads and highways and as weaponry in World Wars I and II. In the late nineteenth century, it was discovered that nitroglycerin could alleviate chest pain by relaxing the blood vessels. Nitroglycerin tablets are placed under patients' tongues, which allows the chemical to be absorbed into the body. The nitroglycerin used in medicine is not explosive.

## Reflect on the Reading

1. *Intern*, the title of the book that this piece is taken from, is subtitled *A Doctor's Initiation*. What is the author being initiated into?

2. Relate this sentence to the rest of the piece: "The middle-of-the-night road trip is an intern rite of passage."

3. In the last paragraph, Jauhar uses the metaphor of a shadow particle. What is he saying about himself in these last few sentences?

4. Immediately after Mrs. Williams's CT scan is concluded, the author writes that he had to "clench his teeth to keep from laughing." What does this temptation to laugh show about his situation?

5. What overall impression of the U.S. medical system did this piece give you?

## Consider Your Viewpoint

1. If you were Steve, the more advanced doctor-in-training who works with Jauhar, what would be your assessment of how well Jauhar dealt with his road trip? What advice would you give Jauhar?

2. What, to you, are the characteristics of a good doctor? To what extent does Jauhar exhibit these characteristics?

3. Think of your own experiences with the U.S. medical system, or the experiences of people you know. To what extent does this piece resemble these experiences?

4. If you're familiar with the health care system of another country, compare how doctors are trained in that country and in the U.S.

5. What do you think would be an ideal way to train new doctors?

# When Life Gives You Potstickers Instead of Wontons, Sharply Verbalize Your Bitterness Until It Fixes Itself

## Sally Mao

In 2005, Sally Mao went from the Bay area of San Francisco to Pittsburgh, Pennsylvania to attend college at Carnegie-Mellon University. She blogged about the first few weeks of college for the website of 826 Valencia, a writing center in San Francisco that offers free writing tutoring for students from age six through high school. This blog is typical of a diary: It is organized according to date, expresses the author's immediate feelings and ideas, and is written in a conversational style.

*826 Valencia in San Francisco*

*08/19/05*

I should be excited, I keep on telling myself. I should be excited. Tonight I will brave a night plane to Pittsburgh and in less than twenty-four hours I will be on a campus on the other side of the country, totally devoid of familiar faces, familiar furniture, and Chinese food.

And so far all of my friends, my mother, my father, and my grandmother have reminded me of this. You should be excited. *You should be so excited. There's absolutely nothing to be terrified about.*

And yet, and yet. Why am I having these feelings so soon? My fingers, as I type this, are almost trembling, with anticipation? Nervousness? Why do I suddenly feel like a plucked cocktail shrimp?

The funny thing is, I've never even had this kind of syndrome before. It's really annoying, not to mention nerve-wracking, as if hundreds of little shockwaves are swimming in my bloodstream. I also don't know why all this seafood imagery is running through my head. Maybe it's because I just came back from China a few weeks ago where I had some of the best fresh-caught fish I've ever tasted. But that's a different story. This story is not about food. It's about queasy feelings that shouldn't exist, and the jubilant feelings that should exist but refuse to appear.

5   Last summer I had gone away to a college campus for CSSSA, the California Summer School for the Arts. And I precisely remember the feelings I had before going away from home by myself for the first time.

They can only be described in two words: "Hell, yeah."

I had absolutely no intention of being homesick, or even missing anyone. I could only silently thank the deities for allowing me a chance to get away from the mundane, suburban existence of Cupertino. I felt that way before going to China this summer, too.

> Mundane: Commonplace, ordinary.

Maybe the terror is that I'm essentially an adult.

I've never much liked the prospect of being one. Most teenage girls want to be older—they want the independence, the maturity. I was never one of these girls. I wanted Neverland. I wanted childhood forever. I wanted to be myself as I was ten years ago—believing in quixotic things, not listening to directions, playing in the dirt, wearing mismatched socks, and not caring about anything. *Insouciance.* That's what I've always wanted. That's what's been on my Christmas list, my birthday list, for many, many years. But, being human and being me, it can never be accomplished. I'm 18, but not a legal adult. I like to say I'm an illegal teenager.

> Quixotic: Impractical, foolish.

*08/20/05, 12:55 AM*

10   The last hour has been spent contemplating certain death. The plane was dimly lit, a pathway of thin neon lights in the center aisle. It was almost pretty, but a little dizzying. I sat next to an emergency exit. Minutes

passed by like the slow descent of thawing winter water. As I tried to doze, I could hear the unstable droning of the plane.

I thought about how it'd be if there were some dire emergency and what it'd feel like to hurtle across the sky with the ruins of a metal bird ripping through my eardrums, all the people and torn belongings floating over me. Sounds romanticized, sure. Maybe too beautiful to be a plane crash. But who really can photograph, document the few moments before death? And even if that were videotaped, who knows what brilliant colors you see when your eyelids shut and wince, in those final few seconds?

We were taking off. The familiar rumble lifted my stomach again. And then we were slowing down. What was going on?

The minutes migrated. The announcer said that there was a problem with the engine and they needed to check things out. Twenty minutes passed. The man to my right snored a slow, soft pattern.

I knew that if we were to take off again, we'd become a meteor in the sky—destined to fall. Yet I thought about death, and this way of dying, and whether I believed in God. The people next to me complained of boredom, while the people in front of me complained of bad service.

15      I guess they just don't think about death. Every time I board a plane, I think about crashing and dying at least once, random thought or whatever.

Finally, the announcer said that we must get off the plane. Part of me was relieved; part disappointed. There was no thrill in safety only boredom.

*Monday, 08/29*

The first day of classes has been a dismal day. It rained. And I'm one of those people who adore the rain. When I think of rain, images of invigorating dewdrops lapping against the black streets come up and I instantly feel like dancing.

Just, not today. It made my sneakers squeal against the sidewalk. Sleepiness overwhelmed me. Caffeine will definitely become my best friend.

The corridors of Porter Hall, where four of my classes were located, looked suspiciously like a high school, with its shiny red lockers and drinking fountains. And this to me is a sort of omen. Maybe it's the pervasive queasiness I get that's reminiscent of my first journal entry. Either way, it's unpleasant. I'll be switching out of a few classes soon, if I cross my fingers.

20      My Interpretation and Argument class, the freshman English requirement, switched topics rather randomly from "Hyphenated American Identities: Native American, Asian American, and Latina/o" to "Paranoia." I don't think I mind. A perfect topic for me, because paranoia has been the definition of my experiences anywhere away from home—like while I was in China for a month and a half, where strangers always had hidden agendas, no matter if they were a small rosy-cheeked child on the street or an old

Paranoia: Distrust of others.

grandma with a walking stick. But since this is supposed to be my new home, I'm going to have to shed that paranoia like last season's ugly teal sweater. Paranoia feels a lot like being inside a sponge. You don't know when you're going to be squeezed into submission and deluged with dirty dishwater.

Speaking of dirty water, August is ending soon, and we have a chance of floods since we live in the basement floor of the Mudge House. Our windows are like gutters—right next to the ground. I haven't been through a flood since the days of mudslides back in California. It's easy enough to imagine a huge roller coaster of steel-like water gushing into our rickety windows.

*Tuesday, 08/30*

We just had an actual fire alarm. I must say it was the most terrifyingly banshee-like bellowing earsplitting screeching noise my eardrums have ever experienced. The smoke smelled like bell peppers stuffed with bad cheese. Some people tried to cook in the kitchen and set off the alarm. Obviously they overestimated their culinary abilities.

The rain still dusted the streets as we rushed out. The police and fire department had arrived already. All of Mudge House was outside. One guy stood there on the wet pavement in a towel, bare-chested and sopping wet. He'd been in mid-shower when the alarm started wailing. How ostentatious. Or maybe it was just bad luck.

The firemen came out, complete in mustard-colored bodysuits. Annoying people smoked cigarettes in front of us. The stuff got into our nostrils. If there is an ideal time to smoke, this sure as hell wasn't it. I shot invisible cannonballs at them.

25     In about five minutes all was over and the firemen left. We could still smell the smoke.

What have been my first few experiences since starting this journal? Dysfunctional planes, possible floods, and cooking fires.

In all reality, I think it's quite beautiful, to have these very faint touches with the absolute sheerness of life. Something about it amazes and terrifies me. I used to shun the excessive fear of death, but now I recognize it: how weightless life is and how heavy death can be. And for once I recognize that my life is only beginning: that now is the time I construct myself, out of time, out of these hands, out of thin air, out of human clay.

Right now our entire country is trying to bear the weight of Katrina, who claws her hands over us like a giant witch, ripping apart our very roots and vomiting on our people. And so I mourn and so I pray . . . for those people down there who dance every day now in their waltz of terror.

*8/31/05*

Since coming to college, I've graduated from doodling on paper. Doodling on my pants is much more fulfilling.

*9/2/05*

30      I am seriously contemplating applying for the BHA program and combining Humanities and Arts. I swear, it's something about that Fine Arts building. Its Romanesque pillars, its music, its elegance, its stature, all as if some invisible moat of beauty surrounded it. Every time I pass by that building, this serenity sweeps over me and I feel like I'm lighter than usual. The orchestra's music always leaks out, drifting into the air in a stream of lovely sound. Inside, there is a huge mural on the ceiling, Sistine-Chapel-esque, that the first graduating Fine Arts class painted.

> **Romanesque:** The architecture of medieval Europe, characterized by round arches, large towers, and massive granite buildings.

I've finally changed my class to Reading Contemporary Poetry. I'm very happy about this. The poetry class I have doesn't involve too many lectures. It's refreshing to hear the familiar voices of Whitman and Dickinson and Plath. Don't get me wrong: I definitely want to try new things. But this is only the first semester. I need my dead poet sisters and brothers to pull me through.

*9/3/05*

I attended my first "frat party" last night. Such escapades, I soon learned, pale in comparison to juggling oranges and running around in the grass.

*9/6/05*

It is an indescribably gorgeous day and CMU is deluged in the radiance that only comes in the very peak of summer when peals of platinum sunshine paint each yellow brick building. I am sitting on a semicircle stone bench at the College of Fine Arts surrounded by engraved wall sculptures of lions persecuting Christians, Eve and the Serpent, a tall and lanky Jesus, and the men of the Last Supper. A few students sit under the trees tossing breadcrumbs at the finches and peeling bananas. Perfection cannot go beyond this.

Unless, of course, I immortalize the scene with magical realism. The sunlight would then paint even the sooty pigeons gold, from their white beaks to their tangerine eyes to their scarlet feet, and all of a sudden the music in the hall would echo higher and faster until the statues start weeping. The students sitting on the grass would burst into song, plastic wings sprouting from their backpacks and unfolding into the light. I would then join them in flight as we hop from building to building. The statues would tear away from walls and stare up at us in awe and stupor, mouths cracking in soundless delight. We would be the ones who stare down at our buildings, our grass, our fence, our University, under a seamless sky.

### 9/08/05

35     Pittsburgh's Asian food really needs reevaluation. I was so deceived.

The menu said "wonton" soup. So I ordered it. And what do they give me? A broth, with potstickers, not wontons. I felt cheated. Maybe it was a psychology thing: all my life I've had many potstickers and not enough wontons. Potstickers were the food I had for lunch, for dinner, always, forever. There are certain distinctions: The potsticker's skin is much thicker than the delicate, thin peel of the wonton, and is loosely in the shape of an orange slice, contrasting the wonton's cubic shape and thin "skirt."

At that moment, once again I felt wonton-deprived.

But then as I explained the grave mistake of the menu to the manager, he gave me the meal for free. Things were happy again in the world.

> **Potstickers and wontons:** Types of Chinese dumplings, consisting of a vegetable or meat filling wrapped in dough and fried or steamed.

### 9/12/05

On Friday, I was supposed to go to a playwriting class. I was very excited to attend, being highly ignorant in the field of playwriting and screenplay in general. Something about the mystery of dialogue still stymies me sometimes in my writing. It's not a dislike of dialogue; it's just that I have other fortes. In conversation I am generally the listener, and in those cases where I'm the speaker nothing I say is particularly whimsical or exciting. Even in my journal entries, which are more colloquial usually than my writings, I tend to be boring. Like the one fact that bothers me insanely is how many "I's" are used. It's a horrible horrible habit, I despise it (there it goes again) but it's like going on a chocolate binge—once you start, nothing will stop you from reaching in that crisp wax wrapper again and taking out a chunk of that raspberry truffle chocolate bar. Indulgence sometimes rips apart my writer's senses. I remember sophomore year and my metaphor binge. Now I'm forever a metaphor-holic. Addictions for me refuse to be cured.

> **Fortes:** Strong points.

40     On to the point: so at 1:30, the time my class was supposed to begin, I showed up to an empty room. It felt positively eerie, with the empty swivel chairs and the wiped blackboard. Ten minutes passed, so I proceeded desperately to the English department, where I discovered that playwriting was actually a part of the Drama department. So after attempting to check whether the class had moved and trying to call the Drama academic advisor a couple of times, I crept into the Drama building, with its wooden panels and winding staircases and high, high ceiling. The academic advisor was cheerful, wore pink lipstick, and had hair the color of sun-dried apricots. Unfortunately, she did not know what was going on.

It felt like a mystery, in which I was to find a missing person who seemed to leave no trace, only it wasn't a person—it was an entire class. The mystique of it built so much tension in my veins. Did I really sign up for a phantom class? What would ghosts discuss anyway? Certainly not the meaning of *life*, right? Ideas about primeval, endless discussions that stay iron solid through the passage of time formulate in my head. But that died when I got an e-mail from the teacher saying the class was cancelled due to an emergency, and that they would meet again next Friday. My spirits somewhat lifted, I accepted the next assignment with glee.

And that assignment was something that really lifted me up: "Overheard dialogue or conversation." So I get to be my own emissary. Rapture!

If only my ears weren't nearly so deaf. . . .

## One Word Spotlight

***Insouciance*** (paragraph 8) means to be lighthearted and carefree. Some young people, such as Mao, prefer to put off accepting the responsibilities of adulthood. Instead they want to remain childlike.

## Reflect on the Reading

1. List five words that you think best describe Mao's emotional state as she wrote the entries in this blog.

2. Mao writes that she is a "metaphor-holic." What does she mean by this expression? Give an example from her blog that shows this characteristic.

3. How well does the title of this piece—"When Life Gives You Potstickers Instead of Wontons, Sharply Verbalize Your Bitterness Until It Fixes Itself"—match the style and content?

4. Select a sentence or two from the piece that best summarizes what Mao is expressing.

5. Mao, a graduate of the writing program of 826 Valencia, wrote this blog specifically for the 826 website. Who is the audience for this website? How well will this blog appeal to this audience?

## Consider Your Viewpoint

1. To what extent can you relate to the emotions and thoughts that Mao expresses in her blog?

2. Mao writes about leaving California to fly across the country to attend college. Many students, however, attend college in their hometown. In what ways would remaining in your hometown affect your experiences as you begin college? How might it be different from moving away to attend college?

3. Mao's blog does not contain photos, videos, links, and other techniques common to digital communication. Describe the kinds of photos, videos,

and links that might be appropriate for this blog, given Mao's writing style and ideas.

4. Mao is the traditional age of a college student—she just graduated from high school. Many college students are older than this. How might their reactions to college be different than the reactions of an eighteen-year-old?

5. Mao doesn't appear to have a job her first semester of college. What are the benefits and difficulties of holding a job while in college?

# WRITING ASSIGNMENT

For this writing assignment, you will explore an event that was important to you. The event can be something you witnessed, something that happened to you, or something that you did. By writing about this event, you'll increase your understanding, create a written record, and communicate something important about yourself to others.

## YOUR EXPLORATION

As the readings in this chapter show, events as mundane as signing up at a gym, as important as learning to stay calm in a crisis, and as life altering as moving away to college can make a good topic for your own exploration. Before beginning this assignment, consider reviewing Chapters 2 and 3 on selecting a topic, analyzing the rhetorical situation, and using a writing process.

### Choosing a Topic

The event you decide to write about should interest you, spark some ideas, and potentially appeal to your readers. Because you'll share your writing with others, avoid selecting a very personal topic. The obvious choices for this assignment are rites of passage, or rituals that signal a new stage of life, and momentous events that are life altering. However, less obvious topics can sometimes lend themselves to more nuanced writing.

> *There are no mistakes, no coincidences. All events are blessings given to us to learn from.*
> —*Elisabeth Kubler-Ross*

One way to think of a topic is to brainstorm a list of major events in your life, such as the following:

a birth or a death

a coming-of-age ritual such as a *quincinera,* a Latin American ceremony that welcomes girls into womanhood

## LANGUAGES and CULTURES

Some people think that to write well you must feel inspired. In many cultures, inspiration is seen to spring from a variety of sources, such as sacred texts, the natural world, dreams, and the individual psyche. While great artists often claim to be inspired, they also constantly practice their craft. When you write, don't wait for lightning to strike. Instead, use techniques for discovering ideas and give yourself enough time to draft, revise, and edit.

a wedding, christening, or graduation

the receipt of a visa for travel or immigration

acceptance into a certain college

Here are some questions to help you get started:

- Select a particular year in your life. What do you remember the most about this year?
- Think of a certain place. What are the first things that come to mind about this place?
- Recall a trip that you have made. What do you picture?
- Think of the last time you experienced a strong emotion, such as joy, anxiety, or fear. What event caused that emotion?
- Consider an important person in your life. What event do you immediately associate with that person?

After you have a topic, be sure to narrow it so you can explore the event in depth. Sandeep Jauhar, for instance, narrowed his topic to a single incident that happened while he was an intern. If you're writing about a trip that you took to another country, at first you might be tempted to write about the airplane ride, and your first meal, and the hotel you stayed at, and the fascinating people you met. However, relating all of these events will result in an essay that remains on the surface. Instead of telling about an entire trip that you made, focus in on a single event that was especially significant.

### Topic Questions for Exploring an Event

- What event am I considering exploring? Why does this event appeal to me?
- Will I be able to explore this event in detail, or does it need to be narrowed down?
- Do I have a preliminary understanding of the importance of this event?
- Am I willing to share my exploration of this event with others?
- Will my audience be interested in reading about this event?

**Activity 5.1**   Select an event you're considering as a topic and spend a few minutes telling the story of the event to several classmates. Afterwards, discuss together why this would or would not make a good topic. Answer these questions: What would be the easiest thing about writing about this event? What would be the hardest thing? Do the same for the other classmates in your group.

**Connect With Others**

## Analyzing the Rhetorical Situation

By analyzing your rhetorical situation, you can respond effectively to the context of this assignment. Your goal is to shape your writing so that your readers understand your message.

**Considering Audience and Purpose.**  When you write about an event, you want your audience to understand your ideas and to find your writing memorable. The more you know about your audience, the greater the chances of this happening.

> ### Audience Questions for Exploring an Event
> - Who would be interested in reading about this topic?
> - What does your audience already know about the topic? What do they need to know?
> - What is their attitude toward the topic?
> - Will their cultural background or gender affect the way they respond to the topic?
> - Will their age or educational level affect their response?

Because your primary purpose in writing this piece is expressive, you'll be writing about your feelings. For instance, in his essay Jauhar shows us his fear that he has harmed his patient, and Mao in her blog communicates her excitement and anxiety about starting college. Gopnik, in writing about the Parisian gym, expresses amusement and frustration. You'll also be informing your readers about the event. Jauhar, for instance, gives enough information for us to understand the possible medical complications of his actions, and Mao fills her blog with details such as what she eats at the Chinese restaurant. Your piece will also be persuasive in the sense that you want your readers to believe what you're saying. In his piece on the French attitude toward athletics, Gopnik shows that he knows his topic by describing the competition for the name of the stadium and the reactions of the gym personnel to his request for frequent gym visits.

## Purpose Questions for Exploring an Event

- What personal thoughts or feelings do I want to share about this event?
- What information am I planning to communicate?
- How will I make my readers believe that I'm knowledgeable about my topic?
- Will my readers' language or cultural background affect their understanding?
- What do I want my readers to take away from this piece?

**Choosing a Genre and Visual Design.** In this chapter you read selections from three genres or forms: an essay, a memoir, and a blog. When you choose one of these genres (or another genre altogether), keep in mind the following distinctions:

> *An essay* will usually have a clear thesis toward the beginning of the piece that expresses the central point. In "The Rules of the Sport" Gopnik's thesis is in the second paragraph:
>
> > The French are prepared to be formally enthusiastic about American-style stadiums and American-style sports, but they are not going to get carried away by it all.
>
> Additionally, an essay most likely will have statements throughout the piece that will indicate what the writer wants you to understand. Throughout his essay Gopnik uses irony to tell us how surprised he is by the French attitude toward sports, as when he writes about asking for a towel and realizes that the request is seen as absurd.
>
> *A memoir,* in contrast, is usually written as a narration told in chronological order. Typically the author suggests the significance of the narration toward the end. For example, in "Road Trip" Jauhar relates the story of his "road trip" without commentary until the last paragraph, when he discusses what he has learned about himself. In particular, his last sentence reveals his central point: "I was beginning to appreciate what it was going to take to make me into a doctor—into a man."
>
> *A blog* is usually organized like a diary, with entries on different days, and the later entries might refer to events in the earlier entries. A blog about an event might be written from a variety of perspectives over different days or weeks. In her blog, for instance, Mao wrote about the plane trip to Pittsburgh, a rainy day, a trip to a Chinese restaurant, and her adventures trying to locate a classroom. A blog is usually more informal than a memoir or an essay

and the language can be similar to a conversation with the reader. A blog, by necessity, will be written about an event that occurs over a stretch of time as opposed to an event that happens quickly.

Depending on the genre that you choose, decide on your visual design, including the layout, font, and other elements such as drawings, photographs, and short videos. Because a blog is by definition on the Internet, its visual display is especially important.

---

### Genre and Visual Design Questions for Exploring an Event

- Which genre will best allow me to communicate with my audience?
- What will be easiest about using this format? What will be hardest?
- What visual design will be best, considering my genre, audience, and purpose?
- What do I already know about using this genre?
- What do I need to learn about writing in this genre?

---

**Reviewing Exigence and Constraints.** As you know, exigence is what makes you want to write a particular piece—what has prompted you to write. Naturally, one exigence for your exploration of an event is that you want to complete an assignment in your writing course. However, what is your exigence for selecting a particular event to write about? You might want to explore what the event means to you, or you might be eager to share the event with your readers. By considering your exigence, you have a better chance of writing an effective exploration of an event.

---

### Exigence Questions for Exploring an Event

- What situation has made me want to write about this event?
- Why do I care about this topic?
- Why do I want my audience to care about this topic?
- Why is it important to have a written record of this event?

---

Constraints include anything that might interfere with you communicating your message to your audience. For example, if you're writing about a very personal event, you might become so emotional it would be hard to focus on the writing. Changing your topic to a less personal event would eliminate that constraint. Another constraint might be your audience's lack of knowledge about the topic. In "Road Trip," for instance, the author had to write about the event in such a way that readers unfamiliar with a CT scan would still understand what was happening. His clear description of the medical procedure helped him overcome this constraint. Constraints can also include a particular length requirement or the need to finish the piece by a certain date.

---

### Constraint Questions for Exploring an Event

- Have I been given any special requirements for this assignment, such as word count, format, and deadlines?
- Will my closeness to my topic constrain my ability to write about it?
- Will I feel constrained about writing on a personal topic to my audience?
- What other constraints do I face in writing this piece?

---

**Connect With Others**

**Activity 5.2**   With a small group, select a potential topic for this assignment. Develop a rhetorical situation for the assignment, including audience, purpose, genre, exigence, and constraints.

## Using the Writing Process

Now that you've analyzed your rhetorical situation, you can begin to write. To ensure the success of your piece, be sure to discover ideas, draft to explore ideas, revise to improve content, and edit to eliminate errors. Keep in mind that the writing process isn't usually as linear as these stages, so you might need to go back to an earlier stage as needed.

### STAGE 1: Discovering Ideas

In Part I of this textbook, you learned a variety of ways to discover ideas. One way that is especially appropriate for an exploration of an event is to list ideas, also known as brainstorming.

**Listing Ideas.**   The purpose of listing isn't to get your *best* ideas down on paper or screen; it's to get *all* of your ideas down. At this early stage of the writing process, you don't want to evaluate your ideas as "good" or "bad." Instead, aim for producing a wealth of material that you can then review to pick out the best parts. As a result, you won't feel too blocked or inhibited. If you wish, you can list ideas in a language other than English, or you can mix languages.

**One Student's Work.**  Student writer Omotayo Olabumuyi was very perturbed about an incident that happened in one of his college courses, so he decided to write about that event. A presenter had come to talk to the class about AIDS in Africa, and as a Nigerian he was offended by some of his fellow students' comments about Africa. Here is what he listed about this event:

> What is WORST thing about Africa? How about the BEST thing about Africa?
>
> My differences from Americans—respect for weak, elders, women, education
>
> Unity of Africa
>
> Obnoxious questions
>
> Diversity, not superior/inferior
>
> People look but don't see, they listen but don't hear
>
> My identity, my culture, my life!

## STAGE 2:  Drafting to Explore Ideas

As you draft, put your ideas down in the genre that you believe is most appropriate for your topic. If you have a clear statement about the significance of your event that you want your readers to understand early in the piece, write in an essay format. Refer to "The Rules of Game" for a model. If, like Sandeep Jauhar, you want to recollect the event as a straightforward story with the significance implied at the end, use a memoir format. The genre of a blog is appropriate if you want to tell about the event in a day-by-day format. A blog also allows you to include images and sound.

**Descriptive Language.**  In expressive writing, descriptive language helps to make your ideas come alive for the readers. Your goal is to help the readers imagine what you are expressing.

One way to do this is by using *sensory words,* or words that appeal to the five senses of sight, smell, taste, touch, and sound. In her blog, Mao uses sensory words when she describes the fire alarm in her dorm:

> I must say it was the most terrifyingly banshee-like bellowing earsplitting screeching noise my eardrums have ever experienced. The smoke smelled like bell peppers stuffed with bad cheese.

By describing the sound of the alarm and the smell of the smoke, Mao lets us experience what she describes.

Another technique for making your language descriptive is to focus in on a particular detail. For example, in "The Rules of the Game," Gopnik describes the reaction of the woman behind the desk when he asks for a towel. He could have simply written, "She didn't know what I was talking about." Instead, he wrote this:

> The girl in the red tracksuit at the desk gave me a long, steady, opaque look. I thought that maybe I had got the word for towel wrong (I hadn't, though), and after I asked again and got the same look in return, I thought it wise to try to describe its function. My description sounded like a definition from Dr. Johnson's dictionary: that thing which is used in the process of removing water from the surfaces of your body in the moments after its immersion. "Ah," she said. "Of course. A towel. We have none yet." She looked off into the middle distance. "This," she said at last, "is envisaged."

A third technique for descriptive language is to use similes and metaphors. A simile is a direct comparison between two things, while a metaphor is an indirect comparison. In a simile, the word *like* is used, as in Mao's statement that "the smoke smelled *like* bell peppers stuffed with bad cheese." Mao uses many similes and metaphors in her blog, so many that she even jokes that she is addicted to metaphors, a "metaphor-holic." These comparisons make her writing more memorable. Here are a few examples from the blog:

> Minutes passed by like the slow descent of thawing winter water.

> I knew that if we were to take off again, we'd become a meteor in the sky—destined to fall.

> And so I mourn and so I pray . . . for those people down there who dance every day now in their waltz of terror.

**Dialogue.** When relating an event, you can use dialogue to move the story along and to convey important ideas. In "Road Trip," Jauhar uses dialogue to convey his growing sense of alarm:

> Now I was in a full-blown panic. "I have to get her back to the unit," I cried. "Can you call Transport?"

> "I already did," the tech replied, nonplussed. "But he said it would take a few minutes."

> "I can't wait. Can you help me bring her back?"

> He looked at me helplessly. "I can't leave, Doc. I'm the only one here and there's another patient on the way."

> I grabbed the IV pole and the back of the stretcher and started racing toward the elevator. "Tell Transport to catch up with me," I shouted.

Like descriptive language, dialogue helps to capture the readers' imagination. However, be sure to use dialogue only when describing important action. Refer to the handbook at the end of this textbook for help with correctly writing dialogue.

**Activity 5.3**   Select an important scene related to the event in your piece and practice using description and dialogue to improve it. Use sensory words, focus on specific details, and experiment with similes and metaphors. If people interact in this scene, write dialogue that will convey an important idea and move the action along.

**Develop Your Understanding**

**Your Emotional Filter and Writing Monitor.** When writing about an event that happened to you or that you observed, you might find yourself becoming emotionally affected by your topic. An emotional connection to your topic helps keep you engaged with the writing process. However, if you find yourself so emotional you can't focus, take a break from writing to allow your feelings to subside. Also, strong emotions might keep you from effectively using your writing monitor to edit your piece for errors. You need a clear head so you can examine your writing carefully.

## STAGE 3:  Revising to Improve Content

When you revise, improve the content of your piece by evaluating how well you have organized and developed your ideas. At this stage you're also ready to review your sentence structure and word choice to make sure that your message is being communicated to your audience. To revise effectively, set aside your writing for a day or two. Ask others to review it and make suggestions for revision. Then return to your piece, review it yourself, and make the changes you think are necessary.

**Clarify the Main Point.** You've probably listened to someone talk about an event and in your head wondered, "So what?" In other words, you can't fathom the point of the story. In order to keep your readers from wondering the same thing, make the significance of your piece clear. In your first draft, you might have been unsure of what the significance actually was, or you might have changed your mind about it. If you're still unsure, spend some time gathering ideas by freewriting, mapping, or using another technique described in Chapter 3. As you revise, keep your main point in mind as you decide how to revise. Delete parts that don't contribute to the main point, and expand those that do.

**Improve Focus.** In your initial draft, you were trying to get your ideas down on paper. Now, however, you need to focus the story that you're telling. Just as a photographer crops a photo or uses a zoom lens, you can use language to direct the readers' attention to certain areas. In "Road Trip," for example, Jauhar gives details that show how inexperienced and

## Rhetorical Situation Questions for an Exploration of an Event

- Audience: Will your audience be interested in reading about this event? Will they learn something from it or be moved in some way?
- Purpose: Have you included enough description and dialogue so that your readers can picture and become involved in what you are relating?
- Genre: Does the format that you decided to use help you achieve your purpose? Have you made the most of this format?
- Exigence: Do you feel that you have communicated what you wanted to? Does the piece meet your expectations? Is there anything more you want to communicate?
- Constraints: What constraints have you encountered as you have drafted this piece? Are there any remaining constraints for you to consider? Develop a plan for overcoming them.

nervous he felt. He describes the tangle of tubes that he inexpertly unwinds, the way he looks to the technician for guidance, his uncertainty about which direction to take down the hallway. All of these details reinforce his point that this "road trip" was a nerve-wracking but necessary part of becoming a doctor.

In addition to clarifying your main point and improving your focus, review the rhetorical situation to help you make further improvements.

To help you revise further, share your draft with your peers. This peer review process gives you alternative perspectives on your piece, which will help you achieve your writing goals.

## Peer Review
## Exploring An Event

1. What is the greatest strength of this piece?

2. What event is being described? To what extent does this topic interest you? What did you already know about this topic? What did you learn?

3. Based on your reading, what do you think is the significance of this piece? How easy or hard was it to understand the significance?

4. Where might I add description or dialogue to make my main point clearer? How can I improve my focus?

5. What parts of the piece could be omitted? Why do they need to be omitted?

6. How well does my topic flow? Where do the ideas seem choppy or jumpy?

7. Underline any words or sentences that you think I should revise because they do not communicate to you.

8. Place a checkmark in the margin next to any punctuation or spelling errors that you discovered while reading this draft.

## STAGE 4: Editing for Correctness

When you drafted and revised your exploration of an event, you focused on content, organization, and development of your piece. Now work on editing your draft to make it readable for your audience. To edit, read your piece word for word. Distinguish between "treatable" and "less treatable" errors. For treatable errors, consult a grammar handbook. Less treatable errors are more idiomatic, such as word choice or colloquial phrases. For less treatable errors, ask a tutor or a classmate for help. If you are fluent in spoken English, read your paper aloud so you can hear your errors.

### To Edit

- Use a dictionary and computer spell-checker.
- For treatable errors, refer to a grammar handbook and follow standard grammatical rules.
- For less treatable errors, ask another student or a tutor to read your writing for errors.
- As you edit, keep an Editing Log, a section in your notebook where you record the errors that you make.

**Activity 5.4**   Once you finish writing this piece, take a moment to look over what you have done. Complete this self-evaluation sheet to help you improve this piece and other writing assignments.

**Evaluate Your Work**

## Self-Evaluation Sheet
### Exploring An Event

1. Have I followed all instructions for this assignment? (Reread the assignment sheet and class notes.)

2. How clear is the significance of the event?

3. How well have I used description and dialogue to help the readers picture what is happening?

4. How well-focused is my writing? Are there any unnecessary or distracting parts that can be omitted?

5. Does each paragraph contribute to developing the main point?

6. Does my opening paragraph make my audience want to continue reading?

7. Do I conclude in such a way that there is a sense of closure?

8. Are my sentences well-written and varied in structure? (Read each sentence beginning with the last one, working backward to the beginning of the paper.)

9. Is my word choice vivid? How well have I used similes and metaphors?

10. Have a checked for grammar, punctuation, and spelling errors? (Use a grammar handbook and the computer spell checker.)

11. If I have used photos, music, or videos, how well do they contribute to the meaning of the piece?

If you're proud of what you have written and want others to read about this event, you will want to share it with a wide audience. In addition to showing it to your classmates and instructor, consider showing it to anyone who participated in the event with you. You can also post it on a website or email it to interested readers.

# ONE STUDENT'S EXPLORATION OF AN EVENT

In Stage 1 of the writing process, we introduced you to Omotayo Olabumuyi, a student who was writing about an event that happened in one of his university classes. Here is the final version of his essay.

## Africa Through the African Eye

### *Omotayo Olabumuyi*

Never have I been so aware of my identity as I was in my Individuals and Societies class when a presenter discussed the issue of AIDS in Tanzania, East Africa. I am one of the two Africans in the class, also the only one who has lived in Africa and not just toured it for a short while. The presenter asked if there were any people who had visited Africa. I looked round—less than one percent had our hands raised. Later on she asked for their general thoughts of what Africa was like. The responses were unbelievable; it then dawned on me that my identity was going to make the class a miserable one for me.

Olabumuyi catches his readers' attention by describing how he feels in class.

The first response was a loud shout from behind. "Primitive!" he yelled; next was "Native!" and then "Uncivilized!" It got worse when I heard a very silent hum sounding like "Animals!" Being an African, I was a little biased and my heart was torn apart until he made it clear that he wasn't calling the people animals. He better qualified himself by saying "Wildlife and the safari." Anyway, this was the sad beginning of the class that was going to disturb my state of mind for hours to come.

The presenter started off by correcting the erroneous responses, stating clearly that there are skyscrapers in the cities, the latest automobiles, cell phones, hotels, and most of the things that are enjoyed in the developed world. Then she proceeded to the crux of the issue but with a twist, knowing that she was speaking to an American audience. She spent most of the time speaking about wildlife and showing pictures of the lions, hippopotamus, all the beautiful animals that make Africa so close to nature. She only spent a little time speaking about the diseases and poverty.

From my understanding, she did this to give the audience a better perception of Africa. She did this so that they may see that Africa has a lot more than we see on TV. But it looked to me like she failed in changing the perceptions of the people. I was riveted in my seat, speechless as my mind raced through the rich culture of the African society made unappealing because of the poor economy. I was motionless as I empathized with the ill fate of the diseased Tanzanian people. But I was alone in this state of melancholy.

Olabumuyi provides description that helps his readers feel what he is feeling.

I managed to keep tears back as I looked around and saw the happy faces who could only imagine the excitement of what it would be like driving so close to a lion in the safari, or having to see a lion tear up a gazelle. The veil that prevented them from showing any sympathy grew thicker as she spoke of her experience while climbing Mount Kilimanjaro. The whole class was blown away, well distracted, and she tried relentlessly to bring the class back to the main health topic of the day. Dolefully, that was now more or less inconsequential.

Eventually, it was a very obnoxious question that captivated them and made them listen to what Africa is, aside from being a land where you visit to see animals in their natural habitat. The question was utterly disheartening. A boy asked the presenter what the WORST thing she had seen in Africa. It seemed to me that the boy could not imagine Africa as a land from which anything good can come out. He was hell bent on seeing more, more gory pictures of hunger and starvation, more stories of the different cultures that he perceived as crude, more disease, more to adorn his superiority. The presenter talked about a woman she had met who had killed herself because her whole family had died of AIDS and her own death was only a matter of months. I looked at the boy's face after the response, and it was initially emotionless—he wasn't impressed, nor was he moved. But then, seconds later, a smile surfaced on his face as he settled in his seat, satisfied, his ego appeased.

In this paragraph, Olabumuyi explains why the events of this class are significant.

The class was slowly coming to an end, far too slowly for my liking. It was unbearable for me—it was too sorrowful. The presenter had done her best and had presented some interesting things about Africa, but the audience had viewed it as only entertainment. Then after she had shown the malnourished kids, the audience felt disdainfully superior. Appalled at this, I asked myself: When would people stop confusing the notion of diversity with that of superiority and inferiority? When will people start to imagine themselves in the shoes of those who are not as privileged as them? When will they think and act to better the plight of others?

On getting home, I continued ruminating. Only my background and upbringing had made me different from them. That was what was responsible for the sharply contrasting reactions we had had. I was brought up in the Yoruba culture of West Africa, and there, like most African tribes, respect was the order of the day. Respect for elders, respect for peers, and respect for people with differences. I remembered how as a little kid I was taught to greet all elders in the traditional way, how I learned the grammatical structures that must be used in addressing adults. This sort of respect allows individuals to appreciate differences. The fact that an old man cannot walk doesn't mean he should not be honored, that my friends speak a different language or have a different accent doesn't change anything, that I am black and you are colored is only a matter of genetics; differences only make us appreciate the world better. Probably this is why one of the most respected men in the world today, Nelson Mandela, is an African.

I thought a little more about the culture, and I realized that my understanding of several delicate issues was also different from those of Americans. And one of these is the issue of women and their rights. Lest I forget, it was in the same Individuals and Societies class that we were told that one of the reasons why AIDS is so widespread in Africa is because of the manner in which women are treated. This struck me as very ridiculous, knowing full well that my mother has perhaps the greatest influence in my own African family and this is true in most homes I know.

It is common to hear in Nigeria that behind every successful man there is a woman. And this, being an eternal truth, prevents any sort of fight for rights. Though the African man tries to be as "manly" as possible, it is always known that his woman is still his soft spot. Women control everything, not by saying, "I am boss," or "I am equal to you," but with their ingenious ability to persuade, convince, and always find their way. No wonder women in Africa hardly fight for their rights—it is something that is already theirs, already bestowed on them by virtue of their strength of character. It is so difficult for anybody to be subservient to any sort of authority; only those fantastic individuals, usually African women, can do this. They help give the family structure in which the father is the head, the wife his assistant, but in some inexplicable way she becomes the head once again. What will Africa be without her women?

Another thing I couldn't avoid thinking about was the perception of the whole of Africa as primitive and uncivilized. Where I come from, education is part of the culture. Learning is mandatory, and even long before formal education began, all the youths went for apprenticeships in trades, sometimes as blacksmiths, and the majority learned to be good farmers, hunters, and family men or women. And with the advent of formal education, the culture that gave so much importance to education continued the trend. Speaking for a small portion of Africa, my nation, Nigeria, I know that we have a very large bank of human resources; the achievers range from Nobel laureates, to pioneers in computer advancements to medical practitioners, Miss World, musicians, footballers, Olympic medalists and talents from all walks of life. The word *primitive* cannot be ideal in qualifying such an eclectic group of people.

Finally, I thought about the unity that abounds among people in my native land. It looks to me like there are no pariahs there. Even psychiatric patients, specifically the extremes—mad men on the street—are still shown love by their family or others who know them. They still eat, and it all comes from well-wishers. There is overwhelming care and affection shown by people. The empathy for a sick person is so high. Family members, neighborhoods, churches, mosques, and communities in general routinely raise funds to help those who are sick. Others who cannot help monetarily at least sympathize; their attitude alone is worth everything.

This was my final thought as I slowly dozed off, my head uneasy, desperately needing a rest. It was a sweet sleep though, the recognition that my upbringing had given me a somewhat better reaction to the presentation in class, that even though we as Africans are looked down upon, it was only ignorance that was responsible for this. Many look but don't see, they listen but don't hear, they choose to believe what they want and neglect those in need. I believe in what is and have pity for those whose chances grow slimmer. My eyes finally closed and I traveled into the world where consciousness is not well defined, a fitting elixir to the initial tension and bitterness that threatened to ruin my day—and then, subconsciously, statements began resonating in my mind saying: "I am different," "I am black," "I am beautiful," "I am intelligent," and "I AM AN AFRICAN."

Olabumuyi provides further detail to support his main point.

Olabumuyi concludes by using the class experience to reaffirm his own identity.

# ADDITIONAL READINGS

## An Immigrant Learns Two New Languages

### Eric Hoover

The *Chronicle of Higher Education,* a newspaper aimed at faculty and staff who work in colleges and universities in the United States, regularly publishes feature articles on students over 50 who are seeking higher education. In the following article, Eric Hoover, a staff reporter for the *Chronicle,* profiles a community college student in Philadelphia.

A desk, a love seat, and a small bookshelf. Little else could fit inside the room Ruth Maldonato calls her sanctuary. Some days, after coming home from class, she closes the door and sits in the quiet, surrounded by four purple walls.

For years she has studied here, on the second floor of the row house she shares with her husband. In this room, she has typed several essays, read many books, and looked up thousands of words.

Ms. Maldonato, a part-time student at the Community College of Philadelphia, learned two languages after emigrating from Colombia 12 years ago. The first was English and the second was law. She plans to graduate in December with an associate degree in paralegal studies. After that, she hopes to find a job, and a way to help immigrants like herself, if only to translate an unfamiliar world.

At 52, Ms. Maldonato has settled in this big, buzzing city, unlike any she once knew. Born in Medellín, she grew up in small towns where people had neither cars nor electricity. As a teenager, she read about the Kennedys and danced to disco, but never imagined living in the United States, which seemed as far away as the moon.

5    Then, while vacationing in Costa Rica in 1997, she met an American with a grin two feet wide. His name was William. She knew no English, but he spoke decent Spanish. They fell in love right then and there.

After returning to the States, William sent her dozens of books, like *Exploring English* and *Easy True Stories,* as well as Spanish-English dictionaries and language cassettes. Months later, he visited her in Colombia, then asked her to come to see him in Philadelphia, where he proposed. At their wedding just weeks later, she knew none of the guests.

His home had a second bedroom. "You can do whatever you want with it," he told her. She decided to turn it into a study, and in that room, she began to redefine herself.

Ms. Maldonato took English courses and eventually became a U.S. citizen. She learned how to drive and how to park on South Philadelphia's narrow streets. She found that she liked Geno's famous cheesesteaks, even American football. She was happy.

Still, something was missing. Ms. Maldonato missed her family, but she felt something deeper than loneliness. She needed a purpose. In Colombia, she had worked in the accounting division of an engineering company, a job she enjoyed. She wanted a routine, a challenge.

10    "I needed to fill that empty hole in my life," she says. "That was my goal—to be somebody."

## 'Another Kind of World'

In 2002, Ms. Maldonato found her first job when a young couple hired her as a nanny. Their first child arrived, then a second. Over the years, she cleaned the house, made the beds, and did the laundry. She changed the children's diapers, took them to the zoo, and played games with them. Sometimes she taught them Spanish words.

The family embraced Ms. Maldonato. In 2005, when she announced that she planned to enroll at the community college, the couple told her they would pay for her courses, which would cost up to $1,700 a semester. She accepted the offer, vowing to study hard. She worked in their home eight hours a day and took classes in the evenings.

Early on, Ms. Maldonato met with an adviser who encouraged her to pursue a career as a paralegal. The idea intrigued her, but she had doubts. To learn a language is to piece together a puzzle that is never quite done. She could read legal cases, but could she interpret them? She could master unfamiliar words, but could she grasp their meaning?

The first novel she read in English was *Foreigner*, by Nahid Rachlin. It tells the story of an Iranian woman who studies in the United States, where she marries and settles down, only to return years later to her native country. Ms. Maldonato filled the book's pages with notes. "It was the same pain," she says. "She knew no English, had no friends. There was different weather, different food. She had to face another kind of world she was not prepared to live in."

Long before Ms. Maldonato came to Philadelphia, she had known the feeling of moving from one place to another. Her mother was a schoolteacher whose job required her to relocate every two or three years. The family's homes changed, but one thing did not: Each night after dinner, her mother would sit everyone down and read to them from the Bible, for they owned few other books.

15    Only later did Ms. Maldonato learn other stories. When she first read *Cinderella*, her mind flooded with fantasies about the many things she would like to own. For a time, she thought a lot about Disneyland.

She grew into a serious student. In 1980 she enrolled at the University of Medellín, where she studied economics. Her family helped pay for her first year, but eventually she decided she could not afford the tuition. After two and a half years, she dropped out and found a job.

For years, Ms. Maldonato looked back in frustration. In Philadelphia, she resolved to graduate, no matter what.

Early on, Ms. Maldonato befriended Clint Gould, a professor at the community college who taught her English 101 course. Over the years, Mr. Gould, who lives just a few blocks away, has talked her through many assignments. Recently, he helped her write her résumé.

Soon she will need it. This spring, she will take a business course for paralegals and a course on wills. In the fall, she plans to complete a legal internship, the last requirement she must fulfill for her degree. If she cannot find a full-time job, she will volunteer, to get some experience.

20    Not long ago, the family for whom Ms. Maldonato worked moved to Connecticut. Since then, she's paid for her courses with money she had saved. She remains close to the couple, who have promised to attend her graduation.

Until then, Ms. Maldonato will study in the room with the purple walls. It contains things she once did not own: a computer, a shelf full of American paperbacks, a copy of *Black's Law Dictionary*. It's a humble study, with an ironing board behind the door and a window overlooking the alley. But in this room, she says, she has everything.

## Reflect on the Reading

1. The author writes that Ruth Maldonato has learned two new languages since emigrating from Columbia: English and the language of the law. In what way is the legal profession a new language?

2. The author begins and ends the article by describing Ms. Maldonato's study room. How does this strategy help to reinforce the author's depiction of Ms. Maldonato?

3. In the middle of this article, the author flashes back to Ms. Maldonato's life in Columbia, and describes some key events in her childhood and early adulthood. How does this flashback contribute to the effectiveness of the article?

## Consider Your Viewpoint

1. In paragraph 13, the author writes that "to learn a language is to piece together a puzzle that is never quite done." Do you agree? Explain your answer.

2. The author describes several key people in Ms. Maldonato's life who helped her achieve her goals, including employers and a teacher. Why is it so important to have these key figures in life?

3. This article is written for U.S. college and university faculty and staff. What do you think the author wants them to learn from this piece?

# Two Languages in Mind, but Just One in Heart

## Louise Erdrich

*America.gov* is a website produced by the U.S. Department of State whose purpose is to educate people worldwide about the U.S. way of life, including its cultural history. In the following piece, Louise Erdrich, an important Native American author, writes about her efforts to learn Ojibwe, which is the language of the Chippewa tribe.

For years now I have been in love with a language other than the English in which I write, and it is a rough affair. Every day I try to learn a little more Ojibwe. I have taken to carrying verb conjugation charts in my purse, along with the tiny notebook I've always kept for jotting down book ideas, overheard conversations, language detritus, phrases that pop into my head. Now that little notebook includes an increasing volume of Ojibwe words. My English is jealous, my Ojibwe elusive. Like a besieged unfaithful lover, I'm trying to appease them both.

Detritus: Small particles or debris.

Appease: To satisfy or relieve.

Ojibwemowin, or Anishinabemowin, the Chippewa language, was last spoken in our family by Patrick Gourneau, my maternal grandfather, a Turtle Mountain Ojibwe who used it mainly in his prayers. Growing up off reservation, I thought Ojibwemowin mainly was a language for prayers, like Latin in the Catholic liturgy. I was unaware for many years that Ojibwemowin was spoken in Canada, Minnesota and Wisconsin, though by a dwindling number of people. By the time I began to study the language, I was living in New Hampshire, so for the first few years I used language tapes.

I never learned more than a few polite phrases that way, but the sound of the language in the author Basil Johnson's calm and dignified Anishinabe voice sustained me through bouts of homesickness. I spoke basic Ojibwe in the isolation of my car traveling here and there on twisting New England roads. Back then, as now, I carried my tapes everywhere.

The language bit deep into my heart, but it was an unfulfilled longing. I had nobody to speak it with, nobody who remembered my grandfather's standing with his sacred pipe in the woods next to a box elder tree, talking to the spirits. Not until I moved back to the Midwest and settled in Minneapolis did I find a fellow Ojibweg to learn with, and a teacher.

## Inspiring Teacher

5 Mille Lac's Ojibwe elder Jim Clark—*Naawi-giizis*, or Center of the Day—is a magnetically pleasant, sunny, crew-cut World War II veteran with a mysterious kindliness that shows in his slightest gesture. When he laughs, everything about him laughs; and when he is serious, his eyes round like a boy's.

*Naawi-giizis* introduced me to the deep intelligence of the language and forever set me on a quest to speak it for one reason: I want to get the jokes. I also want to understand the prayers and the *adisookaanug*, the sacred stories, but the irresistible part of language for me is the explosion of hilarity that attends every other minute of an Ojibwe visit. As most speakers are now bilingual, the language is spiked with puns on both English and Ojibwe, most playing on the oddness of *gichi-mookomaan*, that is, big knife or American, habits and behavior.

This desire to deepen my alternate language puts me in an odd relationship to my first love, English. It is, after all, the language stuffed into my mother's ancestors' mouths. English is the reason she didn't speak her native language and the reason I can barely limp along in mine. English is an all-devouring language that has moved across North America like the fabulous plagues of locusts that darkened the sky and devoured even the handles of rakes and hoes. Yet the omnivorous nature of a colonial language is a writer's gift. Raised in the English language, I partake of a mongrel feast.

**Mongrel:** Mixed breed or origin.

A hundred years ago most Ojibwe people spoke Ojibwemowin, but the Bureau of Indian Affairs and religious boarding schools punished and humiliated children who spoke native languages. The program worked, and there are now almost no fluent speakers of Ojibwe in the United States under the age of 30. Speakers like *Naawi-giizis* value the language partly because it has been physically beaten out of so many people. Fluent speakers have had to fight for the language with their own flesh, have endured ridicule, have resisted shame and stubbornly pledged themselves to keep on talking the talk.

## The Great Mystery

My relationship is of course very different. How do you go back to a language you never had? Why should a writer who loves her first language find it necessary and essential to complicate her life with another? Simple reasons, personal and impersonal. In the past few years I've found that I can talk to God only in this language, that somehow my grandfather's use of the language penetrated. The sound comforts me.

10    What the Ojibwe call the *Gizhe Manidoo*, the great and kind spirit residing in all that lives, what the Lakota call the Great Mystery, is associated for me with the flow of Ojibwemowin. My Catholic training touched me intellectually and symbolically but apparently never engaged my heart.

There is also this: Ojibwemowin is one of the few surviving languages that evolved to the present here in North America. The intelligence of this language is adapted as no other to the philosophy bound up in northern land, lakes, rivers, forests and arid plains; to the animals and their particular habits; to the shades of meaning in the very placement of stones. As a North American writer it is essential to me that I try to understand our human relationship to place in the deepest way possible, using my favorite tool, language.

There are place names in Ojibwe and Dakota for every physical feature of Minnesota, including recent additions like city parks and dredged lakes. Ojibwemowin is not static, not confined to describing the world of some out-of-reach and sacred past. There are words for e-mail, computers, Internet, fax. For exotic animals in zoos. *Anaamibiig gookoosh*, the underwater pig, is a hippopotamus. *Nandookomeshiinh*, the lice hunter, is the monkey.

> Static: Showing little or no change.

There are words for the serenity prayer used in 12-step programs and translations of nursery rhymes. The varieties of people other than Ojibwe or Anishinabe are also named: *Aiibiishaabookewininiwag*, the tea people, are Asians. *Agongosininiwag*, the chipmunk people, are Scandinavians. I'm still trying to find out why.

## Complexity of Ojibwemowin

For years I saw only the surface of Ojibwemowin. With any study at all one looks deep into a stunning complex of verbs. Ojibwemowin is a language of verbs. All action. Two-thirds of the words are verbs, and for each verb there are as many as 6,000 forms. The storm of verb forms makes it a wildly adaptive and powerfully precise language. *Changite-ige* describes the way a duck tips itself up in the water butt first. There is a word for what would happen if a man fell off a motorcycle with a pipe in his mouth and the stem of it went through the back of his head. There can be a verb for anything.

15     When it comes to nouns, there is some relief. There aren't many objects. With a modest if inadvertent political correctness, there are no designations of gender in Ojibwemowin. There are no feminine or masculine possessives or articles.

    Nouns are mainly designated as alive or dead, animate or inanimate. The word for stone, *asin*, is animate. Stones are called grandfathers and grandmothers and are extremely important in Ojibwe philosophy. Once I began to think of stones as animate, I started to wonder whether I was picking up a stone or it was putting itself into my hand. Stones are not the same as they were to me in English. I can't write about a stone without considering it in Ojibwe and acknowledging that the Anishinabe universe began with a conversation between stones.

    Ojibwemowin is also a language of emotions; shades of feeling can be mixed like paints. There is a word for what occurs when your heart is silently shedding tears. Ojibwe is especially good at describing intellectual states and the fine points of moral responsibility.

    *Ozozamenimaa* pertains to a misuse of one's talents getting out of control. *Ozozamichige* implies you can still set things right. There are many more kinds of love than there are in English. There are myriad shades of emotional meaning to designate various family and clan members. It is a language that also recognizes the humanity of a creaturely God, and the absurd and wondrous sexuality of even the most deeply religious beings.

    Slowly the language has crept into my writing, replacing a word here, a concept there, beginning to carry weight. I've thought of course of writing stories in Ojibwe, like a reverse Nabokov. With my Ojibwe at the level of a dreamy 4-year-old child's, I probably won't.

20     Though it was not originally a written language, people simply adapted the English alphabet and wrote phonetically. During the Second World War, *Naawi-giizis* wrote Ojibwe letters to his uncle from Europe. He spoke freely about his movements, as no censor could understand his writing. Ojibwe orthography has recently been standardized. Even so, it is an all-day task for me to write even one paragraph using verbs in their correct arcane forms. And even then, there are so many dialects of Ojibwe that, for many speakers, I'll still have gotten it wrong.

    As awful as my own Ojibwe must sound to a fluent speaker, I have never, ever, been greeted with a moment of impatience or laughter.

Perhaps people wait until I've left the room. But more likely, I think, there is an urgency about attempting to speak the language. To Ojibwe speakers the language is a deeply loved entity. There is a spirit or an originating genius belonging to each word.

Before attempting to speak this language, a learner must acknowledge these spirits with gifts of tobacco and food. Anyone who attempts Ojibwemowin is engaged in something more than learning tongue twisters. However awkward my nouns, unstable my verbs, however stumbling my delivery, to engage in the language is to engage the spirit. Perhaps that is what my teachers know, and what my English will forgive.

## Reflect on the Reading

1. In the last sentence of the first paragraph, Erdrich writes "My English is jealous, my Ojibwe elusive. Like a besieged unfaithful lover, I'm trying to appease them both." What does she mean by this?

2. Relate the title of the article to the author's main points.

3. At the end of her piece, Erdrich writes that fluent speakers of Ojibwe are patient when she mispronounces Ojibwe words. Why are they patient?

## Consider Your Viewpoint

1. If you speak more than one language, have you ever felt torn between two languages? Explain your answer.

2. Why is the Ojibwe language continuing to change by adding new words for technology, exotic animals, and so on?

3. In the beginning of her piece, Erdrich describes how she started learning Ojibwe before she found an Ojibwe teacher. How did you begin to learn your languages? Did you study a language in school, learn two languages at once as a child, or learn another way? Describe this process.

For support in meeting this chapter's objectives, follow this path in MyCompLab: Resources ⇒ Writing ⇒ Writing Purposes ⇒ Writing to Describe. Review the Instruction and Multimedia resources about writing to describe, then complete the Exercises and click on Gradebook to measure your progress.

# CHAPTER

# 6 Making an Observation

## Learning Objectives

In this chapter you will:

- Choose a compelling topic for an observation.
- Determine which genre will be most effective for an observation.

- Draft an effective thesis statement.
- Use key words and transitional words and phrases to improve organization.

*These elderly men are enjoying the pastime of people watching. Where is your favorite place to sit and observe people?*

A ll of us, no matter our age or cultural background, have spent time observing people, places, and things. It can be entertaining to observe people in an airport, watch a soccer match in a neighborhood park, or gaze at a beautiful painting in an art museum. It can be interesting to observe an experiment in biology class or a campus speaker on the topic of how the Supreme Court chooses which cases to hear. Think about the last time you sat and observed something. Did you wish that you could share what you were seeing with someone else? Maybe you even took a photo or telephoned someone to describe what you were seeing. You could also have written down your observation. You might ask, "Why put it in writing when it is so much easier to call or take a photo?" Writing can serve as a lens through which readers see what you see in more detail than a single phone call or photo can capture. What's more, it helps you to learn more about your topic, and it creates a permanent written record of the event that you can return to whenever you wish.

## WRITING TO MAKE AN OBSERVATION

To write an observation, you first select a person, place, or thing to observe. Then you arrange a time to conduct your observation. While observing, take copious notes. Your primary purpose is to use words to paint a picture that helps your readers see what you see, so use all five senses: sight, smell, touch, taste, and hearing. As you observe, look for changes in the person, place, or thing. How is it evolving? What is unusual about it? If needed, when you complete your observation, read about your topic or interview others to gather more detail to add to your piece.

### Questions for Making an Observation

- What am I interested in observing?
- What would my audience want to know about it?
- Which genre and visual design is best for sharing an observation?
- Why is it important to observe and share this information?
- What constraints would prevent me from effectively completing this observation?

## MODEL OBSERVATIONS

Read the following observations to see how authors write about what they observe. Notice how each author uses the five senses—sight, smell, touch, taste, and hearing—to help their readers see what they see.

### Loving Hip-Hop in Morocco

#### Nikki Reyna

In this NYU Livewire article, republished on the website Worldpress.org, Nikki Reyna describes the work of Josh Asen, who received a Fulbright fellowship to study hip-hop music in Morocco. Reyna uses a combination of narration and observation to help her readers see what Asen sees in the culture and politics of Morocco. NYU Livewire is an online site of feature stories written by students of New York University's Arthur L. Carter Journalism Institute. Because the readers for such feature stories scan quickly, authors often use short paragraphs similar to those in newspaper articles.

*H-Kayne, a rap group, signed a deal with Platinum Records, becoming the first Moroccan rap band to be sponsored by a major record label.*

Wandering through the souks of the Marrakech medina, Josh Asen was surprised to hear the hip-hop sounds of Puff Daddy and Eminem over the strains of traditional religious music.

In Morocco on a 2004 Fulbright fellowship to research hip-hop, Asen, then 24, impulsively abandoned the idea of writing a paper—too

Souks: Middle-Eastern marketplaces.

dry—and decided to make a film instead. And that's how a self-described Brooklyn Jew who grew up listening to Sinatra and Ella Fitzgerald came to help found Morocco's first-ever hip-hop festival and, with friend Jennifer Needleman, to make the documentary "I Love Hip Hop in Morocco."

Though he had worked for a year as an international promotions coordinator for Roc-A-Fella records, Asen was surprised at hip-hop's popularity in Morocco. The country isn't included in international marketing or promotions, because of piracy problems there.

Asen asked local rap artists what they needed most in order to promote their music. Concerts, they told him.

5 So Asen appealed to the United States Embassy and Coca-Cola to sponsor a festival, a three-city tour featuring local artists in Casablanca, Marrakech, and Meknes.

"Hip-hop is part of the democratic process. It is the empowerment and the birth of the voice of the oppressed, of the underclass," he said. "This is the young people seizing a voice for themselves, in a way they haven't done since the seventies."

The Moroccan artists put their own twist on the music, with the musicians rapping in Arabic, French, Moroccan Arabic, and English. Complete with D.J.'s, break dancers, and graffiti artists, they've created an underground, indigenous hip-hop movement that has been developing for nearly a decade.

Funding was up in the air and, right to the first night of the festival, the musicians weren't sure they'd go on. Then the embassy's then-cultural attaché in Casablanca, Terry White, got the word that the funds had been approved.

"Our goal was to reach out to a segment of Morocco's youth that we otherwise had trouble reaching, as we really didn't have much they were interested in, and show them another side of America than they were generally seeing on the tube," said White, in an e-mail interview from his current posting in Colombo, Sri Lanka.

10 A triumphant Asen filmed on stage, before 30,000 fans. Hundreds of thousands of other Moroccans also watched the show on TV.

"There were quite a few spontaneous appearances of American flags in the crowds," White said. "And they were right side up and not on fire!"

Moroccans enjoyed the film, and the government seemed tacitly to support it too, said Daoud Casewit, executive secretary of the Moroccan-American Commission for the Educational and Cultural Exchange, which funded Asen's Fulbright.

"They look for ways to reduce extremism and promote diversity," he said. "This is one of them."

The film should likewise give Americans a more nuanced understanding of the Muslim world, Casewit said.

Asen agrees.

15     "You see an Arab kid, a Muslim kid from Morocco on the screen wearing Sean John, or a Yankees cap, rapping or dancing, and you say to yourself, 'well, wow, that's the same thing we do, that looks a lot like us,'" he said.

Hip-hop has certainly succeeded in transcending physical borders, but the themes of American and Moroccan hip-hop are decidedly different.

Achraf Aarab, a member of Fnaire, Morocco's "traditional rap" group that blends American hip-hop and traditional Moroccan music, complains in the film that American hip-hop lyrics are full of whores, cars, and jewelry. The only problem in Morocco is that there is no money, he says, and admits, laughing: "If we had money, we would talk about girls, and everything would be fine."

Political, religious, and social issues are usually addressed discreetly. D.J. Key, founder of Morocco's original hip-hop association, explains in the film that certain practices integral to hip-hop are forbidden to practicing Muslims, especially mixing of the sexes. But he can't explain how he reconciles his religious beliefs with his love of hip-hip. "It's very difficult" he says.

This is a powerful scene in the film, which doesn't otherwise focus on Islam and politics. "We tried not to have a message, not force any kind of conclusion as to what this all means," said Asen, now back in Brooklyn working as an E.S.L. teacher. "This is a part of the world that is largely misunderstood, vilified, and demonized in a lot of ways. [The film] might make people feel a little less estranged from the Muslim world, to see that it's not just all terrorists and fundamentalists. Some kids are just doing hip-hop."

## One Word Spotlight

*Vilified* (paragraph 19) means to make abusive or defamatory statements about someone or something. The word is from the fifteenth-century Latin word *vilis*, meaning vile or cheap. To vilify a group of people, such as the Muslims, is to devalue them.

## Reflect on the Reading

1. Reyna quotes filmmaker Asen, who says, "Hip-hip is part of the democratic process." What does he mean by this? What examples does he use to support his opinion?

2. What sensory details (sight, smell, touch, sound, taste) does Reyna use to help her readers picture the Moroccan hip-hop scene?

3. What are the topics of Moroccan hip-hop music and how do they differ from topics of American hip-hop?

4. How, according to the article, can hip-hop "reduce extremism and promote diversity in the Middle East?"

5. Why, according to Asen, would Americans also benefit from watching his film?

## Consider Your Viewpoint

1. Do you agree with Reyna and Asen that it's important for Morocco to have a hip-hop scene? Explain your answer.

2. Why does Reyna raise the issue of extremism in this article? Do you agree with her decision to do this? Why or why not?

3. Give examples of your favorite music genre. In what other countries is this music played?

4. Analyze the photograph that accompanies this essay. What is the photographer trying to capture? Is this how you pictured a Moroccan hip-hop band? Why or why not?

# Painting Came to My Rescue in a Most Trying Time

## Emily Yoffe

In the following blog posting, published on Slate.com, Emily Yoffe observes life in Prague, Chez Republic, while on an "art vacation." Although this article is about Yoffe's love for art and travel, her profession is as a journalist for *Slate* and the NPR radio show *Day to Day*.

Buildings such as this one contribute to the sense that European cities are dark and gloomy.

It seems insane to fly across the ocean and spend thousands of dollars for the opportunity to make a few pieces of bad art when I could stay home and make reams of pictures no one wants to see. But there I was in Prague in the Czech Republic for a six-day "art vacation" with a company called Artbreak. Unlike the average tourist, who travels simply to consume culture, I would balance my intake by producing culture of my own.

When the urge strikes to go somewhere exotic to do something artistic, there are companies all over the globe, from Guatemala to Greenland, Indonesia to Ireland, that will set you up to draw, paint, pot, sculpt, or weave. Provence and Tuscany are popular destinations, but, perversely, I concluded that their beauty would make me want to wander, not try to capture the scene on canvas. Since I descend from gloomy people who came from gloomy places, I was drawn to Prague, a city where Franz Kafka wrote the story of a man who awoke one morning to find he'd become a bug.

The Artbreak vacation had an appealing structure: making art in the studio each morning, sightseeing in the afternoon, and attending great performances in the evening. This vacation would be possible only if I left my husband and daughter at home. They share a belief that the air in museums does not contain enough oxygen to sustain human life and that our habeas corpus laws prevent involuntary detention at the ballet or opera.

I was an artistic child who thought of the family home as a gallery for my ceramics, paintings, sculptures, and woodcuts. Then I became an adult and let it all go. Occasionally, I would take a class to try to revive my skills, but the classes grew further apart, and what I produced was increasingly disappointing. I hoped that an art vacation would relight that dormant spark.

5      I was also inspired by a slender volume by Winston Churchill, *Painting as a Pastime*. He writes that during a difficult period, he began dabbling with his children's paint box and that "the Muse of Painting came to my rescue." For the rest of his life (even through World War II), he found a restorative "psychic equilibrium" through sketching and painting. This was fortifying advice from the greatest figure of the 20th century, and I was strangely comforted when the book's illustrations revealed that for all his enthusiasm, he remained a mediocre artist.

I wondered whether the atmosphere of Prague would influence my work. My reading about the city didn't so much prepare me as steel me. The very long history of Prague (it was first established in the ninth century) could be summed up as one of domination, defenestration, depression, despair, death, and dumplings. (If you've never tasted a Czech dumpling, believe me, it belongs on this list.) The Czech Republic is a small, landlocked country (about the size of Virginia) that its neighbors seem to think has been affixed with a sign that says, "Invade Me." For hundreds of years, waves of Austro-Hungarians, Germans, and Russians have occupied it. The Czech response is generally not to rise up but to keep their heads down and wait it out until the next invader arrives.

In Simon Mawer's new novel, *The Glass Room*, set in Czechoslovakia on the eve of World War II, one character asks, "Why are Czechs always so mournful?" Another answers, "They have a great deal to be mournful about." In the invaluable *Prague: A Cultural and Literary History*, scholar Richard Burton quotes Albert Camus, who, after a week in Prague, came away saying he was, "emptier and in deeper despair after this disappointing encounter with myself." (It should be noted that if Camus had found himself on a Carnival cruise, it's likely all the fun would have propelled him overboard.)

When I arrived in the fall, the city was, and remained, overcast and gray. But despite the history, despite the weather, maybe even because of this pall—chiaroscuro is a powerful artistic effect—like centuries' worth of visitors, I was stunned and uplifted by the fairy tale splendor of the city. Prague has a lovely setting on the Vltava River, but its real beauty is entirely man-made.

The city's glory is the human impulse to fashion out of raw material something both powerful and delightful. From the constantly varied patterns on the cobblestones beneath your feet, to the pediments that top the buildings, foot by foot, it was the most varied, most breathtaking assemblage of architecture and design I'd ever seen. Denis Dutton, a New Zealand professor of the philosophy of art, believes that the earliest humans got pleasure from making aesthetically beautiful tools and that this "art instinct" is an essential component of human evolution.

10    I met my two fellow Artbreakers. Rachel, a New Yorker in her 30s, is an advertising producer, and Francesco, an Australian in his 40s, is an engineer who specializes in consumer packaging—and I will never look at another box of feminine-care products without thinking of him. Like me, Rachel signed up out of curiosity about Prague and to jump-start her latent creativity. Francesco is a professional-level artist who was on the second leg of a multicontinent art vacation. He had just spent two weeks painting in Morocco, and after Prague, he would be off to Italy, then New York. Our hosts, American expatriate sociologist Douglas Pressman and Czech management consultant (a new profession in a post-Communist world) Richard Furych, took us out for Italian food at a Serbian-run

restaurant, Mirellie, then off to our first cultural event. Later in the week, we were going to the opera, ballet, and symphony, but they like to mix in some funky, locals-only Czech performances. That night, two musicians, Lubos Bena, a Slovak guitarist, and Matej Ptaszek, a Czech harmonica player and singer whose usual venue is the street, performed "The Music of the Mississippi River."

Richard Burton observed that Czechs have a passion for automatons and proto-Frankenstein figures. (More on golem later in the week.) The Czech language is one of the most impenetrable for non-native speakers, but they gave the world the word **robot** from **robota**, or forced laborer, which was introduced in *Rossum's Universal Robots*, a play that premiered in Prague in 1921. I couldn't help thinking of this while listening to Bena and Ptaszek, because their performance was an uncanny channeling of Muddy Waters, Lead Belly, and other Delta greats. The rest of my group found them bizarre, but I loved the creative passion of two white men from Central Europe imagining themselves to be black musicians in the American South 60 years ago. After all, I was there to see whether I could gin up some creative passion of my own.

## One Word Spotlight

*Defenestration* (paragraph 6) is a noun that means that someone has been quickly removed from a political party or office. The word originates from the Latin word *defenestra* which means to throw someone or something out a window. In this article, Yoffe uses "defenestration" to refer to the constant change of power in Prague resulting from repeated foreign invasions.

## Reflect on the Reading

1. Yoffe quotes a character from a novel who describes Prague as "mournful." What does a "mournful" city look like?

2. What other sensory details (sight, smell, touch, sound, taste) does Yoffe use to help her readers see what Prague is like?

3. Who inspired Yoffe's desire to resume painting? What did she learn from this twentieth-century politician?

4. Yoffe says, "The very long history of Prague (it was first established in the ninth century) could be summed up as one of domination, defenestration,

depression, despair, death, and dumplings." Why does she end this alliteration with the word *dumplings*? What is alliteration and why do authors use it?

5. Yoffe concludes by observing "two white men from Central Europe imagining themselves to be black musicians in the American South 60 years ago." How does she tie this observation to her own desire to paint?

## Consider Your Viewpoint

1. Does this article make you want to visit Prague? Why or why not?

2. In spite of the gloomy atmosphere, Yoffe still sees Prague as an interesting place. What is it that she likes about the city?

3. When describing the numerous invasions of their country, Yoffe states, "The Czech response is generally not to rise up but to keep their heads down and wait it out until the next invader arrives." Do you think this analysis of the Czech culture is fair? Explain your answer.

4. In the photo that precedes this short story, analyze the arrangement of the window and the roses. How does this arrangement contribute to the effectiveness of the photo?

# From *In the Shadow of Man*

## Jane Goodall

One of Jane Goodall's most important observations was that of a chimpanzee she named David Graybeard using a stalk of grass to extract termites from a termite mound. Prior to Goodall's observations, scientists thought that only man created tools. This excerpt taken from Goodall's book *In the Shadow of Man* is part of Goodall's written reports. The report genre is similar to that of an essay, but it is usually a more in-depth study of a research topic.

*Jane Goodall, a world-famous naturalist, spent 45 years at Gombe Stream National Park in Tanzania, Africa observing the social interaction of chimpanzees.*

By then it was October and the short rains had begun. The blackened slopes were softened by feathery new grass shoots and in some places the ground was carpeted by a variety of flowers. The Chimpanzees' Spring, I called it. I had had a frustrating morning, tramping up and down three valleys with never a sign or sound of a chimpanzee. Hauling myself up the steep slope of Mlinda Valley I headed for the Peak, not only weary but soaking wet from crawling through dense undergrowth. Suddenly I stopped, for I saw a slight movement in the long grass about sixty yards away. Quickly focusing my binoculars I saw that it was single chimpanzee, and just then he turned in my direction. I recognized David Graybeard.

Cautiously I moved around so that I could see what he was doing. He was squatting beside the red earth mound of a termite nest, and as I watched I saw him carefully push a long grass stem down into a hole in the mound. After a moment he withdrew it and picked up something from the end with his mouth. I was too far away to make out what he was eating, but it was obvious that he was actually using a grass stem as a tool.

I knew that on two occasions casual observers in West Africa had seen chimpanzees using objects as tools: one had broken open palm-nut kernels by using a rock as a hammer, and a group of chimps had been observed pushing sticks into an underground bees' nest and licking off the honey. Somehow I had never dreamed of seeing anything so exciting myself.

For an hour David feasted at the termite mound and then he wandered slowly away. When I was sure he had gone I went over to examine the mound. I found a few crushed insects strewn about, and a swarm of worker termites sealing the entrances of the nest passages into which David had obviously been poking his stems. I picked up one of his discarded tools and carefully pushed it into a hole myself. Immediately I felt the pull of several termites as they seized the grass, and when I pulled it out there were a number of worker termites and soldiers, with big red heads, clinging on with their mandibles. There they remained, sticking out at right angles to the stem with their legs waving in the air.

**Mandible:** Part of an insect's jaw used for biting and cutting food.

5      Before I left I trampled down some of the tall dry grass and constructed a rough hide—just a few palm fronds leaned up against the low branch of a tree and tied together at the top. I planned to wait there the next day. But it was another week before I was able to watch a chimpanzee "fishing" for termites again. Twice chimps arrived, but each time they saw me and moved off immediately. Once a swarm of fertile winged termites—the princes and princesses, as they are called—flew

off on their nuptial flight, their huge white wings fluttering frantically as they carried the insects higher and higher. Later I realized that it is at this time of year, during the short rains, when the worker termites extend the passages of the nest to the surface, preparing for these emigrations. Several such swarms emerged between October and January. It is principally during these months that the chimpanzees feed on termites.

On the eighth day of my watch David Graybeard arrived again, together with Goliath, and the pair worked there for two hours. I could see much better: I observed how they scratched open the sealed-over passage entrances with a thumb and forefinger. I watched how they bit the ends off their tools when they became bent, or used the other end, or discarded them in favor of new ones. Goliath once moved at least fifteen yards from the heap to select a firm-looking piece of vine, and both males often picked three or four stems while they were collecting tools, and put the spares beside them on the ground until they wanted them.

Most exciting of all, on several occasions they picked small leafy twigs and prepared them for use by stripping off the leaves. This was the first recorded example of a wild animal not merely *using* an object as a tool, but actually modifying an object and thus showing the crude beginnings of tool *making*.

Previously man had been regarded as the only tool-making animal. Indeed, one of the clauses commonly accepted in the definition of man was that he was a creature who "made tools to a regular and set pattern." The chimpanzees, obviously, had not made tools to any set pattern. Nevertheless, my early observations of their primitive tool making abilities convinced a number of scientists that it was necessary to redefine man in a more complex manner than before.

# One Word Spotlight

**Emigration** (paragraph 5) means to leave a place to go elsewhere. When we speak of people emigrating, we usually refer to their leaving their native country to settle elsewhere. The word *immigration*, in contrast, means to enter a new country, usually with some kind of official document review at the border. One way to remember the difference is that emigration starts with an "e" for "exit from" and immigration starts with an "i" for "introduce to."

## Reflect on the Reading

1. How does Goodall's description of her surroundings in the first few sentences help the readers picture the scene?

2. Throughout the report, what other sensory details (sight, smell, touch, sound, taste) does Goodall use to help her readers observe what she sees?

3. What constraints does Goodall describe about the process of observing animals in the wild?

4. Since others before her observed chimpanzees using tools, what was so special about Goodall's observation?

5. How did Goodall's observation and discovery result in a redefinition of the word *man*?

## Consider Your Viewpoint

1. What personality traits are required to work as a naturalist? Would this line of work appeal to you? Why or why not?

2. What additional details could Goodall have provided on David Graybeard's activities?

3. Do you agree with Goodall that "The chimpanzees, obviously, had not made tools to any set pattern." Explain your answer.

4. How does the photo of Jane Goodall make it easier to picture what she was like as a researcher? As a person?

# WRITING ASSIGNMENT

For this writing assignment, you will observe a person, place, or thing. Consider first whether you are required to conduct an observation for one of your other classes. Are you required, for example, to observe people in a public setting for a sociology class or animals in their natural setting for a biology lab? If yes, then use this assigned topic for your observation piece. If you are not required to write an observation for another class, then you or your instructor for this class may choose what you will observe.

# YOUR OBSERVATION

Now it's your turn to write an observation. The model observations in this chapter may give you some ideas for what to observe, but you will do your best writing if you choose something of special significance to you. If needed, before beginning this assignment, review Chapters 2 and 3 to refresh your memory on choosing a topic and analyzing the rhetorical situation and completing the stages of the writing process.

---

### Writing Assignment Checklist

☐ Carefully read the assignment.
☐ Look for key words that describe what you must do.
☐ Determine whether the topic is assigned or free choice.
☐ Ask your instructor any questions that you have about the assignment.

---

## Choosing a Topic

If you are free to choose your topic, identify a person, place, or thing that interests you, that you are curious to learn more about, and that you think your readers will be interested in reading about, too. For example, you might choose to observe fans at your favorite sporting event, a place on campus that you have wanted to visit, or a piece of sculpture you admire in the local art gallery. If you are not sure what to observe, use the following questions to help you choose a topic:

### People

Where do people like to gather in your community?
Where do they go for fun and relaxation?
Where can you find people doing interesting things?

### Place

Is there a new place such as a restaurant or nightclub that you might observe?
What is your favorite place to spend time?
Where could you go to observe animals, birds, or insects?

### Thing

What do you use regularly that might be of interest to your readers?
What interesting items can you find in an art or history museum?
Is there new construction of a building, road, or other structure that you might observe?

After choosing a topic, be sure to narrow it so you can describe the subject in depth. For example, it would be impossible to observe an athlete's activities over a lifetime, but you could observe that person participating in a big game.

> ## Topic Questions for Making an Observation
>
> - Is this an assigned topic? If so, what are the requirements?
> - Is this topic free choice? If so, what would I like to observe?
> - Will readers be interested in my choice of topic?
> - Does my topic choice offer enough sensory detail to be interesting?
> - Will I be able to arrange to observe this person, place, or thing?

**Connect
With Others**

**Activity 6.1** With your instructor serving as a referee, conduct a creative brainstorming session. Divide into groups of three or four students with each group brainstorming a list of people, places, and things to observe. Your instructor may want to set a time limit such as five or ten minutes. Then ask one member of each group to read the group's list aloud. Each time that group has listed a topic that the other groups *do not* have on their lists, that group receives a point. Once all groups have read their lists, the group with the most points is the winner: the most creative at finding topics for observation.

## Analyzing the Rhetorical Situation

Now that you have chosen a topic, analyze the rhetorical situation to ensure that you and your readers are interested in the topic of your observation. The better your rhetorical analysis, the more effective your writing will be.

**Considering Audience and Purpose.** Begin by choosing an audience that you think will be interested in "seeing" what you observe. The more you know about your audience, the easier it will be for you to choose details and present them in a way to appeal to this audience.

> ## Audience Questions for Making an Observation
>
> - Who would be interested in learning about this topic?
> - How much do these readers already know about what I will observe? How much do they need to know?
> - What is the average age of these readers?
> - Does my readers' gender or cultural backgrounds affect my choice of topic?
> - What is their educational level?
> - What is their political orientation: conservative, moderate, liberal?

Although your primary purpose is to inform your readers of what you observe, you may include some expressive writing if you have personal experience with the topic of your observation. You'll notice that in the model observation readings, Reyna only reports what she observes without including her own personal opinion of the Moroccan hip-hop scene. Yoffe, on the other hand, shares her personal reaction to Prague, and Goodall describes her excitement at the discovery that chimpanzees create tools. Your personal experience and enthusiasm for the topic can help your readers generate enthusiasm, too. Don't try to persuade your readers to believe one way or another about what they are seeing, though. You are simply the lens through which they see what you see. Let them draw their own conclusions about the topic.

---

### Purpose Questions for Making an Observation

- What information do I hope to share through this observation?
- What personal thoughts or feelings can I include in this informative piece?
- Does the language and cultural background of my readers affect my purpose?
- What do I want my readers to think or feel about this topic once they have read my observation?

---

**Choosing a Genre and Visual Design.**  Once you analyze your audience and purpose, you are ready to choose the genre or format that best fits the message that you are communicating. When writing observations, authors usually choose essays, memoirs, short stories, blogs, newspaper articles, or reports. Depending on the genre you choose, you decide which layout, font, and visual elements to use. In a report, for example, authors often use headings, subheadings, and bullets to organize their ideas. They may also include visuals such as graphs, charts, drawings, or photographs to help readers understand what they are observing. For more help with visual design, see Chapter 14.

---

### Genre and Visual Design Questions for Making an Observation

- Which format will best communicate my topic to my chosen audience?
- How will the format help me inform my readers?
- What visual design elements will strengthen my observation?
- What do I know about the genre I've chosen?
- What do I need to learn to write in this genre?

**Reviewing Exigence and Constraints.** In this assignment, you might want to observe a person, place, or thing because it's an assigned topic by a professor or employer, to improve your own understanding of it for a research project you are working on, or simply to have a permanent record of what you have observed.

---

### Exigence Questions for Making an Observation

- What is important about this observation?
- Given their gender and culture, will the audience be receptive to this observation?
- Will this observation change the readers' ideas about this person, place, or thing?
- Why is it important to have a *written* record of this observation?

---

Constraints include anything that might interfere with your ability to complete your observation. For example, you might not be able to get permission to observe something by the deadline for completing this assignment. Try to anticipate as many constraints as you can and plan ways to work around them before you begin this assignment. Dr. Goodall, for example, was constrained by the very chimpanzees she observed. She comments in her report that she had to wait a week before she could observe the chimpanzees again because when they spotted her watching them, they simply left.

---

### Constraint Questions for Making an Observation

- Does the assignment itself impose any restrictions such as an assigned topic or word limit?
- What will influence the success of my observation?
- Will my audience have certain expectations that I might not be able to fulfill?
- Do I need to conduct research to complete my observation?
- What other constraints do I face to completing this piece?

---

**Connect With Others**

**Activity 6.2**   With a small group, select one of the creative topics chosen in Activity 6.1 and develop a rhetorical situation for it, including audience, purpose, genre, exigence, and constraints.

# Using the Writing Process

You're now ready to begin the stages of the writing process: discovering ideas, drafting to explore ideas, revising to improve content, and editing to eliminate errors. Writing is a recursive process, so you may find yourself moving back and forth as you work through these steps. As you write, try to keep your audience and purpose in mind.

### STAGE 1: Discovering Ideas

In Chapter 3 you learned various ways of discovering ideas. One that works especially well for an observation piece is freewriting. Before you begin your observation, take a few moments to freewrite what you already know about the topic.

**Freewriting.** When freewriting, you write nonstop for a certain amount of time, such as ten to fifteen minutes, or until you have written a specified number of pages. Since you have already chosen a topic, you'll do what is called a focused freewriting, where you try to stay on the topic of your observation while writing whatever comes into your mind about that topic.

*Where observation is concerned, chance favors only the prepared mind.*

*—Louis Pasteur*

**One Student's Work.** Student writer Susana Cruz received an assignment requiring her to observe someone in the profession she hoped to pursue upon graduation. Since Susana wanted to be a television news anchor, she began by freewriting what she already knew about this profession prior to observing actual news anchors at a local television station. Here is an excerpt from her freewriting:

> I'm not quite sure why I want to be a television news anchor because there is such a negative perception of them. What is an anchor? In the movies they are portrayed as airheads who don't really investigate or write the news. Instead, like the anchor in the movie *Network*, they are simply good-looking people who *read* the news from a teleprompter. Someone else actually goes out and gets the story and writes it up. The news anchor is seen as a "pretty" boy or girl who isn't really serious about journalism.
>
> So, then, why *do* I want to be a news anchor? I'm hoping that this perception is wrong. When I observe a real news anchor at a local television station, maybe it will dispel this sense that anchors

aren't serious. I want to be both. I want to be a good reporter, and I want to be on the air delivering the news. I guess there is a part of me that likes the fact that as an anchor not only will I do the hard investigative work, but once I sit behind that camera and deliver what I've written, my work will be recognized by the public. I think it would be fun to walk into a store and be recognized by the customers. If I am good enough, I might land a job at a network such as MSNBC or CNN—that would be a dream come true!

## STAGE 2: Drafting to Explore Ideas

As you draft, try to get your ideas on paper in the format of the genre you chose while completing your rhetorical analysis. If you plan to write a report, for example, the chart below will help you understand the difference between the report and the essay.

|  | Report | Essay |
|---|---|---|
| **Topic** | ■ a problem or case study with topic selected by professor or employer | ■ a single idea or question with topic chosen by author or professor |
| **Audience and Purpose** | ■ usually a distant audience<br>■ usually informative: to investigate, present, and analyze | ■ can be a personal or distant audience<br>■ can be expressive, informative, or persuasive |
| **Genre and Visual Design** | ■ comprised of lengthy paragraphs, often with headings and subheadings to divide sections<br>■ includes a summary or abstract at beginning<br>■ often includes bullet points<br>■ formal word choice | ■ written in complete sentences and paragraphs, but usually without headings and subheadings<br>■ sometimes includes bullets<br>■ varied word choice depending on audience and purpose |
| **Exigency and Constraints** | **Effectiveness depends upon:**<br>■ the demonstration of good research skills<br>■ the objective presentation and analysis of relevant information | **Effectiveness depends upon:**<br>■ how well the content supports the thesis statement<br>■ how well-developed and organized the essay is |

While drafting, you may realize that although you took notes while observing, you still don't have enough information to write an informative piece on your topic. You may decide to interview someone who is knowledgeable about it. To conduct an interview:

- Request an interview in a place where the interviewee feels comfortable.
- Explain the purpose and format of the interview.
- Take notes or ask permission to record.
- Ask one question at a time and give the interviewee plenty of time to answer.
- Try to remain neutral to the responses.
- Provide transitions between topic changes.
- Keep the interviewee on topic.
- Offer a phone number or email where the interviewee can contact you.
- After the interview, write down your observations.
- Send a thank-you note to the interviewee.

See Chapter 18 "Field Research" for additional help with conducting an interview.

**Thesis Statements.** Before beginning your draft, write a thesis statement to guide your writing. For this piece, you want what is most important about the observation to be clear to your readers. To write an effective thesis statement, state the topic of your piece, list or suggest the main points you will make, and indicate why the topic is important. Be sure that it is specific to what you will observe and that it will capture your readers' attention. After writing your observation, you can always revise the thesis statement, if needed, to match the content of your paper.

Thesis statements may be one or two sentences and are usually near the beginning of your piece. Look at the thesis statements in each of the model observation pieces to see how the authors projected what their pieces would be about:

> In Morocco on a 2004 Fulbright fellowship to research hip-hop, Asen, then 24, impulsively abandoned the idea of writing a paper—too dry—and decided to make a film instead.
>
> —*Nikki Reyna, "Loving Hip-Hop in Morocco"*

In this thesis statement, Reyna makes it clear that the topic of her observation will be Asen's research in Morocco. From this thesis, her readers also understand that the main point of her article will be to show what Asen learns during his filming of hip-hop. Because Asen is in Morocco on a Fulbright fellowship, readers know that this is an important project.

It seems insane to fly across the ocean and spend thousands of dollars for the opportunity to make a few pieces of bad art when I could stay home and make reams of pictures no one wants to see. But there I was in Prague in the Czech Republic for a six-day "art vacation" with a company called Artbreak.

—*Emily Yoffe, "Painting Came to My Rescue*
*in the Most Trying Time"*

In this two-sentence thesis statement, Yoffe lets her readers know that the observation will be of Prague, with an emphasis on her art vacation there. Because Yoffe refers to this as an "insane" adventure, her readers understand that this is no ordinary trip.

Suddenly I stopped, for I saw a slight movement in the long grass about sixty yards away. Quickly focusing my binoculars I saw that it was single chimpanzee, and just then he turned in my direction. It was David Graybeard.

—*Jane Goodall, From* In the Shadow of Man

In this excerpt from her book, Goodall signals her readers that she will observe the chimpanzee, David Graybeard. Because she describes *quickly* stopping and focusing her binoculars, her readers understand that this is an important observation.

## LANGUAGES and CULTURES

Writers from different cultures organize writing differently. Standard Written English (SWE), for example, uses a linear style with careful placement of key words and transitions that quickly and effortlessly guide readers from beginning to end.

Writers from other countries can contribute to the U.S. culture, however, by sharing their own preferred styles for a discussion of similarities and differences across cultures.

**Your Emotional Filter and Writing Monitor.** When writing an observation, you may want to draft on the spot, getting as much information as possible on paper while you are observing. If, however, you find that you are having difficulty getting everything down, you can always jot down your observations in phrases and fill in the blanks when you finish the observation. While you observe, try to keep your writing monitor low by simply letting your ideas flow. When you revise and edit, you can fill in the blanks if you aren't able to get everything down.

### STAGE 3: Revising to Improve Content

To revise, improve the content of your paper by looking at how you have organized and developed your ideas, and review your sentence structure and word choice to ensure that they communicate effectively for the audience you have chosen. To help you revise, set aside your writing for a day or two, reread, and then rewrite it.

**Improve Organization.**  As you rewrite, focus on the organization of your piece. Especially if you are writing a lengthy piece such as report, organization is important to helping your readers follow your meaning. Reyna, Yoffe, and Goodall all use a chronological organization to describe what happened first, next, and last. As you revise your piece, read each paragraph, and if necessary, reorder your paragraphs to ensure that the organization moves your readers effortlessly from the beginning to the end.

One way to check the organization of your paper is to try *reverse* outlining. On a sheet of paper, for each paragraph of your paper, write down the topic of that paragraph in ten words or less. Then, for each paragraph, briefly describe how it contributes to the overall organization and logic of the paper. If you find paragraphs that don't contribute to the paper, remove them.

**Key Words and Transitions.**  Key words and transitions can also improve the organization of your piece, helping your readers move from one idea to the next more easily. Key words are important words or phrases that you repeat to link ideas together. In Reyna's article, for example, she repeats the words "hip-hop," "Morocco," "film," "rap," and "music" throughout the article to help her readers understand that she is still on the topic of hip-hop in Morocco.

In addition to key words, you may want to add transitional words and phrase to improve the organization of your paper. These transitional words alert your readers to the organizational structure of your piece.

> *One doesn't discover new lands without consenting to lose sight of the shore. . .*
> —Andre Gide

## Transitional Words and Phrases

**To add one thought to another**

| | | | |
|---|---|---|---|
| in addition | besides | furthermore | next |
| moreover | again | likewise | and |
| last | and then | too | further |

**To emphasize**

| | | | |
|---|---|---|---|
| surely | indeed | without a doubt | in fact |
| certainly | undoubtedly | to be sure | truly |

**To show an example will follow**

| | | |
|---|---|---|
| for example | specifically | for instance | to illustrate |

**To compare ideas**

in the same way     similarly          likewise

**To contrast ideas**

| but | nevertheless | in spite of | still |
| on the contrary | notwithstanding | though | although |
| yet | conversely | on the other hand | in contrast |

**To show results**

| as a result | since | therefore | thus |
| then | consequently | because | accordingly |

**To summarize**

| therefore | in short | consequently | as a result |
| finally | in conclusion | accordingly | to sum up |

## Connect With Others

**Activity 6.3**   Divide into groups with each group taking one of the model readings at the beginning of this chapter. For each reading, create a reverse outline of the organization of the piece. Then underline the key words and transitions. Discuss what you have found with your classmates.

Once you improve the organization of your piece, review what you have written in light of your original plans for the rhetorical situation.

### Rhetorical Situation Questions for Making an Observation

- Audience: Will your audience be interested in reading this observation? Will they learn something of significance by reading it? Is there anything more you can do to appeal to the audience you have chosen?
- Purpose: Have you included enough detail to inform your readers of what you have observed? Have you refrained from trying to convince them to believe as you do about what you observed?
- Genre: Does the format you chose help the audience understand your points? Would this be a more powerful piece if you changed to another genre?
- Exigence: Do you feel that you have shared what is important to you about what you have observed? Is there anything more you need your audience to know?
- Constraints: Are there any remaining constraints to your success in completing this observation?

Now share your draft with your peers to get some other opinions for ways to continue to improve your piece. Here is an example of a peer review sheet that you might use for an observation piece.

## Peer Review
## Making an Observation

1.  What is this observation's greatest strength?

2.  What is being observed? Is this a topic that you would like to learn more about? Why or why not?

3.  Where might I add details to better support the main points? Which sections or sentences would you like me to clarify? How well did the ideas flow? Where do you suggest I add transitions to help you move from one idea to another?

4.  If I used research or interviews to support my observation, how well was this research used? How well did I avoid simply cutting and pasting information into the piece? How well are quotations and paraphrases used? How well did I indicate the sources of the research in the text of the piece and at the end?

5.  What more would you like to know about this topic?

6.  Underline any words or sentences that you think I should revise because they do not communicate to you.

7.  Place a checkmark in the margin next to any punctuation or spelling errors that you discover while reading this essay.

### STAGE 4: Editing for Correctness

When you drafted your observation piece, you were busy getting what you were observing on paper, so your sentences probably contain some mistakes. You will now want to edit your draft for readability and correctness to be sure that you have eliminated those errors. Read your revised essay carefully, word for word, looking for awkward sentences and errors in spelling, punctuation, and grammar. Consult a handbook and a dictionary to help you edit. If English is not your first language, consult ESL resources such as an English Learner's Dictionary for help.

### To Edit

- Use a dictionary or computer spell checker.
- Refer to a grammar handbook and follow standard grammatical rules.
- Ask another student to read your writing for errors.
- As you edit, keep an Editing Log, a section in your notebook where you record the errors that you make.

**Evaluate Your Work**

**Activity 6.4**    Once you complete the writing process, take a moment to look over what you have done. Complete the self-evaluation sheet to help you improve your observation.

## Self-Evaluation Sheet
## Making an Observation

1. Have I followed all instructions for this assignment? (Reread the assignment sheet and class notes.)

2. Does my paper make the importance of what I observed clear?

3. Are my thoughts well-ordered?

4. Is my paper written clearly and concisely? (Reread your paper out loud.)

5. Does it have a controlling idea?

6. Does each paragraph contribute to the overall organization?

7. Do I introduce my topic in such a way that readers are engaged?

8. Do I conclude in such a way that there is a sense of closure?

9. Is the paper written in my own words?

10. Are my sentences well-written and varied? (Read each sentence beginning with the last one, working backward to the beginning of the paper.)

11. Is my word choice appropriate for the audience and purpose?

12. Have I checked for grammar, punctuation, and spelling errors? (Use a grammar handbook and the computer spell-checker.)

13. If I used other sources of information, did I give credit to them both in the text and on a Works Cited page?

Share your final observation piece with your instructor and classmates, either by distributing printed or emailed copies or posting it to a class website.

## ONE STUDENT'S OBSERVATION

In the Discovering Ideas stage of the writing process, you met Susana Cruz, a student who used freewriting to discover ideas for an assignment that required her to observe someone in the profession she hoped to pursue some day. Even though Susana's freewriting was about why she would like to be an anchor, after she completed her observation of TV anchors, she shifted the focus to what news anchors do on the job.

## From Anchor to Viewer

### *Susana Cruz*

What is an anchor? Is he or she a newscaster who is selected on looks and reads horrifying news prepared for him or her to frighten the audience? Sad as it sounds, that is most viewers' stereotype of an anchor. Viewers see and hear anchors without imagining the long hours of work they put into a report. Sometimes stories even take weeks before they are finished. When viewers observe professional anchors at KFOX presenting the news in the most relaxing way, it is amazing to know what anchors go through during the preparation. It entails long hours of dedicated work, such as research, writing, or interviewing, to develop great news for the viewers.

I arrived at KFOX without imagining the hours of hard work both anchors had ahead of them. The long, slender body of a fairly-complected woman named Audra Schroeder sits comfortably in her chair, fixing her large, blue eyes on the computer screen in front of her. She is wearing a black, long sleeved shirt with light denim jeans, and her feet are bare, exposing the tiny red nails on each toe. The whole outfit looks comfortable on her. Schroeder glances at her black wristwatch, and sees it is 5:06 p.m. Ben Swann is on the other side of the room, sitting in his chair as well. With a great deal of work left to do, both anchors realize they have only a few hours left until they go live on the nine o'clock KFOX nightly news.

"Anchors need to find the story of the day to capture the viewer's attention," Schroeder says, swinging her chair from side to side, causing her short, blond hair to move with the same motion. She continues, "People think that we only fix ourselves to look good on camera and that we read the news from the teleprompter, but they don't understand that we do a lot more other work. Our image is a big part of being an anchor, but we do lots of writing and look for a story that affects people in the most serious way." According to Schroeder, anchors need to be able to work with different elements such as visuals, finding ways of showing the story, not just telling it. Other elements used are sound, pictures, storytelling, and finding people to offer different opinions. She explains, "KFOX anchors also conduct interviews, set up appointments, and have communication with producers, editors, broadcast engineers, and camera people. We need to be able to work as a team with everyone." While printing out a document, Schroeder also points out that anchors are connected with the fire department, police department, and several hospitals, so that these departments can provide information on news occurring daily.

Susana begins her essay by asking the same question that she asked in her freewriting.

From her observation of actual anchors, Susana begins to reshape her definition.

Susana now understands that anchors go out to find the story.

Observing and interviewing news anchors provides Susana with new material.

Anchors also need to center their attention on the camera operator's hand signals and movements while they are on the air and must look natural. "We need to be able to control our emotions. I have been working for at least two years at KFOX, and I still get nervous before the live news roll. Not only do anchors look for a story, write the story, but they also edit the story with the help of KFOX editors. Then we have to practice, practice, and practice before we go live," she mentioned laughing. She also explains that newscasters need to have a loud and clear voice and read with a pleasant tone. "Taking care of your voice and health are important, to be flexible is another. I've been here since two o'clock, and sometimes our lunch consists of water. Anchors need to learn to work under stress, especially if there's a last-minute news shooting," she concluded.

Swann is still cheerfully sitting in his chair. The black, dressy, long sleeve shirt he is wearing does not match the torn, worn-out jeans and old Nike sneakers he has on. He repeatedly rewinds and fast-forwards the tape that was shot earlier about a child molester on the run. On the screen appears a middle-aged man who is being interviewed regarding what he thinks about the child molester. Swann transcribes the interview to help him write reports and capture his thoughts. He finishes revising the tape and starts typing the story. The clicking of the keyboard is heard with each stroke. Some of the captions on the computer screen read, "He is after young girls . . ." and "The phone rings at your house, you answer and . . ." Swann stops and grabs the office phone next to the computer screen, dialing a number. While the tape is still playing, Swann asks to speak to a person on the other end. He immediately sets up an appointment to meet with him. He quickly jots down the appointment day and time on a notepad. He hangs up the phone with a flashing smile and stares at the clock on the wall.

Five o'clock has come and gone. Now it is seven o'clock. Schroeder busily hurries to Ernie Miranda, a KFOX story editor, to review the "story of the day." In a matter of less than ten minutes, Miranda looks it over and agrees with Schroeder's findings. Satisfied, she runs into one of the four editing rooms located off a small hallway connected to the broadcast engineering room, the graphics room, the studio, and the production control room. Once inside one of the editing rooms, Schroeder swiftly starts editing the story.

Throughout her essay, Susana observes how much work is involved in being a news anchor.

From the narrow hallway, Swann can be seen practicing the leading story about the child molester. He appears very confident in front of the intimidating, massive camera. Swann stands up hastily with a new idea. He looks up quickly, away from the papers he is holding, and smiles. He asks, "Susana, my I borrow you for a second?" He has an idea for a dramatization that includes me. I will be playing the teenage girl who gets a phone call from the anonymous child molester, who is being played by the broadcast engineer. My supposed "father," a KFOX director, hands the phone to me. We all pretend to talk while the camera man records us. Sometimes anchors create such dramatizations to get a point across. At times, effects are added to dramatizations through editing. Swann says, "You guys were great! All I have to do now is edit the story." Ben and an editor work on combining the three tapes containing the dramatization, the man who was interviewed, and the one with Ben talking into the camera. I look at the clock and notice that it is getting close to eight o'clock. Ben and Audra get together to review what is going to be said and done that night.

At eight o'clock, Audra grabs her belongings, consisting of two hangers, a pair of black high heels, and quite a large handbag. She runs upstairs to the second floor dressing room and changes from her black shirt into a sky blue form-fitting sleeveless shirt. Audra buttons up the last three buttons of her shirt, and she throws her black shirt and empty hanger onto the chair next to the door. She unzips her handbag and takes out a blow dryer, a brush, and a cosmetic bag. The light coat of powder makes her face look radiant and less shiny. She puts on neutral lip liner that matches her nude lipstick and quickly teases her straight shiny hair with the brush and a mist of hairspray. She applies a very light blush to her cheekbones, making them stand out slightly. Her final task is to put on brownish eye shadow, a layer of mascara, and a dab of concealer. She puts her heels on, making her look even taller. I notice all this takes only a matter of a few minutes. Audra grabs her belongings and runs downstairs. Ben just had to go to his car to get his suit jacket and run his hands through his hair. He even jokes about how naturally beautiful he is; he needs no makeup.

The dim studio set has been lit with extremely bright spotlights. Four metal chairs accompany the arched desk where the anchors are seated. Two of them contain a cushion to elevate whoever will be sitting there shortly. The desk has a built-in TV covered with glass to show the anchors how the live show is being presented to viewers. From their desk, the anchors see the three-labeled prompters with oversized white writing so that they can easily follow along with their script. Prompter number one is located to the left of the long arched desk. Prompter number two is centered, and prompter number three is to the far right of the desk. Behind the prompters three weighty cameras are lined up. Next to one of the prompters is a small desk where the prompter operator controls the captions displayed on the prompters.

Audra gets into her black jacket, locates her "interruptible foldback earpiece" (IFB); a small device fitted into her ear and through the back of her jacket. The IFB connects her to the control room where she can get instructions from the KFOX crew. From the front, the device is barely visible. Audra gets seated into one of the cushioned chairs and starts practicing what she is about to say in approximately fifteen minutes, constantly licking her lips, a sign that she is getting nervous. Ben will not be anchoring tonight. Instead, he is concentrating on the child molester report.

There are five minutes left for the show to start, and Audra clips a tiny microphone on her jacket. In the production control room, the KFOX staff is getting ready as well. In there the director and other staff members control the show to

*Susana adds description to help her readers see what she sees.*

make sure everything is coming together by giving instructions to the anchors and the crew through headsets. After the five minutes, the KFOX identifying song plays, and she starts off the live news. A clear and loud voice fills the studio. Her appearance looks confident and professional as she is looking straight into the center camera. Ben is seen next on the screen, where he speaks in front of the camera for a few minutes in a tranquil way while adding inflections to his words. The tape that was put together by the editor and Ben is being played. At this moment, Ben and Audra are off air.

Susana's observation is much more detailed than her freewriting.

Ben gets up from his seat and leaves the set. Audra's tense appearance emerges again. The tape of the man who was interviewed is being played, and the next ten seconds shows the dramatization. I see myself answering the phone in the dramatization on one of the many TV's that are in the production control room. On the other TV monitor, Audra can be seen fixing her hair and earpiece every ten seconds. Again she is back on screen following the hand signals from the person behind the camera. The camera operator signals for her to look to the left camera, then to the right, and back to the center camera. She looks natural as she changes directions. After a few minutes, they are off to commercials.

Audra relaxes, retouches her hair and earpiece, sips from her water bottle, and breathes deeply. The commercial break is over, and Audra starts reading other news. After a few more commercial breaks, she finally ends the live broadcast with "Thanks for watching KFOX News at nine, and see you next weekend." All the studio equipment is shut down. She sits on the chair for a few minutes removing all the devices and gathering her belongings. It was all a long process, and I realize that both anchors did not have a lunch break today. Ben is busy looking for next week's story. The whole staff, including anchors, gets together to review the broadcast. The show went over by three minutes, but overall they did a great job. Audra gets her handbag, hangers, and clothes, waves goodbye, and heads to the door. Ben and the KFOX staff follow her. Now the studio is silent, waiting for tomorrow's anchors to arrive for another busy day at work.

Susana brings her essay full circle by again mentioning the stereotype about news anchors. She, too, has come full circle in her thinking about what a news anchor does.

KFOX anchors are not just pretty faces reading prepared news. Viewers would be surprised to know how much preparation is devoted to putting a story together. From teamwork, to interviews, to commuting from place to place, researching, creating stories, editing stories, and practicing to have adequate news is not an unusual process for anchors. Without a doubt it is hard to achieve superior audience levels and demonstrate calmness and smiles to the audience after long hours of intense work. To be an anchor is devotion and long hours of work, even if they look appealing and relaxed in the eyes of viewers.

# ADDITIONAL READINGS

## Stranded in Paradise

### Mary Kay Magistad

This article, written for *Foreign Policy* magazine, is about Uighur Muslims released from Guantánamo, Cuba, and sent to the Republic of Palau. Palau is an island nation in the Pacific Ocean near Australia. Considered a paradise by tourists, it is simply a place of confinement for these Muslims. The reporter, Mary Kay Magistad, is an award-winning correspondent who regularly covers East Asia. In this article she observes what life is like for these Guantánamo prisoners who must adjust to confinement in Palau.

Life on a tropical island with sandy white beaches and swaying palm trees might not seem like the worst option, if you've just spent eight years as a prisoner in Guantánamo. But for the six ethnic Uighur Muslims from China's western region of Xinjiang who were released last November from Guantánamo to the Pacific island state of Palau, the prospect of an eternity in a small island country, with no passport and no Uighur community other than themselves, is its own kind of confinement.

> Uighur: A Turkish ethnic group.

The amenities aren't bad. The Uighurs live together in a spacious apartment with water views, on the second floor of a white villa, owned by President Johnson Toribiong's brother Joe. Downstairs is a bank. Next door and across the street are Joe's liquor store, bar and restaurant—perhaps not the best neighbors for devout Muslims. From the street, you can see that a blanket covers one window of the Uighurs' apartment; they told journalists shortly after arriving that they would turn one room into a prayer room. They have also joined the one humble mosque on the island, frequented by Bangladeshi migrant workers, with whom they're said to get along fine. Palau Community College even built a special washroom for them, so they can wash and pray between their English classes. But they'd still rather be someplace else.

"We came here to Palau, because it's close to Australia," Ahmad Tourson, one of the six Uighurs, said to Australia's SBS *Dateline* program, upon arriving in Palau. They've since grown weary of talking to journalists, and now refuse almost all requests for interviews. "While we're here, if we apply again to settle in Australia, we are hoping it'll be accepted."

The Uighurs liked the idea of Australia because it has a sizable Uighur community and, they thought, was beyond China's reach. But Australia has still not agreed to accept any Uighurs, despite repeated requests from the United States. The Chinese government has applied considerable pressure, saying it sees the 22 Uighurs who'd been in Guantánamo as terrorist suspects, who must be returned to face justice. Several of the Uighurs admitted under interrogation that they did receive limited arms training in Afghanistan—but said they were only ever interested in using it against China, not against the United States. No evidence has surfaced linking any of them to combat or to a terrorist attack.

5    And yet, when the Uighurs arrived at Palau's airport in the early hours of Nov. 1, a local newspaper, *Tia Belau*, went sensationalist: "As if lifted from a spy movie thriller, a plane arrived in wee hours at an airport in darkness without knowledge of the sleeping country, and emerged six bearded Muslim terrorists, in shackles and guarded by many armed commandos." Leave aside the fact that the Uighurs aren't terrorists. Footage of their arrival shows they weren't guarded on the ground by armed commandos, and their ankles were only tied while they were on the plane. Once they stepped onto Palauan soil, they were free.

Palau's President Toribiong told me during my visit to Palau in late February that he tried from the beginning to make the Uighurs feel at home. He threw an island picnic for them shortly after their arrival. They requested and sacrificed a goat, in thanks for their freedom, and offered Toribiong the first plate. He says the men have tried to fit in, and people have grown to accept their presence, including some of their fellow students at Palau Community College.

"They don't cause any trouble. They just do what they do, and we do what we do, and we welcome anybody and everybody," said Susan Rideb, an electronics student, taking a break from listening to her friends play the ukelele around a shaded picnic table. "They were accused of something they did not do, and now our government is giving them another chance."

Not everyone sees it that way. Student Elizabeth Cruz said she has chatted with the Uighurs, and she's impressed with how fast their English has improved. But she says they still make her uncomfortable. "It's just, sometimes when you hear about terrorists in Palau, this is a really small island; you get afraid," she told me. "Six people could ruin the whole island of Palau."

The Uighurs might argue that it's their lives that have been ruined. They say they fled Xinjiang almost a decade ago to escape the Han Chinese-dominated government's harassment and persecution of Uighurs, and went to Afghanistan because it was the only neighboring country at the time that wasn't returning Uighurs to China. When the bombing started, the Uighurs say they first took shelter in caves, then fled to Pakistan where, they've told journalists, bounty hunters who had seen U.S. posters offering $5,000 a head for terrorist suspects, turned them in.

10    In the first stretch of their incarceration in Afghanistan, Ahmad Tourson told SBS, his leg was beaten and cut, and then he was made to stand in water for days. By the time he got to Guantánamo, his leg was so infected it had to be amputated. He said he and the other Uighurs were then kept in small cages with almost no natural light.

At one point early on, U.S. guards at Guantánamo allowed Chinese officials to come and interrogate and threaten the Uighurs, and take their pictures. The Uighurs worried how this would affect their families back home.

Finally, when a U.S. court in 2008 ordered their release for lack of evidence, a public outcry at the prospect of allowing the 22 Uighurs to live in the United States prompted first the George W. Bush and then the Obama administrations to seek homes for the Uighurs elsewhere. Albania took five Uighurs. Bermuda took four. Switzerland just agreed to take two, who are still in Guantánamo. Palau has offered to take the rest—including the six already there, plus another five still in Guantánamo.

But those five have refused; they're instead pursuing a case in U.S. courts asking to be granted residence in the United States. Others are looking to the case to set precedent not only for all the Uighurs, but also for other foreign prisoners wrongfully detained by the United States. A federal court ruled in their favor; an appeals court overturned it on a technicality, saying the judicial branch doesn't have the authority to decide who can be released onto U.S. territory. The case was supposed to have been heard by the Supreme Court on March 23. But the Uighurs' initial argument was that they had nowhere else to go. Now that they have an offer to be resettled elsewhere, the Supreme Court in early March sent the case back to a lower court to consider these new facts.

Meanwhile, Palau's offer to take all the remaining Uighurs stands. Toribiong says the decision was made as a humanitarian gesture and as a favor to the United States, which has given Palau more than $800 million in aid over the past 15 years for its 20,000 people, along with a pledge to defend it if attacked, in exchange for U.S. military access to Palauan territory and waters. Palau is also one of the 23 countries that recognize the government of Taiwan rather than that of the People's Republic of China, putting it more or less out of reach of Chinese pressure—although, Toribiong says, China has made its displeasure known to Palau's representative at the United Nations.

15    "When we accepted the United States' request, I conveyed to them that they should be here temporarily, until they find a permanent place for them to resettle," Toribiong said. "The United States agreed to that. But of course, there's no limit to what's temporary. So they'll be here as long as it's temporary. I think it's a matter of mindset, rather than intent."

Toribiong says though the Uighurs have made an effort to fit in, he does worry about what will happen once they finish their English studies and start looking for work.

"They're Muslim, so it's hard to find them jobs in hotels where ladies are sunning on the beach or something," Toribiong said. "They cannot be working in restaurants where they serve liquor, or where waitresses are walking around. So these are conditions I didn't understand [when agreeing to grant them asylum], that these are people with a unique culture."

There's also the fact that the Uighurs are still mentally adjusting after years of incarceration, says Ted Glenn, a former U.S. corrections officer who'd been assigned by Toribiong as a coordinator for the Uighurs to help them settle in. Glenn says he tried to organize them, to structure their time and give them a sense of purpose. The Uighurs resented the control. After a couple of months, Toribiong told me, they asked that Glenn be relieved of his duties; they said he reminded them too much of their guards at Guantánamo.

When I chatted with Glenn in late February in Palau, he was sympathetic to the Uighurs' perspective. "You're dealing with the psychology of a captive," he said. "If you're a captive, you're a captive. It doesn't matter how good the amenities are. You're not free. They don't have passports, they can't go anywhere. In their minds, they are not free."

20        Still, the Uighurs feel restless and out of place. They'd rather live somewhere bigger, with a Uighur community, out of China's reach. But with the U.S. court case moving slowly and no expressed interest yet from Australia or other countries in giving the Uighurs a permanent home, Toribiong says he's starting to think of the long-term happiness of his country's Uighur guests, because they might be there a good long while. They've been told that while they won't be offered citizenship or passports, they could get travel documents—although none have been issued yet. And Toribiong says he's thinking of another way to help the Uighurs feel free.

"It is my personal belief that people may be freed from imprisonment, may experience physical freedom, but unless they are in an environment where they are culturally acclimated, and where they have the opportunity to find wives, spouses, their freedom is incomplete," Toribiong told me. "So I'm trying to find ways for them to realize the fullness of their freedom. The pursuit of happiness means marital happiness, a family, a community where they belong."

Two of the Palau Uighurs have wives and families back in Xinjiang—but have had a hard time communicating with them, because the Chinese government cut off most telephone and Internet communications into Xinjiang after last July's riots. The other four Uighurs, all in their 30s, are single. Toribiong joked that he may end up becoming a matchmaker for them. That assumes that they're willing to settle down and make a life in a place that, however alluring, still feels far from home.

## Reflect on the Reading

1. Why, according to Magistad, are these six ethnic Uighur Muslims from China's western region of Xinjiang in Palau? Where would they prefer to be? Why can't they leave Palau?

2. From her observation, Magistad concludes that these Uighur Muslims feel uncomfortable living in this vacation paradise. What is it about Palau that makes them uncomfortable?

3. The Uighur Muslims find it difficult to find a job in Palau. Why?

4. Why, according to Magistad, is Palau's President Toribiong trying so hard to help these Muslims fit in?

## Consider Your Viewpoint

1. Do you agree with the decision to send these Guantánamo prisoners to Palau? Explain your answer.

2. Why do you think Magistad describes Palau as a paradise? What do you know about Palau? Is it a place you would like to live? Why or why not?

3. Do you agree with President Toribiong's statement, "It is my personal belief that people may be freed from imprisonment, may experience physical freedom, but unless they are in an environment where they are culturally acclimated, and where they have the opportunity to find wives, spouses, their freedom is incomplete?" What does Toribiong mean by "culturally acclimated"?

4. Magistad relies heavily on interviews to support what she observes. How does this use of quotes from her interviews strengthen her piece?

## Troubled Teens

### Dawn Stover

This article written by Dawn Stover for *Conservation Magazine* is an observation of what happens when young male animals are left to their own devices because of laws that allow their fathers to be hunted and killed. *Conservation Magazine*, as its name suggests, takes on environmental issues, but in an unbiased way. This observation relates both sides of the issue.

On a dark night last fall, 11-year-old Joe Hess was playing a backyard game of hide-and-seek with his younger brother and two friends near Grand Coulee Dam in eastern Washington. Lying face-down in the grass, Joe thought he saw Magellan—a huge housecat that lived next door—out of the corner of his eye. When the cat pounced on the boy's head, Joe leaped to his feet and yelled, "No!" But it wasn't Magellan—Joe was staring at a cougar that looked a little bigger than a German shepherd.

Joe slowly backed away from the animal, then turned and ran inside the house. He had a few shallow scratches but was otherwise unharmed. The wildlife agents who responded to the scene told Joe's parents that the cougar was probably a young animal, about a year old, that had recently left home to begin life on its own. Joe's lack of serious injuries might have meant the cat was just playing with him. Or maybe it was simply an inexperienced predator, unsure of whether a boy belonged on the menu.

Cougar encounters like this one are becoming increasingly common in the United States. Most people assume that's because cougar populations are growing, or because the big cats are coming into closer contact with the expanding web of human suburbs. But Robert Wielgus, director of the Large Carnivore Conservation Lab at Washington State University, believes there is something far more complex at work.

In research that has stirred controversy in academic and policy circles, Wielgus argues that poorly designed hunting policies might be triggering an increase in cougar-human conflicts. As hunters kill disproportionate numbers of mature, male cougars, a generation of disorderly teenage cats is taking over their turf. Without adults to keep them in check, Wielgus believes, the unruly juveniles are more likely to run afoul of humans, livestock and pets.

5    Cougars aren't the only species with troubled teens. Off the Florida coast, small sharks attack swimmers more often than large ones do. In Africa, orphaned male elephants have killed humans and rhinoceroses. And in the southwestern U.S., young California condors have destroyed roof tiles and torn off windshield wipers after being released into the wild. The naughty condor behavior decreased markedly when researchers began a "mentoring" program that houses puppet-reared chicks with an adult condor for about a year before they are released. And the marauding elephants calmed down when older bulls were introduced. In a provocative theory that suggests adolescent wildlife may be surprisingly similar to human teenagers, some scientists believe adult supervision could be the key to better behavior for cougars, too.

**Marauding:** To roam about causing damage.

"Sometimes they hiss at you as you're climbing," says Hugh Robinson, a University of Montana researcher who, as a graduate student, helped Wielgus track down cougars. For more than a decade, Wielgus's research teams have been fitting the big cats with radio collars and monitoring their movements. To locate the cougars, researchers get up at 4:30 on winter mornings and set out on snowmobiles. If they find fresh tracks in the snow, the researchers bring in a houndsman with trained dogs to follow the scent and drive the cougar into a tree. Once the cat is treed, the team moves in and shoots it with a tranquilizer dart. If the cougar doesn't then jump—or fall—out of the tree, a researcher climbs up and lowers the cat to the ground with a rope.

From 1998 to 2003, Wielgus's team turned up some unexpected findings as they tracked a group of cougars in northeastern Washington, northern Idaho, and southeastern British Columbia. At the time, cougar populations were believed to be exploding across the U.S. This perception was driven in part by an increase in cougar attacks. Beginning in the 1970s, cougar attacks on humans went from about four per decade in the U.S. and Canada to about 18 per decade, says Paul Beier, a Northern Arizona University professor who studies cougar attacks. Although such altercations are rare compared with, say, attacks by domestic dogs— which kill about 16 Americans every year and send another 386,000 to the emergency room—they generate a lot of media coverage, which builds an outsized impression of cougars' presence.

> **Altercation:** A heated argument.

In Wielgus's home state of Washington, this perception was furthered by a 1996 ban on using hounds to hunt cougars—which many believed would reduce the number of cougars killed by hunters—as well as a rising number of cougar complaints. In 1995, the Washington Department of Fish and Wildlife registered 247 cougar complaints. By 1998, that number had skyrocketed to 927.

Wielgus's study—published in 2006, three years after the radio-collar monitoring was completed—found that the cougar population was actually declining rapidly. (1) What really struck Wielgus's team was that they found almost no male cougars older than four years of age.

10    Wielgus suspected hunting policies were the culprit. Wildlife managers have long seen hunting as a way to keep cougar populations in check, placating ranchers and homeowners who worry the cats will prey on livestock or children. Wielgus thought hunters might be picking off most of the big, mature males, which make the best trophies. To test his theory, Wielgus added two more groups of cougars to the tracking program—one in a heavily hunted area and another in a comparable but lightly hunted area. In a recent study in *Ecology*, he and his coauthors concluded that heavy hunting indeed decimates older males. (2) Another study showed the size of the cougar population in the heavily hunted area did not change, but the population structure shifted toward younger animals. (3)

Conventional wisdom holds that eliminating large male cougars keeps people and livestock safe. But Wielgus believes this paves the way for a bigger threat: unruly young males who move in from nearby areas and, unlike mature cougars who have learned to avoid humans, don't always mind their manners.

The life of a male cougar is not an easy one. Raised by a single mom, he is forced to leave home by the age of two. His father, who marks and patrols a territory that may include the home ranges of several females and cover hundreds of square miles, does not tolerate other adult males in the area. So the son strikes out on his own, traveling long distances in search of a new home where he can find food and females. Only about 40 percent of young males survive their first winter alone, sometimes by occupying the loosely defended fringes of an older male's territory. A young male lucky enough to find an unoccupied territory will spend the rest of his life guarding the boundaries established by the previous occupant. "It's like a home going up for sale," says Wielgus. "The property remains the same; there's just a new owner."

These homeowners are elusive creatures. Harley Shaw, who spent 27 years as a wildlife biologist working in cougar country for the Arizona Game and Fish Department, has seen only four cougars without the help of tracking collars or hounds. But studies using GPS collars have found that cougars spend a surprising amount of time cruising the edges of suburban neighborhoods, undetected. Some biologists cite this as proof that humans and cougars can peacefully coexist. "Usually they are inclined to avoid us," Shaw says. "If they didn't, we would have a lot more attacks and encounters."

Wielgus worries that these elusive tendencies are breaking down. When older males die, they leave behind an open territory that's often within range of human settlements. The males who move in are younger, unaccustomed to humans, and—possibly—more brazen and curious. But can this really make them more likely to run afoul of people and livestock?

15      This question weighs heavily on the mind of Ben Maletzke, a WSU graduate student who is comparing cougar complaints from the heavily hunted and lightly hunted areas. His preliminary findings suggest that the heavily hunted area has five times as many complaints per capita, and eight times as many livestock predations, as the lightly hunted area—even though the density of cougars and livestock is about the same in both areas. Wielgus suspects that teenage immigrants in the heavily hunted area may be responsible for most of the trouble.

In other words, hunting policies that allow a disproportionate number of males to be killed may be exacerbating the very problem they set out to solve. Paul Beier's studies of attacks on humans support this counterintuitive notion. Beier says that at least half of the cougars involved in these attacks are juvenile animals, typically around a year old. "The older ones are smarter and know how to behave better," Beier says.

The scientists have also discovered that, in the heavily hunted area, the home ranges of the new arrivals are much larger and overlap more than in the lightly hunted area, because the animals are not old enough to maintain strict boundaries. "It's territorial chaos," Wielgus says. "Instead of one old cougar that keeps his nose clean, you've got three teenagers wreaking havoc."

Havoc: General destruction, confusion, or disorder.

Wielgus's ideas don't sit well with everyone. His critics and even some of his own former graduate students are not completely convinced that age is a key factor in human-cougar conflicts. "Hunting definitely does cause an influx of juvenile males," says the University of Montana's Robinson, but he doesn't yet see solid proof that juveniles are more trouble-prone than older cats. "It's still just a hypothesis," he says.

Maybe increased attacks have nothing to do with a cougar's age but instead simply result from the cats' being new to the area. In many cases, the new arrivals have been squeezed out of remote wilderness habitat and forced into areas where they are more likely to encounter humans. "There's so much more to the equation than just being a young cat," says Mat Alldredge, a researcher at the Colorado Division of Wildlife who is studying cougar demographics and human interactions along the Front Range. And with few cats surviving to a ripe old age, there may be no way to know whether older animals would be better behaved than youngsters. "I think humans are primarily responsible for all the interaction you see," Alldredge says. "We're moving into these areas where cougars and deer are."

20   As a possible solution, Alldredge is testing scare tactics, which he euphemistically refers to as "aversive techniques." The idea is to teach cougars to be apprehensive about approaching populated areas. Some of the cougars Alldredge traps and relocates are being released with a special sendoff: beanbag rounds fired from a noisy, 12-gauge shotgun. "It's an 'extra' to see whether it helps keep them away" from populated areas, he explains.

A bigger fix might be to revise hunting policies in a way that ensures older, wiser males remain in the cougar population. In a recent study in *PLoS ONE*, University of Minnesota professor Craig Packer and his coauthors estimated that killing only males that are at least four years old would ensure that they live long enough to produce offspring and protect them from other males. (4) Perhaps there should be a minimum "catch size" for cougars, Packer says, similar to the laws that require sport fishermen to release small fish so that they can grow up to be big fish.

"You cannot manage animals like chess pieces," says Gay Bradshaw, an expert on animal psychology and neuroscience who heads The Kerulos Center in Jacksonville, Oregon. Bradshaw has written extensively about how elephants, lions, and other species have distinct cultures that humans are only starting to glimpse. Until these cultures are understood and respected, she believes, it will be virtually impossible to live peaceably with cougars and other wildlife.

It's a controversial idea that raises a provocative question: Instead of just eradicating "problem" cougars or other animals, should we try to understand them in the same way we understand humans who come from broken homes or violent neighborhoods?

Bradshaw has documented how witnessing a shooting—or living in daily fear of being shot—can trigger posttraumatic stress disorder in lions and elephants. These animals have the same brain structures and mechanisms that in humans are responsible for intelligence, emotion, and culture, Bradshaw says. And young male elephants seem to behave better when there are mature bulls around.

25 Wielgus has no doubt that cougars follow a similar dynamic, even though this makes him an outlier among his colleagues. Cougars are solitary animals, but Wielgus notes they do come into contact with each other. He believes these interactions may teach youngsters to distinguish between appropriate and inappropriate prey and behavior. In turn, Wielgus thinks it's time to consider how hunting and other human activities can cause social chaos among these animals. Older male cougars may not be role models, says Wielgus, "but they certainly serve as a police force."

If this seems like a bizarre idea, think of it in human terms: imagine what any community would be like if most of the adult men disappeared. We may not understand what makes 18-year-old males more likely than 48-year-old men to do dangerous things, Wielgus says, but we know that the world would be a different place if teenagers were in charge.

## Literature Cited

1. Lambert, C.M.S. et al. 2006. Cougar population dynamics and viability in the Pacific Northwest. *Journal of Wildlife Management* 70(1):246–254.

2. Cooley, H.S. et al. 2009. Does hunting regulate cougar populations? A test of the compensatory mortality hypothesis. *Ecology* 90(10):2913–2921.

3. Robinson, H.S. et al. 2008. Sink populations in carnivore management: Cougar demography and immigration in a hunted population. *Ecological Applications* 18(4):1028–1037.

4. Packer, C. et al. 2009. Sport hunting, predator control and conservation of large carnivores. *PLoS ONE* 4(6):e5941.

## Reflect on the Reading

1. Why according to Robert Wielgus, director of the Large Carnivore Conservation Lab at Washington State University, is there an increase in conflicts between humans and cougars? Does his hypothesis sound plausible to you? Why or why not?

2. What is the value of setting up "mentoring" programs for teenage animals? What examples of such programs does Stover provide?

3. Stover describes the life of a young cougar male. How does this observation of their living conditions contribute to the point of the article?

4. Stover concludes, "In other words, hunting policies that allow a disproportionate number of males to be killed may be exacerbating the very problem they set out to solve." What research does she cite to support this view? Do you agree with her? Why or why not?

## Consider Your Viewpoint

1. How effective is Stover's observation? Her research? How do these two work together to create a stronger article?

2. Not everyone agrees that young cougars are more "trouble-prone" than older ones. Why does Stover introduce this opposing view? Does it change the way you think about Wielgus's hypothesis? Explain your answer.

3. Stover also interviews Gay Bradshaw, an expert on animal psychology and neuroscience, who claims that we must understand animal culture better. Do you agree that animals have distinct cultures? Can you describe other animal cultures?

4. Stover concludes her article by quoting Wielgus, who compares the cougar situation to that of letting human teenagers take over a community. How effective is this comparison?

mycomplab

For support in meeting this chapter's objectives, follow this path in MyCompLab: Resources ⇒ Writing ⇒ Writing Purposes ⇒ Writing to Reflect. Review the Instruction and Multimedia resources about observing and reflecting, then complete the Exercises and click on Gradebook to measure your progress.

# 7 Explaining a Concept

## Learning Objectives

In this chapter you will:

- Write to explain a concept.
- Use an outline to discover ideas.

- Learn strategies to effectively explain a concept.
- Revise to improve focus and provide clear definitions.

A young fan tearfully hugs Major League Baseball player Rickey Henderson of the Oakland Athletics. What is the concept behind such sports hero worship?

**E**ach field of study has its own general ideas or
concepts, and the more you know about these concepts, the
better you will do in your classes. If, for example, you are an
education major, you learn concepts such as standardized tests, at-risk
students, and lesson plans. If you are a psychology major, you learn
concepts such as cognition, reinforcement, and personality. In this
writing class, you are learning concepts such as rhetorical analysis,
writing process, and genre. Understanding concepts and being able to
use the specialized vocabulary associated with them
is one way you demonstrate your knowledge and
communicate effectively with others in the same
field of study. The knowledge of concepts also helps
you become a member of the culture of a field.

Concept: A
thought or
general idea
derived from
specific knowledge.

> *Words are tools which*
> *automatically carve*
> *concepts out of experience.*
> —*Julian Sorrell Huxley*

# WRITING TO EXPLAIN A CONCEPT

To explain a concept, you start by choosing a thought or general idea that
interests you and that you would like to explain to someone else. For example, you might be interested in explaining the concept of democracy as
a political system or in comparison to a dictatorship. Or you might be interested in explaining how DNA fingerprinting works. You review what you
already know about the concept. If you need specific knowledge, you read
more about it online or at the library and interview people who are knowledgeable about the topic. When explaining a concept, your primary purpose is informative: to share the information that you know and have
gathered about the idea with your audience.

## Questions for Explaining a Concept

- What concept would I like to explain? Is this a concept people
  generally agree on?
- Where can I find information on this concept?
- Is this concept controversial? What would my audience want to know
  about it?
- Which genre and visual design would provide the best format for
  sharing this information? How complex is this concept and how could
  visual design simplify it?
- Why is it important for my audience to understand this concept?
- What constraints would prevent me from effectively explaining this
  concept?

# MODEL EXPLANATIONS OF CONCEPTS

As you read the following explanations of concepts, consider how you might use some of these authors' strategies in your own writing. For each reading, notice how the author introduces the topic. Label the thesis statement and mark the different writing patterns the author uses to develop the piece. Then notice how the author concludes the piece.

## The "Trophy Kids" Go to Work

### Ron Alsop

A concept that many people agree on is that different generations have unique characteristics. In the United States, for example, many people believe that "Baby Boomers," people born between 1946–1964, are workaholics who are defined by their professions, and "Generation X," people born between 1964–1980, are people who crave adventure more than a secure job. In this *Wall Street Journal* article, Ron Alsop describes the characteristics of the "millennials," people born between 1981–2001, and how their employers struggle to adjust to their unique characteristics.

*Millennials depend on their cell phones for personal and professional communication.*

When Gretchen Neels, a Boston-based consultant, was coaching a group of college students for job interviews, she asked them how they believe employers view them. She gave them a clue, telling them that the word she was looking for begins with the letter "e." One young man shouted out, "excellent." Other students chimed in with "enthusiastic" and "energetic." Not even close. The correct answer, she said, is "entitled." "Huh?" the students responded, surprised and even hurt to think that managers are offended by their highfalutin opinions of themselves. If there is one overriding perception of the millennial generation, it's that these young people have great—and sometimes outlandish—expectations. Employers realize the millennials are their future work force, but they are concerned about this generation's desire to

Highfalutin: Pretentious or exaggerated.

shape their jobs to fit their lives rather than adapt their lives to the workplace.

Although members of other generations were considered somewhat spoiled in their youth, millennials feel an unusually strong sense of entitlement. Older adults criticize the high-maintenance rookies for demanding too much too soon. "They want to be CEO tomorrow," is a common refrain from corporate recruiters.

More than 85% of hiring managers and human-resource executives said they feel that millennials have a stronger sense of entitlement than older workers, according to a survey by CareerBuilder.com. The generation's greatest expectations: higher pay (74% of respondents); flexible work schedules (61%); a promotion within a year (56%); and more vacation or personal time (50%).

"They really do seem to want everything, and I can't decide if it's an inability or an unwillingness to make trade-offs," says Derrick Bolton, assistant dean and M.B.A. admissions director at Stanford University's Graduate School of Business. "They want to be CEO, for example, but they say they don't want to give up time with their families."

5    Millennials, of course, will have to temper their expectations as they seek employment during this deep economic slump. But their sense of entitlement is an ingrained trait that will likely resurface in a stronger job market. Some research studies indicate that the millennial generation's great expectations stem from feelings of superiority. Michigan State University's Collegiate Employment Research Institute and MonsterTrak, an online careers site, conducted a research study of 18- to 28-year-olds and found that nearly half had moderate to high superiority beliefs about themselves. The superiority factor was measured by responses to such statements as "I deserve favors from others" and "I know that I have more natural talents than most."

For their part, millennials believe they can afford to be picky, with talent shortages looming as baby boomers retire. "They are finding that they have to adjust work around our lives instead of us adjusting our lives around work," a teenage blogger named Olivia writes on the Web site Xanga.com. "What other option do they have? We are hard working and utilize tools to get the job done. But we don't want to work more than 40 hours a week, and we want to wear clothes that are comfortable. We want to be able to spice up the dull workday by listening to our iPods. If corporate America doesn't like that, too bad."

Where do such feelings come from? Blame it on doting parents, teachers and coaches. Millennials are truly "trophy kids," the pride and joy of their parents. The millennials were lavishly praised and often received trophies when they excelled, and sometimes when they didn't, to avoid damaging their self-esteem. They and their parents have placed a high

Accolade: Praise or award for doing a good job.

premium on success, filling résumés with not only academic accolades but also sports and other extracurricular activities.

Now what happens when these trophy kids arrive in the workplace with greater expectations than any generation before them? "Their attitude is always 'What are you going to give me,'" says Natalie Griffith, manager of human-resource programs at Eaton Corp. "It's not necessarily arrogance; it's simply their mindset."

Millennials want loads of attention and guidance from employers. An annual or even semiannual evaluation isn't enough. They want to know how they're doing weekly, even daily. "The millennials were raised with so

Affirmation: Praise.

much affirmation and positive reinforcement that they come into the workplace needy for more," says Subha Barry, managing director and head of global diversity and inclusion at Merrill Lynch & Co.

10    But managers must tread lightly when making a critique. This generation was treated so delicately that many schoolteachers stopped grading papers and tests in harsh-looking red ink. Some managers have seen millennials break down in tears after a negative performance review and even quit their jobs. "They like the constant positive reinforcement, but don't always take suggestions for improvement well," says Steve Canale, recruiting manager at General Electric Co. In performance evaluations, "it's still important to give the good, the bad and the ugly, but with a more positive emphasis."

Flounder: Struggle.

Millennials also want things spelled out clearly. Many flounder without precise guidelines but thrive in structured situations that provide clearly defined rules and the order that they crave. Managers will need to give step-by-step directions for handling everything from projects to voice-mail messages to client meetings. It may seem obvious that employees should show up on time, limit lunchtime to an hour and turn off cellphones during meetings. But those basics aren't necessarily apparent to many millennials.

Gail McDaniel, a corporate consultant and career coach for college students, spoke to managers at a health-care company who were frustrated by some of their millennial employees. It seems that one young man missed an important deadline, and when his manager asked him to explain, he said, "Oh, you forgot to remind me." Parents and teachers aren't doing millennials any favors by constantly adapting to their needs, Ms. McDaniel says. "Going into the workplace, they have an expectation that companies will adapt for them, too."

Millennials also expect a flexible work routine that allows them time for their family and personal interests. "For this generation, work is not a place you go; work is a thing you do," says Kaye Foster-Cheek, vice president for human resources at Johnson & Johnson.

Although millennials have high expectations about what their employers should provide them, companies shouldn't expect much loyalty in return. If a job doesn't prove fulfilling, millennials will forsake it in a flash. Indeed, many employers say it's retention that worries them most. In the Michigan State/MonsterTrak study, about two-thirds of the millennials said they would likely "surf" from one job to the next. In addition, about 44% showed their lack of loyalty by stating that they would renege on a job-acceptance commitment if a better offer came along. These workplace nomads don't see any stigma in listing three jobs in a single year on their resumes. They are quite confident about landing yet another job, even if it will take longer in this dismal economy. In the meantime, they needn't worry about their next paycheck because they have their parents to cushion them. They're comfortable in the knowledge that they can move back home while they seek another job. The weak job market may make millennials think twice about moving on, but once jobs are more plentiful, they will likely resume their job-hopping ways.

15    Justin Pfister, the founder of Open Yard, an online retailer of sports equipment, believes he and his fellow millennials will resist having their expectations deflated. If employers fail to provide the opportunities and rewards millennials seek, he says, they're likely to drop out of the corporate world as he did and become entrepreneurs. "We get stifled when we're offered single-dimensional jobs," he says. "We are multi-dimensional people living and working in a multi-dimensional world."

These outspoken young people tend to be highly opinionated and fearlessly challenge recruiters and bosses. Status and hierarchy don't impress them much. They want to be treated like colleagues rather than subordinates and expect ready access to senior executives, even the CEO, to share their brilliant ideas. Recruiters at such companies as investment-banking firm Goldman Sachs Group Inc. and Amazon.com describe "student stalkers" who brashly fire off emails to everyone from the CEO on down, trying to get an inside track to a job.

Companies have a vested interest in trying to slow the millennial mobility rate. They not only will need millennials to fill positions left vacant by retiring baby boomers but also will benefit from this generation's best and brightest, who possess significant strengths in teamwork, technology skills, social networking and multitasking. Millennials were bred for achievement, and most will work hard if the task is engaging and promises a tangible payoff.

Clearly, companies that want to compete for top talent must bend a bit and adapt to the millennial generation. Employers need to show new hires how their work makes a difference and why it's of value to the company. Smart managers will listen to their young employees' opinions, and give them some say in decisions. Employers also can detail the career opportunities available to millennials if they'll just stick around awhile. Indeed, it's the wealth of opportunities that will prove to be the most effective retention tool.

In the final analysis, the generational tension is a bit ironic. After all, the grumbling baby-boomer managers are the same indulgent parents who produced the millennial generation. Ms. Barry of Merrill Lynch sees the irony. She is teaching her teenage daughter to value her own opinions and to challenge things. Now she sees many of those challenging millennials at her company and wonders how she and other managers can expect the kids they raised to suddenly behave differently at work. "It doesn't mean we can be as indulgent as managers as we are as parents," she says. "But as parents of young people just like them, we can treat them with respect."

# One Word Spotlight

***Entitlement*** (paragraph 2) is the concept that a person is owed something. For example, the phrase "culture of entitlement" is used by conservatives to define some U.S. citizens' beliefs that the government owes them retirement, health care, and unemployment benefits. In the article "The 'Trophy Kids' Go to Work," entitlement refers to the millennials' belief that they are owed certain benefits when they are hired by a company.

## Reflect on the Reading

1. According to Alsop, why do "millennials" feel entitled?

2. Underline the one sentence in the piece that you think best states the author's main point about millennials and work. Explain why you chose this sentence.

3. Explain how the phrase "Trophy Kids" connects to the concept. Make a list of other concepts that are related to work. Which of these concepts might you write about?

4. What evidence does Alsop use to explain the "millennials"? How convincing is this evidence?

5. Why do you think that Alsop chose to end his article with a quote from the mother of a "millennial"? How effective is this closing?

## Consider Your Viewpoint

1. Do you believe that "millennials" are spoiled? Explain your answer.

2. Do the millennials have a right to feel entitlement? Why or why not?

3. In which generation were you born? Baby Boomers? Generation X? Millennial? Using Google or another search engine, look up the characteristics of your generation. Do you agree with the characterization? Why or why not? Is one of these concepts a potential topic for your paper?

4. A photograph is more interesting if the subject is close, but not exactly centered. Does the photograph of the cell phone at the beginning of this article follow this principle? Is it interesting? Why or why not? Are there other concepts related to photography that interest you?

# How Farmers Are Going to Save Civilization

## Jenn Hardy

Many people take a keen interest in media reporting about the need to protect our planet. But when it comes to taking action on the concept, most people don't do more than look for the "organic" label on the foods that they buy in the supermarket. An exception is Trent Rhode, a young person who is taking action by advocating permaculture. This magazine article, written by Jenn Hardy, a freelance writer who lives in Montreal, Canada, describes Trent and others like him who are determined to make a difference by living by the principles of permaculture.

*A Central American farmer displays a handful of coffee beans.*

Trent Rhode looks great in a suit. The 27-year-old resident of Peterborough, Ont., seems perfectly comfortable standing before a long table of elected officials twice his age, lecturing them on the importance of environmental sustainability. His message is simple but powerful: he tells his audience they are not separate from the environment—they are the environment. Natural resources are dwindling, he says, and now is the time to act.

Rhode sits on the steering committee of Transition Town Peterborough, a non-profit organization that is working toward building a self-sufficient community less dependent on fossil fuels; at this particular meeting he is outlining some of the group's ideas for Peterborough's municipal officials and bureaucrats. His power suit says he belongs in this boardroom—but it's not actually where he prefers to be.

When his business there is done, Rhode slips into a comfortable pair of trousers and an old blue t-shirt and digs his hands deep into the soil. In his job as a natural gardener, Rhode works the land at several properties in Ontario. He spends his time not only designing, but also implementing edible "forest gardens" at an eco-education centre in Colborne, a farm in Cobourg, and a residential property near Belleville. His hometown, which he obviously holds dear to his heart, has hired him to maintain gardens in Peterborough.

As a five-year-old horsing around on his grandfather's Belleville farm, Rhode couldn't be bothered with the ins and outs of growing vegetables— he was much more interested in chasing the pigs and geese. But 12 years later, while researching agriculture for his journalism program at Loyalist College, he stumbled across a concept that would become the foundation of his future career and virtually every aspect of his life. The idea was permaculture.

5    "I became aware of how fragile agriculture is, and how it's dependent on so many things," he says. "I began to see how fragile the economy is for the same reasons. I became interested in what seemed to be a necessity. The future is uncertain—but what is certain is we need to eat."

Rhode has applied to a master of science in integrative ecosocial design at Gaia University, a program that specializes in teaching people already involved in the "regeneration and world change fields." Rhode is helping to organize an Ontario-wide permaculture convention to take place in Toronto in the fall, and evangelizes the principles of permaculture to just about anyone who will listen.

"The grocery store is the big box we go into and we buy our food," he says. "There is no connection between the farm and our refrigerator. In this culture we take food for granted; it isn't seen as the

**Evangelizes:**
Preaches a particular gospel or belief.

necessity it is. The way we think is fragmented and everything is disconnected, but permaculture seeks to integrate—it has a more holistic view."

In other words, Rhode believes that putting these ideas into practice on the farm and in the garden can fix our ailing food supply; moreover, he believes permaculture can transform every aspect of our lives for the better. And he's not alone.

So what exactly is permaculture? The term was coined in the 1970s by Bill Mollison and co-originated with another Australian academic, David Holmgren. Originally it stood for "permanent agriculture": at a time when the burgeoning environmental movement was rediscovering ancient concepts like pesticide-free agriculture, Mollison and Holmgren bundled together these ideas into a complete design system for environmentally friendly food production.

10　　Decades later, that design system has spread to many other fields, including architecture, economics, education, and spirituality, so that permaculture now really stands for permanent culture—a design philosophy for making every aspect of our lives truly sustainable. It advocates a dozen key principles, which include caring for the earth, caring for people, using and valuing renewable resources, integration rather than segregation, and using small and slow solutions.

And if there's one thing a permaculture advocate can't stand, it's waste. The throwaway, wasteful society we live in now, they say, can't last: idling in the drive-thru to get a coffee from Starbucks, driving in our gas guzzlers the few blocks from home to the grocery store, all to purchase onions from Egypt, apples from Chile, and broccoli from Spain. Then, when we get home, it all goes in a power-sucking refrigerator to keep it from going bad.

"People often think, 'The first thing I need to do is to change the way I move around in a vehicle or how I heat my house,'" says David Holmgren from his home in Victoria, Australia. "And those things are important. But we eat every day, and our decisions in what we eat, and how we eat, and how we get that food, are enormously powerful. Permaculture aims to redesign the whole food-production chain."

That means more household self-reliance, such as growing some of our own food and doing some of the chores our grandparents did—food growing, canning, clothes mending, and DIY of all sorts—in order to reduce our environmental footprint and cut back on the wastefulness that has brought us to the brink of dangerous and irreversible environmental decline. Permaculture means changing more than just the contents of your fridge: it means altering some fundamental aspects of the way you live your life.

DIY: Do-it-yourself.

Which all seems like a bit of an undertaking, to say the least. But not to worry: permaculture is based on slow-and-steady change, starting, literally, in your own backyard.

15    The modern farm is an industrial marvel, a factory for growing as much food as possible in the smallest space at the lowest cost. But it can't last: plants and animals aren't cogs in a machine, and industrial farming is beginning to run up against some fundamental limits of nature. Drive around in the country, and you'll pass rows and rows of monoculture crops planted horizontally. Behind the scenes, huge amounts of chemically manufactured nitrogen and phosphorous are pumped into the soil to prevent it from becoming infertile—these chemicals then leak into the groundwater and, inevitably, into the ocean. Modern farming requires about 10 calories of energy for every calorie of food produced, which means growing food isn't actually production at all, it's just another type of consumption.

If you wander into your nearest grocery store right now, the answer to this problem appears to be to label everything "organic." See that well-heeled yuppie in the checkout line buying $10 organic oatmeal? Her great-grandmother would probably scoff at the label (and the cost) because the term would have been meaningless: organic was all she ever knew, and it didn't need a fancy name. Her apples had spots on them because the chemicals and hormones that now bathe modern fruits and vegetables just didn't exist. The "organic" label is a modern invention, a backlash against industrial farming. As a marketing tool, the word has been very successful.

> Organic: Food grown without the use of chemicals or hormones.

But saying something is organic doesn't automatically mean it's sustainable. Permaculture and organic agriculture share some obvious traits, but it is possible to have one without the other. For example, those carrots at the supermarket might be labeled "organic," but if they're packed in a plastic bag and shipped from South America, they're hardly environmentally friendly. You'd be better off buying non-organic produce from your local farmers' market, because the food you buy there has less packaging and burned less gas to get to you. Similarly, you'd be better off buying the pork chop of a local free-roaming pig that got a few injections than you would that of a pig that has all the paperwork required to label it "organic," but that lived in a barn eating processed feed pellets.

What this means, say permaculture activists, is that it's simply not enough to throw some organic instant waffles in your shopping cart and get on with your life: it's our responsibility to truly know what we're eating and how it got to our plate. Individually, culturally, economically, spiritually, we really are what we eat.

The reason these questions are so important right now is that it is becoming increasingly obvious that the world as we know it is in big trouble.

20    The chief scientific adviser of the U.K., professor John Beddington, recently said we are facing a "perfect storm," where shortages of water, food, and energy sources will take a devastating toll on the world. He reckons we have about 20 years.

Holmgren, however, says the storm is already upon us. "We are in a continuous economic, energetic climate crisis," he says. "The way that unfolds will be difficult to predict, but I think most of these statements that are being made by even well-meaning people at higher levels are enormously underplaying things."

Steve Jones, an ecologist and permaculture teacher in Wales, agrees that the crisis is already here. He has a scary name for this historical period we're entering: "descent culture"—a perilous time of scarce resources, declining standards of living, and social breakdown. What goes up, he says, must come down.

"It is a basic law of physics and therefore inescapable," he says. "It will change everything. It will change the way we think. The next generation will look back at us thinking we were crazy or naive. At best we will be leaving them a world scarred by fossil fuel use and dependent on cheap energy that is no longer there. It is going to be very tough over the next few decades whilst we figure out how to respond."

Jones emphasizes that oil is at the root of the problem. He says no other energy source can rival petroleum in terms of energy density, ease of access, and sheer usefulness.

25    But it is not sustainable. He doesn't believe we'll run out of oil entirely, he says, but "we have probably used half the available supply that is in the ground, the easy half to get hold of. So at some point, possibly quite soon, the world supply will peak, and the rate at which it can be extracted from the ground will go into a decline that cannot and will not be reversed."

Permaculture advocates say we'd be better off modifying our way of life now than waiting for nature to do it for us. Holmgren, for instance, doesn't see much point in trying to build an environmentally friendly car when the sanest choice would be to, well, just drive less. The point isn't to build a better rat race—it's to get out of it altogether. We might as well accept these changes with a positive outlook, Holmgren says, because "whatever we do in the future, we're going to have a lot more success by figuring out how to not do things than desperately trying to create ways to maintain current patterns of living that just aren't going to work."

Two-and-a-half hours walk up a mountain in Vilcabamba, Ecuador, lives a 34-year-old red-headed farmer named Yves Zehnder. He is a farmer in every sense of the word: this is no side project, and he has no additional day job. He works hard every day from sunrise to sunset (and sometimes beyond) managing the 10 hectares of land he lives on.

*The view at Yves Zehnder's Sacred Sueños farm in Vilcabama, Ecuador.*

Eco-terrorist:
A person who does harm to others who harm the environment.

Fearing that his frustration with our society might turn him into an eco-terrorist, Zehnder left his home in northern Ontario 14 years ago, and five years ago decided to live sustainably in the south of Ecuador. A mere $1,400 in his bank account gave him residency and home became a tent on top of an Andean mountain. He lived in the tent for six months while he single-handedly built the adobe brick communal facilities the farm laborers now use.

At first, life at the farm, called Sacred Sueños, was hard. When he arrived at his mountainside property nothing would grow except bracken fern. The soil, because of the unsustainable slash-and-burn farming in the area, was basically infertile. In retrospect, would he have chosen land with better soil? "No," he says. "It taught me patience and perseverance. It was an ethical decision to change poor soil into something fertile. I didn't want to be a frivolous white boy who buys good land and has it all. This way I have been able to find solutions to big problems and share that knowledge."

30    Slowly, but surely, he put permaculture's techniques to work on the farm. For example, he uses a composting toilet. One of the permaculture principles is that in nature, there is no such thing as waste. So Zehnder has a "humanure" system, turning every bit of human feces back into soil. Once a guest uses the lovely mountainside-view toilet (a glorified bucket under a seat) he or she scoops up a coconut shell of sawdust (happily donated to Zehnder by a sawmill down the hill) and covers the mess. The last to fill the bucket empties it in the appropriate pile. He also uses a "chicken tractor." His five hens don't have to do much heavy lifting, but they are penned in a large area, and their natural scratching and digging for grubs turns the soil under their feet. Chicken poop is also an excellent fertilizer that prepares the ground for plants when the "tractor" is relocated a week later.

Zehnder strategically plants trees to help him create shade during the four-month dry season and others that prevent erosion during the rainy season.

*Yves Zehnder with Sacred Sueños' two donkeys, Bonne and Posito.*

He and his partner, Jennifer Martin, keep chickens for eggs, donkeys, a horse, and goats for milk and cheese. They grow delicious native fruit like *naranjillas*, which often come from "volunteers" as he calls them—seeds that blossom out of the "humanure." (He has also had the help of human volunteers who come to work on the farm.)

The homemade shower is heated by a black tube coiled to attract the sun, and it has the same beautiful valley view as the toilet—which leaves everyone fighting over the opportunity to be naked outside.

Natural building is a part of the permaculture design system that often uses a material called "cob," traditionally made of clay, sand, straw, water and earth, an easy combination to find when building a straw-bale house somewhere like Canada or the U.K. Finding straw up top a mountain in Ecuador, however, is more of a challenge. True to the system he follows, Zehnder has gone one step further with cob. He sees the use of an organic material such as straw as a waste and instead uses shredded plastic bags to bind the material together.

35    Though he now has much better soil, his work is far from finished. A friend has recently purchased the 40 hectares of neighboring land, and Zehnder will make use of it for rotating pastures and reforestation. Aside from the daily chores that come with running such a large piece of land, Zehnder is building an educational centre at Sacred Sueños, where he will teach permaculture not only to rich Westerners who can make their way down there, but also to locals who can take the course with scholarships.

It's easy to see that permaculture puts an emphasis on human manual labor. This is why critics often call it uneconomical or impractical when it comes to large-scale farming. But the manual labor is exactly what permaculture adherents like about it. For them it's about taking your life into your own hands.

Grégoire Lamoureux is another farmer who is putting permaculture into practice. On Spiral Farm in Winlaw, B.C., where he has lived for

> Hectares: 100 acres.

almost two decades, Lamoureux says permaculture is "looking at design issues and implementing them in human habitat—where people live and taking into account places for every living being as well. It doesn't exclude other living creatures."

Growing up on a dairy farm in southern Quebec, Lamoureux quickly learned what he didn't want to do when he grew up. He didn't want to be involved with large monoculture farming. He first learned about permaculture in the '80s, and now on his farm, on the western bank of the Slocan River, he grows a diversity of plants, fruits, nuts, useful trees, and vegetables, mostly for his own use. He dries and cans food to keep himself going all year round. Lamoureux teaches other people at Spiral Farm, but also takes his knowledge on the road and teaches courses across the country.

The movement has spread through such courses taught by people like Lamoureux. They are now available all over the world, adapted to different climates and skill levels. Some introductory courses are taught in a day, although there are also two-week intensive design courses that grant certificates and qualifications to teach.

40    A typical permaculture design course covers the essential principles and elements, as well as some hands-on experience. In the two-week course, you learn about the ethics of sustainability, building soil fertility, natural building design, waste recycling and treatment, and water harvesting, among others.

And it's not all about back-to-the-land living of the type Yves Zehnder is doing; some courses are designed for curious urbanites. Lamoureux, for instance, teaches one for people who want to start a container garden on their balcony. "Some people feel the negative sides of living in a city," he says. "The course can empower you to feel more comfortable where you live. People can take information home and apply the ideas."

For Sandra Storr, who runs Romany Rest, a 120-year-old farmhouse bed and breakfast, using permaculture principles in P.E.I., it made the most sense to get her certification online. She says online study was not only economical, but it meant she didn't have to fly across the world to do it. (Anyone who is serious about the environment, she says, avoids flying as much as possible.) Storr isn't only concerned about reducing her carbon emissions, but *reducing*—period. That was her first aim when she and her husband, Fred, immigrated to Canada from Wales in 2006.

The bed and breakfast uses solar power for showers and the swimming pool. While a solar electricity system is a bit out of range at the moment, they have looked to low-tech permaculture solutions such as passive solar—renovating their farmhouse to include big windows that face the sun, and, in true DIY fashion, they made reflectors out of plywood and aluminum emergency blankets, which double or triple the amount of sunlight, and therefore heat, that enters the building. The property features 26 micro wind turbines.

Storr says her solutions are "cheap and cheerful": she's covered some of the non-essential windows in bubble wrap to keep heat in.

45     The couple rarely visit the grocery store, even to keep the B&B operating. They keep a few chickens running around and some sheep. Like Lamoureux, Storr teaches on-site and does her own bottling, canning, and dehydrating. She is most interested in beans, cooked grains, wheat, and seeds, and she keeps a root cellar. And thanks to the provincial government's forest regeneration scheme, the property now has a hectare of new native trees in its backyard. "I had heard of permaculture years ago, but thought of it as simply another form of gardening," says Storr. "We already had an organic garden in Wales and I couldn't see what all the fuss was about. It wasn't until five years ago that I realized it was about so much more—a whole system designed to mimic natural systems and function efficiently." She explains that it was studying permaculture more intensely that taught her to bring everything together.

"When we first got here we didn't think five acres was big enough. But, because permaculture is such an efficient system, now I think, what do we do with all this space?" In a permaculture garden, you don't see row upon row of the same crop. The system discourages monocultures and promotes the use of vertical space. That means that permaculture gardens often end up like a chaotic mess, with plants tangled in amongst each other—the way they are in nature. "Instead of transforming the environment to fit your needs," Lamoureux says, "you have to use the existing environment and adapt *your* needs to *it*."

What a lovely idea this permaculture is. Lovely perhaps, but maybe not too practical. We don't all have the time or money to leave our lives behind and start a full-scale farm. Even if we could afford it, not everyone has a burning desire to be a farmer and live off the land. Similarly, many people living in an apartment or a house with a small garden just don't have time to grow tomatoes. We like eating grapefruit, mangos, and bananas year-round. We like to listen to our iPods and drink Starbucks from disposable cups. Plenty of us like our Land Rovers! This is normal life for most of us, and the general feeling is no one has the right to take that away. And no one is taking it away—just yet. But no matter how you slice it, big changes in energy and economics are coming soon. If we clue in to the idea that capitalism, and all the wonderful things that come with it, are not sustainable as they now exist, we may be able to make small changes in our individual lives that could mitigate the crises still to come.

Mitigate: To relieve or make less painful.

It may require some effort, but there are many ways to implement permaculture into your life now. Changes can be made slowly and relatively painlessly. Don't want to grow your own food? Then why not participate in Community Supported Agriculture and buy a weekly food basket from a local farmer? Or challenge yourself at the grocery store to search for food that was produced in your own country. If it ain't broke, don't buy a new one. If it is broke, fix it. For too long we have lived as if we were characters in Aldous Huxley's *Brave New World*, happily reciting, "Ending is better than mending. The more stitches, the less riches."

To the chagrin of Greenpeace activists everywhere, not everyone actually cares about the environment. Not everyone believes the earth has a soul and we should worship her in all her glory. What most people do care about, however, is their wallets, and the truth is, virtually everything about permaculture is about saving cash. (Saving trees, seeds, and the world might come next on the list.)

50    Permaculture devotees generally come in two camps: the ones who see it as a kind of spiritual devotion and the ones who see it as a scientifically rigorous system.

23-year-old Sara Bresee is definitely in the first category. She learned about permaculture while going on a spiritual retreat in Spain. On top of a mountain, she lived in a teepee, sat in sweat lodges, and danced barefoot with her hippie self. While building a mandala in the garden, she met a man who introduced her to a few permaculture techniques. "I thought, 'That's the smartest thing in the world,'" she says. And it was something she could take back with her to her urban life in Montreal, where she is studying to be a nutritionist and a yoga teacher, and works at a raw vegan restaurant.

Bresee and her three roommates share a community garden a five-minute walk from home, where they grow their own vegetables. They also support Community Supported Agriculture, a world-wide network which gives urbanites the opportunity to support local food growers. The roommates opt for a family-sized vegetable basket, which provides them with local organic food year-round. Bresee says it is the perfect way to create community links between the city and the country.

It is this spiritual connection that interests Bresee most: "Permaculture, as a way of life, has acknowledged that no man or woman can do everything on their own, and thus community is undeniably important. This holistic view, to me, is what makes permaculture sustainable, what makes everything come together in the end."

As a basis for spirituality, Bresee says permaculture's spiritual message is "let's care for ourselves, care for each other, and care for the earth. It's simple, beautiful, and true." Across the Atlantic, 27-year-old Faye Tomson falls into the science camp. Tomson, who is completing her master's in environmental engineering at the University of Leeds, is specializing in renewable energy and low-energy housing "in a bid to try and restore the balance," she says.

55    "Working in such a field is twofold," she says. "Not only is it useful—and necessary in the transition to a low-carbon economy—it's also lucrative. My family has no money and is unlikely to in the near future. My dream is to earn enough to move us all away to some far-flung place away from the masses when it all goes tits up—which I don't think is going to be very long from now."

She jokes that she's anticipating some Armageddon-style scenario—but she's only half kidding. "When the shelves are empty," she says, "people are going to fight and riot and steal and hurt each other. I want to be far away by then. With my family." For Tomson, it isn't only new technologies that will be important in the future, but long-lost crafts and trades like horsemanship, woodwork, knitting, sewing, and leather tanning.

"People of like minds really need to get together—leave egos at the door, and start building arks," she says. There is urgency in her tone. "Save seeds that haven't been messed up by companies like Monsanto, and learn as many skills as possible. Learn how to keep bees and preserve and store food for winter months. This is serious. Agriculture is dying, and the old ways have gone. We must relearn them—and fast."

Trent Rhode can't argue with Tomson's desire for immediate change, although he doesn't share her survivalist viewpoint. But while Tomson and Yves Zehnder may choose to build lives outside the city limits, right now Rhode is comfortable working in an urban setting. "How can you be a hermit and live by yourself in the forest, when your air and water quality is affected by people on the other side of the world?" he asks. "We are not independent in that sense. We drink the same water and breathe the same air." Rhode believes it would be possible for people to grow almost all of their own food within city limits, if all the available land were put into productive use.

"If cities were actually consciously designed to take into account all human needs through time, the possibilities would be endless," he says. "There's this idea that somehow human civilization is diametrically opposed to a healthy environment and that somehow we are separate from the natural world."

60    His goal is to help urbanites realize that our cities are as much a part of the natural world as a beaver dam or beehive: "It's the very perception that we are somehow separate from the environment around us, and that

our actions toward the environment have no consequences to us, that leads to the creation of such destructive human habitats."

Rhode would like to own a farm one day. But he hopes to own it collectively, with the thought that you can learn so much from other people and their experiences. Like a natural ecosystem, he says, living in a community makes everything stronger and more resilient.

"It's exciting and energizing to be with people who understand what's going on in the world and understand what we need to do to live in harmony and to live, period," he says. "The most important thing is to give people hope."

## One Word Spotlight

*Sustainability* (paragraph 1) means to use a resource in such a way that it isn't harmed or depleted. The concept of environmental sustainability began in the 1700s when European loggers realized that if they didn't replant trees that they cut down, they would not be able to continue logging in the future. In the past couple of decades, as the media has reported on global warming and other threats to our environment, the concept of sustainability has gained popularity, with more and more people trying to live in such a way that they don't deplete resources needed by future generations.

## Reflect on the Reading

1. According to Hardy's article, what is permaculture and why should we care about this concept? What other concepts related to the environment interest you?

2. Explain this quote from the reading, "The modern farm is an industrial marvel, a factory for growing as much food as possible in the smallest space at the lowest cost. But it can't last: plants and animals aren't cogs in a machine, and industrial farming is beginning to run up against some fundamental limits of nature." Connect this statement to the main idea of the article.

3. In her article, Hardy uses examples of people who have adopted a sustainable lifestyle. How do these examples help support her explanation of the concept of permaculture?

4. Which group of readers might agree most with concept of permaculture? Which might disagree? Explain your answer.

## Consider Your Viewpoint

1. After reading this article, do you plan to change anything about the way you consume food? Drive your car? Treat the environment? Why or why not? Could you use one of these concepts for your paper?

2. Do you agree with this dire prediction made by a permaculture advocate: "When the shelves are empty," she says, "people are going to fight and riot and steal and hurt each other. I want to be far away by then. With my family." Explain your answer.

3. What is the concept of "capitalism"? Do you agree that it is not sustainable and that we need to make changes if we wish to sustain our current lifestyles?

4. How well do the photographs work within the context of this article? Do they aid your understanding? What other photos would you like to see?

# The *Avatar* Age

## Karrie Jacobs

How would you describe the concept of beauty? What do you think of when you think of something beautiful? In this article, published online at *MetropolisMag.com*, Karrie Jacobs takes issue with the *New Yorker* film critic who called the movie *Avatar* "beautiful." Jacobs explains her own concept of beauty in film and videogames. You can read more of Jacob's work on her blog at karriejacobs.com.

"James Cameron's *Avatar* is the most beautiful film I've seen in years," wrote the *New Yorker* film critic David Denby, going on to call the $280 million showcase of the latest in computer graphics and 3-D entertainment "lovely," "luscious," "freewheeling," "bounteous," and "strange." And so, with visions of unprecedented aesthetic experiences in my head, I braved the mob at the neighborhood megaplex, donned stylish 3-D glasses, and prepared myself to be wowed.

Aesthetic: Pleasurable or beautiful to the senses.

I was initially captivated when the hero, Jake Sully—a paraplegic whose consciousness had been transplanted into a lanky, blue alien body—made his foray into the jungles of the planet Pandora and discovered the magical flora, like those pinkish flowers that telescope out and suddenly shrink down to nothing. Pretty, I thought. And then came the first chase scene, in which Sully was pursued by a saber-toothed tiger or the local variant of a mastodon (I can't remember which). But once the action took off and the clichéd plot kicked in, I grew less impressed. The 3-D was kind of cool. But not beautiful.

In the *New York Times*, Dave Itzkoff wrote that *Avatar* "has been criticized by social and political conservatives who bristle at its depictions of religion and the use of military force; feminists who feel that the male avatar bodies are stronger and more muscular than their female counterparts; antismoking advocates who object to a character who lights up cigarettes." He quoted Rebecca Keegan, author of a biography of Cameron: "It's really become this Rorschach test for your personal interests and anxieties."

Me? I walked out of the theater concerned about the devaluation of the word *beauty*. I felt cheated. At first I thought maybe beauty wasn't truly attainable in an animated film. After all, Pixar-style animation annoys me, and I bet if I watched *Fantasia* today I'd be disappointed. But then I remembered Richard Linklater's 2001 film *Waking Life*, in which a young man appears to walk through an unending lucid dream, having deep conversations with everyone he meets. It didn't shatter any box-office records, but, God, was it beautiful. And Ari Folman's 2008 animated documentary, *Waltz with Bashir*, about his experience during the 1982 Israeli invasion of Lebanon, was devastating, brutal—and beautiful. What those films have in common with *Avatar* is that they use technologically sophisticated animation techniques to make them more lifelike. *Waking Life* was made with an old process called "rotoscoping"—first used by Max Fleischer and in vintage Disney cartoons—that was jazzed up with Macintosh computers. A new software allowed animators to easily draw on top of live video footage, creating an uncannily lifelike cartoon. *Bashir* was also based on live footage, but it was reinterpreted, rather than drawn over, by the animators, who used software like Flash for special effects.

Cameron relied on something he called "captured performance," in which the physical movements and facial expressions of live actors are fed into an animation system so that the inhabitants of the computer-generated world are made convincingly alive. But though Linklater and Folman succeeded in making the real world look exotic, Cameron managed to make an alien world look oddly familiar.

5    And that was the real problem. I'd been to Pandora, or someplace a lot like it, before. Maybe Denby, like most grown-ups, hasn't had much contact with the world of computer games. If he had, he would have understood that the world depicted in *Avatar* is not so special. He might have recognized the weird veracity and equally uncanny soullessness of the graphic approach. I'm not a gamer, but I've visited some postapocalyptic worlds on an Xbox and know that many of the best games employ the same technique as Cameron's, although it's more commonly called "motion capture."

Still, I'm not sure that beauty, per se, exists in the computer-generated world, but I remember a time when I thought it might. About 20 years ago, the term "virtual reality" was coined, and we started seeing pictures of the computer pioneer Jaron Lanier, a roly-poly, dreadlocked man wearing a strange piece of headgear and waving a pair of awkwardly gloved hands. He was experiencing life inside a computer-generated environment for the first time. Lately, the only people I've seen hooked up to computers in that rather cumbersome way were the actors in *Avatar*. HBO's behind-the-scenes documentary about the movie shows Sam Worthington and Zoë Saldana saying their lines while wearing goofy electronic helmets.

Lanier himself has just resurfaced. I heard him on the radio the other day promoting his new book, *You Are Not a Gadget*, and arguing that online social networking is inherently dehumanizing. I picked up the book and noticed that Lanier waxes nostalgic about the dawn of VR, when he and his cyber pals coaxed rudimentary digital worlds into being. "Of course, there were bugs," he reminisces. "I distinctly remember a wonderful bug that caused my hand to become enormous, like a web of flying skyscrapers." Back then, it was all free-form, open-ended— experience for the sake of experience. And there was no plot. Now, Lanier complains, "Full-blown immersive VR is all too often done with a purpose these days. If you are using VR to practice a surgical procedure, you don't have psychedelic clouds in the sky."

Maybe what Lanier experienced during the early days was beauty, but we don't hear much about VR anymore. It has been displaced by things with more clearly commercial applications, like computer-generated imagery. The world Lanier thought he was making, where free spirits in clunky headsets would frolic among the polygons, didn't happen. What we

VR: Virtual reality.

got instead were millions of moviegoers wearing 3-D glasses, deeply immersed in a very creaky, manipulative story. Or millions more kids, engrossed in computer games.

The one game I actually enjoy is Grand Theft Auto. Now in its fourth iteration, this game is hugely and justifiably controversial for its casual violence. In it, you pick an avatar—perhaps the gangster Tony Prince or his bodyguard, Luis Lopez—and roam the streets of an obsessively detailed New York City, stealing cars, shooting people at will, and creating mayhem. Despite the violence, I'm fascinated by the game, because of its depth and, yes, beauty. As in *Waking Life* and *Waltz with Bashir*, the creators of Grand Theft Auto take the world we know and recast it with such manic ingenuity that we are able to see the city, its architecture and its street culture, in startling new ways.

10    Recently, my favorite 15-year-old gave me a master class in Grand Theft Auto, and I tried my best to steal cars and shoot people. But the thing that really gave me a thrill was finding the Roosevelt Island tram and riding it across the East River. (Typical, right? I play Grand Theft Auto and wind up taking the loopiest form of mass transit.) My instructor liked the helicopter that could be called up at will. He made Lopez put on a parachute, fly to the top of the Empire State Building (called Rotterdam Tower in the game), and jump off without opening his chute. He sailed through the air and went splat on the pavement. Which was not a problem, because, like the pivotal figures in Cameron's movie, Luis was just an avatar.

The movie *Avatar* is breaking box-office records because it takes the computer game—a $20-billion-a-year industry in the United States alone—to the next level, trading in the handheld game controller for a direct cortical hookup. It's successful because it reflects and amplifies the already familiar experiences of every adolescent gamer. Jake Sully, the paraplegic hero, stands in for the legion of couch potatoes who can only perform amazing acts of physical bravery and prowess through computer magic.

> Cortical: The section of the brain that processes sensory information.

# $O$ne $W$ord Spotlight

*Waxes nostalgic* (paragraph 7) is a phrase that means to become more thoughtful about or long for an earlier time or past event. "Waxes" is an Old English word, dating before the twelfth century, that means to grow in size or intensity. Today, it is most often used when describing the waxing (increasing in size) and waning (decreasing in size) of the moon.

## Reflect on the Reading

1. How does Jacobs define the concept of beauty in this piece?

2. What examples and description does she use as evidence to support her concept of beauty?

3. Why, according to Jacobs, isn't *Avatar* beautiful? Why does she say *Avatar* is so successful?

4. Jacobs describes several animation methods including "rotoscoping." Define the differences in these methods in more detail.

5. Jacobs quotes a Cameron biographer on the movie: "It's really become this Rorschach test for your personal interests and anxieties." What does this mean?

## Consider Your Viewpoint

1. Give at least three words or phrases that describe how you define the concept of beauty. Has this article changed your concept of beauty in films or videogames? Why or why not? Is there another concept related to films or videogames which you could write about?

2. Jacobs says that the *New Yorker* reviewer, "like most grown-ups, hasn't had much contact with the world of computer games. If he had, he would have understood that the world depicted in *Avatar* is not so special." Do you agree? Why or why not?

3. Jacobs compares *Avatar* to two other films, *Walking Life* and *Waltz with Bashir,* and one videogame, *Grand Theft Auto.* She believes that these are more beautiful than *Avatar.* Are there movies or computer games that you think are visually beautiful? Describe them to your classmates.

4. How original is the photograph at the beginning of this article? How does the originality contribute to your enjoyment of the photo?

# WRITING ASSIGNMENT

For this writing assignment, you will explain a concept. To select a topic, consider concepts of personal interest to you. For example, if you enjoy using Facebook, you might explain the concept of using social networking sites. Or consider a concept related to your major. If you are an Art major, for example, you might explain the concept of using color in an oil painting. You may also consider concepts related to societal issues such as the environment, globalization, or immigration. What are some important societal concepts that you would like to explain to others?

# YOUR EXPLANATION OF A CONCEPT

Now it's your turn to explain a concept. The readings in this chapter may give you topic ideas, but because there are so many concepts to choose from, you will probably choose to explain a concept that is of special significance to you. Before beginning this assignment, review Chapters 2 and 3 to refresh your memory on choosing a topic, analyzing the rhetorical situation, and completing the stages of the writing process.

---

### Writing Assignment Checklist

- ☐ Carefully read the assignment.
- ☐ Look for key words that describe what you must do.
- ☐ Determine whether the topic is assigned or free choice.
- ☐ Ask your instructor any questions that you have about the assignment.
- ☐ Develop a timeline for completing the assignment.

---

## Choosing a Topic

When choosing a concept to explain, identify a concept that not only interests you, but that you are willing to take apart and explore in depth so that you can explain it well to your reader. To generate topics for explaining a concept, ask yourself, "What does it mean?" "Why is it important?" "Who needs to know?" "Can I explain it in a unique way?" Here are some examples:

**School**

education

intelligence

service learning

a concept specific to your own field of study

**Work**

employment

stress

technology training

family-friendly policies

**Community**

homelessness

freedom

marriage

literacy

Concepts can be complex, with readers holding different opinions about them. Whatever concept you choose to explain, do more than just define it. Question and examine your concept carefully so that you can describe the specific details that make up the general thought or idea of the concept.

---

### Topic Questions for Explaining a Concept

- Is this an assigned topic? If so, what are the requirements?
- Is this topic free choice? If so, what concept would I like to explain?
- Is this concept complex enough to need explanation?
- Will readers be interested in this concept?
- Can I find information on this topic?

---

**Activity 7.1**    Divide into groups of three or four students and brainstorm a list of concepts that group members would like to learn more about. Share your list with the rest of your classmates to determine which concepts are of most interest.

**Connect With Others**

## Analyzing the Rhetorical Situation

Now that you have chosen a topic, analyze the rhetorical situation to ensure that you and your readers can reach a mutual understanding of the concept that you are explaining. The better your rhetorical analysis, the more effective your explanation of a concept will be.

**Considering Audience and Purpose.**  Begin by choosing an audience that will be interested in learning more about the concept that you will explain. Remember, you are the expert on this topic, so you want to write this essay as the authority. Your audience will be looking to you to explain a concept that they may know little about, so be sure to explain the concept clearly, using vocabulary that your readers will understand.

## Audience Questions for Explaining a Concept

- Who would be interested in learning about this concept?
- How much do these readers already know about the topic? How much do they need to know?
- What is the average age of these readers?
- Do their gender or cultural backgrounds affect my choice of topic?
- What is their educational level?
- What is their attitude toward this topic?

Although you already know your primary purpose is to inform, you'll notice that neither Alsop in "The 'Trophy Kids' Go to Work" nor Hardy in "How Farmers Are Going to Save Civilization" share any of their own personal experiences about the concepts of millennials or permaculture. They may not have personal experience with these topics or just prefer to keep the focus of their articles on others' experiences. You may still include some expressive writing if you have personal experience with the concept you are explaining. In her article, "The *Avatar* Age," Jacobs shares her personal experience with watching *Avatar* and other movies and playing the videogame *Grand Theft Auto*. However, she doesn't rely only on her personal experience. She also provides plenty of other specific details to explain her concept.

## Purpose Questions for Explaining a Concept

- Why do I want to explain this concept, and what are some specific details that I can share to help explain it?
- Do I have any personal history, thoughts, or feelings that I should include in this informative piece?
- How does my cultural background affect the way I view this concept?
- What do I want my readers to understand as a result of reading this piece?

**Choosing a Genre and Visual Design.**   Most writing that you do for class is informative, so you may already have experience with a number of informative genres, including textbooks, essays, lab reports, research papers, and short exam answers. In the workplace, informative genres include memos, letters, reports, and newspaper or magazine articles.

In collaboration with your instructor, decide the genre that you will use for this assignment. Refer to Chapter 14 for specific help with the page layout, font, and visual elements of the genre you choose.

## Genre and Visual Design Questions for Explaining a Concept

- Which genre will be most effective to explain a concept?
- How will the format help me clarify the concept?
- What visual design elements will strengthen my explanation?
- What do I know about this format?
- What do I need to learn to write in this format?

**Reviewing Exigence and Constraints.** As with any writing, you will do a better job of writing if you identify the reasons for communicating this information. You may have a passion for a certain concept that you want to explain to your readers. On the other hand, sometimes the exigency is simply that it is an assignment for class or a request from your manager at work. Whatever the reason, putting it in writing will help you understand the concept.

## Exigence Questions for Explaining a Concept

- Why do I want to explain this concept? Are there complexities that I wish to share with my readers?
- How can I share my enthusiasm for this concept with my readers?
- Given their gender and culture, will the audience be receptive to this concept?
- How would an understanding of this concept change my readers' lives?

Constraints include anything that might interfere with your ability to convey your message to your audience. A primary constraint for explaining a concept is that concepts are often abstract, general ideas. It can be difficult to explain them in a way that your reader can understand. To explain abstract concepts, you must use easily understood, concrete details as evidence.

## Constraint Questions for Explaining a Concept

- How can I find the specific details needed to explain an abstract concept?
- Will my audience have certain attitudes or beliefs that I must overcome?
- What more do I need to learn to truly inform my audience about this concept?
- What other constraints do I face to completing this piece?

**Connect With Others**

**Activity 7.2**   With a small group, select one of the topics chosen in the previous group work and develop the rhetorical situation. Include audience, purpose, genre, exigence, and constraints.

## Using the Writing Process

You are now ready to write, using the stages that you learned in Chapter 3: discovering ideas, drafting to explore ideas, revising to improve content, and editing to eliminate errors.

### STAGE 1:  Discovering Ideas

You already know that you can use various ways to discover ideas for your concept paper, but because clearly explaining a concept can be difficult, you may want to develop an outline of your ideas to ensure that you present the specific details in a logical way to help your reader understand the general idea of the concept.

**Outlining.**  Develop a topic or sentence outline to record your ideas, the importance of each, and the relationship between the main ideas, sub-ideas, and specific details that explain your concept. A traditional outline uses this format:

    I.
        A.
        B.
            1.
            2.
                a.
                b.
    II.
        A.
        B.

Your ideas are divided into main ideas (I., II.), sub-ideas (A., B.), details (1., 2.), and even more specifics details (a., b.). In a traditional outline, each heading and subheading must have at least two parts and should be stated in either complete sentences or phrases, but not both. It's not necessary to outline the introduction or conclusion.

**One Student's Work.**  This is part of an outline drafted by student writer Angela D'Onofrio to gather ideas for a concept essay on the topic of "wanderlust." She chose this topic because she would like to write a travel book that includes descriptions of American wanderers, including herself.

I.   A number of authors have had wanderlust
   A.  Chris McCandless in *Into the Wild*
   B.  John Steinbeck in *Travels with Charley*
      1.  Describes his own and others' propensity to wander
      2.  Wanted to get to know Americans
         a.  Discovered that Americans have a burning desire to travel
         b.  Felt that this may result from our ancestors' settling of America
   C.  David Thoreau in *Walden*
      1.  Went to Walden Pond
      2.  Lived in isolation
II.  My wanderlust inspired by these authors
   A.  Embarked on my own trip from Chicago
   B.  Decided to make wanderlust a way of life, not just a vacation

## STAGE 2:  Drafting to Explore Ideas

As you draft, expand your outline into a complete draft. If you are writing an essay, for example, write in complete sentences and paragraphs. Begin by writing a tentative thesis statement that introduces your reader to the concept and describes why it is important. If you already know your main points, you may briefly list them in phrases as part of the thesis statement.

If you find it too difficult to write an introduction, leave it for now and draft all of your other paragraphs, including the conclusion. Then go back and write the introduction that matches your essay. If necessary, revise your thesis statement to match as well.

**Strategies for Development.**  Writers use strategies for development to help make their text convincing, interesting, and easy to remember. To develop your paragraphs, consider using one or more of these writing patterns described in detail in Chapter 13:

- Narrating—describe a series of events related to your concept.
- Describing—use your five senses to paint a picture in words.
- Giving Examples—provide facts, statistics, quotations, or other details that explain the general idea.
- Describing a Process—explain how something key to your concept works.
- Defining—simplify an abstract idea by providing a definition of key words.
- Comparing and Contrasting—explain how your concept is similar to or different from other concepts that your reader may be more familiar with.

- Classifying—explain how your concept fits within a larger scheme or group.
- Using Cause and Effect—describe the relationship between something that happened and the result.

**One Student's Work.** Angela, whose outline you read above, knew she wanted to use McCandless, Steinbeck, and Thoreau as examples to explain her concept of wanderlust, but she also wanted to explain her own need to travel. When she drafted her outline, she planned to write about the authors' wanderlust in the first half of the paper and then talk about her own in the second half. By the time she began drafting she decided to use comparison and contrast to explain how her experiences compared with each of the authors' wanderlust. Here is Angela's first draft.

## Wanderlust

On October 21st, 2008 at 4pm on a chilly afternoon in Chicago, I embarked on my own grand adventure. Until then my lifelong wanderlust had been expressed by a path worn into the carpet of the travel section at Borders Bookstore. Desire and impulse were not alone enough to inspire me to take action and become a vagabond. I had to actually say goodbye to all I had known and embrace the unknown as I attempted to join the ranks of those who had gone before me. I had traveled around the world already, but this time it was different. My wanderlust was not going to be expressed by a vacation, but as real life.

My journey began with the simple act of ridding myself of all extraneous keys. Well, perhaps my method is not the only method and may not be quite as universal as the impulse itself; after all, what worked for me was certainly not the path Henry David Thoreau chose to appease his nagging voice within. He describes his journey in his book *Walden*. He did not go into the wild, or hit the open roads as our two previous heroes did; he went, simply, to Walden Pond. Although the thought of going to the pond doesn't necessarily conjure up images of dangerous wilderness journeys or daring feats of bravery, his adventure was wild and brave. For Thoreau, the journey was not so much about where he was going as it was about what he left. He lived primarily off the land, in seclusion, and close to nature. His choice to live as a free human and apart from the safety, comfort and confines of organized society, could be likened to a skydiver jumping out of a plane without a parachute. What is known, what is comfortable is always easier. However, those who are bent towards wandering instinctively know that comfort is not enough, and that safety does not a life make. Whether embarking to learn, to create, or to adventure, there is one common theme to all heroes of the open road—that which can be obtained out there, in the unknown, cannot be had here. Thoreau believed a person to be capable of fulfilling their dreams. He learned through his "experiment" on Walden Pond that "if one advances confidently in the direction of his dreams, and endeavors to live the life which he has imagined, he will meet with a success unexpected in common hours" (Thoreau 87).

**Your Emotional Filter and Writing Monitor.** Writing to explain a concept can be intimidating because you are presenting information that can be hard to understand. The most effective way to keep your emotions and writing monitor in check is to plan this concept piece carefully, thinking constantly about how you can organize your thoughts in a way to clearly communicate information about your concept to your audience. In other words, try to put yourself in the place of your reader. How can you best help your reader understand this concept?

## STAGE 3: Revising to Improve Content

To revise your explanation of a concept, look again at how you have organized and developed your ideas, and review your sentence structure and word choice to ensure that they contribute to the explanation. When writing about concepts, there are two areas that require special attention:

**Focus.** When writing to explain a concept, one of the challenges is to determine what to include and what to leave out. Your choices will largely determine how well your reader understands the concept. As you draft, keep your audience in mind. Who will read your explanation of a concept? What will they need to know and why? Choose specific details that will help your audience understand the concept.

"How Farmers Are Going to Save Civilization" is a lengthy piece because Hardy is writing for an audience who knows little or nothing about the concept of permaculture. She uses numerous examples to help her readers fully understand this topic. On the other hand, "The *Avatar* Age" is a shorter piece because Jacobs is writing for an audience that already has an understanding of the concepts of beauty, movies, and videogames. She simply wants to present her views on the concept of beauty in the movie *Avatar.*

**Definition.** While drafting your concept piece, consider whether you have adequately defined all vocabulary terms to help your reader understand your explanation of a concept. If your readers don't understand the key terms, they won't understand the concept.

In "The 'Trophy Kids' Go to Work," Alsop carefully defines his key terms, including *millennials, trophy kids,* and *entitlement.* In "The *Avatar* Age," Jacobs doesn't have to define the words *beauty, movies,* or *videogames,* but she does define difficult terms such as *rotoscoping* and *motion capture.*

## Connect With Others

**Activity 7.3**   Divide into groups and reread "The 'Trophy Kids' Go to Work." As you read, label the ways Alsop develops his concept of the millennials in the workplace. Indicate which of these strategies you could add to your draft.

Once you improve the development, review the rhetorical situation to help you make further improvements.

### Rhetorical Situation Questions for Explaining a Concept

- Audience: Will your audience be interested in reading about the concept that you explain? Will your audience learn something new from your piece?
- Purpose: Have you included enough detail to inform your readers about the concept that you discuss? Develop those paragraphs that need additional detail.
- Genre: Does the format that you chose help the audience understand your concept?
- Exigence: Do you feel that you have explained everything you want to about this topic?
- Constraints: What constraints have you encountered in explaining this concept? Develop a plan for overcoming them.

If you can, ask others to review your revised draft. Following is an example of a peer review sheet that you might use for this piece.

## Peer Review
### Explaining a Concept

1. What is this concept paper's greatest strength?

2. What concept is explained? Did you already know about this concept or was it new to you?

3. Where might I add details to better support the main points? Which sections or sentences would you like me to clarify? How well did the ideas flow? Where do you suggest I add transitions to help you move from one idea to another?

4. If I used library or Internet research to support my explanation, how well was this research used? How well did I avoid simply cutting and pasting information into the piece? How well are quotations and paraphrases used? How well did I indicate the sources of the research in the text of the piece and at the end?

5. How interesting is my concept? What more would you like to know about it?

6. Underline any words or sentences that you think I should revise because they do not communicate to you.

7. Place a check mark in the margin next to any punctuation or spelling errors that you discovered while reading this Explaining a Concept piece.

## STAGE 4: Editing for Correctness

You check for correctness by looking for errors in spelling, punctuation, and grammar. When reading about a concept that can be difficult to understand, it is important that your reader focus on your explanation, rather than on errors in your writing.

### LANGUAGES and CULTURES

Common cultural beliefs and values affect the way a writer writes about a concept and the way a reader understands it. When explaining a concept to someone from another culture, careful revising and editing can help you conform to a different cultural understanding. Asking someone from the target culture to read and respond to the piece can ensure that the complexities of the concept are understandable.

### To Edit

- Use a dictionary or computer spell-checker.
- For treatable errors, refer to a grammar handbook and follow standard grammatical rules.
- For less treatable errors, ask another student to read your writing for errors.
- As you edit, keep an Editing Log, a section in your notebook where you record the errors that you have made.

**Activity 7.4**   Once you complete the writing process, take a moment to look over what you have done. Complete the self-evaluation sheet to help you further improve your work.

**Develop Your Understanding**

# Self-Evaluation Sheet
## Explaining a Concept

1. Have I followed all instructions for this Explanation of a Concept assignment? (Reread the assignment sheet and class notes.)

2. Have I identified an interesting concept to explain?

3. Are my thoughts about the concept well-ordered?

4. Is my paper written clearly and concisely? (Reread your paper out loud.)

5. Is each paragraph developed and does each contribute to the overall organization?

6. Do I introduce my concept in such a way that the reader is engaged?

7. Do I conclude in such a way that there is a sense of closure and my reader feels informed about the concept?

8. Is the paper written in my own words?

9. Are my sentences well-written and varied? (Read each sentence beginning with the last one, working backward to the beginning of the paper.)

10. Is my word choice appropriate for the audience and purpose?

11. Have I checked for spelling, punctuation, and grammar errors?

12. If I used other sources of information in this investigation, did I give credit both in the text and on a Works Cited or References page?

If you're passionate about your concept, you will be eager to share it with readers who can learn about it. If you wrote about a concept related to school, for example, you might share it with a group of students or publish it in a newsletter related to the topic. If you wrote about a work-related concept, you might e-mail it to your colleagues or manager, and if you wrote about a community-related concept, consider sending it to the local newspaper for publication.

# ONE STUDENT'S EXPLANATION OF A CONCEPT

In the earlier stages of the writing process, we introduced you to Angela D'Onofrio, a student who wrote on the concept of "wanderlust." She revised her thesis statement and developed, revised, and edited her draft into this final version of an essay. She worked to develop her literary and personal examples and to compare famous authors' wanderlust with her own.

## Wanderlust: The Great American Trait

### *Angela D'Onofrio*

> Angela creates a more interesting title.

In our society there are those who are plagued by wanderlust, the impulse and desire to adventure and to explore. To spot these wanna-be-nomads look for these tell tale signs: the reading and rereading of Alpine adventure books and other travel narratives, the endless fascination with maps of all kinds, the frequent checking of the price of a plane ticket to Malaysia, and the ever growing collection of *Lonely Planet* travel guides on the shelf. For these unfulfilled vagabonds (there may be one in the cubicle next to you), regular life seems like something you do while you are waiting for your next adventure. For most of them, the adventure never happens; 2.5 children happen, a white picket fence happens and a mountain of financial, professional and personal responsibilities buries them and their dream. However, there are a heroic few, a small percentage who make it. Their wanderlust doesn't just whisper in their ear, it screams and throbs until it gets what it wants—adventure, wildness . . . to roam. It is irresistible; they must go. Those that go are the saints in the cannon of the true traveler, and they are revered by those whose great desire to roam goes unfulfilled. Rather than the pursuit of happiness, one could argue our great American trait is our wanderlust, and we salute our American saints.

> Angela introduces her concept and defines it.

> Angela describes what wanderlust feels like.

> With this thesis statement, Angela explains why her concept is important to understand.

Alexander Supertramp, idealistic young man known to his friends and family as Chris McCandless, gave away his money, possessions, and name and headed out *Into the Wild*. Jon Krakauer's book of that name follows his journey from a college educated, middle class kid, to a dreamer daring to put his ideas to the test and make his philosophy his reality. With Tolstoy, London and Thoreau as his travel mates, his wanderlust poked and prodded him across the country, and into the wilds of Alaska. He left a life of money, society and responsibilities seeking to find a more pure and honest way. Alex died alone in the wild. It is not his end that ranks him among the saints, but his journey. Whether readers regard his story as tragedy or as inspiration, he was nothing if not brave. To leave the comforts of home and embark on an unknown road is difficult, but necessary to still the voice of wanderlust inside. Those who set their sail for the great unknown may never reach a holy grail (Alex did not), but their journey gives the rest of us hope that we too may someday ditch our neckties and high heels and hit the open road.

> Angela begins by narrating the events of *Into the Wild*.

At age 58, a self-proclaimed old man, John Steinbeck outfitted a pickup truck with a small camper, books, a full bar and his dog to discover America. Arguably one of our country's greatest writers, Steinbeck himself sought to fulfill his own wanderlust. In *Travels with Charley*, Steinbeck talks not only about his own propensity to wander, but the wanderlust of those he met on his travels. As he roamed the country with his dog Charley, he attempted to know the collective America. He writes

> Angela then introduces a great American author and describes his wanderlust.

At this point, Angela begins to compare and contrast her own wanderlust to that of the authors she introduced.

that he sees something "over and over in every part of the nation—a burning desire to go, to move, to get under way, anyplace, away from any Here"(Steinbeck 178). He sees a characteristic, a longing to explore the unknown and leave the past behind and forge a new future. Perhaps the spirit of those who explored and settled this great land of ours lives in each of us, prodding us forward. My own journey to fulfill my wanderlust was greatly inspired by these daring pioneers.

On October 21st, 2008 at 4pm on a chilly afternoon in Chicago, I embarked on my own grand adventure. Until then my lifelong wanderlust had been expressed by a path worn into the carpet of the travel section at Borders Bookstore. Desire and impulse were not alone enough to inspire me to take action and become a vagabond. I had to actually say goodbye to all I had known and embrace the unknown as I attempted to join the ranks of those who had gone before me. I had traveled around the world already, but this time it was different. My wanderlust was not going to be expressed by a vacation, but as real life.

Angela further develops her paper by describing a process for becoming a wanderer.

My journey began with the simple act of ridding myself of all extraneous keys. It can be duplicated by following these five simple steps:

**Five easy steps to fulfilling your wanderlust and hitting the road**

Step One: Decide to leave your "real life" (bye bye to jobs, to house, to normality).

Step Two: Buy a $300 house you can take with you (homemade camper trailer towed behind 1997 Dodge Intrepid).

Step Three: Pack (some clothes, food, camp stove, laptop and some books. Don't forget husband and guinea pig).

Step Four: Hit the road (become friends with the map).

Step Five: Learn, live and dream.

Angela introduces another author.

Well, perhaps my method is not the only method and may not be quite as universal as the impulse itself; after all, what worked for me was certainly not the path Henry David Thoreau chose to appease his nagging voice within. He describes his journey in his book *Walden*. He did not go into the wild, or hit the open roads as our two previous heroes did; he went, simply, to Walden Pond. Although the thought of going to the pond doesn't necessarily conjure up images of dangerous wilderness journeys or daring feats of bravery, his adventure was wild and brave. For Thoreau, the journey was not so much about where he was going as it was about what he left. He lived primarily off the land, in seclusion, and close to nature. His choice to live as a free human and apart from the safety, comfort and confines of organized society, could be likened to a skydiver jumping out of a plane without a parachute. What is known, what is comfortable is always easier. However, those who are bent towards wandering instinctively know that comfort is not enough, and that safety does not a life make. Whether embarking to learn, to create, or to adventure, there is one common theme to all heroes of the open road—that which can be obtained out there, in the unknown, cannot be had here. Thoreau believed a person to be capable of fulfilling their dreams. He learned through his "experiment" on Walden Pond that "if one advances confidently in the direction of his dreams, and endeavors to live the life which he has imagined, he will meet with a success unexpected in common hours" (Thoreau 87).

Inspired not only by my own nagging wanderlust but also by the example of these heroes I, in reexamining my own life and in the great tradition of Americans who left before me, became a vagabond. In doing so I stumbled upon an equation to assist in "advancing confidently in the direction of my dreams":

> Begin with *Wanderlust* (impulse and desire to explore)
> subtract –
> *Old Life* (House, job, responsibilities, and the tediousness of the mundane)
> add +
> *Life on the Road* (Homelessness, adventure and surprise)
> to equal =
> *Real Life* (Being awake to the life one was always meant to live)

*The Free Dictionary by Farlex* describes the state of wanderlust as "itchy feet." This desire, this urge and nagging within, weaves through the landscape of our country's collective unconscious from our earliest settlers, to Lewis and Clark, Neil Armstrong and even to myself. Our wanderlust just may be our one true and great American trait. Although we as Americans do not all fulfill our wanderlust by becoming vagabonds that travel the open road, there is evidence that perhaps this desire lurks more often than not under the surface of our workaday worlds, and the safety of our gated neighborhoods. To those willing to raise their hands and admit to their own inner lust to wander, I submit you look to the heroes and saints in the cannon of the American adventure. Look to those who, in acknowledging their itch, sought to scratch by ceasing to accept the mundaneness, the mediocrity, the sameness of everyday life. For these brave souls, it was not the destination that inspired their explorations, but rather the simple of act of going . . . of leaving behind the safety and familiarity of home to adventure into a life of unknown. For these heroes, and for myself, fulfilling the inner wanderlust is not about where you end up, but simply that you embark.

### Works Cited

Krakauer, Jon. *Into the Wild*. New York: First Anchor Books, 1996. Print.

Steinbeck, John. *Travels with Charley*. New York: Penguin Books, 1986. Print.

Thoreau, Henry David. *Walden*. Mount Vernon: Classic Books America, 2009. Print.

Wanderlust. *The Free Dictionary by Farlex*. Farlex, 2009. Web. 2 Nov. 2009.

Angela classifies her own wanderlust as part of a greater tradition.

Angela uses cause and effect to show what happens to a wanderer.

Angela provides another definition of wanderlust.

Angela concludes by predicting the future for those who dare to follow her example.

# ADDITIONAL READINGS

## How to Fall 35,000 Feet— and Survive

### Dan Koeppel

In this *Popular Mechanics* article, reporter Dan Koeppel explains how to survive a fall from an airplane, using this extreme scenario to describe concepts like *terminal velocity, fate, luck,* and *fear.* Using the second person "you," he gives his reader detailed instructions for what to do during each of four stages of the fall. He creates a narrative tension between humor and sordid details, compelling the reader to continue reading even while experiencing a growing feeling of panic.

You have a late night and an early flight. Not long after takeoff, you drift to sleep. Suddenly, you're wide awake. There's cold air rushing everywhere, and sound. Intense, horrible sound. *Where am I?*, you think. *Where's the plane?*

You're 6 miles up. You're alone. You're falling.

Things are bad. But now's the time to focus on the good news. (Yes, it goes beyond surviving the destruction of your aircraft.) Although gravity is against you, another force is working in your favor: time. Believe it or not, you're better off up here than if you'd slipped from the balcony of your high-rise hotel room after one too many drinks last night.

Or at least you will be. Oxygen is scarce at these heights. By now, hypoxia is starting to set in. You'll be unconscious soon, and you'll cannonball at least a mile before waking up again. When that happens, remember what you are about to read. The ground, after all, is your next destination.

Hypoxia: Oxygen deficiency.

5    Granted, the odds of surviving a 6-mile plummet are extraordinarily slim, but at this point you've got nothing to lose by understanding your situation. There are two ways to fall out of a plane. The first is to free-fall, or drop from the sky with absolutely no protection or means of slowing your descent. The second is to become a wreckage rider, a term coined by Massachusetts-based amateur historian Jim Hamilton, who developed the Free Fall Research Page—an online database of nearly every imaginable human plummet. That classification means you have the advantage of being attached to a chunk of the plane. In 1972, Serbian flight attendant Vesna Vulovic was traveling in a DC-9 over Czechoslovakia when it blew up. She fell 33,000 feet, wedged between her seat, a catering trolley, a

section of aircraft and the body of another crew member, landing on—then sliding down—a snowy incline before coming to a stop, severely injured but alive.

Surviving a plunge surrounded by a semiprotective cocoon of debris is more common than surviving a pure free-fall, according to Hamilton's statistics; 31 such confirmed or "plausible" incidents have occurred since the 1940s. Free-fallers constitute a much more exclusive club, with just 13 confirmed or plausible incidents, including perennial Ripley's Believe It or Not superstar Alan Magee—blown from his B-17 on a 1943 mission over France. The New Jersey airman, more recently the subject of a *MythBusters* episode, fell 20,000 feet and crashed into a train station; he was subsequently captured by German troops, who were astonished at his survival.

Whether you're attached to crumpled fuselage or just plain falling, the concept you'll be most interested in is *terminal velocity*. As gravity pulls you toward earth, you go faster. But like any moving object, you create drag—more as your speed increases. When downward force equals upward resistance, acceleration stops. You max out.

Depending on your size and weight, and factors such as air density, your speed at that moment will be about 120 mph—and you'll get there after a surprisingly brief bit of falling: just 1500 feet, about the same height as Chicago's Sears (now Willis) Tower. Equal speed means you hit the ground with equal force. The difference is the clock. Body meets Windy City sidewalk in 12 seconds. From an airplane's cruising altitude, you'll have almost enough time to read this entire article.

By now, you've descended into breathable air. You sputter into consciousness. At this altitude, you've got roughly 2 minutes until impact. Your plan is simple. You will enter a Zen state and decide to live. You will understand, as Hamilton notes, "that it isn't the fall that kills you—it's the landing."

Zen state: Completely focused on how things are in the moment.

10    Keeping your wits about you, you take aim.

But at what? Magee's landing on the stone floor of that French train station was softened by the skylight he crashed through a moment earlier. Glass hurts, but it gives. So does grass. Haystacks and bushes have cushioned surprised-to-be-alive free-fallers. Trees aren't bad, though they tend to skewer. Snow? Absolutely. Swamps? With their mucky, plant-covered surface, even more awesome. Hamilton documents one case of a sky diver who, upon total parachute failure, was saved by bouncing off high-tension wires. Contrary to popular belief, water is an awful choice. Like concrete, liquid doesn't compress. Hitting the ocean is essentially the same as colliding with a sidewalk, Hamilton explains, except that pavement (perhaps unfortunately) won't "open up and swallow your shattered body."

With a target in mind, the next consideration is body position. To slow your descent, emulate a sky diver. Spread your arms and legs, present your chest to the ground, and arch your back and head upward. This adds friction and helps you maneuver. But don't relax. This is not your landing pose.

The question of how to achieve ground contact remains, regrettably, given your predicament, a subject of debate. A 1942 study in the journal *War Medicine* noted "distribution and compensation of pressure play large parts in the defeat of injury." Recommendation: wide-body impact. But a 1963 report by the Federal Aviation Agency argued that shifting into the classic sky diver's landing stance—feet together, heels up, flexed knees and hips—best increases survivability. The same study noted that training in wrestling and acrobatics would help people survive falls. Martial arts were deemed especially useful for hard-surface impacts: "A 'black belt' expert can reportedly crack solid wood with a single blow," the authors wrote, speculating that such skills might be transferable.

The ultimate learn-by-doing experience might be a lesson from Japanese parachutist Yasuhiro Kubo, who holds the world record in the activity's banzai category. The sky diver tosses his chute from the plane and then jumps out after it, waiting as long as possible to retrieve it, put it on and pull the ripcord. In 2000, Kubo—starting from 9842 feet—fell for 50 seconds before recovering his gear. A safer way to practice your technique would be at one of the wind-tunnel simulators found at about a dozen U.S. theme parks and malls. But neither will help with the toughest part: sticking the landing. For that you might consider—though it's not exactly advisable—a leap off the world's highest bridge, France's Millau Viaduct; its platform towers 891 feet over mostly spongy farmland.

15    Water landings—if you must—require quick decision-making. Studies of bridge-jump survivors indicate that a feet-first, knife-like entry (aka "the pencil") best optimizes your odds of resurfacing. The famed cliff divers of Acapulco, however, tend to assume a head-down position, with the fingers of each hand locked together, arms outstretched, protecting the head. Whichever you choose, first assume the free-fall position for as long as you can. Then, if a feet-first entry is inevitable, the most important piece of advice, for reasons both unmentionable and easily understood, is to clench your butt.

No matter the surface, definitely don't land on your head. In a 1977 "Study of Impact Tolerance Through Free-Fall Investigations," researchers at the Highway Safety Research Institute found that the major cause of death in falls—they examined drops from buildings, bridges and the occasional elevator shaft (oops!)—was cranial contact. If you have to arrive top-down, sacrifice your good looks and land on your face, rather than the

Banzai: A reckless act.

back or top of your head. You might also consider flying with a pair of goggles in your pocket, Hamilton says, since you're likely to get water eyes—impairing accuracy—on the way down.

Given your starting altitude, you'll be just about ready to hit the ground as you reach this section of instruction (based on the average adult reading speed of 250 words per minute). The basics have been covered, so feel free to concentrate on the task at hand. But if you're so inclined, here's some supplemental information—though be warned that none of it will help you much at this point.

Statistically speaking, it's best to be a flight crew member, a child, or traveling in a military aircraft. Over the past four decades, there have been at least a dozen commercial airline crashes with just one survivor. Of those documented, four of the survivors were crew, like the flight attendant Vulovic, and seven were passengers under the age of 18. That includes Mohammed el-Fateh Osman, a 2-year-old wreckage rider who lived through the crash of a Boeing jet in Sudan in 2003, and, more recently, 14-year-old Bahia Bakari, the sole survivor of last June's Yemenia Airways plunge off the Comoros Islands.

Crew survival may be related to better restraint systems, but there's no consensus on why children seem to pull through falls more often. The Federal Aviation Agency study notes that kids, especially those under the age of 4, have more flexible skeletons, more relaxed muscle tonus, and a higher proportion of subcutaneous fat, which helps protect internal organs. Smaller people—whose heads are lower than the seat backs in front of them—are better shielded from debris in a plane that's coming apart. Lower body weight reduces terminal velocity, plus reduced surface area decreases the chance of impalement upon landing.

20    The ground. Like a Shaolin master, you are at peace and prepared. *Impact*. You're alive. What next? If you're lucky, you might find that your injuries are minor, stand up and smoke a celebratory cigarette, as British tail gunner Nicholas Alkemade did in 1944 after landing in snowy bushes following an 18,000-foot plummet. (If you're a smoker, you're *super extra lucky*, since you've technically gotten to indulge during the course of an airliner trip.) More likely, you'll have tough work ahead.

Follow the example of Juliane Koepcke. On Christmas Eve 1971, the Lockheed Electra she was traveling in exploded over the Amazon. The next morning, the 17-year-old German awoke on the jungle floor, strapped into her seat, surrounded by fallen holiday gifts. Injured and alone, she pushed the death of her mother, who'd been seated next to her on the plane, out of her mind. Instead, she remembered advice from her father, a biologist: To find civilization when lost in the jungle, follow water. Koepcke waded from tiny streams to larger ones. She passed crocodiles and poked the mud in front of her with a stick to scare away stingrays. She had lost one shoe in the fall and was wearing a ripped miniskirt. Her only food was a bag of candy, and she had nothing but dark, dirty water to drink. She ignored her broken collarbone and her wounds, infested with maggots.

On the tenth day, she rested on the bank of the Shebonya River. When she stood up again, she saw a canoe tethered to the shoreline. It took her hours to climb the embankment to a hut, where, the next day, a group of lumberjacks found her. The incident was seen as a miracle in Peru, and free-fall statistics seem to support those arguing for divine intervention: According to the Geneva-based Aircraft Crashes Record Office, 118,934 people have died in 15,463 plane crashes between 1940 and 2008. Even when you add failed-chute sky divers, Hamilton's tally of confirmed or plausible lived-to-tell-about-it incidents is only 157, with 42 occurring at heights over 10,000 feet.

But Koepcke never saw survival as a matter of fate. She can still recall the first moments of her fall from the plane, as she spun through the air in her seat. That wasn't under her control, but what happened when she regained consciousness was. "I had been able to make the correct decision—to leave the scene of the crash," she says now. And because of experience at her parents' biological research station, she says, "I did not feel fear. I knew how to move in the forest and the river, in which I had to swim with dangerous animals like caimans and piranhas."

Caimans: Central or South American crocodiles.

Or, by now, you're wide awake, and the aircraft's wheels have touched safely down on the tarmac. You understand the odds of any kind of accident on a commercial flight are slimmer than slim and that you will likely never have to use this information. But as a courtesy to the next passenger, consider leaving your copy of this guide in the seat-back pocket.

## Reflect on the Reading

1. Koeppel claims that to survive a fall from an airplane, you must understand the concept of *terminal velocity*. What is it, and how will it help you survive a fall?

2. What research does Koeppel cite as evidence that you can survive a fall from an airplane? How convincing is this research?

3. Why, according to Koeppel, are children under the age of four more likely to survive such falls?

4. According to Koeppel, what is the best way to make contact with the ground?

## Consider Your Viewpoint

1. Give examples of where Koeppel uses humor in this article. Is this article funny or gruesome? Explain your answer.

2. Why do you think Koeppel describes Juliane Koepcke's survival at such great length? What lessons do you take from Koepcke's experience?

3. Why do you think Koeppel suggests the reader carry eye goggles while flying? Is he serious?

4. Does your explanation of a concept lend itself to humor? If yes, where could you insert it?

# When Employers Make Room for Work-Life Balance

## Jennifer Ludden

In this National Public Radio (NPR) *Morning Edition* report, Jennifer Ludden, a National Correspondent for NPR, explains the concept of "work-life" balance.

For years, Katie Sleep's life was dominated by a grueling commute. She remembers never eating dinner before dark, never getting to watch her kids play in the yard. When she lived in San Francisco, she would drop her kids off at day care at 6:00 a.m. in order to get to the office on time. When Sleep launched her own software development company, she felt passionately that her employees should not suffer as she had.

"Work cannot be everything," Sleep says. "People who have their lives are far better workers."

In a large majority of families with children, both parents work, and women now hold half of all jobs. Sleep's company, List Innovative Solutions, is among a growing number of American firms adapting to the needs and wants of a changing workforce.

The company is located amid a tangle of highways in Northern Virginia—a real commuter nightmare. So Sleep lets employees largely set their own hours and telecommute at will. And it's not just mothers but also fathers who take advantage of these flexible work options.

## 'People End Up Getting Their Job Done'

5 "They want the ability to go to their children's play, which is usually at 3; it's never at 5 or 6," Sleep says. "And what you find out is, people end up getting their job done."

Sleep has nearly 100 employees, but on a recent early afternoon visit, many offices are empty. Human Resources Director Kristy Stumpf prepares to head out in time to beat rush hour traffic and to meet her children's school bus.

"When I'm in the office, that's my face time," Stumpf says. "Today were my meetings, filing, that kind of stuff." At home, she works on self-guided projects.

Stumpf's dad was a long-suffering commuter, and she used to think that's just the way life was.

"Now that I've worked here, I realize I would never in a million years be able to be in an office 40, 50 hours a week and commute forever. It just wouldn't work." Stumpf starts to laugh, then seems to catch herself, almost as if she feels guilty about her own good luck.

## Work Time Revolution

10 U.S. labor laws are perfectly suited to 1960, says University of Minnesota sociologist Phyllis Moen. The 40-hour workweek and 9-to-5 workday were all codified in an era when men went off to an assembly line and women stayed home.

"We're really in the middle of something like an industrial revolution," Moen says. "But it's a work time revolution."

First, more and more employers are discovering that loosening the traditionally rigid work schedule pays off. Sleep says her retention rate over 16 years is an astonishing 95 percent. And study after study shows productivity also shoots up. More than half of companies now say they offer flextime, and one-third allow telecommuting at least part-time.

On the other hand, research also shows that employees don't find their workplaces nearly as flexible as managers report. Work-family experts say arrangements often appear more generous on paper than in practice and can be highly dependent on the generosity of immediate supervisors. What's more, the bad economy has led some employers to take away flex benefits.

So, what about that revolution? Well, work-life experts say another force is building: working parents are no longer the only ones who want flexible hours.

## Millennials Want Balance

15 "When you talk about Gen-X or Gen-Y or the millennials, they've taught us that we can't necessarily say work-family balance," says Lisa Horn of the Society for Human Resource Management. The preferred term now is work-life, because young workers apparently value their flexibility just as much as a working mom.

You may have heard that millennials in the workplace are lazy and "entitled," but sociologist Moen says that's a bad rap. She says young workers simply don't want to wait decades until retirement for their quality of life—an attitude that has been reinforced by the recession, as they've seen parents and boomer relatives lose their jobs.

"They no longer believe in the myth that working in rigid ways for long hours necessarily pays off," Moen says. "That's a real change."

Another change is the degree of mobile technology young workers have grown up with.

"This generation is completely untethered. They have laptops in grade school," says Jody Thompson, a co-founder of Culture Rx, a consulting firm that promotes a completely flexible work style. Thompson says young people today are used to getting stuff done—on their laptops, cell phones, iPods—wherever they are, whenever they want.

20    "Then we bring them into the work environment and we say, 'Here's this 6x6 square you're going to work in, with a desktop computer,' which to them, by the way, is a gaming computer," Thompson says. "'And here's your phone with your cord. You come in at 8 and you leave at 5, and between 10 and noon, that's when we're creative.'"

Thompson says young workers simply can't relate to such a system.

## Signs Point to Flexibility

If moms and millennials united aren't enough to loosen rigid work rules, experts say yet another push for flexibility will come from an unlikely source: the very baby boomers who defined 9-to-5 culture in their prime. Sociologist Moen says as they grow older, many will want or need to keep working well past traditional retirement age.

"And older workers who you may want to keep on because of their skills or contacts will want to work differently—more flexibly and less," Moen says.

It's hard to find the case against flexible work these days. Even the staunchly pro-business Chamber of Commerce promotes it, though Marc Freedman, the chamber's director of labor law policy, says it only works for some employees and jobs.

25     "You can imagine certain jobs where you have to be at the workplace," he says. "And if you're not there, somebody else is going to have to pick up the load, and that won't be fair to them."

In fact, researchers are looking into ways to bring more flexibility to the hardest case low-wage and hourly jobs.

But even at her software development company, Sleep agrees, all flex arrangements are not for everyone. In fact, she says she could never work at home.

"It's not good for me. I like being around the people!" she says.

Sleep has also had to fire employees who took advantage of the flexibility she offers. But she says it's worth finding those who can handle the freedom, even if it makes her job more difficult.

30     "There's not a day that I don't kind of panic when I know that my workforce is all working from home," she says. "So it's not like you've got it all wrapped up and the answers are simple. It's whether or not you can let loose of that anxiety and really trust in people."

## Reflect on the Reading

1. Ludden uses a short narrative to introduce her topic. How does this draw the reader into her report?

2. In addition to providing examples of companies that have successfully implemented flextime, Ludden cites a number of authorities on work-life balance. How does this add credibility to her report?

3. How does Ludden conclude this report?

## Consider Your Viewpoint

1. How important is the concept of "work-life" balance and flextime to you? Do you currently work for a company that has flextime? If yes, describe your experience. If no, would you like to work for such a company? Why or why not?

2. According to Ludden, millennial workers prefer the term "work-life" to "work-family." Why? Do you agree that this is an important distinction? Explain your answer.

3. Why would the "stanchly pro-business Chamber of Commerce" oppose flextime? What abuses of the system are possible?

4. Are you the type of person who could work from home? Why or why not?

For support in meeting this chapter's objectives, follow this path in MyCompLab: Resources ⇒ Writing ⇒ Writing Purposes ⇒ Writing to Inform. Review the Instruction and Multimedia resources about writing to inform, then complete the Exercises and click on Gradebook to measure your progress.

PEARSON
mycomplab

# 8 Investigating a Cause

## Learning Objectives

In this chapter you will:

- Write an investigation of a cause.

- Discover ideas through questioning.
- Learn to write effective body paragraphs.
- Revise to improve development.

*This photo was taken in the American Southwest. Notice the rainbow and the shot-out sign. What do you make of this juxtaposition?*

**H**ave you ever been with a child who keeps asking "why"? As in, why is it raining, or what causes a rainbow, or why is my sweater red? Adults also want to know "why" though our questions might be more practical: We wonder why some people recycle and others don't, or why neighborhood crime in our city has suddenly decreased, or why countries near the equator are among the poorest on earth. Fortunately, finding causes is easier than ever before because of Internet search engines such as Google. You might discover that the people who recycle the most are those in cities where recycling is convenient. Neighborhood crime has decreased because more police are riding bikes rather than driving cars. Countries close to the equator tend to be poor because the climate makes it hard to grow crops. When you use Google or another form of research to find out why something happens, you are investigating causes.

# WRITING TO INVESTIGATE A CAUSE

To investigate a cause, you start by asking a question. Then you begin to collect information by reviewing what you already know, reading about your topic either online or at the library, interviewing people who are knowledgeable about the topic, or conducting a survey of people who may be interested. Although you might share some personal thoughts and feelings about the topic, your primary purpose is informative: to share the information that you have gathered for your specific audience and purpose.

## Questions for Investigating a Cause

- What question do I need to answer?
- Where can I find information to answer this question?
- What would my audience want to know about this topic?
- Which genre and visual design would provide the best format for sharing this information?
- Why is it important for my audience to understand this information?
- What constraints would prevent me from effectively communicating this information?

# MODEL INVESTIGATIONS

You can find investigative writing in many different contexts, from brochures published by a chamber of commerce to lengthy tomes published by scholars. The following examples of investigative writing come from a book, a magazine, and a website.

## My Freshman Year: Worldliness and Worldview

### Rebekah Nathan

Rebekah Nathan is the pseudonym of an anthropology professor, Cathy Small, who was curious about the experiences of freshmen college students. Though she was in her 50s, she enrolled at Northern Arizona University, lived in a dorm, and attended classes. The result of her research is a book, *My Freshman Year*, in which she sympathetically describes the stresses and challenges of students' lives. In the following excerpt, Nathan describes international student complaints about the causes of U.S. students' ignorance of the world.

*An internationally oriented student union.*

**Informant:** Person who gives cultural information to an anthropologist.

The single biggest complaint international students lodged about U.S students was, to put it bluntly, our ignorance. As informants described it, by "ignorance" they meant the misinformation and lack of information that Americans have both about other countries and about themselves. Although most international students noted how little other students asked them about their countries, almost all students had received questions that they found startling: "Is Japan in China?" "Do you have a hole for a bathroom?" "Is it North Korea or South Korea that has a dictator?" "Where exactly is India?" "Do you still ride elephants?" "Do they dub American TV programs into British?"

These are just a few of the questions American students actually asked of international students. While they no doubt came from the less sophisticated of their classmates, it was clear that international students across the board felt that most Americans—even their own friends—are woefully ignorant of the world scene. It is instructive to hear how students from diverse countries discuss their perceptions of American students' views of themselves and the world.

Japan: Really, they don't know very much about other countries, but maybe it's just because a country like Japan is so far away. Japanese probably don't know about the Middle East. Sometimes, students keep asking about ninjas.

UAE: American students are nice, but they need to stop being so ignorant about other countries and other cultures. Americans need to look at the world around them, and even the cultures around them in their own country.

Mexico: The U.S is not the center of the world. [Americans] don't know anything about other countries. Many of them don't have an interest in learning about other cultures. The only thing students ever ask me about in my culture is food.

China: Americans know very little about China or its culture. Most people think China is still very poor and very communist-controlled, with no freedom. There is a very anticommunist feeling, and people know little about today's China, which is quite changing and different. New Zealanders know much more about China—perhaps it's their proximity. I think that older people here have more of a sense of history, and that history, about the wars, about the cold war, makes them understand more about the world. Younger people seem to have no sense of history.

England: People here know surprisingly little about England, and they assume a lot of things, some true, some not. People's impressions of me when I say I'm from England is that I might drink tea off a silver tray, and maybe live in a castle, and use a red telephone box. That's the honest truth. The questions that I've been asked are unbelievable.

Malaysia: I tell people that I am Muslim, and they take for granted that I'm an Arab. How can they not realize that not all Muslims are Arabs when they have many Muslims who are American?

Germany: American students are much more ignorant of other countries and cultures. I suppose it's because it's so big, and knowing about California for you is like us knowing about France. It's a neighbor. The U.S. is less dependent on other cultures, and maybe that's why they need to know less. Still, Americans come across as not interested in other cultures, like they don't really care about other countries. So they think things like Swedish people are only blonds.

India: Somebody asked me if we still ride on elephants. That really bothered me. If I say I'm Indian, they ask which reservation? I say

I'm from Bombay. "Where is Bombay?" Some people don't even know where India is. A friend of mine and I tried to make these Americans see what it was like and we asked them where they're from. They said California. And we said, Where was that?

France: People here don't know where anything is. For World War II, the teacher had to bring in a map to show where Germany and England are—it was incredible! I read somewhere a little research said only 15 to 20 percent of Americans between the ages eighteen to twenty-five could point out Iraq on a map. The country will go to war, but it doesn't know where the country is!

**Consensus:** General agreement.

Despite the critical consensus in these comments, it would be unfair of me to represent international students' perspectives as roundly negative. In general, students from outside the United States warmly appreciate the American educational system as well as the spirit of the American college student. The criticisms that they did have, though, were pointed and focused. Taken together, they amounted to nothing less than a theory of the relationship among ignorance and ethnocentrism in this country, one that international eyes saw bordering on profound self-delusion. When I asked the linked questions, "What would you want American students to see about themselves?" and "What advice would you give them?" one German student stated succinctly what many students communicated to me at greater length: "Americans seem to think that they have the perfect place to live, the best country, the best city, I hear that all of the time. I used to think that you just got that from politicians, but now I see it's from regular people too. The patriotism thing here really bothers me."

It is sobering to hear these words from a German student, whose country's historical experience in the 1930s and 1940s taught him the dangers of hypernationalism. To his fellow U.S. students he offered this recommendation: "I'd give them advice to live elsewhere. They should recognize that the way of living in the U.S. is fine, but it isn't necessarily the best way for everyone. I don't like to evaluate, and I'd like that applied to me. Be more informed. Information leads to tolerance."

5 It bothered a Chinese student who read in an article that American students don't want to study a foreign language because they believe that the world language will be English. "I think they need to learn about the world, to learn a foreign language," he urged. It bothered a British student, who lamented how much of world music American students seem to miss. "Everything here [on his corridor] is either black gangster rap or punk rock, and that's basically it. They don't want to hear other music—contemporary music from around the world."

The connection between lack of information and intolerance translated occasionally into personal stories of frustration, hitting home in the lives of some students. "I wish they [his hall mates] were accepting of more different music" said an Indian student. "I play my own music. I play it loud just like they do—Arabic and Punjabi and other stuff—and they complain to the R.As. But it's my right to play that too. Why don't they understand that?"

"They don't accept other cultures," speculated one Japanese student.

Once I was eating the food I made—Japanese noodles—and we Japanese eat noodles with a noise. Somebody else in the kitchen area looked at me funny. She asked, "Why are you making so much noise?" I told her that's the way Japanese eat their noodles, and I can see by her face that she is disapproving. It hurt me to see that. Some Americans don't care about other worlds.

One key toward creating a more positive cycle of information, self-awareness, and tolerance was for many the university and university education itself. Learn a foreign language and study overseas, many recommended for individual students. Use your education to expand your purview beyond your own country. For the university, other students recommended a greater emphasis on self-awareness, including a more critical eye directed to our own institutions and history.

> Purview: Scope or range of knowledge.

10    For one Chinese student, the need to be more reflective about the media representation of news and issues was critical: "Media coverage has a very great influence here. In China, it has less influence because everyone knows it's propaganda. Here it is not seen that way because there is a free press. But it's curious." In American newspaper articles and TV news, "the individual facts are true often, but the whole is not sometimes. I can see how Americans need to question the way stories are being presented to them."

A French student beseeched us to examine our own educational system:

Americans teach like the only important thing is America. There is no required history course in college. The history course I took on Western Civ. at AnyU was middle-school level, and it was very biased. I mean they taught how, in World War II, America saved France and saved the world, how they were so great. The courses don't consider what Americans have done wrong. All the current events here is news about America and what America is doing. If it's about another country, it's about what America is doing there. There's nothing about other countries and their histories and problems. [In France] we had lots of history and geography courses, starting very young. I learned about France, but then we had to take a course in U.S. industrialization, in China, Russia, Japan, too. We got the history and geography of the world, so we could see how France now fits into the bigger picture.

For the international students I interviewed, American college culture is a world of engagement, choice, individualism, and independence, but it is also one of cross-cultural ignorance and self-delusion that cries out for remediation. It was a Somali student who summed up all of their hopes for "America": "You have so much here, and so many opportunities. I wish America would ask more what this country can do to make the world a better place."

## One Word Spotlight

*Ethnocentrism* (paragraph 3) means to evaluate other cultures according to the values of one's own culture. For example, people from a culture that highly values saving money will be critical of a culture where most people don't put money aside. Another meaning of *ethnocentrism* is the belief that one's own culture is superior to others'. People in all cultures are likely to be ethnocentric to some degree.

## Reflect on the Reading

1. According to the international students interviewed by Nathan, what makes U.S.-born college students ethnocentric?

2. Underline the one sentence in the piece that you think best states the author's main point. Explain why you chose this sentence.

3. Explain how the title "Worldliness and Worldview" connects to the essay.

4. What type of evidence does Nathan give about the ways that international students view U.S.-born college students? How persuasive is this evidence?

5. Why do you think that Nathan chose to use a pseudonym for her book?

## Consider Your Viewpoint

1. Do you believe that U.S. college students are ethnocentric? Explain your answer.

2. Nathan assumes that her readers will agree that ethnocentrism is a bad thing. To what extent do you agree with this?

3. Give several examples of ethnocentrism in your own culture(s).

4. Internationally speaking, what are some of the effects of ethnocentrism?

# Miles to Go: Why Automakers Don't Sell a Car That Gets 50mpg

## Keith Naughton

In the following article, published in *Newsweek*, Keith Naughton explains the causes that led U.S. automakers to avoid manufacturing 50mpg cars. *Newsweek* was first published in 1933, when it cost 10 cents a copy. Currently it has a circulation of 4 million readers and publishes some of the most influential writers in the United States. Because readers of magazines scan articles quickly, authors tend to use photos, such as this one of a SmartCar, and short paragraphs with the most important facts presented early in the piece.

*This SmartCar gets 46 miles per gallon in the city, 70 on the freeway.*

So gas just hit another miserable milestone. Unleaded regular is averaging a record $3.30 a gallon and seems likely to blast past $4 by Memorial Day. Wouldn't it be great if you could drive a car that gets 50 miles per gallon? Well, you can. Just hop on a plane and fly to Europe, where all new cars average 43mpg, or Japan, where the average hits 50mpg. Here in the United States, we're stuck at 25mpg in our considerably larger and more powerful cars, trucks and SUVs. So why can't we do better? Here's the dirty little secret: we can. "If you want better fuel economy, it's just a question of when auto companies want to do it and when consumers decide they want to buy it," says Don Hillebrand, a former Chrysler engineer who is now director of transportation research for Argonne National Labs. "Auto companies can deliver it within a year."

A 50mpg car would certainly put a tiger in the tank of the moribund U.S. auto industry. But don't get your checkbook out quite yet. The reality is that you won't see a car on a showroom floor in America with 50mpg on the window sticker for at least three years and maybe longer. Sure, all auto companies are focusing on jacking up fuel economy, especially since Congress just mandated that all new autos sold by 2020 must average 35mpg. The new mileage mantra also is motivated by the fact that car sales are weak, partially because of panic at the pump. But putting out a 50mpg

> **Mantra:** Sacred word or chant.

car any time soon is daunting even to the maker of America's mileage champ, the 48mpg Toyota Prius. "We're close enough to spit at that now," says Bill Reinert, Toyota's national manager of advanced technologies. "It's not an incredible stretch, but it's an incredible stretch to do it on a mass-market basis."

It might seem ludicrous to you that there isn't a mass market right here and now for a 50mpg car. For crying out loud, we've entered the age of the $128 fill-up. (The cost of topping off a Chevy Suburban.) But here's the problem: to get to 50mpg in the near future, consumers would have to trade off at least one of three very important things—cost, drive quality or safety. That's because the quickest way to make a car more fuel-efficient is to make it smaller, lighter and equip it with some high-tech (a.k.a. costly) propulsion system like a plug-in gas-electric system.

Consider the exercise Ford just went through. It ran a computer simulation on what would happen to the mileage of a Ford Focus small car if you built it entirely out of lightweight aluminum. Losing the steel allowed the Focus to drop 1,000 pounds—30 percent of its body weight. That enabled Ford to outfit it with a tiny one-liter engine, half the size of its old engine, but far more fuel efficient because of new technology. Best of all, the small motor goes just as fast as the big one because the car is so much lighter. The result: fuel economy on this fabulous Focus went from 35mpg to 50mpg. What's stopping Ford from moving this car from pixels to pavement? The cost of an all-aluminum car could top $50,000—not a sum the typical economy-car buyer is willing to pay. "What's going to be the cost acceptance for this much improvement in fuel economy?" asks Dan Kapp, director of Ford's advanced engines and transmissions. "We don't know yet."

5       Still, all the major automakers are putting their cars on a crash diet. Ford wants to drop 250 to 750 pounds in all its models by 2012. Toyota and Nissan want to cut the fat by 10 to 15 percent. But this slim-fast campaign is running into the drive for more safety features in automobiles. Back in the 1980s, the Honda CRX-HF and the Geo Metro each got more than 50mpg, but they didn't have airbags or steel beams in their doors to protect occupants in a crash. These days, cars are equipped with six air bags, steel safety cages and electronic stability control to prevent spinouts. That makes cars much safer—but a lot fatter. "We are working in two directions," says Toyota's Reinert. "One is to make cars as safe as possible, and that generally makes them heavier. And the other is to make cars as fuel efficient as possible."

Downsizing also has its drawbacks. For starters, U.S. highway statistics show the smallest cars have death rates 2.5 times higher than the biggest. What's more, wimpy engines often (under) power small cars and that's a drawback many Americans won't abide. I recently drove the diminutive Smart car for a week. While it's certainly cute, its puny 70-horsepower

Diminutive: Very small.

engine and slow-shifting transmissions made me feel like Fred Flintstone could outrun me. That might be enough power for twisty Old World roads, but here in America, we have a need for speed. "Going zero to 60 in 15 seconds doesn't fit the average American consumer's idea of mobility today," says Reinert. "That's too doggy."

> Doggy: Slow as a dog.

Another quick way to improve fuel economy—and chase away customers—is to strip out stuff that makes the ride comfortable. For example, engineers could remove the soundproofing material that keeps road and engine noise out of the cockpit. Back in the '90s, when Detroit was fond of noting that gasoline was cheaper than bottled water, Hillebrand worked on the popular Chrysler minivan. They were having problems making the cabin quiet, so they sacrificed mileage to add sound insulation. "We just sprayed penny a pound asphalt into it to quiet it down because that was what the customer wanted," recalls Hillebrand. "Another mile per gallon would not make *Car and Driver* headlines. But having no wind noise did."

These days, though, more mpg makes news. And GM has certainly been getting plenty of mileage out of the Chevy Volt plug-in electric car it hopes to have on the market by 2010. On Thursday, they took reporters inside their Volt lab for another in a series of updates—unusual for a work in progress. And next week, GM will conduct a global online discussion with journalists to address the question: "Why don't automakers produce a 100mpg car?"

So when I called to ask why there are no 50mpg cars, Volt chief engineer Frank Weber practically scoffed at me. "Fifty miles per gallon is not the target," he said in his German accent. "We are working in the three-digit range." All hype aside, analysts say GM just might be the first to achieve 50mpg with the Volt, which Weber assured me will get well over 100mpg. Crackling with confidence, he "guaranteed" the car's advanced lithium-ion battery is ready for the road. Many automakers are racing to develop lithium-ion batteries (like those used in laptops), which juice up faster and go farther on a charge. But only GM is claiming to have cracked the code. Weber also said there is "no doubt" the Volt will deliver on GM's promise of driving for the first 40 miles on pure electric power. After that, a tiny engine kicks in, but only to recharge the battery, not to turn the wheels like conventional hybrids. "Our goal," says Weber, "is to avoid the usage of gasoline completely."

10    Wouldn't that be nice? But at what price? Analysts predict the Volt will top $30,000, and consumers might have to pay an additional $100 to $200 a month to lease that advanced, but unproven, battery pack. Weber dismissed battery leasing as "an old idea," but declined to divulge pricing on the Volt so far from its launch. Any new technology like this, though, comes with a hefty premium, which takes years to pay off in savings at the gas pump. So taking the high-tech road to high mileage comes down to a

question of pay now or pay later. (In the case of some high-priced hybrids, like the late and not-so-great Honda Accord hybrid, the payoff never came.)

In the end, what I found most fascinating about raising this 50mpg question is just how nervous it's made Honda and Toyota. Honda wouldn't even speak to me about it. Perhaps that's because Honda has a Prius competitor in the works that it has promised will have better mileage when it hits the road next year. Let's see, what's better than 48mpg? And Toyota is in the midst of creating an entire lineup of Prius models, which will include a wagon, a family car and a tiny urban runabout beginning in 2010. So if you take the Prius power plant and put it into a Smart-size car, what do you get? Toyota isn't saying, but there could be a hint in Reinert's assessment of Mercedes's mighty mite. "The Smart is incredibly attractively packaged," he says. "It could be the iPhone version 1 of cars." Version 2.0 could roll into a Toyota showroom in a few years—with a window sticker well above 50mpg. And not a moment too soon.

## One Word Spotlight

*Hype* (paragraph 9) means to strongly promote or advertise. It usually implies exaggeration, even deception. It can also refer to something that receives excessive attention or publicity, such as a sensational trial. The word is believed to have originated in the United States around 1925 to 1930 and to be a shortened form of *hyperbole*, which means exaggeration. This is a good example of a word that started out as slang but now is generally accepted as part of standard English.

## Reflect on the Reading

1. According to Naughton's article, why don't we yet have 50mpg cars in the United States?

2. How does the phrase "Miles to Go" in the title relate to the rest of the piece?

3. Explain this quotation: "I recently drove the diminutive Smart car for a week. While it's certainly cute, its puny 70-horsepower engine and slow-shifting transmissions made me feel like Fred Flintstone could outrun me." Connect this statement to the main idea of the essay.

4. In his essay, Naughton often uses statistics and quotations to support his points. In your view, where does he do this most effectively?

5. Which group of readers might agree most with the author? Which might disagree? Explain your answer.

## Consider Your Viewpoint

1. Would you buy a 50mpg car even if it were more expensive and less powerful? Explain your answer.

2. Naughton's essay implies that there was a time when "Detroit was fond of noting that gasoline was cheaper than bottled water." Will it ever be that cheap again? Explain your answer.

3. Do you think the American culture places too much attention on the size and performance of its cars? Why or why not?

4. In many countries, small cars are very popular. Why is this so?

# Immigration and U.S. History

## Hasia Diner

Throughout the history of the United States, the topic of immigration has been contentious. Each successive group of immigrants who came to the United States was often met with suspicion and even hostility. What caused this reaction to immigrants? In her investigation of immigration and the United States, Hasia Diner, a professor of history at New York University, describes the successive waves of peoples who settled in the United States. This essay originally appeared on america.gov, produced by the U.S. State Department, as a part of an e-journal called *Immigrants Joining the Mainstream.*

*Immigration is celebrated in an exhibit on a college campus.*

Millions of women and men from around the world have decided to immigrate to the United States. That fact constitutes one of the central elements in the country's overall development, involving a process fundamental to its pre-national origins, its emergence as a new and independent nation, and its subsequent rise from being an Atlantic outpost to a world power, particularly in terms of its economic growth. Immigration has made the United States of America.

Like many other settler societies, the United States, before it achieved independence and afterward, relied on the flow of newcomers from abroad to people its relatively open and unsettled lands. It shared this historical reality with Canada, South Africa, Australia, New Zealand, and Argentina, among other nations.

In all of these cases the imperial powers that claimed these places had access to two of the three elements essential to fulfilling their goal of extracting natural resources from the colony. They had land and capital but lacked people to do the farming, lumbering, mining, hunting, and the like. Colonial administrators tried to use native labor, with greater or lesser success, and they abetted the escalation of the African slave trade, bringing millions of migrants, against their will, to these New World outposts.

Immigration, however, played a key role not only in making America's development possible but also in shaping the basic nature of the society. Its history falls into five distinct time periods, each of which involved varying rates of migration from distinctly different places in the world. Each reflected, and also shaped, much about the basic nature of American society and economy.

## Settlers of the New World

5 The first, and longest, era stretched from the 17th century through the early 19th century. Immigrants came from a range of places, including the German-speaking area of the Palatinate, France (Protestant Huguenots), and the Netherlands. Other immigrants were Jews, also from the Netherlands and from Poland, but most immigrants of this era tended to hail from the British Isles, with English, Scottish, Welsh, and Ulster Irish gravitating toward different colonies (later states) and regions.

These immigrants, usually referred to as settlers, opted in the main for farming, with the promise of cheap land a major draw for relatively impoverished northern and western Europeans who found themselves unable to take advantage of the modernization of their home economies. One group of immigrants deserves some special attention because their experience sheds much light on the forces impelling migration. In this era, considerable numbers of women and men came as indentured servants. They entered into contracts with employers who specified the time and conditions of labor in exchange for passage to the New World. While they endured harsh conditions during their time of service, as a result of their labors, they acquired ownership of small pieces of land that they could then work as independent yeoman farmers.

## Mass Migration

The numbers who came during this era were relatively small. That changed, however, by the 1820s. This period ushered in the first era of mass migration. From that decade through the 1880s, about 15 million immigrants made their way to the United States, many choosing agriculture in the Midwest and Northeast, while others flocked to cities like New York, Philadelphia, Boston, and Baltimore.

Factors in both Europe and the United States shaped this transition. The end of the Napoleonic Wars in Europe liberated young men from military service back home at the same time that industrialization and agricultural consolidation in England, Scandinavia, and much of central Europe transformed local economies and created a class of young people who could not earn a living in the new order. Demand for immigrant labor shot up with two major developments: the settlement of the American Midwest after the inauguration of the Erie Canal in 1825 and the related rise of the port of New York, and the first stirrings of industrial development in the United States, particularly in textile production, centered in New England.

Immigrants tended to cluster by group in particular neighborhoods, cities, and regions. The American Midwest, as it emerged in the middle of the 19th century as one of the world's most fertile agricultural regions, became home to tight-knit, relatively homogeneous communities of immigrants from Sweden, Norway, Denmark, Bohemia, and various regions of what in 1871 would become Germany.

10    This era saw the first large-scale arrival of Catholic immigrants to the largely Protestant United States, and these primarily Irish women and men inspired the nation's first serious bout of nativism, which combined an antipathy to immigrants in general with a fear of Catholicism and an aversion to the Irish. Particularly in the decades just before the U.S. Civil War (1861–1865), this nativism spawned a powerful political movement and even a political party, the Know Nothings, which made anti-immigration and anti-Catholicism central to its political agenda. This period also witnessed the arrival of small numbers of Chinese men to the American West. Native-born Americans reacted intensely and negatively to their arrival, leading to the passage of the only piece of U.S. immigration legislation that specifically named a group as the focus of restrictive policy, the Chinese Exclusion Act of 1882.

> Nativism: A policy that favors native-born people over immigrants.

## A Wave Becomes a Flood

Gradually over the course of the decades after the Civil War, as the sources of immigration shifted so too did the technology of ocean travel. Whereas previous immigrants had made their way to the United States via sail power, innovations in steam transportation made it possible for larger ships to bring larger loads of immigrants to the United States. The immigrants of this era tended to come from southern and eastern Europe, regions undergoing at the end of the 19th and beginning of the 20th centuries the same economic transitions that western and northern Europe had earlier experienced.

As among the immigrants of the earlier period, young people predominated among the newcomers. This wave of migration, which constituted the third episode in the history of U.S. immigration, could better be referred to as a *flood* of immigrants, as nearly 25 million Europeans made the voyage. Italians, Greeks, Hungarians, Poles, and others speaking Slavic languages constituted the bulk of this migration. Included among them were 2.5 to 3 million Jews.

Each group evinced a distinctive migration pattern in terms of the gender balance within the migratory pool, the permanence of their migration, their literacy rates, the balance between adults and children, and the like. But they shared one overarching characteristic: They flocked to urban destinations and made up the bulk of the U.S. industrial labor pool, making possible the emergence of such industries as steel, coal, automobile, textile, and garment production, and enabling the United States to leap into the front ranks of the world's economic giants.

Their urban destinations, their numbers, and perhaps a fairly basic human antipathy towards foreigners led to the emergence of a second wave of organized xenophobia. By the 1890s, many Americans, particularly from the ranks of the well-off, white, native-born, considered immigration to pose a serious danger to the nation's health and security. In 1893 a group of them formed the Immigration Restriction League, and it, along with other similarly inclined organizations, began to press Congress for severe curtailment of foreign immigration.

> Xenophobia: Fear of foreigners or strangers.

## Legislating Immigration

15 Restriction proceeded piecemeal over the course of the late 19th and early 20th centuries, but immediately after the end of World War I (1914–1918) and into the early 1920s, Congress did change the nation's basic policy about immigration. The National Origins Act in 1921 (and its final form in 1924) not only restricted the number of immigrants who might enter the United States but also assigned slots according to quotas based on national origins. A complicated piece of legislation, it essentially gave preference to immigrants from northern and western Europe, severely limited the numbers from eastern and southern Europe, and declared all potential immigrants from Asia to be unworthy of entry into the United States.

The legislation excluded the Western Hemisphere from the quota system, and the 1920s ushered in the penultimate era in U.S. immigration history. Immigrants could and did move quite freely from Mexico, the Caribbean (including Jamaica, Barbados, and Haiti), and other parts of Central and South America. This era, which reflected the application of the 1924 legislation, lasted until 1965. During those 40 years, the United States began to admit, case by case, limited numbers of refugees. Jewish refugees from Nazi Germany before World War II, Jewish Holocaust survivors after the war, non-Jewish displaced persons fleeing Communist rule in eastern Europe, Hungarians seeking refuge after their failed uprising in 1956, and Cubans after the 1960 revolution managed to find haven in the United States because their plight moved the conscience of Americans, but the basic immigration law remained in place.

## The Hart-Celler Act

This all changed with passage of the Hart-Celler Act in 1965, a by-product of the civil rights revolution and a jewel in the crown of President Lyndon Johnson's Great Society programs. The measure had not been intended to stimulate immigration from Asia, the Middle East, Africa, and elsewhere in the developing world. Rather, by doing away with the racially based quota system, its authors had expected that immigrants would come from the "traditional" sending societies such as Italy, Greece, and Poland, places that labored under very small quotas in the 1924 law. The law replaced the quotas with preference categories based on family relationships and job skills, giving particular preference to potential immigrants with relatives in the United States and with occupations deemed critical by the U.S. Department of Labor. But after 1970, following an initial influx from those European countries, immigrants began to hail from places like Korea, China, India, the Philippines, and Pakistan, as well as countries in Africa. By 2000 immigration to the United States had returned to its 1900 volume, and the United States once again became a nation formed and transformed by immigrants.

Now in the early 21st century, American society once again finds itself locked in a debate over immigration and the role of immigrants in American society. To some, the new immigrants have seemed unwilling or unable to assimilate into American society, too committed to maintaining their transnational connections, and too far removed from core American values. As in past eras, some critics of contemporary immigrants believe that the newcomers take jobs away from Americans and put undue burdens on the educational, welfare, and health care systems. Many participants in the debate consider a large number of illegal immigrants to pose a threat to the society's basic structure.

The immigrants, however, have supporters who point out that each new immigrant wave inspired fear, suspicion, and concern by Americans—including the children and grandchildren of earlier immigrants—and that Americans claimed, wrongly, that each group of newcomers would somehow not fit in and would remain wedded to their old and foreign ways. So too advocates of immigration and most historians of immigration argue that immigrants enrich the United States, in large measure because they provide valuable services to the nation.

20    In every era of U.S. history, from colonial times in the 17th century through the early 21st century, women and men from around the world have opted for the American experience. They arrived as foreigners, bearers of languages, cultures, and religions that at times seemed alien to America's essential core. Over time, as ideas about U.S. culture changed, the immigrants and their descendants simultaneously built ethnic communities and participated in American civic life, contributing to the nation as a whole.

## One Word Spotlight

*Great Society Programs* (paragraph 15) refers to the legislation enacted by President Lyndon Johnson the first few years after he became president in November 1963. These programs included Medicare, Medicaid, the Job Corps, and major civil rights legislation. Educational programs that were established during this time included Upward Bound, Head Start, and federal student loans.

## Reflect on the Reading

1. What is the main point of this essay, and where is it expressed?
2. Early immigrants to the U.S. were usually farmers, but beginning in the 1800s many immigrants began to live in urban areas. Why was this so?
3. How did some immigrants' religious affiliations affect the way they were received in the United States?
4. How was immigration restricted after World War I?
5. According to the author, what criteria are used today to admit people into the United States?

## Consider Your Viewpoint

1. If you are an immigrant or descended from immigrants, in which of the five immigration time periods described by the author do you or your ancestors belong?

2. What are some factors that make people hostile to immigrants?

3. The author does not mention illegal immigration in this essay. Why do you think this is so?

4. African-American slaves were the victims of forced immigration because they were brought to the United States against their will. How did this enslavement affect their descendants?

5. In the future, do you predict there will be more, less, or the same restrictions on immigrants coming to the United States?

# WRITING ASSIGNMENT

For this writing assignment, you will investigate the cause or causes of a particular fact, event, or occurrence to inform an interested audience of what you have learned. To select a topic, consider your interests, such as music, movies, gaming, sports, pets, gardening, hobbies, and so on. Then think about the parts of your life that consume a great deal of your time, such as school, work, and family. Finally, consider the societal issues that you're concerned about, such as the environment, globalization, or the economy.

# YOUR INVESTIGATION OF A CAUSE

Now it's your turn to investigate a cause. The model investigations in this chapter may give you topic ideas, or you may choose to investigate something else entirely. Before beginning this assignment, review Chapters 2 and 3 to refresh your memory on choosing a topic, analyzing the rhetorical situation, and completing the stages of the writing process.

### Writing Assignment Checklist

- ☐ Carefully read the assignment.
- ☐ Look for key words that describe what you must do.
- ☐ Determine whether the topic is assigned or free choice.
- ☐ Ask your instructor any questions that you have about the assignment.
- ☐ Develop a timeline for completing the assignment.

## Choosing a Topic

When choosing a topic to investigate, identify a question that interests you, that you are curious to learn more about, and that you think will interest others, too. For investigating a cause, try to use the phrase "What causes" or "Why is this" with some of your interests, activities, and societal issues. Here are some examples:

**Sports**

What causes professional athletes to take steroids?

Why is Phil Mickelson one of the best golfers in the world?

**Business**

What causes some small businesses to be profitable and others not?

Why is organic produce becoming so popular?

**Education**

What causes college students to drop out of school?

Why are community colleges more popular than universities?

**Family**

What caused U. S. divorce rates to stabilize in the past decade?

Why are many prospective parents not interested in adopting older children?

**Economy**

What causes homes to drop in value?

Why are unemployment rates increasing?

**Environment**

What has caused the increase in hurricanes in the United States in recent years?

Why does pollution in China affect other countries?

**Technology**

What caused the creation of the World Wide Web?

Why do people want to participate in social networking sites such as Facebook?

After choosing a topic, be sure to narrow it so you can explain the subject in depth. For instance, if you want to write about why home values have dropped, you could narrow it to home values in Los Angeles, California from 2008 to 2009.

---

### Topic Questions for Investigating a Cause

- Is this an assigned topic? If so, what are the requirements?
- Is this topic free choice? If so, what would I like to investigate?
- Can I state the topic in such a way that there is a fact, event, or occurrence with related causes?
- Will readers be interested in this investigation of causes?
- Can I find information for this investigation?

---

**Activity 8.1**    Divide into groups of three or four students and brainstorm a list of topics that interest the members of your group. Select several of these topics and discuss how you might narrow them to explain them in depth.

**Connect With Others**

## Analyzing the Rhetorical Situation

Now that you have chosen a topic, analyze the rhetorical situation to ensure that you and your readers can reach a mutual understanding of the message that you are communicating. The better your rhetorical analysis, the more effective your writing will be.

**Considering Audience and Purpose.** Begin by choosing an audience that will be interested in learning more about the topic that you are investigating. The more you know about your audience, the easier it will be for you to choose details and present them in a way to appeal to the audience of your investigative piece.

---

### Audience Questions for Investigating a Cause

- Who would be interested in learning about this topic?
- How much do these readers already know about the topic?  How much do they need to know?
- What is the average age of these readers?
- Will their gender or cultural backgrounds affect how I present my topic?
- What is their educational level?
- What is their attitude toward this topic?

---

Although you already know your primary purpose is to inform, you may still include some expressive writing if you have personal experience with the topic you are investigating. Try to remain objective, though, and not include too much personal information. Similarly, don't turn this piece into an argument for your position on the topic. Instead, let the strength of the information you present convince your readers to agree with what you learned through investigation.

In her essay, "My Freshman Year: Worldliness and Worldview," for example, Nathan wrote to inform her students, colleagues, and the general public of what causes college students to behave in ways that on the surface appear to be superficial or inappropriate. Nathan's article includes her own experience as a college student, and she wants her American readers to be convinced of what she is saying, but her primary purpose is still informative. She is simply pointing out what she has observed. For instance, when students fall asleep in class people might assume it's because they have been up late partying. Nathan points out, however, that it is more likely that the students are exhausted because they are working their way through college.

---

### Purpose Questions for Investigating a Cause

- Why am I investigating this topic, and what is the key information I plan to share?
- What personal history, thoughts, or feelings can I include in this informative piece?
- How does the cultural background of my readers affect my purpose?
- What do I want my readers to take away from this piece?

---

**Choosing a Genre and Visual Design.** Once you analyze your audience and purpose, choose the genre or format that best fits the message that you are communicating. For informative writing, authors often choose essays, newspaper articles, reports, websites, or video documentaries. In "Miles to Go: Why Automakers Don't Sell a Car That Gets 50mpg," Naughton, a reporter who covers the auto industry, chose to write a magazine article because, after all, he is a news reporter who publishes his writing where millions of people can read it.

Remember, the genre you choose often dictates the content and style of your message. You will decide which layout, font, and visual elements to use. The design includes those visual elements that will strengthen your communication. For example, could you use headings, bullets, and font styles and sizes to help you make your points more effectively? Are there visuals such as graphs, charts, drawings, or photographs that could help make your writing more convincing? If you use visual elements from other sources such as the web, be sure to request permission before using them in your writing. Refer to Chapter 14 for more help with visual design.

---

### Genre and Visual Design Questions for Investigating a Cause

- Which format will best communicate my topic to my chosen audience?
- How will the format help me inform my readers?
- What visual design elements will strengthen my message?
- What do I know about this format?
- What do I need to learn to write in this format?

---

Reviewing Exigence and Constraints. You remember that exigence is what makes you *want* to communicate something. In this assignment, you might choose to investigate a topic to improve your own understanding, to share with others who might also be interested, and to have a permanent record of what you learn through your investigation. You will do a better job of writing if you identify the reasons for communicating this information.

---

### Exigence Questions for Investigating a Cause

- What investigative topic and causes am I trying to explain?
- Why do I care about this topic?
- Given their background, will the audience be receptive to my topic?
- What change would I like to see in my audience as a result?
- Why is it important to put this investigation of causes in writing?

---

Constraints include anything that might interfere with your ability to convey your message to your audience. For example, constraints might include a limited knowledge of the topic, information that is available only in another language, or deadlines for getting things written. As you write your investigation, you'll want to remove as many of these constraints as possible.

In "Immigration and U.S. History," Hasia Diner was constrained by the limited amount of space she had to develop such a broad topic. As a result, she organized her topic into five time periods, which made it easier for her readers to follow.

---

### Constraint Questions for Investigating a Cause

- What will influence the success of my investigation?
- Will my audience have certain expectations of me?
- What more do I need to learn to write this investigative piece?
- What other constraints do I face to completing this piece?

---

**Activity 8.2**  With a small group, select one of the topics chosen in Activity 8.1 and develop the rhetorical situation. Include audience, purpose, genre, exigence, and constraints.

**Connect With Others**

# Using the Writing Process

Once you complete your rhetorical analysis, you are ready to write. To do your very best writing, follow the stages that you learned in Chapter 3: discovering ideas, drafting to explore ideas, revising to improve content, and editing to eliminate errors.

## STAGE 1: Discovering Ideas

You have learned numerous ways of discovering ideas that you may use for this assignment. One that can be especially useful in an investigation of causes is questioning.

**Questioning.** Ask a series of questions about the topic, such as Who? What? When? Where? Why? How? For example, in the article "Miles to Go: Why Automakers Don't Sell a Car That Gets 50mpg," Naughton might have asked these questions prior to writing his article:

1. Who is in favor of a car that gets 50mpg? Who is opposed?
2. What alternatives are there to cars that get poor gas mileage?
3. When will the United States develop a 50mpg car?
4. Where can the consumer learn more about cars and their mileage?
5. Why is low gas mileage a problem?
6. How would a 50mpg car solve the problem?

---

### Idea Questions for Investigating a Cause

- Where can I read more about my topic, either online or at the library?
- Who can I interview who is knowledgeable about the topic?
- Would a survey of people willing to share their ideas on this topic be helpful for discovering ideas?

---

**One Student's Work.** Erik Vasquez, a Mexican-American student who converted to Islam, wanted to educate his classmates about his religion, so he chose to write an investigative essay on the causes of the stereotypes about Muslims and their religion, Islam. He began by asking these questions to help him discover ideas:

1. Why is there a backlash against Muslims in the United States?
2. Is it possible to overcome the stereotype that Islam is a militant religion?
3. What do my classmates need to know to understand this religion?
4. Why is it important that they know the meaning of the word *jihad*?

5. Why are these stereotypes a problem?

6. What sources can I use to help me explain Islam to my classmates?

Once Erik had written these questions, he began to research the answers to discover ideas for what to say in his essay. Erick's completed essay is at the end of the chapter.

## STAGE 2: Drafting to Explore Ideas

As you draft, try to get your ideas on paper in the format of the genre you have chosen. If, like Erik, you are writing an essay, follow the essay format introduced in Chapter 3. If, like Naughton, you are writing a news article, use the format of his piece as a model. Drafting styles vary widely. Some writers draft quickly and spend considerable time revising; others draft slowly, going back and forth as they write until they feel confident that they are expressing their meaning.

As you draft, you might struggle to find the right words. Here are some strategies:

- Consult dictionaries or use a thesaurus.
- Use a language other than English.
- Leave a blank space. You can fill in the right word later.
- Talk about your ideas with others to get their feedback.
- Draw a picture.

Before beginning your draft, brainstorm a list of words related to your topic that you can refer to while you're writing. Here are some key words and phrases that you might use in a draft that investigates causes:

## LANGUAGES and CULTURES

Research in the writing processes of second-language writers has suggested that many second-language writers, when they draft, prefer to draft-redraft-draft-redraft. In other words, they write a couple of sentences, pause to read over the sentences, make changes to those sentences and then move on to draft a few more sentences, repeating the process. According to the research, one of the writers' primary concerns at this point is thinking of the right words in English to express their meaning. If this process works for you, use it. But if you find yourself stuck on a certain word or phrase, express that idea in your first language so that you can move on and finish the draft in a reasonable amount of time. You will have time to alter your word choice when you revise and edit.

| | | |
|---|---|---|
| cause of | due to | lead to |
| make | be responsible for | promote |
| as a result of | because of | produce |
| this is why | as a consequence | |

Body Paragraphs. In Chapter 3, you learned that body paragraphs include a topic sentence and information to support it. For an investigation of causes, your introductory paragraph describes what you plan to investigate

## LANGUAGES and CULTURES

In the United States, there is a cultural assumption that a piece of writing is the author's personal property and someone who copies a portion of the text is stealing it. This view may seem reasonable in an individualistic society, but this is not a view shared by writers in all societies. In other countries, such as China and India, the traditional assumption is that it is more valuable to reproduce texts written by others to demonstrate knowledge of others' teachings. The ability to write something original is not as valuable as passing on traditional knowledge. It is important to note, however, that Western cultural assumptions about knowledge have greatly influenced non-Western cultures.

and why it is important. Your body paragraphs provide the causes and explain them. In "My Freshman Year: Worldliness and Worldview," Nathan starts her essay by describing what she plans to investigate: why international students think American students are ignorant of the world outside of the United States. Her body paragraphs each describe a cause for this opinion and provide enough detail to convince her readers that international students do indeed consider American students uninformed.

**Your Emotional Filter and Writing Monitor.** When you draft, you want to focus on getting your ideas down on paper. If you feel anxious, bored, or hurried, you might not be able to focus and the task will take longer than necessary. At this point, your writing monitor should be low, so you shouldn't be overly worried about grammar rules. Let your ideas flow. When you revise and edit, you can select your best writing from the material you have produced.

**Preventing Plagiarism.** It is likely that you might conduct research for your topic. When doing this, beware the temptation to simply cut and paste information into your paper. To use information from outside sources, you need to

- quote or paraphrase (put into your own words) any information you found in your research
- indicate in the text where the information came from by giving the author and page number
- include a "Works Cited" or "References" page at the end of the piece in which you give bibliographic information about all of your sources
- use the reference tools in your word processing program to help you manage and correctly cite your sources

### STAGE 3: Revising to Improve Content

To revise, improve the content of your paper by looking at how you have organized and developed your ideas, and review your sentence structure and word choice to ensure that they communicate effectively for the audience you have chosen. To help you revise, set aside your writing for a day or two, reread, and then rewrite it.

**Improving Development.** As you rewrite, focus on improving the development of your piece. Simply stating the topic you are investigating and listing the causes will not be sufficient to convince your readers that it is important to pay attention or to take action on this topic. For example, in the newspaper article "Miles to Go: Why Automakers Don't Sell a Car That Gets 50mpg," it wouldn't be enough for Naughton to ask the question about American automakers, "So why can't we do better?" and then to simply list the reasons why. To write an informative magazine article, Naughton develops each of the reasons with plenty of detail. Reread his article and you will find that he used every method of development in his article: narration, description, examples, comparison/contrast, classification, definition, and cause and effect.

**Activity 8.3**   Divide into groups and reread "Miles to Go: Why Automakers Don't Sell a Car That Gets 50mpg." As you read, label the various methods of development Naughton uses to develop his article. Discuss what you have found with your classmates and suggest which methods you might add to your writing.

**Connect With Others**

Once you improve the development, review the rhetorical situation to help you make further improvements.

> ## Rhetorical Situation Questions for Investigating a Cause
>
> - Audience: Will your audience be interested in reading about the cause that you explain? Will your audience learn something new from your piece?
> - Purpose: Have you included enough detail to inform your readers about the cause that you discuss? Develop those paragraphs that need additional detail.
> - Genre: Will your audience approve of the format and design that you chose for your piece? Does the format help the audience understand your points?
> - Exigence: Do you feel that you have explained everything you want to about this topic?
> - Constraints: What constraints have you encountered? Develop a plan for overcoming them to complete this assignment.

Even more effective than rereading your own draft is to ask others for help, a strategy known as peer review. Following is an example of a peer review sheet that you might ask someone to complete for an investigation of causes piece:

## Peer Review
## Investigating a Cause

1. What is this piece's greatest strength?

2. What causes are investigated in this piece? Did you already know about these causes, or are some of them new to you? Are there any causes that I omitted that you think should be included? Are there any causes that should be deleted?

3. Where might I add details to better support the main points? Which sections or sentences would you like me to clarify? How well did the ideas flow? Where do you suggest I add transitions to help you move from one idea to another?

4. If I used library or Internet research to support the investigation of causes, how well was this research used? How well did I avoid simply cutting and pasting information into the piece? How well are quotations and paraphrases used? How well did I indicate the sources of the research in the text of the piece and at the end?

5. How interesting is my topic? What more would you like to know about it?

6. Underline any words or sentences that you think I should revise because they do not communicate to you.

7. Place a checkmark in the margin next to any punctuation or spelling errors that you discovered while reading this investigation of causes piece.

As you read the reviewers' comments and begin revising your draft, consider the following areas for improvement: organization, development, and correctness.

### STAGE 4: Editing for Correctness

*Self-knowledge is the beginning of self-improvement.*
—*Baltasar Gracián*

When you edit, you check for correctness by looking for errors in spelling, punctuation, and grammar. Distinguish between "treatable" errors and "less treatable" errors. Treatable errors are those that you can consult a grammar handbook to find out the correct form, such as subject-verb agreement and verb tense. Less treatable errors are those that are more idiomatic, such as word choice. If you are fluent in spoken English, read your paper aloud so you can hear your errors.

## To Edit

- Use a dictionary or computer spell-checker.
- For treatable errors, refer to a grammar handbook and follow standard grammatical rules.
- For less treatable errors, ask another student to read your writing for errors.
- As you edit, keep an Editing Log, a section in your notebook where you record the errors that you have made.

**Activity 8.4**  Once you complete the writing process, take a moment to look over what you have done. Complete the self-evaluation sheet to help you improve your work.

**Develop Your Understanding**

# Self-Evaluation Sheet
## Investigating a Cause

1. Have I followed all instructions for this investigation of causes assignment? (Reread the assignment sheet and class notes.)

2. Have I identified a fact, event, or occurrence to investigate?

3. Are my thoughts about the causes of this well-ordered?

4. Is my paper written clearly and concisely? (Reread your paper out loud.)

5. Is each paragraph developed and does each contribute to the overall organization?

6. Do I introduce my investigative topic in such a way that the reader is engaged?

7. Do I conclude in such a way that there is a sense of closure?

8. Is the paper written in my own words?

9. Are my sentences well-written and varied? (Read each sentence beginning with the last one, working backward to the beginning of the paper.)

10. Is my word choice appropriate for the audience and purpose?

11. Have I checked for grammar, punctuation, and spelling errors? (Use a grammar handbook and the computer spell-checker.)

12. If I used other sources of information in this investigation, did I give credit both in the text and on a Works Cited or References page?

If you're proud of what you have written, you will be eager to share it with your intended audience. For this investigative piece, consider reading it aloud in class or sending it to your school or area newspaper. If you have access to the Internet, you might also publish your work by emailing it to interested readers or making it available on websites.

## ONE STUDENT'S INVESTIGATION OF A CAUSE

In Stage 1 of the writing process, we introduced you to Erik Vasquez, a student who investigated the causes of stereotypes about Muslims and Islam. After he answered the questions he wrote to discover ideas, Erik drafted, revised, and edited an essay on this topic to inform his fellow students about this topic. Here is his final version of the essay.

By beginning his piece with these questions, Erik captures his readers' attention and begins to advance his main point.

### Measure Muslims on their Merits

*Erik Vasquez*

Is your mother Arab? Is your family from the Middle East? These are the types of questions I get when somebody finds out that I am Muslim. I suppose it is a surprise for many to hear that a Chicano would become Muslim, especially since we are a people known for holding on to tradition—part of that tradition includes being Catholic. We hear of an individual becoming a Mormon, a Jehovah's Witness, or even Jewish, but a Muslim is out of this world. The Israeli and Palestinian conflicts, the unfortunate events of 9/11, and the current war in Iraq have all contributed to a large amount of backlash against Muslims and Islam in the United States, and this probably adds to the shock one gets when they are aware of the decision I made four years ago. I didn't embrace Islam for the shock factor, but it was because I found it to be a very logical and peaceful religion.

This explanation of Islam shows Erik's audience awareness: He knows his readers most likely know little about the religion. He is also careful to point out commonalities with religions that are better known to his readers.

It is important for people to understand what Islam is before a solid conclusion is made about the religion. Islam means the complete surrender to the will of God, and through that surrender one finds peace; the Muslim is the one who surrenders to that will. It is a strict monotheistic religion, and it is the third of the three major Abrahamic faiths (the other two being Judaism and Christianity). Muslims believe that the Prophet Muhammad was the last of a series of prophets who were sent to deliver God's message; prior prophets include Noah, Abraham, Moses, and Jesus. I have had several conversations with people who assumed that Muslims worshiped something else, and that Allah was some other kind of strange deity. In fact, Allah is the Arabic word for God, and it is the same word used by Arab Christians and Jews.

Moreover, people assume that Islam preaches violence and hatred. One of my mistaken beliefs prior to my conversion was that Islam was a militant religion for the angry and oppressed black man, and my only reference for a Muslim was the very vexed civil rights activist, Malcolm X. This controversial figure eventually saw the reality of what Islam is about, and his prejudiced views were transformed when he saw that there were all sorts of Muslims, even those of the white race, when he made the pilgrimage to the Muslim holy city of Mecca—a requirement all Muslims must make once in their lifetime if they are physically and financially capable.

The concept of *jihad* is also misunderstood among non-Muslims. The most popular meaning for *jihad* in the Western World is "holy war." One can find this term abused by the media on a regular basis, but the true meaning of jihad is to struggle for the cause of Allah. A Muslim faces *jihad* in different ways. Muslims are required to pray five times a day, and my *jihad* is finding a quiet place to worship without being stared at in the UTEP library. Muslim women also must confront *jihad* daily when they are scrutinized for dressing modestly and wearing the Islamic head cover, the *hijab*. Being a Muslim in America is a *jihad* in itself. Attempting to eradicate the stereotypes forced on the followers of Islam may also fall under the category of *jihad*.

Stereotypes are a plague for cultures and societies everywhere, and Muslims are no exception to this. Mexican-Americans can relate to the stereotypes people have about their culture and Mexican ethnicity. Common stereotypes for Mexicans are that they all eat beans; they are low class, uneducated, and are only fit for positions as maids, gardeners, or burrito ladies; the majority of the youth are gang bangers who are strung out on drugs. These are obviously unfair and ignorant statements about Mexicans, and no civil rights group would let such comments slide, yet generalizations about Muslims go uncontested every day.

> By comparing stereotypes between Muslims and Mexicans, Erik is helping his readers understand his point by appealing to knowledge they already have.

The most popular stereotype is the infamous terrorist label. Extremist, radical Islamic groups like the Taliban and Al Qaeda have committed abhorrent and detestable acts of violence on the innocent in the name of Islam. The overwhelming majority of Muslims do not condone these terrorist actions, and the Qur'an, the holy book of the Muslim, emphasizes the value for human life. One specific verse says that "if anyone killed a person . . . it would be as if he killed all mankind, and if anyone saved a life, it would be as if he saved the life of all mankind" (*The Noble Qur'an,* Al Maida 5.32). The United States has also had its fair share of terrorist attacks. The Unabomber Ted Kaczynski terrorized people with mail bombs, and Timothy McVeigh bombed a building in Oklahoma City in 1995. What's more, a number of disgruntled youth have taken out their aggressions by shooting their fellow classmates; the Columbine High School and Virginia Tech massacres were instances of domestic terrorist acts, and there are a list of others. Should all Americans be characterized as terrorists for these incidents that were driven by sheer fanaticism? In addition to terrorism, many of the people limit Muslims to being Arabs. Those who spread the message of Islam were Arab, but over time, people of different ethnicities came to adopt the faith as their own. Arabs only make up a small portion of Muslims; the largest Muslim population happens to be in Indonesia (Bowen 3). The religion of Islam was sent to all of mankind, and it is not limited to a select group. This has helped to make it the fastest growing religion in the country.

> This information about Muslims adds to Erik's credibility because it shows he is knowledgeable about his topic.

Islam is also labeled as an oppressive faith toward women. Many non-Muslims feel that women are abused and are limited in their freedoms because they must stay covered. If freedom and liberation are defined by the amount of clothing a woman wears, then women in the West are also oppressed when compared to women in the remote places of Africa where they wear almost nothing at all. Muslim women who wear the *hijab* are wearing it out of modesty and piety, for they are only practicing their faith. Catholic nuns wear very similar garb to that of Muslim women, yet they are not persecuted nor are they regarded as oppressed—they are observing piousness. Non-Muslim women in this community should take the time to ask Muslim women whether they are oppressed or not.

Muslims should no longer be singled out in our communities; we need to step up and represent the nation as a community that is tolerant to those of the Islamic faith. Muslims are valuable assets in our communities. They are doctors, engineers, college professors, and business owners. Americans, in general, are unaware of what Islam actually is. Additionally, the generalizations that surround the religion do not do it any justice. This is the bottom line: all communities, nations, and religions have good people and bad people. Do not blame Islam, a religion of peace, for the actions of the extremist Muslims.

> This last sentence reveals Erik's exigence: He was motivated to write this essay because of some people's reactions when they discovered he was a Muslim.

### Works Cited

Bowen, John R. *Islam, Law, and Equality in Indonesia: An Anthropology of Public Reasoning.* New York: Cambridge UP, 2003. Print.

*The Noble Qur'an.* Riyadh: Darussalam Publishers and Distributors, 2001. Print.

# ADDITIONAL READINGS

## The Truth About Change

### Walt Wolfram

Language is always in a process of change. Often words, phrases, and grammatical constructions that are originally considered improper or slang become accepted into the standard language. But how and why does language change? In the following essay, Walt Wolfram, a professor at North Carolina State University, focuses on the importance of social class in language change. This essay appeared on the website accompanying the PBS series *Do You Speak American?*

Twenty-five years ago, speakers who used *like* in *she's like, "Don't leave the house!"* were largely confined to Southern California and strongly associated with a stereotypical Valley Girl way of speaking. Today, the specialized use of *like* to introduce a quote (what linguists call the "quotative *like*") has spread throughout the English-speaking world. The rapid, expansive spread of "quotative *like*" among speakers under the age of 40 is truly exceptional. It also raises important questions about the nature of language change.

The common myth in American society is that the English language is now following a single path of change under the irrepressible, homogenizing influence of mass media. However, the truth is that language is far too resourceful and social structure far too complicated to follow any single path.

Change is one of the inevitable facts in the life of any language. The only language not in a perpetual state of flux is a dead language. Language itself provides the seeds of change, and social circumstances provide fertile ground for their growth and spread. Yet the truth about language change may be different from the popular conception. People often assume that change begins with the upper class, modeling language for other social groups to follow. In fact, most language change starts subtly and unconsciously among middle-class speakers and spreads to other classes— and women often lead the way.

Pressure to change comes both from within language itself and from its role in society. Because language is a highly patterned code for communication, people collectively pressure it to change in ways that preserve its patterning or enhance its communicative efficiency. (More on this later.) At the same time, we use language as a social behavior, to solidify or separate different social groups.

5    Social context, including the social evaluation of language differences, is as important in language change as the inner workings of language. The reason that *oxen* has not yet given way to *oxes* throughout the English language cannot be found within language itself, but in the social sanctions that have been placed on the use of this form by socially dominant groups. By the same token, one can only speculate as to why *mouses* (as in, *"We asked the IT department to order some new mouses"*) would become an acceptable plural for a computer device by the same middle-class speakers who resolutely chastise any speaker who might call rodents *mouses*. Social evaluation of language may seem inconsistent and arbitrary, but this does not lessen its role in language change.

Most language change actually starts subtly and unconsciously among the lower classes and spreads. Extremes in social strata, for example, the highest and the lowest classes, tend to be marginal to this process. Instead, the middle-class groups, who have the strongest loyalty to the local community while being connected to other groups, are the most sensitive to language innovation.

On the other side of language innovation lies resistance. Even when certain changes seem natural and reasonable, they are resisted by socially dominant classes who want to avoid being affiliated with subordinate groups that have already adopted these changes. The regularization of irregular past forms such as *knowed* and *growed* or the regularization of such words as *hisself* and *theirselves*, which have made some inroads among vernacular speakers of English, tend to be resolutely resisted by the middle classes despite their linguistic reasonableness. Higher-status groups may often suppress natural changes taking place in lower-status groups to maintain their social distinction through language. The acceptance and rejection of language changes are constrained by the social interpretation of those changes and the relationships that exist among social groups.

## The Spread of Language Change

Language change can spread via several paths. In American society, one prominent pattern of language change is the cascade or hierarchical model, in which change starts in heavily populated metropolitan areas that serve as cultural focal points. From these areas, the change spreads first to moderately sized cities that fall under the influence of these urban areas, and then to yet smaller cities and communities, affecting the rural areas lastly. The Northern Cities Vowel Shift is following this pattern of diffusion, which is facilitated by the cultural status of metropolitan areas and by the more extended social networks of cities with larger populations.

Other paths of diffusion in language change show that it is not simply a matter of population dynamics. In Oklahoma, for example, the structure *fixin' to* for "intend to" in a sentence such as *They're fixin' to move* has spread from its rural roots to larger urban areas rather than the converse. This contrahierarhical model of change is explained in terms of cultural identity and trends in population movement. As more non-Southerner transplants move to large cities in Oklahoma, native residents want to assert their Southern identity to distinguish themselves from outsiders. By adopting a language feature associated with rural Southern speech, natives can counteract the influx of the newer transplants through this symbolic use of language.

10    A third diffusion pattern follows a wave-like pattern in geographical space. In this instance, the pattern of diffusion is explained primarily in terms of physical distance—the farther the location is from the site of the innovation, the later the change will take place. The merger of the vowels in *field* and *filled* or *steal* and *still* in some areas of the South illustrates this pattern of contagious diffusion.

Different diffusion patterns are not necessarily exclusive; they may co-exist in the same region depending on the language differences involved. Population dynamics, social structure and the social meaning ascribed to changing structures help us to understand the paths of language change.

## Language Change and the Media

It is sometimes assumed that the language of the media is homogenizing English. After all, everyone watches the same television networks, in which a dialectally neutral English has become the norm. Doesn't this common exposure affect language change and the level of dialect differences? It can be quite difficult to assess the precise role of the media in language change, but a couple of observations are appropriate.

Although TV shows have clearly contributed some words to the vocabulary and facilitated the rapid spread of some popular expressions, including perhaps the use of quotative *like*, media influence is greatly exaggerated because people do not model their everyday speech after media personalities with whom they have no interpersonal interaction. In ordinary, everyday conversation, most people want to talk like their friends and acquaintances.

Commonplace conversation, interpersonal interaction and social networks are the venues through which language change takes place, not impersonal media characters. Furthermore, the current evidence on language change and variation indicates that language diversity is alive and well. Some historically isolated dialects are receding due to outside influences, but other dialects are intensifying and accelerating in their rate of language change. If the media were so influential, that wouldn't happen. Part of this trend toward maintaining diversity is due to the fact that language change is inevitable. And part of it may be due to a renewed sense of place and region that attaches social meaning to some of the language changes taking place in American society.

## The Nuts & Bolts of Change and the Language System

15 Languages are highly patterned cognitive systems. Within the system of English, irregular noun plurals such as *oxen* for the plural of *ox* and *sheep* for the plural of *sheep* go against the dominant grain of forming the plural by adding *-s* or *-es*, creating pressure to change these plurals to *oxes* and *sheeps*. Vernacular dialects throughout the English-speaking world have succumbed to this linguistic tendency even as standard English has withstood this internal pressure.

At the same time, the plural of *mouse—mouses—*would have seemed unthinkable to any standard English speaker a few decades ago, but this regularized plural is now commonly used to refer to the hand-held computing device, as in "We purchased new *mouses* for all of our computers." Over time and place, language itself will pressure exceptions into conforming with dominant patterns.

There is also pressure to expand patterns of application. Lexical items (*words*), for example, tend to extend their meaning to cover new references; grammatical forms tend to become more general in their application. The term *holiday*, once limited to a religious event, now refers to any day away from work. In a similar way, the shape associated with the nautical vessel *submarine* was extended to refer to the fast-food sandwich based on the shape of the roll wrapped around the contents. The use of the word *like* to introduce a quote as in, "He's like, What are you doing?" simply extends this grammatically versatile word, already used as a noun, verb, adverb, adjective and conjunction, to set off quoted statements. The human mind organizes language and uses it to communicate thought in a way that predisposes it to certain types of change.

Change within language is also shaped by our ability to produce and perceive language sounds. The sound of *th* in *think* and *that*, for example, is more difficult to produce and to perceive than the *t* of *tea* or the *d* of *dip*, one of the reasons that *th* is not nearly as common in the world's languages as *t* or *d*. Not surprisingly, throughout the English-speaking world, the *th* sounds show phonetic variation and change, with pronunciations that range from *t* or *d* (*tink* for *think*, *dat* for *that*) to *f* or *v* (*baf* for *bath*, *brover* for *brother*). Similarly sequences of consonant sounds such *mpt* in *attempt* or *sts* in *tests* are much more phonetically complex than a single consonant at the end of a word (*top* or *this*), and therefore subject to change over time and geographical space.

Sounds may also change based on their relation to other sounds in the system. Vowels, for example, are primarily differentiated from one another by where the tongue is positioned in the mouth, somewhat like the different sounds created by whistling into bottles filled with various amounts of water. A slight shift in the position in one vowel closer to the position of another vowel may make it more difficult to hear the difference between the neighboring vowels, triggering one of two effects. It may create a domino-like effect, a chain shift, among a series of vowels in which other vowels move to preserve phonetic distance between them, or it may cause adjacent vowels to merge and become one sound. Both chain shifts and mergers have played an important role in past and present-day changes in English language vowels.

20    One important chain shift taking place in the vowels of American English, the Northern Cities Vowel Shift (in Chicago, Detroit, Cleveland, Syracuse, Rochester and more), involves the sound of *coffee* shifting so that it is produced more like (though not identical to) the sound of *cot*. This in

turn triggers a shift in the pronunciation of a word like *pop* so that it is produced more like *pap*, which, in turn, triggers a shift in the pronunciation of *bat* so that it sounds a bit more like *bet*. But the shift doesn't end there, as the sound of *bet* moves back, closer to the sound of *butt*, and the sound of *butt* moves closer to that of *bought*, the place vacated by the original shift of the vowel in *bought* or *caught*. This shift of the vowels in the mouth looks somewhat like the following rotation.

This subtle and elaborate shift in vowel production is not conscious, but rather the natural outcome of the rotational force of vowels. Meanwhile, Southern vowels rotate in a completely different format, resulting in growing divergence in the vowels of Southern and Northern speech in the United States.

Vowels also shift by merging into one sound. In Eastern New England, including Boston, and in most of the Western United States, a shift in vowels of *caught* and *cot* and *dawn* and *Don* has resulted in their identical production. Similarly, before a nasal sound, the vowel of *pin* and *pen* are merged in the South. Though there may be different responses to the movement of vowels, it is natural for them to shift their position over time, affecting other vowels. Though often unnoticed, language change is by guided the pressures of the language system working in tandem with societal divisions that assign social meaning to these changes.

## Reflect on the Reading

1. What does social class have to do with people's resistance to language change?

2. According to the author, what role does the media play in language change?

3. Explain the last sentence of the essay: "Though often unnoticed, language change is guided by the pressure of the language system working in tandem with societal divisions that assign social meaning to the changes."

## Consider Your Viewpoint

1. When you speak, to what extent do you use "like" to introduce a quote?

2. Have you observed any changes in the way you speak when you are with different groups of people? If so, why do you think this occurs?

3. In your opinion, why do some people resist language change?

# What's New? The Effect of Hip-Hop Culture on Everyday English

## Emmett G. Price III

Hip-hop culture, originally excluded from the cultural mainstream, now has become so accepted that its influence is seen in corporate advertising and in the language spoken by people from all ages and all parts of life. In the following essay, Emmett G. Price III, a professor at Northeastern University, traces the influence that hip-hop has had on English in the United States and around the world. This essay originally appeared on America.gov.

Language is the product of society. As a society changes, so does its language. One of the greatest signs of a changing language is the rapid expansion of its lexicons. Over the past 30 years, American dictionaries have grown at unprecedented levels. Words attesting to the rich contribution of global cultures to American culture, words created for scientific use, words recognizing technological advances, and, of course, words representing contemporary culture have expanded the English language. Yet, it is this last category that has altered the English language more rapidly than any other influence.

These changes are sparked by words created by youth and young adults who feel empowered to codify and label their own realities with new expressions: words that represent the new ponderings, new searches, new desires, and new ideas (even if the ideas really are not so new). In *The Hip Hop Generation*, Bakari Kitwana establishes the birth years of 1965–1984 as the criterion for admission into the hip-hop generation. It is obvious that Kitwana's closing year of 1984 is not wide enough, as we have witnessed the emergence of multiple hip-hop generations, each birthing new additions and approaches to the English language.

## Hip-Hop Culture

During the 1960s and 1970s—as the streets of New York City erupted in violence, social decay, and economic demise—young, multiethnic, inner-city kids devised their own solution to the traumatic challenges that they continually faced. Unifying the preexisting elements of rapping, graffiti, dancing, and deejaying (a method of using sound equipment and records to create totally new sounds and combinations from those originally recorded—scratching, rapid repeats of segments, remixes, etc.), these diverse youth created an alternative to the hopelessness found in their neighborhoods.

During the mid-1970s, this local phenomenon was ignored by mainstream America; yet by the 1980s, not only did hip-hop culture have a national presence, it was sought globally. Movies such as *Wild Style*, *Style Wars*, and, later, *Beat Street* and *Breakin'* allowed international audiences to experience the many facets of hip-hop culture, including the unique approach to speaking and writing English. By the 1990s, print and broadcast media and even video games were dominated by the presence and effect of hip-hop culture. Corporations such as Burger King, Coca-Cola, America Online (AOL), Nike, and Reebok launched advertising and marketing campaigns featuring hip-hop culture, responding to the popular/hip image of these elements and, at the same time, helping integrate them into the broader culture. Amidst the dancing, fashion, and numerous musical elements, what quickly struck the ears of many were the new rules for speaking, reading, and writing English.

## Hip-Hop Language

5 Popular culture in the United States has had a unique effect on everyday English for many generations. African-American music, in many ways, has played a demonstrative role in this evolution. From the days prior to the emergence of the spirituals and the blues, African-American music has informed its listeners (early on, mostly black) of the current events and liberation strategies, using alternative language understood only by those within the cultural network.

Through the years, many of the words and phrases became integrated and used by outside communities who had figured out the context and definitions of these words. This process of cultural adaptation happened in many of the ethnic communities and enclaves within America, yet it was African-American music, containing much of this language, that informed much of American mainstream culture.

The language of hip-hop culture is an extension of past and recent vernacular. Words like "hot" (1920s), "swing" (1930s), "hip" (1940s), "cool" (1950s), "soul" (1960s), "chill" (1970s), and "smooth" (1980s) have been redefined and usurped into hip-hop language. Hip-hop language is the next generation's answer to the age-old question—What's new?

## The Impact of Hip-Hop Culture

The greatest impact of hip-hop culture is perhaps its ability to bring people of all different beliefs, cultures, races, and ethnicities together as a medium for young (and now middle-aged) people to express themselves in a self-determined manner, both individually and collectively. Hip-hop culture has influenced not only American English, but numerous languages around the world. Multicultural nations have vibrant hip-hop communities who have had to figure out what to do with these new words and phrases. From German Hip-Hop to Australian Hip-Hop to Pinoy Rap (Philippines) to Azeri Rap (Azerbaijan) to Rap Nigerien (Niger), hip-hop has had its effect on the languages of these nations and cultures.

Whether it is the addition of the phrase "bling-bling" to the *Oxford English Dictionary* in 2003 or the inclusion of the term "crunk" in the 2007 volume of the *Merriam-Webster Collegiate Dictionary*, hip-hop culture is changing the nature, the sound, and the rules of the English language. Words such as "hood" (short for neighborhood), "crib" (which translates as place of residence), and "whip" (meaning car) have become commonplace within everyday conversation. Phrases such as "what's up" (hello), "peace out" (good-bye), and the extremely popular "chill out" (relax) are frequently used in television shows, movies, and even commercials for Fortune 500 corporations. American English is a living organism, and with vibrant mechanisms such as hip-hop culture and the rapid growth of technology, who's to say what we will be saying or writing in the next 30 years. Whether the United States is a "Hip-Hop Nation," as declared on the cover of the February 5, 1999, issue of *Time* magazine, or not, it is clearly evident that English has been greatly influenced by hip-hop culture.

## Reflect on the Reading

1. What are some characteristics of hip-hop music as it was originally created during the 1960s and 1970s?

2. How has hip-hop penetrated mainstream society?

3. What are some common words that originally were a part of hip-hop culture?

## Consider Your Viewpoint

1. In your view, has hip-hop become passé, or is it still a viable form of music?

2. Do you use any hip-hop expressions in your everyday language? If so, give some examples.

3. Do you agree with the author that the greatest effect that hip-hop culture has had is the way that it has brought together people of diverse backgrounds and interests? Explain your answer.

For support in meeting this chapter's objectives, follow this path in MyCompLab: Resources ⇒ Writing ⇒ Writing Purposes ⇒ Writing to Analyze. Review the Instruction and Multimedia resources about writing to analyze, then complete the Exercises and click on Gradebook to measure your progress.

# CHAPTER

# 9 Evaluating an Experience

## Learning Objectives

In this chapter you will:

- Choose a performance, place, product, or idea to evaluate.

- Analyze how to persuade your audience to agree with your judgment.

- Draft a convincing evaluation that includes criteria and evidence.

- Revise and edit to improve coherence.

*How would you evaluate these baskets? Would you buy one?*

To evaluate something is to make a judgment about it. We evaluate what's around us all of the time without even realizing it. You name it, and we pass judgment on it: books, restaurants, college classes, other people's ideas. We don't usually feel the need to write down our evaluations because we're judging only to make decisions for ourselves. This can change, though, when we want to convince someone else to agree with our evaluation. For example, imagine that you love your home country, Japan, and want to convince others to visit it. Or possibly you're involved in a community political campaign where you would like voters to agree with your assessment of the mayoral candidates. Imagine your boss asking you to evaluate one technology solution over another to make a recommendation for which one to buy. In all of these scenarios, you must convince someone else to accept your evaluation, so you take the time to organize your thoughts and share them in a convincing way. One of the best ways to do this is to put your evaluation in writing.

# WRITING TO EVALUATE AN EXPERIENCE

To write an evaluation, you choose something to evaluate such as a performance, place, product, or idea and then learn as much as you can about it. Because you want your audience to accept your viewpoint, you present your judgment and then provide a convincing argument based on criteria or standards typically used to evaluate this topic. Once you determine the criteria, you provide the necessary details to convince your reader to accept your viewpoint.

For an evaluation, your primary purpose is persuasive: to convince your readers to accept your view about the value of something. To be convincing, however, you also need to include plenty of information. If you have personal experience with what you are evaluating, you may include that as well.

---

### Questions for Evaluating an Experience

- What will I evaluate?
- What is my judgment of this topic?
- What do I know about this topic? What more do I need to learn?
- Which genre and visual design will provide the best format for sharing my judgment?
- Why is it important for my readers to agree with my judgment of this topic?
- What could prevent me from convincing my readers to agree with me?

# MODEL EVALUATIONS OF EXPERIENCES

As you read these model evaluations, notice how the authors present their judgment, what criteria and types of evidence they include to support their position, and what they ask readers to do with this information.

## Cinematic Riches in "Millionaire"

### Ty Burr

In the following movie review from the *Boston Globe* website, boston.com, Ty Burr reviews the movie *Slumdog Millionaire*. Filmed in Mumbai, India, by a British film director, the movie has come under fire for its use of British English and its negative portrayal of India and Hinduism. Nevertheless, it's a wildly popular movie, with a number of awards including eight 2009 Oscars, one for Best Picture. A movie review often starts with the reviewer's judgment of the movie, a short synopsis of the film's plot, and a summary of what the reviewer thinks of the cinematography, acting, and directing.

*Dharavi Slum in Mumbai, India.*

Fetid: Foul or disgusting odor.

I'll keep this simple: Cancel whatever you're doing tonight and go see "Slumdog Millionaire" instead. Yes, you, the girl obsessed with "Twilight" and the guy still hung up on "The Dark Knight." Take the grandparents, too, and the teenagers. Everyone can play.

You've never heard of the actors. A third of the film is in Hindi. Much of it takes place in the most fetid, poverty-ridden corners of the Indian subcontinent, and most of it isn't nice. Yet this sprawling, madly romantic fairy-tale epic is the kind of deep-dish audience-rouser we've long given up hoping for from Hollywood. "Slumdog" is a soaring return to form for director Danny Boyle ("Trainspotting"), but mostly it's just a miracle of mainstream pop moviemaking—the sort of thing modern filmmakers aren't supposed to make anymore. Except they just did.

Unfolding with the scope and brisk energy of a Dickens novel transplanted to Asia, "Slumdog Millionaire" is the tale of Jamal Malik (Dev Patel), a lanky, sad-faced Mumbai slum kid who, when we first meet him, is poised to win 20 million rupees on India's version of "Who Wants to Be a Millionaire." He has already aced the first rounds; tonight, the entire country will be tuning in to hear his final answer. The show's host, a blow-dried slickster played by Bollywood superstar Anil Kapoor, is not happy. So much so, in fact, that he has arranged for the local cops to give the kid a working-over.

> **Mumbai:** The most populated city in India.

Is Jamal a genius? Is he a cheat? How would a young man with no education and a life on the streets know whose picture is on a US $100 bill? That's what a police lieutenant (Irrfan Khan, the father in "The Namesake") hopes to beat out of him. When torture doesn't work, he sits the boy down in front of a videotape of his appearances on the show and demands to know, question by question, how Jamal did it. And thus an entire life unfurls before us, as does the history of modern India itself.

5    Boyle, working from Simon Beaufoy's adaptation of a novel by Vikas Swarup, gives us Jamal's unsentimental education in head-spinning, vertiginous flashbacks that become the main story line. Each answer on the TV show becomes a key that unlocks another chapter of the boy's past, a pat narrative device kept from cliché by the deft, vital filmmaking.

The first sequence, prompted by a question involving a famous Indian movie star—the sort of factoid any Mumbai kid would know—shows the hero's early years as both horrifying and exuberant. Jamal (played as a child by Ayush Mahesh Khedekar) and his brother Salim (Azharuddin Mohammed Ismail) take their desperate existence as merely the soup in which they swim; Boyle and cinematographer Anthony Dod Mantle visualize that soup with an astonishing pullback that reveals the vastness of Mumbai's tin-roof chaos.

The siblings' innocence, such as it is, ends when their mother (Sanchita Choudary) is killed in the anti-Muslim riots of 1992–93 and they take to the streets, picking up an urchin girl named Latika (Rubina Ali) in the process. The three small musketeers are taken in by a smiling villain (Ankur Vikal) who runs a school for child beggars; what this Fagin does to create an extra-special line of underage street singers marks the grueling nadir of "Slumdog Millionaire," yet the movie, knowing such things happen, doesn't let us look away.

> **Nadir:** The lowest point.

The trio grow into adolescence and young adulthood, by which point the brothers have chosen their respective paths. The adult Salim (Madhur Mittal) has gone for quick cash and gangster glory; Latika (Freida Pinto) is the kept plaything of a mobster boss (Mahesh

Manjrekar). Jamal has found work as a gofer at one of the new Mumbai's energetic, youthful call centers. He serves tea, absorbs everything around him, and, when needed, dons the headset to deal with cranky old ladies in Scotland.

Good brother, bad brother, childhood sweetheart torn between the underworld and true love: We've all been here before. Warner Brothers and MGM used to dine out on this stuff in the 1930s, with actors like Jimmy Cagney and Pat O'Brien and Ann Sheridan in the roles. Boyle cherishes the tale's popcorn durability, though—it's an old story because it works—and his team retrofits it, polishes it up, and sets it careening.

10      Mantle's images and Chris Dickens' editing are infused with the go-go colors and rhythms of the subcontinent; the co-direction by Loveleen Tandan adds to the sense of teeming sensory overload; the music keens with beauty and corn. (Even the subtitles feel fresh, popping up like speech balloons all over the screen.) The characters are archetypes draped with specifics of time and place and, in Jamal's case, of character. As Patel plays him, he seems too studious—too inward-directed—to be the hero of such a big movie, yet that's why we come to love him. In the rushing slipstream of "Slumdog Millionaire," he's our anchor.

This sort of headlong melodrama has long since dropped out of fashion in our irony-drenched age, and some audiences, I'm sure, will turn up their noses. There have been grumblings that the film's just too pretty, and that a movie about India directed by an Englishman can't be taken seriously. Allow me to float the idea that it's possible to talk yourself out of intense movie going pleasure.

And "Slumdog Millionaire" is a pleasure, as Jamal negotiates every obstacle before him (including, in one nerve-wracking turn of events, a psychological showdown with Kapoor's preening host), and teeters between intelligence, luck, and a destiny that he has in large part made for himself. In his story, the movie implies, is that of an entire modern nation. After the dust has settled, the Bollywood dance scene that explodes under the closing credits feels both incongruous and earned: Young India kicking up its heels.

You may even feel like dancing in the aisles yourself. Sure, the real world doesn't always work this way. Have you forgotten that this is one of the reasons why we go to movies in the first place?

> Preening: Grooming oneself excessively.

# One Word Spotlight

***Archetype*** (paragraph 10) is something that serves as a model or ideal. For example, Superman serves as the archetype of all superheroes. In *Slumdog Millionaire*, Burr notes that the main characters, Jamal, Salim, and Latika, are modeled after the movie archetypes of "good brother, bad brother, childhood sweetheart." The problem with archetypes, though, is that they can also become stereotypes. Superman, for example, is a tall, handsome, muscular, white male. Many people cannot picture a superhero who doesn't fit this model.

## Reflect on the Reading

1. What is Burr's judgment of the movie *Slumdog Millionaire?* At what point in the review do you know his viewpoint?

2. What criteria does he use to make this judgment?

3. What details does he provide to convince you to agree with his judgment? How persuasive is this evidence?

4. What opposition to his viewpoint does he acknowledge? How does he address this opposition?

## Consider Your Viewpoint

1. If you haven't seen the movie, does Burr's review make you want to see it? If you have seen the movie, do you agree with his review? Why or why not?

2. What does Burr mean when he says that the director's "team retrofits it, polishes it up, and sets it careening"? What other movies does he use as a comparison? Have you seen any of these movies? Do you agree that they are similar to *Slumdog Millionare?*

3. Give several examples of movies that you have seen that you would like others to see.

4. In the photograph that precedes this evaluation, how does the visual image help you understand the meaning of the word *slum?*

# Second Life: Is There Any There There?

## Gary Anthes

*Second Life* is a virtual world accessible anywhere through the World Wide Web. Users, called Residents, create three-dimensional representations of themselves to interact with other users. In this highly interactive Internet world, people can do just about anything they do in the real world; some have even married

*A* Second Life *screen shot.*

in *Second Life*, although they have never met in real life. In this evaluation of *Second Life*, written for *COMPUTERWORLD*, an online site for information technology professionals, Gary Anthes evaluates *Second Life* to let his readers know whether he would recommend it to them.

Until recently, I thought "second life" referred to one of those places the Bible says we'll go after we depart this life.

Now I know it's a virtual place, a vast collection of electrons on computers all over the world and, more to the point, a state of mind and a place for adventure, romance, business and just plain fun for millions of users.

My editor made me do it. I never would have given Second Life (SL) a second look had she not asked me to write a story about it. I considered myself too old and too serious to dive into something I imagined was designed for twentysomethings looking for virtual sex.

I had two fears. One was that in SL I would be persuaded to reveal—maybe even invent—secrets about myself that would horrify my neighbors, jeopardize my marriage and cost me my job.

5    My second fear was that I'd get utterly consumed by the experience. I'm already at the ragged edge of addiction to e-mail and ordinary Web surfing, and I didn't want to find myself up at 3 a.m. navigating my avatar through cyberspace.

So I posed that time-worn question to my editor: Where's the corporate IT angle in this? Wouldn't she rather I wrote a story like "How to Replace Windows with Linux on 1,000 Servers Without Breaking a Sweat," or "The Top 10 Ways to Sort a VSAM File"?

But Bill Gates and others have appeared at respectable IT conferences via Second Life, and HP has conducted job interviews in its virtual offices, so there must be something there, she said. Just do it, and we'll figure out the angles later.

*MONDAY: Square One*

So I did it. I started with some background reading. Yes, there is virtual sex in SL, I learned, but that's not the main point for most users. And I was shocked to learn that you can, and many people do, spend real money in SL.

When I went to Secondlife.com, the type was so small I couldn't read it without enlarging it two times in Firefox. So it *was* designed for twentysomethings, after all!

10    I signed up and downloaded the client software. I declined to use my non-virtual credit card to buy the virtual currency called Linden dollars (after SL's creator, Linden Research Inc.), and I declined to buy a headset and mike, which is what you need if you want to talk to your fellow residents rather than type to them.

I was presented a longish list of last names from which to choose. You can then pick any first name, so I became Icon Silverspar. I was assigned a plain vanilla avatar by default, based on gender, but apparently nearly everyone but me changes theirs.

Newbies are required to start out doing four simple tutorial exercises in a place called Orientation Island. Well, three were simple and one was impossible. I finally had to call a colleague for assistance, which I hated to do.

I spent a lot of time stuck on this beginning step, and it was quite frustrating—a little like trying to get Microsoft Word to stop doing those annoying autoformatting things.

But even at this beginning stage, I had my first emotional experience in the virtual world. The pretty young female Asian avatar of a woman who said she was Chinese stopped to say hello. We exchanged a few pleasantries until my (real) telephone rang. When I came back to my PC five minutes later, she had shouted, in apparent frustration, "PLEASE TALK TO ME!" I apologized, and I meant it, but by then, she had walked away.

15    I had inadvertently dissed this nice woman—or at least I think she was a woman—and I felt bad about it. But it was a good reminder of something that I guess I knew but had not really thought about: Behind the two-dimensional avatars on my screen were real human beings.

> Dissed: Insulted or showed disrespect toward.

*TUESDAY: Square 1.01*

My colleague couldn't help me with the tutorial. "Second Life's user interface sucks sometimes," he explained, not to my surprise, and he advised me to just move on. I decided to quit trying so hard to learn how to do everything and just chat with the people I met. Maybe they could teach me things.

I moved rather easily from Orientation Island to Help Island, where I found no help and from which I could not escape. I ran into a fellow newbie there, and I asked her if she knew how I could get to a more interesting place, like a big city.

She said she had read somewhere that newbies had to wait for "greeters" to take them off the island. She was waiting for a greeter, and I was welcome to wait with her. We waited, but nothing happened. I logged off and immediately ordered *A Beginner's Guide to Second Life* from Amazon.com, paying extra for one-day shipping.

*WEDNESDAY: Dawn*

Advice to readers: Buy a book on SL or get some tutoring from an experienced user. With the help of the book and sheer persistence, I painfully—but, it must be said, with some fun—guided my avatar down the learning curve. I discovered how to get from place to place (yes, you can fly in SL), how to change my appearance (most residents of SL, both men and women, are young and gorgeous), how to search for things, how to read maps and so on.

20    But now that I had mastered the basics and had overcome much of my initial frustration, some important questions moved from the back burner to the front of the stove: Just why am I here, and what will I do here? What are my definitions of "success" or "happiness" in SL, and how will I find them?

Knowing my editor would ask me about practical IT applications, I sought out a virtual island owned by IBM. To get an idea of how exciting this place is, imagine a 1950s-era IBMer in a starched white shirt and tie with a "THINK" sign hanging on his wall.

I walked into a huge, round auditorium called IBM Theatre I. The seats were all empty, and the stage was bare save for a big white board with some semi-interesting techno-items written on it, each followed by an ordinary Web address. Problem was, the addresses were grayed out, and when I clicked on them, nothing happened. Advice to vendors: If you are going to play this game, make sure it works.

Undaunted, I made my way to a Sears store, where I found crude images of Sears appliances. It was possible to click on them and go to Sears' regular Web site. Wow! And it was possible to get and save a "card" with appliance product specs written on it in plain text. Double wow! I saw no other visitors at the IBM or Sears sites.

*THURSDAY: Déjà vu*

> Déjà vu: Feeling that you have experienced an event before.

While booting up, I remembered buying the pioneering PC game *King's Quest* for my daughter in 1987. It ran under DOS, and of course my

PC had no mouse, so we had to navigate Sir Graham by tedious and clumsy taps on the four arrow keys. Now, 20 years later, SL is barely better. The images are still crude and flat, and the arrow keys no easier to use.

25    There's a reason for that. There are usually tens of thousands of users on SL at any given time, and Linden's servers deliver a dynamic and unique view to each one. (Although some of it does come from the local client software and images.)

Rendering 3-D images realistically in real time is incredibly computer and bandwidth-intensive, more than we have a right to expect from SL. Still, scenes download painfully slowly, often taking more than a minute on my PC, a high-end, dual-core model that has 3GB of memory and is attached to the Internet at 15Mbit/sec. I worried about the life of my disk, which made little I/O noises nonstop whenever I was logged on.

*FRIDAY: Looking for Commerce*

I returned to IBM's main island determined to find an IBMer who could answer some questions. I didn't find such a person, but I had a long chat with a well-dressed wolf who said he was from FurNation. He said he was only there to use the public "sandbox," which is provided by IBM, to build things. There are a number of such sandboxes in SL, where residents can go and unpack the bits and pieces in their "inventories" and then work to assemble them into useful objects, such as furniture, vehicles or fashion accessories.

I told him I was trying to find out if companies in SL made any money. Virtual companies make real money, he said, "selling furry avatars, sexual bits, weapons and the like," while real companies like IBM only advertise and recruit. The wolf was not applying for a job at IBM, it seemed, but he thanked IBM for providing the sandbox. I asked if I might photograph him in front of it, but he refused.

Still fretting about bandwidth, I traveled next to the Cisco Virtual Campus and walked into the Cisco Training Center. A sign indicated that it was for use only by Cisco partners and employees, which raises the question of why it's on the public Internet and not on a Cisco intranet.

30    In any case, I found neither partners nor employees in any of the training rooms, and no books, computers or training materials of any kind. Never had it seemed so reasonable to ask if there really was a there there.

*SATURDAY: Looking for Romance*

I can't share all the details with you. Suffice it to say I found two choices. I could go to some more or less respectable place and approach some more or less respectable-looking women and chat them up. I did that. Some just walked away, and some made polite small talk and then walked away. I think one problem was I had not taken the time to tweak my appearance, so I still looked like a boring nerdy newbie—no tattoos, no jewelry, no big muscles, no flashy, body-defining clothes.

The other choice was to go to some raunchy place devoted to orgies and just join in. I didn't do that. OK, I went to some but I didn't join in. That wouldn't have been "romance," would it?

*SUNDAY: Reflection*

To say I tried everything in SL would be almost as ludicrous as saying I have tried everything in my first life. Readers who are experienced SLers will argue that if I had only done this or tried that, or joined such and such a group, I would have seen the magic in this virtual world—which, after all, has attracted 10 million registered users. Perhaps. But I can only report the disappointments as I encountered them, as seen by a real person during a short sojourn in a virtual world.

The user interface is slow, clunky and primitive, at least compared with what's available in the best computer games today. Graphics are flat and poorly nuanced, and image downloads would try the patience of Job. But perhaps my biggest disappointment, since I write for corporate IT managers, is that the corporate presence in SL is so tentative and rudimentary, in most ways inferior to the companies' own Web sites.

35     To be fair, most of these companies are experimenting, and their islands in SL are nascent works in progress. But I will now reveal to these companies what they need to do, so they can then buy huge numbers of Linden dollars with the real dollars they save on focus groups.

Nascent: Recently come into existence.

Each major company location in SL should be staffed with a real person, at least during business hours. If some friendly and attractive avatar at the Cisco center had approached me and said, "Yes, sir, how may I help you?" and then had given me useful answers to my typed in questions about training, employment opportunities or products, I would have fallen out of my chair with amazement and delight.

Yes, I know that would cost serious bucks. One or more real people would have to be paid real dollars to do that. But if a company can't make its virtual experience substantially better—and I mean really head-and-shoulders better—than its existing Web capabilities, it might as well not bother.

Because my wolf friend isn't going to buy an IBM computer because he spotted it through the window while playing in the IBM sandbox, the IBM island must be a destination deliberately sought out by people with an interest in IBM, with the knowledge that they will have a really cool virtual experience there while being treated like a real human by a real human.

So will I return to SL? I probably will one day. But first I have to knock out that Windows/Linux story.

# One Word Spotlight

*Avatar* (paragraph 11) is a Sanskrit word meaning the incarnation or personification of a Hindu god into human or animal form. In the online environment, it refers to a two- or three-dimensional computer image used to represent a human or animal. Online programs such as *Second Life* require users to create an avatar to embody the traits and qualities that the user would like to possess while in the site.

## Reflect on the Reading

1. Which sentence or sentences express Anthes' judgment about *Second Life*?
2. How does the title relate to this judgment?
3. Anthes often uses description and examples to support his viewpoint. In your view, where does he do this most effectively?
4. What is Anthes' judgment about the companies doing business in *Second Life*? What advice does he give to them?
5. Which group of readers might agree with Anthes' viewpoint? Which might disagree? Explain your answer.

## Consider Your Viewpoint

1. Anthes admits that he is not a twentysomething user of *Second Life*. Does this affect the way you view *his* evaluation?
2. Anthes provides a rebuttal to *Second Life* users who might say that he didn't take advantage of all that the program offered or do the right things while in the program. How effective is this rebuttal?
3. Do you agree with Anthes that programs such as *Second Life* keep people from enjoying all that is available to them in their first life, or do these programs enhance their first life?
4. Analyze the *Second Life* home page screen capture that precedes this evaluation. Does the home page make the purpose and navigation of *Second Life* clear? Why or why not?

# Start Your Engines: Remote Possibilities

## Steve Campbell

In this magazine article written for *Consumers Digest*, Steve Campbell reviews the remote starter, a device that can start a car, turn on the heater, or charge the battery from inside your house—all at the push of a button. Campbell has a great deal of credibility with his readers because he has written for automotive magazines for over thirty years.

*A remote starter could be useful during a New York City blizzard.*

Likely scenario: You run to your car to escape the heat or cold only to be reminded once inside you are either on the hot seat or are able to give a first-hand account of what freezer burn is all about.

The ability to control climate in nasty weather is the obvious benefit of a remote starter, whether in the deep-freeze of January or the blistering temperatures of August. But the devices—increasingly popular in all but the most temperate regions—offer convenience that is undeniable. With a remote starter, the vehicle is ready to roll from the moment you ease into the seat. In fact, numerous automakers now offer remote starters as dealer options on selected models. If you don't plan to buy a new car or truck soon, however, remote starters can be added to your present ride at a reasonable cost.

Remote starters allow you to fire the engine with the press of a button from hundreds or perhaps thousands of feet away, letting pre-set climate controls bring the interior to balmy perfection before you even walk out the door. The distance from which devices operate varies based on transmitter type and the effects of radio interference, especially in urban areas or by AM radio towers. "Real world, it depends on climate, surroundings and elevation," adds Link Ahlers, owner of Audio Concepts in Simi Valley, Calif. "The newer systems use radio-frequency transmitters and operate at higher bandwidths, kind of like your cordless phone at home, so they can go through buildings and get better range." The transmission frequency has jumped from 305 MHz to 433 MHz.

The newest systems also offer automatic starting—where the system will actually start the car at predetermined times so your car doesn't die—when severe weather hits.

5   **Back at Ya'.** The newest innovation in remote starters is the *two-way* system. Like *one-way* systems, it can operate all the functions of a remote fob, including keyless entry, trunk release, arming and disarming an alarm, turning on lights and activating a siren or horn to serve as a "car finder" if you forget where the car is parked. (While that functionality has been around for some time, today's microprocessors allow much more information to be stored in physically smaller units.) However, those systems are hush-hush about whether the mission was accomplished, unless you can actually see or hear the vehicle.

With a two-way system, the remote fob and the car contain transponders (devices, often not much bigger than a matchbook, that both transmit and receive). When a remote-starter signal is sent and the car's engine is successfully fired, the car's transponder sends a signal back to the remote to indicate that the action was completed. It takes the guesswork out of the equation.

Anyway, two-way remotes are most commonly fitted with either liquid-crystal displays (LCDs) or light-emitting-diode (LED) displays. LCDs provide graphic representations of the vehicle, its systems and their current status. For instance, a vehicle icon might include a blinking smoke puff at the tailpipe if the car is running. The LCD will also alert the owner if the alarm is triggered. With the LED display, the various start, entry and alarm functions are indicated by light flashes and, in some cases, sound codes.

**Good Timing.** A number of automatic remote starters now have timers. In many of the more advanced units, the system can be programmed to start the car at predetermined times and run for durations of 5 to 30 minutes. Additionally, auto starters can be linked with engine block heaters in the coldest climates to keep engines from freezing.

The remote starter can be set to activate the heater either at specific times or, with a temperature sensor, when the mercury drops below a set point, preheating the engine's lubricant so the car is ready to go to the show when you are. In the absence of a block heater, the remote starter can be programmed to fire the engine based on either time or temperature and run every 2 or 3 hours during the night.

10   Of course, this should go without saying but if you park your car in a garage, it's imperative to remember to shut the mechanism off. In some of the newer systems, there is also a battery-monitoring function that will start the car to charge the battery if its voltage limbos below a certain level.

**Anything to Add?** If you already have a vehicle with a fob for opening doors and such, there are programmable add-on systems for your remote-starting enjoyment, which can be integrated into your vehicle's existing remote. If the owner hits the lock button three times in succession, for instance, the car starts. That doesn't add any security, but it provides a remote-starter capability for those climate-control and engine heat-up or cool-down features.

Also, beyond the basic safety and security functions, remote starters can now accommodate diesel engines. Many systems now incorporate wait-to-start features that power the diesel's glow plugs for a warm-up period before activating the starter. Similarly, a shut-down delay is used on systems that are added to turbocharged engines—both gasoline and diesel—because turbocharged engines should be run at idle speed and allowed to cool before they are shut down.

**Installing Confidence.** The prices of remote starters vary dramatically from $100 to $500 or more and can be affected by an assortment of options and requirements. Installation charges are substantial, ranging from $100 to $250 depending on your car and what features you purchase, but a knowledgeable technician is critical to proper operations.

"I can't imagine anybody doing it who doesn't do it for a living," Ahlers says. "I have guys you've been doing it for 2 or 3 years and still have to spend a full day getting the security system to adapt to the car. Getting the car to recognize the system and setting up all of the integration is really tough."

## One Word Spotlight

*MHz* (paragraph 3) is the abbreviation for the word *megahertz*, named for German physicist, Heinrich Rudolf Hertz. A hertz is a transmission frequency measure for one cycle completed in one second. One MHz is one million cycles completed per second.

## Reflect on the Reading

1. How does Campbell introduce his review of remote starters? Is it an effective introduction?

2. List the criteria Campbell uses to review remote starters. What other criteria could he have chosen? Are the criteria explicitly stated or implied?

3. What exactly is Campbell's judgment on remote starters? Where is his judgment stated?

4. What evidence does Campbell provide to support his judgment?

5. The piece concludes with a bit of cautionary advice to purchasers of remote starters. Does this conclusion undermine his evaluation? Why or why not?

## Consider Your Viewpoint

1. Based on this review, would you purchase a remote starter? Why or why not?

2. What, to you, would be the characteristics of a good remote starter? If you could give advice to a manufacturer, what would it be?

3. What more would you like Campbell to discuss in his review of remote starters?

4. Does the photo of a New York blizzard increase your interest in this topic? Why or why not?

# WRITING ASSIGNMENT

For this writing assignment, choose an experience such as a performance, place, product, or idea to evaluate. You should evaluate something of importance to you: It may be something on your campus, in your workplace, or community, or you may choose a national or international topic that you think others would be interested in learning about. Your goal is to persuade your readers to agree with your evaluation.

# YOUR EVALUATION OF AN EXPERIENCE

Now that you have read the model evaluations, you have some examples of what an evaluation looks like. Possibly, you have even thought of something to evaluate. Remember that simply stating your opinion may not be enough to convince others to agree with you. By first analyzing the rhetorical situation and then following the stages of the writing process, you will write an evaluation that will change even skeptical readers' views about your topic.

## Choosing a Topic

To select a topic, think back over the past year. Have you viewed a performance that you would recommend to others, visited a place that you particularly liked, or purchased a product that you think others should try? When choosing a topic to evaluate, identify a topic that is important to you and that others might be convinced to agree with you about.

Here are some examples of topics you might choose for each category:

**Performance**

Live: play, sporting event, dance, concert
Recorded: CD, DVD, podcast, website

Film: movie, either fictional or documentary
Print: book, magazine, graphic novel

### Place

College: study place, bookstore, research lab
Workplace: computer firm, retail store, service provider
Community: restaurant, nightclub, amusement park
National: park, tourist attraction
International: city, country, continent

### Product

College: courses, website
Workplace: equipment, technology, projects
Community: websites, services, playgrounds
National: social networking sites, government services
International: products, services

### Idea

College: tuition increase, value of a degree
Workplace: customer service, family-friendly policies
Community: proposed legislation, road improvements
National: government policy, congressional actions
International: world issues, cultural traditions

> *I write to discover what I know . . .*
> *—Flannery O'Connor*

Once you choose a topic, narrow it so that you can give your judgment, criteria, and sufficient evidence to convince your readers of your viewpoint. For example, it isn't possible to evaluate everything about the college you attend for this assignment, but you could evaluate one policy, course, or website.

---

## Topic Questions for Evaluating an Experience

- What will I evaluate? A performance? Place? Product? Idea?
- Is this a topic for which I have a strong opinion?
- Are there readers who can be convinced to agree with me on this topic?
- What are the criteria for evaluating this topic?
- Can I find evidence to support my position?

**Activity 9.1**   Spend a few minutes telling several classmates what you plan to evaluate. Discuss why this would or would not make a good topic. Answer these questions: Would this topic be interesting to these class members? What are the criteria for evaluating this topic? What evidence do you have? What more would you need to have to convince these classmates to agree with your evaluation?

**Connect With Others**

## Analyzing the Rhetorical Situation

Now that you have chosen something to evaluate, analyze the rhetorical situation to ensure that you have all of the information necessary to convince your readers to agree with your position.

**Considering Audience and Purpose.** Begin by choosing readers who might be interested in your topic and can be convinced to agree with your judgment. For example, Ty Burr published his *Slumdog Millionaire* review on boston.com, the web version of the *Boston Globe* newspaper. Readers of boston.com tend to be young adults, many of whom attend local universities. This is a group of readers looking for good movie entertainment and interested in reading movie reviews.

### Audience Questions for Evaluating an Experience

- Who would be interested in my evaluation?
- Do these readers have any background knowledge of this topic?
- Do age, gender, and/or cultural background affect attitudes toward this topic?
- If my readers don't agree with my judgment, how difficult will it be to convince them to agree with me?

Although your primary purpose for this assignment is persuasive, your secondary purpose is informative. You want to provide enough information to convince your readers that you know your topic well. You may also include some personal experience to lend credibility to your evaluation. In Anthes' evaluation of *Second Life*, for example, he provides detailed information about the website, but relies heavily on his personal experience visiting this virtual world to provide evidence to support his judgment.

### Purpose Questions for Evaluating an Experience

- Why am I evaluating this topic?
- What key information should I share to help convince my readers of my viewpoint?
- What personal history, thoughts, or feelings can I include?
- How does the cultural background of my readers affect my purpose?
- What do I want my readers to take away from this piece?

**Choosing a Genre and Visual Design.** Once you analyze your audience and purpose, choose the genre or format that best fits the message that you're communicating. For persuasive writing, authors often choose essays, reviews, white papers, editorials, and articles. Consider adding visuals to your evaluation to increase your readers' understanding and to make the piece more appealing to read. If you plan to publish your piece on the web, it's important that the visuals are appealing to the online reader. If used properly, visuals can increase readability.

---

### Genre and Visual Design Questions for Evaluating an Experience

- Which format will best communicate my evaluation to my chosen audience?
- How will the format help persuade my readers?
- What visual design elements will strengthen my persuasive message?
- What do I know about this format?
- What do I need to learn about this format?

---

**Reviewing Exigence and Constraints.** Most often, we evaluate something in writing because we want to convince others to agree with us. In some cases, though, the motivation to write is the result of a class or job assignment. Anthes, the author of the *Second Life* review, says, "My editor made me do it." He explains that he would never have chosen to review or even to log on to *Second Life* otherwise.

---

### Exigence Questions for Evaluating an Experience

- What is my judgment of this topic?
- Why do I care about this topic?
- Will gender and culture affect my audience's reaction to my topic?
- What opinion would I like to see my audience have after reading this piece?
- Why is it important to put this evaluation in writing?

---

Constraints include anything that might interfere with your ability to convey your message to your audience. Anthes' constraints, as he describes them in his evaluation, include a limited interest in and little knowledge of his topic. He overcame these constraints by reminding himself that his editor wanted him to write this evaluation.

**Constraint Questions for Evaluating an Experience**

- What will influence the success of my evaluation?
- What expectations will my audience have for this piece?
- What do I need to know to write this evaluation?
- What other constraints do I face to completing this piece?

**Activity 9.2**   In newspapers, magazines, or on the web, find examples of evaluations of performances, places, and products. Answer the following questions about these evaluations:

**Develop Your Understanding**

1. What is being evaluated and why?
2. What is the author's judgment? How is the author trying to persuade you to agree with this judgment?
3. What criteria and evidence does the author use to support the judgment?
4. If there are visuals, how do these help to influence your opinion?

# Using the Writing Process

Once you complete your rhetorical analysis, you're ready to put your evaluation into writing. To do your best evaluation, follow the stages of the writing process: discovering ideas, drafting to explore ideas, revising to improve content, and editing to eliminate errors.

### STAGE 1:  Discovering Ideas

In Chapter 3, you learned a variety of ways to discover ideas that you may use for this assignment. One that is especially useful for an evaluation is mapping.

Mapping.  Mapping requires that you write down your topic on a page or computer screen and place a circle or box around it. Then as you think of specific ideas, circle them, and draw lines to connect them to the larger circle. Imagine, for example, that you decide to evaluate Solio, a solar-powered device that charges your handheld electronic devices. Figure 9.1 shows what your map might look like.

### STAGE 2:  Drafting to Explore Ideas

Whatever genre you choose, write a draft evaluation that includes an introduction, a thesis statement, body paragraphs, and conclusion.

**FIGURE 9.1**

Sample map to discover ideas

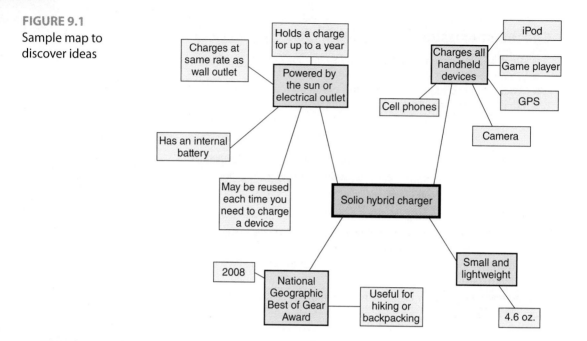

## LANGUAGES and CULTURES

The way authors write introductions varies by culture. In some countries, such as Japan and Mexico, writers often begin by complimenting the reader, asking about the reader's family, or wishing the reader good luck. In the United States, this style of introduction may be viewed as a waste of the reader's valuable time. Be aware that different writing styles exist and match your introduction to the audience you have chosen.

**Introductions.** The introduction to your evaluation gets your readers' attention and announces your thesis statement. For an evaluation, this is the sentence or sentences that state your judgment. By presenting your judgment as part of your thesis, you immediately let your readers know where you stand and what to expect from your evaluation.

So how do you get your readers' attention and present your judgment in a thesis statement? One way is to hook your readers first and then present your judgment. Notice how in the *Slumdog Millionaire* review Burr gets his readers' attention by beginning with this statement:

> I'll keep this simple: Cancel whatever you're doing tonight and go see "Slumdog Millionaire" instead.

The effect is to cause readers to ask the question, "What is so important about this movie that I should cancel my plans?" Burr answers this question by providing his judgment in the second paragraph of the review:

> You've never heard of the actors. A third of the film is in Hindi. Much of it takes place in the most fetid, poverty-ridden corners of the Indian subcontinent, and most of it isn't nice. Yet this sprawling, madly romantic fairy-tale epic is the kind of deep-dish

audience-rouser we've long given up hoping for from Hollywood. "Slumdog" is a soaring return to form for director Danny Boyle ("Trainspotting"), but mostly it's just a miracle of mainstream pop moviemaking—the sort of thing modern filmmakers aren't supposed to make anymore. Except they just did.

> *The last thing one discovers in composing a work is what to put first.*
>
> —*T. S. Elliot*

To introduce your evaluation, consider using one or more of these strategies:

- Begin with an interesting story or anecdote about what you are evaluating.
- State a startling fact or statistic about the evaluation topic.
- If you are evaluating a difficult topic, define what it is that you will evaluate.
- Quote what someone else has said about your topic.
- Ask a question about your topic.

While writing a discovery draft, you are also writing a draft of your introduction. Later, when you revise, you may wish to strengthen it by improving the hook and judgment. If you find that you simply can't draft an effective introduction at this point in the process, you may want to leave the introduction until you finish the draft.

**Criteria.** To convince your readers to agree with your judgment, you must include criteria. Criteria are the benchmarks or standards against which you compare a performance, place, product, or idea. For example, Campbell's criteria for evaluating remote starters includes convenience, safety, features, innovation, and cost. Although the topic you choose will dictate the specific criteria, consider these broad categories: usefulness, appearance, and value. Include each to demonstrate that you have thoroughly researched your topic.

**Usefulness.** Useful criteria are those that highlight the practical aspects of your topic. For example, in the map of the Solio solar-powered device, usefulness includes whether Solio works as described, the length of the battery charge, cost of the product, and ease of use.

**Appearance.** Appearance refers to the aesthetic beauty of what you're evaluating. In the Solio evaluation map, some appearance criteria include the attractive shape and color, small size, and light weight.

**Value.** Value refers to those criteria that highlight whether the topic of your evaluation is valuable to others who have reviewed it. In the Solio evaluation, some value criteria include the *National Geographic* award, the potential savings in electricity, and the use of the product to help you explore nature.

As you draft your evaluation, look for evidence that includes facts: names, dates, numbers, statistics, and other data about your topic to support your criteria. See Chapter 13 "Writing Patterns" for additional ways to develop your evaluation. It's also important to mention opposing viewpoints and explain why you disagree with them. By doing this, you demonstrate that you know your topic well and have considered other people's views before forming your own.

To use criteria effectively, try one or more of these strategies:

- Include usefulness, appearance, and value criteria to support your judgment.
- Be clear how these criteria contribute to your judgment.
- Where possible, use comparison and contrast to establish standards.
- Introduce and address any opposing viewpoints.
- Use a fair and impartial tone throughout your evaluation.

**Conclusions.** As you draft, you also write an effective conclusion. The reader should know that your evaluation is drawing to an end. In the *Slumdog Millionaire* review, for example, Burr uses his concluding paragraph to restate his judgment, provide a brief summary, and to make a prediction about India's future.

> And "Slumdog Millionaire" is a pleasure, as Jamal negotiates every obstacle before him (including, in one nerve-wracking turn of events, a psychological showdown with Kapoor's preening host), and teeters between intelligence, luck, and a destiny that he has in large part made for himself. In his story, the movie implies, is that of an entire modern nation. After the dust has settled, the Bollywood dance scene that explodes under the closing credits feels both incongruous and earned: Young India kicking up its heels. You may even feel like dancing in the aisles yourself. Sure, the real world doesn't always work this way. Have you forgotten that this is one of the reasons why we go to movies in the first place?

To conclude your evaluation, use one of these strategies:

- Restate your judgment.
- Provide a summary.
- Make a recommendation.
- Include a call for action.
- Use an effective quotation.
- Ask a question.
- Predict the future.

**Group Work.** On occasion, you may have the opportunity to collaborate with other classmates on a writing project. To improve your group experience:

- Stay in touch and communicate often.
- Divide the project into manageable parts and set deadlines.
- Do your part well and on time.
- Listen actively to others' suggestions.
- Don't put down others' work. Say something positive about every contribution.
- Revise and edit to ensure that the writing is cohesive.
- Review group processes to improve next time.

**A Student Group Project.** A team of students—Laura Mendez, Christina Munoz, Rosa Orozco, and Stella Owens—worked together to write this white paper on the performance of the Federal Emergency Management Agency's (FEMA) response to Katrina. A white paper is a report that argues a position to readers outside of the author's organization. Most often used by government and business, white papers have become an important way to evaluate and sell ideas and products to the general public.

Not sure that all of their readers were familiar with FEMA, the students drafted an introduction that includes a definition of this government agency:

> FEMA's mission is to reduce the loss of life and property and protect communities nationwide from all hazards, including natural disasters, acts of terrorism, and other man-made disasters.

Their introduction also includes their judgment of the agency's performance during Katrina:

> As a result of September 11, 2001, FEMA is now a branch of Homeland Security which brings together all the organizations related to national natural or man-made disasters and emergencies. President George W. Bush signed The Post-Katrina Emergency Reform Act of 2006 as a result of numerous errors made when the most devastating disaster in U.S. history, Hurricane Katrina, occurred in August 2005.

The rest of their white paper, which you can read at the end of this chapter, establishes the criteria and details that lead to this call for action:

> Our country should resolve to avoid the previous mistakes made by FEMA and resort to breaking down barriers. This includes barriers of communication, race, age, and income. Together we can make a difference.

**Your Emotional Filter and Writing Monitor.**  When evaluating an experience, ensure that your emotional filter doesn't interfere with a fair evaluation. If you are too emotional about a topic, you may not effectively monitor your writing, but instead let your emotions dictate what you say. Student writer Stella Owens, for example, had a difficult time working with her group on this white paper because of the emotions stirred by memories of Hurricane Katrina. As a result of Katrina, her parents were forced to leave Stella's childhood home to move to Dallas, Texas. To balance her negative emotions, Stella made a point of researching FEMA's strengths and improvements. This addition to the paper also had the effect of adding credibility to the evaluation; readers could see that it was written in a fair and impartial way.

## STAGE 3:  Revising to Improve Content

To revise your evaluation, improve the content by looking at how you have organized your writing, including how you have developed your judgment, criteria, and evidence. Review your sentence structure and word choice to ensure that they communicate effectively.

**Improve Coherence.**  A coherent evaluation is critical if you want your readers to agree with your opinion. Your evaluation is coherent if your readers are able to see the relationship between your judgment, the criteria, and the evidence to support it. You can improve the coherence of your overall paper by ensuring that your introduction includes your judgment and that each paragraph contains criteria and evidence to support that judgment. Coherence also means that each paragraph is unified, with each sentence within the paragraph supporting the topic sentence of that paragraph. You can improve the coherence of each paragraph by repeating key words and using pronouns, transitional words, and a variety of sentence patterns.

**Repetition of Key Words.**  Repeat key words within each paragraph so that your readers know that you are still on the same topic. In this paragraph from "Start Your Engines: Remote Possibilities," Campbell repeats the words *remote starter* four times to ensure that his readers know that he is still describing this particular device.

> The ability to control climate in nasty weather is the obvious benefit of a *remote starter*, whether in the deep-freeze of January or the blistering temperatures of August. But the devices—increasingly popular in all but the most temperate regions—offer convenience that is undeniable. With a *remote starter*, the vehicle is ready to

roll from the moment you ease into the seat. In fact, numerous automakers now offer *remote starters* as dealer options on selected models. If you don't plan to buy a new car or truck soon, however, *remote starters* can be added to your present ride at a reasonable cost.

**Synonyms.** If, however, you would prefer not to repeat the exact words again, you can also use synonyms, words that mean the same or almost the same thing. Campbell uses two synonyms, *devices* and *systems*, in place of the phrase *remote starters* in this paragraph:

> Remote starters allow you to fire the engine with the press of a button from hundreds or perhaps thousands of feet away, letting pre-set climate controls bring the interior to balmy perfection before you even walk out the door. The distance from which devices operate varies based on transmitter type and the effects of radio interference, especially in urban areas or by AM radio towers. "Real world, it depends on climate, surroundings and elevation," adds Link Ahlers, owner of Audio Concepts in Simi Valley, Calif. "The newer systems use radio-frequency transmitters and operate at higher bandwidths, kind of like your cordless phone at home, so they can go through buildings and get better range." The transmission frequency has jumped from 305 MHz to 433 MHz.

**Pronouns.** You can also use pronouns such as *this, that, these, those, he, she, it, they,* and *we* to refer to something previously mentioned. Campbell uses pronouns in this paragraph:

> Of course, this should go without saying but if you park your car in a garage, it's imperative to remember to shut the mechanism off. In some of the newer systems, there is also a battery-monitoring function that will start the car to charge the battery if its voltage limbos below a certain level.

**Activity 9.3**  With a small group, reread one of the model evaluations in this chapter. Underline and label each key word, synonym, and pronoun. Discuss how effectively the author used these words to improve the coherence of the piece. Share what you learned with the class.

**Connect
With Others**

Once you have improved your draft, you can also ask others to review it. Following is an example of a peer review sheet for an evaluation piece:

# Peer Review
## Evaluating an Experience

1. What is this piece's greatest strength?

2. What is being evaluated? What is my judgment? What are the criteria for this evaluation? Are there criteria that I should add or delete?

3. Where might I add details to better support my judgment? Which sections or sentences would you like me to clarify? How well did the ideas flow? Where do you suggest I add transitions to help you move from one idea to another?

4. If I used library or Internet research to support my evaluation, how well was this research used? How well did I indicate the sources of the research in the text of the piece and at the end?

5. How interesting is my evaluation? What more would you like to know about it?

6. Underline any words or sentences that you think I should revise because they do not communicate to you.

7. Place a checkmark in the margin next to any punctuation or spelling errors that you discovered while reading this evaluation.

As you read the reviewers' comments and begin revising your draft, consider the following areas for improvement: organization, development, and correctness.

## To Edit

- Use a dictionary or computer spell-checker.
- For treatable errors, refer to a grammar handbook and follow standard grammatical rules.
- For less treatable errors, ask another student to read your writing for errors.
- As you edit, keep an Editing Log, a section in your notebook where you record the errors that you have made.

## STAGE 4: Editing for Correctness

When you edit, you check for correctness by looking for errors in spelling, punctuation, and grammar. Since you have worked so hard to persuade your readers to agree with your evaluation, don't spoil the effect with distracting errors. Too many errors will cause your readers to pay attention to the errors instead of what you have to say.

**Activity 9.4**   Once you complete the writing process, take a moment to look over what you have done. Complete this self-evaluation sheet to help you improve your work.

## Self-Evaluation Sheet
### Evaluating an Experience

1. Have I followed all instructions for this evaluation assignment? (Reread the assignment sheet and class notes.)

2. Are my criteria for evaluating this experience well-established?

3. Is my paper written clearly and concisely? (Reread your paper aloud.)

4. Is each paragraph developed and does each contribute to the overall organization?

5. Do I introduce my evaluation in such a way that the reader is engaged?

6. Do I conclude in such a way that there is a sense of closure?

7. Is the paper written in my own words?

8. Are my sentences well-written and varied? (Read each sentence beginning with the last one, working backward to the beginning of the paper.)

9. Is my word choice appropriate for the audience and purpose?

10. Have I checked for grammar, punctuation, and spelling errors? (Use a grammar handbook and the computer grammar and spell-checker.)

11. If I used other sources of information in this evaluation, did I give credit both in the text and on a Works Cited or References page?

When you have completed your evaluation, consider sending it to a newspaper or magazine or posting it to a blog or other website where people go to read evaluations on this topic. If you receive comments about your evaluation, share them with your instructor and class.

# STUDENT GROUP'S EVALUATION OF AN EXPERIENCE

In Stage 2 of the writing process, we introduced you to a group of students who wrote a white paper on FEMA. They discovered ideas, drafted, revised, and edited their paper to persuade their readers to agree with their evaluation of FEMA. Here is their final version:

## Breaking Down the Barriers: Evaluating the Federal Emergency Management Agency (FEMA) Response during Hurricane Katrina

*Laura Mendez, Christina Munoz,
Rosa Orozco, Stella Owens*

The students began their white paper by expanding on the definition that they wrote in the drafting section of the process.

FEMA is the Federal Emergency Management Agency of the United States. Its mission is to reduce the loss of life and property and protect communities nationwide from all hazards, including natural disasters, act of terrorism, and other man-made disasters (FEMA, Home page). FEMA leads and supports the nation in a risk-based, comprehensive emergency management system of preparedness, protection, response, recovery and mitigation.

In this paragraph, the students added a brief history to help readers understand FEMA.

FEMA was established in 1979 as a result of an executive order which combined all disaster relief programs into one organization. As of 2007, FEMA had assisted in more than 2,700 disasters. Disaster relief began in 1803 when a fire broke out in New Hampshire, devastating the town. Since then federal approaches began when disasters occurred by distributing disaster loans for public facilities damaged by any disaster such as earthquakes, floods, and hurricanes. More than 100 federal agencies were developed for disaster and emergency relief. In 1979, President Carter combined all disaster relief programs into what is now known as FEMA. The organization has assisted in the disasters or crisis such as the Cuban refugee crisis, accident at Three Mile Island nuclear plant, the Loma Prieta earthquake of 1889, the California earthquake 1971, Hurricane Andrew in 1992, and Hurricane Katrina in 2005.

In 2001 the United States suffered a terrorist attack on September 11 and FEMA concentrated on national preparedness and Homeland Security. As a result of September 11, FEMA is now a branch of Homeland Security which brings together all the organizations related to national natural or manmade disasters and emergencies. President George W. Bush signed The Post-Katrina Emergency Reform Act of 2006 as a result of numerous errors made when the most devastating disaster in U.S. history, Hurricane Katrina, occurred in August 2005 (FEMA, Home page). Hurricane Katrina's storm resulted in fifty-three levee breaches flooding 80% of the city. As of 2006 the death total resulting from Katrina was approximately 1,577 and 705 people remain missing.

The students now state the judgment that they wrote during drafting.

Hurricane Katrina was one of the five deadliest hurricanes in the United States. On August 26 computer simulations predicted the shift in the Hurricane heading directly for New Orleans, a potential catastrophe as parts of New Orleans and the metro area are located below sea level ("Effects"). On August 29 New Orleans Mayor Ray Nagin ordered a mandatory evacuation of the city, and set up refuges for individuals who could not leave the city in time. The Louisiana Superdome provided shelter and food and water was provided to an estimated 26,000 people.

The lack of communication on behalf of FEMA impacted three vulnerable populations the most. Due to late response during the Hurricane Katrina devastation, many more casualties resulted. Could this have been avoided? Could these populations have been alerted sooner? Could response time have come sooner? These are questions that were asked during the aftermath and have still kept America wondering how well this natural disaster was handled.

The first vulnerable population impacted was the elderly community, particularly those who resided in "assisted medical/living" homes. Most of the elderly did not know where to go or how to get there. Many of these people were immobile and therefore without someone there to lend assists, they were not going to be helped. This may be a pattern for this particular population. The senior community seems to be easily forgotten during natural crisis and their lack of knowledge ends in devastation.

> At this point in the white paper, the students begin to provide their criteria and evidence for their judgment.

The second to be impacted was the group whose socioeconomic status is so low they did not have the means to evacuate or have access to mainstream media to remain updated on the status of Hurricane Katrina. Due to New Orleans' social and economic status the storm had the biggest impact on the poor and the African American because they are the biggest population residing. Many of those in this population were not aware of the hurricane coming, how strong it would be, and the massive devastation it could possibly cause. Many were just not alerted and could not evacuate in time. The strength of the storm caused many power outages which cut off landlines and cell phone usage. The information was then broadcasted and published on the internet for the evacuees; however, many did not have access to the internet.

The third was those who were evacuated and sent to temporary locations but were forgotten there without any further assistance. Many of those rescued from New Orleans and neighboring cities were sent to Houston, Dallas, San Antonio, even to Louisiana's Superdome for refuge. Once they arrived, they waited without having a next plan of action. Having so many people in such close proximity with one another caused many types of disturbances. These evacuees may have been physically safe but far from being mentally stable. Populations grew and grew especially in the Superdome and formed chaotic living areas for the evacuees. Many drug overdosed, committed suicide, stole, raped or caused harm to those around them. Violence erupted at these temporary evacuation sites. Maybe if better organization took place and plans of action had been created, communicated, and implanted these evacuees would not have suffered as many did. Permanent placement should have been created so as not to have the evacuees shuttled from the Superdome to the Astrodome located in Houston, Texas. That type of living was not healthy. Many were exposed to tainted flood water and mosquito diseases. Many died of dehydration and exhaustion while medical staff was shorthanded and sometimes could not give proper medical care when needed. For these entities that received evacuees, they were given initial directions on receiving and temporarily housing evacuees, but received no further communication or direction on how to integrate this group back into society.

In this paragraph, the students show that they can see both sides of the issue.

FEMA has much to offer when it comes to serving disaster victims. FEMA's top priority is to provide disaster assistance to all individuals and communities who are eligible for the services. The agency works closely with federal, tribal, state, and local government and other agencies to integrate preparedness. It prepares to create an operational and preparedness plan and organizes incident management to train and certify staff in emergency management skill and techniques. FEMA also has disaster logistics, hazard mitigation, emergency and public disaster communications in place.

Several reports indicate of those who died, almost half were 75 or older. In an article written by the Associated Press, Chicago, *"elderly residents may have thought the warnings were a false alarm, feared that abandoning their homes would lead to looting, or who simply didn't want to leave their familiar surroundings for the unknown"* (Associated Press). In addition, older people are more vulnerable and frail and simply were unable to fight the massive storm. Why might the elderly have believed the warnings were a false alarm? In the wake of the aftermath, Joan Brunkard, lead author and researcher at the federal Centers for Disease Control and Prevention, was quoted as saying, "just shows us where we need to direct our disaster preparedness effort," and "we must reach these populations before, during, and after storms, and provide the assistance and reassurance they need to be willing to evacuate." It appears no one took the steps necessary to address the issues of the elderly during the evacuation process. This vulnerable group was quickly forgotten and as a result, made up the largest pool of victims.

Quotes from authorities and statistics provide evidence.

In a poll conducted by *Time* magazine, 57% blame the victims themselves, but according to an article written by Spencer S. Hsu in the *Washington Post* February 12, 2006, delays in ordering evacuations were revealed as the first order by the federal government to evacuate New Orleans was not issued until August 31 at 1:30 a.m. In addition to this delay, Louisiana politicians failed to prepare and make decisions regarding the 100,000 residents who they knew had no cars and relied on public transportation. "The city's failure (and not the victims) to complete its mandatory evacuation, ordered August 28, led to hundreds of deaths."

Further investigation condemned "hyped media coverage of violence and lawlessness for increasing security burdens, scaring away rescuers and heightening tension in the city." It was later determined few cases of gunshots and violence had been confirmed. Perhaps the "hyped" up media coverage also gave the elderly reason to believe their homes would be looted if they left. In addition to these findings, the investigation also revealed that when rescuers were needed, the National Guard was unavailable for rescue and security missions due to high numbers of deployment in Iraq.

Using highly technical communication methods is not the best solution for communicating important information, especially to vulnerable populations as those mentioned above. Groups that live in low income housing or reside in low socioeconomic areas may not have access to mainstream media. FEMA may believe they are in fact reaching these groups when in reality they may not own a television or radio or as was the case with the elderly, may believe the warnings are a false alarm. Having to regress to word of mouth, a written plan of evacuation, or having authority figures step in and take command is necessary. Great care and consideration must also be given before, during, and after a natural disaster in disseminating information such as a federally issued order to evacuate because the loss of telecommunications and electricity is inevitable.

The United States General Accounting Office provided a report to Congressional Requesters in 1993 titled *Disaster Management: Improving the Nation's Response to Catastrophic Disasters* in which several important points were made in light of responding to natural disasters (USGAO). It seems as though the report may have been disregarded as none of the information was taken into consideration in responding to Hurricane Katrina. Members of business team five endorse the report in addition to providing additional information on formulating the best solutions to assist these vulnerable populations during dire times.

Providing the funding and a written plan of action practiced by mock drills is absolutely necessary. Without the funding for food, shelter, transportation, and other essential services, preparing for a natural disaster and/or mass evacuation is highly unlikely. "Identifying quantities, locations, and transportation requirements for mass care supplies" should be made in advance regardless of the future disaster. In the El Paso area, for example, Fort Bliss military officials not dealing with matters of national security could assist our state, local, and federal law enforcement agencies in determining the best locations for temporary and even permanent shelters for people displaced as a result of a natural disaster. This requires oral and written communication that establishes a "command center" and commanding officer to take charge and direct the operation during a critical incident. The plan must be written, practiced in the form of mock drills and modified if necessary. In the event of telecommunications or electricity failures, a door-to-door method must be employed in order to alert and evacuate people much as is done during a SWAT call out. As tedious as this task may be, identifying those areas housing the highest volume of elderly and low socioeconomic populations *in advance* should be a priority and disseminating this information to all agencies involved should not be hindering or confusing, but rather carried out systematically if every agency involved knows what their role is.

Having the medical community, first responders and housing authority involved, particularly those who work in nursing homes and/or assisted living communities. Each entity should be required to implement a plan of action in anticipation of a storm or natural disaster. The housing authority should be able to provide statistics at any given time of those residing in government assisted residential properties and assist other agencies by sharing this information during a critical incident. The statistics should include, but not be limited too, the size of the families and ages of all members. If the property happens to house an elderly population, management should be aware and take special care in ensuring they are notified of mandatory orders to evacuate. Emergency contacts should be reviewed and updated on a regular basis for residents in nursing homes and/or assisted living communities and evacuation drills and/or fire drills should be conducted on a regular basis. Emergency contacts should be notified and asked to participate.

The medical community should have a proper and updated inventory of medical supplies, and occupancy should be checked in area hospitals on a continual basis. In addition, each member of the medical community should have the proper training in handling victims' care in a catastrophic situation. Each entity should be fully aware of the role each assumes during critical incidents and this requires a great deal of lateral communication.

Post Hurricane Katrina, the biggest resettlement in American history took place. According to an article written by Peter Grier for the *Christian Science Monitor*, the states which saw the largest numbers of evacuees were Arkansas with 50,000 and Texas with 200,000 in shelters and homes. "Many evacuees are putting down roots in new areas and say they'll never return." How do receiving communities proceed? Receiving communities such as Houston, Texas, and Baton Rouge, Louisiana, are concerned. They have seen an increase in crime, traffic, long lines at post offices, and empty grocery shelves. Some indicated they are worried refugees will take existing jobs. Not only are existing jobs a concern for the receiving communities, housing, legal aid, public schools, medical care and the rise in crime rates are also a concern. Once it is determined a number of displaced people will stay in a receiving community, incentives to improve their quality of life as well as the welfare of a receiving community should be offered. In addition, written communication and guidance should allow a receiving community to apply for federal grants that cover public housing and schooling, health care and additional law enforcement officers for a period not to exceed five years to ensure a fairly smooth integration of the displaced population into the new society. Adding conditions such as attending job training and/or continuing education classes in order to receive grant money only benefits everyone involved.

Our politicians can make a difference by communicating with all agencies at different levels and deploying resources such as law enforcement officers for security details and conveyances for those who do not have transportation. Congress must also guarantee reimbursement in advance for the reception of elderly into other area hospitals or assisted living centers and more importantly, taking into consideration to reach those who lack the latest technological advances.

Before, during, and after a massive storm such as Hurricane Katrina, a great deal of coordination is required between state, local, military, and federal officials. While the country does its best to *react* to such events, we should begin taking a *proactive* approach. Coordination requires an enormous amount of communication, both oral and written, to avoid confusion and lack of direction. As demonstrated by this natural disaster, the country was ill prepared for what ensued after the storm hit and many lives were lost as a result. The elderly, the poor, and those communities that received evacuees in particular suffered a great

The students begin to wrap up their evaluation of FEMA with a call to action.

deal. In the GAO Disaster Management Report, they found "inadequate damage and needs assessments, miscommunication, unclear legislative authority, and unprepared, untrained state and local responders" to be the most problematic with the federal strategy for catastrophic disasters. This is a clear indication of what we are up against in responding to a natural disaster and the need for improvement in this area is evident. Agencies should coordinate their efforts in advance and practice lateral and vertical communication. Practice by means of mock evacuation drills conditions the body to react in a time of need and this could be said of first responders or the average citizen who may need to evacuate their home one day.

Our country should resolve to avoid the previous mistakes made and resort to breaking down barriers. This includes barriers of communication, race, age and income. Together we can make a difference.

The students conclude with the statement that they drafted.

Works Cited

Associated Press. "Half of Katrina Victims Were 75 or Older."
      MSNBC, 28 Aug. 2008. Web. 16 Apr. 2009.

"Effects of Hurricane Katrina in New Orleans." *Wikipedia*.
      Wikimedia Foundation, April 2009. Web. 16 Apr. 2009.

Federal Emergency Management Agency/U.S. Department of
      Homeland Security (FEMA). "Home Page." FEMA, April 2009.
      Web. 16 Apr. 2009.

Grier, Peter. "The Great Katrina Migration." The Christian Science
      Monitor, 12 Sept. 2005. Web. 16 Apr. 2009.

Hsu, Spencer S. "Katrina Report Spreads Blame." *Washington
      Post*. The Washington Post, 12 Feb. 2006. Web. 16
      Apr. 2009.

"Poll Results: Hurricane Katrina." *Time*. TIME, 10 Sept. 2005.
      Web. 16 Apr. 2009.

United States General Accounting Office (USGAO). "*Disaster
      Management: Improving the Nation's Response to
      Catastrophic Disasters*." USGAO Archive, 23 July 1993. Web.
      16 Apr. 2009.

# ADDITIONAL READINGS

## When the Media Is the Disaster

### Rebecca Solnit

In this *Huffington Post* Internet newspaper article, Rebecca Solnit evaluates how media sensationalism interfered with rescue efforts in the aftermath of the earthquake in Haiti and Hurricane Katrina in New Orleans. By focusing on property rather than people, the media drew attention from survivors' needs during these disasters. Rebecca Solnit is a freelance writer who wrote a book, *A Paradise Built in Hell*, about Hurricane Katrina.

Soon after almost every disaster the crimes begin: ruthless, selfish, indifferent to human suffering, and generating far more suffering. The perpetrators go unpunished and live to commit further crimes against humanity. They care less for human life than for property. They act without regard for consequences.

I'm talking, of course, about those members of the mass media whose misrepresentation of what goes on in disaster often abets and justifies a second wave of disaster. I'm talking about the treatment of sufferers as criminals, both on the ground and in the news, and the endorsement of a shift of resources from rescue to property patrol. They still have blood on their hands from Hurricane Katrina, and they are staining themselves anew in Haiti.

Within days of the Haitian earthquake, for example, the *Los Angeles Times* ran a series of photographs with captions that kept deploying the word *looting*. One was of a man lying face down on the ground with this caption: A Haitian police officer ties up a suspected looter who was carrying a bag of evaporated milk. The man's sweaty face looks up at the camera, beseeching, anguished.

*Looters make off with rolls of fabric goods from an earthquake-wrecked store in downtown Port-au-Prince.*

Another photo was labeled: Looting continued in Haiti on the third day after the earthquake, although there were more police in downtown Port-au-Prince. It showed a somber crowd wandering amid shattered piles of concrete in a landscape where, visibly, there could be little worth taking anyway.

5   A third image was captioned: A looter makes off with rolls of fabric from an earthquake-wrecked store. Yet another: The body of a police officer lies in a Port-au-Prince street. He was accidentally shot by fellow police who mistook him for a looter.

People were then still trapped alive in the rubble. A translator for Australian TV dug out a toddler who'd survived 68 hours without food or water, orphaned but claimed by an uncle who had lost his pregnant wife. Others were hideously wounded and awaiting medical attention that wasn't arriving. Hundreds of thousands, maybe millions, needed, and still need, water, food, shelter, and first aid. The media in disaster bifurcates. Some step out of their usual objective roles to respond with kindness and practical aid. Others bring out the arsenal of clichés and pernicious myths and begin to assault the survivors all over again.

> **Bifurcates:** Divides into two parts.

The looter in the first photo might well have been taking that milk to starving children and babies, but for the news media that wasn't the most urgent problem. The looter stooped under the weight of two big bolts of fabric might well have been bringing it to now homeless people trying to shelter from a fierce tropical sun under improvised tents.

The pictures do convey desperation, but they **don't** convey crime. Except perhaps for that shooting of a fellow police officer—his colleagues were so focused on property that they were reckless when it came to human life, and a man died for no good reason in a landscape already saturated with death.

In recent days, there have been scattered accounts of confrontations involving weapons, and these may be a different matter. But the man with the powdered milk? Is he really a criminal? There may be more to know, but with what I've seen I'm not convinced.

## What Would You Do?

10   Imagine, reader, that your city is shattered by a disaster. Your home no longer exists, and you spent what cash was in your pockets days ago. Your credit cards are meaningless because there is no longer any power to run credit-card charges. Actually, there are no longer any storekeepers, any banks, any commerce, or much of anything to buy. The economy has ceased to exist.

By day three, you're pretty hungry and the water you grabbed on your way out of your house is gone. The thirst is far worse than the hunger. You can go for many days without food, but not water. And in the improvised encampment you settle in, there is an old man near you who seems on the edge of death. He no longer responds when you try to reassure him that this ordeal will surely end. Toddlers are now crying constantly, and their mothers infinitely stressed and distressed.

So you go out to see if any relief organization has finally arrived to distribute anything, only to realize that there are a million others like you stranded with nothing, and there isn't likely to be anywhere near enough aid anytime soon. The guy with the corner store has already given away all his goods to the neighbors. That supply's long gone by now. No wonder, when you see the chain pharmacy with the shattered windows or the supermarket, you don't think twice before grabbing a box of PowerBars and a few gallons of water that might keep you alive and help you save a few lives as well.

The old man might not die, the babies might stop their squalling, and the mothers might lose that look on their faces. Other people are calmly wandering in and helping themselves, too. Maybe they're people like you, and that gallon of milk the fellow near you has taken is going to spoil soon anyway. You haven't shoplifted since you were 14, and you have plenty of money to your name. But it doesn't mean anything now.

If you grab that stuff are you a criminal? Should you end up lying in the dirt on your stomach with a cop tying your hands behind your back? Should you end up labeled a looter in the international media? Should you be shot down in the street, since the overreaction in disaster, almost any disaster, often includes the imposition of the death penalty without benefit of trial for suspected minor property crimes?

15    Or are you a rescuer? Is the survival of disaster victims more important than the preservation of everyday property relations? Is that chain pharmacy more vulnerable, more a victim, more in need of help from the National Guard than you are, or those crying kids, or the thousands still trapped in buildings and soon to die?

It's pretty obvious what my answers to these questions are, but it isn't obvious to the mass media. And in disaster after disaster, at least since the San Francisco earthquake of 1906, those in power, those with guns and the force of law behind them, are too often more concerned for property than human life. In an emergency, people can, and do, die from those priorities. Or they get gunned down for minor thefts or imagined thefts. The media not only endorses such outcomes, but regularly, repeatedly, helps prepare the way for, and then eggs on, such a reaction.

## If Words Could Kill

We need to banish the word looting from the English language. It incites madness and obscures realities.

Loot, the noun and the verb, is a word of Hindi origin meaning the spoils of war or other goods seized roughly. As historian Peter Linebaugh points out, at one time loot was the soldier's pay. It entered the English language as a good deal of loot from India entered the English economy, both in soldiers' pockets and as imperial seizures.

After years of interviewing survivors of disasters, and reading first-hand accounts and sociological studies from such disasters as the London Blitz and the Mexico City earthquake of 1985, I don't believe in looting. Two things go on in disasters. The great majority of what happens you could call emergency requisitioning. Someone who could be you, someone in the kind of desperate circumstances I outlined above, takes necessary supplies to sustain human life in the absence of any alternative. Not only would I not call that looting, I wouldn't even call that theft.

20    Necessity is a defense for breaking the law in the United States and other countries, though it's usually applied more to, say, confiscating the car keys of a drunk driver than feeding hungry children. Taking things you don't need is theft under any circumstances. It is, says the disaster sociologist Enrico Quarantelli, who has been studying the subject for more than half a century, vanishingly rare in most disasters.

Personal gain is the last thing most people are thinking about in the aftermath of a disaster. In that phase, the survivors are almost invariably more altruistic and less attached to their own property, less concerned with the long-term questions of acquisition, status, wealth, and security, than just about anyone not in such situations imagines possible. (The best accounts from Haiti of how people with next to nothing have patiently tried to share the little they have and support those in even worse shape than them only emphasize this disaster reality.) Crime often drops in the wake of a disaster.

**Altruistic:** Considerate of others' needs.

The media are another matter. They tend to arrive obsessed with property (and the headlines that assaults on property can make). Media outlets often call everything looting and thereby incite hostility toward the sufferers as well as a hysterical overreaction on the part of the armed authorities. Or sometimes the journalists on the ground do a good job and the editors back in their safe offices cook up the crazy photo captions and the wrongheaded interpretations and emphases.

They also deploy the word *panic* wrongly. Panic among ordinary people in crisis is profoundly uncommon. The media will call a crowd of people running from certain death a panicking mob, even though running is the only sensible thing to do. In Haiti, they continue to report that food is being withheld from distribution for fear of stampedes. Do they think Haitians are cattle?

The belief that people in disaster (particularly poor and nonwhite people) are cattle or animals or just crazy and untrustworthy regularly justifies spending far too much energy and far too many resources on control—the American military calls it security—rather than relief. A

British-accented voiceover on CNN calls people sprinting to where supplies are being dumped from a helicopter a "stampede" and adds that this delivery risks sparking chaos. The chaos already exists, and you can't blame it on these people desperate for food and water. Or you can, and in doing so help convince your audience that they're unworthy and untrustworthy.

25     Back to looting: of course you can consider Haiti's dire poverty and failed institutions a long-term disaster that changes the rules of the game. There might be people who are not only interested in taking the things they need to survive in the next few days, but things they've never been entitled to own or things they may need next month. Technically that's theft, but I'm not particularly surprised or distressed by it; the distressing thing is that even before the terrible quake they led lives of deprivation and desperation.

In ordinary times, minor theft is often considered a misdemeanor. No one is harmed. Unchecked, minor thefts could perhaps lead to an environment in which there were more thefts and so forth, and a good argument can be made that, in such a case, the tide needs to be stemmed. But it's not particularly significant in a landscape of terrible suffering and mass death.

A number of radio hosts and other media personnel are still upset that people apparently took TVs after Hurricane Katrina hit New Orleans in August 2005. Since I started thinking about, and talking to people about, disaster aftermaths I've heard a lot about those damned TVs. Now, which matters more to you, televisions or human life? People were dying on rooftops and in overheated attics and freeway overpasses, they were stranded in all kinds of hideous circumstances on the Gulf Coast in 2005 when the mainstream media began to obsess about looting, and the mayor of New Orleans and the governor of Louisiana made the decision to focus on protecting property, not human life.

A gang of white men on the other side of the river from New Orleans got so worked up about property crimes that they decided to take the law into their own hands and began shooting. They seem to have considered all black men criminals and thieves and shot a number of them. Some apparently died; there were bodies bloating in the September sun far from the region of the floods; one good man trying to evacuate the ruined city barely survived; and the media looked away. It took me months of nagging to even get the story covered. This vigilante gang claimed to be protecting property, though its members never demonstrated that their property was threatened. They boasted of killing black men. And they shared values with the mainstream media and the Louisiana powers that be.

**Vigilante:** A self-appointed group to fight crime.

Somehow, when the Bush administration subcontracted emergency services—like providing evacuation buses in Hurricane Katrina—to cronies who profited even while providing incompetent, overpriced, and much delayed service at the moment of greatest urgency, we didn't label that looting.

30    Or when a lot of wealthy Wall Street brokers decide to tinker with a basic human need like housing. . . . Well, you catch my drift.

Woody Guthrie once sang that some will rob you with a six-gun, and some with a fountain pen. The guys with the six-guns (or machetes or sharpened sticks) make for better photographs, and the guys with the fountain pens not only don't end up in jail, they end up in McMansions with four-car garages and, sometimes, in elected—or appointed—office.

## Learning to See in Crises

Last Christmas a priest, Father Tim Jones of York, started a ruckus in Britain when he said in a sermon that shoplifting by the desperate from chain stores might be acceptable behavior. Naturally, there was an uproar. Jones told the Associated Press: The point I'm making is that when we shut down every socially acceptable avenue for people in need, then the only avenue left is the socially unacceptable one.

The response focused almost entirely on why shoplifting is wrong, but the claim was also repeatedly made that it doesn't help. In fact, food helps the hungry, a fact so bald it's bizarre to even have to state it. The means by which it arrives is a separate matter. The focus remained on shoplifting, rather than on why there might be people so desperate in England's green and pleasant land that shoplifting might be their only option, and whether unnecessary human suffering is itself a crime of sorts.

Right now, the point is that people in Haiti need food, and for all the publicity, the international delivery system has, so far, been a visible dud. Under such circumstances, breaking into a U.N. food warehouse—food assumedly meant for the poor of Haiti in a catastrophic moment—might not be violence, or looting, or law-breaking. It might be logic. It might be the most effective way of meeting a desperate need.

35    Why were so many people in Haiti hungry before the earthquake? Why do we have a planet that produces enough food for all and a distribution system that ensures more than a billion of us don't have a decent share of that bounty? Those are not questions whose answers should be long delayed.

Even more urgently, we need compassion for the sufferers in Haiti and media that tell the truth about them. I'd like to propose alternative captions for those *Los Angeles Times* photographs as models for all future disasters:

Let's start with the picture of the policeman hogtying the figure whose face is so anguished: Ignoring thousands still trapped in rubble, a policeman accosts a sufferer who took evaporated milk. No adequate food distribution exists for Haiti's starving millions.

And the guy with the bolt of fabric? As with every disaster, ordinary people show extraordinary powers of improvisation, and fabrics such as these are being used to make sun shelters around Haiti.

For the murdered policeman: Institutional overzealousness about protecting property leads to a gratuitous murder, as often happens in crises. Meanwhile countless people remain trapped beneath crushed buildings.

40 And the crowd in the rubble labeled looters? How about: Resourceful survivors salvage the means of sustaining life from the ruins of their world.

That one might not be totally accurate, but it's likely to be more accurate than the existing label. And what is absolutely accurate, in Haiti right now, and on Earth always, is that human life matters more than property, that the survivors of a catastrophe deserve our compassion and our understanding of their plight, and that we live and die by words and ideas, and it matters desperately that we get them right.

## Reflect on the Reading

1. Authors use irony to convey the *opposite* meaning of the literal words on the page. How does Solnit use irony in her introduction? Is it effective?

2. What is Solnit's judgment of the media's coverage of Haiti and Katrina? At what point in the review do you know her opinion?

3. What evidence does she provide to convince you to agree with her judgment? How persuasive is her evidence?

4. What opposition to her viewpoint does she acknowledge? How does she address this opposition?

5. In her conclusion, Solnit states, "We live and die by words and ideas, and it matters desperately that we get them right." What does she mean by this?

## Consider Your Viewpoint

1. Do you agree with Solnit's judgment of the media's coverage of disasters? Why or why not?

2. Can you think of other examples of where the media has sensationalized an event and, as a result, harmed people? Explain your answer.

3. What justifications does Solnit give for people looting during a disaster? Do you agree with her that it is justified and so shouldn't be punished?

4. Do you agree with Solnit when she says, " . . . human life matters more than property . . . ?" Are there any situations in which property could be more important?

# Why I Still Watch *Lost*

## Bao Phi

Bao Phi originally published this piece on the *Star Tribune's* Your Voices blog. He is a performance poet, one who writes poetry that he can perform in public. This blog posting, however, is a departure from his poetry. Instead, he evaluates the TV program *Lost* and its depiction of Asians.

For much of my adult life, I didn't watch television. Except for the *Simpsons* and *X-Files*, I had not been a big fan of television since my early addictions to *Robotech, Reading Rainbow,* and *Transformers.* I missed out on shows that a lot of my peers seemed to be into, like *Cheers, Seinfeld, Friends, The Cosby Show* and *The Fresh Prince.* Mostly because I didn't have time to dedicate myself to a weekly viewing schedule, and I hated the idea of missing an episode if I did happen to fall in love with a series. Added to this my growing unease with the lack of, or problematic depictions of, Asians and Asian Americans in media, and television became a pop culture blind spot I was more than willing to have.

With the invention of the DVD and being able to rent series from the video store, I began to rent shows and see what I had been missing. One show that was getting considerable buzz in the Asian American community was *Lost.* Until I started hearing murmurs from my peers about the show, I had dismissed it as that show about being stranded on an island starring that hobbit from *Lord of the Rings.* But some very impassioned community members kept arguing about how great the writing was, the fantastic premise, and above all, the nuanced characters played by Daniel Dae Kim and Yunjin Kim. Despite all the positive buzz, I couldn't quite believe it.

Asian Americans have good reason to be skeptical, when it comes to representation in film and television. You either get racially or, if Asians are portrayed at all, it's usually as a male martial arts villain/punching dummy for a Caucasian hero, or a female victim in need of love and being saved from her war-torn homeland/her oppressive patriarchical culture by a white knight. Pun intended. Even in shows like *E.R.,* where you'd think since it was based in Chicago hospitals that there'd be lots of Asians, there were just a token one or two. You know those online quizzes where you answer a series of questions and it tells you what character you'd be on a television show or movie? I don't take those quizzes, because usually "Asian delivery boy #2" is not one of the outcomes.

Patriarchical: From *patriarchy,* a culture where men are in charge.

What's especially perplexing is the failure of American media, mainstream and alternative, to mention issues of race and representation when it comes to Asians. As a person who reads pop culture reviews from Roger Ebert to the Onion's AV Club to local papers such as the *Star Tribune* or *City Pages,* seldom have I found any American reviewer or commentator, regardless of race or gender, mention issues of representation when it comes to Asians and Asian Americans. From movies like *The Painted Veil* where Asians are relegated to mere backdrop, to films like *Rambo* and *The Last Samurai* where a white hero is inserted to save/slaughter Asians, to pop culture blockbuster shows like *Battlestar Gallactica* with its loaded and problematic Asian female character, to films like *21* and *Avatar: The Last Airbender*, where Asians are outright replaced by whites, one cannot find many instances where reviewers and commentators think race regarding Asians and Asian Americans is worth mentioning or discussing.

5    To be honest, the first few episodes of *Lost* didn't help the cause. Here was a patriarchal, abusive and domineering Korean husband and his docile Korean wife, two characters seemingly tailor-made for that type of condescending, patronizing and self-congratulatory first-world liberation story that seems so popular in Hollywood. There was also the problematic depiction of the Iraqi character Sayid, played by Naveen Andrews, and though he is a thoroughly amazing actor and his presence brings the number of primary Asian cast members in the show to an unprecedented *three*(!), there was that nagging feeling that maybe the role should have gone to an Iraqi or at least Arab actor, and the fact that the dude was a torturer didn't exactly break any stereotypes.

Behest: An urgent request.

But at the behest of my peers, I stuck with the series and dutifully plowed through season 1, DVD after DVD even though many of the early episodes honestly made me cringe, and *still* make me cringe: Jin slapping Sun's hand, Sun strutting in a bathing suit as if it was the most liberating act in the world (considering how men and women dress in Seoul, which is where Jin and Sun are supposedly from, one wonders if a bathing suit is really a big deal). And then there was the show's embarrassing (though thankfully brief) depiction of the antagonism between Jin and one of the few Black male characters in the show, Michael (played by Harold Perrineau). In an episode, the show hints at a chemistry between Sun and Michael, a sub-plot that would continue through several episodes. In that same episode, Jin violently attacks Michael, and later Michael violently retaliates against Jin. At one point Michael tells his son Walt that, where he comes from, Koreans do not like Black people. Of course the Asians get no say in this matter. These superficial and sensationalized depictions of race and gender conflict struck me as irresponsible and tired. To tell you the truth, it all seemed quite dreadful, and I hurried through season 1 waiting for the drastic turnaround that my community members promised me would be there if I was just patient.

It was a long time later, in the penultimate episode of season 1, where at last the character arcs of Jin, Sun, and Sayid finally allowed them to be thoroughly complicated, and sympathetic characters. But what a punishing ordeal the makers of *Lost* made us endure for, finally, an earned moment of beauty and a kiss between two Asian characters on prime time American television. If at this point you would accuse me of being nauseatingly hetero, let me ask you to put this in context: in your viewing of American television and film, how often have you seen two Asian characters kiss? Now compare that number to everyone else. See?

> Penultimate: Next to the last.

Maybe that's why since then I've become, and have remained, a loyal but critical *Lost* fan. Things have gotten better regarding representation. Sayid has emerged as one of the most compelling characters in television, and is by far the most sympathetic Iraqi character in American pop culture. Daniel Dae Kim and Yunjin Kim have garnered critical acclaim for bringing their nuanced and well-loved characters to life. The addition of the great Ken Leung bumps the number of primary Asian cast members up to four. Four! For those of you who are laughing, imagine how rough it must be for Asian American viewers, let alone Asian American actors, if an American show with four Asian and Asian American major cast members is a lot. It is, in fact, a ton. Add to that number the supporting character Pierre Chang (played by Francois Chau) and you have one of the largest Asian casts in popular American television history. One of my fellow *Lost* viewers reminded me of a wonderful scene in season 5 with Jin, Miles, Pierre, and Hurley—perhaps one of the few scenes in pop American culture featuring four men of color that was at once well-written, funny, and effortless.

"*Lost* is significant in that it proved that it was not only possible to conceive a show with a large, diverse, well-rounded cast of characters, but you could also make it intelligent and challenging—and people would watch it," remarks Phil Yu, creator of the insightful pop culture website Angry Asian Man (angryasianman.com) and *Lost* fan. "Yes, America will watch Asians on TV! Both subtitled and English-speaking Asians alike."

10    It is telling that, at a moment in time where we are told that race doesn't matter anymore, *Lost* has a substantial following amongst Asian Americans. Sure, it may not be the only reason many of us watch *Lost*, but it also cannot be denied that the large number of complex, sympathetic Asian characters on the show has something to do with our loyalty.

At the same time, there's still plenty of room for improvement. There is still a shortage of other characters of color in the show, and while I applaud the relatively large number of Asian actors, It'd be great if they were joined by actors from other communities of color. The newer actors introduced in recent years, such as Michelle Rodriguez, Adewale

Akinnuoye-Agbaje, Said Taghmaoui, and the ill-fated Kiele Sanchez and Rodrigo Santoro, have for some reason or other have had bad "luck," shall we say, with the show and its fans.

And aspects of the Asian characters as well as other characters of color sometime toe the line towards stereotype. Season 3's episode *Stranger in a Strange Land*, guest starring Bai Ling, manages to portray every ugly stereotype of a Southeast Asian country as seen through a white male tourist—and not in a way that was remotely critical or even interesting.

Some aspects of the character Sayid remain troubling. "Sayid's career as a torturer reinforces the idea that violence comes naturally to him, and thus much of his character is to redeem himself as a 'good Arab'—one that works for the good of all people," observes University of Minnesota grad student and *Lost* fan Charlotte Karem Albrecht. "Clearly, the show tries to complicate this stereotype, but because Sayid's violent past still keeps popping up in ways that signal he has to control violent impulses, it seems to be linked to the notion of an inherently violent culture or an inherently violent essence, which because he is Muslim and Arab are presented as one in the same."

And it doesn't escape me that bad-boy white heartthrob to middle America, Sawyer, reserves his racial quips for the Asians (sure, he makes fun of everybody, but he doesn't make fun of everybody *racially*).

15    But my loyalty and hope for *Lost,* as well as greater change, can be compared to one of my favorite scenes in the entire series, the last episode of season 1. By that episode, Losties had seen 24 hour-long episodes of back-story, drama, and lots and lots of characters with daddy issues. There was a smoke monster that liked to munch on tourists, a mysterious band of enemies known enigmatically as the others, the deaths of several castaways, and a long and well-earned reunifying kiss (yay!). But then, seemingly out of nowhere, there is a simple montage scene set to music, of all the characters getting onto the plane before it takes off and flies them to their fate. There's Charlie trying to stuff his guitar into a closet, there's Hurley with a Spanish-language comic book, there's Sayid trying to stay cool as a white dude looks at him wordlessly and assumes he's a terrorist. This simple, effective scene seems to urge us to pause and examine a moment, getting onto a plane, that many of us take for granted, that could change our lives forever. It's a bittersweet moment illuminating that many of our lives are connected in ways we don't even understand, that our lives can be connected in ways both beautiful and tragic. So even if a blog about a show like *Lost* at this moment seems trivial, superficial, and unnecessary, it's my hope that it has its own place in this mundane moment and may one day lead to something quite fantastic.

Or at least, a bunker full of Dharma ranch dip and some Apollo bars.

**Mundane:** Ordinary or commonplace.

## Reflect on the Reading

1. What reasons does Phi give for not having watched much TV as an adult? Does this disqualify him from evaluating a TV show? Why or why not?

2. What is Phi's judgment of *Lost*? Why is he willing to watch this TV show?

3. What evidence does Phi provide to show that Asians are stereotyped in most TV shows? What evidence does he provide that Asians are not stereotyped on *Lost*?

4. Why does Phi believe that *Lost* is a good TV show? What improvements would he still like to see in *Lost*?

5. What is Phi referring to in his closing sentence, "Or at least, a bunker full of Dharma ranch dip and some Apollo bars?"

## Consider Your Viewpoint

1. Have you watched the TV show *Lost*? If you have, do you agree with Phi's evaluation of the show? Why or why not?

2. What other criteria could Phi have used to evaluate this show? Explain your answer. What is your favorite TV show? Describe the criteria you use to evaluate TV shows.

3. Phi says, "It is telling that, at a moment in time where we are told that race doesn't matter anymore, *Lost* has a substantial following amongst Asian Americans." What does Phi mean by this sentence? Do you agree or disagree that "race doesn't matter anymore"?

4. What is the significance of the *Lost* airplane scene, according to Phi?

---

For support in meeting this chapter's objectives, follow this path in MyCompLab: Resources ⇒ Writing ⇒ Writing Purposes ⇒ Writing to Evaluate. Review the Instruction and Multimedia resources about writing to evaluate, then complete the Exercises and click on Gradebook to measure your progress.

mycomplab

# CHAPTER

# 10 Arguing a Position

## Learning Objectives

In this chapter you will:

- write an argument with a convincing claim, reasons, and evidence.
- avoid logical fallacies.
- use logos, pathos, and ethos effectively.

Political opponents Barack Obama and John McCain shaking hands

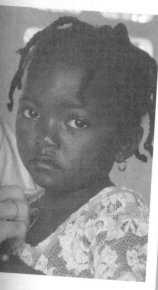

When you think of an argument, you might imagine a dispute between spouses or a television personality railing against a political opponent. However, an argument can also be a rational discussion between well-informed people that leads to mutual agreement or compromise. The American philosopher and rhetorician Kenneth Burke focused on argument as a way for people to understand each other better, which can lead to everything from happier relationships to world peace. Arguments range from the everyday, such as when you convince a friend to not drive drunk, to the momentous, as when congressional leaders debate major legislation. In this chapter you'll learn the basic frameworks of written arguments so that you can argue a position that will lead to a beneficial effect.

## WRITING TO ARGUE A POSITION

To argue a position, consider the range of convictions that you hold. These convictions can be related to your everyday life: Should college tuition continue to increase? Should contributions to political campaigns by corporations be limited? Should your employer be forced to provide health insurance? Should schoolteachers be allowed more freedom in the classroom? They can also concern regional, national, or international issues, such as immigration, banking regulation, or climate change. You'll research multiple sides of the issue that you select in order to understand all viewpoints, and then you'll make and justify your claim. Your primary purpose is persuasive: You are trying to get readers who disagree with you or who are neutral about the topic to see the validity of your perspective. To be persuasive, you'll need to be well-informed about the topic so that you can present information that supports your ideas. If you have personal experience with the topic, you can provide that as well as information that you learned from experts.

*If you wish to win a man over to your ideas, first make him your friend.*

*—Abraham Lincoln*

> ## Questions for Arguing a Position
>
> - What position will I argue?
> - Is my position reasonable?
> - Will some people agree with me and others disagree?
> - What kind of information will I need to justify my claim?
> - What might my audience already know about this topic, and what information do I need to provide them?
> - Which genre and visual design will be most suitable for convincing my audience?
> - What constraints might prevent me from writing an effective argument?

# MODEL ARGUMENTS THAT TAKE POSITIONS

Arguments take a variety of forms, depending on the writer's audience, purpose, and context. The following arguments demonstrate different strategies to consider.

## Why Greens Must Learn to Love Nuclear Power

### Mark Lynas

In the following column from the British magazine *New Statesman,* originally published in 2008, columnist and environmental activist Mark Lynas directly addresses "greens," or his fellow environmentalists, telling them that nuclear power should be part of the answer to global climate change. This position on nuclear power contradicts one of the long-held convictions in the environmental movement that nuclear power is too dangerous. Because of this controversial opinion, Lynas assumes his readers will disagree with him, and he structures his argument accordingly.

*Steam rises from a nuclear power plant.*

"If nuclear power is the answer, it must have been a pretty stupid question," went an oft-cited slogan of the 1970s environmental movement. But the question was not stupid, and it is even less so today when the challenge is even blunter: how are we going to provide for our energy needs in a way that does not destroy, via global warming, the capacity of our planet to support life? The hard truth is that if nuclear power is not at least part of the answer, then answering that challenge is going to be very difficult indeed.

Unfortunately, just by writing the sentence above, I will already have prompted many readers to switch off. Being anti-nuclear is an article of faith (and I use that word intentionally) for many people in today's environmental movement and beyond, just as it was during the 1970s. That the Green Party, Friends of the Earth and Greenpeace have held the same position on the subject for 30 years could show admirable consistency—but it could also be evidence of dogmatic closed-mindedness.

> Dogmatic: Opinionated.

When I first broached the issue in these pages three years ago, the reaction was extraordinary. A close acquaintance sent me a tearful email saying that I had "destroyed" her motivation for environmental campaigning. Other friends here in Oxford accused me—jokingly, of course—of having formed a romantic liaison with BNFL's spokeswoman. Just last week, after tackling the subject once again, I received a one-line email from a well-known environmentalist accusing me of having "done a considerable disservice to the cause of combating climate change."

> Broached: Mentioned for the first time.

> BNFL: British Nuclear Fuels Limited.

So why does the nuclear issue evoke such strong reactions? For answers, I think we need to look to nuclear's past, when today's entrenched positions were first formed. Civil nuclear power began life as a heavily state-subsidised industry largely designed to produce plutonium for bombs. Civil nuclear power was part of the military-industrial complex and shrouded in secrecy. An association with the mushroom cloud has tainted the nuclear industry ever since—and clearly continues to be an issue in countries such as Iran, North Korea and Pakistan.

> Subsidised: The British spelling for "subsidized." This column contains other British spellings, such as "programme" instead of "program."

5    Then there is radiation. Most people are terrified of radiation precisely because it is invisible, making it all the more threatening, and because of its potential to cause cancer and genetic deformities. (Many other cancer-causing agents such as food or smoke seem innocuous by comparison.) Nuclear accidents and near-meltdowns—such as Three Mile Island in 1979—provoke scary headlines throughout the media, as did popular treatments such as the film *The China Syndrome* (released, by an extraordinary stroke of luck for the film-makers, just 12 days before Three

Mile Island), in which a sinister nuclear cabal covers up evidence of an accident.

It is undeniable that nuclear fission generates radioactive by-products, some of which will inevitably enter the environment. It is also undeniable that exposure to radiation increases the risk of cancer (though radiation can also be employed to treat cancers). But it is the level of risk that counts, and here the story is less fearsome than many would have us believe. Take Three Mile Island, which exposed local populations to one millirem of radiation on average. This equates to roughly what we all receive from natural sources (cosmic rays and naturally occurring radioactive elements in the ground) every four days. The number of deaths from Three Mile Island—the worst civil nuclear accident ever in a western country, and one that ended the U.S. nuclear programme (not a single reactor has been built since)—is therefore officially estimated to be zero.

Even Chernobyl, surely the worst-imaginable case for a nuclear disaster, was far less deadly than most people think. In the immediate aftermath of the explosion, 28 people died due to acute radiation sickness—all firemen and power plant workers, some of whom had been exposed to radiation doses as high as one million millirems. By comparison, 167 men were killed during the Piper Alpha disaster on a North Sea oil rig in 1988. But it is the long-term effects from Chernobyl that tend to scare people most. In a 2006 report, Greenpeace claimed that "60,000 people have additionally died in Russia because of the Chernobyl accident, and estimates of the total death toll for the Ukraine and Belarus could reach another 140,000."

These figures, if correct, would make Chernobyl one of the worst single man-made disasters of the last century. But are they correct? The United Nations Scientific Committee on the Effects of Atomic Radiation reports 4,000 cases of thyroid cancer in children and young people in Belarus, Russia and Ukraine, but very few deaths (thyroid cancer is mostly treatable). Indeed, it concludes, "There is no evidence of a major public health impact attributable to radiation exposure 20 years after the accident," and no evidence of any increase in cancer or leukaemia among exposed populations. The World Health Organisation concludes that while a few thousand deaths may be caused over the next 70 years by Chernobyl's radioactive release, this number "will be indiscernible from the background of overall deaths in the large population group." Without wishing to downplay the tragedy for the victims—especially the 300,000 people who were evacuated permanently—the explosion has even been good for wildlife, which has thrived in the 30km exclusion zone.

## A Plentiful Supply of Free Fuel

One way of statistically assessing the safety of nuclear power versus other technologies is to use the measure of deaths per gigawatt-year. This technique is cited by Cambridge University's Professor David MacKay in his book *Sustainable Energy—Without the Hot Air* (available free on the web), and shows that in Europe, nuclear and wind power are the safest technologies (about 0.1 death per GWy), while oil, coal and biomass the most dangerous (above 1 per GWy).

10      A focus on statistics is also useful when assessing the financial costs of nuclear power. The high price for nuclear waste disposal and decommissioning—with a hefty chunk always payable from public funds—is surely one of the environmental lobby's strongest arguments, particularly if any subsidy from taxpayers means taking money away from investment in renewables. Helen Caldicott's book *Nuclear Power Is Not the Answer* discusses the finances of nuclear under a chapter subheaded "Socialised Electricity," quoting figures for nuclear's subsidy in the U.S. over recent decades of $70bn. To make a direct cost comparison, the International Energy Agency in a 2005 study looked at life-cycle costs for all power sources—including construction costs, operations, fuel and decommissioning—and concluded that nuclear was the cheapest option, followed by coal, wind and gas.

But how about nuclear power's potential contribution to mitigating global warming? One persistent myth is that once construction and uranium mining are taken into account, nuclear is no better than fossil fuels. However, according to the Intergovernmental Panel on Climate Change (IPCC), total life-cycle greenhouse-gas emission per unit of electricity is about 40g $CO_2$-equivalent per kilowatt-hour, "similar to those for renewable energy sources."

But why not ditch nuclear and focus only on renewables, as the greens suggest? MacKay calculates that even if we covered the windiest 10 percent of the UK with wind turbines, put solar panels on all south-facing roofs, implemented strong energy efficiency measures across the economy, built offshore wind turbines across an area of sea two-thirds the size of Wales, and fully exploited every other conceivable source of renewables (including wave and tidal power), energy production would still not match current consumption.

This is rather different to Britain being the "Saudi Arabia of wind power" as many in the environmental movement are fond of asserting. Indeed, MacKay concludes that we will need to import renewable electricity from other countries—primarily from solar farms in the North African desert—or choose nuclear, or both. Indeed, it is vital to stress that neither I nor MacKay nor any credible expert suggests a choice between renewables and nuclear: the sensible conclusion is that we need both, soon, and on a large scale if we are to phase out coal and other fossil fuels as rapidly as the climate needs. As MacKay told me: "We need to get building."

The UK's Sustainable Development Commission, in its 2006 report on nuclear power, argued that new plants should be ruled out until the existing waste problem could be solved. But what if a new generation of nuclear plants could be designed that, instead of producing more waste to leave as a toxic legacy for our grandchildren, actually generated energy by burning up existing waste stockpiles? This is the solution proposed by Tom Blees, a U.S.-based writer, in his upcoming book *Prescription for the Planet*. Blees focuses particularly on so-called fourth-generation nuclear technology—better known as fast-breeder reactors. While conventional thermal reactors use less than 1 percent of the potential energy in their uranium fuel, fast-breeders are 60 times more efficient, and can burn virtually all of the energy available in the uranium ore.

15     This gives these fourth-generation reactors a big advantage. As Blees puts it: "Thus we have a prodigious supply of free fuel that is actually even better than free, for it is material that we are quite desperate to get rid of." Moreover, fast-breeder reactors can also run on the "depleted" uranium left behind by conventional reactors, and help reduce the proliferation threat by burning up plutonium stockpiles left over from decommissioned nuclear weapons. Blees estimates that supplies of nuclear waste and depleted uranium are sufficient to "provide all the power needs of the entire planet for hundreds of years before we need to mine any more uranium." Although these reactors produce plutonium—which might be used for nuclear weapons, and could therefore pose a proliferation threat—weapons-grade material is never isolated in the fuel-cycle process, making fast-breeders less dangerous to international stability than conventional reactors, and relatively simple to inspect.

But what about the waste these reactors themselves produce? Since the by-products of fast-breeder reactors are highly radioactive, they have much shorter half-lives—rendering them inert in a couple of centuries, instead of the longer time over which conventional nuclear waste remains dangerous. (Once again there is a powerful myth here—that high-level waste from reactors remains dangerous for enormous lengths of time. Greenpeace states that "waste will remain dangerous for up to a million years." In fact, almost all waste will have decayed back to a level of radioactivity less than the original uranium ore in less than a thousand years.) Fourth-generation nuclear technology is also inherently safer than earlier designs. The Integral Fast Reactor (IFR), discussed at length by Blees, operates at atmospheric pressure, reducing the possibility of leaks and loss-of-coolant accidents. It is also designed to be "walk-away safe," meaning that if all operators stood up and left, the reactor would shut itself down automatically rather than overheat and suffer a meltdown.

So why, given the purported advantages in safety and fuel use, have fast-breeders not been developed commercially? The U.S. Integral Fast Reactor programme was shut down in 1994, possibly—Blees suggests—because of political pressure levied on the Clinton administration by anti-nuclear campaigners. (Even so, fourth-generation nuclear power plants are being built in India, Russia, Japan and China.) Ironically, the Clinton administration may have inadvertently killed off one of the most promising solutions to global warming in an attempt to please environmentalists. Even if the decision were to be reversed immediately, 20 years has been lost.

It is worth remembering the contribution that nuclear power has already made to offsetting global warming: the world's 442 operating nuclear reactors, which produce 16 percent of global electricity, save 2.2 billion tonnes of carbon dioxide per year compared to coal, according to the IPCC. Blees agrees that "the most pressing issue is to shut down all coal-fired power plants" and urges a "Manhattan Project-like" effort to convert the world's non-renewable power to IFRs by the thousand. This sounds daunting but it is not unprecedented: France converted its power supply to 80 percent nuclear in the space of just 25 years by building about six reactors a year.

An anti-nuclear report published by the Oxford Research Group in 2007 concluded that an additional 2,500 reactors would need to be built by 2075 to significantly mitigate global warming. The report's authors suggested that this was a "pipe-dream." But it sounds eminently achievable to me, given that it is only a five-times increase from today. The question is this: are those who care about global warming prepared to reconsider their opposition to nuclear power in this new era? We are no longer living in the 1970s. Today, the world is more threatened even than it was during the Cold War. Only this time nuclear power—instead of being part of the problem—can be part of the solution.

# One Word Spotlight

**Mushroom cloud** (paragraph 4) is a reference to the cloud of smoke, dust, and debris that follows an explosion, in particular a nuclear explosion. Shaped like a mushroom, such clouds often are associated with the terror and destruction that follows a nuclear bomb. The symbol of the mushroom cloud was famously invoked in 2003 by Dr. Condoleezza Rice, President Bush's National Security Advisor, about the possibility of Saddam Hussein having a nuclear weapon: "We don't want the smoking gun to be a mushroom cloud."

## Reflect on the Reading

1. What is Lynas's main point (or claim), and where is it stated?

2. Who is Lynas's audience, and why does he assume that many readers will disagree with him?

3. The author begins several paragraphs with questions, such as this one from paragraph 11, "But how about nuclear power's potential contribution to mitigating global warming?" Why does he use this strategy to begin these paragraphs?

4. Throughout his argument Lynas describes the views of environmentalists toward nuclear power in the 1970s. How well does he support his perspective that these views are no longer valid?

5. In this piece Lynas describes the destruction caused by the nuclear plant Chernobyl in the 1980s. How well does this information help the author support his claim?

## Consider Your Viewpoint

1. What opinion, if any, about the safety and feasibility of nuclear power did you have before you read this piece?

2. Were you persuaded by the author's argument by the time you finished reading the piece? Explain your answer.

3. What was the author's strongest supporting point or evidence in this piece? What was the weakest? Explain your answer.

4. To what extent do you identity with the environmentalist (or "green") movement? How did this identification (or lack of identification) affect your reaction to this piece?

5. In your view, how important is the issue of climate change when you compare it to other pressing international issues, such as poverty and war?

# You Have No Friends

## Farhad Manjoo

Facebook and other social media sites have grown popular within an amazingly short period of time—just a few years. In contrast, the newly invented landline telephone, which was patented in 1876, took decades before it became common in U.S. households. Social media has its fans and its detractors— on the one hand, it has made communication amazingly easy,

*Facebook homepage.*

but on the other hand it can suck up your time and make your private information widely available. In "You Have No Friends," published in 2009, Farhad Manjoo, a technology columnist for the online magazine *Slate*, addresses the concerns of Facebook skeptics.

---

At 1:37 a.m. on Jan. 8, Mark Zuckerberg, the 24-year-old founder and CEO of Facebook, posted a message on the company's blog with news of a milestone: The site had just added its 150-millionth member. Facebook now has users on every continent, with half of them logging in at least once a day. "If Facebook were a country, it would be the eighth most populated in the world, just ahead of Japan, Russia and Nigeria," Zuckerberg wrote. This People's Republic of Facebook would also have a terrible population-growth problem. Like most communications networks, Facebook obeys classic network-effects laws: It gets better—more useful, more entertaining—as more people join it, which causes it to grow even faster still. It was just last August that Facebook hit 100 million users. Since then, an average of 374,000 people have signed up every day. At this rate, Facebook will grow to nearly 300 million people by this time next year.

If you're reading this article, there's a good chance you already belong to Facebook. There's a good chance everyone you know is on Facebook, too. Indeed, there's a good chance you're no longer reading this article because you just switched over to check Facebook. That's fine—this piece is not for you. Instead I'd like to address those readers who aren't on Facebook, especially those of you who've consciously decided to stay away.

Though your ranks dwindle daily, there are many of you. This is understandable—any social movement that becomes so popular so fast engenders skepticism. A year ago, the *New York Observer* interviewed a half-dozen or so disdainful Facebook holdouts. "I don't see how having hundreds or thousands of 'friends' is leading to any kind of substantive friendships," said Cary Goldstein, the director of publicity at Twelve Publishers. "The whole thing seems so weird to me. Now you really have to turn off your computer and just go out to live real life and make real connections with people that way. I don't think it's healthy." I was reminded of a quote from an *Onion* story, "Area Man Constantly Mentioning He Doesn't Own a Television": "I'm not an elitist. It's just that I'd much rather sculpt or write in my journal or read Proust than sit there passively staring at some phosphorescent screen."

Friends—can I call you friends?—it's time to drop the attitude: There is no longer any good reason to avoid Facebook. The site has crossed a threshold—it is now so widely trafficked that it's fast becoming a routine aid to social interaction, like e-mail and antiperspirant. It's only the most recent of many new technologies that have crossed over this stage. For a long while—from about the late '80s to the late-middle '90s, *Wall Street* to *Jerry Maguire*—carrying a mobile phone seemed like a haughty affectation. But as more people got phones, they became more useful for everyone— and then one day enough people had cell phones that everyone began to assume that you did, too. Your friends stopped prearranging where they would meet up on Saturday night because it was assumed that everyone would call from wherever they were to find out what was going on. From that moment on, it became an affectation *not* to carry a mobile phone; they'd grown so deeply entwined with modern life that the only reason to be without one was to make a statement by abstaining. Facebook is now at that same point—whether or not you intend it, you're saying something by staying away.

> Affectation: Pretense.

5   I use Facebook every day, and not always to waste time. Most of my extended family lives in South Africa, and though I speak to them occasionally on the phone, Facebook gives me an astonishingly intimate look at their lives—I can see what they did yesterday, what they're doing tomorrow, and what they're doing right now, almost like there's no distance separating us. The same holds true for my job: I live on the West Coast, but I work in an industry centered on the East Coast; Facebook gives me the opportunity to connect with people—to "network," you might say—in a completely natural, unaggressive manner. More than a

dozen times, I've contacted sources through Facebook—searching for them there is much easier than searching for a current e-mail or phone number.

In fact, Facebook helped me write this story. The other day I posted a status update asking my Facebook friends to put me in touch with people who've decided against joining. The holdouts I contacted this way weren't haughty—they were nice, reasonable people with entirely rational-sounding explanations for staying off the site. Among the main reasons people cited was that Facebook looked like it required too much work. Chad Retelle, a network systems administrator in Madison, Wis., said he'd seen how his wife—my friend Katie—had taken to the site. But at the same time, it had changed her: "Now she's obligated to spend time maintaining her Facebook page. She's got to check it every morning. I have no desire to do that."

Retelle and other Facebook holdouts also protested that the site presents numerous opportunities for awkwardness—there's the headache of managing which people to friend and which to forget, the fear that one of your friends might post something on your wall that will offend everyone else, the worry that someone will find something about you that you didn't mean to share. Naomi Harris, a magazine photographer in New York, says that, for all that trouble, Facebook seems to offer little in return. "Why?" she asks. "I'm on the computer enough as it is for work. I don't really want to be there for recreation purposes, too. I have no interests in someone from fifth grade contacting me and saying, 'Hey, I sat behind you in class—wanna chat?'"

Finally, I heard what must be the most universal concern about Facebook—*I don't want people knowing my business!* Kate Koppelman is a 23-year-old New Yorker who works in the fashion industry. She was on Facebook all through college, and she concedes that the site has many benefits. And yet, the whole thing creeped her out: "I had friends from back home knowing what was going on with my friends from college—people they had never met—which was weird," she told me. "I found friends knowing things about what was on my 'wall' before I'd had a chance to see it—which was also weird." Koppelman quit Facebook last year. She still uses it by proxy—her roommates look people up for her when she's curious about them—but she says she'll never sign up again.

Yet of the many concerns about Facebook, Koppelman's is the most easily addressed. Last year, the site added a series of fine-grained privacy controls that let you choose which friends see what information about you. Your college friends can see one version of your profile, your high-school friends another, and your family yet another; if you want, you can let everyone see essentially nothing about you.

10      Retelle's worry that Facebook demands a lot of work is also somewhat misguided. It's true that some people spend a lot of time on it, but that's because they're having fun there; if you're not, you can simply log in once or twice a week just to accept or reject friends. Even doing nothing and waiting for others to friend you is enough: You're establishing a presence for other people to connect with you, which is the site's main purpose.

That brings us to Harris' argument: What's the social utility to Facebook—why should you join? Like with e-mail and cell phones, there are many, and as you begin to use it, you'll notice more and different situations in which it proves helpful. In general, Facebook is a lubricant of social connections. With so many people on it, it's now the best, fastest place online to find and connect with a specific person—think of it as a worldwide directory, or a Wikipedia of people. As a result, people now expect to find you on Facebook—whether they're contacting you for a job or scouting you out for a genius grant.

True, you might not want people to be able to follow your life—it's no great loss to you if your long-lost college frenemy can't find you. But what about your old fling, your new fling, your next employer, or that friend-of-a-friend you just met at a party who says he can give you some great tips on your golf swing? Sure, you can trade e-mail addresses or phone numbers, but in many circles Facebook is now the expected way to make these connections. By being on Facebook, you're facilitating such ties; without it, you're missing them and making life difficult for those who went looking for you there.

Skeptics often suggest that online social networks foster introverted, anti-social behavior—that we forge virtual connections at the expense of real-life connections. But only someone who's never used Facebook would make that argument. Nobody avoids meeting people in real life by escaping to the Web. In fact, the opposite seems true: Short, continuous, low-content updates about the particulars of your friends' lives—Bob has the flu, Barbara can't believe what just happened on *Mad Men*, Sally and Ned are no longer on speaking terms—deepen your bonds with them. Writer Clive Thompson has explored this phenomenon, what social scientists call "ambient awareness." Following someone through his status updates is not unlike sitting in a room with him and semiconsciously taking note of his body language, Thompson points out. Just as you can sense his mood from the rhythm of his breathing, sighing, and swearing, you can get the broad outlines of his life from short updates, making for a deeper conversation the next time you do meet up.

It's this benefit of Facebook that seems to hook people in the end: Their friendships seem to demand signing up. Last year, Darcy Stockton, a fashion photographer in New York, held nothing back in describing her hatred of Facebook to the *Observer*. "If you have time to network through a site like that, you aren't working enough," she said. "I just don't have the *time* or the *ability* to keep up with yet another social networking site in my free time. I feel there's other things and real experiences I could be having in real life instead of wasting my free time on Facebook."

15    Stockton now has 250 Facebook friends. In an e-mail, she explained that she'd decided to join the site when her friends migrated over from MySpace. She added, "Thank you for making me eat my words!"

## One Word Spotlight

A *milestone* (paragraph 1) refers to a significant event that marks some sort of progress. The word was first used in 1746 to refer to stones set on pillars on roadways to indicate the passage of each mile. The development of this word is typical of many English-language words, which begin as names for specific things but eventually refer to abstract concepts.

## Reflect on the Reading

1. What is Manjoo's main point about Facebook?

2. Manjoo, in his first paragraph, refers jokingly to "The People's Republic of Facebook," reminiscent of China's official name, "The People's Republic of China." How is Facebook like—and not like—a nation?

3. Manjoo has a rebuttal for the arguments of people who dislike Facebook. In other words, he responds to their objections. In your view, which objection to Facebook is the most important? How well does he respond to this objection?

4. Manjoo compares the growing popularity of Facebook to the popularity of cell phones in the 1980s and 1990s. How logical is this comparison?

5. Manjoo frequently uses his own experiences with Facebook to support his point. How effective is this strategy?

## Consider Your Viewpoint

1. Describe your experiences with Facebook. How similar are these experiences with Manjoo's?

2. To what extent do you agree with Manjoo that Facebook and other social media sites can be helpful in the workplace? To what degree do you use it in your workplace?

3. Estimate the amount of time you use social media sites such as Facebook every week. In your view, is this a reasonable amount of time? In other words, are you getting enough out of this interaction to warrant the amount of time you put into it?

4. The creators of new communication technology tend to be young adults who are often in their twenties. Mark Zuckerberg was twenty when he and a few friends created Facebook, and Sergey Brin and Larry Page were both 25 when they created Google. The creators of Yahoo and Twitter were also young adults. Why do you think young adults (as opposed to middle-aged or older people) have tended to create new communication technology?

5. Manjoo quotes one Facebook skeptic as saying, "'I don't see how having hundreds or thousands of 'friends' is leading to any kind of substantive friendships. . . . The whole thing seems so weird to me. Now you really have to turn off your computer and just go out to live real life and make real connections with people that way. I don't think it's healthy.'" To what extent do you share this person's viewpoint? Explain your answer.

# Health Is a Human Right

## Paul Farmer

From 2005 to 2009, *All Things Considered,* a popular radio show on National Public Radio, invited listeners to submit personal essays titled "This I Believe." Based on a radio show from the 1950s, this feature aired hundreds of short essays read out loud by their authors that focused on the authors' core values and beliefs. In 2008, Paul Farmer, a physician who has worked for many years in Haiti and other countries helping the poor, submitted this personal essay. More "This I Believe" pieces can be heard at npr.org.

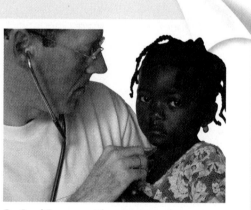

*Dr. Paul Farmer with a young patient in Haiti after the 2010 earthquake.*

I believe in health care as a human right. I've worked as a doctor in many places, and I've seen where to be poor means to be bereft of rights.

Bereft: Deprived.

I saw early on, still just a medical student, the panicky dead-end faced by so many of the destitute sick: a young woman dying in childbirth; a child writhing in the spasms of a terrible disease for which a vaccine has existed—for more than a century; a friend whose guts were irreparably shredded by bacteria from impure water; an 8-year-old caught in cross-fire. *Li mouri bet*—what a stupid death, goes one Haitian response.

Destitute: Poverty-stricken.

Fighting such "stupid deaths" is never the work of one, or even of a small group. I've had the privilege of joining many others providing medical care to people who would otherwise not be able to get it. The number of those eager to serve is impressive, and so is the amount that can be accomplished. I believe that stupid deaths can be averted; we've done it again and again. But this hard and painful work has never yet been an urgent global priority.

The fight for health as a human right, a fight with real promise, has so far been plagued by failures. Failure because we are chronically short of resources. Failure because we are too often at the mercy of those with the power and money to decide the fates of hundreds of millions. Failure because ill health, as we have learned again and again, is more often than not a symptom of poverty and violence and inequality—and we do little to fight those when we provide just vaccines, or only treatment for one disease or another. Every premature death, and there are millions of these each year, should be considered a rebuke.

5     I know it's not enough to attend only to the immediate needs of the patient in front of me. We must also call attention to the failures and inadequacy of our own best efforts. The goal of preventing human suffering must be linked to the task of bringing others, many others, into a movement for basic rights.

The most vulnerable—those whose rights are trampled, those rarely invited to summarize their convictions for a radio audience—still believe in human rights, in spite of—or perhaps because of—their own troubles. Seeing this in Haiti and elsewhere has moved me deeply and taught me a great deal.

I move uneasily between the obligation to intervene and the troubling knowledge that much of the work we do, praised as "humanitarian" or "charitable," does not always lead us closer to our goal. That goal is nothing less than the refashioning of our world into one in which no one starves, drinks impure water, lives in fear of the powerful and violent, or dies ill and unattended.

Of course such a world is a utopia, and most of us know that we live in a dystopia. But all of us carry somewhere within us the belief that moving away from dystopia moves us towards something better and more humane. I still believe this.

## One Word Spotlight

*Dystopia* (paragraph 7) means the opposite of *utopia,* or a perfect world. Referring to a world of suffering and oppression, this word was formed in the mid-nineteenth century by adding the Greek word "dys," meaning bad, to the word "utopia." Many science-fiction movies depict dystopias, such as *The Matrix, Doomsday, Brazil,* and *Blade Runner.*

## Reflect on the Reading

1. Farmer says that "health is a human right." According to him, what has prevented this from happening? How can "stupid deaths" be avoided?

2. Unlike many arguments, Farmer's piece does not contain statistics or other types of data. To what extent is this a strength or weakness of the piece?

3. Farmer gives several examples to support his point. In your view, which example is most notable, and why?

4. In the fourth paragraph of this piece, Farmer gives three sentence fragments that begin with the word "failure." In many rhetorical situations sentence fragments are considered incorrect. Why does Farmer include these fragments, and what effect do they have on his listeners and readers?

5. Based on this piece, what can be some of the differences between a persuasive piece written for radio listeners and a persuasive piece that is intended for readers?

## Consider Your Viewpoint

1. How convincing did you find Farmer's radio essay? Explain your answer.

2. Farmer's piece was broadcast during the time that the U.S. Congress was debating health care reform, yet he never refers directly to the health care debate. Why do you think this is so?

3. Though Farmer says at the end of his piece that "we live in a dystopia," he goes on to affirm his belief that human beings do care about the welfare

of others. How do you think a person like Farmer—who sees so much human suffering—maintains this belief?

4. Farmer writes that "our goal" is "nothing less than the refashioning of our world into one in which no one starves, drinks impure water, lives in fear of the powerful and violent, or dies ill and unattended" (par. 6). To what extent do you think this is possible?

5. If you were to write a radio essay called "This I Believe," what would you write about?

# WRITING ASSIGNMENT

In this chapter you'll select a topic that interests you and argue a position on that topic in order to try to alter your readers' perspectives. After analyzing the rhetorical situation, you'll narrow your topic and draft a claim, create supporting points, including reasons and evidence, and anticipate the arguments against your points. You'll also study ways to avoid faulty logic that might weaken your points. Part of the success of your argument depends on how well you understand your readers and how effectively you acknowledge their views while at the same time attempting to shift their perspectives.

## YOUR ARGUMENT OF A POSITION

If you've ever debated an issue with a family member or friend, you've used argumentative strategies such as stating your claim, supporting your points, and refuting the opposition. In this chapter you'll study these strategies so that you're more aware of how to argue effectively to persuade others.

### Choosing a Topic

It's important to select a topic that interests you, that you know something about, and that makes you want to persuade others. Here are some general ideas to get you started, but keep in mind that you'll need to narrow the topic in order to develop it in detail.

*I have spent many years of my life in opposition, and I rather like the role.*

—*Eleanor Roosevelt*

## National Topics

Should English be the "official" language of the United States?

Is recycling economically feasible?

Are bilingual or dual-language programs effective for children?

Should the United States open its doors to more (or fewer) immigrants?

What is "language discrimination" and should people be protected against it?

How effective are efforts to protect airline passengers from terrorists?

Should any kind of profiling play a role in law enforcement?

## Regional Topics

Should restaurants in your community be required to list nutritional information?

Should green spaces (such as parks) be protected in your community, and if so, how?

Should taxpayers pay for free WiFi access in your community?

Should children not be exposed to television or the Internet until a certain age?

Should billboards be eliminated on city highways to promote beautification?

Should drivers pay a fine for talking on cell phones or texting while they drive?

## Education Topics

Should college campuses sell apparel made in international "sweat shops"?

Should guns be allowed on college campuses?

Should your college have separate classes for students who speak English as a second language?

Should all college students be required to know how to speak at least two languages?

Should international students pay more for college tuition in the United States than domestic students?

Should tuition at your campus be capped at a certain level to make college more affordable to students?

In order to develop your points in detail, you'll need to narrow your topic. Arguing that your community should require all restaurants to provide nutritional information to their customers is a good start. However, what about small, family-owned restaurants? To comply with this ordinance, they would have to invest some money in having everything on their menu analyzed, as well as pay for brochures listing all of the information. On the other hand, this ordinance will most likely not be a burden on chain restaurants. Narrowing your topic to a particular kind of restaurant will help you explain the effect of the ordinance on business.

One technique for narrowing your topic is to ask the questions *who, what, where, when why,* and *how.*

> Topic: "Should guns be allowed on college campuses?"
>
> *Who:* Who should carry guns? Students, faculty, visitors, staff?
>
> *What:* What kinds of guns, if any, should be allowed?
>
> *Where:* Where should they be allowed—in classrooms, the union, the library?
>
> *When:* When should such a law be enacted, if ever?
>
> *Why:* Why should this law be passed, or why shouldn't it be passed? Will it make campuses safer, cause no difference, or make campuses more dangerous?
>
> *How:* How would such a law come to pass? Through the state legislature, for instance?

---

### Topic Questions for Arguing a Position

- Does my topic interest me?
- Do I have a position on it?
- Do I already know something about this topic?
- What might I need to find out about my topic?
- Is my topic narrow enough so that I can go into detail about it?

---

**Activity 10.1**   With several classmates, brainstorm several topics for an argument in which you take a position. For each topic you brainstorm, narrow it so that it can be developed in detail using the questions *who, what, where, when, why,* and *how*. Refer to Chapter 3 for additional strategies for narrowing a topic. Share your list of narrowed topics with the class.

**Connect With Others**

## Analyzing the Rhetorical Situation

Understanding the rhetorical situation is important for every type of writing, but it is particularly important for arguments. If you don't understand your audience, your argument will be ignored by your readers. In his argument in favor of nuclear power, Mark Lynas responded thoroughly to the beliefs of those in the environmental movement who typically have campaigned against nuclear power. Without understanding his audience's perspective, Lynas would have had little chance of changing his readers' minds.

**Considering Audience and Purpose.** In an argument, you have to assume that your readers either disagree with your point or are neutral about it. If they already agree with you, then why read what you have to say? Farhad Manjoo, in his argument in favor of Facebook, interviewed Facebook skeptics and included their ideas in his piece. That way he was sure to respond directly to their opposing points.

---

### Audience Questions for Arguing a Position

- What arguments will people who oppose my position have?
- What can I say in response to these opposing viewpoints?
- What background knowledge will my readers have about the topic?
- What information will I need to provide my readers?
- Will my readers' age, gender, language, or cultural background affect the way they respond to my position? If so, how can I best respond to these reactions?

---

Your purpose for writing might be obvious—to persuade your readers to change their minds or at least reconsider their views about your position. However, how this purpose is expressed can be subtle. In Paul Farmer's radio essay, for example, his purpose as expressed by his title is to convince people that health is a human right. By the end of his essay, though, his position had shifted: By noting that people's health is directly connected to "poverty, violence, and inequality," he is really arguing for a totally changed world.

---

### Purpose Questions for Arguing a Position

- What is my purpose in arguing a position? To change people's minds, to get them to understand my position is a valid one, or to get them to do something?
- Where in my piece will my purpose be evident?
- To what extent do I anticipate readers will resist accepting my position?

---

**Choosing a Genre and Visual Design.** When arguing a position, you want to choose a genre that will reach your intended readers. Mark Lynas, for example, expressed his views about nuclear power in the format of a news magazine opinion piece, which allowed him to express himself in some detail to thousands of readers of the *New Statesman,* a British newspaper with an online version that is free and therefore read by many readers. Paul Farmer, who wrote about health as a human right, also chose a venue with a wide audience—National Public Radio. However, his genre of a radio essay suited his approach, which featured more passion because of his experiences treating poor people around the world. Your genre will affect the visual design that you develop. For help with visual design, see Chapter 14.

## Genre and Visual Design Questions for Arguing a Position

- What genre, or format, will allow me to reach a wide audience?
- To what extent will this format allow me to develop my ideas in detail?
- What do I need to learn about this format?
- What visuals (such as photographs or drawings) will help me argue my position?
- If I use visuals, where will I find them?
- Where will the visuals be placed in my text?

**Reviewing Exigence and Constraints.** Your exigence is what pushes you to write about your position—what sparks your desire to persuade your readers. For example, Farhad Manjoo, as the technology editor of *Slate,* an online magazine with a wide circulation, is naturally interested in new media and other technological innovations. Because he uses Facebook himself, it is likely he was motivated to convince others that Facebook is a worthwhile social application.

## Exigence Questions for Arguing a Position

- What has made me interested in this topic?
- How long have I had a position on this topic?
- Why do I want to persuade others about my position?

Constraints consist of limitations that you impose upon yourself or that others impose upon you. One of Paul Farmer's constraints, for instance, was that the "This I Believe" radio essays are short, which probably led him to express his conviction that health is a human right in the title of the essay because he had so little room. In his case, the genre of a radio essay led him to express his points in a concise, straightforward way.

**Constraint Questions for Arguing a Position**

- To what extent does the format that I've chosen for my argument limit my freedom in terms of space or format?
- How long do I have to research and write this piece?
- How can I work to make sure that this piece is a success?

**Develop Your Understanding**

**Activity 10.2**   Go to the op-ed section of a newspaper's website (this section is where the newspaper publishes opinion pieces on different topics). Read an opinion piece and answer the following questions:

1. Who is the audience for the piece?
2. What is the writer's purpose?
3. What claim is the writer making?
4. How well is the argument supported with reasons, facts, and examples?
5. If there are visuals, how do these help to influence your opinion?

## Using the Writing Process

Once you complete your rhetorical analysis, you're ready to begin composing an argument. Follow these stages to do your best work: discovering ideas, drafting to explore ideas, revising to improve content, and editing to eliminate errors.

### STAGE 1: Discovering Ideas

To begin composing your argument, you need to draft a claim, or the main point you're arguing. Your claim should:

- express a strong belief or conviction that reasonable people can either agree or disagree with
- avoid purely personal opinion that cannot be supported with logical reasons and evidence
- be narrow enough so that you can argue your position in sufficient detail considering the length of the assignment

How effective are the following claims?

*Bilingual education programs have been eliminated in several states.* Because this is a verifiable fact, no one can disagree with this, so it's not a good claim.

*Bilingual education programs are the answer to all of the problems in our educational system.* Reasonable people will not agree with this, so it's not a good claim.

*I know bilingual education works because I was a bilingual education student and it worked for me.* This statement comes from the personal experience of one person rather than from a position that can be supported through logical reasons and evidence, so it's not a good claim.

Here are some claims about bilingual education that satisfy the criteria of a good claim:

> Because research shows that dual-language programs are more effective than bilingual education programs, our school should adopt a dual-language program.

> Dual-language programs should be adopted only with the support of students' parents.

> Until more research is completed, dual-language programs should not be widely used in elementary schools.

**Activity 10.3**   With several classmates, revise the following weak claims so that they satisfy the criteria for an effective claim for an argument.

**Connect With Others**

1. Tuition at this college has increased the previous four years in a row.
2. I have been a victim of language discrimination.
3. Our city's biggest shopping mall should be razed and made into a park.
4. Immigration foes are ignorant fools.
5. The president should abolish the death penalty.

## STAGE 2: Drafting to Explore Ideas

In arguing a position, you need to include reasons and evidence, respond to the objections of your readers, and avoid mistakes in logic.

**Identifying Reasons and Evidence.** To successfully argue your position—in other words, to get your readers to see your perspective—you need to give reasons that are supported with evidence. In "Health Is a Human Right," Paul Farmer says that he wants to stop "stupid deaths," to use the Haitian descriptor of deaths that could be easily prevented with good health care. This is one of his reasons for believing that everyone should have access to health care. In "You Have No Friends," Farhad Manjoo gives several reasons to support his conviction that Facebook is a worthwhile

### LANGUAGES and CULTURES

To the classical Greek scholar Aristotle, who lived around 350 B.C.E., rhetoric was "the faculty of observing in any given case the available means of persuasion." In other words, the most important part of making an argument was employing strategies that would give you reasons and evidence to make your point. Aristotle also paid particular attention to audience and taught his students the types of arguments that appealed to different groups of people.

enterprise. He shows that Facebook can help people keep in touch with friends and family, succeed at their jobs, and improve their social lives. According to Mark Lynas, the reasons that "Greens Must Learn to Love Nuclear Power" is that nuclear power is safe, economical, and effective in weaning the developed world off of dirty, expensive energy sources.

While you may be able to think of several reasons to support your claim, how do you know if these reasons are effective? Make sure that they directly support the claim, can be supported with credible evidence, and are logically stated. Use freewriting, listing, mapping, or another discovery method from Chapter 3 to discover reasons to support your claim.

The evidence that you use to support your reasons is a key component of the success of your argument. Evidence can consist of examples, facts, and statistics gathered from research that you conduct on your own, such as surveys and case studies, or from research published by reputable sources. This evidence should be directly connected to your reasons and clearly explained.

**Offering Objections and Rebuttals.**  At first glance it might seem odd to include in your argument the objections of people who disagree with your claim. After all, won't that weaken your argument? In actuality, discussing your opponents' points strengthens your position because it shows that you understand all sides of the argument. It also adds to the impression that you are seeking to come to a common understanding on the topic. Finally, it gives you the opportunity to note weaknesses in the other person's position. While at times you can acknowledge the soundness of an argument that goes against your conviction, most of the time you will refute—or offer a rebuttal—to your opponents' ideas.

Farhad Manjoo's article argument about Facebook is notable because for the most part it is an extended rebuttal to people who believe that Facebook is a waste of time. Manjoo begins early in his piece, "Friends—can I call you friends?—it's time to drop the attitude: There is no longer any good reason to avoid Facebook." The bulk of his piece consists of his responses to people he's interviewed who have refused to join Facebook. To people who say that

**LANGUAGES and CULTURES**

Nowadays most business people communicate with others from across the globe, and as a result cross-cultural conflicts are likely to occur. What happens, for instance, when business people from a culture that values directness and clarity (such as Israel) work with people from a culture that values politeness, indirectness, and humility (such as India)? Unless people make an effort to understand each other's communication styles, misunderstandings will occur.

Facebook takes too much time, Manjoo points out that you only need to check it a couple of times a week. When someone worries about the lack of privacy, he notes that Facebook's privacy settings let you control how much of your information is released. When people claim that Facebook replaces more meaningful face-to-face interaction, he refers to research that suggests that online social interactions can be equally meaningful. Because he so thoroughly anticipates and refutes people who disagree with him, his argument is convincing.

**Activity 10.4**    With several classmates, develop and refute arguments that go against your claim. Then outline your pro and con points to help you develop your ideas without confusing your readers.

**Connect With Others**

**Analyzing Logical Fallacies.**  An effective argument, especially one written in an academic setting, should be based primarily on reason and logic. Therefore, it's important to avoid logical fallacies, or faulty logic. In general, logical fallacies consist of some type of overgeneralization. Here are some common types of logical fallacies.

**Faulty Comparison.**  The phrase "comparing apples to oranges" refers to a faulty comparison. For instance, suppose someone is criticizing your college for not having graduation rates equal to those of Harvard. Most likely, this is an example of faulty comparison because your college (indeed, most colleges) are very different from Harvard where most students come from affluent backgrounds and don't hold jobs while attending school. In contrast, people who attend your college may have to work to support themselves through college. As a result, it may take some students at your school more than four years to graduate. This comparison between your college and Harvard is faulty because the schools are so different.

**Slippery Slope.**  In the slippery slope fallacy, one thing inevitably leads to another thing, which inevitably leads to something else, and so on. Here are some examples of slippery slope arguments from the past:

>   If we let girls wear miniskirts to school, next thing you know they'll want to go without clothes altogether.
>   If we don't ban rock music, young people will start to riot in the streets.
>   Forcing people to wear seat belts when they drive will lead to the government telling us which cars we have to drive or where we have to go.

The problem with slippery slope arguments—what makes them illogical—is that the claim that one thing will lead to another thing is usually too extreme to be credible.

**Either-Or Reasoning.**  This logical fallacy occurs when it is assumed that there are only two sides to an issue when in actuality other options exist. For example, someone might argue that without the death penalty, criminals will be out on parole in just twenty years. However, there are other options besides the death penalty or early parole, such as sentencing someone to life in prison without the option of parole. Politicians often use either-or reasoning, as in "Without this health care reform package, your mother will end up without insurance." There are more than two sides to an issue as complex as health care reform.

**False Causes.**  Many superstitions are a result of the fallacy of false causes. A ball player might win a game wearing a particular pair of socks, so she continues to wear that pair of socks for the rest of the season. A student might get a good test grade after drinking a large cup of coffee, so he continues to drink coffee before taking a test. A related logical fallacy is confusing correlation with causation. For example, a research study might find that people who live a long time like to eat broccoli; however, this doesn't prove that eating broccoli will lead to longevity.

**Straw Person.**  When you misrepresent your opponent's argument, you're using the straw person fallacy. For example, suppose you're arguing in favor of making English the official language of the United States, and you claim that people who oppose this idea don't want people to learn English at all. This assertion misrepresents what most people believe about the issue.

*Ad hominem.*  Meaning "against the person" in Latin, an *ad hominem* argument is a personal attack on your opponent. "My opponent didn't go to college, so he's too ignorant to hold office" is an example of the *ad hominem* fallacy.

**Universal Generalization.**  A universal generalization occurs when you say or imply that something is true for everyone, or when you claim that something occurs all of the time. "College students don't want their tuition to increase" is an example of a universal generalization: not all college students feel this way. Qualify this statement by saying that "*most* college students don't want their tuition to increase" or "*many* college students don't want their tuition to increase."

**Using Argumentative Appeals.**  When writing an argument, consider how you're appealing to your audience. Are you trying to argue by appealing to your readers' reason? Or are you trying to convince your readers by making them become emotional about the topic? You also need to consider how to make your readers believe that you know and care about your topic.

**Logos.**  When you use logos, or the logical appeal, you use reasons, evidence, and data to support your points. Most arguments written in academic settings rely on the logical appeal.

**Pathos.**  You use pathos when you get your audience to "feel" what you are describing. Paul Farmer, in writing about his work as a doctor in Haiti, relied on pathos when he described the illness and poverty he encountered in that part of the world.

**Ethos.**  To be convincing, you have to make your readers believe that you are knowledgeable about the topic and are sincerely engaged with it. In other words, you have to create an effective ethos. You can do this by referring to your personal experiences with the topic. In some cases, letting your readers know about your credentials and educational background can help you create your ethos. Paul Farmer, in describing his work in Haiti, enhanced his ethos and made his argument more convincing.

For more help with logos, pathos, and ethos, see Chapter 11.

**Your Emotional Filter and Writing Monitor.**  As you're writing your argument, be sure that you're not too emotional about the topic. You want to feel involved in your topic but not to the point where you can't maintain some distance. At the same time, you want to believe that your topic is important so that you are engaged as you research and write. Avoid overmonitoring your writing as you're drafting your ideas; you'll have the chance to revise and edit further along in the writing process.

**One Student's Work.**  Priscilla Duran, while writing an argument on language discrimination that appears at the end of this chapter, found that she had to control her emotional filter while she was writing because she became emotionally involved in the topic.

> When I first started writing about language discrimination, I didn't know much about the topic. But as I began reading about the topic, it suddenly occurred to me that I had been the victim of language discrimination. One of my former supervisors was always threatening to fire her employees for speaking Spanish on the job, even when we were just talking to each other and not to customers. At first I became angry when I realized what had happened, but then I was able

*to control my emotions by telling myself that I would become a better writer because I cared about the topic. And I think that's what happened.*

## STAGE 3: Revising to Improve Content

When you revise, examine your claim, reasons, and evidence to ensure that they are clear, logical, and developed. Be sure that you have included objections and rebuttals, as well as avoided logical fallacies. In addition to content, review your word choice and sentence structure and revise as needed.

**Using Effective Evidence.** In supporting your points, be sure that your evidence is credible. Avoid sources that are irrelevant, too old, lack substance, or are biased. In "Why Greens Must Learn to Love Nuclear Power," Mark Lynas uses information from the United Nations—a credible source—to question a claim made by Greenpeace, an advocacy organization that might be potentially biased. His other sources include the Intergovernmental Panel on Climate Change, a nonpartisan organization that won the Nobel Peace Prize in 2007.

Your own research or experience can also serve as effective evidence. Farhad Manjoo used his own survey results to develop some of his ideas, while Paul Farmer referred to his own experiences as a doctor in Haiti and around the world to give his points credibility and substance. Consult Chapter 18, "Conducting Field Research," for help with conducting your own research.

**Connecting Reasons and Evidence.** To avoid gaps in your argument, explicitly connect your reasons and evidence. Here's an example where the reason and evidence lack connection:

> According to *Today's Environment,* hybrid and electric cars can significantly reduce carbon emissions (Jonas 95). Consumers who buy hybrid and electric cars should receive tax credits.

Here's the same reason and evidence with the connection explicitly made:

> According to *Today's Environment,* hybrid and electric cars can significantly reduce carbon emissions (Jonas 95). *Therefore, more hybrid and electric cars should be purchased. To encourage this purchasing,* consumers who buy hybrid and electric cars should receive tax credits.

By explicitly showing the connection between the reason and evidence, you help your reader understand your point, which makes your argument stronger. How do you know when you need to show this connection? Ask someone to review it. See the example of a peer review sheet for an argument essay.

# Peer Review
## Arguing a Position

1. What is this argument's greatest strength?

2. What is the claim being argued? How clearly is this claim stated?

3. Evaluate my reasons and evidence. How effective are they? Are there other reasons and evidence I could give? How well I have included arguments that go against my claim? How persuasive are my rebuttals? Have I avoided logical fallacies and connected the evidence to my reasons?

4. If I used research to support my points, how well was this research used? How well did I indicate the sources of the research in the text of the piece and at the end?

5. How interesting is my argument? What more would you like to know about the topic?

6. Underline any words or sentences that you think I should revise because they do not communicate to you.

7. Place a check mark in the margin next to any punctuation or spelling errors that you discovered while reading this evaluation.

STAGE 4:  **Editing for Correctness**

When you edit, you look for errors in spelling, punctuation, and grammar. These errors can be distracting for readers who want to focus on your argument.

## To Edit

- Use a dictionary. This can be a monolingual dictionary, a language learner's dictionary, or a bilingual dictionary. Also use your computer spell-checker.
- For rule-governed errors, refer to a grammar handbook and follow standard English-language rules.
- For more idiomatic errors, ask another student or a writing tutor to read your writing and give you feedback.
- As you edit, keep an Editing Log where you record and correct your errors. Refer to this Editing Log to help keep you from making these same errors again.

**Develop Your Understanding**

**Activity 10.5** Complete the self-evaluation sheet to help you improve your work.

## Self-Evaluation Sheet
## Arguing a Position

1. Have I followed all instructions for this assignment? (Reread the assignment sheet and class notes.)

2. Is my claim stated clearly? Are my arguments well-supported with reasons and evidence?

3. Have I included arguments that go against my claim? Have I refuted these arguments?

4. Have I used good logic and effective evidence?

5. Are my points organized well?

6. Is my introduction interesting? Do I conclude in such a way that there is a sense of closure?

7. If I used research, did I give credit both in the text and on a Works Cited or References page at the end of the piece?

8. Are my sentences well-written and varied? (Read each sentence beginning with the last one, working backward to the beginning of the paper.)

9. Is my word choice appropriate for my audience?

10. Have I checked for grammar, punctuation, and spelling errors?

11. Is my piece formatted appropriately according to my audience's expectations?

Consider submitting your argument to a newspaper or posting it to a blog or other website on your topic. If you receive comments about your argument, share them with your instructor and class.

## ONE STUDENT'S ARGUMENT

In Stage 2 of the writing process, we introduced you to Priscilla Duran, a student who wrote an argument on language discrimination. Priscilla discovered ideas, drafted, revised, and edited her paper to persuade her readers to agree with her position. Here is her final version.

## Language Discrimination: A Common Theme in Education and the Work Place

### *Priscilla Duran*

Our world is full of diversity, and each continent, country, and city carries its own set of people, beliefs and language. The United States, which has often been called a melting pot, is filled with people from all over the world. They come here to fulfill the "American dream," to find fulfillment and a better life for themselves and their families. In a place that professes so much freedom, one would think that diversity would be gladly accepted and welcomed: that is not the case. Although there are laws that forbid discrimination on the basis of race, sex, religion or national origin, language and accents have caused many people heartache. Language discrimination has caused children to lose out on a good education while adults have lost jobs or have been refused jobs because of their "inability" to speak "proper" English.

Language discrimination must first be defined and understood. According to the U.S. Equal Employment Opportunity Commission, it is illegal to discriminate against people based on their particular place of origin, such a certain country, or on their national origin group, which includes ethnic groups such as Arabs or Hispanics. While discrimination is often thought of in physical terms, it can also relate to linguistic characteristics ("EEOC"). According to the Legal Aid Society, "Language discrimination occurs when a person is treated different because of that person's native language or other characteristics of that person's speech." Such characteristics include accent, grammar, and pronunciation.

While language discrimination is illegal, it is not always easy to identify, as the following case illustrates. Manuel T. Fragante was a man with a heavy Filipino accent who applied for a job at the Honolulu office of the Department of Motor Vehicles. Fragante's test scores and written exams were nearly perfect; he was first out of 721 applicants. However, he was denied the position. He received a letter with the following:

> As to the reason for your non-selection, we felt the two selected
> applicants were both superior in their verbal communication ability. As
> we indicated in your interview, our clerks are constantly dealing with
> the public and the ability to speak clearly is one of the most important
> skills required for the position. Therefore, while we were impressed
> with your educational and employment history, we felt the applicants
> selected would be better able to work in our office because of their
> communication skills. (Piatt 40–41)

Believing that he was discriminated against, Fragante filed a lawsuit. He lost the suit and lost the appeal of the decision (Piatt 41). Was he, in fact, a victim of

---

While writing this argument, Priscilla had to refrain from becoming too emotionally involved in the topic because she had been a victim of language discrimination. She made sure that her argument focused on logos, or reason, and as a result made sure to clearly define "language discrimination."

language discrimination? In this case, he was not. The ability to communicate well with the public was an essential part of the job. In his interview, Fragante was difficult to understand, and because a key criterion of the position was clear oral communication, he was rightfully denied (Piatt 41–42).

In many other instances, however, language discrimination has been a factor in the workplace. This most often occurs in workplaces with "English Only" rules even though speaking a language other than English does not hurt business. In one instance, a Rochester, New York, gas station required its employees to speak only English while working or else face discipline or even loss of their jobs. The employees sued and won because speaking a language other than English did not affect how well they did their jobs ("Hess"). In another instance, a casino in Colorado implemented an English Only policy with its employees that even required workers who didn't speak English, such as those employed in the housekeeping department, to speak only English. Essentially, these employees were not allowed to speak at all. The casino reached a $1.5 million settlement with the government as a penalty for this policy ("Language Discrimination").

Clearly, employers need to follow the law and not enact "English Only" policies that unnecessarily restrict their employees' choice of language in the workplace. Language discrimination, however, needs to be considered in contexts broader than simply the workplace. In particular, language discrimination can be harmful in schools.

Children spend on average seven hours a day at school. They interact not only with fellow students but also with faculty from a different range of backgrounds and culture. Although many schools are implementing programs to accept and celebrate cultural diversity, there is still animosity towards students who do not speak what many consider "standard English." As sociolinguist Rosina Lippi-Green has stated, "When asked directly about language use, most people will draw a very solid basic distinction of 'standard' (proper, correct) English vs. everything else" (166). Vernacular English is often stigmatized, and as a result children who come to school speaking a vernacular will be looked down upon. In fact, what is considered "correct" or "good" English is simply the type of English spoken by people from higher socioeconomic backgrounds.

The effect of language discrimination in our educational systems is shown in a study conducted by Sherry Marx of Utah State University. She focused on a school in the small town of Cherry Creek, which had recently experienced an increase in Latino students. Marx studied white and Latino students, as well as the faculty, to determine the different perspectives that these groups had of each other (Marx 69–72).

What she found was shocking. "For every item of the questionnaire, White students responded more positively than did Latino students, with more positive thoughts about the school and their own experiences in the school . . . there were clear differences in Latino and White students regarding the quality of their schooling"(Marx 74). Many Latino students responded negatively when asked if their culture and home language was respected by their school. One comment by a student mentioned that "' . . . people still look at you and tell you 'stupid Hispanics' . . . teachers/student/school board don't seem to care. I think this school is so strict & racist & does not understand students'" (Marx 76–77). It is sad and even frightening to think that this is the environment that surrounds children seven or more hours a day.

Fortunately, efforts are being made to fight language discrimination. A recent public service announcement shows a man calling to ask if an apartment is still available. He uses a total of eight different accents and names ranging from Juan Hernandez, Sanji Kumar and Chang Li. Each time he asks about the apartment the manager tells him that it has been rented. It is only when he uses the name Graham Wellington and speaks in a non-vernacular English that the manager gladly says that the apartment is available. The announcer mentions that this is discrimination and that there are Fair Housing laws that do not allow this (*"Accents"*).

In addition to raising awareness of laws against language discrimination, we should encourage opportunities for students to broaden their cultural experiences. Carol Gilmore and Martha A. Broderick suggest in their article "English Only? Rethinking Language requirements in a Multicultural Work World" that "a reassess-ment of the importance of foreign language and cultural experiences should be sought, perhaps even preferred . . . this will create a more 'international flavor'" (334). Because the business world is rapidly becoming globalized, students should be given the opportunity to study abroad and learn foreign languages. As a result, they will be more appreciative of the wide range of language accents they will encounter in the workplace.

Language discrimination must be closely looked at and studied in order to make the work place and school environment a wonderful and nurturing place for people of all different skin colors, backgrounds and ethnicities. The studies and research being conducted are not enough. Somehow, people must move beyond a binary way of thinking and accept that there are more different ethnicities and languages than there are colors of the rainbow. Only then will diversity, flavor and culture be truly welcomed not only in the United States but globally.

By relying on peer-reviewed research, Priscilla gives credible evidence while at the same time developing her topic in more detail.

Priscilla wanted to offer solutions to the problem of language discrimination so that her readers would understand that they could do something about this problem.

## Works Cited

*"Accents" (Fair Housing PSA). YouTube.* 3 March 2008. Web. 30
    Dec. 2009.

Bergman, Mindy E., Kristen M. Watrous-Rodriguez, and Katherine
    M. Chalkley. "Identity and Language: Contributions to and

Consequences of Spanish Speaking in the Workplace."
*Hispanic Journal of Behavioral Sciences* 30.1 (2008): 40–68.
*HAPI.* Web. 30 Dec. 2009.

Funkhouser, Vegosen, Liebman, & Dunn. "Language
Discrimination in the Workplace." Funkhouser, Vegosen,
Llebman, & Dunn, July 2006. Web. 15 Apr. 2010.

Gilmore, Carol, and Martha A. Broderick. "English Only? Rethinking
Language Requirements in a Multicultural Work World."
*Journal of Individual Employment Rights* 12.4 (2007):
329–336. *EBSCO.* Web. 28 Dec. 2009.

"Hess Settles Language Discrimination Case." *Convenience Store
News.* 11 July 2008. Web. 15 Apr. 2010.

Kahlenberg, Jessica. "Professor Explores Effects of Language
Discrimination." *The Flat Hat.* N.p., 20 Mar. 2009. Web. 28
Dec. 2009.

Legal Aid Society. "Language Discrimination: Your Legal Rights."
N.d. Web. 27 Dec. 2009.

Lippi-Green, Rosina. "Accent, Standard Language Ideology, and
Discriminatory Pretext in the Courts." *Language in Society*
23.2 (1994): 163–198. *JSTOR.* Web. 28 Dec. 2009.

Marx, Sherry. "'Not Blending In': Latino Students in a
Predominantly White School." *Hispanic Journal of Behavioral
Sciences* 30.1 (2008): 69–88. *HAPI.* Web. 27 Dec. 2009.

Piatt, Bill. *Language on the Job: Balancing Business Needs and
Employee Rights.* Albuquerque: University of New Mexico
Press, 1993. Print.

U.S. Equal Employment Opportunity Commission (EEOC). "Section
13: National Origin Discrimination." *Compliance Manual.* 2
Dec. 2002. Web. 15 Apr. 2010.

# ADDITIONAL READINGS

## CCCC Guideline on the National Language Policy

### Conference on College Composition and Communication (CCCC), March 1988, Updated 1992

Because language is so closely connected to identity, it is often a contentious issue, especially in a country as multicultural as the United States. During the last hundred years, people have debated whether English should become the "official" language. The Conference on College Composition and Communication, the largest professional organization of English-language writing teachers in the country, has issued the following statement against the Official English movement. Though published in 1992, its arguments are still commonly debated today.

## Background

The National Language Policy is a response to efforts to make English the "official" language of the United States. This policy recognizes the historical reality that, even though English has become the language of wider communication, we are a multilingual society. All people in a democratic society have the right to education, to employment, to social services, and to equal protection under the law. No one should be denied these or any civil rights because of linguistic differences. This policy would enable everyone to participate in the life of this multicultural nation by ensuring continued respect both for English, our common language, and for the many other languages that contribute to our rich cultural heritage.

## CCCC National Language Policy

Be it resolved that CCCC members promote the National Language Policy adopted at the Executive Committee meeting on March 16, 1988. This policy has three inseparable parts:

> To provide resources to enable native and nonnative speakers to achieve oral and literate competence in English, the language of wider communication.

To support programs that assert the legitimacy of native languages and dialects and ensure that proficiency in one's mother tongue will not be lost.

To foster the teaching of languages other than English so that native speakers of English can rediscover the language of their heritage or learn a second language.

Passed unanimously by both the Executive Committee and the membership at the CCCC Annual Meeting in March 1988, the National Language Policy is now the official policy of the CCCC.

## What Raised the Need for the Language Policy?

The English Only movement began in 1981 when Senator S. I. Hayakawa sponsored a constitutional amendment to make English the official language of the United States. Variations on his proposal have been before Congress ever since; there were five proposals in 1988 and three in 1990. The Language of Government Act has been pending before the House and Senate since 1991.

5      In 1983 an organization called "U.S. English" was founded by Senator Hayakawa and Dr. John Tanton, an ophthalmologist. That organization promotes English Only legislation, both in Congress and state legislatures. By June 1992, sixteen states had declared English the official language.

Some states, however, have taken stands against language protectionism. In 1989, New Mexico, Washington, and Oregon passed "English Plus" laws that protect the use of languages other than English and encourage the study of foreign languages. Both Hawaii and Louisiana have official policies aimed at preserving languages and cultures.

In February 1990, a federal district judge in Arizona ruled that the state's constitutional amendment making English the official language violated the First Amendment's protection of free speech.

## What's Wrong with English Only?

**It's unnecessary.** English, the global lingua franca and the language of wider communication in this country, is not threatened. For two centuries, most immigrants learned English within a generation without any laws compelling them. Current immigrants are doing the same.

**It's unrealistic.** Thousands of people are on waiting lists to enroll in English classes. Laws making English the official language do nothing to increase the number of such classes, nor do they teach a single person English.

**It's educationally unsound.** English Only opposes bilingual and similar programs that help students build on their linguistic skills. When students cannot use their strengths, they experience alienation and failure. Prohibiting or discouraging diversity limits rather than expands learning opportunities.

**It's unfair and dangerous.** When we pass laws that forbid health and safety information, street signs, court trials, and marriage ceremonies in languages people can understand, we deny them legal protection and social services.

**It's invasive.** English Only laws violate the privacy of speakers of other languages. When Filipino hospital employees are told they cannot speak Tagalog in the lounge, or when a college employee is told he must not speak Spanish during lunch break, they are denied free expression.

**It's counterproductive.** As members of the global community, we need speakers of different languages. It's shortsighted, anti-immigrant, and racist to demean and destroy the competencies of bilingual people.

**It's unconstitutional.** The First Amendment guarantees freedom of speech. The Fourteenth Amendment forbids abridging the privileges and immunities of naturalized citizens. English Only laws violate these constitutional rights.

## Who Else Opposes English Only?

The English Plus Information Clearinghouse (EPIC) was born in the fall of 1987. Housed at the headquarters of the Joint National Council on Languages in Washington, D.C., EPIC serves as a national repository for information helpful to the increasing number of scholarly, ethnic, and civil liberty organizations that oppose English Only legislation. *EPIC Events*, a bimonthly newsletter, keeps subscribers informed. According to EPIC's Statement of Purpose, the English Plus concept "holds that the national interest can best be served when all persons of our society have access to effective opportunities to acquire strong English proficiency *plus* mastery of a second or multiple languages."

More than forty civic, religious, and professional organizations have passed resolutions opposing the English Only movement and supporting English Plus. Supporters include NCTE, NEA, TESOL, MLA, American Council of Teachers of Foreign Languages, the Center for Applied Linguistics, the American Psychological Association, the National Council for Black Studies, and the National Council of Churches of Christ. Both NCTE and NEA have published books that explain their positions on English Only legislation and that provide background material necessary to guard against language restrictionism (see Selected Titles). For more information, contact EPIC, 220 I Street, NE, Suite 220, Washington, DC 20002.

## Support the National Language Policy: What You Can Do

10    **Strive** to include all citizens of all language communities in the positive development of our daily activities.

**Provide** education, social services, legal services, medical services, and protective signing for linguistic minorities in their own languages so that basic human rights are preserved.

**Emphasize** the importance of learning second and third languages by all Americans so that we can:

participate more effectively in worldwide activities

unify diverse American communities

enlarge our view of what is human

**Recognize** that those who do not speak English need time and encouragement to learn, but that their ability to prosper over the long term requires facility in the dominant American language.

**Encourage** immigrants to retain their first languages, to pass them on to their children, and to celebrate the life-supporting customs of their parents in the company of other Americans of differing backgrounds.

## Selected Titles

Adams, Karen L., and Daniel T. Brink, eds. *Perspectives on Official English: The Campaign for English as the Official Language in the USA.* New York: Mouton de Gruyter, 1990.

Baron, Dennis E. *The English Only Question.* New Haven: Yale University Press, 1990.

Butler, Melvin A., chair, and the Committee on CCCC Language Statement. "Students' Right to Their Own Language." Special Issue of *College Composition and Communication* 25 (Fall 1974): 1–32.

Crawford, James, ed. *Language Loyalties: A Source Book on the Official English Controversy.* Chicago: The University of Chicago Press, 1992.

Daniels, Harvey A., ed. *Not Only English: Affirming America's Multicultural Heritage.* Urbana, IL: NCTE, 1990.

*Official English/English Only: More than Meets the Eye.* Prepared for the National Education Association by John Trasvina. Washington, DC: National Education Association, 1988.

Piatt, Bill. *Only English? Law and Language Policy in the United States.* Albuquerque: University of New Mexico Press, 1990.

Smitherman-Donaldson, Geneva. "Toward a National Public Policy on Language." *College English* 49.1 (1987): 29–36.

## Reflect on the Reading

1. Why does the Conference on College Composition and Communication oppose the "English Only" movement?

2. How well does this statement refute the opposition's points?

3. In what way is this statement a call to action?

## Consider Your Viewpoint

1. In your view, should the United States have a national language policy? If so, what should it be?

2. To what extent have recent immigrants been learning English, in your experience?

3. The CCCC language policy statement claims that it's unrealistic to have an English Only policy. Do you agree? Why or why not?

# Why the U.S. Needs an Official Language

## Mauro E. Mujica

Controversial topics, such as language policy, often lead to the formation of advocacy groups that attempt to influence people and shape policy. One such advocacy group is the U.S. English Foundation, led by Mauro E. Mujica. In an effort to sway government leaders and the general public, Mujica has made numerous television appearances and spoken to many groups throughout the United States. He has also written about the topic. In "Why the U.S. Needs an Official Language," he develops his argument for English as the official language of the United States.

In June, the Pew Research Center announced the results of an extensive survey on global trends such as the spread of democracy, globalization, and technology. Titled "Views of a Changing World," it was conducted from 2001 to 2003 and polled 66,000 people from 50 countries. The survey received some publicity in the United States, mainly because it showed that anti-American sentiments were on the upswing around the world. Less publicized was the fact that there is a now a global consensus on the need to learn English.

One question in the Pew survey asked respondents to agree or disagree with the statement "Children need to learn English to succeed in the world today." Many nations showed almost unanimous agreement on the importance of learning English. Examples include Vietnam, 98 percent; Indonesia, 96 percent; Germany and South Africa, 95 percent; India, 93 percent; China and the Philippines, 92 percent; Honduras, Japan, Nigeria, and Uganda, 91 percent; and France, Mexico, and Ukraine, 90 percent.

To an immigrant like myself (from Chile), these results come as no surprise. Parents around the world know that English is the global language and that their children need to learn it to succeed. English is the language of business, higher education, diplomacy, aviation, the Internet, science, popular music, entertainment, and international travel. All signs point to its continued acceptance across the planet.

Given the globalization of English, one might be tempted to ask why the United States would need to declare English its official language. Why codify something that is happening naturally and without government involvement?

## The Retreat Of English

5 In fact, even as it spreads across the globe, English is on the retreat in vast sections of the United States. Our government makes it easy for immigrants to function in their native languages through bilingual education, multilingual ballots and driver's license exams, and government-funded translators in schools and hospitals. Providing most essential services to immigrants in their native languages is expensive for American taxpayers and also keeps immigrants linguistically isolated.

Historically, the need to speak and understand English has served as an important incentive for immigrants to learn the language and assimilate into the mainstream of American society. For the last 30 years, this idea has been turned on its head. Expecting immigrants to learn English has been called "racist." Marta Jimenez, an attorney for the Mexican American Legal Defense and Educational Fund, speaks of "the historical use of English in the United States as a tool of oppression."

Groups such as the National Association for Bilingual Education complain about the "restrictive goal" of having immigrant children learn in English. The former mayor of Miami, Maurice Ferre, dismissed the idea of even a bilingual future for his city. "We're talking about Spanish as a main form of communication, as an official language," he averred. "Not on the way to English."

Perhaps this change is best illustrated in the evolving views of the League of United Latin American Citizens (LULAC). Started in 1929, the group was originally pro-English and pro-assimilation. One of the founding aims and purposes of LULAC was "to foster the acquisition and facile use of the Official Language of our country that we may hereby equip ourselves and our families for the fullest enjoyment of our rights and privileges and the efficient discharge of our duties and obligations to this, our country." By the 1980s the executive director of LULAC, Arnoldo Torres, could proudly proclaim, "We cannot assimilate and we won't!"

The result of this is that the United States has a rapidly growing population of people—often native born—who are not proficient in English. The 2000 Census found that 21.3 million Americans (8 percent of the population) are classified as "limited English proficient," a 52 percent increase from 1990 and more than double the 1980 total. More than 5 million of these people were born in the United States.

10    Citing census statistics gives an idea of how far English is slipping in America, but it does not show how this is played out in everyday life. Consider the following examples:

> The *New York Times* reports that Hispanics account for over 40 percent of the population of Hartford, Connecticut, and that the city is becoming "Latinized." Last year, Eddie Perez became Hartford's first Hispanic mayor. The city Web page is bilingual, and after-hours callers to the mayor's office are greeted by a message in Spanish. Half of Hartford's Hispanics do not speak English. According to Freddy Ortiz, who owns a bakery in the city, "In the bank, they speak Spanish; at the hospital, they speak Spanish; my bakery suppliers are starting to speak Spanish. Even at the post office, they are Americans, but they speak Spanish." Even Mayor Perez notes that "we've become a Latin city, so to speak. It's a sign of things to come."

> In May, about 20 percent of the students at Miami Senior High School, where 88 percent of the students speak English as a second language, failed the annual Florida Comprehensive Assessment Test (FCAT) exam, which is required for graduation. The poor results prompted protests and demands for the test to be given in

Spanish as well as English. Over 200 students and teachers gathered outside the school waving signs and chanting "No FCAT." A state senator from Miami introduced a bill that would allow the FCAT to be given in Spanish.

Just a day before the Pew survey was released, Gwinnett County in Georgia announced it will provide its own staff translators for parents of students who speak Spanish, Korean, and Vietnamese. The school board approved $138,000 for the new translators despite a tight budget. Donna Robertson, a principal at an elementary school in the county, claimed the translators are only a short-term solution. The real solution, she claims, is a multilingual school staff. There are 46 languages spoken among students in Gwinnett County.

In May, a poll taken by NBC News and the *Sun-Sentinel* newspaper of Fort Lauderdale, Florida, found 83 percent of Hispanics in south Florida agreeing that "it is easy to get along day in and day out without speaking English well/at all."

## The Costs Of Multilingualism

Multilingual government is not cheap. Bilingual education alone is estimated to cost taxpayers billions of dollars per year. The federal government has spent over $100 million to study the effectiveness of bilingual education, only to discover that it is less effective at teaching English than English immersion programs are. Much of the cost for court and school translators, multilingual voting ballots, and multiple document translations is picked up at the local level. Even during good economic times, this is a burden. In lean years it is a budget breaker, taking funds away from education, health care, transportation, and police and fire services.

For example, Los Angeles County spent $3.3 million, 15 percent of the entire election budget, to print election ballots in seven languages and hire multilingual poll workers for the March 2002 primary. The county also spends $265 per day for each of 420 full-time court interpreters. San Francisco spends $350,000 per each language that documents must be translated into under its bilingual government ordinance. Financial officials in Washington, D.C., estimate that a proposed language access would cost $7.74 million to implement. The bill would require all city agencies to hire translators and translate official documents for any language spoken by over 500 non-English-speaking people in the city.

The health-care industry, already reeling from a shortage of nurses and the costs of treating the uninsured, was dealt another blow by

President Clinton. Executive Order 13166 was signed into law on August 11, 2000. The order requires private physicians, clinics, and hospitals that accept Medicare and Medicaid to provide, at their own expense, translators for any language spoken by any patient. The cost of an interpreter can exceed the reimbursement of a Medicare or Medicaid visit by 13 times—costing doctors as much as $500 per translator.

15    Of course, there are also nonmonetary costs associated with a multilingual America. These expenses often have a human cost.

A 22-year-old immigrant won a $71 million settlement because a group of paramedics and doctors misdiagnosed a blood clot in his brain. The man's relatives used the Spanish word *intoxicado* to describe his ailment. They meant he was nauseated, but the translator interpreted the word to mean intoxicated.

Six children were killed when a loose tailgate from a tractor trailer fell off on a Milwaukee highway. The driver of the family's SUV could not avoid the tailgate, which punctured the gas tank and caused the vehicle to explode. An investigation found that other truckers had tried to warn the driver of the tractor trailer about his loose tailgate, but the driver did not understand English.

An immigrant in Orange County, California, died from a fall into a 175-degree vat of chemicals at an Anaheim metal-plating shop. Though the company's instructions clearly forbade walking on the five-inch rail between tanks, they were printed in English, a language that the worker did not understand. An inquiry into the accident found that many of the recent hires were not proficient in English.

Hispanics accounted for nearly one-third of Georgia's workplace deaths in 2000, despite making up only 5.3 percent of the state's population. The National Institute for Occupational Safety and Health, a branch of the U.S. Centers for Disease Control and Prevention, blamed "misunderstandings arising from language barriers" for the deaths and said they "could be prevented and don't have to happen."

## The Dis-United States

20 We need only look to Canada to see the problems a multilingual society can bring. America's northern neighbor faces a severe constitutional crisis over the issue of language. In 1995, the predominately French-speaking province of Quebec came within a few thousand votes of seceding from Canada. The secessionist Parti Quebecois ruled the province until this year. The national government must cater to Quebec to preserve order and maintain a cohesive government. This has spurred secessionist movements in English-speaking western Canada on the grounds that the Canadian government favors French speakers.

Of course, battles over language rage across the globe, but since Canada is so similar, it offers the most instructive warning for the United States. While the policy of official multilingualism has led to disunity, resentment, and near-secession, it is also very costly. Canada's dual-language requirement costs approximately $260 million each year. Canada has one-tenth the population of the United States and spent that amount accommodating only two languages. A similar language policy would cost the United States much more than $4 billion annually, as we have a greater population and many more languages to accommodate.

Unless the United States changes course, it is clearly on the road to a Canadian-style system of linguistic enclaves, wasteful government expenses, language battles that fuel ethnic resentments, and, in the long run, serious ethnic and linguistic separatist movements.

What is at stake here is the unity of our nation. Creating an American-style Quebec in the Southwest as well as "linguistic islands" in other parts of the United States will be a disaster far exceeding the Canadian problem. Now, over 8 percent of the population cannot speak English proficiently. What happens when that number turns to 10 percent, 20 percent, or more?

The American assimilation process, often called the melting pot, is clearly not working. Declaring English to be our official language would bring back the incentive to learn it. Specifically, this step would require that all laws, public proceedings, regulations, publications, orders, actions, programs, and policies are conducted in the English language. There would be some commonsense exceptions in the areas of public health and safety, national security, tourism, and commerce.

25      Of course, declaring English the official language would only apply to government. People can still speak whatever language they choose at home and in private life. Official English legislation should also be combined with provisions for more English classes for non-English speakers. This can be paid for with a fraction of the money saved by ending multilingual government.

A bill in Congress would make this a reality. The English Language Unity Act of 2003, H.R. 997, was introduced by Rep. Steve King (R-Iowa) earlier this year. The bill already has over 90 cosponsors and is starting to make some waves on the talk radio circuit. If it passes, we can start to rebuild the American assimilation process and lessen the amount of linguistic separation in the United States. If it fails, we might have lost the last best chance for a sensible and cohesive language policy in this country. If that happens we can say hasta la vista to the "United" States and Adelante to Canadian-style discord over the issues of language and ethnicity.

## Reflect on the Reading

1. Evaluate the author's reasons and evidence in support of making English the official language of the United States. In your view, where does the author best develop and support his argument?

2. Why does the author point out toward the beginning of his article that he is an immigrant from Chile?

3. How effective is the comparison between Canada's language policy and the language policy in the United States?

## Consider Your Viewpoint

1. What was your opinion of making English the official language of the United States before you read this article? To what extent did the author make you shift your opinion?

2. The author makes the case that having a single language helps to unite a country. What is your opinion about this assertion?

3. Should ballots be written in only one language? Explain your position.

---

PEARSON
mycomplab

For support in meeting this chapter's objectives, follow this path in MyCompLab: Resources ⇒ Writing ⇒ Writing Purposes ⇒ Writing to Argue or Persuade. Review the Instruction and Multimedia resources about writing to argue or persuade, then complete the Exercises and click on Gradebook to measure your progress.

## Learning Objectives

In this chapter you will:

- Write about how to solve a particular problem.

- Learn to develop ideas with logos, pathos, and ethos.

- Focus on a feasible solution.

One of the most intractable human problems has been war. Do you think the world is a safer place now than ten years ago? Five years ago?

A problem can be as minor as what to have for dinner and as major as finding a solution for the effect of climate change. The first thing you might do when faced with a problem is consider your options. For dinner you have the option of cooking, eating leftovers, ordering in, or going out. For solving problems related to climate change, individuals can cut down on their carbon footprint, governments can set policies and enact laws, companies can find ways to make energy conservation profitable, and scientists can work toward technological improvements. Often the solution to a particular problem lies in how you're imagining the problem in the first place. Many people, for instance, are worried about paying for college. As a result, people's conception of what it means to "go to college" has changed. Instead of moving away from home to live in a dorm or an apartment, it can mean starting off at a two-year college and living with your family while going to school. It can also mean enrolling in online courses, taking college classes while still in high school, and studying abroad in a country where higher education is less expensive.

> *We can't solve problems by using the same kind of thinking we used when we created them.*
> —*Albert Einstein*

## WRITING TO SOLVE PROBLEMS

When you write about solving a problem, your first step (or problem!) is to find an appropriate topic for the assignment. You can focus on a problem in your own life, such as in your workplace, school, or family. Alternatively, you might prefer to deal with a problem from a wider realm of life, such as education, the environment, health care, or the economy. This type of problem might entail doing some research. Then you'll consider different solutions to the problem and select a solution that you can support with logic, facts, and reasons. You'll also need to anticipate drawbacks to your solution, as well as any difficulties in implementing it. The problem that you select needs to be sufficiently focused so that you can explain the solution in detail.

## Questions for Solving a Problem

- What problem do I want to write about?
- What solution to this problem am I considering?
- Why is it important for me to tell about this problem and solution?
- Why would my audience be interested in this problem?
- What genre and visual design is best for communicating this topic to my audience?
- What constraints would keep me from effectively communicating my ideas about this topic?

# MODEL SOLUTIONS

Problem-solution texts exist in many contexts. When you listen to the news driving into work, you might hear political leaders propose solutions to major issues such as the economy, health care, or foreign affairs. In your workplace, your supervisor might ask you to propose a solution to a drop in profits. In a kinesiology class, your professor might require that you write a proposal for implementing a physical education program for preschool children. The following are several examples of problem-solution texts and their contexts.

# Remarks by the President to the Ghanaian Parliament

## Barack Obama

In the summer of 2009, President Barack Obama visited Africa to encourage the stable development of African nations. On July 11, 2009, he gave a major speech to the Ghanaian Parliament in Accra, Ghana. In order to reach the widest audience possible in Africa and across the world, portions of the speech were sent out to SMS (short message service) subscribers who could access it from their cell phones. On the White House website (www.whitehouse.gov), the speech was transcribed in English, French, Arabic, Portuguese, and Swahili, which are some of the most commonly spoken languages in Africa.

*President Obama addressing the Ghanaian Parliament.*

Good afternoon, everybody. It is a great honor for me to be in Accra and to speak to the representatives of the people of Ghana. I am deeply grateful for the welcome that I've received, as are Michelle and Malia and Sasha Obama. Ghana's history is rich, the ties between our two countries are strong, and I am proud that this is my first visit to sub-Saharan Africa as President of the United States of America.

I want to thank Madam Speaker and all the members of the House of Representatives for hosting us today. I want to thank President Mills for his outstanding leadership. To the former Presidents—Jerry Rawlings, former President Kufuor—Vice President, Chief Justice—thanks to all of you for your extraordinary hospitality and the wonderful institutions that you've built here in Ghana.

I'm speaking to you at the end of a long trip. I began in Russia for a summit between two great powers. I traveled to Italy for a meeting of the world's leading economies. And I've come here to Ghana for a simple reason: The 21st century will be shaped by what happens not just in Rome or Moscow or Washington, but by what happens in Accra, as well.

This is the simple truth of a time when the boundaries between people are overwhelmed by our connections. Your prosperity can expand America's prosperity. Your health and security can contribute to the world's health and security. And the strength of your democracy can help advance human rights for people everywhere.

5    So I do not see the countries and peoples of Africa as a world apart; I see Africa as a fundamental part of our interconnected world—as partners with America on behalf of the future we want for all of our children. That partnership must be grounded in mutual responsibility and mutual respect. And that is what I want to speak with you about today.

We must start from the simple premise that Africa's future is up to Africans.

I say this knowing full well the tragic past that has sometimes haunted this part of the world. After all, I have the blood of Africa within me, and my family's—my family's own story encompasses both the tragedies and triumphs of the larger African story.

Some you know my grandfather was a cook for the British in Kenya, and though he was a respected elder in his village, his employers called him "boy" for much of his life. He was on the periphery of Kenya's liberation struggles, but he was still imprisoned briefly during repressive times. In his life, colonialism wasn't simply the creation of unnatural borders or unfair terms of trade—it was something experienced personally, day after day, year after year.

My father grew up herding goats in a tiny village, an impossible distance away from the American universities where he would come to get an education. He came of age at a moment of extraordinary promise for Africa. The struggles of his own father's generation were giving birth to new nations, beginning right here in Ghana. Africans were educating and asserting themselves in new ways, and history was on the move.

10    But despite the progress that has been made—and there has been considerable progress in many parts of Africa—we also know that much of that promise has yet to be fulfilled. Countries like Kenya had a per capita economy larger than South Korea's when I was born. They have badly been outpaced. Disease and conflict have ravaged parts of the African continent.

In many places, the hope of my father's generation gave way to cynicism, even despair. Now, it's easy to point fingers and to pin the blame of these problems on others. Yes, a colonial map that made little sense helped to breed conflict. The West has often approached Africa as a patron or a source of resources rather than a partner. But the West is not responsible for the destruction of the Zimbabwean economy over the last decade, or wars in which children are enlisted as combatants. In my father's life, it was partly tribalism and patronage and nepotism in an independent Kenya that for a long stretch derailed his career, and we know that this kind of corruption is still a daily fact of life for far too many.

Now, we know that's also not the whole story. Here in Ghana, you show us a face of Africa that is too often overlooked by a world that sees only tragedy or a need for charity. The people of Ghana have worked hard to put democracy on a firmer footing, with repeated peaceful transfers of power even in the wake of closely contested elections. And by the way, can I say that for that the minority deserves as much credit as the majority. And with improved governance and an emerging civil society, Ghana's economy has shown impressive rates of growth.

This progress may lack the drama of 20th century liberation struggles, but make no mistake: It will ultimately be more significant. For just as it is important to emerge from the control of other nations, it is even more important to build one's own nation.

So I believe that this moment is just as promising for Ghana and for Africa as the moment when my father came of age and new nations were being born. This is a new moment of great promise. Only this time, we've learned that it will not be giants like Nkrumah and Kenyatta who will determine Africa's future. Instead, it will be you—the men and women in Ghana's parliament—the people you represent. It will be the young people brimming with talent and energy and hope who can claim the future that so many in previous generations never realized.

15    Now, to realize that promise, we must first recognize the fundamental truth that you have given life to in Ghana: Development depends on

good governance. That is the ingredient which has been missing in far too many places, for far too long. That's the change that can unlock Africa's potential. And that is a responsibility that can only be met by Africans.

As for America and the West, our commitment must be measured by more than just the dollars we spend. I've pledged substantial increases in our foreign assistance, which is in Africa's interests and America's interests. But the true sign of success is not whether we are a source of perpetual aid that helps people scrape by—it's whether we are partners in building the capacity for transformational change.

This mutual responsibility must be the foundation of our partnership. And today, I'll focus on four areas that are critical to the future of Africa and the entire developing world: democracy, opportunity, health, and the peaceful resolution of conflict.

First, we must support strong and sustainable democratic governments.

As I said in Cairo, each nation gives life to democracy in its own way, and in line with its own traditions. But history offers a clear verdict: Governments that respect the will of their own people, that govern by consent and not coercion, are more prosperous, they are more stable, and more successful than governments that do not.

20    This is about more than just holding elections. It's also about what happens between elections. Repression can take many forms, and too many nations, even those that have elections, are plagued by problems that condemn their people to poverty. No country is going to create wealth if its leaders exploit the economy to enrich themselves—or if police—if police can be bought off by drug traffickers. No business wants to invest in a place where the government skims 20 percent off the top—or the head of the Port Authority is corrupt. No person wants to live in a society where the rule of law gives way to the rule of brutality and bribery. That is not democracy, that is tyranny, even if occasionally you sprinkle an election in there. And now is the time for that style of governance to end.

In the 21st century, capable, reliable, and transparent institutions are the key to success—strong parliaments; honest police forces; independent judges; an independent press; a vibrant private sector; a civil society. Those are the things that give life to democracy, because that is what matters in people's everyday lives.

Now, time and again, Ghanaians have chosen constitutional rule over autocracy, and shown a democratic spirit that allows the energy of your people to break through. We see that in leaders who accept defeat graciously—the fact that President Mills' opponents were standing beside him last night to greet me when I came off the plane spoke volumes about Ghana; victors who resist calls to wield power against the opposition in unfair ways. We see that spirit in courageous journalists like Anas

Aremeyaw Anas, who risked his life to report the truth. We see it in police like Patience Quaye, who helped prosecute the first human trafficker in Ghana. We see it in the young people who are speaking up against patronage, and participating in the political process.

Across Africa, we've seen countless examples of people taking control of their destiny, and making change from the bottom up. We saw it in Kenya, where civil society and business came together to help stop post-election violence. We saw it in South Africa, where over three-quarters of the country voted in the recent election—the fourth since the end of Apartheid. We saw it in Zimbabwe, where the Election Support Network braved brutal repression to stand up for the principle that a person's vote is their sacred right.

**Apartheid:** A policy of separating people according to race.

Now, make no mistake: History is on the side of these brave Africans, not with those who use coups or change constitutions to stay in power. Africa doesn't need strongmen, it needs strong institutions.

25    Now, America will not seek to impose any system of government on any other nation. The essential truth of democracy is that each nation determines its own destiny. But what America will do is increase assistance for responsible individuals and responsible institutions, with a focus on supporting good governance—on parliaments, which check abuses of power and ensure that opposition voices are heard; on the rule of law, which ensures the equal administration of justice; on civic participation, so that young people get involved; and on concrete solutions to corruption like forensic accounting and automating services—strengthening hotlines, protecting whistle-blowers to advance transparency and accountability.

And we provide this support. I have directed my administration to give greater attention to corruption in our human rights reports. People everywhere should have the right to start a business or get an education without paying a bribe. We have a responsibility to support those who act responsibly and to isolate those who don't, and that is exactly what America will do.

Now, this leads directly to our second area of partnership: supporting development that provides opportunity for more people. With better governance, I have no doubt that Africa holds the promise of a broader base of prosperity. Witness the extraordinary success of Africans in my country, America. They're doing very well. So they've got the talent, they've got the entrepreneurial spirit. The question is, how do we make sure that they're succeeding here in their home countries? The continent is rich in natural resources. And from cell phone entrepreneurs to small farmers, Africans have shown the capacity and commitment to create their own opportunities. But old habits must also be broken. Dependence on

**Entrepreneurs:** People who start their own businesses.

commodities—or a single export—has a tendency to concentrate wealth in the hands of the few, and leaves people too vulnerable to downturns.

So in Ghana, for instance, oil brings great opportunities, and you have been very responsible in preparing for new revenue. But as so many Ghanaians know, oil cannot simply become the new cocoa. From South Korea to Singapore, history shows that countries thrive when they invest in their people and in their infrastructure; when they promote multiple export industries, develop a skilled workforce, and create space for small and medium-sized businesses that create jobs.

As Africans reach for this promise, America will be more responsible in extending our hand. By cutting costs that go to Western consultants and administration, we want to put more resources in the hands of those who need it, while training people to do more for themselves. That's why our $3.5 billion food security initiative is focused on new methods and technologies for farmers—not simply sending American producers or goods to Africa. Aid is not an end in itself. The purpose of foreign assistance must be creating the conditions where it's no longer needed. I want to see Ghanaians not only self-sufficient in food, I want to see you exporting food to other countries and earning money. You can do that.

30 Now, America can also do more to promote trade and investment. Wealthy nations must open our doors to goods and services from Africa in a meaningful way. That will be a commitment of my administration. And where there is good governance, we can broaden prosperity through public-private partnerships that invest in better roads and electricity; capacity-building that trains people to grow a business; financial services that reach not just the cities but also the poor and rural areas. This is also in our own interests—for if people are lifted out of poverty and wealth is created in Africa, guess what? New markets will open up for our own goods. So it's good for both.

One area that holds out both undeniable peril and extraordinary promise is energy. Africa gives off less greenhouse gas than any other part of the world, but it is the most threatened by climate change. A warming planet will spread disease, shrink water resources, and deplete crops, creating conditions that produce more famine and more conflict. All of us—particularly the developed world—have a responsibility to slow these trends—through mitigation, and by changing the way that we use energy. But we can also work with Africans to turn this crisis into opportunity.

> **Mitigation:** The act of lessening in force or intensity.

Together, we can partner on behalf of our planet and prosperity, and help countries increase access to power while skipping—leapfrogging the dirtier phase of development. Think about it: Across Africa, there is bountiful wind and solar power; geothermal energy and biofuels. From the Rift Valley to the North African deserts; from the Western coasts to South

Africa's crops—Africa's boundless natural gifts can generate its own power, while exporting profitable, clean energy abroad.

These steps are about more than growth numbers on a balance sheet. They're about whether a young person with an education can get a job that supports a family; a farmer can transfer their goods to market; an entrepreneur with a good idea can start a business. It's about the dignity of work; it's about the opportunity that must exist for Africans in the 21st century.

Just as governance is vital to opportunity, it's also critical to the third area I want to talk about: strengthening public health.

35    In recent years, enormous progress has been made in parts of Africa. Far more people are living productively with HIV/AIDS, and getting the drugs they need. I just saw a wonderful clinic and hospital that is focused particularly on maternal health. But too many still die from diseases that shouldn't kill them. When children are being killed because of a mosquito bite, and mothers are dying in childbirth, then we know that more progress must be made.

Yet because of incentives—often provided by donor nations—many African doctors and nurses go overseas, or work for programs that focus on a single disease. And this creates gaps in primary care and basic prevention. Meanwhile, individual Africans also have to make responsible choices that prevent the spread of disease, while promoting public health in their communities and countries.

So across Africa, we see examples of people tackling these problems. In Nigeria, an Interfaith effort of Christians and Muslims has set an example of cooperation to confront malaria. Here in Ghana and across Africa, we see innovative ideas for filling gaps in care—for instance, through E-Health initiatives that allow doctors in big cities to support those in small towns.

America will support these efforts through a comprehensive, global health strategy, because in the 21st century, we are called to act by our conscience but also by our common interest, because when a child dies of a preventable disease in Accra, that diminishes us everywhere. And when disease goes unchecked in any corner of the world, we know that it can spread across oceans and continents.

And that's why my administration has committed $63 billion to meet these challenges—$63 billion. Building on the strong efforts of President Bush, we will carry forward the fight against HIV/AIDS. We will pursue the goal of ending deaths from malaria and tuberculosis, and we will work to eradicate polio. We will fight—we will fight neglected tropical disease. And we won't confront illnesses in isolation—we will invest in public health systems that promote wellness and focus on the health of mothers and children.

40    Now, as we partner on behalf of a healthier future, we must also stop the destruction that comes not from illness, but from human beings—and so the final area that I will address is conflict.

Let me be clear: Africa is not the crude caricature of a continent at perpetual war. But if we are honest, for far too many Africans, conflict is a part of life, as constant as the sun. There are wars over land and wars over resources. And it is still far too easy for those without conscience to manipulate whole communities into fighting among faiths and tribes.

These conflicts are a millstone around Africa's neck. Now, we all have many identities—of tribe and ethnicity; of religion and nationality. But defining oneself in opposition to someone who belongs to a different tribe, or who worships a different prophet, has no place in the 21st century. Africa's diversity should be a source of strength, not a cause for division. We are all God's children. We all share common aspirations—to live in peace and security; to access education and opportunity; to love our families and our communities and our faith. That is our common humanity.

That is why we must stand up to inhumanity in our midst. It is never justified—never justifiable to target innocents in the name of ideology. It is the death sentence of a society to force children to kill in wars. It is the ultimate mark of criminality and cowardice to condemn women to relentless and systemic rape. We must bear witness to the value of every child in Darfur and the dignity of every woman in the Congo. No faith or culture should condone the outrages against them. And all of us must strive for the peace and security necessary for progress.

Africans are standing up for this future. Here, too, in Ghana we are seeing you help point the way forward. Ghanaians should take pride in your contributions to peacekeeping from Congo to Liberia to Lebanon—and your efforts to resist the scourge of the drug trade. We welcome the steps that are being taken by organizations like the African Union and ECOWAS to better resolve conflicts, to keep the peace, and support those in need. And we encourage the vision of a strong, regional security architecture that can bring effective, transnational forces to bear when needed.

45    America has a responsibility to work with you as a partner to advance this vision, not just with words, but with support that strengthens African capacity. When there's a genocide in Darfur or terrorists in Somalia, these are not simply African problems—they are global security challenges, and they demand a global response.

And that's why we stand ready to partner through diplomacy and technical assistance and logistical support, and we will stand behind efforts to hold war criminals accountable. And let me be clear: Our Africa Command is focused not on establishing a foothold in the continent, but on confronting these common challenges to advance the security of America, Africa, and the world.

In Moscow, I spoke of the need for an international system where the universal rights of human beings are respected, and violations of those rights are opposed. And that must include a commitment to support those who resolve conflicts peacefully, to sanction and stop those who don't, and to help those who have suffered. But ultimately, it will be vibrant democracies like Botswana and Ghana which roll back the causes of conflict and advance the frontiers of peace and prosperity.

As I said earlier, Africa's future is up to Africans.

The people of Africa are ready to claim that future. And in my country, African Americans—including so many recent immigrants—have thrived in every sector of society. We've done so despite a difficult past, and we've drawn strength from our African heritage. With strong institutions and a strong will, I know that Africans can live their dreams in Nairobi and Lagos, Kigali, Kinshasa, Harare, and right here in Accra.

50     You know, 52 years ago, the eyes of the world were on Ghana. And a young preacher named Martin Luther King traveled here, to Accra, to watch the Union Jack come down and the Ghanaian flag go up. This was before the march on Washington or the success of the civil rights movement in my country. Dr. King was asked how he felt while watching the birth of a nation. And he said: "It renews my conviction in the ultimate triumph of justice."

Now that triumph must be won once more, and it must be won by you. And I am particularly speaking to the young people all across Africa and right here in Ghana. In places like Ghana, young people make up over half of the population.

And here is what you must know: The world will be what you make of it. You have the power to hold your leaders accountable, and to build institutions that serve the people. You can serve in your communities, and harness your energy and education to create new wealth and build new connections to the world. You can conquer disease, and end conflicts, and make change from the bottom up. You can do that. Yes you can—(applause)—because in this moment, history is on the move.

But these things can only be done if all of you take responsibility for your future. And it won't be easy. It will take time and effort. There will be suffering and setbacks. But I can promise you this: America will be with you every step of the way—as a partner, as a friend. Opportunity won't come from any other place, though. It must come from the decisions that all of you make, the things that you do, the hope that you hold in your heart.

Ghana, freedom is your inheritance. Now, it is your responsibility to build upon freedom's foundation. And if you do, we will look back years from now to places like Accra and say this was the time when the promise was realized; this was the moment when prosperity was forged, when pain was overcome, and a new era of progress began. This can be the time when we witness the triumph of justice once more. Yes we can. Thank you very much. God bless you. Thank you.

# One Word Spotlight

*Colonial map* (paragraph 11) refers to the establishment of colonies in Africa in the nineteenth century by Great Britain, Portugal, France, Germany, Belgium, Spain, and Italy, who raided and exploited the continent for its natural resources and manpower. In carving out most of the continent for their own rule, these countries did not follow traditional African boundaries, and as a result people united by a common language or culture often were separated by artificially imposed borders. By the time colonial powers pulled out of Africa in the twentieth century, these borders were so ingrained that they were generally maintained by the newly independent African nations.

## Reflect on the Reading

1. Analyze the rhetorical situation for this speech: audience(s), purpose(s), topic, exigence, and constraints.

2. Summarize Obama's message in a few sentences.

3. Why do you think Obama chose to address the Ghanaian Parliament instead of another group of Ghanaians?

4. Ethos refers to the believability of a writer or speaker—the background, knowledge, and credentials that make the communicator credible to the audience. What is Obama's ethos in this speech? Compare his ethos in speaking to an African audience to the ethos of previous U.S. presidents.

5. At the end of the speech Obama refers to the "dreams" of Africans and then refers to Martin Luther King's visit to Africa. What effect is Obama trying to achieve with this strategy?

## Consider Your Viewpoint

1. Obama proposes four areas of concern for Africans: democratic governments, economic development, public health, and conflict resolutions. What are some of the connections between these four areas? In your view, which one is most important?

2. In this speech Obama promises billions of dollars to Africans for food programs and health care. Given its recent economic troubles, should the United States be giving money to Africa? Explain your answer.

3. Refer to Africa's history in explaining this sentence from Obama's speech: "For just as it is important to emerge from the control of other nations, it is even more important to build one's own nation."

4. Obama asserts that in order for nations to succeed they need "strong parliaments; honest police forces; independent judges; an independent press; a vibrant private section; [and] a civil society." Are these universal values, or can some countries succeed without all of these characteristics?

5. According to Obama, terrorism in Somalia and genocide in Darfur are global problems, not just local concerns. Do you agree? Explain.

# America Must Rethink Its Attitude about Teenage Drinking

## Robert Rowley
## Italian translation by Gianni Latronico

The following editorial was published in *La Fenice*, a bimonthly online literary journal published in Colobraro, Italy, a small town in the southern part of the country. Its writer, Robert Rowley, contributes a regular column called "Una Voce dall' America," ("A Voice from America") in which he compares the U.S. and Italian cultures. The column is published in both English and Italian. Rowley, whose maternal grandparents immigrated to the United States from Colobraro, is a freelance writer living in Las Cruces, New Mexico. This piece is typical of editorials, which are short columns published in newspapers and magazines that argue for a particular perspective.

*In many cultures, people of all ages enjoy drinking beer or wine with a meal.*

For many colleges around the United States, "Spring Break" has ended. Spring Break is, generally, a one-week vacation from study during the spring semester. Unfortunately, many American college students use spring break to engage in excessive drinking, a behavior that is known as "binge drinking." According to recent research by the National Center on Addiction and Substance Abuse at Columbia University, 70% of American college students drink alcohol, and 49% of those surveyed engage in binge drinking—a clear sign of substance abuse and dependence. This growing problem among American youth can be attributed, in large part, to our society's unenlightened attitude toward teenage alcohol consumption.

In Italy—and in many other European countries—societal attitudes are more mature concerning teen drinking. Young people, at an early age, are introduced to alcohol consumption as a part of everyday life. Liquor, usually in the form of wine, is present at the dinner table, and children are permitted to drink it with meals. This is a healthy attitude because it fosters the understanding among the young that alcohol is not a "forbidden fruit," a substance that adults withhold from children because it contains some magical elixir that allows for escape from the mundane aspects of living. Because of this healthy attitude toward alcohol, Italy—although consuming nearly as much alcohol as any other country in the world—has a decidedly lower rate of alcohol abuse.

According to Dr. David J. Hanson, a sociology professor at the State University of New York, Potsdam, "Italian young people look down on friends who drink too much." In an article titled "Italian Teens Frown On Binge Drinking," Hanson cites Dr. Enrico Tempesta, a research scientist from the

Per molte università degli Stati Uniti, si è appena concluso lo "Spring Break = Intervallo di Primavera." Lo "Spring Break" è, generalmente, una settimana di vacanza dagli studi, durante il semestre della primavera. Purtroppo, molti studenti americani usano lo "Spring Break" per darsi al bere eccessivo, con un comportamento, che è conosciuto come "binge drinking = esagerazione nel bere." Secondo una recente ricerca del National Center on Addiction and Substance Abuse at Columbia University = Centro Nazionale sull'assuefazione e l'abuso di sostanze nocive, all'Università della Colombia), il 70% degli studenti universitari americani beve alcool e il 49% di quelli esaminati è soggetto all'esagerazione nel bere—segno chiaro di abuso e di dipendenza. Questo problema, in aumento fra la gioventù americana, puóessere attribuito, in gran parte, al nostro atteggiamento tollerante verso il consumo dell'alcool, da parte degli adolescenti. In Italia—e in molti altri paese europei—gli atteggiamenti sociali sono più maturi riguardo al bere degli adolescenti.

I giovani, ad un'età adeguata, sono introdotti al consumo dell'alcool, come a un aspetto della vita di tutti i giorni. Il liquore, solitamente consistente in vino, è presente a tavola, durante il pranzo, e ai ragazzi è consentito berlo con i pasti. Questo è un atteggiamento sano, perché promuove la comprensione, fra i giovani, che l'alcool non è "un frutto proibito," una sostanza che gli adulti sottraggono ai ragazzi, perché contiene un certo elisir magico, che permette la fuga dagli aspetti quotidiani della vita. A causa di questo atteggiamento sano, nei confronti dell'alcool, l'Italia—pur consumando quasi lo stesso alcool di qualunque altro paese al mondo-ha decisamente un tasso più basso di abuso di alcool.

government-sponsored Permanent Observatory on Alcohol and Youth, who says: "Here, children and teenagers disapprove and tend to exclude from their circle a contemporary who gets drunk." This attitude toward drunkenness is a direct result of a more mature understanding of the role of alcohol in society.

The attitude is different here in America. For young people, alcohol is taboo. It is against the law to buy or consume alcoholic beverages if you are under the legal age—twenty-one years in most states. Needless to say, many teenagers find a way around the law, drinking illegally and often facing the consequences for their lawbreaking. Others who wait until they reach legal age frequently abuse themselves because of a mistaken attitude about alcohol use: that it is a substance used by adults to signify adulthood. Therefore, many young people come to view the legal consumption of alcohol as a benchmark that marks the passage from youth to adulthood. This distorted tenet—that alcohol is only to be consumed by adults—often leads young people to celebrate their age of legality by participating in a dangerous rite-of-passage: the overindulgence of alcohol to celebrate their birth into adulthood. One particularly dangerous ritual requires that young people who are turning twenty-one begin drinking at midnight of their birthday and consume one shot of hard liquor for each year of their age. Anybody who knows anything about the potency of whisky or other hard liquors understands that twenty-one shots are enough to kill a young person. And, indeed, several college students here at New Mexico State University in Las Cruces have tragically died from binge drinking.

5    In order to change this dangerous trend in American society, adults in the United States must set a responsible example regarding alcohol use. Adults, themselves, must not abuse alcohol. They must refuse to condone public

Secondo il Dott. David J. Hanson, professore di sociologia all'università di Stato di New York, Potsdam, "i giovani italiani guardano dall'alto in basso gli amici che bevono troppo." In un articolo intitolato "Italian Teens Frown On Binge Drinking" ("Gli adolescenti italiani disapprovano l'esagerazione nel bere"), Hanson riporta il Dott. Enrico Tempesta, ricercatore scientifico del governo, finanziato dall'osservatorio permanente sull'alcool e sulla gioventù, che dice: "Qui, i bambini e gli adolescenti disapprovano e tendono ad escludere dal loro gruppo un coetaneo che si ubriaca." Questo atteggiamento nei confronti dell'ubriachezza è un risultato diretto di una comprensione più matura del ruolo dell'alcool nella società.

L'atteggiamento è differente qui, in America. Per i giovani, l'alcool è tabù. È illegale comprare o consumare le bevande alcoliche, se si è al di sotto della maggiore età—ventun anni nella maggior parte degli Stati Uniti. È superfluo dire che molti adolescenti trovano una scappatoia alla legge, bevendo illegalmente ed affrontando spesso le conseguenze del loro reato. Altri, che attendano fino al raggiungimento della maggiore età, ne abusano frequentemente a causa di un atteggiamento erroneo sull'uso dell'alcool: che è una sostanza usata dagli adulti, per indicare l'età adulta. Di conseguenza, molti giovani arrivano a considerare il consumo legale di alcool come segno di riferimento che segna il passaggio dalla gioventù all'età adulta. Questo principio distorto—che l'alcool deve essere consumato soltanto dagli adulti—spesso porta i giovani a festeggiare l'età della legalità, partecipando ad un rito-di-passaggio pericoloso: l'abuso di alcool, per celebrare il loro ingresso nell'età adulta. Un rituale particolarmente pericoloso richiede ai giovani che diventano ventunenni di cominciano a bere alla mezzanotte del loro compleanno e di consumare un bicchierino di

drunkenness. And—as in the Italian example—they must adopt a more mature attitude concerning teenage drinking. Allowing young people to consume modest amounts of alcoholic beverages with meals at home will strip away the mystique surrounding drink, thereby encouraging a reasoned approach to the consumption of beer, wine and hard liquor.

superalcolici, per ogni anno della loro età. Chiunque sappia qualcosa sulla potenza del whiskey, o di altri liquidi inebrianti, capisce che ventuno bicchierini sono abbastanza, per uccidere un giovane. E, infatti, parecchi studenti universitari qui, nel New Mexico State University (l'università di Stato del Nuovo Messico) a Las Cruces sono morti tragicamente, per l'esagerazione nel bere.

10    Per cambiare questa tendenza pericolosa, nella società americana, gli adulti degli Stati Uniti devono dare un esempio responsabile, per quanto riguarda l'uso dell'alcool. Gli adulti stessi non devono abusare dell'alcool. Devono rifiutare di perdonare l'ubriachezza pubblica. Ésulll'esempio italiano-devono assumere un atteggiamento più maturo riguardo al bere degli adolescenti. Permettere che i giovani consumino una quantità modesta di bevande alcoliche, durante i pasti a casa, metterà a nudo il mistero, che circonda le bevande; quindi bisogna consigliare un metodo ragionato per il consumo di birra, vino e di liquidi inebrianti.

## One Word Spotlight

***Spring break*** (paragraph 1) for U.S. college students began in 1936, when the swim coach of Colgate University in New York began taking his team to Fort Lauderdale, Florida, for spring practice at the Casino Pool, the first Olympic-size swimming pool in Florida. The practice caught on with other college swim teams, and by the mid-1950s thousands of college students headed to Fort Lauderdale to swim in pools and on the beach. The 1960s movie *Where the Boys Are*, starring George Hamilton, and other beach movies of the era further connected spring break with beach partying. Now spring break is a tradition throughout the world, including Japan, southern Africa, Canada, China, and Mexico.

## LANGUAGES and CULTURES

The translated version of Rowley's piece illustrates the challenge that translators often face. Obviously, there is no word-for-word correspondence between two languages because of different idioms, grammars, and contexts. Translators need to decide how to express ideas unique to the original text. The translator of Rowley's piece, for example, uses the strategy of giving certain phrases in their original English and then translating them into Italian. He does this in the beginning by writing "Spring Break = Intervallodi Primavera."

## Reflect on the Reading

1. How does Rowley define "a mature attitude concerning teenage drinking"?

2. How does Rowley accommodate his message to an Italian audience? What does he assume Italians already know about the topic and what they don't know?

3. Assume that you disagree with Rowley's message. What are several arguments against his position?

4. How well do you think Rowley supports his points?

5. Rowley asserts that "America must rethink its attitude about teenage drinking," yet he is writing to an Italian audience. Why might Italian readers be interested in this topic?

## Consider Your Viewpoint

1. Rowley writes that in the United States people believe that alcohol is "a substance used by adults to signify adulthood." To what extent do you agree? Explain your answer.

2. When you were growing up, did you view alcohol as a "forbidden fruit," or did you view it another way? Looking back, how healthy was this viewpoint? Is there anything you would have liked to change?

3. Rowley cites a survey that found that 49% of college students engage in binge drinking. How well does this finding correspond to your own experiences?

4. Recently, several presidents of well-known colleges, including Duke, Ohio State, and Morehouse, have recommended that lawmakers consider lowering the legal drinking age to eighteen. They argue that the law keeping people from drinking until twenty-one is routinely ignored and actually encourages binge drinking. Do you agree with this proposal? Why or why not?

5. At the end of his editorial, Rowley writes, "Adults in the United States must set a responsible example regarding alcohol use." To what extent is this goal realistic? How might adults be encouraged to set such an example?

# Asylum and Acceptance: Seeking Peace in Charlottesville, Virginia

## Michael Keller

In 2007, Michael Keller, a student at the College of the Atlantic, applied for a $10,000 grant from 100 Projects for Peace, a philanthropy established by Kathryn Wasserman Davis on her one-hundredth birthday. The goal of 100 Projects for Peace, according to Davis, is to "bring new thinking to the prospects of peace in the world" by encouraging college students in the United States to propose ways to bring mutual understanding to different parts of the world through grassroots activities. For his project, Keller produced what he called a photo-narrative peace project focusing on the lives of refugees living in Charlottesville, Virginia. He has published a book about his experiences on

*Clothing illustrates the mixing of new and old cultures.*

this project, *Streets, Boundaries, and Other Places: Stories of Asylum.* The following is his grant proposal for the project. As you read, note the way that the proposal is divided into different sections for ease of reading.

## Project Overview

Interacting with international refugees has been a life-changing experience—an experience that introduced me to the personal horrors of war, famine, and persecution as well as the resiliency of the human spirit and the importance of community support for disrupted families seeking peace. I propose to collect, record, archive, and share refugee stories of asylum and acceptance through documentary photography and digital recordings in Charlottesville, Virginia, the city where I was born and grew up. Since middle school my life has intersected with the lives of refugees whose stories have spilled out as I helped a Congolese teammate write a poem in English, shared Orthodox Christmas with a Bosnian family, learned Serbo-Croatian on the soccer pitch, and drove a Burmese family to the health department for DPT shots. I learned about the concerns of international families, first as a public school student and youth soccer player, and later as an International Rescue Committee volunteer and English as a Second Language (ESL) mentor.

## Peace Through Shared Experience

As I listened to refugee stories, I heard painful but brave narratives of leaving native lands to begin life in a new country. Although some have lived in Virginia for almost a decade, refugees are often invisible in the Charlottesville area although they present educational, employment, housing, transportation, and even public health challenges. As we shared a ride, chased a ball, or roasted a freshly slaughtered lamb on an outdoor spit, I have considered how most families in our country, including my own, were new here once and that all of us have significantly more in common than we have apart. Because peace demands understanding, empathy, and respect for what others value, *Asylum and Acceptance* will concentrate on our similarities, not our differences, highlighting the historical shared experience of life in a new land. Since simply arriving in a new place does not automatically restore peace to lives that have been involuntarily and often violently interrupted, the project will also help reveal ways to develop more equitable policies that creatively respond to legitimate refugee needs and concerns.

Now re-settled, refugee families pursue peace in their personal lives as they confront different customs and new cultural, racial, economic, and political tensions. Two public officials elected to represent Virginia in the U.S. Congress—deriding what they do not understand—recently made inflammatory remarks about immigrants and minorities. Former Senator George Allen addressed a Virginia student of Indian ancestry as "macaca," and Congressman Virgil Goode, of the 5th Congressional District where I live, criticized Congressman Ellison of Minnesota for using the Koran in his swearing-in ceremony even though that particular

Koran was previously owned by Thomas Jefferson, Charlottesville's most famous citizen and the author of not only the Declaration of Independence but also the Virginia Statute for Religious Freedom. Such remarks are especially ironic as Virginia begins observing the 400th anniversary of the immigration of 108 Europeans who crossed the Atlantic and founded Jamestown in 1607. Today's immigrants, like the Jamestown settlers, are resilient and entrepreneurial despite the hardships and challenges.

## Project Details

To demonstrate a continuum of migration over four centuries, I will document 108 refugees living in Charlottesville, VA, the smallest U.S city with a chapter of the International Rescue Committee (IRC). The IRC, which in 2008 will mark ten years in Charlottesville and seventy-five years internationally, helps to resettle refugees and has made my city a more diverse and multicultural community. Charlottesville is a city where a grassroots initiative can make a difference in community relations and foster a spirit of peaceful cooperation and mutual respect, instead of hostility and suspicion. My project is grassroots and local, yet global with the involvement of refugee families from at least three continents. In Summer 2007, I will use skills developed and knowledge gained at college by courses such as *Advanced Documentary Photography, Intercultural Education,* currently *Europe: Old Continent, New World* (an advanced seminar on the EU and immigration issues), and an independent study in research methodology, a summer working as an architectural photographer, as well as my previous experience as a mentor at the IRC, as an ESL tutor in a summer ESL immersion program for incoming COA students, and as a regular writing tutor during the academic year. I will document refugees' struggles and successes through personal interviews and photography, and include their stories of leaving their own countries and the important legacies and memories of former lives, as well as the transitions to Virginia and an ongoing acceptance of new careers and pursuits. Recognizing that refugees are a vulnerable population, I will develop safeguards and minimize risks to ensure that participants control their own narratives. All participants will be fully informed about the project and appropriate consents and approvals for public use will be digitally recorded before proceeding with interviews, photography, exhibition, or publication. All participants will receive cds of their interviews and copies of their photographs; ongoing consultations will occur throughout the summer. Documentary photography and digitally recorded interviews will occur in different work, study, and home contexts rather than as individual portraiture. The exhibition will highlight local refugee-owned businesses and entrepreneurs and provide a forum to disseminate information about refugee skills and potentials.

## Timeline

5 Prior to setting up an office in week 1 beginning June 4th, I will review human subjects protocols, complete consultations with an oral historian and documentary photographer on project ethics, establish a project website, and begin gaining consents from participants suggested by IRC. In Week 2, in addition to scheduling interpreters for interviews where English is insufficient, I will begin interviews and photography that will continue through Week 8. Since refugees sometime have a unique sense of belongings and possessions, I will ask each participant to select a significant object that can be photographed or exhibited as a contemporary archeological artifact. During the photo-narration process, I will ask several participants to co-curate a community-wide exhibition based on the Peace Project photographs and interviews: all curators will be credited. In Weeks 9–13, we will design, install, and open the exhibition, and edit/revise/archive all products. In Week 14, I will prepare the final report and open two exhibits: one at C'ville Coffee, a meeting place owned and operated by a former Vietnamese immigrant, and the other hosted by the Charlottesville Community Design Center in a downtown pedestrian mall. In addition, I will seek out exhibit space at other local venues and at College of the Atlantic. I will invite public and private school administrators, ESL teachers, affordable housing and public health officials, advocates, and elected officials to participate in the opening of the exhibit to foster cross-cultural understanding and to disseminate the stories of the 108 refuges and policies that will facilitate their acceptance into the community.

## Anticipated Outcomes

Project outcomes include increased awareness of refugee issues and contributions, improved public relations, refugee services, and public policies as well as an enhanced sense of identity, belonging, and ownership for a group that is often forgotten, misunderstood, criticized, or neglected. *Asylum and Acceptance* will have lasting effects through a strengthened community voice articulating refugee issues, struggles, successes, and contributions. These refugee stories will provide models and inspiration for new arrivals struggling to create peaceful lives. Expanded awareness within the broader Charlottesville community should increase sponsorships and donations to the IRC and broaden refugee educational and employment opportunities. All profits from the sale of any photos will be donated to IRC. The project celebrates the entrepreneurship of the many refugee families with new businesses or educational successes. Project materials will be archived at COA and Albemarle Charlottesville Historical Society; anonymity and confidentiality will be ensured where requested. Designed as a seed project, the Peace Project will conclude in September, but I will pursue the topic for a panel discussion at the Virginia Festival of the Book as well as develop a COA senior project that will address refugees, xenophobia, and policies that influence integration.

# One Word Spotlight

*Asylum*, which comes from the classical Greek word for "sanctuary," refers to the practice of nations (including the United States) offering refuge to people undergoing persecution in another part of the world. The persecution can be on the basis of politics or some form of oppression. At one time in the Western world, churches could offer asylum to political prisoners and even criminals.

## Reflect on the Reading

1. What does Keller do to persuade his readers that he is qualified to carry out this project?

2. Summarize what Keller says about the need for his project. How persuasive is he on this topic?

3. How clearly does he state what he will do for this project? What questions do you have, if any, about how he will carry this out?

4. Keller compares Charlottesville's recent immigrants to the Jamestown settlers. Why does he make this comparison? How well does this comparison help him make his point?

5. In the "Anticipated Outcomes" section, Keller writes, "*Asylum and Acceptance* will have lasting effects through a strengthened community voice articulating refugee issues, struggles, successes, and contributions." To what extent has he convinced you that this will happen?

## Consider Your Viewpoint

1. The goal of "100 Projects for Peace" is to "bring new thinking to the prospects of peace in the world." What, if anything, is the "new thinking" in Keller's project?

2. Would some refugees resist participating in this project? Why or why not?

3. Keller writes that the participants in this project will "control their own narratives." Why is this important?

4. What are your experiences—directly or indirectly—with issues related to refugees or immigrants? To what extent are your experiences similar to or different from Keller's experiences?

5. Keller assumes that disseminating the refugees' stories about their experiences is beneficial. Do you agree? How important is it to give people an opportunity to create and display stories about their lives?

# WRITING ASSIGNMENT

For this writing assignment, you will persuade your readers about how to solve a particular problem. The problem can come from experiences in your own life, such as from your workplace, school, or family, or it can come from the wider world around you, such as the environment, education, health care, or the economy. In order to propose a feasible and logical solution, you will need to select a problem sufficiently narrow to be developed in a fairly short piece. You'll consider different solutions to the problem and select a solution that can be explained with logic, facts, and reasons. As a result of proposing how to solve a problem, you will have practiced effective persuasive strategies and be given the opportunity to solve an important problem.

## YOUR SOLUTION TO A PROBLEM

The readings in this chapter exemplified different approaches to writing about problems and their solutions—Obama's speech about developing nations in Africa, an online editorial about attitudes toward alcohol, and a proposal to help immigrants express their identities. Now it's your turn. As always, you want to select a topic that interests you and that fits the constraints of the assignment. Review Chapters 2 and 3 on selecting a topic, analyzing the rhetorical situation, and using a writing process before beginning this assignment.

# Choosing a Topic

As with most writing assignments, a good topic is critical to the success of your piece. While you might be tempted to write about the first topic that comes to you, take the time to consider a variety of topics. For this assignment, focus on finding a problem that is sufficiently narrow in scope to allow you to propose a solution that doesn't take many pages to explain.

You might start by considering topics related to your everyday experiences.

### Workplace

Problem:   Work schedules that don't accommodate the needs of new parents

Solution:  More opportunities to work from home, daycare at workplace

### School

Problem:   Unadvertised scholarship and grant opportunities

Solution:  Weekly email bulletins, "help desk" in financial aid office

### Transportation

Problem:   Traffic jams when classes start and end at the same time

Solution:  Varied class schedules, more online classes, traffic bulletins

You can also reflect on topics that are less focused on your everyday experiences but which still significantly affect you. Here are several examples:

### Humane Treatment of Animals

Problem:   Animal shelters euthanizing thousands of cats and dogs

Solution:  Organize school students to raise money to pay for spaying and neutering animals

### Healthy Lifestyles

Problem:   Growing obesity rates in children

Solution:  Increase number of hours spent in physical education every week

### Environment

Problem:   Reliance on cars for transportation

Solution:  Raise by $1.00 the tax on gasoline; use this money to fund the development of renewable energy

Once you choose a topic, be sure that it is narrow enough to discuss in detail. For example, a proposal to reduce greenhouse gas by requiring each state to increase wind energy by 20 percent is too technical to be discussed in a fairly short piece. This proposal also isn't very feasible because it would be so controversial. However, you could propose that the city council in your community offer tax incentives to encourage businesses to develop and/or use wind energy.

---

### Topic Questions for Solving a Problem

- ▪ Will my readers be interested in my topic?
- ▪ Do I feel engaged with this topic?
- ▪ Is the problem and solution narrow enough to be discussed in detail?
- ▪ Will the solution make sense to the audience?
- ▪ Will I be able to find enough reasons and evidence to support my ideas?

---

**Connect With Others**

**Activity 11.1**    With several classmates, list a series of problems in different areas of your life, such as the workplace and school. Also consider several social problems. Next, brainstorm as many solutions as you can for each problem, writing them down as they come to you. Finally, review the solutions that you have gathered and discuss which ones would be most appropriate for this assignment. Which solutions can be supported in just a few pages? Which ones seem most reasonable and can be backed with reasons and evidence?

---

## Analyzing the Rhetorical Situation

Now that you have selected a problem/solution topic, you need to examine your rhetorical situation to ensure the effectiveness of your piece.

**Considering Audience and Purpose.**   Start by imagining readers who care about the problem you're examining and who will be interested in your solution. Depending on your topic, your readers might be people who can actually implement the solution you're proposing. For instance, if you're discussing a problem in your workplace, your audience could be your immediate supervisor. If you're proposing a change in your community, your audience might be the mayor and/or the city council. The audience for President Obama's speech to the leaders of Ghana was political leaders who could initiate the changes he proposed. The readers of Michael Keller's grant proposal were the directors of 100 Projects for Peace charged with distributing the organization's funds. Your audience could also be people who are simply interested in the topic, similar to the Italian readers of Robert Rowley's piece on binge drinking in the online journal *La Fenice*.

## Audience Questions for Solving a Problem

- Who will care about the problem I'm discussing?
- Who will be able to implement the solution that I'm proposing?
- What background knowledge do these readers have about the topic?
- Will their cultural background, age, or gender affect their reaction to my proposal?
- What will my readers' attitudes be? Will they tend to agree, disagree, or be neutral about my ideas?

For this assignment, your primary purpose for writing is persuasive: You want to convince your readers to agree with your ideas. However, your secondary purpose will be informative because you'll need to provide your readers with sufficient information for them to understand your points. By providing good reasons and enough information, you can make your readers take your ideas seriously. Your own experiences with the topic can enhance your credibility as well. In Michael Keller's grant proposal, for instance, he provided information about his previous experiences working with immigrants to persuade his readers that he had the background to successfully complete his project.

## Purpose Questions for Solving a Problem

- What reasons will be most persuasive for my audience?
- What kinds of evidence will my readers want me to provide?
- What personal experience can I include that will be persuasive?
- What do I want my readers to take away from this piece?

**Choosing a Genre and Visual Design.**  After analyzing your audience and purpose, you're ready to select the most suitable genre or format. In some instances the audience determines a particular format; for instance, the directors of 100 Projects for Peace required that applicants submit their grant applications as electronic files, which is typical for grant proposals. Other times, though, you can determine the genre based on the purpose of the message. President Obama, for example, could have written a letter to the Ghanaian Parliament. However, his message had much greater impact because he appeared in person. Consider adding visuals to your problem/solution piece if they will add to its persuasiveness. See Chapter 14 for more information about visual design.

## Genre and Visual Design Questions for Solving a Problem

- Has my audience given me a particular format to follow?
- If I can choose my format, which one would be best for persuading my readers to agree with my ideas?
- What visual design elements will make my piece more readable and persuasive?
- What can I do to increase my knowledge of this format and visual design?

**Reviewing Exigence and Constraints.**   Usually we think of ways to solve problems so that our lives, and the lives of others, can be improved. The desire for improvement is why people write letters to the editor, volunteer in the community, and run for political office. Of course, a class or work-place assignment is another motivation to write.

## Exigence Questions for Solving a Problem

- What are your motivations for writing this piece?
- Why do you care about the topic?
- What do you want your readers to think after they read your piece?
- Why is it important to write out your ideas for solving a problem?

Constraints include anything that might present challenges, such as the need to find evidence to support your point or to interview someone about the feasibility of your solution. They can also include practical matters such as fitting this assignment into your busy schedule and finding a fast Internet connection to help you do research.

## Constraint Questions for Solving a Problem

- What concerns me the most about completing this piece?
- How might I arrange my schedule so I can have enough time for writing?
- To what extent will the page limit constrain me in communicating my ideas?
- What steps can I take to meet these challenges?

**Activity 11.2**   Analyze examples of problem/solution pieces. Find these pieces by consulting the "op/ed" sections of newspapers, the websites of political leaders, or correspondence in your workplace about policies and procedures. Analyze these examples by responding to the following questions:

1. How well do the authors convince you that a problem needs to be solved?
2. How logical and sensible is the proposed solution?
3. How persuasive are the reasons and evidence?
4. If there are visuals, how do they help convey the author's message?

# Using the Writing Process

Now that you have analyzed the rhetorical situation, you're ready to begin writing by following the stages of the writing process: discovering ideas, drafting to explore ideas, revising to improve content, and editing to eliminate errors.

### STAGE 1: Discovering Ideas

As you learned in Chapter 3 , you can discover ideas by using a variety of techniques. One of the best techniques for a problem/solution piece is charting.

Charting.  An advantage of using a chart when discovering ideas is that it can show the relationship between ideas. Your word processing program offers a variety of different kinds of charts to select from, including pie charts, bar charts, and area charts. If, for instance, you had decided to write about the problem of teenagers dropping out of school, you could chart various solutions for this problem, as shown in Figure 11.1.

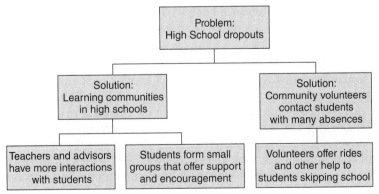

**FIGURE 11.1**  Charting to analyze a problem

## STAGE 2: Drafting to Explore Ideas

In a persuasive piece of any genre—speech, editorial, proposal, and so on—you will use a combination of logos, ethos, and pathos as you develop your ideas. Aristotle, the Greek philosopher who lived around 350 B.C.E, referred to logos, ethos, and pathos as the three appeals that communicators make to persuade their audiences.

**Logos.** The word *logic* is derived from the classical Greek word *logos*, which originally meant "word." When you use logos, you try to persuade your reader through reasons, evidence, and (naturally) logic. When you appeal to your reader's intellect, you often use facts and statistics, as Rowley did in his opinion piece on binge drinking:

> According to recent research by the National Center on Addiction and Substance Abuse at Columbia University, 70% of American college students drink alcohol, and 49% of those surveyed engage in binge drinking—a clear sign of substance abuse and dependence.

Notice that Rowley connects the percentage of drinking among college students to the main topic of his piece—the problem of binge drinking—so that his readers understand how the evidence supports his main topic.

Logos can also consist of factual examples, as in President Obama's speech in Ghana:

> So across Africa, we see examples of people tackling these problems. In Nigeria, an Interfaith effort of Christians and Muslims has set an example of cooperation to confront malaria. Here in Ghana and across Africa, we see innovative ideas for filling gaps in care—for instance, through E-Health initiatives that allow doctors in big cities to support those in small towns.

Examples such as these are persuasive because they illustrate to the audience how Obama's recommendations can be implemented.

**Ethos.** At first glance, "ethos" might appear to refer to "ethics" because of the similarity of the two words. However, Aristotle used ethos in a broader way: to refer to the writer's believability or credibility. To be persuasive, you need to show your readers that you know what you're talking about, as demonstrated by the quality of your ideas and information. Your previous experiences and any research that you conduct can also enhance your credibility. Aristotle also emphasized that you need to be seen as trustworthy, which can be shown by your willingness to examine your opponent's position objectively.

To strengthen your ethos, show that you know about the topic through personal experience or research. In his grant proposal, Michael Keller establishes his ethos quickly in his first paragraph:

> Since middle school my life has intersected with the lives of refugees whose stories have spilled out as I helped a Congolese teammate write a poem in English, shared Orthodox Christmas with a Bosnian family, learned Serbo-Croatian on the soccer pitch, and drove a Burmese family to the health department for DPT shots.

These references to his previous experiences make Keller appear knowledgeable and engaged, which helps him convince his readers to invest money in his project.

Your ethos is also expressed visually. A document that is formatted according to appropriate genre conventions demonstrates your knowledge of the rhetorical situation. When you give a speech, your preparation, appearance, and mannerisms can make you more (or less) convincing to your audience. If you give a formal presentation to a group of business leaders while wearing shorts and a t-shirt, your ethos will suffer. Political leaders often surround themselves with patriotic images such as the flag to convince the audience that they have the best interests of the country at heart.

**Pathos.** When you appeal to your audience's emotions, you are using pathos. Advertisers use pathos when they make you feel inadequate if you don't have the latest trend. Lovers use pathos when they write romantic notes to their beloved. Charities draw on your sympathy when they show pictures of disadvantaged people while soliciting for donations. Aristotle believed that pathos was potentially the strongest appeal but also the most dangerous because pure emotion could mislead people to do wrong.

Despite Aristotle's caution, pathos is an excellent persuasive tool when used skillfully and ethically. In his address in Ghana, Obama used pathos when he reminded his audience of Martin Luther King:

> You know, 52 years ago, the eyes of the world were on Ghana. And a young preacher named Martin Luther King traveled here, to Accra, to watch the Union Jack come down and the Ghanaian flag go up. This was before the march on Washington or the success of the civil rights movement in my country. Dr. King was asked how he felt while watching the birth of a nation. And he said: "It renews my conviction in the ultimate triumph of justice."

Obama is appealing to his audience's patriotism by referring to the birth of modern Ghana, an event that naturally fills his audience with pride. At the same time, Obama connects the birth of this nation with the widely respected King, which helps to intensify this pride. As a result, Obama's audience is more likely to agree with his argument about the path that African nations should follow.

When he discussed logos, ethos, and pathos, Aristotle stressed that you need to know which appeals are best suited to particular audiences. Ethos is critical for every audience because you need to appear trustworthy in order to be persuasive. Logos is important for academic audiences because of the high value placed on reason and logic. Pathos is used for many different audiences because at times everyone is swayed more by emotion than by rationality.

**Your Emotional Filter and Writing Monitor.** If you have chosen a topic about which you have strong feelings, you might need to detach yourself from the topic as you draft so you can marshal your best arguments. You want to energetically argue your position but not to the point where you forget to anticipate how your audience will respond. On the other hand, if you find yourself wavering about your position, you might be too indecisive to take a convincing stand. In this case, do more research to discover the best position to take. Because you're still focusing mostly on content, do not overly monitor your writing. Focus on getting your ideas down on paper in an organized way. If you can't think of the right word to express an idea, leave it blank or write it down in another language. You'll be able to fix these problems as you revise.

## STAGE 3: Revising to Improve Content

Before your revise your piece, set it aside for a day or two. When you take it up again, you'll have a fresher perspective. When revising to improve content, focus on how you have organized and developed your ideas, as well as on sentence structure and word choice. As you rewrite, try to imagine the piece from the perspective of a reader: How convincing would that reader find your solution to the problem you're discussing?

**Find a Feasible Solution.** The word *feasible* comes from the Latin word *facere,* or "to do." To be persuasive, the solution that you propose should seem doable. In his proposal for 100 Projects for Peace, Michael Keller could have claimed that he would get every immigrant he worked with a well-paying job. However, this would have been an unreasonable claim because he simply didn't have the resources or authority to make this happen. In contrast, his proposal to document refugees' struggles and successes was something that he had the skills to complete in a limited time period.

**One Student's Work.** In her composition class, student writer Daniele Arat was asked to write an online editorial for the class website. She had been concerned about the hip-hop music her younger siblings liked to listen to because of lyrics that she believed were degrading to women. But what could be done? She freewrote some possible solutions.

> I find some hip-hop music to be misogynist, and I worry about how that affects listeners, especially girls and boys who might think that these lyrics are cool. So what can be a solution to these lyrics? How to get hip-hop to be more respectful to women? I can suggest that such lyrics should be censored, but that's pretty unrealistic. I bet some artists would say that censorship violates their right of freedom of expression, and they might be right about that. I can imagine all sorts of court cases that don't lead anywhere except maybe to more publicity for some of the hip-hop musicians.
>
> The music industry basically encourages lyrics that degrade women because it sells more records. They only care about the bottom line. Is there a way to change the record industry? Ha! I doubt it. Is there a way to educate people about the effects of these lyrics on hip-hop fans? So that they don't buy the music? Perhaps if they knew about hip-hop that was really good but wasn't degrading to women. That might make a lot more sense.

**Activity 11.3**  Divide into groups with each group selecting one of the readings at the beginning of the chapter. Discuss the ways that logos, ethos, and pathos are developed in the reading. Consider the writer's overall approach to the topic as well as specific paragraphs. Keep in mind that the three appeals work together to achieve a particular purpose and as a result cannot be viewed in isolation.

**Connect
With Others**

## Rhetorical Situation Questions for Solving a Problem

- Audience: Will your audience understand that the problem is important and worth reading about? Have you appropriately used logos, ethos, and pathos to appeal to your audience?
- Purpose: Have you proposed a feasible solution to the problem? Have you explained the problem in sufficient detail to be persuasive?
- Genre: Is the format that you have chosen appropriate for your audience and purpose? Would your message be more persuasive if you used another genre?
- Exigence: Do you feel that you have shared an important idea with your audience? Is there anything more that you want your audience to know?
- Constraints: Are there any remaining obstacles to finishing this piece? If so, how do you plan to overcome them?

To further help you revise your piece, ask someone to read it and give suggestions for revision. This peer review will help you gauge how potential readers will react to your writing.

## Peer Review
### Solving a Problem

1. What is the greatest strength of this piece?

2. What problem is being described and how important does it seem? How well do I make you concerned about the problem?

3. What is the proposed solution to the problem? To what extent is the solution feasible and realistic? Can you suggest an improvement?

4. How effective is my ethos? Do I appear to be knowledgeable about the topic?

5. Taking my intended audience into consideration, how effectively do I use logos and pathos?

6. How well are my ideas connected together? Point out any sentences that seem choppy.

7. Underline any words or sentences that you had trouble understanding.

8. Put a checkmark in the margin when you see an error in punctuation or spelling.

## STAGE 4: Editing for Correctness

In the previous stages you have focused on content, organization, and development. As you did this, you probably improved your sentences and word choice. When you edit, you want to make your piece more readable for your audience by eliminating distracting errors. Remember that some errors are governed by rules, and the rules to correct these errors can be looked up in a grammar handbook such as the one at the end of this book. You might have made other errors, such as the incorrect use of a word or phrase, where there's no rule that determines its correctness. Ask someone to read your piece to help you correct these errors. If you are fluent in spoken English, reading your piece aloud will help you recognize any errors you might have made.

## To Edit

- Use a dictionary and a computer spell-check.
- Refer to a grammar handbook for treatable errors such as verb tense, sentence fragments, and so on.
- Ask a tutor or friend to help you with errors such as prepositions and idioms.
- As you edit, keep an Editing Log, a section in a notebook or a computer document in which you record your errors and show how they should be corrected. Refer to this Editing Log frequently as a reminder.

# ONE STUDENT'S SOLUTION TO A PROBLEM

In the revising section of this chapter you read part of Daniele Arat's on-line editorial draft in which she worked toward developing a feasible solution to the problem of misogyny in hip-hop. Here is Arat's final version.

### Misogyny in Hip-Hop and Rap

#### *Daniele Arat*

For some time the entertainment industry, particularly the part of the industry that produces and markets hip-hop and rap, has been criticized for the alarmingly offensive, disparaging, and even violent ways that women are portrayed. The lyrics of some songs refer to black women as "bitches" and "hos" as the singers boast about how they are going to beat up or even kill them; some CD covers and music videos depict women wearing almost nothing while performing sexually degrading acts on the artists. The hip-hop and rap entertainment industry is a powerful global institution which continues to earn millions of dollars at the expense of women. The best way to stop this exploitation is through local, grassroots efforts that emphasize that misogyny is a violation of the rights and dignity of women *and* men.

It is important to acknowledge that not all hip-hop music is negative toward women. Artists such as Mary K. Blige and MC Lyte have created music that focuses on women's need for self-respect and control over their own lives. When asked about the way women are portrayed in rap videos, Lyte replied that "There are ways to be sexy and classy without being borderline disgusting" (Morgan 192). And hip-hop music in general can be a positive force for change. Hip-hop artists have worked together to encourage young people to stay away from crime (Schaeffer-Duffy 10a), to promote environmentalism (De Simone), and to encourage young

Arat arrived at this claim after freewriting about feasible solutions to misogyny in hip-hop.

By noting that not all hip-hop is negative toward women, Arat is enhancing her ethos. She appears even-handed and objective about her topic.

people to vote (Chang). In fact, when hip-hop began early in the 1970s in the South Bronx it was a political as well as musical movement because the artists were bringing to light the drugs, poverty, and violence that they encountered (Jackson and Anderson 23). The misogyny and violence in hip-hop increased only after record companies realized that they could make money from it.

It's likely that hip-hop music can affect how people behave. A study by the Pacific Institute for Research and Evaluation conducted by Meng-Jinn Chen and two colleagues surveyed over a thousand young people to see if there was any relationship between people's behavior and the type of music they listened to. Chen writes that the study found that

> Compared with other music genres, rap music was consistently and positively associated with use of alcohol, malt-liquor, potential alcohol-use disorder, marijuana, club drugs, and aggressive behaviors. (Chen, Miller, and Grube 3)

By supporting her points with peer-reviewed scholarly research, Arat is using logos, a credible strategy for her audience.

Similarly, interviews with young people in forty focus groups in ten cities revealed that young black girls had low self-esteem and often tried to act like the women portrayed in music videos (Britt). These studies suggest that the rap music and rap videos negatively affect both young women and young men.

Censorship of hip-hop (or any kind of music) is not the answer because the U.S. Constitution protects freedom of speech. Education and persuasion are much better approaches. Artists, producers, and music company executives need to come together to save hip-hop from misogyny and violence toward women. Some action has already been taken toward this goal. In 2004 a hip-hop political convention was held in Newark, New Jersey, in which students, artists, and political activists focused on trying to direct hip-hop energy toward political action. The topics of women's rights and misogyny were discussed (Raimist). In 2005 Spelman College and *Essence* magazine held a town hall meeting called "Take Back the Music" which dealt with how women were portrayed in hip-hop videos. Some attendees included music industry executives (Spelman College). Princeton University held a symposium on rap music in 2006 that included rap artist TalibKweli, U.S. Rep. Maxine Waters of California, and Cornell West ("Hip-Hop"). Events such as these allow discussions about effective ways to change the negative messages of hatred and violence toward women.

By noting that misogyny in hip-hop affects men as well as women, Arat is appealing to a broad audience.

Attitudes about sexuality in hip-hop affect men as well as women. Filmmaker and social activist Byron Hurt has criticized the "hyper-aggression" in rap that leads to homophobia and misogyny ("Behind the Mask" 86). He points out that rap promotes violence against men as well as against women. Hurt created a documentary, *Hip-Hop: Beyond Beats and Rhymes*, in which he calls on the hip-hop music industry to take responsibility for negative images of men (as well as women). He writes, "I made this film for all of the Hip-Hop fans who, like me, are conflicted about Hip-Hop and can't let it go" (Hurt 2). The movie has been shown at community centers around the country where young people and community leaders together discuss its message.

Hip-hop and rap are important musical traditions that developed toward the end of the twentieth century as a way to represent the experience of young African-Americans in inner cities. However, this music can also devalue women and men. We need to educate people to pressure the music industry to stop sexual exploitation in music.

## Works Cited

"Behind the Mask." *Bitch Magazine: Feminist Response to Pop Culture* 41 (Fall 2008): 86–87. *Academic Search Complete.* Web. 22 Oct. 2009.

Britt, Donna. "A Devastating Loss of Self-Esteem." *The Washington Post* 13 Feb. 2004: B01. Web. 15 Oct. 2009.

Chang, Jeff. "Fight the Power." *Mother Jones* 32.6 (2007). *Academic Search Complete.* Web. 21 Sept. 2009.

Chen, M. J., B. A. Miller, and J. W. Grube. "Influence of Music on Youth Behaviors." *Brown University Child and Adolescent Behavior Letter* 22.6 (2006): 3–4. *Academic Search Complete.* Web. 1 Oct. 2009.

De Simone, Claudia Sara. "Hip Hopping Mad." *Alternatives Journal* 34.1 (2008): 7. *Academic Search Complete.* Web. 12 Oct. 2009.

"Hip-Hop Symposium Joins Academics and Activists." *Princeton University.* Trustees of Princeton U, 2 Oct. 2006. Web. 22 Oct. 2009.

Hurt, Byron. "A Resource Guide for Community Organizers and Educators." *Hip-Hop: Beyond Beats & Rhymes.* Byron Hurt, 2007. Web. 15 Oct. 2009.

Jackson, Brenda, and Sharon Anderson. "Hip Hop Culture Around the Globe: Implications for Teaching." *Black History Bulletin* 72.1 (2009): 22–32. *Academic Search Complete.* Web. 12 Oct. 2009.

Morgan, Joan. "Mc lyte." *Essence* 36.2 (2005): 192. *Academic Search Complete.* Web. 15 Oct. 2009.

Raimist, Joan. "Activists, Scholars, Artists and Students Gather to Talk about Hip-Hop." *New York Amsterdam News* 1 July 2004. *Academic Search Complete*. Web. 29 Sept. 2009.

Schaeffer-Duffy, Claire. "Rappers Promote Peace in Song." *National Catholic Reporter* 20 Oct. 2006: 10a. *Academic Search Complete*. Web. 22 Oct. 2009.

"Spelman College and *Essence* Magazine Co-Host 'Take Back the Music' Town Hall." Spelman College, 25 Feb. 2005. Web. 22 Oct. 2009.

# ADDITIONAL READINGS

## Lose 300 Million Tons of $CO_2$ in Just Three Weeks!

### Kate Sheppard

Environmental issues such as air pollution, greenhouse gases, and climate change have been discussed for several decades, and while progress has been made in some areas, much needs to be done. In "Lose 300 Million Tons of $CO_2$ in the Just Three Weeks!" Kate Sheppard, an environmental reporter, tries to attract attention to this issue by proposing that a common technique used by people who are cutting calories can also help with cleaning up the environment and reducing greenhouse gases.

I've been known to indulge in a few potato chips now and then—and by a few, I mean the whole bag. But it wasn't until my doctor asked me to keep a diary of my dietary habits that I began to realize I might have a fried-potato problem. It's one thing to mindlessly munch on Kettle Chips while watching the cast of *Glee* bust out a racy rendition of Salt-n-Pepa's "Push It." It's another to document every single indulgence for the inspection of your disapproving doc. As it turns out, the diet diary is a tried-and-true weight-loss technique, as a 2008 study in the *American Journal of Preventive Medicine* discovered. It worked for me: After two weeks of guiltily recording every time I popped a Pringle, I started eating a lot more carefully.

This simple tool may be useful for tackling problems more momentous than my potato-chip habit. Take the heat-trapping greenhouse gases that are changing life on Earth as we know it. As it happens, a collection of agencies and regulators are about to require large swaths of the economy to record and disclose their emissions—basically the equivalent of a carbon diary. Could the country's biggest polluters be shamed into going on a greenhouse gas diet?

Soon, major emitters that account for roughly 85 percent of the country's greenhouse gas output will be required to report their emissions to the Environmental Protection Agency. Electric utilities, oil and chemical refineries; major manufacturers; and iron and steel producers will start submitting data by 2011, with heavy-duty vehicle and engine manufacturers to join in the following year. And any public company—from banks like Bank of America to department stores like Wal-Mart to software companies like Microsoft—will have to report its impact on the climate, as well as potential liabilities arising from global warming, under new guidelines from the Securities and Exchange Commission. A growing number of businesses are even fessing up voluntarily, via initiatives like the Carbon Disclosure Project, whose 2,500 member companies document both their own emissions and potential financial risks arising from environmental changes.

The model for the new wave of carbon disclosure rules is the Toxics Release Inventory, which was created by Congress in the 1980s to discourage the use of harmful chemicals in industrial production. The program didn't force companies to cut back on the chemicals they released (amendments to the Clean Air Act would later do so). It simply mandated that they document them. But then something unexpected happened. When the first year's worth of data was released in 1987, it made the front pages of newspapers around the country. Chemical manufacturers, oil refiners, and paper mills, it turned out, had pumped out nearly 3 billion pounds of toxic air pollution that year—and the inventory identified the worst offenders. Richard Mahoney, CEO at the agribusiness giant Monsanto—which had released 374 million pounds of toxins into the air over the preceding 12 months—vowed to cut the company's toxic emissions by 90 percent over five years. "Our overall goal is zero effect on public perceptions," Mahoney told *Financial World*.

5    In the first year of reporting from 1987 to 1988, toxic releases dropped by 548.8 million pounds. Between 1988 and 1989, they fell by

another 720.8 million pounds—a 19 percent decrease in just two years. Some companies "really didn't know what they were emitting," said David Doniger, climate policy director at the Natural Resources Defense Council. Others "didn't want to lose the perception of being clean." The principle at work was what psychologists call "social proof"—the human tendency to adjust behavior to those around them. Companies, like people, don't want to stand out for the wrong reasons.

Early adopters of carbon disclosure credit the practice with helping them identify bad habits. 3M, maker of the ubiquitous Scotch tape as well as other adhesives, building materials, and medical and office supplies, started counting and disclosing its greenhouse gas emissions in 2002. In the process, it discovered that its thermal oxidizers—which are used to keep hazardous toxics out of the air—were responsible for a significant portion of their carbon emissions. By adopting a new system, the company was able to cut emissions 54 percent by 2006, says 3M's manager of environmental initiatives and sustainability, Keith Miller.

Putting emissions data in the public domain can also bolster legal efforts to tackle climate change. In 2005, lawyers for a group of states suing electric utilities over their carbon output used EPA records to calculate the five biggest polluters—American Electric Power, Southern Co., Cinergy (now merged with Duke Energy), the Tennessee Valley Authority, and Xcel Energy. After losing in district court, the states won on appeal. (The utilities are seeking Supreme Court review.) Expect to see more such lawsuits: The various new disclosure rules under development will gather data from many more companies and make it widely accessible.

Of course, just as a diet diary alone won't magically evaporate unwanted pounds, carbon disclosure alone is not the answer to our over-emitting problem. But if my potato chip consumption is any guide, it's a surprisingly effective place to start.

**Ubiquitous:** Appearing everywhere.

## Reflect on the Reading

1. The author compares keeping a diet diary with requiring emitters to keep track of and publish their emissions. How effective is this analogy?

2. The author relies on logos to develop her points. How effective is her use of facts, data, and other evidence?

3. What strategies does the author use to develop her ethos?

## Consider Your Viewpoint

1. In the fifth paragraph, the author refers to "social proof": "the human tendency to adjust behavior to those around them." What is an example of social proof that you have encountered?

2. Are you more likely to buy products from companies that have cut their toxic emissions? Why or why not?

3. To what extent should the government regulate toxic emissions and to what extent should companies regulate themselves?

## Attention Whole Foods Shoppers

### Robert Paarlberg

Eating organic, going vegan, growing your own food—these are recent food trends in the developed world as people focus on healthy lifestyles. In the developing world, in contrast, millions of people go hungry on a regular basis. In the following selection, Robert Paarlberg, a professor at Wellesley College, discusses this paradox as he focuses on the global politics of food.

From Whole Foods recyclable cloth bags to Michelle Obama's organic White House garden, modern eco-foodies are full of good intentions. We want to save the planet. Help local farmers. Fight climate change—and childhood obesity, too. But though it's certainly a good thing to be thinking about global welfare while chopping our certified organic onions, the hope that we can help others by changing our shopping and eating habits is being wildly oversold to Western consumers. Food has become an elite preoccupation in the West, ironically, just as the most effective ways to address hunger in poor countries have fallen out of fashion.

Helping the world's poor feed themselves is no longer the rallying cry it once was. Food may be today's cause célèbre, but in the pampered West, that means trendy causes like making food "sustainable"—in other words, organic, local, and slow. Appealing as that might sound, it is the wrong recipe for helping those who need it the most. Even our understanding of the global food problem is wrong these days, driven too much by the single issue of international prices. In April 2008, when the cost of rice for export had tripled in just six months and wheat reached its highest price in 28 years, a *New York Times* editorial branded this a "World Food Crisis."

> Cause célèbre: A cause that gets great public attention.

World Bank President Robert Zoellick warned that high food prices would be particularly damaging in poor countries, where "there is no margin for survival." Now that international rice prices are down 40 percent from their peak and wheat prices have fallen by more than half, we too quickly conclude that the crisis is over. Yet 850 million people in poor countries were chronically undernourished before the 2008 price spike, and the number is even larger now, thanks in part to last year's global recession. This is the real food crisis we face.

It turns out that food prices on the world market tell us very little about global hunger. International markets for food, like most other international markets, are used most heavily by the well-to-do, who are far from hungry. The majority of truly undernourished people—62 percent, according to the U.N. Food and Agriculture Organization—live in either Africa or South Asia, and most are small farmers or rural landless laborers living in the countryside of Africa and South Asia. They are significantly shielded from global price fluctuations both by the trade policies of their own governments and by poor roads and infrastructure. In Africa, more than 70 percent of rural households are cut off from the closest urban markets because, for instance, they live more than a 30-minute walk from the nearest all-weather road.

Poverty—caused by the low income productivity of farmers' labor—is the primary source of hunger in Africa, and the problem is only getting worse. The number of "food insecure" people in Africa (those consuming less than 2,100 calories a day) will increase 30 percent over the next decade without significant reforms, to 645 million, the U.S. Agriculture Department projects.

5      What's so tragic about this is that we know from experience how to fix the problem. Wherever the rural poor have gained access to improved roads, modern seeds, less expensive fertilizer, electrical power, and better schools and clinics, their productivity and their income have increased. But recent efforts to deliver such essentials have been undercut by deeply misguided (if sometimes well-meaning) advocacy against agricultural modernization and foreign aid.

In Europe and the United States, a new line of thinking has emerged in elite circles that opposes bringing improved seeds and fertilizers to traditional farmers and opposes linking those farmers more closely to international markets. Influential food writers, advocates, and celebrity restaurant owners are repeating the mantra that "sustainable food" in the future must be organic, local, and slow. But guess what: Rural Africa already has such a system, and it doesn't work. Few smallholder farmers in Africa use any synthetic chemicals, so their food is de facto organic. High transportation costs force them to purchase and sell almost all of their food locally. And food preparation is painfully slow. The result is nothing to celebrate: average income levels of only $1 a day and a one-in-three chance of being malnourished.

**Synthetic:**
Developed by humans through a chemical process.

If we are going to get serious about solving global hunger, we need to de-romanticize our view of preindustrial food and farming. And that means learning to appreciate the modern, science-intensive, and highly capitalized agricultural system we've developed in the West. Without it, our food would be more expensive and less safe. In other words, a lot like the hunger-plagued rest of the world.

## Reflect on the Reading

1. What does the author mean when he writes that food has become "an elite preoccupation"?

2. According to the author, why is focusing on food prices an inaccurate way of determining how many people go hungry?

3. What are preindustrial farming methods and why are they inadequate for producing enough food in many parts of the world?

## Consider Your Viewpoint

1. Explain how the title of this piece helps to develop the author's main point.

2. How well has the author used logos, ethos, and pathos? In other words, how well has he supported his points and to what extent do you find him credible?

3. Do you agree with the author that we have romanticized preindustrial methods of producing food?

For support in meeting this chapter's objectives, follow this path in MyCompLab: Resources ⇒ Writing ⇒ Writing Samples ⇒ Writing Samples: Proposals. Review the Instruction and Multimedia resources about proposals, then complete the Exercises and click on Gradebook to measure your progress.

# CHAPTER 12 Advocating for Change

## Learning Objectives

In this chapter you will:

- Support or defend a cause to improve the lives of others.
- Consider how including visual content can strengthen your argument.
- Use sentence variety to draft a strong argument.
- Revise and edit to improve word choice.

*What change would you like to see on your campus?*

Have you ever asked yourself why things can't be different: why more countries don't do something about global warming, why there aren't more women engineers in the United States, why California freeways can't withstand an earthquake, or why more people in your community don't recycle? Have you ever wanted to do something to change the situation? To advocate for change means to support or defend a cause that will improve the lives of others. To effectively champion a cause and educate others about the necessity for action, you must first educate yourself. Then, once you fully understand the situation, you're in a position to develop an argument to advocate for change.

When you develop an argument, you have the opportunity to persuade others to think as you do and, in turn, to take action. When used in rhetoric, an argument is not a quarrel; it is a carefully crafted piece of writing intended to persuade an audience.

# WRITING TO ADVOCATE FOR CHANGE

To advocate for change, start by identifying a cause that you would like to support. You may already have a passion for a particular cause, but if not, begin by reading some online local, national, or international newspapers or reading websites such as slate.com or salon.com. What are some community, state, national, and international causes in the headlines? Can you identify a cause that you would be willing to support in an effort to bring about change? When advocating for change, your primary purpose is persuasive: to change your readers' minds and to get them to take action. In addition, you provide information to support your position and provide some of your own personal thoughts and feelings to demonstrate your commitment.

---

### Questions for Advocating for Change

- What cause would I like to support?
- Can I gather enough information to convince others?
- What would my audience want to know about this cause?
- Which genre and visual design would provide the best format for persuading my audience to take action?
- What constraints would prevent me from persuading my audience?

# MODEL ADVOCACIES FOR CHANGE

As you read these models, notice what change is advocated and how the authors develop their arguments to convince their readers to take action.

## Education: It's Not Just about the Boys. Get Girls into School

### Jonathan Alter

In this *Newsweek* article, Jonathan Alter advocates for educating girls in developing countries. He explains that in too many countries, parents still don't see the importance of sending their girls to school. He concludes by asking readers to take action through support of the United Nations Millennium Development Goals. Development goal #2 reads: "Ensure that, by 2015, children everywhere, boys and girls alike, will be able to complete a full course of primary schooling." By publishing this article in *Newsweek*, Alter knows that it will be widely read by an educated, sympathetic audience.

*Can you imagine what your life would be like if you hadn't attended school?*

Who wants more poor children around the world to go to school? Raise your hand. Yep, everyone's hand is up. Education is the ultimate mom-and-apple-pie (or rice-and-beans) issue. Everyone's for it. But our best efforts to get more impoverished kids into schools aren't always effective. Despite some recent progress in China and India, 73 million children worldwide don't go to primary school. Three times as many never go to secondary school. Though they can sometimes be trained later in life, their shortened time in school is often a major impediment to advancement. These kids are mostly doomed to a life of poverty, and so are their families.

The way out is not just to champion education generally but to focus intently on one subset of the problem: girls, who make up nearly 60 percent of the kids out of school. In parts of sub-Saharan Africa, only one in five girls gets any education at all. Here's where to zero in on the challenge: most of the benefits that accompany increased education are attributable to girls, who use their schooling more productively than boys. Women in the developing world who have had some education share their earnings; men keep a third to a half for themselves.

"The reason so many experts believe educating girls is the most important investment in the world is how much they give back to their families," says Gene Sperling, a former top economic adviser to President Bill Clinton (and currently advising Barack Obama). Sperling's book, *What Works in Girls' Education* (with Barbara Herz), is simultaneously disturbing and encouraging. It's disheartening to think of how far we have to go to get all kids into school—one of the United Nations Millennium Development Goals launched in 2000 to accelerate progress on fighting poverty, disease and other social ills. But it's also hopeful: at least we can focus on a specific solution.

When girls go to school, they marry later and have fewer, healthier children. For instance, if an African mother has five years of education, her child has a 40 percent better chance of living to age 5. A World Health Organization study in Burkina Faso showed that mothers with some education were 40 percent less likely to subject their children to the practice of genital mutilation. When girls get educated, they are three times less likely to contract HIV/AIDS.

5      Unfortunately, many African parents still don't know that their own lives can be greatly improved if their daughters go to school. They're often uncomfortable when their girls have to travel long distances to school (making them more subject to sexual predators). Girls themselves grow uncomfortable in school when they have no separate latrines. They fear being spied on by boys; their parents agree and withdraw them. This is the kind of everyday impediment to progress that aid organizers notice on the ground but rarely becomes part of the debate.

The biggest barrier to primary and secondary education in the developing world remains the fees that too many countries continue to charge parents for each child in school. Sometimes it's a flat fee; sometimes it's barely disguised as a fee for books or school uniforms. The practical effect is that poor families (disproportionately in rural areas, where school attendance is lightest) send their two oldest, healthiest boys to school with the hope that they will support their parents in their old age. This often deprives girls—the ones actually much more likely to help their families— of the chance to go to school.

The waste of human capital is incalculable. Consider that only 5 percent of children with disabilities get any education at all in the developing world. Countries like Kenya and Uganda, which have abolished fees, have seen a flood of new students, with enrollments surging by 30 percent or more. So why haven't other developing nations followed their example? It's not the loss of fee revenue but the absence of a large-enough education infrastructure to sustain the influx of new students. Five years after abolishing fees, Kenya still needs 40,000 new teachers. Officials there say they can't meet the need without more consistent funding.

Donor nations and NGOs are increasingly reaching a consensus that global education, especially for girls, is the keystone to the arch of development. The Millennium Development Goals of universal primary education with gender equity are among the hottest topics at international conferences. But Sperling calls these "the world's most ambitious and pathetic goals—ambitious because so many countries are not on track to reach them; pathetic because of the idea that five or six years of primary education will suffice when there's no real demonstrable advantage without eight."

The challenge extends beyond funding to changing the culture of the developing world. Fathers must be convinced that if their daughters go to school, they will learn enough math to help them in the market. Mothers must learn that while sending their daughters to school might mean one fewer pair of hands to help around the house, their families will be better off in the long run.

10    "This is not a disease without a known cure," says Sperling. "These things work everywhere." If these become the mom-and-apple-pie values of the developing world, we'll all win.

## One Word Spotlight

**NGO** (paragraph 8) is the abbreviation for the term *nongovernmental organization*. NGOs consist of people who work together to provide services or to advocate for change locally, nationally, or internationally. Most are nonprofit and work in the area of human rights, disaster relief, or public assistance. NGOs are usually financed by private donations, governments, and international organizations.

## Reflect on the Reading

1. According to the experts, why do girls use their education more productively than boys?

2. Underline the one sentence in the piece that you think best states Alter's main point. Explain why you chose this sentence.

3. What are some reasons that girls in developing nations don't go to school?

4. What evidence does Alter give to convince his readers that there is a waste of human capital because girls aren't educated? How persuasive is this evidence?

5. What changes would Alter like to see so that more girls can attend school?

## Consider Your Viewpoint

1. In your culture, do girls use their education more productively than boys? Why or why not?

2. Alter assumes that his readers will agree that lack of education is a bad thing. Do you agree with this assumption? Give several examples of the effects of education on your family or community.

3. What are some other ways for encouraging more education in developing countries?

4. Analyze the photograph that precedes this essay. A photograph is more interesting if the subject is close, but not exactly centered. Has the photographer followed this guideline? How does the photograph relate to the article?

# Reviewing Applicants: Research on Bias and Assumptions

## Women in Science & Engineering Leadership Institute

A brochure is a multipage document that communicates through both image and text to either inform or persuade readers. To be effective, brochures should be visually appealing as well as rhetorically effective. This brochure, published by the Women in Science & Engineering Leadership Institute (WISELI) at the University of Wisconsin–Madison, advocates for change in the way people view applicants for positions. It explains how biases and assumptions about gender, race, and ethnicity affect hiring decisions and it gives suggestions for what readers can do to monitor their own biases.

# Reviewing Applicants

## Research on Bias and Assumptions

We all like to think that we are objective scholars who judge people solely on their credentials and achievements, but copious research shows that every one of us has a lifetime of experience and cultural history that shapes the review process.

> *"To evaluate other people more accurately we need to challenge our implicit hypotheses...we need to become explicitly aware of them."*
>
> VIRGINIA VALLAN

The results from controlled research studies demonstrate that people often hold implicit or unconscious assumptions that influence their judgments. Examples range from expectations or assumptions about physical or social characteristics associated with race, gender, and ethnicity to those associated with certain job descriptions, academic institutions, and fields of study.

It is important to note that in most studies examining evaluation and gender, the sex of the evaluator was not significant; both men and women share and apply the same assumptions about gender.

Recognizing biases and other influences not related to the quality of candidates can help reduce their impact on your search and review of candidates.

**Examples of common social assumptions or expectations:**

- When shown photographs of people of the same height, evaluators overestimated the heights of male subjects and underestimated the heights of female subjects, even though a reference point, such as a doorway, was provided (Biernat et al.).

- When shown photographs of men with similar athletic abilities, evaluators rated the athletic ability of African American men higher than that of white men (Beirnat and Manis).
- When asked to choose counselors from among a group of equally competent applicants who were neither exceptionally qualified nor unqualified for the position, students more often chose white candidates than African American candidates, indicating their willingness to give members of the majority group the benefit of the doubt (Dovidio and Gaertner).

These studies show that we often apply generalizations that may or may not be valid to the evaluation of individuals (Bielby and Baron). In the study on height, evaluators applied the statistically accurate generalization that on average men are taller than women to their estimates of the height of individuals who did not necessarily conform to the generalization. If generalizations can lead us to inaccurately evaluate characteristics as objective and easily measured as height, what happens when the qualities we are evaluating are not as objective or as easily measured? What happens when the generalizations are not accurate?

> *"Even the most well-intentioned person unwittingly allows unconscious thoughts and feelings to influence apparently objective decisions."*
>
> MAHZARIN R. BANAJI

**Examples of assumptions or biases that can influence the evaluation of applications:**

- When rating the quality of verbal skills as indicated by vocabulary definitions, evaluators rated the skills lower if they were told an African American provided the definitions than if they were told that a white person provided them (Biernat and Manis).
- Randomly assigning different names to résumés showed that job applicants were more likely to be interviewed for open positions than were equally qualified applicants with "African American-sounding names" (Bertrand and Mullainathan).

> *"To respond without prejudice... an individual must overcome years of exposure to biased and stereotypical information."*
>
> PATRICIA DEVINE ET AL.

- When symphony orchestras adopted "blind" auditions by using a screen to conceal candidates' identities, the hiring of women musicians increased. Blind auditions fostered impartiality by preventing assumptions that women musicians have "smaller techniques" and produce "poorer sound" from influencing evaluation (Goldin and Rouse).
- Research shows that incongruities between perceptions of female gender roles and leadership roles cause evaluators to assume that women will be less competent leaders. When women leaders provide clear evidence of their competence, thus violating traditional gender norms, evaluators perceive them to be less likeable and are less likely to recommend them for hiring or promotion (Eagly and Karau; Ridgeway; Heilman et al.).

**Examples of assumptions or biases in academic job-related contexts:**

- A study of over **300** recommendation letters for medical faculty hired by a large U.S. medical school found that letters for female applicants differed systematically from those for males. Letters written for women were shorter, provided "minimal assurance" rather than solid recommendation, raised more doubts, portrayed women as students and teachers while portraying men as researchers and professionals, and more frequently mentioned women's personal lives (Trix and Psenka).
- In a national study, **238** academic psychologists (**118** male, **120** female) evaluated a curriculum vitae randomly assigned a male or a female name. Both male and female participants gave the male applicant better evaluations for teaching, research, and service experience and were more likely to hire the male than the female applicant (Steinpreis et al.).
- A study of postdoctoral fellowships awarded by the Medical Research Council of Sweden found that women candidates needed substantially more publications to achieve the same rating as men, unless they personally knew someone on the panel (Wennerás and Wold).

---

*When we assume "that cultural, racial, ethnic, and gender biases are simply nonexistent [in] screening and evaluation processes, there is grave danger that minority and female candidates will be rejected."*

CAROLINE S. V. TURNER

---

**Advice for minimizing the influence of bias and assumptions:**

- **Strive to increase the representation of women and minorities in your applicant pool.** Research shows that gender assumptions are more likely to negatively influence evaluation of women when they represent a small proportion (less than **25%**) of the pool of candidates (Hellman).
- **Learn about and discuss research on biases and assumptions and consciously strive to minimize their influence on your evaluation.** Experimental studies show that greater awareness of discrepancies between the ideals of impartiality and actual performance, together with strong internal motivations to respond without prejudice, effectively reduces prejudicial behavior (Devine et al.).
- **Develop evaluation criteria prior to evaluating candidates and apply them consistently to all applicants.** Research shows that different standards may be used to evaluate male and female applicants and that when criteria are not clearly articulated before reviewing candidates evaluators may shift or emphasize criteria that favor candidates from well-represented demographic groups (Biernat and Fuegen; Uhlmann and Cohen).
- **Spend sufficient time (at least 20 minutes) evaluating each applicant.** Evaluators who were busy, distracted by other tasks, and under time pressure gave women lower ratings than men for the same written evaluation of job performance. Sex bias decreased when they were able to give all their time and attention to their judgments, which rarely occurs in actual work settings (Martell).
- **Evaluate each candidate's entire application; don't depend too heavily on only one element such as the letters of recommendation, or the prestige of the degree-granting institution or postdoctoral program.** Recall the study showing significant patterns of difference in letters of recommendation for male and female applicants (Trix and Psenka).

- **Be able to defend every decision for eliminating or advancing a candidate.** Research shows that holding evaluators to high standards of accountablility for the fairness of their evaluation reduces the influence of bias and assumptions (Foschi).
- **Periodically evaluate your judgments, determine whether qualified women and underrepresented minorities are included in your pool, and consider whether evaluation biases and assumptions are influencing your decisions by asking yourself the following questions:**
  - ❏ Are women and minority candidates subject to different expectations in areas such as numbers of publications, name recognition, or personal acquaintance with a committee member? *(Recall the example of the Swedish Medical Research Council.)*
  - ❏ Are candidates from institutions other than the major research universities that have trained most of our faculty being undervalued? *(Qualified candidates from institutions such as historically black universities, four-year colleges, government, or industry, might offer innovative, diverse, and valuable perspectives on research and teaching.)* Have the accomplishments, ideas, and
  - ❏ findings of women or minority candidates been undervalued or unfairly attributed to a research director or collaborators despite contrary evidence in publications or letters of reference? *(Recall the biases seen in evaluations of written descriptions of job performance.)* Is the ability of women or minorities to run
  - ❏ a research group, raise funds, and supervise students and staff of different gender or ethnicity being underestimated? *(Recall social assumptions about leadership abilities.)* Are negative assumptions about whether
  - ❏ women or minority candidates will "fit in" to the existing environment influencing evaluation? *(Recall students' choice of counselor.)*

**References:**

M.R. Banaji et al., *Harvard Business Review* 81 (2003).
M. Bertrand, S. Mullainathan, *American Economic Review* 94 (2004).
W.T. Bielby, J.N. Baron, *American Journal of Sociology* 91 (1986).
M. Biernat et al., *Journal of Personality and Social Psychology* 60 (1991).
M. Biernat, M. Manis, *Journal of Personality and Social Psychology* 66 (1994).
M. Biernat, K. Fuegen, *Journal of Social Issues* 57 (2001).
P. Devine et al., *Journal of Personality and Social Psychology* 82 (2002).
J.F. Dovidio, S.L. Gaertner, *Psychological Science* 11 (2000).
A.H. Eagly, S.J. Karau, *Psychological Review* 109 (2002).
M. Foschi, *Social Psychology Quarterly* 59 (1996).
C. Goldin, C. Rouse, *American Economic Review* 90 (2000).
M.E. Hellman, *Organizational Behavior and Human Performance* 26 (1980).
M.E. Hellman et al., *Journal of Applied Psychology* 89 (2004).
R.F. Martell, *Journal of Applied Social Psychology* 21(1991).
C.L. Ridgeway, *Journal of Social Issues* 57 (2001).
R. Steinpreis et al., *Sex Roles* 41 (1999).
F. Trix, C. Psenka, *Discourse and Society* 14 (2003).
C.S.V. Turner, *Diversifying the Faculty: A Guidebook for Search Committees* (Washington, DC: AACU, 2002).
E.L. Uhimann, G.L. Cohen, *Psychological Science* 16 (2005).
V. Vallan, *Why So Slow? The Advancement of Women* (Cambridge, MA: MIT Press, 1999).
C. Wennerás, A. Wold, *Nature* 387 (1997).

For full references please see:
**http://wiseli.engr.wisc.edu/hiring/BrochureReferences.pdf**

**W I S E L I**
*Women in Science and Engineering Leadership Institute*
*University of Wisconsin-Madison*

http://wiseli.engr.wisc.edu

Preparation of this document was made possible by grants from the National Science Foundation (NSF #**0123666** and #**0619979**). Any opinions, findings, and conclusions or recommendations expressed in this material are those of the author(s) and do not necessarily reflect the views of the National Science Foundation.

# One Word Spotlight

**Bias** (paragraph 4) is a personal judgment. You have the heard saying, "Don't confuse me with the facts." To be biased is to hold a belief without thoroughly examining the facts. Bias can be conscious or unconscious. Unconscious bias is a prejudice that we don't even know we have.

## Reflect on the Reading

1. According to the WISELI brochure, both men and women make the same assumptions about gender when hiring. Why is it important to note this?

2. What are some examples of biases mentioned in this brochure? Have you ever experienced such biases?

3. Explain this quotation: "Even the most well-intentioned person unwittingly allows unconscious thoughts and feelings to influence apparently objective decisions." Connect this statement to the main idea of the brochure.

4. The authors of this brochure often use the results of research studies as evidence to support their main points. In your view, is this an effective way to convince their readers? What other types of evidence could they add?

5. Which group of readers might agree most with the authors of this brochure? Which might disagree? Explain your answer.

## Consider Your Viewpoint

1. Are you aware of any biases that you have? What, if anything, are you doing to monitor and eliminate them?

2. The WISELI brochure concludes with suggestions for overcoming bias when hiring. Can you think of other ways to ensure that you don't let biases and assumptions affect your view of other people?

3. Do you think the American culture places too much or too little attention on diversity in hiring decisions? Explain your answer.

4. Analyze the photograph on the front of the brochure. The woman in this photograph is in double jeopardy when she applies for a job because she is female and African American. Why is she a good candidate for the front cover of this brochure?

# PARK(ing) Day: Rethinking Urban Infrastructure Around the World

## Collin Dunn

A photo essay is a slideshow that communicates through image, text, and sometimes sound to inform or persuade readers. Created by Collin Dunn for Earth Watch, this photo essay persuades readers to organize a PARK(ing) Day. Earth Watch (earthwatch.org) is an organization that encourages people to become involved in changing their environment.

In cities around the globe today, artists, activists and citizens will temporarily transform metered parking spaces into public parks and other social spaces, as part of an annual event called PARK(ing) Day.

*Invented in 2005 by Rebar, a San Francisco art and design studio, PARK(ing) Day challenges people to rethink the way streets are used and reinforces the need for broad-based changes to urban infrastructure.*

*"In urban centers around the world, inexpensive curbside parking results in increased traffic, wasted fuel and more pollution," says Rebar's Matthew Passmore. "The strategies that generated these conditions are not sustainable, nor do they promote a healthy, vibrant urban human habitat. PARK(ing) Day is about re-imagining the possibilities of the metropolitan landscape."*

*Wanna create your own PARK(ing) Day installation? It's pretty straightforward—just follow these instructions. All you need is a parking space, some quarters (or whatever coin currency you need to feed parking meters), your park setup, and maybe some sunscreen.*

*Many PARK(ing) installations involve grass—it goes well with the "park" theme. Maybe somewhat surprisingly for some, it isn't that hard to install sod in a parking space. Just don't forget your tarp.*

*Since 2005, the project has blossomed into a worldwide grassroots movement: in 2008, PARK(ing) Day included more than 500 "PARK" installations in more than 100 cities across four continents. This year, the project will expand to urban centers across the globe, including first-time PARK installations in South Africa, Poland, Norway, New Zealand and South Korea.*

PARK(ing) Day installations can take many different shapes and forms. In Berkeley, some landscape architecture students decided to build a park in a parking spot for people to picnic in.

Here's the finished picnic PARK(ing) Day spot in Berkeley—looks like way more fun than driving, no?

At another PARK(ing) Day spot in Berkeley, a group of architects set up this "urban living room" where a few of them could park and catch up on some reading.

Last year in Grand Rapids, Michigan, leaders of the Green Grand Rapids initiative headed up West Michigan's first celebration of PARK(ing) Day with a little homage to Herman Miller.

Back in San Francisco, Rebar took PARK(ing) Day to the streets with the "Parkcycle," a mobile parking spot that serves to expand the notion of how the space can be used. "From public parks to free health clinics, from art galleries to demonstration gardens, PARK(ing) Day participants have claimed the metered parking space as a rich new territory for creative experimentation, activism, socializing and play," says Blaine Merker of Rebar.

This year, the Parkcycle will be outfitted with a new kind of park. "We are keeping the details secret, but we'll be out pedaling around and visiting other PARK(ing) Day installations around the city," says Rebar's Teresa Aguilera. "If you live or work in San Francisco, keep your eyes open for a twenty-two foot long park pedaling through the street." It'll be pretty hard to miss.

*Get out there and get PARK(ing)!*

# One Word Spotlight

***Grassroots*** (slide 4 text) is a commonly used term that means to originate at the most basic level. An adjective that dates back to 1907, "grassroots" often refers to political support or to a new organization formed by everyday people.

## Reflect on the Reading

1. According to the photo essay, who created PARK(ing) Day and why?
2. What environmental change does PARK(ing) Day advocate?
3. Why do you think Dunn included photos from a variety of cities?
4. What additional information about PARK(ing) Day would you like to see provided?

## Consider Your Viewpoint

1. Would you advocate for PARK(ing) Day in your community? Why or why not?
2. Dunn states that PARK(ing) Day will change the way people look at urban infrastructure. Does this photo essay cause you to look at parking spaces differently? Explain your answer.
3. This piece relies heavily on photos to advocate for change. What do you find attractive about these photos? What could be improved?
4. Go to the Earth Watch website (earthwatch.org) and view other photo essay slideshows. What do they all have in common?

# WRITING ASSIGNMENT

For this assignment, you will write an argumentative piece that advocates for change to improve the lives of others. You may choose a current issue or a long-standing one. To select a topic, consider the societal issues that you're concerned about such as immigration, environment, globalization, or expanding technology and how they affect you and your community, state, country, or the world. Your purpose is to persuade your readers to accept your position and take some action.

# YOUR ADVOCACY FOR CHANGE

It can be difficult to get people to agree with your idea for change and even more difficult to get them to respond to your call for action, so preparation is important when advocating for change. To do your best, you need to choose a topic that you really care about and that is sufficiently narrow to fit the genre that you choose.

# Choosing a Topic

When choosing a topic to advocate for change, you can't rely solely on your personal opinion to persuade readers who don't already agree with you. You need reliable evidence such as facts and statistics to change their minds, so choose a topic for which you can find such evidence. To choose a topic, ask, "What cause do I care about?" and "Is there an action that will create change?" Here are some examples:

**Community:** What is it about your community that you would like to change? You might want more street lights or a place for young people to gather, or you might want to encourage your neighbors to recycle or your city council to vote to build a convention center. If you choose to write on a community topic, here is an example of how you could describe a community cause and action:

> *Cause*: Even though we live in a region of abundant sunshine, the citizens of this community don't use solar power.
>
> *Action*: Educate local citizens on how to convert their homes to solar power and convince City Council to provide incentives for doing so.

**State:** You may know of a cause that is not limited to just your community, but instead requires statewide action. Examples of statewide causes might include improving tourism, lowering sales taxes, requiring a balanced state budget, or developing a light rail system. Here is an example of how you could describe a statewide cause and action:

> *Cause*: The state legislature has passed a law that makes English the official language of the state and requires English only on all state documents and forms.
>
> *Action*: Persuade state citizens to write their legislators with a request to repeal this law.

**Country:** You might also want to write about a national problem such as unemployment, health care, national security, or the war in Afghanistan.

Here is an example of how you could describe a national cause and action:

> *Cause*: Not enough U.S. students, especially women and members of underrepresented groups, see the value of majoring in science or engineering in college.

> *Action*: Persuade U.S. students to major in science or engineering.

**World:** Your advocacy for change might be about a global issue such as world hunger, climate change, drug trafficking, or space exploration. Here is an example of how you could describe a global cause and action:

> *Cause*: Is the Amazon rain forest still endangered? Did public information and advocacy campaigns save it?

> *Action*: If the Amazon rain forest is still in danger, persuade readers to take action.

---

### Topic Questions for Advocating Change

- Is this an assigned topic? If so, what are the requirements?
- Is this topic free choice? If so, what is the cause that I would like to support?
- Will readers be interested in this cause?
- Is there an action that readers can take to effect a change?
- Can I find evidence for my position and specific actions to recommend?
- Can I explain why my action is better than others that may be proposed?

---

Before doing anything else, narrow your topic to something that you can handle in a short written piece. You can't solve all societal problems with this assignment, but you can make it clear where you stand on one single issue.

**Connect With Others**

**Activity 12.1**  Divide into groups of three or four students. Each group member should brainstorm a list of three or four causes for which you would like to advocate a change. Read your lists aloud to your group members to see if any causes turned up on more than one list. Select one of the topics and discuss how you would narrow it and what actions you would propose to address the issue.

## Analyzing the Rhetorical Situation

Now that you have chosen a topic, analyze the rhetorical situation to ensure that you have selected a cause that is important to you and your readers and for which there is sufficient evidence of the problem and an adequate solution to suggest.

**Considering Audience and Purpose.** As you know, the more you know about your audience and purpose, the easier it will be for you to write a piece that convinces your readers to take action.

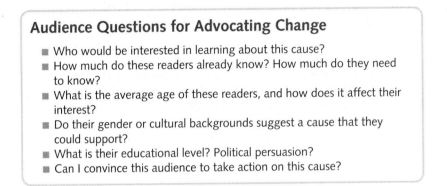

## Audience Questions for Advocating Change

- Who would be interested in learning about this cause?
- How much do these readers already know? How much do they need to know?
- What is the average age of these readers, and how does it affect their interest?
- Do their gender or cultural backgrounds suggest a cause that they could support?
- What is their educational level? Political persuasion?
- Can I convince this audience to take action on this cause?

Although you already know your primary purpose is to persuade, you may still include some expressive writing if you have personal experience with the cause. Try to remain objective, though, and not include too much personal information. Let the strength of the informative evidence you include convince your readers to agree with your position on the cause.

In his article "Education: It's Not Just About the Boys. Get Girls into School," Alter uses a variety of evidence to convince his readers, including defining the problem, relating events, providing examples such as facts and statistics, showing similarities across countries, and using cause and effect to show what happens when girls attend school.

## Purpose Questions for Advocating Change

- Why am I convinced that I can persuade others to take action on my cause?
- What personal history, thoughts, or feelings can I include to convince my readers to agree with me?
- Can I adequately inform my readers about this cause?

**Choosing a Genre and Visual Design.** For a persuasive piece such as this one, authors often choose essays, newspaper or magazine articles, brochures, blogs, photo essays, or video documentaries. In "Reviewing Applicants: Research on Bias and Assumptions," the WISELI staff chose to write a brochure because they wanted a visually-attractive persuasive piece that they could distribute widely. If you choose a brochure or other genre with high visual content, pay close attention not only to the content, but to the layout, font, and visual elements.

### Genre and Visual Design Questions for Advocating Change

- Which genre will best communicate my topic to my chosen audience?
- How will the format help me to persuade my readers?
- What visual design elements will strengthen my message?
- Will this format make a clear, logical argument?
- Will the argument be easily understood?
- What do I know about this format?
- What do I need to learn to use this format?

**Reviewing Exigence and Constraints.** In this assignment, more than any other, it is important that you select a topic that you truly want to communicate. It is difficult to change people's minds, but if your sense of urgency comes through in your writing, you increase your chances that your readers will also get excited about the change you advocate.

### Exigence Questions for Advocating Change

- Why do I feel I must communicate this need for change?
- Why is it important to put it in writing?
- What action would I like my audience to take after reading my piece?

Constraints include anything that inhibits your ability to persuade your readers. For example, constraints to advocating for change might include lack of evidence to support your position on the cause, a tendency to be overly emotional in writing about it, or an audience that doesn't share your passion. As you write, you'll want to remove as many of these constraints as possible. For example, you can choose a topic for which you can find plenty of evidence of a problem, you can monitor your tendency to be too emotional, and you can choose an audience that you feel certain will be interested in what you have to say.

In "PARK(ing) Day: Rethinking Urban Infrastructure Around the World," for example, Dunn is constrained by the fact that only a few cities are currently participating in PARK(ing) Day and by the general public's apathy toward environmental change. He is further constrained by his choice of genre. The photo essay places most of the emphasis on the photographs, leaving him little opportunity to write persuasively.

> "Writing is an act of faith, not a trick of grammar."
>
> —E. B. White.

**Constraint Questions for Advocating Change**

- What will influence the success of my piece?
- What more do I need to do to advocate this change?
- What other constraints do I face to completing this piece?

**Activity 12.2**   With a small group, select one of the topics chosen in Activity 12.1 and develop the rhetorical situation. Include audience, purpose, genre, exigence, and constraints.

**Connect With Others**

## Using the Writing Process

When you have completed your rhetorical analysis, you are ready to advocate for change by putting your ideas into writing, using the stages of the writing process: discovering ideas, drafting to explore ideas, revising to improve content, and editing to eliminate errors.

### STAGE 1:  Discovering Ideas

One way of discovering ideas that can be especially useful in advocating for change is by using key words to help you conduct secondary research. Secondary research is the collection of data from websites, databases, books, and journals. In other words, someone else has already conducted research and written about their results. You will then summarize or paraphrase what they have written. For more help conducting research, see Chapter 19, "Using Sources."

Using Key Words.  You can always Google your topic on the web, but then you must also evaluate the accuracy of the information. To find information that you know is reliable, search your college library online databases instead. For example, you can search the database *Periodical Abstracts* to find articles related to your topic. According to their website, they provide "indexing and abstracting of articles in more than 1,800 general-reference publications, including 635 periodicals related to the social sciences, 396 related to the humanities, 169 in the general-sciences, 212 business titles, and 239 general-interest publications. The database now includes full-text articles from approximately 600 of the indexed titles."

When consulting a database, use *key words,* or words that pertain to your topic, to help locate information. In his article, "Education: It's Not Just About the Boys. Get Girls into School," key words that Alter may have used are "education," "girls" and "developing countries." For more information on how to use key words to conduct research, see  Chapter 19, "Using Sources."

> ## Finding Key Words for Advocating Change
>
> - Where can I read more about my topic, either online or at the library?
> - Where can I find a librarian who can help me identify key words and locate databases?
> - Would a survey of people willing to share their ideas on this topic be helpful for discovering key ideas and words?

## STAGE 2: Drafting to Explore Ideas

If you plan to develop a brochure, photo essay, or video documentary, first draft the content and then develop the design of the piece. For the content, concentrate on making an interesting, clear, and logical argument. Then turn your attention to creating the visuals to persuade your readers and to help them quickly and easily understand what you are advocating and how they can take action.

**Sentence Variety.** One way to keep your writing interesting is to vary your sentences and punctuation marks. It is hard to say why certain arrangements of words ignite readers' interest more than others, but it is similar to music, where different people respond to different sounds. It is certain, though, that one simple sentence pattern quickly bores your readers. Try varying your sentences by using short, simple sentences to make important points and longer, more complex sentences to provide the evidence to support your argument. In "Reviewing Applicants: Research on Bias and Assumptions," for example, the authors make an important point with this short imperative sentence: "Be able to defend every decision for eliminating or advancing a candidate." When describing the research, however, they use longer, more complex sentences.

As you draft, look at your sentence pattern and length to determine whether you have written them in an interesting way. You are more likely to keep your readers' attention if you vary your sentence length and use a variety of sentence patterns. Here are some ways to vary your sentences.

Begin with an introductory word or phrase:

> Yes, the movie was one of my favorites.
> Of course, I can't recommend that you visit the museum at this time.

Begin with an adverb:

> Personally, I prefer to visit Costa Rica.
> Certainly, you can always change your mind if you don't like the concert.

Begin with a parenthetical expression:

> To say the least, I am not willing to recommend this book to you.
> To tell the truth, it was my first time to enroll in this course.

Begin with a prepositional phrase:

*From our seats, we could see behind the stage.*
*During our visit, they had an earthquake.*

Write a question:

*Would you like to attend a wonderful play?*
*Is this government policy in the action?*
*Does this compare with your favorite cultural tradition?*

Write an imperative sentence:

*Let me tell you about this wonderful restaurant we visited.*
*Permit me to explain what is so special about this candidate.*

**Your Emotional Filter and Writing Monitor.** Your emotional filter may be high and your writing monitor low as you draft about a cause that is important to you. Be careful not to let your emotions dictate what you write. You know that to be persuasive, you use a combination of logos, ethos, and pathos as you develop your ideas. Ethos helps you to be believable. Logos is important to demonstrate reason and logic. Pathos sways your readers through emotion. If, however, you rely too much on emotion, your readers may begin to doubt your ability to be reasonable, logical, or believable. The key is to use a combination of logos, ethos, and pathos.

## STAGE 3: Revising to Improve Content

In the revision process, you are concerned with how well you have communicated your message to your readers. When advocating for change, your primary concern is whether you have convinced your readers to take action. When revising, focus on how you have organized and developed your ideas to convince your readers to make a change. Look, too, at your sentence variety and word choice. Finally, review your format and visuals to ensure that they contribute meaningfully to your message.

**Word Choice.** Try rewriting this sentence: "These are the times that try men's souls." It's difficult to rewrite because this particular choice of words works so well. There is a certain rhythm and cadence because of the alliteration: Five of the eight words begin

### LANGUAGES and CULTURES

Have you ever wondered about the different structures of words? Some words in English such as "I" are as short as one letter, but words in other languages can be as long as the alphabet. For example, in the Western Desert Language of Australia, "palyamunurringkutjamunurtu" is a single word that means "he/she definitely did not become bad." As linguist David Crystal notes in *How Language Works*, in some languages an individual word can convey the type of information that in English is usually conveyed in a sentence.

with the letter "t." It is likely that Thomas Paine chose to use these particular words knowing the effect that they would have. As you revise, look closely at the words you have chosen to be sure that you have selected correct, clear, and concise words.

Correctness. Correctness is selecting the right word to convey the meaning you intend.

> *Incorrect*: The *principle* finding of my study is that learning a new language can improve your chances of finding a job.
>
> *Correct*: The *principal* finding of my study is that learning a new language can improve your chances of finding a job.

The word *principle* means a rule or standard. The word *principal* means primary or leading.

Clarity. Clarity is choosing words that communicate exactly.

> *Unclear*: We discovered that Nepal was great.
>
> *Clear*: We discovered that Nepal has eight of the world's ten highest mountains, including the highest mountain in the world, Mt. Everest.

The first sentence isn't clear because the reader learns no useful information about Nepal.

Conciseness. Conciseness is choosing the fewest words you need to convey your meaning.

> *Not Concise*: I believe that it is really important that you understand the importance of not drinking bottled water due to the fact that it is no healthier than tap water.
>
> *Concise*: Bottled water is no healthier than tap water.

**Connect With Others**

**Activity 12.3** Divide into groups and reread "Interviewing Applicants: Research on Bias and Assumptions." As you read, label the methods of development and highlight any interesting word choices that you find. Discuss what you have found with your classmates and suggest ways that you could improve your word choice in your piece to advocate for change.

Once you improve your word choice, review the rhetorical situation to help you make further improvements.

## Rhetorical Situation Questions for Advocating Change

- Audience: Will your audience be interested in reading about the cause that you advocate? Will your readers be willing to take action as a result?
- Purpose: Have you included enough detail to persuade your readers about the cause? Develop those paragraphs that need additional detail.
- Genre: Does the genre that you chose contribute to the persuasion? Does the format help the audience understand your points more clearly?
- Exigence: Do you feel that you have had the opportunity to take a stand on this cause? Have you said what you wanted to say?
- Constraints: What constraints have you encountered? Develop a plan for overcoming them to complete this assignment.

Ask classmates to read your piece and to answer these questions on how you might more effectively persuade them to take action.

## Peer Review
### Advocating for Change

1. What is this piece's greatest strength?

2. What is this piece advocating? Did you already know about this cause or is it new to you?

3. Where might I add details to convince you to take action? Which sections or sentences would you like me to clarify? How well did the ideas flow? Where do you suggest I add transitions to help you move from one idea to another?

4. If I used library or Internet research to gather evidence, how well was this research used? How well did I avoid simply cutting and pasting information into the piece?

5. How does my choice of genre contribute to the readability and to your understanding of my cause? Do the visuals help clarify the text? How might I improve the layout of the piece?

6. Are you persuaded by my piece? What more could I do to persuade you?

7. Underline any words or sentences that you think I should revise because they do not communicate to you.

8. Place a check mark in the margin next to any punctuation or spelling errors that you discovered while reading this piece.

## STAGE 4: Editing for Correctness

When you edit, you check for correctness by looking for errors in spelling, punctuation, and grammar.

**One Student's Work.**   Here is an excerpt from a paper titled "Childhood Obesity" written by student writer Theresa Cast. You'll notice that throughout her paper she made a number of errors (italicized in this excerpt) in spelling, punctuation, and grammar that she corrected in her final paper at the end of the chapter.

> With this new *intiative*, changes are already coming into play from a vast array of companies that have committed their resources to helping "Let's Move" achieve *it's* goals:

- The American Beverage Association

  This association will put clear calorie labels on cans, bottles, and vending machines within two years.

- The American Academy of Pediatrics

  This association will ask physician-members to monitor the body mass index on our children that are 2 years old and up on a regular basis.

- School *Cafeteria's*

  Major food suppliers to our *cafeteria's* have committed to cut the sugar, salt, and fat as well as increase whole grains and produce that is supplied to school *cafeteria's*.

- Food Producers/Agribusiness

  Executives from approximately 40 major companies will promote healthful eating. Participants are from *Kraft, Foods,* Sara Lee, and other major food companies. Combined, these companies have already developed more than 10,000 products with reduced fat, trans fat, sugar, salt, and calories.

- Major Media Companies

  *Agreed to join efforts by showing public service announcements to promote bettereating/exercise choices companies that have committed to this initiative include the Walt Disney, NBS, Universal, and Viacom.*

---

### To Edit

- Use a dictionary or computer spell-checker.
- For treatable errors, refer to a grammar handbook and follow standard grammatical rules.
- For less treatable errors, ask another student to read your writing for errors.
- As you edit, keep an Editing Log, a section in your notebook where you record the errors that you have made.

**Activity 12.4**   Once you complete the writing process, complete the self-evaluation sheet to help you further improve your work.

## Self-Evaluation Sheet
### Advocating for Change

1. Have I followed all instructions for this assignment? (Reread the assignment sheet and class notes.)

2. Have I identified a cause for which I can find sufficient evidence?

3. Are my thoughts well-ordered?

4. Is my paper written clearly and concisely? (Reread your paper out loud.)

5. Is each paragraph developed and does each contribute to the overall organization?

6. Do I support my cause in such a way that the reader is engaged?

7. Do I provide a solution and ask my readers to take action?

8. Is the paper written in my own words?

9. Are my sentences well-written and varied? (Read each sentence beginning with the last one, working backward to the beginning of the paper.)

10. Is my word choice appropriate for the audience and purpose?

11. Have I checked for spelling, punctuation, and grammar errors? (Use a grammar handbook and the computer spell-checker.)

12. If I used other sources of information, did I give credit both in the text and on a Works Cited or References page?

   If you're proud of what you have written, you will be eager to share it with your intended audience. For this advocacy piece, consider offering it to an organization that could use it to affect change.

# ONE STUDENT'S ADVOCACY FOR CHANGE

Running Head: CHILDHOOD OBESITY                                    1

Childhood Obesity

Theresa Cast

CHILDHOOD OBESITY                                           2

## Abstract

Childhood obesity has many causes and effects. This report will take a snapshot of childhood obesity along the border area and then will compare statistics from our region to that of the country as a whole. A look at some of the current initiatives underway will be included as well. A broad range of sources were used for this report to provide a well-rounded view on the issue of childhood obesity. My report will begin with a brief background on childhood obesity, some statistics from our area as compared to our nation and globally, actions that have been taken or are being implemented, and a brief conclusion. A reference list for information contained in this report will be included at the end. Readers are encouraged to use these references for self-education. The goal of this report is to simply bring awareness to this health condition and measures that are underway to reduce childhood obesity.

CHILDHOOD OBESITY                                              3

## Childhood Obesity

Childhood obesity has reached epidemic proportions across the nation. The statistics on obesity and the resulting health factors to our children is astounding. In her address to the U.S. Conference of Mayors, First Lady Michelle Obama states that one in three children in

*Childhood obesity along the border-land is a common problem that is shadowed by diabetes.*

the United States are indeed overweight and that one-third of our children will develop diabetes as a result. For the El Paso area, the statistics indicate a much higher percentage of our population, specifically children, at risk of becoming obese and will have resulting health factors such as diabetes. Living in a border area, it is difficult to determine who is at risk for diabetes and who, according to our cultural standards, is overweight or obese. The lack of affordable healthcare for screening, education in our schools, nutritional support, and basic knowledge of health standards all contribute to this cause and effect. Fast food and hectic lifestyles along the border create an easy, almost irresistible gateway to feeding our children as we hurry from one place to another in our daily lives. By the time we realize we have a problem with obesity, the health factors have already settled in. Without proper education we don't know who or where to turn to for assistance. For some families, food choices aren't a matter of nutritional availability as much as the necessity to put food on the table. Most families in the border region struggle to provide their children with the bare necessities.

CHILDHOOD OBESITY                                           4

Statistics

According to the El Paso Diabetes Association (2010) estimates
show that more than 85,000 people in the El Paso area have
diabetes and of those, as many as 25% may not even know they
have this potentially deadly disease. The Paso del Norte Health
Foundation Executive Summary (2010) states that El Paso County
has the highest rate of diabetes among all U.S. Counties and that
obesity rates in this region are at 37% of our population for the El
Paso area alone. Children in the El Paso area with diabetes is just
short of double in numbers compared to the nation as a whole.
The number one cause of diabetes is attributed to obesity and
while diabetes is just one resulting factor across the United
States, it is the prevalent health factor for our region.

Global

The chart below is taken from Perspectives in Health Magazine (2010)
and gives us an idea where we stand compared to other countries
with illustrated trends and sub-trends from the global perspective.

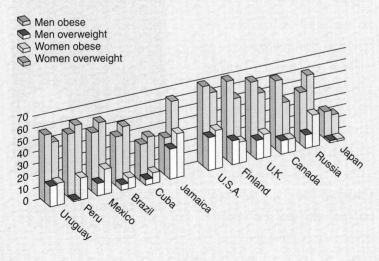

CHILDHOOD OBESITY                                                                5

While obesity is on the rise globally, its underlying dynamics vary across regions. In poor countries people tend to get fatter as their incomes rise, while in developed and transitional economies, higher income correlates with slimmer shapes.

Studies on the relationship between poverty and overweight have identified a number of socioeconomic factors at work. Some have linked low stature and growth stunting due to fetal and early malnutrition with obesity in later life. Cultural factors are also important: many minority and lower income groups associate fatness with prosperity, a perception not shared in better off and better educated sectors of society.

Gender differences further complicate the picture. In general, women tend to have higher rates of obesity than men. But rates of overweight are higher for men in developed countries yet higher for women in developing ones. Moreover, in many developing countries, the relationship between socioeconomic status and obesity is positive for men but negative for women.

Actions

On February 9, 2010, First Lady Michelle Obama announced a new initiative "Let's Move" to address childhood obesity in the United States. This announcement was posted the following day, February 10, 2010, in the *El Paso Times*. Citing the leading known causes for obesity as being poor nutritional choices and a lack of physical activity, Mrs. Obama will

*First Lady Michelle Obama speaks to schoolchildren on the importance of the "Let's Move" initiative.*

CHILDHOOD OBESITY                                          6

work hand-in-hand with agencies such as the American Diabetes Association, the federal government, local mayors, foundations, and nonprofit organizations of all sorts. The goal will be to decrease the increasingly growing number of children who fall into poor health due to obesity factors such as diabetes, heart disease, etc. With this new initiative, changes are already coming into play from a vast array of companies that have committed their resources to helping "Let's Move" achieve its goals:

- The American Beverage Association
  Will put clear calorie labels on cans, bottles, and vending machines within two years.
- The American Academy of Pediatrics
  Will ask physician-members to monitor the body mass index on our children that are 2 years old and up on a regular basis.
- School Cafeterias
  Major food suppliers to our cafeterias have committed to cut the sugar, salt and fat as well as increase whole grains and produce that is supplied to school cafeterias.
- Food Producers/Agribusiness
  Executives from approximately 40 major companies will promote healthful eating. Participants are from Kraft Foods, Sara Lee, and other major food companies. Combined, these companies have already developed more than 10,000 products with reduced fat, trans fat, sugar, salt, and calories.
- Major Media Companies
  Agreed to join efforts by showing public service announcements to promote better eating/exercise choices. Companies that have committed to this initiative include Walt Disney Co., NBC, Universal, and Viacom.

Theresa corrected the spelling of *initiative*.

Theresa corrected *its*.

Theresa removed the apostrophe from *cafeterias*.

Theresa corrected typo by removing comma between Kraft and Foods.

Theresa corrected run-on sentences.

CHILDHOOD OBESITY                                                    7

In addition, many communities have already begun their own initiatives to decrease obesity and will no doubt draw resources from Mrs. Obama's program to assist in reaching their goals. Some of the better known agencies include the following:

- The Robert Wood Johnson Foundation is a major contributor to these initiatives across the country and has funded various projects, programs and studies in the El Paso region. These resources will be vital to the success of bringing obesity under control.

- The Paso del Norte Health Foundation (PdNHF) conducts strategic planning initiatives and tracks the majority of progress along the border area. This, along with educational projects, community involvement, and lots of volunteer hours from local health professionals, seem to be the best resource our area has for local, hands-on action with positive results. The PdNHF has several projects underway that address health as it relates to obesity within our culture. These initiatives can be found in the PdNHF strategic health intelligence report titled "Determinants of Health in the PdNHF Region." In this region-specific report, consideration is given to the areas we live in, the availability of education, resources, medical care, etc. This organization is very meticulous in monitoring the programs they provide. Adjustments are made as needed and action taken.

- The El Paso Diabetes Association tracks obesity as the number one cause of diabetes. EPDA provides well-rounded medical assistance, education, resources, and counseling to help families make better choices in food, exercise, and overall health. The work this organization puts into helping others is astronomical and in large supported by volunteers within the community.

CHILDHOOD OBESITY                                                    8

Conclusion

Globally, obesity is an issue that needs to be addressed. Here in the
United States, we are seeing progress. With the "Let's Move" initiative
it will be important to focus on a healthy diet which includes regular
exercise, better choices in food, and intervention at the school level
to teach our children about the importance of proper diet and
exercise. At home it will be vital to this initiative that we, as parents,
support our children in the knowledge they may bring from the
classroom. We must take responsibility for the health and well being
of our children, ourselves, and our community as a whole. By active
involvement in the "Let's Move" initiative, we will no doubt achieve our
goals of better health for our children and for ourselves.

CHILDHOOD OBESITY 9

### References

Eberwine, D. (2002). Globesity: The crisis of growing
proportions. *Perspectives in Health Magazine*, 7(3),
Retrieved from http://www.paho.org

El Paso Diabetes Association. (2010). What is diabetes.
Retrieved from www.epdiabetes.org

Paso del Norte Health Foundation. (2009). Assessment of
determinants of health in the PDNHF region: A review
of select health indicators for the counties of El
Paso. Retrieved from http://www.pdnhf.org

ScienceDaily. (2009). El Paso county serves as a model
for obesity prevention. Manuscript submitted for
publication, School of Public Health, University of
Texas at Houston, Houston, Texas. Retrieved from
http://www.sciencedaily.com

Skiba, K. (2010, February 10). First lady's goal to
overcome childhood obesity gets help. *El Paso
Times*, p. A1.

# ADDITIONAL READINGS

## The Church of Please and Thank You

### Julie Traves

In this article, published in *This Magazine*, author Julie Traves advocates for a greater awareness of local culture when teaching English as a foreign language. Although English can be invaluable in business, teachers shouldn't assume that speaking and writing American English is more valuable in every way. In this piece, for example, Traves uses the British spelling of words such as "storey" and "cheque" because she lives in Canada where these words are spelled this way.

Michelle Szabo smiles encouragingly as a young businessman talks about his hobbies in broken English. She is a Canadian teacher at Aeon's language school in Kawagoe, Japan. He is a prospective student she's charged to recruit as part of her job. The two meet in a drab five-storey office building outside the train station. The room is so small it fits only a table and two chairs. But making the sell to would-be learners has little to do with décor. What counts is Szabo's final handshake.

More than contact with an attractive young woman, her personal touch symbolizes a grasp on a better life. In the competitive marketplace of Japan, English test scores make or break job applications. Getting ahead means getting into classes with teachers like Szabo. "I would ask so many people, 'do you expect to use English in your life?' And most people would say 'No, no, no, I just need this test score,'" says Szabo. "I think it's sort of a given for all families—it's like food, shelter, English." Some sarariiman (salarymen) were so excited they trembled when they took her hand.

In addition to the 380 million people worldwide who use English as their first language, it's estimated there are 350 million to 500 million speakers of English as a foreign language (EFL)—and the number is growing. For people from affluent and developing nations alike, it is clear that the secret passwords to safety, wealth and freedom can be whispered only in English. Even 66 percent of French citizens, linguistic protectionists *par excellence*, agreed they needed to speak English in a 2001 Eurobarometer poll. While thinkers such as John Ralston Saul proclaim the death of globalization, locals from countries around the world are clamouring for English training.

> Eurobarometer poll: European public opinion surveys.

Enter thousands of Westerners who spread the English gospel overseas each year. Like the Christian missionaries who came before them, many are young, have a blind faith in the beliefs they've grown up with and are eager to make their mark on the world. Unlike the 19- to 26-year-olds who proselytize for the Latter-day Saints, however, these new missionaries are also out for adventure, good times—and hard cash. Part of a $7.8-billion industry, instructors can earn $400 a month plus room and board in China and up to $4,000 a month in Japan. That's a lot more than a McJob back home.

Proselytize: To recruit others to join a faith or cause.

5    But students expect more than lessons in syntax and style. EFL teachers are also hired to share Western customs and values. "'Let's have lunch sometime' doesn't mean stop by my office tomorrow and we'll go out and have lunch. It means something more general, like 'It's been nice talking to you and maybe at some point I'd like to continue the conversation,'" says Diane Pecorari, a senior lecturer at the University of Stockholm. "When you're teaching formulae like 'Please,' 'Thank you,' 'Can I split the cheque?' you also have to teach the context in which they come up. That means teaching culture."

But what is the effect of that culture on students' dialects, customs—their very identity? Ian Martin, an English professor at York University's Glendon College in Toronto, points to a troubling precedent for the current explosion of EFL. "One of the big moments in the spread of English took place in India in 1835. [British politician] Thomas Babington Macaulay proposed that English be used to create a class of Indian middlemen who would be sympathetic to British interests, without the necessity of large numbers of British citizens coming out and running the show." Instead of invading India at great economic and human cost, English allowed the British to transform the country from within. With English on the tip of their tongues, Indians could much more easily swear allegiance to England.

Today's linguistic imperialism has a similar goal. Where once English facilitated the staffing of colonial offices, now it helps fill the cubicles of multinational corporations. Teaching locals Western speech and when it's appropriate to use it no longer transforms them into perfect Englishmen, it makes them into perfect businessmen and women. The politics of English haven't changed—the language simply serves a new corporate master.

To be sure, even those who are fascinated by the countries where they teach sometimes can't help transforming "the natives" as part of their work abroad. Canadian Michael Schellenberg, who taught in Japan more than a decade ago, loved learning about Japanese customs but also sheepishly admits he urged students to express themselves—quite against the Japanese grain. "One of the sayings in Japan is that the nail that sticks up will get pounded down. They wanted people to conform," he says. "I remember classes where I'd be like, 'Just be yourself!' As someone in my early 20s, I had a pretty good sense of how I thought the world should be. I felt pretty confident being forthright about that."

Teaching materials subtly suggest the superiority of Western values. Produced primarily in the US and UK, textbooks propagate the advantages of materialism, individualism and sexual liberation. For example, Ian Martin recalls an Indian friend's reaction to one textbook that showed Jack and Jane meeting in lesson one and dancing alone together by lesson three. "Where are the parents?" his friend wondered.

> **Propagate:** To cause to spread.

10    Some newer textbooks are more culturally sensitive. But in many of the books currently in circulation, says Martin, "there's nothing about environmentalism, nothing about spirituality, nothing about, say, respecting non-native [English] speakers. And there's very little realism in any of the language learning material that I've seen. It's this mythic world of dream fulfillment through consumerism and Westernization." The Aeon language franchise in Japan uses Cameron Diaz and Celine Dion as its poster girls.

Of course, not all teachers aggressively peddle a mythic world—some have their soapbox thrust upon them. In her book *The Hemingway Book Club of Kosovo*, California writer Paula Huntley chronicles her experience teaching English to the survivors of the area's brutal ethnic clashes. Huntley doesn't believe her language and culture are better than any other. She wants to learn from the Kosovars as much as they want to learn from her. It's her students who are convinced that the American way is the way forward, that English is the true language of progress.

Before leaving for Kosovo, Huntley crams for four weeks to complete an English as a second language instructors' certificate. But this is not what impresses the owner of the Cambridge School in Kosovo, a man named Ahmet whose house and library of 5,000 books were destroyed by the Serbs. Barely looking at her CV, he tells her she's hired. "'You are an American,'" he says. "'So you can teach our students more than English. You can teach them how to live together, with others, in peace. You can teach them how to work, how to build a democracy, how to keep trying no matter what the odds.'"

Then there is the conflicted experience of Kathy Lee. She teaches at Guangdong Industry Technical College in China. In a suburb called Nanhai, the school is putting up satellite facilities eight times larger than the main campus. Teaching labs have banks of computers and a plasma screen TV. But like so much of the country, there is such impatience to forge ahead that Lee conducts her three classes a week amid construction because the school is expanding so fast.

Her pupils are equally anxious to take part in the country's massive business boom. Though most of them have been studying English since primary school, their fluency is strained. They tell her: "The world is growing and many people speak English. If I want to do business with them, I must speak English well too!" What students want is a foreign teacher to help them get up to speed. That's why the college has hired the 23-year-old Canadian at 4,000 RMB a month, two to three times the average salary for Chinese teachers.

15    The payoff is more than just monetary for Lee. Born in China but raised in Canada, she accepted the job so she could live in Hong Kong, within a short train ride from her sick grandmother. But now, her feelings have deepened. "When the schools were asking me why I wanted to teach in China, I BS'd and said it's because I wanted to learn about my 'other' culture," she says. "But the more I said it, the more I believed it. Now, I feel that I need to be here and learn what it means to be a Chinese person."

Yet the way of life Lee is trying to understand is challenged by her methodology in the classroom. By the end of term, her students will be well practised in communication modes that are entirely un-Chinese. Lee worries about this—and the general English fever sweeping the country that even includes television programs that aim to teach English.

"I know that if everyone spoke English in the world there would still be cultural differences, but the differences between cultures will become less and less," she says. "Why is China pushing English so hard? [My students] get the sense that their own language is not good enough. To prosper, they need English. What was wrong with the way it was before? Why do you have to be Western to be competitive in business?"

If it is tough for teachers to come to terms with these questions, it is even more complex for students. While some are in what Martin calls a "process of self-assimilation," others are much more ambivalent about the course they are on. These students may be struggling with the political implications of learning English in places where the language is associated with American or British hegemony. Or they may simply recognize that as English proliferates, the survival of their own customs and dialects is under threat.

Take 27-year-old Sanghun Cho of South Korea. He is a graduate student in Toronto and has a Canadian girlfriend. But when he thinks of English he also thinks of the U.S. "It's a kind of dilemma for Koreans," he says. "I don't like America in Korea because they want to control the Korean government, but to survive in this kind of competitive environment I have to speak English and I have to know what English culture is."

20    Another South Korean student puts it even more bluntly. Part of a multinational research project Martin has been conducting over the past five years to examine why students study English as a foreign language, the student was asked to draw a picture of his future with English, and describe the picture. He sketched Uncle Sam extending a fishing line from the U.S. across the Pacific Ocean, a hook dangling above the student's

open mouth. His description: "English is the bait that Americans are using to catch Koreans in their net."

Marta Andersson is a part of the last generation of Poles forced to learn Russian in school. When she was able to study English after the fall of communism, she was thrilled. On the one hand, it paid off: she got a good job in Poland, is now studying abroad and speaks English at home with her husband. On another level, though, Andersson is aware that using English is eroding part of what her people fought for. "I have just started to lose the sense of my native language and just wait when it will become moribund," she says, "Yet I cannot imagine my future without the presence of English."

Swede Hélène Elg is also concerned about the fate of her language as English words invade it the way they do in "Chinglish" and "Franglais." "I think it's important to separate the languages in order to 'protect' our own," she says. "I realize that languages evolve, allowing new words to come into use, but we should be aware of that development and be cautious about it. The reason I feel this is because languages are so much more than just words. Words have cultural connotations. As with languages, cultures evolve, but that development should not be about adopting another culture."

Can students fight back? It's arguable that withdrawing from English would exact too high a cost for those who want to be a part of a global economy. Instead, what's changing is how people from around the world use English. Rather than simply conforming to an English steeped in Western values, many students are co-opting the language for themselves.

On an internet discussion board for EFL teachers, one teacher writes: "I feel the need of reminding our students and young colleagues that the purpose of learning English is not for us to 'speak and act' like an English person . . . but to 'speak English' as an educated Indonesian." Similarly, one Cuban who participated in Martin's project drew a picture of a rocket being launched into the sky with the description: "English is the rocket which will allow Cuba to tell its own stories to the world."

25 A new "global" English is emerging that is a bridge language between cultures, not simply a language that supplants other cultures. As Salman Rushdie is quoted as saying in the best-selling history *The Story of English*, "English, no longer an English language, now grows from many roots; and those whom it once colonized are carving out large territories within the language for themselves. The Empire is striking back."

Along with students, many teachers are joining the fight to create a more egalitarian English. They do not want to be cultural colonialists. As David Hill, a teacher in Istanbul, writes in *The Guardian Weekly*: "English is global for highly dubious reasons: colonial, military and economic hegemony, first of the British, now of the US . . . If we are not to be imperialists then we must help our students to express themselves, not our agenda."

To do that, new programs are emerging, like the Certificate in the Discipline of Teaching English as an International Language, which Martin coordinates at Glendon College. It pays close attention to issues of cultural sensitivity and autonomy when training teachers. As Martin says, "We're trying to come to grips with the effect of globalization on language teaching. Do we want a globalization that is going to be assimilationist to Western models of communication only? Or, do we want to help people gain a voice in English?"

Michelle Szabo is one teacher who has tried to give her students a voice. After her stint in Japan, she took a job at Chonbuk National University in South Korea from 2003 to 2004. On one November morning, she recalls encouraging discussion about the power of English. Her hope was to give pause to students who'd never considered the impact of studying English on their lives—as well as a place for those who had thought about it—a rare place to vent.

And there was plenty of venting as students heatedly debated face-to-face from desks arranged in a conversation-friendly horseshoe configuration. "One side was feeling very pressured and resentful," says Szabo, "and one side was saying, 'No, [English is] opening doors for us.'" Szabo tried to "equalize" the class by sitting among the students. She also said little. She wanted a forum that conveyed the message, "I'm not here to change you, to acculturize you, to force my beliefs on you," she says.

30      But even Szabo's new self-consciousness about what it is she is selling to her students along with English grammar has limits. English has irrevocably changed and acculturated the world already. Even if locals don't want to participate in the global capitalist machine, they need English to truly challenge it. As one of Szabo's students couldn't help but point out during the debate, "Isn't it ironic we're discussing the effect of English—in English?"

## Reflect on the Reading

1. Why do some Japanese say that they don't need to speak English; they simply need the "test score"?

2. Traves quotes an English professor who says, "One of the big moments in the spread of English took place in India in 1835." What was this big moment and how did it affect the study of English worldwide?

3. One of Traves' concerns about teaching English as a foreign language is that teachers also teach Western culture and traditions. What evidence does Traves provide to support this claim? What change is she advocating?

4. In this article, Salman Rushdie is quoted as saying, "English, no longer an English language, now grows from many roots; and those whom it once colonized are carving out large territories within the language for themselves. The Empire is striking back." What does this mean?

## Consider Your Viewpoint

1. Consider your own language experiences. When you learned a foreign language, did you also learn about the culture and traditions of native speakers? How did you assimilate this information with what you know of your own culture?

2. Do you speak English at school and another language at home? If so, why do you think this occurs?

3. In your opinion, should English be the only language spoken in the United States? Explain your answer. Should English be the language of business worldwide? Why or why not?

4. One of Traves's students points out, "Isn't it ironic we're discussing the effect of English—in English?" How effective is this statement as part of the conclusion?

# Blue Collar Brilliance

## Mike Rose

In this excerpt, taken from his book *The American Scholar*, Mike Rose advocates for a change in the way we view intelligence, work, and class. Rose, the son of Italian immigrants, has written ten books and numerous articles on the topics of language and literacy.

My mother, Rose Meraglio Rose, shaped her adult identity as a waitress in coffee shops and family restaurants. When I was growing up in Los Angeles during the 1950s, my father and I would occasionally hang out at the restaurant until her shift ended, and then we'd ride the bus home with her. Sometimes she worked the register and the counter, and we sat there; when she waited booths and tables, we found a booth in the back where the waitresses took their breaks.

There wasn't much for a child to do at the restaurants, and so as the hours stretched out, I watched the cooks and waitresses and listened to what they said. At mealtimes, the pace of the kitchen staff and the din from customers picked up. Weaving in and out around the room, waitresses warned *behind you* in impassive but urgent voices. Standing at the service window facing the kitchen, they called out abbreviated orders. *Fry four on two*, my mother would say as she clipped a check onto the metal wheel. Her tables were *deuces*, *four-tops*, or *six-tops* according to their size; seating areas also were nicknamed. The *racetrack*, for instance, was the fast-turnover front section. Lingo conferred authority and signaled know-how.

> Lingo: Specialized vocabulary.

Rosie took customers' orders, pencil poised over pad, while fielding questions about the food. She walked full tilt through the room with plates stretching up her left arm and two cups of coffee somehow cradled in her right hand. She stood at a table or booth and removed a plate for this person, another for that person, then another, remembering who had the hamburger, who had the fried shrimp, almost always getting it right. She would haggle with the cook about a returned order and rush by us, saying, *He gave me lip, but I got him*. She'd take a minute to flop down in the booth next to my father. *I'm all in*, she'd say, and whisper something about a customer. Gripping the outer edge of the table with one hand, she'd watch the room and note, in the flow of our conversation, who needed a refill, whose order was taking longer to prepare than it should, who was finishing up.

I couldn't have put it in words when I was growing up, but what I observed in my mother's restaurant defined the world of adults, a place where competence was synonymous with physical work. I've since studied the working habits of blue-collar workers and have come to understand how much my mother's kind of work demands of both body and brain. A waitress acquires knowledge and intuition about the ways and the rhythms of the restaurant business. Waiting on seven to nine tables, each with two to six customers, Rosie devised memory strategies so that she could remember who ordered what. And because she knew the average time it took to prepare different dishes, she could monitor an order that was taking too long at the service station.

5    Like anyone who is effective at physical work, my mother learned to work smart, as she put it, *to make every move count*. She'd sequence and group tasks: What could she do first, then second, then third as she circled through her station? What tasks could be clustered? She did everything on the fly, and when problems arose—technical or human—she solved them

within the flow of work, while taking into account the emotional state of her coworkers. Was the manager in a good mood? Did the cook wake up on the wrong side of the bed? If so, how could she make an extra request or effectively return an order?

And then, of course, there were the customers who entered the restaurant with all sorts of needs, from physiological ones, including the emotions that accompany hunger, to a sometimes complicated desire for human contact. Her tip depended on how well she responded to these needs, and so she became adept at reading social cues and managing feelings, both the customers' and her own. No wonder, then, that Rosie was intrigued by psychology. The restaurant became the place where she studied human behavior, puzzling over the problems of her regular customers and refining her ability to deal with people in a difficult world. She took pride in being among the public, she'd say, *There isn't a day that goes by in the restaurant that you don't learn something.*

Intelligence is closely associated with formal education, and most people seem to move comfortably from that notion to a belief that work requiring less schooling requires less intelligence. These assumptions run through our cultural history, from the post–Revolutionary War period, when mechanics were characterized by political rivals as illiterate and therefore incapable of participating in government, until today. Generalizations about intelligence, work, and social class deeply affect our assumptions about ourselves and each other, guiding the ways we use our minds to learn, build knowledge, solve problems, and make our way through the world.

Although writers and scholars have often looked at the working class, they have generally focused on the values such workers exhibit rather than on the thought their work requires—a subtle but pervasive omission. Our cultural iconography promotes the muscled arm, sleeve rolled tight against biceps, but no brightness behind the eye, no image that links hand and brain.

> **Iconography:** Traditional images or symbols.

One of my mother's brothers, Joe Meraglio, left school in the ninth grade to work for the Pennsylvania Railroad. From there he joined the Navy, returned to the railroad, which was already in decline, and eventually joined his older brother at General Motors, where, over a 33-year career, he moved from working on the assembly line to supervising the paint-and-body department. When I was a young man, Joe took me on a tour of the factory. The floor was loud—in some places deafening—and when I turned a corner or opened a door, the smell of chemicals knocked my head back. The work was repetitive and taxing, and the pace was inhumane.

10    Still, for Joe the shop floor was a school. He learned the most efficient way to use his body by acquiring a set of routines that were quick and preserved energy. Otherwise he never would have survived on the line.

As a foreman, Joe constantly faced new problems and became a consummate multitasker, evaluating a flurry of demands quickly, parceling out physical and mental resources, keeping a number of ongoing events in his mind, returning to whatever task had been interrupted, and maintaining a cool head under the pressure of grueling production schedules. In the midst of all this, Joe learned more and more about the auto industry, the technological and social dynamics of the shop floor, the machinery and production processes, and the basics of paint chemistry and of plating and baking. With further promotions, he not only solved problems but also began to find problems to solve: Joe initiated the redesign of the nozzle on a paint sprayer, thereby eliminating costly and unhealthy overspray. And he found a way to reduce the energy costs of the baking ovens without affecting the quality of the paint. He lacked formal knowledge of how the machines under his supervision worked, but he had direct experience with them, hands-on knowledge, and was savvy about their quirks and operational capabilities. He could experiment with them.

In addition, Joe learned about budgets and management. Coming off the line as he did, he had a perspective of workers' needs and management's demands, and this led him to think of ways to improve efficiency on the line while relieving some of the stress on the assemblers. He had each worker in a unit learn his or her coworkers' jobs so they could rotate across stations to relieve some of the monotony. He believed that rotation would allow assemblers to get longer and more frequent breaks. It was an easy sell to the people on the line. The union, however, had to approve any modification in job duties, and the managers were wary of the change. Joe had to argue his case on a number of fronts, providing him a kind of rhetorical education.

Biographical accounts of the lives of scientists, lawyers, entrepreneurs, and other professionals are rich with detail about the intellectual dimension of their work. But the life stories of working-class people are few and are typically accounts of hardship and courage or the achievements wrought by hard work.

Eight years ago I began a study of the thought processes involved in work like that of my mother and uncle. I catalogued the cognitive demands of a range of blue-collar and service jobs, from waitressing and hair styling to plumbing and welding. To gain a sense of how knowledge and skill develop, I observed experts as well as novices. From the details of this close examination, I tried to fashion what I called "cognitive biographies" of blue-collar workers.

15    Our culture—in Cartesian fashion—separates the body from the mind, so that, for example, we assume that the use of a tool does not involve abstraction. We reinforce this notion by defining intelligence solely on grades in school and numbers on IQ tests. And we employ social biases pertaining to a person's place on the occupational ladder. The distinctions among blue, pink, and white collars carry with them attributions of character, motivation, and intelligence. Although we rightly acknowledge and amply compensate the play of mind in white-collar and professional work, we diminish or erase it in considerations about other endeavors— physical and service work particularly. We also often ignore the experience of everyday work in administrative deliberations and policymaking.

> Cartesian: The philosophy of René Descartes. Descartes believed that the unconscious mind and the conscious brain were distinct entities that were not always in agreement.

Here's what we find when we get in close. The plumber seeking leverage in order to work in tight quarters and the hair stylist adroitly handling scissors and comb manage their bodies strategically. Though work-related actions become routine with experience, they were learned at some point through observation, trial and error, and, often, physical or verbal assistance from a coworker or trainer.

The use of tools requires the studied refinement of stance, grip, balance, and fine-motor skills. Workers must also know the characteristics of the material they are engaging—how it reacts to various cutting or compressing devices, to degrees of heat, or to lines of force. Some of these things demand judgment, the weighing of options, the consideration of multiple variables, and, occasionally, the creative use of a tool in an unexpected way.

Carpenters have an eye for length, line, and angle; mechanics troubleshoot by listening; hair stylists are attuned to shape, texture, and motion. Sensory data merge with concept, as when an auto mechanic relies on sound, vibration, and even smell to understand what cannot be observed.

Planning and problem solving have been studied since the earliest days of modern cognitive psychology and are considered core elements in Western definitions of intelligence. To work is to solve problems. The big difference between the psychologist's laboratory and the workplace is that in the former the problems are isolated and in the latter they are embedded in the real-time flow of work with all its messiness and social complexity.

20    Verbal and mathematical skills drive measures of intelligence in the Western Hemisphere, and many of the kinds of work I studied are thought to require relatively little proficiency in either. Compared to certain kinds of white-collar occupations, that's true. But written symbols flow through physical work.

Numbers are rife in most workplaces: on tools and gauges, as measurements, as indicators of pressure or concentration or temperature, as guides to sequence, on ingredient labels, on lists and spreadsheets, as markers of quantity and price. Certain jobs require workers to make, check, and verify calculations, and to collect and interpret data. Basic math can be involved, and some workers develop a good sense of numbers and patterns. Consider, as well, what might be called material mathematics: mathematical functions embodied in materials and actions, as when a carpenter builds a cabinet or a flight of stairs.

A simple mathematical act can extend quickly beyond itself. Measuring, for example, can involve more than recording the dimensions of an object. As I watched a cabinetmaker measure a long strip of wood, he read a number off the tape out loud, looked back over his shoulder to the kitchen wall, turned back to his task, took another measurement, and paused for a moment in thought. He was solving a problem involving the molding, and the measurement was important to his deliberation about structure and appearance.

In the blue-collar workplace, directions, plans, and reference books rely on illustrations, some representational and others, like blueprints, that require training to interpret. Esoteric symbols—visual jargon—depict switches and receptacles, pipe fittings, or types of welds. Workers themselves often make sketches on the job. I frequently observed them grab a pencil to sketch something on a scrap of paper or on a piece of the material they were installing.

> Esoteric: Understood by only a few.

Though many kinds of physical work don't require a high literacy level, more reading occurs in the blue-collar workplace than is generally thought, from manuals and catalogs to work orders and invoices, to lists, labels, and forms. With routine tasks, for example, reading is integral to understanding production quotas, learning how to use an instrument, or applying a product. Written notes can initiate action, as in restaurant orders or reports of machine malfunction, or they can serve as memory aids.

25    True, many uses of writing are abbreviated, routine, and repetitive, and they infrequently require interpretation or analysis. But analytic moments can be part of routine activities, and seemingly basic reading and writing can be cognitively rich. Because workplace language is used in the flow of other activities, we can overlook the remarkable coordination of words, numbers, and drawings required to initiate and direct action.

If we believe everyday work to be mindless, then that will affect the work we create in the future. When we devalue the full range of everyday cognition, we offer limited educational opportunities and fail to make fresh and meaningful instructional connections among disparate kinds of skill and knowledge. If we think that whole categories of people—identified by class or occupation—are not that bright, then we reinforce social separations and cripple our ability to talk across cultural divides.

Affirmation of diverse intelligence is not a retreat to a softhearted definition of the mind. To acknowledge a broader range of intellectual capacity is to take seriously the concept of cognitive variability, to appreciate in all the Rosies and Joes the thought that drives their accomplishments and defines who they are. This is a model of the mind that is worthy of a democratic society.

## Reflect on the Reading

1. Rose describes places like the restaurant where his mother worked as "a place where competence was synonymous with physical work." What does he mean by this statement?

2. Rose challenges the assumption that "Intelligence is closely associated with formal education, and most people seem to move comfortably from that notion to a belief that work requiring less schooling requires less intelligence." What evidence does he provide to support his viewpoint?

3. What change is Rose advocating in this piece? Underline the sentence where he first states his position.

4. Rose says that the meaning of work is to "solve problems." What examples does he give of this? And how does he differentiate the work of the educated and uneducated?

5. Rose claims that he is not being "softhearted" when he proposes that we recognize a diversity of intelligences. What does he mean by this?

## Consider Your Viewpoint

1. Do you agree with Rose's claim, "If we think that whole categories of people—identified by class or occupation—are not that bright, then we reinforce social separations and cripple our ability to talk across cultural divides?" Explain your answer.

2. Rose states that "life stories of working-class people are few and are typically accounts of hardship and courage or the achievements wrought by hard work." Do you agree? What life stories of working-class people have you read?

3. In your opinion, should we recognize a diversity of intelligences? Why or why not? How would such recognition help us bridge cultural divides?

4. Rose uses expressive writing—writing where he shares his own personal experiences—with the reader. How effective is this to help him advocate for change?

PEARSON
mycomplab

For support in meeting this chapter's objectives, follow this path in MyCompLab: Resources ⇒ Writing ⇒ Writing Purposes ⇒ Writing to Argue or Persuade. Review the Instruction and Multimedia resources about writing to argue or persuade, then complete the Exercises and click on Gradebook to measure your progress.

# 13 Writing Patterns

## Learning Objectives

In this chapter you will:

- Learn to use writing patterns and details to develop ideas.
- Read examples of student writing that include these patterns.
- Practice using writing patterns in your own writing.

*As you look at the bricks in this photo, the first thing you notice is that they are in a pattern. Do you know what this pattern is called?*

A fter you notice the pattern of the bricks in the photo on the chapter opening page, you see other details such as the writing on the bricks and the grass growing between them. Just as this photographer created an interesting and memorable photograph by focusing her lens on the pattern and details of the bricks, you can improve your writing by focusing attention on the patterns and details that you use to develop your ideas.

## WRITING PATTERNS TO DEVELOP IDEAS

What are the patterns that writers use to help them develop their ideas and how do they use them to add interest to their writing? You were introduced to these eight common patterns in Chapter 3:

- narration
- description
- examples
- process
- definition
- comparison and contrast
- classification
- cause and effect

Writers use these patterns to help make their text convincing, interesting, and easy to remember, and they often use more than one pattern in a piece of writing. In some cases, writers use most or all of the patterns listed. By including each method of development, they are providing their readers with a variety of interesting ways to understand the topic.

*Good writers are those who keep the language efficient. That is to say, keep it accurate, keep it clear.*
*—Ezra Pound*

**Activity 13.1**   In discussion with your classmates, share what you already know about the writing patterns listed above. Which ones work best for you? How will learning additional writing patterns improve the way you write in the future?

**Connect With Others**

As you read the following descriptions of writing patterns, make a note of the ones you would like to try in your own writing. Would you be willing to try all of them in one piece? The more patterns you can use, the more interesting your writing will be.

# Narration

Narration tells a story or relates a series of events as they happened in time. Sharing your personal stories defines who you are and helps your readers get to know you better. Writing about other people's stories helps you to understand them and their unique cultural experiences.

**One Student's Narration.** Student writer Margaret Henderson narrated these events as part of an autobiographical essay. In choosing to relate these particular events about her early life in Germany, Margaret is not only telling a story about herself, but also about her experience living within another culture.

> "Sprechen Sie Deutsch?" My first memories are of a blond, plump toddler being pulled on a small, wooden sled across the snowy grounds of an apartment complex in Bamberg, Germany by an even blonder, plumper German housekeeper. When I was just eighteen months old, my father, a sergeant in the Army, was stationed in an area flecked with tall pines and post–World War II foxholes. Because he and my mother saw this overseas assignment as a chance to see Europe, I spent weeks at a time with our housekeeper: a kind, middle-aged woman, who spent hours lovingly tending to her family and me. When I was six, my father was transferred to Ft. Bliss, Texas, a stark contrast to Germany. El Paso truly was a parched, arid town with frequent sandstorms that stung my bare legs as I walked or rode a Schwinn bike to Hughey Elementary School. Because of the time I had spent with our German housekeeper and her family, my English was limited, so I was placed in an ESL classroom for my first year of primary school. I was a shy student who enjoyed school and who spent countless hours on school-related activities. I spent weekends playing with paper dolls, cutting pictures out of a Sears catalog, and, of course, playing school. I realize now that school and friends became a refuge of sorts—a place where I knew I could do well—and so it remained through my high school years.

---

## Narration Checklist

*Characteristics of effective narration include:*

☐ topic of interest for the chosen audience

☐ clear context for the story

☐ well-chosen, vivid details used to relate the events

☐ chronological sequence of events to help the reader easily follow the story

☐ consistent point of view

# Description

Description uses words to paint a picture for your readers so that they can see, hear, touch, smell, or taste what you are describing. You use description to help your readers experience what you are writing. Through this experience, they come to more fully understand and appreciate your message.

**One Student's Description.** Student writer Charles Lujan wrote this description of the local homeless shelter as a way to discover ideas for a report on the homeless in his city. While making this observation, he discovered things about the homeless community that profoundly affected his view of this subculture.

As I drive to observe the homeless shelter, I can't help but wonder what to expect. Driving closer to the shelter I notice small groups of what I think to be homeless people just blocks away from the shelter. I begin to wonder if I'll see them inside the shelter later, or will they just spend the evening outdoors? I park my vehicle about a block away. This is the closest parking I can find to enter an alley that leads to the main entrance. While walking through the alley I observe a few tired faces, people who appear to have been walking for days. Their clothes look just as tired. Making my way through the alley and entering the doorway, a distinct odor penetrates my sense of smell. We had similar odors in our school lockers after a game. Many people notice my entrance all at once. The faces vary from old to young, with every type of culture carrying the same look of tired eyes just wanting a place to sleep for the night. Many have backpacks that look like they've been dragged through miles of dirt roads. Some of the individuals are already sleeping on a mat placed on the floor, while others are looking for a bald spot to place their belongings for a night of rest themselves. Unbelievably, each individual is side by side with just a couple of inches between them, each lying on a mat provided by the shelter. As I make my way through a path of floor space made clear by the staff to provide the shelter employees and patrons a walking trail to move from one room to another, I notice only a few homeless talking with each other. The others seem pleased to take a quiet moment to themselves.

### Description Checklist

*Characteristics of effective description include:*

☐ creation of a mood, atmosphere, or dominant impression

☐ vivid sensory details that include the five senses

☐ clear organizational pattern

☐ enough detail to illustrate the main point

☐ no details to distract from the main point

## Examples

Examples make ideas clear and concrete through specific details. Examples can be facts, statistics, quotations, or other details that explain a general topic more specifically. The examples you add also help make your point and hold your readers' attention.

**One Student's Examples.** Lisa Estala, a student writer, suggests ways to overcome writer's block. Imagine if Lisa had simply written, "At times you pick up a pen and suddenly your mind is blank. All you need to break through your own writer's block is within you, the writer." Fortunately, Lisa provided examples to help her readers understand what she means by her opening and closing sentences.

> At times you pick up a pen and suddenly your mind is blank, you can't think, you're unsure of how to start, and minutes go by with nothing to write. Try thinking of something else, a completely different topic, start writing a poem, or just describe something you see outside the window. At this point, all you want to do is write *something* to stimulate your mind. Look out the window and write about what the woman may be thinking as she carries her groceries home. Write about how heavy her bags look or invent a storyline of how she is upset that her daughter didn't pick her up at the store as she promised. Once you start writing, it should be easier to change the subject. At this point, you are feeling creative, inspired, and ready to write. Now, try writing on the assigned topic. These examples might not work for everyone, but the trick is to find what works for you. All you need to break through your own writer's block is within you, the writer.

## Examples Checklist

*Characteristics of effective examples include:*

☐  specific and concrete details

☐  interesting and informative models

☐  each example effectively supports the main idea

☐  enough examples to help readers understand the main point

☐  no off-the-topic examples

# Process

A process gives directions for how to do something or provides information on how something works. By explaining the process steps in order, you help your readers understand what you are describing.

**One Student's Process.**  In these paragraphs from an essay entitled "Boot Camp," student writer Kebba Khan describes the beginning of an initiation process used in his culture to prepare boys for manhood.

> The process commenced with the "elders" collecting me from our house in the middle of the night, and taking me and approximately two dozen boys to an unknown body of water for a cleansing ceremony. From the moment I left my house up until the moment we arrived at the cleansing site, my whole body was covered with a dark piece of cloth, and an unknown "elder" led me by the hand. The procession to the cleansing site was accompanied by drumbeats and chants. The cleansing ceremony was followed by a long trek, in total silence, into the wilderness where we established our base camp—our home for the next eight weeks.
>
> We arrived at the campsite at the crack of dawn, exhausted and disoriented; the air was humid, dense and stiflingly hot. Upon our arrival, I had an opportunity to look around and realized that our entourage was comprised mostly of complete strangers. The elders immediately instructed us to clear an area to build our grass huts, kitchen, toilets and bathrooms. The camp had a circular layout; the elders' huts formed the perimeter around that of the "Njulies" (*initiates* in my dialect). We built the kitchen and dining area between the huts for the elders and that of the initiates. A campfire marked the center of the camp; we lit it upon completion of the construction of all the camp structures, and extinguished it

only after the demolition of the camp. We finished the erection of
the required structures around noon and settled down in our
temporary home.

---

**Process Checklist**

*Characteristics of effective process analysis include:*

☐ sufficient background information to help the reader understand
the process

☐ clear definitions of specialized vocabulary

☐ consistent explanation of the process steps

☐ transitional words used to guide the reader step by step

☐ clear results of the process

---

**Connect
With Others**

**Activity 13.2**   In a group of four classmates, select an item such as a cell
phone, keys, or wallet from one group member's pocket. Each member
should then draft a paragraph, using one of the four writing patterns already
presented. One group member, for example, will narrate a story about how
the item got into the pocket, another one will describe the item, the third one
will provide examples of similar items, and the fourth member will describe a
process for using the item. Share your writing patterns within the group and
select one to read to the entire class.

---

## Definition

Definition tells what a word or concept means. Often when we write, we
use words or concepts that are unfamiliar or open to various interpretations. To ensure that your readers understand exactly what you mean, you
can provide a formal dictionary definition, a synonym, or an extended description of the meaning of a word.

**One Student's Definition.**   Student writer Miriam Aziz used this definition of Hezbollah in a research paper that she wrote for a Political
Science class.

Hezbollah or the "Party of God" is a combination of radical Islamic groups
and organizations under one banner, Islamic Jihad. Hezbollah has come
to be one of the most recognized and notorious terrorist organizations
in the world. Created by a group of clerics in southern Lebanon, the group

has not only gained military strength, but they have also entered the political arena as well, having gained considerable popular support in southern Lebanon. According to the U.S. Department of Justice website's information on foreign terrorist organizations, Hezbollah is strongly anti-West and anti-Israel. What is interesting about the group is the dichotomy of their behavior: while they are viewed as terrorists in the West and Israel, they are a powerful political force within Lebanon because of the philanthropic benefits they provide the public.

---

### Definition Checklist

*Characteristics of effective definition include:*

- ☐ specific and concrete description
- ☐ easily understood words used to describe the word or concept
- ☐ enough detail to make the meaning clear
- ☐ consistent focus on the meaning of what is being defined
- ☐ support for the main idea

---

## Comparison and Contrast

Comparison and contrast shows how ideas are alike and how they are different. When comparing and contrasting, choose between two organizational strategies: (1) write about how two things are alike, followed by how they are different, or (2) show the similarities and differences between each, point by point.

**One Student's Comparison and Contrast.** In this letter to her college dean, student writer Judith Almodovar compares and contrasts to persuade the dean to allow her to minor in a foreign language rather than minor in business.

The more educated students are the more competitive and attractive they become to potential employers. Because of this, the College of Business requires students to both major and minor in business-related fields. For example, they might major in finance and minor in economics or major in marketing and minor in management. I would like to propose a better-suited alternative to meet employers' demands: allow business majors to minor in a foreign language instead. Long gone are the days when the United States only conducted domestic business. Foreign direct investment and the removal of trade barriers have led to a more global economy. In today's market, multinational enterprises are in need of culturally sensitive individuals to conduct business all over the world. Completing a minor in a foreign language would require the same time and effort as a major and minor in business fields. The difference, however, is that with a minor in a foreign language, students would be prepared for today's business environment. According to a survey conducted by Korn Ferry International, 66 percent of American recruiters agree that being bilingual is a vital skill. Therefore, I believe allowing students to pursue a minor in a foreign language rather than a minor in business would only make them a stronger potential asset to an employer and ultimately translate into greater career success.

---

### Comparison and Contrast Checklist

*Characteristics of effective comparison and contrast include:*

☐ clear presentation of similarities and differences

☐ examples of each included

☐ only information that is relevant

☐ consistent order of both comparison and contrast details

☐ transitional words that help readers see relationships

---

# Classification

Classification sorts things into groups to help your readers organize the material and remember what you say. Occasionally, you may also classify to convince your readers of the superiority of one group over another. For example, you might classify fuel-efficient cars such as the Ford Fusion, Toyota Prius, Honda Insight, and Mini Cooper and then go on to argue that the Mini Cooper is the best choice because it has excellent safety features and it looks cute and is fun to drive.

**One Student's Classification.** In this journal entry, student writer Chris Morris classifies his various discourse communities.

There are really only three major discourse communities in which I am involved. These include (1) my family, (2) my friends, and (3) church. When communicating with my family, I use genres such as speaking face to face, texting, email, and talking on the phone. The subjects covered in our conversation are usually family matters, current events, politics, or sports. I use Standard English to communicate in all genres and in all subjects, though I do use some text lingo when texting, but not as much as my family members do. I communicate with my friends in much the same way as my family. In addition to speaking face to face, texting, and talking on the phone, we communicate on Facebook through messages, chat, and status updates, although we don't typically use regular email at all. My friends and I discuss the same types of subjects that I discuss with my family, except for family matters. The language we use is similar to that which I use to communicate with my family, though we tend to use a bit of slang in the conversations as well. When I communicate with the people at church, it is usually face to face. We also communicate through Facebook and email. The subjects discussed are much different from those discussed with my family and friends. In this community, the subjects are usually Bible study topics and church events with a little bit of casual conversation thrown in here and there.

---

### Classification Checklist

*Characteristics of effective classification include:*

- [ ] clear focus on what is being classified
- [ ] effective organizational pattern used throughout
- [ ] uniquely described categories
- [ ] details that further delineate categories
- [ ] transitional words that help readers see relationships among categories

---

# Cause and Effect

Cause and effect describes the relationship between something that happened (cause) and the result (effect). The relationship should be clear. In other words, the effect should be a direct consequence of what happened and not just a subsequent event.

**One Student's Cause and Effect.**  Student writer Gilbert Serna describes the effects of cultural values on his beliefs and goals.

Two traditional American cultural values I identify with are individualism and equality. As a Hispanic growing up in the United States, I was educated to be self-sufficient and to set my own

## LANGUAGES and CULTURES

Ideally, multilingual writers should not be expected to give up writing patterns used in other discourse communities, but should instead add new ones. Along with this should come a knowledge of how and when to use each within a variety of cultural and societal situations. For example, texting can be valuable within a particular discourse community, but not appropriate in others; for example, texting would not work for a graduate school application.

goals in life. I was taught that I control my own destiny and not to count too much on others. The effect of these teachings is that I am now more content when I achieve my goals. My work ethic is the same as the rest of the American society when it comes to living the American dream such as working hard and seeking prosperity. The other effect is that I now believe that everyone "is created equal" and has the same rights; this includes children, men, women of all ethnic and cultural groups living in the United States.

Two Mexican cultural values I identify with are family bonding and pride. Hispanics normally have large families, and the Hispanic culture believes that family is very important. The effect of this is the knowledge that no matter what happens, Hispanics can always go back to their parents' house for comfort, advice, and whatever else they need. The other element I can identify myself with is pride. Hispanics tend to be patriotic and carry the flag of their beloved country, favorite team, or neighborhood. As a result, I take very much pride in my education, work, and family. My education will help me attain my goal to get the job I need to support my own family and their educational needs.

## Cause and Effect Checklist

*Characteristics of effective cause and effect include:*

☐ clear distinction between what happened and the result

☐ logical organization of details within each category

☐ details further explain events

☐ transitional words that help reader see cause and effect relationships

**Activity 13.3**   With a small group of students, select a student model from one of the Part II chapters and label the different patterns of development the student used. Present your findings to the class and explain how the writing patterns make the piece convincing, interesting, and easier to remember.

**Connect With Others**

Any developed piece of writing such as an essay, report, or newspaper article will undoubtedly include more than one writing pattern. Each pattern connects to the next pattern and contributes to the readers' understanding of the whole. Effective communication occurs when authors use a variety of patterns and details to convey their message to their readers.

# WRITING ASSIGNMENT

Find a speech, essay, newspaper article, movie review, or brochure that interests you and that you would like to spend some time analyzing for writing patterns. You may choose a favorite piece from this class, a daily newspaper, or an article from a website. Read the piece looking for writing patterns that the author used to develop it. When you find a writing pattern such as narration or classification, label it in the margin.

Once you have labeled your selection, write a short essay describing the writing patterns and how they increased your understanding of the selection. As you write, use a variety of writing patterns in your own essay.

For support in meeting this chapter's objectives, follow this path in MyCompLab: Resources ⇒ Writing ⇒ Writing Purposes. Review the Instruction and Multimedia resources about writing patterns and purposes, then complete the Exercises and click on Gradebook to measure your progress.

# CHAPTER
# 14 Visual Design

## Learning Objectives

In this chapter you will:

- Analyze the rhetorical situation to add visuals.
- Learn the principles of good visual design.
- Learn effective page design.
- Practice evaluating visuals.
- Learn to create an effective PowerPoint presentation.

*The caption on the side of this truck reads, "What do we have to do to get your attention?" How does this photograph get your attention?*

A  s you learned in Chapter 1, literacy is the way we
use language to speak, listen, view, and think about the world
around us. *Visual* literacy is the way we use images, as well as
language, to interpret and create meaning. In Figure 14.1, the cartoonist
uses both language and image to make a statement about the importance
of literacy.

**FIGURE 14.1** Editorial cartoon

**Activity 14.1**    Analyze the cartoon in Figure 14.1 by answering these
questions:

1. What is happening in this cartoon?
2. What is the relationship between the words and the image?
3. What is the author's message about literacy?
4. Would readers of all cultures understand this cartoon? Why or why not?

**Develop Your
Understanding**

In the past, when we used the word *literacy* or *writing* we usually referred to the written word. Today, we seldom see the written word without
some type of visual design to accompany it. Reports are full of charts and
graphs, newspapers include colorful photos, and websites, too, are full of
electronic images. All of them take advantage of a variety of text font styles
and sizes. To be an effective reader and writer, it's not enough to understand the printed word; we must also understand how visuals work to influence our understanding. Once we recognize the effect that visuals have
on us, we can use words and images to help us communicate our own
messages more successfully.

Design: To plan
something in a
skillful or artis-
tic way.

# READ AND WRITE ABOUT VISUAL DESIGN

Part of the challenge of learning about visual design is that there are no
hard and fast rules. If there were universal rules, there would be no need
for talented graphic designers who know how to create visual designs that
appeal to various audiences. Even if we aren't graphic designers, however,
we can learn the basics of good design, how to recognize it when we see it,
and how to incorporate it into our own writing.

## Analyzing the Rhetorical Situation to Create a Visual Design

Visual design includes the text fonts, white space, color, borders, and images such as illustrations and photos that we use in a written or electronic
document. Just as we analyze the rhetorical situation before beginning to
write words, we can also use these same elements to ensure that we
choose the most effective visual design to enhance our message.

**Considering Audience and Purpose.**  The more you know about your audience and purpose, the easier it is for you to design a written or electronic document that appeals to them, and the more you know about your
audience's visual preferences, the easier it is to choose design details and
present them in a way to appeal to this particular audience. Readers bring
different cultural values, beliefs, and background knowledge to what they
see in a design, so a thorough audience analysis is critical to the success
of your communication.

> ### Visual Design Audience Questions
>
> - Who is the audience?
> - Does this audience's gender or culture suggest visual design
>   preferences?
> - How can the visual design attract and hold the readers' attention?
> - How can the visual design facilitate the communication for this
>   particular audience?

You should choose a visual design that supports your chosen purpose: (1) to express, (2) to inform, or (3) to persuade. For example, if you
keep a blog to describe your trip to Israel, you would undoubtedly include photographs to give your readers a richer sense of your experience.
If, on the other hand, you are writing a report on the gender and ethnicity of your college student population, you might include tables and

graphs to show the numbers and percentages of each. Finally, if you are writing a letter to persuade your boss to improve workflow in your office, you might include a flowchart or other illustration to underscore the persuasive argument.

## Visual Design Purpose Questions

- What is the primary purpose of this communication?
- Are there ways the visual design can enhance this purpose?
- What aspects of the communication are best presented through visuals?
- Which visuals would be most effective?

**Choosing a Genre.** In this textbook you have the option to write in a variety of genres, including the essay, memoir, blog, report, brochure, newspaper editorial, pamphlet, website, and photo essay. If you are free to select the genre for your work, consider which one is most effective to deliver your message. Then read or visit online examples of works in your chosen genre to learn the design elements associated with it.

## Genre Questions

- Is one genre more effective than another for communicating this information?
- Does my audience have expectations that I will use a particular genre?
- Are there ways that the genre can facilitate understanding for nonnative speakers of English?
- What do I know about creating the visual elements for this genre?

**Reviewing Exigence and Constraints.** When something happens that causes you to want to communicate, you have the exigence to act. If you choose to communicate in writing, you must determine how this exigence affects the visual design as well as the written message.

## Visual Design Exigence Questions

- Why is it urgent to communicate this message?
- How can I use visual design to underscore this urgency?
- How do I hope the audience will respond to my words and visual design?

Depending on how much experience you have working with visual design, you may find many or few constraints to using visual elements in your documents. Whatever your level, though, you can improve your understanding and use of visuals.

---

**Visual Design Constraint Questions**

- Am I able to find or create these visuals within the timeframe I have to produce this document?
- Where can I learn more about creating visuals for this document?
- Are there visual design elements that I shouldn't use because they might offend readers from other cultures?

---

**Connect With Others**

**Activity 14.2**   Divide into small groups, with each group assigned to find examples of writing in various genres such as a memoir, blog, article, or report. Examine each document and discuss how the author used visual design to increase the impact of the message on a particular audience and for a specific purpose. Share what your group discovered with the class.

---

# PRINCIPLES OF GOOD VISUAL DESIGN

Even if you have no experience as a graphic designer, you already have a good sense of visual design. You make decisions based on your design preferences every day. You choose to read one news site over another with similar content because you prefer the layout of one. You pay attention to certain billboards and ignore others because of your reaction to their design. Just how important is good design? Design contributes to an overall first impression of a document and can influence a reader's decision to continue reading.

Once you have analyzed the rhetorical context, use the following basics to help you recognize and plan an effective *overall* page design.

*Effective rhetoric is . . . a two-pronged strategy of verbal/visual persuasion, showing while it tells, illustrating its claims with powerful examples, making the listener see and not merely hear. . . .*

—W. J. T. Mitchell

- context
- proportion
- arrangement
- emphasis
- originality

# Context

When working with visual design, every design element should relate to the context of the message including its topic, audience, purpose, and genre. We have all seen instructional leaflets that scream at us in all capital letters and PowerPoint presentations with cute barking dog clip art that has nothing to do with the topic of the presentation. Let's admit it, sometimes our enthusiasm for using design tools interferes with delivering a clear and convincing message. Simplicity and coherence in design are best. Always strive for a balance between the appearance and the content of your message and be sure that every design element contributes meaningfully to the communication.

Context: The environment within which something takes place.

Figure 14.2 includes two slides from different PowerPoint presentations on the same topic. The PowerPoint slide on the left is text-heavy and has cartoonish clip art. The slide on the right has a simpler design, is more professional in appearance, and, as a result, is more visually appealing.

FIGURE 14.2  Ineffective and effective PowerPoint slides

## Visual Design Context Questions

- Which design elements (fonts, white space, color, borders, backgrounds, and images) will help my readers more easily understand my message within the context of my chosen topic and genre?
- Are my design element choices simple and clear?
- Which design elements should I omit because they do not contribute to the meaning?

Proportion:
Relative size.

# Proportion

Determine the size of all design elements by their relative importance on the page. Important design elements should have more emphasis and appear more prominent on the page or screen than less important ones. Varying the sizes of type or graphics adds contrast and helps readers see the major divisions in a document. Titles and headings in a newsletter, for example, should be larger in font size, made bold, or underlined to stand out from the regular text because these elements help readers navigate your document.

In Figure 14.3, the sample from a student article for a newsletter on the left does not include proportion or spacing. The sample on the right, which uses proportion and spacing for titles and headings, is much easier to read.

---

Taxing Our Sins

The newest weapon against obesity is a controversial plan to impose a "sin tax" on sodas and other sweet beverages. Local and state governments are eager to try taxing soda to generate revenues that could be used to educate citizens about obesity and its related health risks. Although this tax will have to overcome much resistance in order to be put into law, many medical experts are endorsing the idea. The Argument for Taxing Soda

In a number of cities and states, politicians who support the idea of a tax on soda see it as a way to reduce consumption of unhealthy products and to pay for the high costs of obesity. As the medical costs of obesity-related diseases skyrocket, local governments must look to manage and minimize this expense. In New York City, for example, the tax revenue could support new programs to fight the childhood obesity epidemic. The goal of such education programs would be to encourage families to learn about healthier choices; including how to avoid sweetened drinks.

---

**Taxing Our Sins**

The newest weapon against obesity is a controversial plan to impose a "sin tax" on sodas and other sweet beverages. Local and state governments are eager to try taxing soda to generate revenues that could be used to educate citizens about obesity and its related health risks. Although this tax will have to overcome much resistance in order to be put into law, many medical experts are endorsing the idea.

**The Argument for Taxing Soda**

In a number of cities and states, politicians who support the idea of a tax on soda see it as a way to reduce consumption of unhealthy products and to pay for the high costs of obesity. As the medical costs of obesity-related diseases skyrocket, local governments must look to manage and minimize this expense. In New York City, for example, the tax revenue could support new programs to fight the childhood obesity epidemic. The goal of such education programs would be to encourage families to learn about healthier choices; including how to avoid sweetened drinks.

---

**FIGURE 14.3** Ineffective and effective document formatting

**Visual Design Proportion Questions**

- Does my choice of genre dictate specific proportions?
- What are the most important elements of this communication?
- How can I use proportion to help me highlight those important elements?

# Arrangement

Just as transitional words and phrases serve as a guide to help readers move from one idea to another, arrangement helps readers move from idea to idea with an understanding of the relative importance of each section. Effective visual design in many Western cultures guides readers through a document by following readers' tendency to read from left to right, top to bottom. Arrangement also refers to the consistency of elements within the document. Use restraint, for example, by choosing only a couple of font styles and sizes and applying them consistently. Align all similar elements in a document consistently, and use white space to separate chunks of information consistently. For print documents, it is easy to check alignment using your word processor's rulers and print layout view.

Arrangement: Organized in a way that is pleasing to the eye.

Figure 14.4 shows two similar kinds of web pages. The *Craigslist* page is difficult to read because there is little variation in proportion, and within the major columns the headings are sometimes followed by a single column of items, sometimes by multiple columns. The headings group chunks of information, but there are few cues to help readers know which direction to go. *Angie's List*, on the other hand, is easier to read because these visual cues are used consistently.

**Visual Design Arrangement Questions**

- Are the visual design elements logically arranged to guide readers across and down the page?
- Do I use consistent fonts, sizes, and spacing for text, headings, and captions?
- Do I use graphic elements such as lines, columns, and borders consistently?
- Do I present all images in a consistent way?

**FIGURE 14.4** Ineffective and effective use of arrangement

Emphasis:
Force of
expression to
indicate
importance.

## Emphasis

Give balance and contrast to your document with the emphasis you place on each of the design elements. With text, use titles, headings, and fonts to show emphasis. With images, use composition to create balance and guide the readers' attention to what is most important. Different genres require different emphases.

Principles of Good Visual Design

As is typical of the genre, the business letter in Figure 14.5 has little change in emphasis. Pamphlets, such as the one in Figure 14.6, use design elements such as borders, white space, and light and dark areas to show emphasis.

**Tia Palsole**
PMB 200 · 315 Montana · El Paso, TX · 79901
915.555.1111
palsole@gmail.com


February 13, 2009

Ms. Barbara Walker, Chair
Graduate School Committee
Department of Art
The University of Texas at El Paso
500 West University
El Paso, TX  79968

Dear Ms. Walker:

As you consider my application for acceptance in the Masters of Fine Arts in Studio Arts program at UTEP, I know that my portfolio is probably of more importance than my words; however, I would appreciate your consideration of my enclosed resume and statement of purpose, as well as my portfolio.

Through my portfolio, you can see the development of my art and the transition from being a beginner to finding my own style. You can also see that I would benefit greatly from the further honing of my knowledge, skills and foundation in becoming an artist who is representative of the art education provided by UTEP.

I ask that you consider my work, my words and my commitment when reviewing my portfolio and documentation. It would be my great honor to complete a Masters of Fine Arts in Studio Arts under the Art Department of The University of Texas at El Paso.

Sincerely,


Tia Palsole

**FIGURE 14.5** An example of a business letter

CODE OF BEST PRACTICES IN FAIR USE FOR MEDIA LITERACY EDUCATION

but also on how it affects media making. In particular, educators should explore with students the distinction between material that should be liscensed, material that is the public domain or otherwise openly available, and copyrighted material that is subject to fair use. The ethical obligation to provide proper attribution also should be examined. And students should be encouraged to understand how their distribution of a work raises other ethical and social issues, including the privacy of the subjects involved in the media production.

## CONCLUSION

**Educators need to be leaders, not followers, in establishing best practices in fair use.**

Most "copyright education" that educators and learners have encountered has been shaped by the concerns of commercial copyright holders, whose understandable concern about large-scale copyright piracy has caused them to equate any unlicensed use of copyrighted material with stealing. The situation has been compounded by the—again, understandable—risk-aversion of school system administrators and lawyers. So-called fair use guidelines that institutional stakeholders have negotiated with some copyright holders have had similar results, intensifying fear and creating confusion among educators. These approaches have not responded directly to the actual needs of educators and learners, nor have they fully expressed or recognized the legal rights that educators and learners have.

This code of best practices, by contrast, is shaped by educators for educators and the learners they serve, with the help of legal advisors. As an important first step in reclaiming their fair use rights, educators should employ this document to inform their own practices in the classroom and beyond. The next step is for educators to communicate their own learning about copyright and fair use to others, both through practice and through education. Learners mastering the concepts and techniques of media literacy need to learn about the important rights that all new creators, including themselves, have under copyright to use existing materials. Educators also need to share their knowledge and practice with critically important institutional allies and colleagues, such as librarians and school administrators. ■

14

**FIGURE 14.6** An example of a pamphlet design

Originality:
Not done
before, novel,
unusual.

# Originality

Strive to create documents that are consistent, but not boring. This is the most difficult skill to master because it requires practice to achieve a balance. To achieve consistency, repeat certain elements such as headings and rules. Design all the pages of your document so that elements are used regularly. For documents such as brochures or websites that include a distinctive first page, repeat elements such as headings or rules that give your document consistency and coherence. Look for relevant yet unusual or original images to engage readers. Choose images that have a clear purpose or connection to your text. Take care to position an image near the text it supports.

While the community newsletter in Figure 14.7 may not use original layout or images, its consistency is appropriate for its audience, who expect a simple, formal document. The *Oatmeal CookieBlog* (Figure 14.8), on the other hand, uses proportion, arrangement, and emphasis effectively and includes some original elements such as the banner design and the red font to match the strawberries.

**Connect
With Others**

**Activity 14.3**    Divide into small groups, with each group assigned a different publication such as a brochure, newspaper editorial, Wiki, or pamphlet. Using the principles of good visual design (context, proportion, arrangement, emphasis, and originality), evaluate each document to determine how the overall design affects your first impression of the document. Share what your group has discovered with the class.

august 2009   issue 7   volume 3

# HealthMatters

your columbia/boone county department of public health & human services resource for better living

## From The Director

Welcome to the August edition of Health Matters, your source for healthier living. On page 2, you'll find the third installment in our series of summer safety articles, featuring tips for playing it safe in and around the water.

School starts this month, and we've included an article covering the top 5 reasons kids are absent from school and child care. When flu season arrives this year, we may make recommendations on staying home from school (and work) if you become ill with the flu. These recommendations will be made for your safety, and the safety of others in the community.

Our staff continues to meet and discuss the upcoming flu season with representatives from our schools and medical community, ensuring they understand and are following current Centers for Disease Control and Prevention (CDC) guidance regarding seasonal flu and H1N1 influenza.

Finally, don't forget to check out Stacia Reilly's delicious Cheese Stuffed Zucchini recipe and our Employee Spotlight, where this month we feature Shawna Victor from the Office of Community Services.

Live Well!
Stephanie

## Why Do Kids Miss School?

*Geni Alexander, Public Information Officer*

School will soon be back in session and your child's immune system will be put to the test. After all, young children in large groups are breeding grounds for the organisms that cause illness. Here, we list the top 5 illnesses that cause the most school and child care absences — and tell you how to prevent and treat them.

### COMMON COLD
*Spreads easily through contact with infected respiratory droplets coughed or sneezed into the air.*
Signs and symptoms may include runny or stuffy nose, itchy or sore throat, cough, sneezing and low-grade fever. There's no cure for the common cold, and cough and cold medicines aren't recommended for young children — but you can help your child feel better while he or she toughs it out:

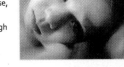

- Offer plenty of fluids, such as water, juice and chicken soup.
- Encourage your child to rest as much as possible.
- Run a humidifier in your child's bedroom or have your child sit in a steamy bathroom.
- Try over-the-counter saline nose drops.
- For an older child, soothe a sore throat with hard candy, cough drops or by gargling salt water. An over-the-counter pain reliever — such as acetaminophen (Tylenol) or ibuprofen (Advil, Motrin) — can reduce a fever and ease the pain of a sore throat or headache. Remember, however, low-grade fevers don't need treatment. If you give your child a pain reliever, follow the dosing guidelines carefully. Don't give aspirin to anyone age 18 or younger.

### STOMACH FLU (viral gastroenteritis)
*Stomach flu typically develops after contact with an infected person or after eating or drinking contaminated food or water. Signs include vomiting and diarrhea. There's no effective treatment for viral gastroenteritis, but while the illness runs its course:*

*continued on page 3*

**FIGURE 14.7**  An engaging community newsletter

**FIGURE 14.8**  An engaging blog design

# PAGE DESIGN

Once you know the principles of good visual design, it's time to turn to the specifics of page design, starting with the format, fonts, and color. Many page design decisions depend on the type of document you are creating. In academic documents, these decisions are often made for you by style manuals such as those published by the Modern Language Association (MLA) or the American Psychological Association (APA). (See Chapter 20 for more information about these academic styles.)

# Format

The format of your text includes orientation, margins, justification, and paragraphing. The following guidelines can help you make basic design choices:

- Orientation: Academic writing such as the essay typically uses a vertical orientation and an 8½ × 11-inch page. Other documents such as the brochure may use a horizontal orientation with nonstandard page sizes.
- Margins: Academic writing typically uses 1-inch margins as the default, which can be set in word processing programs. Other documents use a variety of margin sizes.
- Justification: Academic writing typically uses left-justification and a ragged right edge, while other genres such as a newspaper article use full-justification, with the text justified on both the left and the right margins.
- Paragraphing: For most genres, the paragraph is the basic unit of text. Most academic writing requires a paragraph indent of one-half inch. Consider also using bulleted or numbered lists to convey information more quickly. Use numbered lists when the listed items must occur in the order presented (such as when giving directions).

# Fonts

Fonts are the text letters in your document. Using your word processing program, you can select a font style and size. You can make it bold, put it in italics, or add a shadow. The following are some basic design principles for selecting fonts for your documents:

Serif: A horizontal or vertical line at the top of a letter (N). Sans serif is a letter without such a line (N).

**Readability.** Select a font style that is easy to read. For a printed document such as an essay or pamphlet, a serif font such as Times New Roman is easiest to read. For online text such as a website or blog, a sans serif font such as Syntax is easier to read. Because they can be difficult to read, avoid using italicized fonts such as *Alexa* in the body of a text.

**Size.** Font size is also important. For print text, use a 12-point font in the body of the text. For a website or blog, use a larger font such as 14-point, and for a PowerPoint presentation, use 30-point or higher.

Point: A unit of measure used to indicate font size. In most word processing programs, the point sizes run from 8 (smallest) to 72 (largest).

Use bold, italics, or underlining to distinguish headings and subheadings from the rest of the text. You can also increase the font size somewhat to provide emphasis. For example, if your body text is a 12-point font, consider using a 14-point font for your headings.

Use restraint by selecting no more than two fonts for any one document and using them consistently throughout. For example, if your first

## LANGUAGES and CULTURES

Be aware that if your document will be shared with an international audience, colors often have different associations in different cultures. The meanings for colors around the world vary, and so having a sense of how a particular color choice will be received by readers can be helpful. For example, while readers in the United States associate red with anger, danger, or passion, in Asian cultures red may be associated with happiness, good luck, and marriage. While white may be associated with mourning for some Hindu readers and with death for Asian readers, American readers associate black with these meanings. Test your color selections with readers to be sure that the color scheme you choose has the intended effect.

heading is a centered 14-point bold font, then each heading of that kind throughout your document should also be a centered 14-point bold font.

## Color

For academic writing such as an essay or report, the preferred colors are black for fonts and white space to organize the parts of your text. You can also add additional space after a heading, around images, and between an image and a caption. Include color only if it contributes to your readers' understanding of the topic. A heading or an example printed in color can provide emphasis that helps guide the readers' attention. Consider which colors work best for the genre you have chosen. Red or blue work well in professional documents such as reports or business letters, but hot pink is probably not appropriate. Hot pink, however, could work well in a website designed to appeal to an audience looking for a good time. Use color for important elements in your document, and remember to maintain contrast between color used for type and the background. In general, darker colors are more legible on a light background.

Other genres, such as cartoons, blogs, and websites, include a variety of colors. To learn to use color effectively, examine the latest color trends in magazines and online documents. Experiment with them in your own work.

## Connect With Others

**Activity 14.4** Divide into small groups, with each group assigned to find several examples of writing in various genres such as an essay, instructional leaflet, and a photo essay. Examine each document and discuss how the format, fonts, and color change within each genre. Share what your group has discovered with the class.

# ADD VISUALS

The best way to learn how to incorporate visuals into your print and electronic documents is to first analyze the effects of visuals on you as a reader. As you look through the visuals and text on the next few pages, use the principles of good visual design to help you think about how these visuals deliver a more complex message than just words alone and how you might use similar visuals in your own writing.

Some of the more commonly used and effective visuals include tables, charts, graphs, cartoons, and photographs.

## Tables, Charts, and Graphs

Depending on the type of information you are presenting, select tables, charts, and graphs that provide additional information to support your text.

**Table.** A table organizes complex or large amounts of numerical data or text in rows and columns. Tables can help your readers clarify concepts and trends that you are discussing in the text. Your word processor includes many easy-to-use tools to create and format tables.

Tabel 1. The Benefits of Exercise
The impact of exercising for physical fitness on...

| How much do you think exercising can impact... | Long and Healthy Life | Attractiveness |
|---|---|---|
| | % | % |
| A lot | 86 | 59 |
| A little | 11 | 31 |
| Not at all | 1 | 6 |
| It depends | 1 | 2 |
| Don't know | 1 | 2 |
| | 100 | 100 |

FIGURE 14.9 An effectively designed table

To create effective tables:

- Present accurate data.
- Identify each table with a number and title. (The MLA and APA have specific guidelines for numbering and captioning tables and other visuals.)
- Include a label or brief description of the contents.
- Use clear, concise labels for each row and column.
- If applicable, cite the source of the table or of the data you used to create the table.

**Flowchart.** Flowcharts show the relationship of the parts to the whole and/or the directional steps in a process.

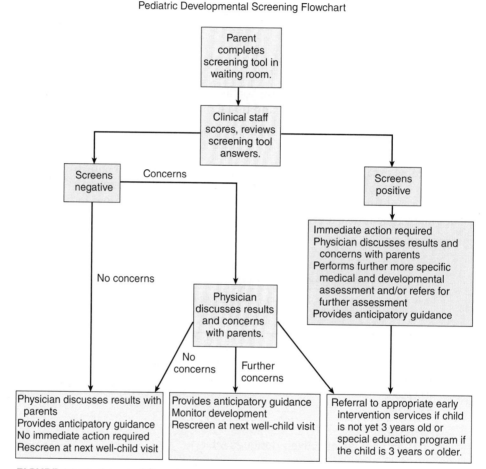

Pediatric Developmental Screening Flowchart

**FIGURE 14.10** A typical flowchart

To create a flowchart:

- Provide a title and label each part of the flowchart.
- Use arrows to show the direction of the flow.
- Do not crowd the steps. Leave plenty of white space between them.
- If needed, cite the source of the flowchart.

**Pie Charts.** Pie charts give a picture of how pieces of data fit into a whole.

To create effective pie charts:

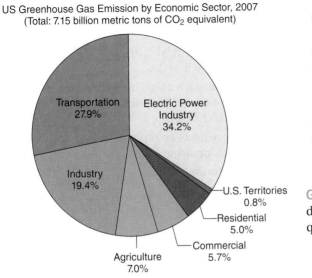

US Greenhouse Gas Emission by Economic Sector, 2007
(Total: 7.15 billion metric tons of $CO_2$ equivalent)

FIGURE 14.11 A pie chart showing how a whole is divided

■ Use pie charts to depict data that add up to a meaningful total.

■ Provide a title.

■ Label each piece. Or, provide a key at the side or bottom that explains what each slice represents.

■ Be sure the pieces add up to the total.

■ If needed, cite the source of the data in your chart.

**Graphs.** Bar graphs (Figure 14.12) depict data in bars and columns to show how quantities make up a percentage of a whole.

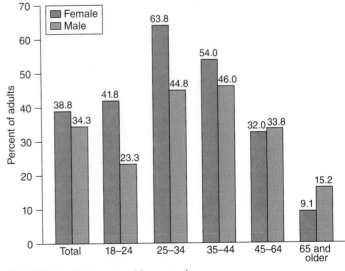

FIGURE 14.12 A typical bar graph

Figure 1. Uninsured Children by Age: 1987–2001

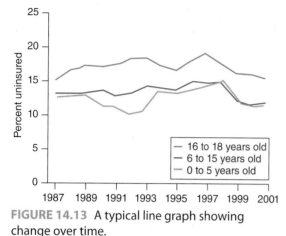

Line graphs (Figure 14.13) depict data that change over time.

To create a graph:

- Provide a title.
- Show the relationship between two or more sets of data.
- Label each axis. The vertical axis should represent the amount and the horizontal axis the category.
- Provide a key at the bottom to define symbols or visual cues.
- If needed, cite the source of the graph.

**FIGURE 14.13**  A typical line graph showing change over time.

**Maps.**  Maps represent geographical areas and can be used to provide data about regions, information about distances or locations, and other insights.

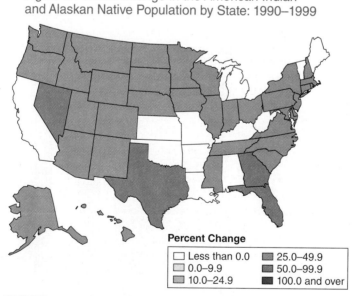

**FIGURE 14.14**  A map showing demographic information

**Activity 14.5**   Working with classmates, gather several documents that include tables, charts, graphs, maps, diagrams, or other illustrations of data. You might include newsletters, brochures, websites, or other documents from school, work, or home. Using the advice in this chapter, choose one document that includes a table, graph, or other element that you think is not entirely successful. Try drafting an improved version. Then bring your draft to class, and be ready to explain what was unsuccessful in the original and what you did to improve it.

**Connect With Others**

## Cartoons

Cartoons offer valuable social commentary. The audience varies depending upon where the cartoon is published, but the purpose is almost always to persuade readers to accept the author's viewpoint. The editorial cartoon in Figure 14.15 delivers a compelling message about the dangers of texting while driving. Notice the components of the visual design. The first panel is humorous. The final panel shows the grim reaper texting a response. This cartoon uses white space to direct the eye to the most important details: the image of the grim reaper, light against the darkness, laughing at the driver who seems oblivious to the danger he's in. The arrangement of these components provides a context and adds variety and interest to the cartoon.

Social commentary: An opinion on the nature of society.

FIGURE 14.15   An editorial cartoon

**Develop Your Understanding**

**Activity 14.6**   Analyze the cartoon in Figure 14.15 by answering these questions:

1.  What is this editorial cartoon's message?
2.  What is the ethnicity, age, socioeconomic class, and gender of the character in the first panel?
3.  Why did the artist choose to use caricatures instead of realistic images?
4.  Who is the intended audience for this cartoon?
5.  What is the relationship between the words and the image? Are the words or the image more important to the context of the message? Why?

## Photographs

With the popularity of digital cameras and the availability of software and scanners, more people are learning to recognize good photographs when they see them and, in some cases, are taking their own photographs to include with their writing. Good photographs add information, interest, and familiarity to documents. For example, the photo of the cookie on the *Oatmeal CookieBlog* (Figure 14.8) is familiar because it reminds us of how fond we are of cookies. The addition of this visual clarifies the written language because it is much easier to imagine what a cookie looks like from a photo than a recipe. Choose images that have a clear purpose in your document. When evaluating a photographic image, look specifically at two aspects: composition and quality.

**Composition.**   Most photographers will tell you that the most important decision a photographer makes is what's important and what's not important to include. When analyzing a photograph, look to see if it's obvious what's important and if the photographer has eliminated all elements that distract from this point of interest. Objects or people in a photograph are bound to seem more important if they are closer to the viewer, or seem large. Then look at the arrangement of the elements. A photograph is more interesting if the subject is close, but not exactly centered. In a portrait, the person should be just to the left or right, and in a landscape, the point of interest should be just above or below the center. Consider how the objects or people in a photograph are positioned, whether they are close together and related or distant. As a viewer, consider the perspective or point of view in the photograph: are you looking down at the subject, or does it seem the photograph presents objects straight on? Look at the setting of the photograph and other details such as body language and facial expressions and consider what responses these evoke as well.

## LANGUAGES and CULTURES

When selecting photographs for an international audience, avoid using photographs of people with bare arms, legs, and feet. In some Middle Eastern cultures, depictions of other body parts are also considered offensive. Although in the United States most readers are accustomed to images that show modest amounts of bare skin, images that depict nudity are considered graphic and shocking, while in western Europe they may be more widely accepted. Also keep in mind that body language and gestures may have different meanings for readers in other cultures. You might want to check with a variety of readers that your photographs do not interfere with your intended message.

*Photographs showing the soles of the feet send an entirely different message in some cultures than they do in the United States, where walking barefoot outside is common.*

**Quality.** When analyzing a photograph, look for images that are in focus, have clear colors, and have a resolution that prevents a degraded appearance. Effective use of light also improves the quality of a photograph by providing clear contrasts. A photographer took the two photographs in Figure 14.16 from the same spot in a fishing village in Nova Scotia, but one is a better photograph. Can you tell which one?

To use photographs effectively:

- Choose photographs that reinforce your point or that help readers understand your document. Avoid using photographs simply for decoration.
- Provide a caption.
- Position the photograph near the text it accompanies.

**FIGURE 14.16**  An ineffective and effective photograph

- Avoid making alterations to photographs you haven't taken yourself that would change the meaning or mislead readers about their original context.
- Avoid clip art.
- Cite the source of the photograph. Request permission to reuse images, if necessary.

**Develop Your Understanding**

**Activity 14.7**   Analyze the two photos by answering these questions:

1. What is the photographer's point of interest in these two photographs?
2. How did the photographer use proportion, arrangement, and emphasis more effectively in the photo on the right?
3. How did the photographer use color more effectively in the photo on the right?
4. In what written context might an author use such a photo?
5. Is the photograph appropriate for all cultures? Why or why not?

# PRESENTATIONS

## PowerPoint Presentations

Guy Kawasaki, a venture capitalist and columnist for *Entrepreneur Magazine*, recommends the 10/20/30 rule when creating PowerPoint presentations: no more than 10 slides for a 20-minute presentation, with no font size smaller than 30 point. This is a good rule of thumb for evaluating and creating presentations using PowerPoint or other presentation software. You can also use some of the principles of good visual design that you learned earlier in the chapter to analyze and create slides for presentations:

- Context: Every piece of information is relevant to the topic.
- Proportion: Important elements such as headings are larger.
- Arrangement: Use only a few words and consistent fonts and graphic elements.
- Emphasis: Include high-quality graphics, video, and audio when appropriate. If possible, test to be sure the graphics will display properly and do not cause your presentation to run slowly.
- Originality: Do not use Microsoft PowerPoint templates without adapting them for your specific purposes. Avoid cartoonish clip art. If you use visuals from other sources, as in Figure 14.17, be sure to include a caption or credit line.

FIGURE 14.17  An effective PowerPoint slide

**Develop Your Understanding**

**Activity 14.8** Analyze this PowerPoint slide by answering these questions:

1. What is this slide's message?
2. How does the author use proportion, arrangement, emphasis, and originality to convey the message?
3. How does the photograph contribute to the message?
4. Would this PowerPoint slide communicate effectively to readers of various cultures? Why or why not?

# WRITING ASSIGNMENT

Using the principles of good visual design outlined in this chapter along with the elements of effective page design, create a literacy narrative describing your experiences with visuals that itself makes use of visuals or other media. Using photographs, audio, video, or web text, create a brief document that reveals something about you as a reader and writer of visual texts. You might focus your literacy narrative on one or two questions about your personal history working with visuals or your experiences designing something for school or work.

Before you begin your visual literacy narrative, write a few paragraphs in response to some of these questions to help you gather ideas:

- In what media do you like to read and write?
- Describe a document in which you added visuals. What visuals did you add and why?
- How did you learn to use visuals? In class? From friends? From the web?
- What are some examples of visual images that represent your particular group, culture, or country?
- To what extent do you consciously apply rules and guidelines when you include visuals in your writing?

Finally, after you have completed your visual literacy narrative, write a one-page reflection on your sense of your strengths as a visual designer. What are your weaknesses? Which aspects of working on visual design would you avoid if you could, and which ones do you enjoy, and why?

mycomplab

For support in meeting this chapter's objectives, follow this path in MyCompLab: Resources ⇒ Writing ⇒ Writing and Visuals ⇒ Writing and Visuals. Review the Instruction and Multimedia resources about using and analyzing visuals, then complete the Exercises and click on Gradebook to measure your progress.

# 15 Writing in the Workplace

## Learning Objectives

In this chapter you will:

- Use rhetorical knowledge to communicate effectively in business contexts.
- Choose the best genre for specific business documents.
- Apply the writing process for workplace documents.

*How might effective writing strategies help these two professionals?*

Whatever your career choice, you will probably spend time communicating in writing: reading and writing application letters, résumés, memos, business letters, and email. Employers often rank "effective communication skills" as one of the most important qualities they look for in prospective employees. They want employees who can:

- analyze the rhetorical situation for a variety of workplace writing tasks
- gather and interpret data and think critically about sources
- write clear, concise documents
- write collaboratively, including tactfully evaluating others' work
- demonstrate personal integrity through writing
- use technology to enhance writing and presentations

> *If you can't explain something simply, you don't understand it well.*
>
> —*Albert Einstein*

When writing résumés, memos, and business letters, use the same writing process that you learned in this course: analyze the rhetorical situation, discover ideas, draft, revise, and edit. When writing email, you may not use the entire writing process, but revise and edit before sending.

It is especially important to select the appropriate genre for each workplace writing situation. Your audience will regard you as a professional only if you can demonstrate that you have learned the conventions of the workplace formats used in their environment.

## Business Communication Genre Checklist

- ☐ Use business letters for official communication to readers outside of the organization.
- ☐ Use résumés to apply for employment or graduate school.
- ☐ Use application letters with résumés to further explain interest and qualifications.
- ☐ Use memos for official communication to readers inside an organization.
- ☐ Use email for quick communication with readers inside and outside of an organization.
- ☐ Use instant messaging for communication with close colleagues.

Because workplace readers also have expectations for the format of workplace genres, learn how the following design elements work in each document:

- white space
- fonts
- headings
- bullets and lists
- graphics

In view of how essential communication skills are, workplace writing requires special attention to exigency. When you write for the workplace, it is important to focus on *why* you are writing, along with whom you are writing to and what you hope will be the result. Indeed, many forms of workplace writing require answers to these questions be spelled out clearly, as in the headings and subject lines of email. The exigence for much workplace writing will be determined for you, as when your supervisor requires you to submit a memo or email a client. Other times, the exigence for writing will be something you create, as when you decide to switch jobs and must update your résumé and write a cover letter.

Exigence: A situation or circumstance that makes you want to communicate something to someone.

**Activity 15.1** Using the web, look for examples of workplace writing such as letters, memos, or résumés. Discuss why you like a particular format and its design elements with your classmates.

**Connect With Others**

# BUSINESS LETTER

The business letter is an essential part of workplace writing, and the letter you write will leave your readers with an impression not only about what you say but also about you as a writer. For this reason, you want to be careful to analyze your audience, watch your tone and style, and use the correct format.

The format of a business letter includes:

- headings, including return address, date, and inside address (or the name and address of the recipient)
- salutation
- introduction

*I have made this letter longer than usual because I lack the time to make it shorter.*

—*Blaise Pascal*

**LANGUAGES and CULTURES**

When writing for an international business audience, it's important to learn as much as you can about the expectations of your audience. Whether your first language is English or something else, avoid jargon, idioms, and slang that may not be easily translated. Abbreviated terms (*stats* instead of *statistics*) can cause confusion. Instead, learn the format and written customs important to your readers. For example, in the United States, it is typical to begin a business letter by stating the purpose. In Japan or Mexico, it is typical to begin by asking about the well-being of the reader's family.

- body paragraphs
- closing
- signature
- name
- enclosures list (optional)

# Business Letter Visual Design

For a business letter, use one-inch margins all around, single-spacing, with double-spacing between paragraphs and between the heading and the salutation and the last paragraph and the closing. Leave four lines between the closing and your typed name for your signature. Use an 11- or 12-point serif font for the text. A serif font is one that has extra lines (sometimes referred to as tails or feet) at the end of the letters. Times New Roman and Garamond are serif fonts. Use headings only if the letter is more than one page. Use bulleted or numbered lists when needed to list items. Use graphics such as charts, tables, and graphs when needed to illustrate a point. Choose block, modified block, or semi-block letter style and use it consistently throughout the letter.

**Block Style.** Left-justify all parts of the letter, including the heading and closing; no paragraph indentions.

**Modified Block Style.** Left-justify all parts of the letter except the heading and closing, which are placed at the center of the page; no paragraph indentions.

**Semi-block Style.** Left-justify all parts of the letter except the heading and closing, which are placed at the center of the page; indent each paragraph five spaces.

**One Student's Business Letter.** Student writer Jasmine Delgado wrote this business letter as part of a class assignment. Jasmine mailed the letter and got the account.

AzTech Business Supply
7001 Washington Drive, Suite 870
Roanoke, VA 24001

October 8, 2010

Aliyah Dunbar, Purchasing Manager —————————————————————— Inside address
Colefax Medical Supply
145 DeWitt Highway
Dulles, VA 20102

Dear Ms. Dunbar: ——————————————————————————————————— Salutation

——————————————————————————————————————————————————— Block style

When we met on September 17, 2010 to discuss your information technology needs, we ——
discussed the possibility of replacing all of your internal sales force personnel's photocopy
machines. Those machines (most of which were purchased 7 years ago) no longer meet the
needs of your growing business, as they cannot be linked to your internal network and require
employees to leave their desks and queue to make copies. In addition, your current machines
use energy inefficiently and require toner cartridges that cannot be recycled.             Explanation body
                                                                                            paragraphs

I propose that AzTech install, at our expense, a new photocopy machine for a trial period of ——
one month. During this month, we will monitor and compare the energy use of this new
machine compared to your current models, as well as evaluate toner use. We will also connect
the new machine to your internal server and explain to employees how to send documents
directly from their desktop computers to the new photocopier for processing. At the
conclusion of the trial, AzTech will deliver a report to you describing the efficiencies and cost
savings to Colefax should you decide to replace your current photocopy machines with models
identical to the test machine. We will also discuss our technical and on-site service support
options.

After the trial period, if you on behalf of Colefax Medical Supply determine that your business
would like to replace all or some of its current photocopy machines with units identical to that
installed by AzTech, AzTech will procure, install, and train your employees on how to use the
new photocopy machines. Please note that procurement and training can be accomplished
either incrementally or all at once, depending on your business needs.

The estimated cost of replacing 5 photocopy machines and installing appropriate drivers on
your network will be approximately $48,235.00 if purchased as a package. The cost will
increase to approximately ten percent if the machines and installation are purchased
incrementally.                                                                          Conclusion and call
                                                                                         for action
Please contact me at 540–555–4831 to discuss this proposal further. ———————————

                                                                                         Closing
Sincerely,                                                                      ——————————————
                                                                                         Signature
*Jasmine F. Delgado*                                                            ——————————————
Jasmine F. Delgado
External Sales Director
AzTech Business Supply

**Business Letter Checklist**

☐ Include the name of the recipient used in the salutation.

☐ Use the appropriate address such as Mr. or Ms. (not Mrs. or Miss) followed by a colon.

☐ Use a serif font, 11 or 12 point.

☐ Set one-inch margins.

☐ Print on quality bond white, cream, or gray paper, 8½″ × 11″.

☐ Keep correspondence to one or two pages.

☐ First paragraph explains the purpose of the letter.

☐ Middle paragraphs provide the explanation.

☐ Last paragraph concludes with a call for action.

☐ Correct spelling, punctuation, and grammar before sending.

# RÉSUMÉ

A résumé is a summary of your qualifications for a job or for admission to a graduate or professional program. A prospective employer or admission committee will use your résumé to get to know you and to help determine whether to accept you for the job or program. Because this is a competitive process, your résumé should demonstrate your abilities as well as your organizational and writing skills. There are few audiences more important than those who will decide your future.

Many job searches are conducted online; employers search databases and track applicants using key words to find appropriate résumés. While you will want a clean, carefully laid-out print version of your résumé to share, it is very likely that your résumé will also need to be read online or scanned by human resources specialists. After you finalize your formal, print résumé, save a version in a new file, then reformat it for electronic submission. This version will include simple formatting and a helpful list of key words to describe your goals, experience, skills, and training.

Scannable résumés also use few verbs and more nouns and noun phrases to describe experience.

The format for a formal résumé includes:

- a heading that includes your name and contact information
- an objective (optional) that specifically identifies your future goals
- a brief summary of qualifications (optional)
- education
- experience
- other skills
- honors

Many experts suggest omitting reference information from your résumé and suggest instead waiting until a potential employer asks for it. If you omit references, keep a separate references document and be prepared to submit it on request from a potential employer.

An electronic or scannable résumé will also include a keyword section listing job skills, titles, tools, applications, languages, or other key words to help employers find you in a résumé database.

## Résumé Visual Design

Readers expect to spend no more than a minute to read a one- or two-page résumé, and they expect a clean, attractive layout with plenty of white space. Because U.S. readers read from left to right, top to bottom, for this audience include the most important information in the top third of your résumé, the next most important in the middle, and so on. For example, if your education is more impressive or relevant to the job or graduate school to which you are applying, put it first. If, however, your job experience is more impressive or relevant, put it first. Balance your résumé by using major headings to help your readers' eyes move easily down the page. Choose a different font size, boldface, capitalization, italics, or underlining to set your headings apart. Under each heading, use bulleted lists to describe your qualities and skills. Decide whether to use graphics depending on where you will send the résumé. If you are applying to a law school, for example, graphics aren't necessary and may even detract from your message. If you are applying for a job as a graphic designer, however, you should demonstrate your ability with graphics by using them in your résumé.

For the electronic or scannable version of your résumé, you should use a much simpler layout: left-justified without indents and no special formatting for type. Use one easy-to-scan font throughout; set headings off using capitalization and an extra line of space, without boldface, italics, or varying font sizes. Instead of bullets, use a dash or an asterisk and extra space to separate items in lists.

**One Student's Résumé.** Leola Young, a multidisciplinary studies major, wrote this résumé to apply for a position as a group supervisor with the Dozier Corporation, where she already works. Notice how she puts her experience before her education because it is more relevant to the position. Because she was submitting a print copy of her résumé, Leola used boldfaced headings, white space, and bullets to give her résumé a clean, easy-to-read layout.

Heading ——————————————————————

### Leola Young
9142 Dovecreek Street
Columbia, SC 29201
803-777-7777 lyoung@sc.rr.com

Objective ———————————

**Objective:**

Group Supervisor with The Dozier Corporation, where I can use my analytical and communication skills to meet the agency's goal and mission.

Experience ———————————

**Work Experience:**

April 2007 to Present

Information Technologist Specialist, The Dozier Corporation, Regional Office, Columbia, SC

- Provide direction and support to all employees, contractors and members of the public who use our automated and electronic processing systems in South Carolina and North Carolina.
- Point person for receiving new equipment, troubleshooting systems and providing in-house training, both in the form of "hands on" and written "step by step" guidelines and procedures.
- Communicate with employees from various system components to make effective oral recommendations which lead to software modification or upgrade and create a more user-friendly processing tool.

Feb. 1995 to Mar. 2007

System Administrator, The Dozier Corporation, Director's Office, Columbia, SC

- Assisted management in monitoring all electronic file actions to make sure that all evidence was received and added to the file.
- Prepared written guidelines outlining the procedures for docket employees to receive folder-less electronic claims.
- Provided support to the management team by analyzing ARTS and PMSC statistics.

Jun. 1991 to Jan. 1995

Administrative Assistant, The Dozier Corporation, Branch Office Watertown, NY

- Processed personnel actions and performed timekeeping duties.
- Developed automated program for ordering supplies.
- Responsible for training employees in welfare reform program.

**Education:** _____ Education

Bachelor's degree, Multidisciplinary Studies, University of Texas, December 2011; Certification in Microcomputer Applications 2001

**Leadership:** _____ Other skills

Vice President of Zeta Beta Phi Sorority-IotaTau, 1985–1987
Volunteer for Elmwood Senior Citizen Computer Group

Key words:

software operations, user support, troubleshooting, technical support, user training, end-user software applications, web applications, allocation, distribution control, oral and written communications, leadership

# Closing Gaps in Your Résumé

Whether you are a recent graduate or reentering the workforce after time away for military service, unemployment, or other reasons, it is important to be honest and address gaps that you may have in your work history. In most situations you can briefly document your experiences or other activity such as volunteer work or internships in this period and describe it to your advantage. You can also choose to organize your résumé to include more focus on your core skills. Choosing a format with a section to highlight your skills (grouping them into categories) followed by a brief section listing your work history is a good solution, for example, for parents returning to work after an absence.

If you are returning to work after military service, it is essential to focus on translating your military skills and projects into language that civilians can understand. There are many tools online that help take military occupation information and extract civilian language for those work experiences and skills. Avoid using jargon and acronyms that will be unfamiliar to many civilians and focus instead on key words and skills that will be appealing while highlighting your training and experience.

If your experience includes workplaces or institutions outside the United States, list these, keeping descriptions simple. Though educational systems and degree systems vary in different countries, do not attempt to translate these in your résumé. If this information is important to your job search, you may include a brief description of what you accomplished in your cover letter. If your first language is not English, mention your fluency in another language as a special skill. In many fields and at large, multinational companies, language skills are highly desired, so you might consider including this information near the top of your résumé.

## Résumé Checklist

- ☐ Keep to one page, continuing to a second page only if your experience is extensive.
- ☐ Use no more than two font types or sizes, one for headings and the other for text.
- ☐ State contact information clearly, current and permanent address if different.
- ☐ List a clear, focused objective (optional).
- ☐ Give a brief profile or summary of accomplishments, skills, or competencies (optional).
- ☐ Include a keyword list of relevant job titles, skills, languages, tools, software, licenses and certifications, employers, or schools (for electronic or scannable résumés).
- ☐ List education, including graduation date, GPA if over 3.0.
- ☐ List experience using parallel structure, action verbs.
- ☐ Include honors and other skills section showcasing specific honors and skills not already listed.

- ☐ Omit personal data such as marital status, hobbies.
- ☐ Add either "References provided upon request" notation (preferred) or list references.
- ☐ Correct spelling, punctuation, and grammar.
- ☐ If your résumé will be printed:
  - ☐ one-inch margins
  - ☐ quality bond white, cream, or gray paper, 8½" × 11"

# APPLICATION LETTER

Also called a cover letter, an application letter may seem unnecessary now that many job application processes are online, but if you write a letter, you will set yourself apart in a competitive job market. An application letter gives you the opportunity to introduce yourself, highlight your experience, and make yourself memorable to readers.

The format for the application letter is the same as a business letter except that application letters don't usually include bulleted or numbered lists or graphics.

**One Student's Application Letter.** Here is the application letter written by student Leola Young to accompany the résumé on page 484.

September 9, 2010 —————————————————————— Date

9142 Dovecreek Street ————————————————— Return address
Columbia, SC 29201

John Carter ——————————————————————— Inside address
Corporation Director
The Dozier Corporation
18927 Symphony Mall Blvd.
Suite 300
Columbia, SC 29201

Dear Mr. Carter: ——————————————————— Salutation

I am writing to express my interest in the position of Group ————— Introduction
Supervisor. According to the interagency office vacancy web
site, a position is currently available for a Group Supervisor.

*(continued)*

**Interest in position**

I am currently employed with The Dozier Corporation as an Information Technologist, a position which offers unique training opportunities for management. I deal directly with employees and the public every day, either in person or by phone. My duties require that I train people, using written and/or oral methods, and that I follow up to make sure that the employees are correctly using the training that I have provided. I am also a master of identifying, prioritizing, and fixing problems.

**Qualifications**

I am an expert in computer technology among my peers, which will be an asset to your management team as TDC advances into the electronic age. However, another benefit I will provide is my extensive knowledge of the processing procedures, goals and concerns of other TDC components. As my résumé shows, I have worked with both local and regional personnel in the state agency, Services Determination, local offices and all of the other TDC offices. I know you will find my knowledge and contacts to be of great value to your management team as you develop Columbia TDC partnerships.

In December 2011, I will receive my BA in Multidisciplinary Studies from the University of Texas. The program involves business and managerial training, and I am excited to have an opportunity to put my education into practice.

**Conclusion and call for action**

I look forward to meeting you and discussing my qualifications for the Group Supervisor position. You may contact me at (803) 777-7777 or lyoung@gmail.com.

**Closing**

Sincerely,

**Signature**

Leola Young

**Name**

Leola Young

## Application Letter Checklist

☐ Have the name of the person used in the salutation.

☐ Use an appropriate address such as Mr. or Ms. (not Mrs. or Miss) followed by a colon.

☐ Use a serif font, 11 or 12 point.

☐ Print on quality bond white, cream, or gray paper, 8½" × 11".

☐ Keep letter to one page, three to five paragraphs.

☐ Set one-inch margins.

☐ First paragraph explains what impresses you about the company or school.

☐ Middle paragraphs describe your qualifications, explain why you are a good choice, and stress what you can do for this employer or school.

☐ The last paragraph restates your interest, asks for an interview, and provides your contact information.

☐ Correct spelling, punctuation, and grammar before sending.

**Activity 15.2** With a group of your peers, review Leola Young's résumé and application letter. What suggestions would you give to Leola for improving her résumé and application letter? If you were hiring, would you hire her? Why or why not?

**Connect With Others**

# MEMORANDUM

A memorandum (memo) communicates a policy or describes a problem to someone within your organization. A memo is a formal piece of communication, so write it as carefully as you would a business letter. When writing a memo, it's customary to copy your supervisor and anyone else who should know the content of the memo. The format for a memo includes:

- Heading:
    To
    From
    cc
    Date
    Subject (or Re)
- Statement of Purpose
- Discussion
- Closing
- Attachments

## Memo Visual Design

Memos should be no more than one or two pages long, block style, with the heading double-spaced and the rest of the memo single-spaced, with double-spacing between paragraphs. Use headings to divide the major sections. Use a different font size, boldface, capitalization, italics, or underlining to set these headings apart. To help your readers move quickly through the material, use bulleted or numbered lists wherever possible. Use graphics such as charts, tables, and graphs when needed to illustrate a point. If there are attachments, note this at the bottom of the memo and conclude by listing the names and titles of everyone who should receive a copy of the memo.

**One Student's Memo.**  Student writer Emily Conry was required to submit a memo to her instructor and classmates describing the rhetorical situation for a persuasive letter she planned to write.

Title _____    Memorandum

Heading _____    To:    Workplace Writing Class 3355

From:  Emily Conry

Date:  September 27, 2010

Re:    Persuasive Letter Proposal

Purpose _____    Please accept this memo as my description of the rhetorical situation for my persuasive letter.

Discussion with
headings to signal new
direction
_____    **Topic**

My topic is new safety guidelines for exiting and entering my workplace at night. I believe that new safety procedures would empower night employees who may feel nervous with the current safety situation. This policy will not cause a burden to the systems that are already in place. Additionally, this new policy will not cost my workplace any money.

**Audience**
My audience is Human Resources (HR), my supervisor, and the head of security. I believe that these are the individuals who could implement a new policy. Human Resources is a necessary contact as they have the knowledge of all

reported security complaints and concerns, and they work closely with the Security department. I need to include my supervisor in this as well because we work so closely together that this person would be a valuable ally.

### Purpose

My purpose is persuasive. I will write this letter to encourage consideration of a new employee safety policy.

### Exigency

I want to write this letter to improve safety procedures in my workplace and as practice for the future. I am always sizing up the security of anywhere I work. I believe that someday I will find security measures that are less than adequate, and this experience could be very useful.

### Constraints

Even if I convince HR and my supervisor, I still need to convince security. If security believes that I am undermining them or attempting to discredit their current systems, a negative situation could develop. I need to be careful to write my persuasive letter in a way that is nonthreatening to them.

I look forward to writing this persuasive letter. Please let me know if there are any problems with the rhetorical situation for this assignment.

_____ Closing

## Memo Checklist

☐ Keep to one page, continuing to a second page only if absolutely necessary.

☐ Use a serif font, 11 or 12 point.

☐ Set one-inch margins.

☐ Use no more than two font types or sizes, one for headings and the other for text.

☐ Use formal name of the recipient and exact title in heading.

☐ Provide a specific subject in "Subject" line.

☐ Use clear, concise writing throughout the memo.

☐ Make sure that the closing includes a call for action letting readers know what you expect.

☐ Correct spelling, punctuation, and grammar before sending.

# EMAIL

Electronic mail (email) is a quick, easy way to communicate. Although less formal than a business letter or memo, workplace emails are still official communication, so write them as carefully as you would a letter or memo. Remember that email is a public form of communication that can easily be viewed by others. For this reason, never include sensitive workplace information such as credit card account numbers or passwords. Be careful not to put anything in email that you wouldn't want forwarded to others to read. If you have sensitive information to share with someone, it would be better to schedule a phone call or face-to-face meeting.

Email formatting is very similar to the conventions of print memos. The format for an email includes:

- From
- To
- cc
- Subject
- Attachments

The subject line helps your readers determine the urgency of your message. In addition, highly specific subject lines help your readers to file, search, and archive emails appropriately. Be sure that your subject lines concisely and accurately convey the purpose of your message. As with print memorandums, it is customary to copy (or "cc") your supervisor and others who need to be aware of the contents of the email.

## Email Visual Design

Although email formats are set by the software or email service that you use, you may select from a limited number of fonts, backgrounds, and graphics. Use an 11- or 12-point sans serif font (without the extra lines at the end of the letter) such as Arial or Helvetica for the text. Sans serif fonts are easier to read online, while serif fonts are easier to read in print. Include a signature—which can be set to appear at the bottom of all your outgoing messages—that lists your full name, email address, and other contact information. Resist the urge to use colorful backgrounds or busy graphics for business email. Use headings only for longer emails. Include attachments for additional documents or visuals such as charts, tables, and graphs, but keep in mind that attachments with large file sizes can be difficult or time-consuming to download and may annoy your reader.

**One Student's Email.** Student writer Todd Ruecker wrote this email to his fellow students and faculty to gather information for a department website that he was developing. Notice the friendly tone, specific subject line, and clear, concise paragraphs.

From:    Todd Ruecker (truecker@college.edu) —————— *Heading*

To:       Writing Faculty and Students —————— *Email sent to address book group rather than many individual email addresses*

Subject: Personal Profiles for Department Website —————— *Subject line*

Dear Writing Students and Faculty: —————— *Greeting*

Thanks to those of you who have submitted your personal profiles for the department website. I would like to make one —————— *Body paragraphs* change, as well as set a deadline for future submissions. First, although my original example was in third person, I have decided that the profiles should be written in first person so they are more personal. If you have already submitted, I can make the necessary changes.

Second, the deadline to submit your profile is Tuesday, Sept. 15. I should have website access by then and hope to start updating the information around that time. It is important that we update this information ASAP as prospective students will be looking at our website and Wiki over the next several months.

If you have any concerns or questions, please feel free to contact me via email. —————— *Closing*

*Todd Ruecker* —————— *Signature information*
*Writing Department Web Coordinator*
*truecker@college.edu*

## Email Checklist

- ☐ Have a meaningful subject line that clarifies the purpose of the communication.

- ☐ Use an appropriate greeting such as *Mr.* or *Ms.* (not *Mrs.* or *Miss*) followed by a colon.

- ☐ Set font to an 11- or 12-point sans serif font (sans serif is easier to read on the screen).

- ☐ Write clear, concise paragraphs.

- ☐ Correct spelling, punctuation, and grammar before sending.

- ☐ If needed, attach additional files of a reasonable size (less than 1MB).

# WRITING ASSIGNMENT

Choose one of the workplace genres (business letters, résumés, application letters, memos, or email) described in this chapter. Then working alone or with one or two classmates, seek out several examples of that genre on campus, from your mail, online, or your own written work. Analyze these examples and choose one sample document that you think is the most effective.

Next, draft a short list of the key things you have learned about the genre from your review of samples and from your reading in this chapter.

Finally, drawing from the sample document and your written list, write a memo to your instructor and classmates reflecting on what you learned about this genre. Use the advice in this chapter on writing effective memos. How will you use this information to ensure that your audience regards you as a professional?

mycomplab

For support in meeting this chapter's objectives, follow this path in MyCompLab: Resources ⇒ Writing ⇒ Writing Samples: Technical and Workplace. Review the Instruction and Multimedia resources about letters, memos, emails, and career correspondence, then complete the Exercises and click on Gradebook to measure your progress.

# 16 Writing Essay Exams

## Learning Objectives

In this chapter you will:

- Learn how to prepare for essay exams.
- Analyze key essay exam words.
- Use the writing process to take essay exams.
- Learn ways to control your emotional filter and writing monitor.

*What are the advantages and disadvantages of taking in-class essay exams on your laptop?*

An essay exam is a timed writing exam in which you respond to questions by writing in complete sentences and paragraphs. Instructors use them to determine if you understand the course material and, more importantly, if you can think critically and apply what you have learned about a topic. When you imagine yourself taking an essay exam, how do you see yourself? Are you confident and ready to share your knowledge or nervous and afraid that you won't do well? If you see yourself as nervous and afraid, don't be discouraged. Many college students suffer from test anxiety; research suggests that 25 percent to 50 percent of college students feel that their test anxiety interferes with their ability to do well on exams. The encouraging news is that you have already learned how to write an essay. The main difference between writing an essay exam in class and writing an essay outside of class is that in an exam situation you must work through the stages of the writing process (gathering ideas, drafting, revising, and editing) in the short time allocated for the exam rather than over a period of days or weeks.

## LANGUAGES and CULTURES

Student writers understand that instructors *anticipate* a particular answer when evaluating essay exam responses. This can be especially difficult for students from other cultures who have not had practice reading and responding to U.S. essay exam questions. It is important for these students to be sure that they understand not only the language of the exam question but also that they are clear on just what it is that they are expected to write and how it will be evaluated. Similarly, it is important that instructors create essay exam questions that are clearly written, with simple, direct instructions that all students in the class can understand.

## PREPARING FOR AN ESSAY EXAM

The best way to deal with test anxiety is to study the course material to be prepared for exams. Knowing the course material can go a long way toward helping you do well, but you can also take specific steps to prepare for each essay exam. For an essay exam, your audience is your instructor, so throughout the course be thinking about how you can best demonstrate your knowledge to this person.

# Learn What to Expect

You will do your best if you know what to expect on the exam. Find out what type of questions will be on the test, how long you will have to complete it, and how it will be graded. Learn as much as you can about the exam so that you can plan an effective study routine. To learn about the exam:

- Read the syllabus carefully to determine what the instructor considers important.
- Review your notes for information on the exam.
- If the textbook or an accompanying website has a test bank, study the exams.
- Attend all class sessions to hear information about the test.
- Attend review sessions if they are available.
- Ask the instructor any questions that you may have about the exam.

Your instructor will probably ask only a few essay questions, so expect them to cover the most important topics in the course. Most instructors take test items directly from reviews or from study guides, so check these for possible essay questions. Reread your class notes and mark the topics for which you have the most notes. These are also likely essay exam topics.

# Manage Your Study Time

For several weeks prior to the exam, set aside two to three hours of study time a week devoted just to preparing for the exam. During this time, review your lecture notes, catch up on your textbook reading, and begin to make study sheets of the most important material. To make study sheets:

- Create a master study sheet that includes the major topics to be covered on the exam.
- Create study sheets for each of the topics on the master study sheet by outlining the material that you need to learn.
- Create separate study sheets for specialized vocabulary you need to memorize.
- Write practice essay exam responses.

# Form a Study Group

You might also form a study group. Research suggests that studying in groups can increase your knowledge of course material. To form a study group, ask a few of your classmates to meet with you a week or two before a major exam. Share your class notes and discuss the textbook readings.

As a group, discuss and write down what you expect the essay exam questions to be. Then write your individual responses to these questions. Discuss the strengths and weaknesses of each response and decide which would be the best responses to submit for the exam.

**Connect With Others**

**Activity 16.1** With your classmates, reflect on your strengths and weaknesses in preparing for essay exams. How could you improve these preparation skills? In the past, have you formed a study group? If yes, what were the advantages and disadvantages? In no, can you now see a reason to form one? Explain your answer.

## TAKING THE ESSAY EXAM

Once you enter the classroom to take the exam, focus on reviewing your notes and memorizing key points for the exam. Avoid talking with other students who may be venting their fears or frustrations about the exam or the course. Once you receive the exam, analyze the questions, discover ideas, draft, revise, and edit.

### Analyze the Questions

To ensure that you answer the questions correctly:

- Quickly read over the entire exam. Notice the kinds of questions asked and the point value of each.
- Estimate the amount of time you will need to complete each essay response.
- Plan your answers, allowing the most time for the essay questions with the highest point value.
- If you don't understand one of the questions, don't be afraid to ask the instructor for clarification.
- If you have a choice of questions, consider point values and your available knowledge base to help you determine which ones to answer.

As you read each essay question, mark the question to be sure that you understand what is expected of you. This is particularly important if you are nervous about the test. Your nerves may cause you to misread important words. Marking the question forces you to concentrate on what you must write rather than on what you wish you could write. To mark the question, underline the key words that indicate what the essay should be about and then box the words that explain how you should develop and organize your response. If the question has multiple parts, number the parts of the question to ensure that you respond to all parts of the question.

*I never know what I think about something until I see what I've written on it.*

*—William Faulkner*

Here is a multiple part sociology essay exam question marked up by student writer Ivy Walker.

Each of us can name cultures that have influenced who we are and the way that we think. These cultures may include ethnic heritage, family, religion, social organizations, and local or regional customs. (Identify) and (define) a cultural tradition that has special meaning to you. (Describe) the tradition and (explain) its significance.

1.

2.

3.

4.

The words "cultural tradition," "special meaning," and "significance" are all words that indicate what the essay should be about and the words "identify," "define," "describe," and "explain" indicate ways to develop the answer.

> ## Key Essay Exam Words
>
> ▪ Identify—point to the unique characteristics.
> ▪ Narrate—relate a series of events in the order that they happened.
> ▪ Describe—create an image.
> ▪ Explain—provide reasons for.
> ▪ Illustrate—provide examples, facts, statistics.
> ▪ Compare and/or contrast—show similarities and/or differences.
> ▪ Classify—categorize into types.
> ▪ Describe a process—describe how something works.
> ▪ Define—tell what it means.
> ▪ Cause and effect—explain why something happened.

## Discover Ideas

Once you have analyzed and marked the essay question, you might be tempted to begin writing your response right away. Resist the urge, knowing that the time you spend to discover ideas will save you time later. Set aside five minutes to brainstorm a list of the points you want to make. Then number the points in the order that you would like to write about them. By numbering them, you ensure a more organized essay than if you just started writing off the top of your head. Here is an example of the list that Ivy brainstormed as she prepared to respond to the sociology question:

Identify:
   1. Dia de los Muertos or Day of the Dead

Definition:
   2. Dia de los Muertos is a two-day Latin American celebration of various rituals to remember the dead
   3. Dates back to the indigenous people of Mexico

Describe:
    4. Runs November 1–November 2
    5. First day is to remember children who have died
    6. Second day is to remember adults who have died
    7. There is plenty of food and drink on each day
    8. Time is spent with family partying, as well as cleaning and decorating graves

Explain:
    9. Seems macabre to some, but it is beloved tradition in the Mexican and Mexican American culture
    10. It is a way of remembering and honoring the dead

## Draft

Using your brainstormed list, write your essay response just as you would an essay that you write outside of class. Be careful to do exactly what you are directed to do and to answer all parts of the question. Begin with a brief introduction that includes a thesis statement that specifically answers the exam question. Then, sticking to your brainstormed list, write your essay using complete sentences and paragraphs. Each paragraph should include a topic sentence or main idea and specific details to support the topic sentence. Specific details can include facts, statistics, and quotations that demonstrate what you know about the topic. Write a brief conclusion or concluding statement to sum up your essay.

Write only what is relevant to the question; avoid the urge to pad your answers with irrelevant or repeated information. Unless you have unlimited time, don't try to write a rough draft of your response, thinking that you will rewrite it. This will use up valuable time that you may need to write one complete draft.

## Revise and Edit

If possible, allow five minutes at the end of the test to reread the questions and your responses to be sure that you have answered all parts of the question and answered them correctly. If this is a handwritten test and you wish to add content, write it neatly in the margin or at the bottom of the page and use an arrow to point to the place where it belongs. For deletions, draw a line through the material to be deleted and, if needed, write in a correction above the text. Where appropriate, add transitions such as *then, on the other hand, consequently,* or *in conclusion* to help your instructor follow your train of thought.

As you reread your response, also proofread for errors in spelling, punctuation, and grammar because you may be judged not only on the content but also on how clearly you have written the response. Too many surface errors may make it difficult for your instructor to understand what you have written, resulting in a lower test grade. One more thing: be sure your name is on your exam before you turn it in.

## Your Emotional Filter

You know that whenever you write, you're affected by an emotional filter. This emotional filter can help or hinder your performance on an essay exam. If you feel prepared, confident, and interested in sharing what you know, you are emotionally prepared to do your best on an essay exam. However, if you feel unprepared, anxious, or disinterested in the topic, your emotional filter will hinder your performance.

Your previous exam-taking experiences greatly affect your emotional filter. If in the past you received high essay exam grades, your filter is probably positive. However, if you received low essay exam grades, your filter may be negative. With a negative emotional filter, you might put off studying for the test, not read the exam questions carefully, get writer's block during the test, or rush through it and hand it in just to be done with it. Ways to control your emotional filter include the following:

- Prepare for the test.
- Get a good night's sleep the night before the exam.
- Eat healthy foods just prior to the exam.
- Arrive at the exam early and review your notes.
- Eliminate negative self-talk such as "I can't do this," or "I didn't prepare enough."
- Replace negative self-talk with positive comments such as "I can do well" or "I'm doing my best on this test."
- Avoid looking to see how other students are doing.
- Ask the instructor if you are not clear on what the question is asking.

## Your Writing Monitor

Your writing monitor tells you when and how to apply writing rules and guidelines. Because there is little time to revise and edit during an essay exam, your monitor will probably be high to ensure that you have done your best writing in only one draft. Study all returned essay exams, analyze them, and make a note of the errors that you tend to make. Train your writing monitor to check for these common essay exam errors:

- answering with what you know rather than what the question asks
- writing an answer that is too sketchy
- not knowing the key terms required in the response
- not being able to apply the material to new situations
- leaving out important supporting details
- padding the answer with irrelevant or redundant information
- failing to proofread before turning in the exam

**Connect
With Others**

**Activity 16.2**   With a group of your classmates, review the common essay exam errors. Which errors have you committed? How will you use your writing monitor to effectively screen for these errors in the future? Share your group's responses with the entire class to determine if there are common errors unique to your college environment.

**One Student's Writing.**  Earlier in the chapter, we introduced you to Ivy Walker, a student who wrote an essay exam response to this sociology question:

> Cultures define who we are and the way that we think. These cultures may include ethnic heritage, family, religion, social organizations, and local or regional customs. Identify and define a cultural tradition that has special meaning to you. Describe the tradition and explain its significance.

Here is Ivy's final essay exam response:

### Dia de los Muertos

*Ivy Walker*

Ivy identifies the tradition.

   An important Latin American cultural tradition is the Aztec ritual of Dia de los Muertos, translated as Day of the Dead in English. This two-day celebration begins on November 1st with All Saints Day and ends on November 2nd with All Souls Day. Because Dia de los Muertos falls right after Halloween in the United States, a lot of Americans think that this celebration is a Mexican version of Halloween. Dia de los Muertos is not Halloween; instead it's a time to remember friends and family who have died.

She defines the tradition.

The ritual of Dia de los Muertos began thousands of years ago with the Aztecs. When the Spaniards arrived in Mexico in the 15th century, they tried to eradicate it because they saw the celebration as disrespectful to the dead. Many Latin Americans think that the souls of their dead friends and relatives actually visit the cemetery on these two days and this belief, too, bothered the Spaniards. In spite of efforts to end the ritual, it continues today and is practiced by some Hispanic families in the United States.

*Ivy begins to describe the tradition.*

November 1st, or All Saints Day, is reserved for honoring dead children. Friends and family go to the gravesites of deceased children and decorate them with marigolds, candles, and photos and leave *calveras* (sugar skulls) as offerings. Family members might also leave a child's favorite toys on the grave. On November 2nd, or All Souls Day, families return to the cemetery to bring fresh flowers and to clean the area around the gravesites. It isn't unusual to see people having a picnic or a party at the gravesite as a way to remember and celebrate the life of the deceased person. In some cases, people wear masks to chase the souls back to the dead.

Dia de los Muertos may seem macabre in the United States because we tend to avoid the topic of death and are reluctant to celebrate it in any way. In Latin America, however, death is seen as a continuation, not an ending of life, so there is much more willingness to embrace the rituals surrounding Dia de los Muertos. The ritual's significance lies in remembering those who have come before us and acknowledging the importance of death as a continuation of life.

*She concludes by explaining the significance.*

# WRITING ASSIGNMENT

Write an essay for your instructor and classmates that describes how you will use what you learned in this chapter to reduce test anxiety and to prepare for and take essay exams. Read your essay aloud to your classmates to begin a discussion of how to improve essay exam writing skills.

For additional help with writing, reading, and research, go to www.mycomplab.com.

PEARSON mycomplab

# CHAPTER
# 17 Creating Portfolios

## Learning Objectives

In this chapter you will:

- Select materials for a writing portfolio.
- Revise and edit your portfolio.
- Present your portfolio.

*Have you ever created a scrapbook or portfolio to showcase something of importance to you? If you have, what did you enjoy about the experience?*

W hile in this class, you have written on a broad range of topics and in a variety of formats that you can now use to create a portfolio to showcase your writing abilities. A writing portfolio contains a writer's best writing, just as a model's portfolio includes photographs of favorite poses, and an artist's portfolio includes examples of the artist's best art. A well-designed writing portfolio can also emphasize your creative abilities with visual design.

Once you have a portfolio, you can use it for several purposes: to apply for employment, as a writing sample for admission to a graduate program, or as a gift to yourself for all of your commitment, study, and practice.

# SELECT MATERIALS

The contents of your portfolio will vary depending on your audience. If you are using it as part of a job application, for example, you might include more examples of workplace writing. If, however, you are using it as a writing sample for a graduate school, you might include more examples of class assignments. No matter who your audience is, though, your purpose is always to persuade your readers that you are a skilled writer.

In addition to a Table of Contents, your writing portfolio should include the following sections:

- a reflection on your growth as a writer
- samples of your best class writing
- samples of other work

## Reflection

In addition to demonstrating your writing skills, you want your portfolio to show your growth as a writer. You can write a short reflection that describes how your writing has improved during this class. By now, you should have a good idea of what works best for you when gathering ideas, drafting, revising, and editing. Reflect on what you have learned, including your ability to use a variety of genres, to develop visuals, and to work with other students collaboratively.

Use the following questions as a starting point:

1. What is your greatest writing strength?
2. How will you continue to improve any areas of weakness?
3. Which selections in your portfolio were the easiest for you to write? Which were the most difficult?
4. Are there any types of writing that you haven't done, but that you would like to try?

**One Student's Reflection.**    Student writer Hana Hijazi wrote this reflection on what she learned in writing class:

> When I enrolled in this class, I knew it would be difficult for me because English is my second language. I always avoided English classes, but there was no escaping this one because it is a required class! I am happy to say, though, that I have improved as a writer. Because of this class, I have learned not to wait until the last minute to start writing an assignment, to use a process when I write, and to use the correct genre for my purpose and audience. All of these are very important if I want to successfully communicate my ideas.
>
> Before this class, every time I had a writing assignment, I would do it at the last minute. I have learned not to do that because my writing is much better if I take my time and because there was peer review in this class. My group members expected me to have a draft for them to read! Because I don't think my English is very good, I always hated for others to read my work, but I now understand the importance of sharing my drafts with others who can help me improve the message as well as help me eliminate any surface errors. All of this takes time to do well, so I can no longer wait until the night before an assignment is due to start it.
>
> I have also learned to use a process when writing. I learned that all writers work better when they have deadlines and that it's important to set my own deadlines for finishing my work over a matter of days or weeks. I have become more responsible about keeping to the deadlines because I have discovered how much better my writing is if I do that. This has helped me a lot with my fear of writing in English. If I take the time to revise and edit my work, it reads much better.
>
> When I turned in my first assignment, I learned that not every piece of writing is the same. Who knew that we are supposed to

write in different formats for different writing assignments? Because I am a business major, I thought everything was supposed to be in a memo format. I now know that depending on the audience and purpose, I should choose the genre that best suits what I am trying to communicate. In fact, before this course I never even knew about audience. I didn't realize that I should adjust my writing to meet the needs of my particular readers. I wrote the same way every time.

Finally, I am now learning how to do an online portfolio. It's been quite a challenge, but I can see the benefits to me if I can create a portfolio and put it online for graduate school committees and employers to see.

**Activity 17.1** Take a moment to draft a few paragraphs describing your own writing improvement this semester. In which areas have you improved the most and in which areas do you still need improvement? How has your writing changed as a result of the work you have done in this class?

**Develop Your Understanding**

## Samples of Class Writing

Your portfolio should include only your best writing, so choose four or five pieces from your classes as examples. How do you know which pieces to include? Your best writing is probably those pieces you most enjoyed writing and that your peers and instructor told you that they enjoyed reading. To demonstrate your range of writing abilities, select pieces that showcase a variety of audiences, purposes, and genres. Then select pieces that include:

- an effective introduction and thesis statement
- well-developed paragraphs
- good supporting details
- effective transitions
- an effective conclusion
- few or no errors in spelling, punctuation, or grammar

**One Student's Class Writing.** Student writer Maria Cervantes, a sociology major, decided to include this memorandum that she submitted to her English professor as a proposal for the topic she would write about during the semester.

# Memorandum

Date: 02/16/2010
Subject: Domestic Abuse
To: Dr. Gupta, English 1311
From: Maria Cervantes

## The Center Against Family Violence

The Center Against Family Violence initially began as a hotline where victims of domestic abuse were referred to safe houses and private homes. An emergency shelter was created two years later. Visitors to the center are immediately greeted upon entry into the facility by female wooden carved figurines. Attached to the silhouettes are the stories of the women who were victims of domestic abuse and who did not survive the attack. The facility is secured and visitors are buzzed in to the reception area. The hallways are adorned with children's artwork. Counseling sessions are held in small classrooms and are offered throughout the week. The Center Against Family Violence refers victims to agencies that can assist them with legal advice or representation, job placement, and continuing education.

Every year an estimated 1.3 million women are victims of physical assault by an intimate partner in the state of Texas, according to the National Center Against Domestic Violence. It is estimated that one in every four women will experience domestic violence in her lifetime. Boys who have witnessed domestic violence are twice as likely to become abusers themselves as adults. Violence among young teenagers has also increased by 50 percent. There have been more than 2 million emergency calls placed reporting domestic violence in 2009, which was an increase of 25 percent from the previous year.

Family violence is an act committed between family or household members with the intent to cause physical harm, bodily injury, and/or sexual assault. If acts of violence are committed by someone who is not an immediate member of the family or household it would still be considered family violence if the victim and abuser are in a relationship. Dating violence, or dating domestic violence, involves couples who are in a romantic or intimate relationship and one of them commits an act of physical harm, bodily injury, or sexual assault. Teenagers who are charged with domestic violence may be sentenced to two years in jail and one thousand hours of domestic violence counseling. An adult charged with domestic violence may be prosecuted as a third degree felony and could serve 2–5 years in prison.

Acts of domestic violence are planned out by the aggressor over a period of time to gain control and to manipulate the victim. The acts of violence are carried out as a display of power and have less to do with anger. Victims are often emotionally and psychologically victimized as well. The aggressor will punch at walls, destroy belongings, threaten to commit suicide or may display erratic mood swings. Some abusers will threaten to take children away. Victims are under the constant watch of the abuser and are left with limited access to money, vehicles, or forms of communication.

Victims live in constant fear and they often feel emotionally numb or helpless. Often the victims fault themselves and begin to question their own mental stability. Victims will avoid certain topics out of fear that will trigger the abuser. Therefore, the victim will become more submissive to the aggressors' acts of violence.

The goal of the Center Against Family Violence is to provide victims and their families with support groups, counseling, and education to help them cope and overcome from their traumatic ordeal.

## Samples of Other Work

In addition to samples from class, your portfolio may include other types of writing that showcase an even broader range. For example, you might include an editorial you wrote to the newspaper, a report you wrote for work, an entry from your blog, or a poem you wrote for fun.

**One Student's Other Work.** Student writer Matthew Guay included this letter that he wrote to the University of Texas Telecampus upon completion of his online writing class.

Matthew Guay
2001 Place Rd.
Cedar Hill, TX 75104
February 25, 2009

Dr. Darcy Hardy, Executive Director UT TeleCampus
The University of Texas System
702 Colorado Street, Suite 4.100
Austin, TX 78701

Dear Dr. Hardy:

I am a sophomore student with the University of Texas Pan American (UTPA), and I have studied exclusively through the TeleCampus system. I have done most of my courses from Thailand, where my parents are missionaries. The TeleCampus is a great system and enabled me to pursue my dreams even from another country. Though I've enjoyed studying through the TeleCampus, I feel that the TeleCampus needs to make a few changes to its system to make it more accessible to current students and to attract new students in the future.

The largest problem with the TeleCampus is the lack of communication between campuses. Tuition had to be paid at each campus separately, and then leftover grant and scholarship funds were refunded to me by my home campus. Each campus also charged student fees such as registration, athletic activities, and foreign exchange fees. Although some fees were waived after I appealed them, it seemed to be an unnecessary difficulty. Then, each campus required separate email addresses and login credentials for their school's website. Also getting approved for classes that required prerequisites was very difficult due to lack of communication between campuses.

I believe many of these problems could be solved by making the TeleCampus exist as its own "virtual campus" in the UT system. Instead of a traditional campus, it would simply handle all the services for its students. The classes could still be taught through the other UT system campuses, but the process would be invisible to the students. This way, a student enrolled in the TeleCampus would have a TeleCampus email and password, and all payments, grants, and scholarships would go to the TeleCampus and then be distributed to the other UT campuses. Some may feel that the current system is better, since everything is handled by existing departments and systems in the colleges offering the courses. However, I feel the changes would make it much easier and less confusing for students and faculty alike, and both are worth the investment and would eventually save time and money for all involved.

Finally I believe that the TeleCampus can and should increase the number of classes and degree programs that are offered. I believe that the classes I have taken have been as good as their on-site equivalents. Although I would prefer to finish my degree with UT, I am going to be transferring to the University of Phoenix this summer because they offer a software engineering degree fully online. I hope that in the future this will be possible through the TeleCampus, and I firmly believe that the ideas I presented in this letter could help the TeleCampus grow to be one of the largest campuses in the UT system.

Sincerely,

Matthew Guay
Matthew Guay

**Activity 17.2**  With a small group, discuss options for what to include in your writing portfolio. First, describe the audience for your portfolio and how it affects your decision for what to include.

**Connect With Others**

# REVISE AND EDIT YOUR PORTFOLIO

You want to persuade your readers that you're a skilled writer, so review the writing you have selected to include in your portfolio. Reread each selection and make any revisions as needed. For example, you might rewrite an introduction, add details, or revise an awkward sentence. Then edit your work to eliminate any errors in spelling, punctuation, and grammar. Reprint any selections that may need improved formatting or that have instructor comments or grades on them.

> *Writing and rewriting are a constant search for what it is one is saying.*
>
> —John Updike

# PRESENT YOUR PORTFOLIO

Once you make your writing selections, you will need to gather them into a portfolio. Select a binding method that is attractive and holds the pages easily. Use divider pages to mark each section. If you wish, design a creative cover.

If you have access to the web, you may prefer to place your writing portfolio online. One way to do this is to develop a blog or a simple website using online tools. A blog is simply an online journal. Using a blog, you can post and categorize information into a portfolio.

As with any writing assignment, be sure to consider your primary audience and purpose, but remember that web content is public, so you want to include only content that you are willing for anyone to see.

Online portfolios often include more information than a print portfolio. Consider adding the following sections to your online portfolio:

- an introduction or "About Me" section
- visuals that will appeal to your primary audience
- links to favorite sites
- contact information
- a photograph of yourself
- a blog if you wish to keep one
- links to social networking sites where you are a member
- a copyright and/or fair use statement

Use the following guidelines to help you design a visually appealing website:

## LANGUAGES and CULTURES

When viewing online portfolios, watch for cultural preferences for what to include or what to omit. In some cultures, it would not be considered appropriate to include a photograph or a section describing the writer's personal life.

- Start with an attractive logo. Because in the United States we read from left to right, top to bottom, put this logo on the left. If you are designing a website to be read in another country, determine the best placement for that audience.
- In a few words, describe the purpose of your site.
- Use high-quality images, giving credit where appropriate. If you use photographs or other graphics you did not create yourself, you will need to credit the source. Note that to use images you find online—unless they are labeled for reuse—you should obtain permission before publishing them on your site.

- Share interesting information through your links.
- Be friendly but professional in your choice of words and images.
- Be sure that your site is easy to navigate, checking that the navigation links work and that they use consistent wording and design.

**One Student's Online Portfolio.**  Figure 17.1 is an example of the home-page of one student's online portfolio.

FIGURE 17.1  One student's online portfolio

**Connect
With Others**

**Activity 17.3**    Look for examples of online writing portfolios. Using the content and design suggestions provided in this chapter, discuss with your classmates why you like or dislike a particular portfolio format.

# WRITING ASSIGNMENT

Just as you do for all of your writing, think now about your audience and purpose for a writing portfolio. Answer the following questions:

1. Is your portfolio designed to express, inform, or persuade?
2. Who is the primary audience for your writing portfolio?

Given your responses to the preceding questions, ask yourself these questions:

3. What writing qualities would I like to demonstrate through my portfolio?
4. How can I best demonstrate these qualities in my portfolio?
5. What other qualities would I like to demonstrate through my portfolio?
6. How can I best demonstrate these other qualities?

For additional help with writing, reading, and research, go to
www.mycomplab.com.

# PART 4 Expanding Research

# 18 Conducting Field Research

**Learning Objectives**

In this chapter you will:

- Understand and apply the ethics of field research.
- Learn to conduct interviews, surveys, observations, and case studies.

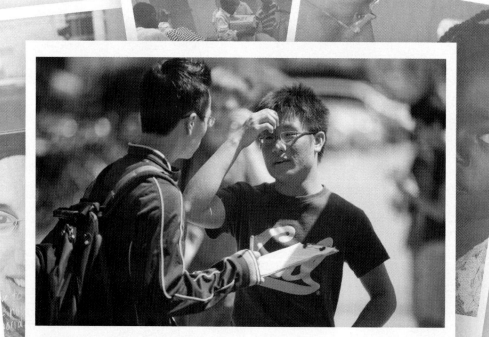

*If a survey were being conducted on your college campus, would you volunteer to take the survey? Why or why not?*

W hen you need to conduct research, you might automatically think of searching for a topic on the Internet or linking into one of your library's databases. However, depending on the question you're trying to answer, research that you conduct yourself might be a better source. Field research (sometimes called primary research) is research that you collect firsthand, such as interviews, surveys, and observations. Suppose you're writing to a college administrator requesting more online sections of writing courses. You could submit a well-reasoned proposal, but the administrator might assume that only one student—you—feels this way. However, after surveying students about this topic, you find that many students also want online classes. By including this information in your proposal, your readers are more likely to agree with you.

---

### Types of Field Research

- Interview—one-on-one conversation conducted in person or by phone or email
- Survey—series of questions on a particular topic given to people in written or oral form
- Observation—careful examination of a place or event using notes, audio, or visual recordings
- Case study—focused research on a single person or place that might include interviews, surveys, and observations

---

## ETHICAL ISSUES IN FIELD RESEARCH

Because field research involves observing, talking to, or collecting data on human subjects, it needs to be conducted as ethically as possible. In fact, colleges and universities typically have an office or department, often called the Institutional Research Board (IRB), charged with making sure that human subject research is conducted according to legal and ethical guidelines.

While field research might seem harmless enough, in actuality people can be hurt unless precautions are taken. For instance, suppose you are upset that your sociology professor has cancelled class three weeks in a row but still expects students to know all the material in the course. You decide to write a proposal to the professor in which you argue that one of the tests should be cancelled. To make your argument convincing, you survey the class and discover that the rest of the students agree with you. In your proposal, you identify these students by name even though you didn't get their permission to do so. As a result, the students could be subject to reprisal even though you are the one writing the proposal.

To ethically conduct field research you need to inform the research participants (the people you're interviewing, surveying, or observing) about the project. In particular, you need to tell them why you're conducting the research, how you will use their contributions, and to what extent their privacy will be kept. This information will help people decide if they want to participate in your project. When conducting the research, try to not intrude on the participants' lives. If you're observing someone, be unobtrusive. When conducting an interview, arrange for a convenient place and avoid unnecessarily taking up someone's valuable time. Be sure to get permission to tape an interview. When appropriate, allow interviewees to review a transcript of their interview so they can correct any misstatements.

---

### Ethical Research Checklist

☐ Tell your research participants why you're conducting the research.

☐ Explain how you'll use the information that you discover.

☐ Maintain the research participants' privacy by not releasing their names.

☐ Get permission from your research participants, preferably in writing.

☐ Avoid intruding on your research participants' personal space.

☐ Do not take up much of the research participants' time.

☐ If audio- or videotaping, be sure to get permission first.

---

## TYPES OF FIELD RESEARCH

Three common types of field research are interviews, surveys, and observations. Some research projects, such as case studies, combine these research methods for more in-depth study.

### Interviews

Interviews can provide you with valuable information and useful insights that you can then include in your writing. The purposes for an interview can vary. By interviewing an expert you can get the most knowledgeable and up-to-date information possible. For instance, if you were writing about affirmative action, you could interview an attorney specializing in this area. You could also interview someone who has had some personal experience with this topic to better understand how affirmative action works. An interview that focuses on personal experiences can give you interesting details for your writing. No matter whom you interview, be sure to prepare questions beforehand, stay focused on the topic, and ask follow-up questions if necessary.

**Open-Ended and Closed Questions.** As you draft your interview questions, consider the type of responses you want. Open-ended questions allow respondents to give opinions and perspectives as well as information. "What is the main benefit of academic advising?" is an open-ended question because interviewees can give a variety of responses. A closed question, in contrast, is designed to elicit a specific answer, such as yes/no or multiple choice. Here's an example:

What is the main benefit of academic advising? Choose one of the following:

**a.** The advisors provide me with career guidance.
**b.** The advisors help me understand degree requirements.
**c.** The advisors keep me on track for graduation.
**d.** The advisors educate me about financial aid.

While open-ended questions provide you with a wealth of responses, closed questions can help you pinpoint people's ideas. Both can be valuable, depending on your purpose. Most interviews consist of both open-ended and closed questions.

> **LANGUAGES and CULTURES**
>
> Nonverbal communication is important in an interview. Your mannerisms, dress, and even the amount of eye contact that you make with your interviewee affect the success of the communication. Cultures differ in their emphasis on eye contact, or the extent to which one person looks into another person's eyes. In the United States, looking someone directly in the eye is a sign of confidence and interest, which is considered a good thing. However, in other cultures extended eye contact can be considered rude. In Japan, for instance, people in a lower status typically avoid extended eye contact to show respect for the person in a higher status. In traditional Middle Eastern countries, women are discouraged from making direct eye contact with men.

**Revise Your Questions.** To make the most of an interview, draft interview questions and practice them on a friend or classmate. Keep in mind the following guidelines:

- Use a logical sequence of questions. Order the questions so that your respondents don't feel that they have to return to a topic they already commented on.
- Determine if the questions should be open-ended or closed. Often interviewers begin with closed questions that elicit basic information and then move on to open-ended questions. An interview about the benefits of academic advising might begin with "How long have you been a student?" and "How often have you sought academic advising?" and then go on to ask the respondents' opinions.

- Limit the number of questions. Do you have five minutes or fifteen minutes? By practicing your interview you can determine its length. Omit questions that are redundant or peripheral to the topic.
- Make your questions clear and unbiased. By practicing the questions on others, you can determine if they are easily understood and don't lead the respondents to predetermined answers.

## Interview Checklist

- ☐ Have in mind the information you want to gather from the interview.
- ☐ Select an appropriate person, such as a professor or an expert from the community.
- ☐ Contact that person through phone or email and explain your purpose.
- ☐ Conduct the interview in person, through email, or via telephone, depending on your purpose and your respondent's availability.
- ☐ Use open-ended questions to elicit a variety of perspectives and closed questions to elicit specific information.
- ☐ Practice your interview to determine if your questions are effectively sequenced, around the right number, and communicate clearly.
- ☐ Take notes or ask permission to tape the interview.
- ☐ Stay focused and don't waste time.
- ☐ Double-check to make sure you spell the person's name correctly.
- ☐ Thank the person for taking the time to help you with your research.

## Surveys

Almost everyone has been surveyed at some time. After you make a purchase you're given a customer satisfaction questionnaire. Around election times pollsters ask for your thoughts on a candidate. At the end of an academic term you are given a survey to evaluate your courses. The purpose of a survey is to gather a particular type of information from a select group of people. Information from surveys can lead to policy changes, improved consumer products, and changes in election outcomes.

When creating a survey, you need to decide who will take it. This depends on your purpose for the survey. If you're interested in people's opinions on a new toll road, should you ask only people likely to use the toll road? Or an assortment of people from the general population, some of whom may not even drive? Your answer will depend on your purpose for research—the question that you're trying to answer.

When giving a survey, identify yourself, explain the purpose of the survey, and describe how you will use the information that you gather. You also need to decide how you will give the survey: in person, by phone, mail-in questionnaires, or email. Consider who will be taking the survey: do they typically pay attention to email messages? Then an email survey might work well. Person-to-person surveys are good if you can capture people's attention and convince them to spend a little time with you. No matter what medium you use, the survey should be short enough so that people can complete it quickly. Try out the questions on friends before giving the survey to make sure it is easily understood. Consider using both open-ended and closed questions so that you gather both specific information and a variety of perspectives. Electronic survey sites can help you distribute the survey widely and quickly compile the results. The more people who complete the survey, the more information you have available to develop and support your writing. If surveying people who speak multiple languages, translate the questions into the most common languages spoken in your area.

A survey can be an effective tool for persuasion. For instance, suppose that you want recent immigrants to your city to more easily be able to take the bus to work or school. You notice that the maps and instructions provided for bus riders are only in English, even though many recent immigrants speak Spanish. You decide to survey bus riders to see if they need bus information in Spanish, so you survey people waiting at bus stops in both Spanish and English, depending on the language spoken. Seventy-nine percent of the surveyed people say that information in Spanish would help them navigate their way around the city. You could then present this information to the local bus company, which might be convinced to include Spanish as well as English on bus maps and instructions.

**One Researcher's Survey.**  Todd C. Ruecker, a scholar who specializes in teaching writing to multilingual students, wanted to learn students' viewpoints about being labeled ESL (English as a Second Language). Students who were labeled "ESL" were placed into different writing classes than students without that label. Here is the survey that he gave to around 250 students in writing classes at his university. Note that he asked a variety of open-ended and closed questions. When he practiced giving the survey with several students, he realized that he needed to define the labels he was asking about. Most students who took the survey reported that they didn't mind how they were labeled because they were satisfied with their writing classes.

1. How many languages do you speak?
2. How well do you think the following labels describe you?

1 = not at all    2 = not very well    3 = somewhat    4 = very well
5 = perfectly

| | | | | | |
|---|---|---|---|---|---|
| Nonnative English Speaker | 1 | 2 | 3 | 4 | 5 |
| ESL Student | 1 | 2 | 3 | 4 | 5 |
| English Language Learner (ELL) | 1 | 2 | 3 | 4 | 5 |
| Limited English Proficiency (LEP) | 1 | 2 | 3 | 4 | 5 |
| Bilingual | 1 | 2 | 3 | 4 | 5 |
| Multilingual | 1 | 2 | 3 | 4 | 5 |
| Monolingual | 1 | 2 | 3 | 4 | 5 |

*Note*

ESL = English as a Second Language
Bilingual = Speaks two languages
Multilingual = Speaks more than one language
Monolingual = Speaks one language

3. How long have you lived in the United States?
4. Were you in a bilingual education program in high school?
5. If given the freedom to choose, would you rather be in a writing course for:

    a. nonnative English speakers.
    b. native English speakers.
    c. a combination of nonnative and native English speakers.

## Survey Checklist

☐ Decide on your purpose for the survey and the kind of information you want from it.

☐ Consider the best people to survey, depending on your purpose and the information you want.

☐ Keep the survey short, no longer than a few minutes.

☐ Decide on the best medium for the survey: in-person, phone, mail, or email. Consider using an electronic survey instrument.

☐ Write the survey in a language that people taking the survey speak.

☐ Give the survey to as many people as possible so you get a large sample size.

☐ Try out the questions first on friends to make sure they are easily understood.

☐ When giving the survey, identity yourself, explain its purpose, and tell how the information will be used.

☐ Maintain the privacy of the survey respondents.

**Activity 18.1**  What do you want to know about the students in your class? Perhaps you're interested in their majors, their work experiences, or their opinions on a controversial topic. With several classmates, design a survey for the rest of the class to take. Share your findings with your classmates, being sure to keep the responses anonymous.

**Connect With Others**

## Observations

By observing people, places, or events, you can discover useful information about a topic. Traffic engineers observe traffic patterns in order to facilitate the flow of cars. Administrators observe teachers in their classrooms as a part of teacher evaluations. Zoologists observe animals in the wild to learn about their habitats and survival strategies.

Suppose you have an assignment in an interior design course to evaluate the effectiveness of the design in your college library. You have noticed a problem with the exit doors on the main floor: adjacent to each door is a decorative panel that looks just like the door. You've noticed that some people try to push open the decorative panels because they confuse them with the real doors. You get permission from the head of the library to conduct an observation. You and several classmates spend several hours observing everyone as they leave through the exit doors. Using clickers, you count both the number of people who try to push open the decorative panels before discovering the actual doors and the number of people who exit the doors without any confusion. Almost 20 percent of people exiting the library confuse the decorative panels with the actual doors. As a result, you can safely conclude that the design of the main library exit is flawed.

---

### Observation Checklist

☐ Decide on your purpose for making the observation. What information will the observation provide?

☐ Get permission before conducting the observation.

☐ Decide exactly what you will observe.

☐ Use a checklist to mark off sightings or use clickers to count particular actions.

☐ Spend enough time observing so you have enough data.

☐ Be unobtrusive.

## Case Studies

A case study is an in-depth examination of an individual in his or her natural environment. Educators, psychologists, and anthropologists often conduct case studies to better understand some aspect of human behavior. An educational researcher who wants to understand how children cope with the stress of taking standardized tests might conduct case studies of several students. The researcher would observe the children in the classroom, examine their schoolwork, and interview the children, their parents, and their teachers. While the results of these case studies can't be generalized to all children, they can suggest ways that children might respond to high-stakes tests.

Case studies are often used in the field of rhetoric and composition. One of the most influential of these case studies was published in 1971 by Janet Emig, who examined the ways that eight high school students approached their writing assignments. She examined all of the writing completed by the students and interviewed them extensively. She found that these students viewed the writing assignments as mechanical, waited until the last minute to compose, and focused mostly on grammatical correctness instead of writing about meaningful topics. As a result of Emig's research, writing teachers began to stress the importance of revising your writing and focusing on content as well as correctness.

---

### Case Study Checklist

☐ Decide on your purpose for conducting a case study and the information you hope to learn from it.

☐ Based on your purpose, select an appropriate person to study.

☐ Get the person's permission.

☐ Interview and observe your research participant closely. Gather relevant materials such as writings and notes.

☐ If possible, audiotape or videotape your research participant (with permission).

☐ Consider sharing your findings with your research participant.

---

**Connect With Others**

**Activity 18.2**   Conduct a simple case study of the way that one of your classmates writes. Find out about this person's writing process, attitude toward writing, experiences with writing, topic preferences, writing concerns, and so on. Interview your classmate about these topics, examine samples of writing, and observe him or her writing. Based on this research, write an analysis of your classmate as a writer. Share this analysis with the individual you studied.

# USING VISUALS TO DISPLAY RESULTS

By visually depicting your field research, you can quickly communicate your results. Charts, tables, graphs, and diagrams help your readers grasp the significance of your findings. However, visuals supplement your explanations; they don't replace them. You still need to analyze your results in language that is clear to your readers.

## Visuals Checklist

☐ Use visuals to supplement your explanations of your research.

☐ Decide on an appropriate visual for your data.

☐ Insert the visual into the text.

☐ Explain the information presented in the visual.

☐ Label the visual clearly.

# WRITING ASSIGNMENT

What kinds of writing will you be asked to do in your profession? How should you prepare to do these kinds of writing? Interview a person who does the kind of work you'd like to do once you graduate. Ask questions about the different forms of writing used, the length of time it takes to write different documents, the kinds of research that is expected, if the writing is done individually or collectively, and so on. Be sure to make an appointment for the interview, come prepared, ask follow-up questions, and be efficient. After the interview, write up your findings and share with your classmates.

For support in meeting this chapter's objectives, follow this path in MyCompLab: Resources ⇒ Research ⇒ The Research Assignment ⇒ Finding Sources. Review the Instruction and Multimedia resources about finding source material, then complete the Exercises and click on Gradebook to measure your progress.

# 19 Using Sources

## Learning Objectives

In this chapter you will:

- Learn to avoid plagiarism.
- Discover how to develop a research plan.
- Learn how to evaluate sources.

- Discover how to locate relevant sources.
- Find out how to use sources effectively in your writing.
- Practice quoting, paraphrasing, and summarizing information.

*Using computers to conduct research and communicate your findings can save time. What are some other advantages of gathering sources electronically?*

**M**ost writing that you do in school or in your workplace uses information from a variety of sources. If you are writing about something based on your direct experience, you are conducting field research. In this case, your sources are firsthand: They are derived from what you observe, from the people you interview, from surveys you develop, or from what you study directly. Often, however, you rely on the research conducted and published by others. Until the age of the Internet, published sources were limited in type: books, magazines, journals, newspapers, encyclopedias, radio, and television. In recent years, scholars have turned to websites, blogs, wikis, and online periodicals and newspapers in addition to traditional sources. However, this increase in the *quantity* of information hasn't necessarily led to more *quality*. Today you face challenges in not only finding sources, but also in evaluating and ethically using sources in your own writing.

> *I'd be happy if I could think that the role of the library was sustained and even enhanced in the age of the computer.*
> —Bill Gates

## DEFINING PLAGIARISM IN THE GLOBAL COMMUNITY

In most U.S. institutions of higher learning, plagiarism is defined as the intentional *or unintentional* use in a paper of sources that have *not been identified* as having been written by someone other than the author of the paper. Plagiarism is borrowing, lifting, stealing, or taking words from another source without acknowledging it. Whether an instance of plagiarism is intentional, or whether it is simply a mistake, it usually results in serious consequences, such as failure, suspension, or even expulsion.

### LANGUAGES and CULTURES

Dr. Charles Juwah, a specialist in problem-based learning and the creator of plagiarisminfo.com, has reported that, in many cultures, quoting materials verbatim is considered the highest form of respect. In some more traditionally based cultures, memorizing is believed to be the very best way to deepen and consolidate learning; analysis and original thought in a paper are seen as egotistical and inappropriate. Blogging about her experience as an American student in India, Jennifer Kumar says it was best to answer questions exactly as the teacher had discussed them, or as the text had discussed them. But, she goes on, her teachers in India did not think of this as plagiarism. It was, instead, the right way to do things. As Jennifer's experience demonstrates, the concept of plagiarism is culturally determined.

When doing source-based writing, keep track of your sources as you do your research. If you don't, you will find it very difficult to later re-create your research path in order to properly cite your sources.

## Using Sources Ethically

When working with sources, you must use quotations, paraphrases, and summaries, all of which need to be cited. When you quote a source, you bor-row the *exact* words of the source, indicated with quotation marks. A para-phrase is when you closely adapt the ideas of a source in your own voice. When summarizing, you boil a source's ideas into a concise statement of the main idea. The one exception to this rule is that you do not have to cite ideas or facts that are widely known among your readers. For example, most basic facts are considered common knowledge, but statistics or interpretations of research are the property of the scholar who created them. If you're unsure if something can be considered common knowledge, cite the source.

## Citation Systems

Over the years, many professions in the United States and Western Europe have developed standard citation systems that are used to explain where sourced information in texts originated. Two of the most common are the ci-tation systems of the Modern Language Association (MLA), widely used in the humanities, and the American Psychological Association (APA), which is used in the social sciences and education. (For more on how to use these ci-tation systems, see Chapter 20.) Using a citation system correctly not only protects you from accidentally committing plagiarism, it also tells your read-ers where they can access the information you used to support your points. Using a citation system to identify your sources also identifies you as a mem-ber of a discourse community by showing how your work belongs to or de-rives from the values and understandings established by that community.

---

### Avoiding Plagiarism

- Understand the standards in the community or institution that you are working in.
- Indicate the source of an idea or expression you obtained from any print or online publication or work.
- Use a standard citation system such as MLA or APA.
- Keep a working bibliography, and be especially careful to keep track of your sources.
- When researching online, use a web-based bookmarking tool like Delicious.com or CiteULike.org to keep track of sources you've consulted.

# DEVELOPING A RESEARCH PLAN

Because so much information is available in so many different areas, it's important to develop a research plan to guide you in your search. Without a plan, you might waste time finding and reading sources that don't pertain to your purpose. Your research plan should take you from a general topic, to a focused research question, to a working thesis. It should also include a strategy for finding and assessing the available sources, formulating a schedule, and developing a system for taking complete and accurate notes. Basically, your research plan is an outline of how you will approach your project; it is a working document that should evolve with your project's needs.

## Analyze the Rhetorical Situation

Often, you will write a research essay in response to an assignment from your instructor. When you receive your assignment, analyze the rhetorical situation: audience, purpose, exigence, genre, visual design, and constraints. If you are allowed to select a topic, gather ideas and get feedback from others. When brainstorming for topics, begin by asking yourself about the audience and purpose of your research project. Who will be interested in these potential topics? What do they need to know about these topics? Do you want to inform this audience of something? To persuade them? Suppose you want to explore the spread of Spanglish, the combination of English and Spanish common in areas of the United States where multilingual Spanish/English speakers live. Your audience for the paper is your professor and your classmates, and your purpose in conducting this research is to educate them about this sociolinguistic phenomenon. Once you have selected a topic, you need to refine it into a manageable project—a project that addresses your topic in sufficient depth within the constraints of your assignment.

## Narrowing Your Broad Topic into a Focused Research Question

You decide to start researching your topic by entering "Spanglish" as a key word in a search engine; the search yields 1,140,000 hits. You realize that you need to narrow your broad topic—Spanglish—into a focused research question. Questions starting with the words *who, what, where, when, why,* and *how* will help you to narrow down your topic.

Topic: Spanglish

- **Research Questions**: What is Spanglish? Who speaks it? Why do people speak Spanglish? When and to whom do they speak it? Where and when is it spoken?
- **Focused Research Question**: Is Spanglish an emerging language or a type of slang?

As you can see, if your question is too general, you may need to further narrow it down in order to focus on a research question that is manageable given your assignment. In this example, the topic was narrowed into a focused research question.

## Creating a Thesis Statement

Narrowing your focus down from a general topic to a focused question will help you to formulate a thesis. After you have a research question, you can do some preliminary research to help you determine what you think the answer may be, which will become your thesis. For example, to answer the research question, "Is Spanglish an emerging language or a type of slang?" a thesis might be "Spanglish is an emerging language because it is developing a standardized syntax and morphology system." Moving forward, your research can provide evidence to support this assertion. While you will need to revise your thesis periodically as new material surfaces, establishing a thesis early on will provide a direction for your research.

## Identifying Types of Sources

Answers to your research questions can come from a variety of sources, so the next step in creating a research plan is to identify the types of sources you'll use. For our research question, you might want to start your paper by defining Spanglish, making print or online dictionaries and encyclopedias a good place to start. If you want to establish the current status of Spanglish as a language for background for your paper, scholarly journal articles written by linguists might be your best source. Or, if you wanted to provide examples of widespread Spanglish usage, websites might be a good place to start. We'll explore search strategies for finding the sources you need later in this chapter.

## Setting a Schedule

After you have decided on a topic, narrowed that topic to a manageable research question, and identified the types of sources that you need, you should establish a schedule for your project. When you receive an assignment, open your calendar and plan your project as a series of small tasks, or goals, that will help you complete your project. For example, if you are given five weeks to complete a research paper, your schedule may look like this:

Week 1: Gather ideas on a possible topic. Select a topic and narrow it to a research question. Do preliminary research and draft a possible thesis. Consult with others to get feedback.

Week 2: Research online by consulting the library's catalog and databases. Visit the library to ask librarians for suggestions on how to access sources. Share your results with classmates and friends.

Week 3: Complete a first draft over the weekend and ask others to read it and make suggestions for revision. Continue library research to fill in holes in your research. Give your draft to peers, tutors, and your instructor for feedback.

Week 4: Revise paper based on feedback. Ask for further suggestions for revision.

Week 5: Edit and proofread several times before due date and submit paper.

## Taking Notes and Keeping an Annotated Bibliography

When developing your research plan, you should also develop a strategy for taking notes throughout the research process. Many students today take notes electronically; however, you can also take notes in a traditional notebook or on index cards (one card per "note"). No matter what format you choose, it is essential to take careful notes throughout the research process. Record facts and ideas from your sources, being careful to note exactly where each piece of information came from. Indicate if you're quoting, paraphrasing, or summarizing. When you begin incorporating your sources into your writing, this diligence will save you from having to revisit your sources later to find the correct citations or, worse, from accidentally committing plagiarism. With each source you consult, be sure to record the publication information that you will need later when creating a citation:

- names of authors or other parties responsible for the document (i.e., editor, translator, and so forth)
- book, journal, magazine, or website title; title of specific article
- page numbers, specific URL, Digital Object Identifier (DOI), volume number, issue number, edition number, date of access (for online sources)

■ publication information: name of publisher, city of publication, copy-right date (or date of publication or most recent update for online sources)

Many instructors will ask you to keep an annotated bibliography, which is a list of sources that you consult that includes the source's citation information, a summary of the source, and sometimes an assessment of the source's role (if any) in your research.

Here is a sample entry for an annotated bibliography, cited in MLA style:

> Stavans, Ilan. *Spanglish: The Making of a New American Language.* New York: Harper Perennial, 2004. Print.
>
> In this book, Stavans explores the spread of Spanglish as a hybrid language that is growing in popularity across all areas of the United States since the early nineteenth century. Stavans traces this development in detail and includes many anecdotes to support his claims. In particular, Stavans creates an interesting analogy between Spanglish and jazz that I would like to integrate into my research paper (3). He also includes a lexicon of 4,500 words from which I can pull specific Spanglish words to use as examples.

While some instructors may require an annotated bibliography, many students also choose to keep one informally—as a type of note taking. You can continue to refine and expand your annotated bibliography throughout your research process.

---

## Research Plan Checklist

☐ Use a research plan to guide and focus your research.

☐ Understand your assignment by analyzing the rhetorical situation (audience, purpose, exigence, genre, visual design, and constraints).

☐ Select a topic and narrow it down to a specific research question.

☐ Turn this question into a preliminary, focused thesis.

☐ Anticipate the kinds of sources that you'll need.

☐ Draft a realistic schedule for completing your project.

☐ Develop a method for taking thorough notes for your project.

**Activity 19.1**   With several classmates, select a concept from one of your classes, such as photosynthesis (biology), gross national product (business), or obsessive compulsive disorder (psychology). Assume that you need to write a definition of this topic for a group of high school students preparing to attend college. Write a series of questions that would help you turn the topic into a thesis. Decide on the type of sources that would be most appropriate for each question.

**Connect With Others**

# EVALUATING YOUR SOURCES

Because of the wealth of resources available in print and online, it is more important than ever before to evaluate your research sources carefully. The sheer amount of information available doesn't make research easier—if anything, it makes it harder. You need to develop a healthy skepticism about the information you encounter when researching a topic. The following checklist will help you assess the relevance, authority, accuracy, objectivity, and currency of a source, particularly on the Internet.

- **Relevance.** Does this information address your research question? How does this source's discussion relate to your thesis?
- **Authority**. Who is the author of this source? How knowledgeable is he or she? Look for credentials such as academic degrees or associations with well-respected institutions. What credentials or titles qualify him or her as an expert on this topic? If there is no author, what organization is responsible for this text? What makes this organization qualified to provide this information?
- **Accuracy.** What is the source of the information? A well-known magazine or newspaper is better than an obscure website. An article from a scholarly journal is more credible than an individual blog.
  - Is information cited in the source? Unless the author is a true expert on the topic, he or she should indicate the source of the information and give proper credit.
- **Objectivity.** How biased is the source? Many sites have particular political slants. The *Huffington Post,* for instance, is a liberal website, whereas the *Drudge Report* is conservative.
- **Currency**. How recent is the source? Typically, you want to find the most up-to-date information on a particular topic. If, however, you need to examine historical texts, you might examine older sources.

**Activity 19.2**   Do an Internet search on the name of a well-known musical group. Select three different sources from the first page of the results and evaluate them according to their reliability. Rank them from most to least credible. Which of them, if any, would be sufficiently reliable to be used in an academic or workplace document?

**Develop Your Understanding**

# FINDING SOURCES

Libraries used to be places with shelves full of books, a few chairs and tables, and a checkout desk with a date stamp. Now most libraries, especially college and university libraries, contain much more—computers, multimedia rooms, virtual databases, art collections, and coffee houses. These changes have made library research both more rewarding and more challenging. While your first instinct when searching for information might be to search the Internet, you would be wiser to start with a library database. Because anyone can put anything on the Internet, sources found online vary widely in quality. Also, the Internet is not organized in a way that is conducive to research. The most widely used search engine, Google, organizes sites according to how frequently they are accessed, not according to their quality. In contrast, librarians sort through and classify sources of information with the primary purpose of helping people conduct research.

## Primary versus Secondary Sources

Before you begin searching for sources, it is helpful to understand the difference between primary and secondary sources. Primary sources are sources that report on a situation firsthand. For example, if you are conducting research in a history course, you may consult official documents from the period you are studying or the journal kept by a participant of a significant event; these are considered primary sources because they are "first-hand" accounts—not filtered and interpreted by another scholar. If you are writing an essay about second language acquisition and you spend time in the language lab at your college interviewing students, you're conducting field or "primary source" research. Libraries and historical organizations often create archives of primary materials. Alternatively, you can gather primary source material on your own by conducting field research, explored in Chapter 18.

Many, if not most, of the sources that you consult as a college student will be secondary sources. Secondary sources are prepared by a scholar in the field; these sources analyze and interpret primary resources and other secondary sources. Secondary sources include scholarly journal articles and books, even your textbooks.

## Using Key Words and Subject Headings to Locate Relevant Sources

Many reference sources, including library catalogs, the Internet, and research databases, can be searched by key words or subject headings. Thus, it is essential to master these two search techniques no matter what type of source you are exploring.

Books and articles are catalogued partly according to key words, which consist of terminology in the text that describes important concepts. For instance, for the research question "Is Spanglish an emerging language or a type of slang?" key words might be "Spanglish" or "mixed languages." Here are some results for a key word search of "Spanglish" using Google Scholar, an Internet search engine that focuses its search on scholarly sources.

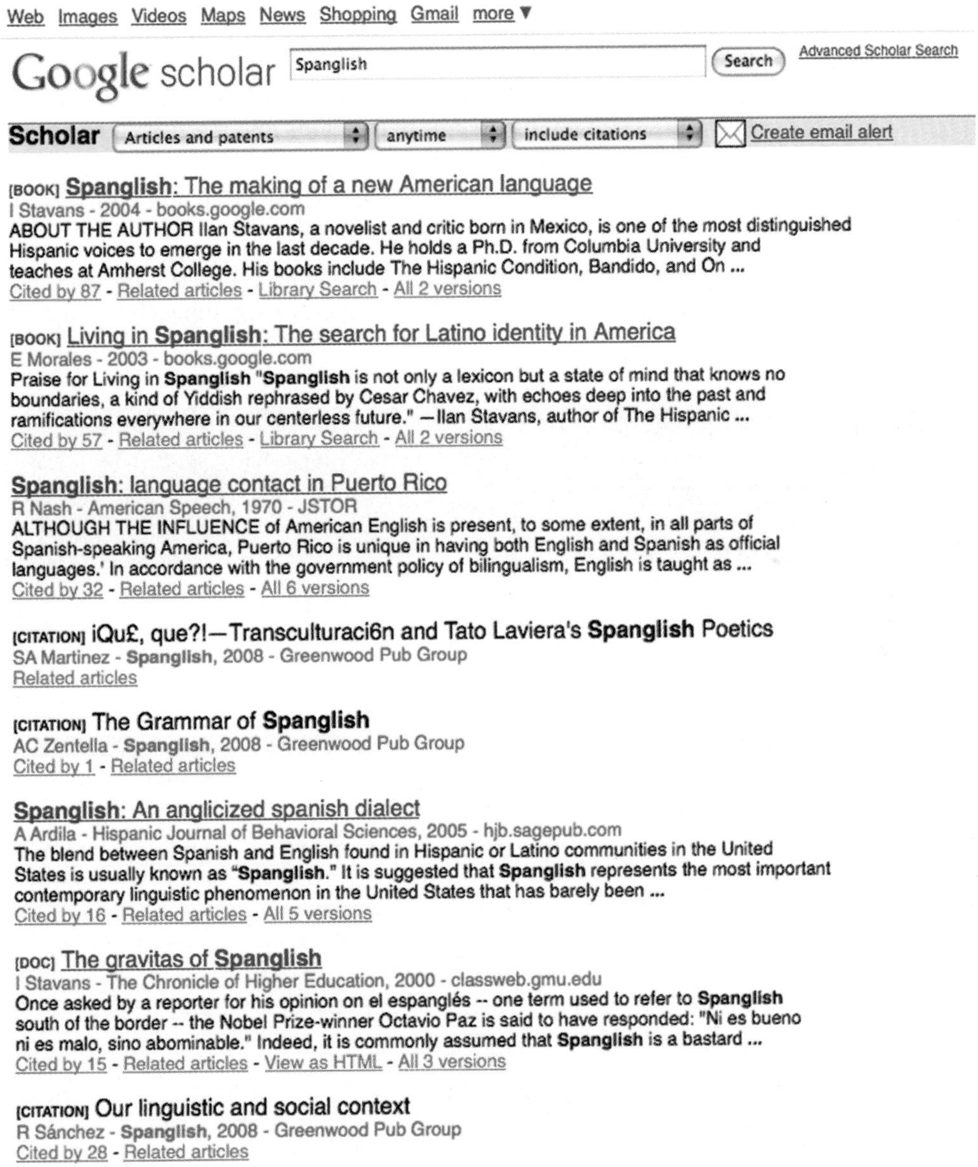

Web  Images  Videos  Maps  News  Shopping  Gmail  more ▼

**Google** scholar  | Spanglish                        | ( Search )   Advanced Scholar Search

**Scholar** | Articles and patents  ◆| | anytime ◆| | include citations ◆| | ☒ Create email alert

[BOOK] **Spanglish**: The making of a new American language
I Stavans - 2004 - books.google.com
ABOUT THE AUTHOR Ilan Stavans, a novelist and critic born in Mexico, is one of the most distinguished Hispanic voices to emerge in the last decade. He holds a Ph.D. from Columbia University and teaches at Amherst College. His books include The Hispanic Condition, Bandido, and On ...
Cited by 87 - Related articles - Library Search - All 2 versions

[BOOK] Living in **Spanglish**: The search for Latino identity in America
E Morales - 2003 - books.google.com
Praise for Living in **Spanglish** "**Spanglish** is not only a lexicon but a state of mind that knows no boundaries, a kind of Yiddish rephrased by Cesar Chavez, with echoes deep into the past and ramifications everywhere in our centerless future." —Ilan Stavans, author of The Hispanic ...
Cited by 57 - Related articles - Library Search - All 2 versions

**Spanglish**: language contact in Puerto Rico
R Nash - American Speech, 1970 - JSTOR
ALTHOUGH THE INFLUENCE of American English is present, to some extent, in all parts of Spanish-speaking America, Puerto Rico is unique in having both English and Spanish as official languages.' In accordance with the government policy of bilingualism, English is taught as ...
Cited by 32 - Related articles - All 6 versions

[CITATION] ¡Qu£, que?!—Transculturaci6n and Tato Laviera's **Spanglish** Poetics
SA Martinez - **Spanglish**, 2008 - Greenwood Pub Group
Related articles

[CITATION] The Grammar of **Spanglish**
AC Zentella - **Spanglish**, 2008 - Greenwood Pub Group
Cited by 1 - Related articles

**Spanglish**: An anglicized spanish dialect
A Ardila - Hispanic Journal of Behavioral Sciences, 2005 - hjb.sagepub.com
The blend between Spanish and English found in Hispanic or Latino communities in the United States is usually known as "**Spanglish**." It is suggested that **Spanglish** represents the most important contemporary linguistic phenomenon in the United States that has barely been ...
Cited by 16 - Related articles - All 5 versions

[DOC] The gravitas of **Spanglish**
I Stavans - The Chronicle of Higher Education, 2000 - classweb.gmu.edu
Once asked by a reporter for his opinion on el espanglés -- one term used to refer to **Spanglish** south of the border -- the Nobel Prize-winner Octavio Paz is said to have responded: "Ni es bueno ni es malo, sino abominable." Indeed, it is commonly assumed that **Spanglish** is a bastard ...
Cited by 15 - Related articles - View as HTML - All 3 versions

[CITATION] Our linguistic and social context
R Sánchez - **Spanglish**, 2008 - Greenwood Pub Group
Cited by 28 - Related articles

FIGURE 19.1  The search results page for the key word "Spanglish" in Google Scholar

It is essential to master the art of inputting key words to get successful search results. If your search term is too general, you may get too many results—many of which may be irrelevant to your research question. Remember to experiment with synonyms and related terms. You can also narrow your search using Boolean commands:

- Use quotation marks around a phrase to search for that exact phrase, as in "language mixing."
- Use "OR" to get a search that will include pages with at least one of the terms, as in "Spanglish OR 'language mixing.'"
- Use "NOT" to eliminate possibilities, as in "Spanglish NOT movie." This will search for documents that include *Spanglish,* while excluding any that also contain *movie.*
- "AND" is a default search term. "Spanglish AND 'language mixing'" is the same as "Spanglish 'language mixing.'"

Subject headings enable you to begin with a broad topic and drill down to increasingly more specific subtopics. Using subject headings can

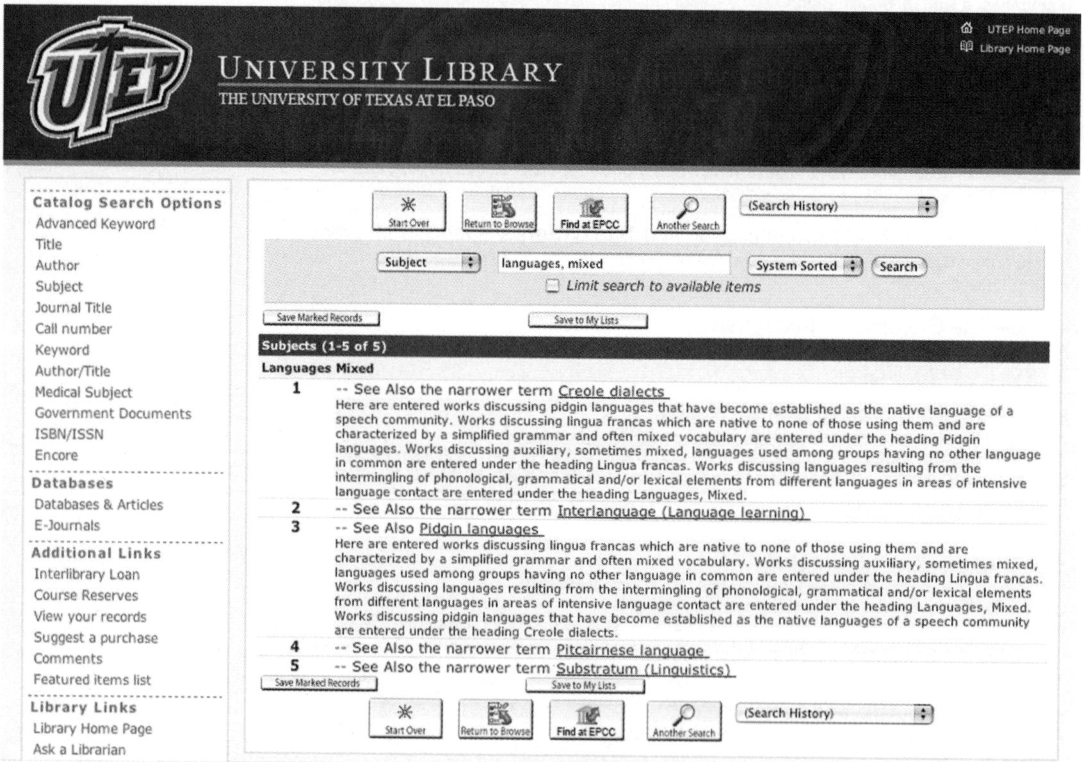

**FIGURE 19.2** Library of Congress subject heading search

lead to a more thorough search, though initially it can be more time consuming. Subject headings are particularly helpful in library searches, as most libraries use the Library of Congress (LOC) classification system, which produces a list of subject headings under which library holdings are classified. Many libraries have the LOC subject headings available in print, and they are available online. A similar concept is applied by Internet directories, such as the Yahoo! or Google Directories.

The Library of Congress subject heading "language" leads to the term "languages, mixed," a narrower and therefore more useful approach for the topic of Spanglish.

## Library Catalog

A library catalog is a systematically arranged record of the items in the library: books, journals, multimedia, and so on. Before computers, the library catalog consisted of cabinets of alphabetized cards, but now you can usually find the catalog on a link on the library's home page. The catalog can be searched using author, title, key words, or subject headings.

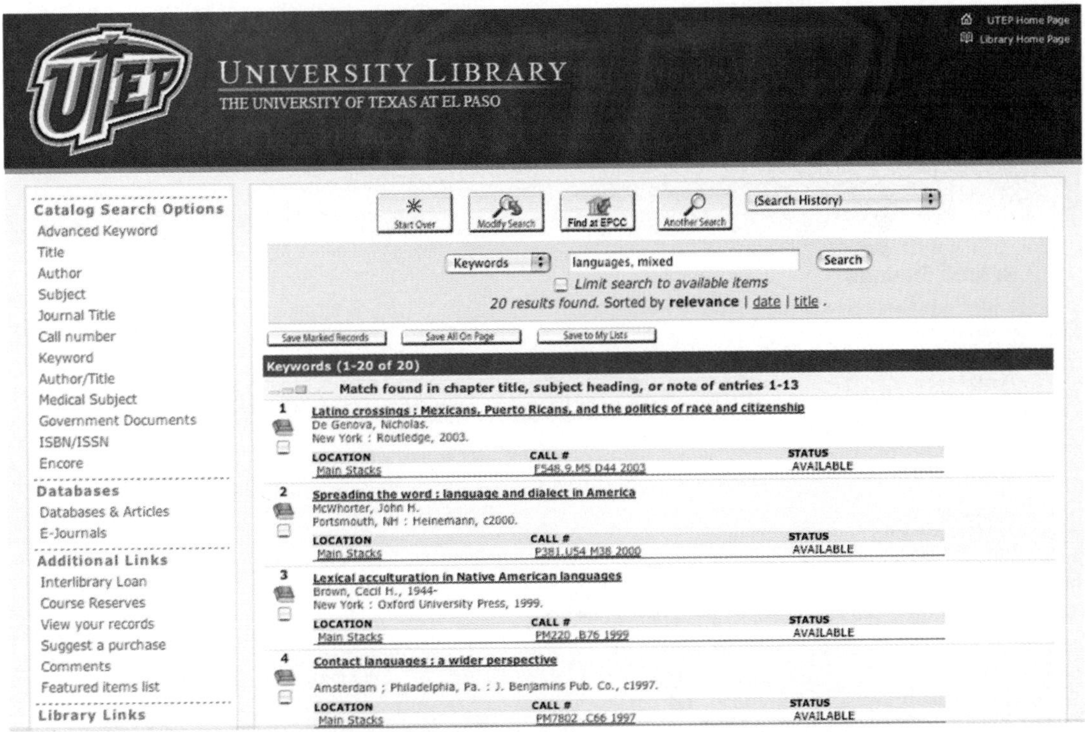

FIGURE 19.3 The search results from the library catalogue of a major university on the term "mixed languages"

# Research Databases

A research database is an electronic index that lists the publication information for items in magazines, newspapers, scholarly journals, and other materials. Many databases feature abstracts, which are short summaries of an article's content that help you determine if this content is relevant enough for you to seek out and read the article. While some databases provide just the information you need to locate a particular article, most also provide you with a copy of the article itself.

Most databases can be searched by the author, title, or publisher of a source, or according to a key word or subject heading search. Typically, you can limit your search according to date, type of source, language of source, and so on. You can also limit your search to peer-reviewed articles, which are scholarly articles that have been reviewed by experts in the field, ensuring high quality. While some databases are multidisciplinary, many of them focus on particular fields such as business, engineering, or history.

You can access databases online through your college library, typically through a link on the library home page.

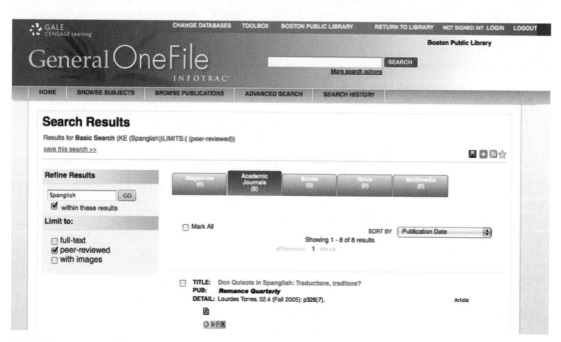

**FIGURE 19.4** Search results on the term "Spanglish," limited to peer-reviewed sources in the GeneralOneFile database

## Library Research Checklist

- [ ] For the best research results, use libraries rather than the Internet.
- [ ] Search for particular library sources by using key words and subject headings.
- [ ] Use library catalogs to find library holdings.
- [ ] Examine library databases to locate information in magazines, newspapers, scholarly journals, and other materials.
- [ ] Rely on peer-reviewed scholarly journals for the most expert information.

**Activity 19.3**   Select a particular language or dialect you're interested in and conduct a database search for articles on that topic. Consider using both multidisciplinary databases as well as databases that focus on aspects of language behavior. Search several times, each time limiting your search in a different way, such as by language, year, or whether or not the articles are peer-reviewed.

**Develop Your Understanding**

# The Internet

The Internet is an international system of interconnected computer networks—essentially, a network of networks—used by billions of people. Unlike a library, the information on the Internet hasn't been sifted through for quality or topic—it simply is out there. You sort through the Internet yourself according to the type of search engine that you use and the key words that you enter into it.

As Figure 19.5 shows, the Internet can lead and mislead you at the same time. First of all, "Spanglish" gets some 9,080,000 hits—far too many to sort through. If you look at the first listing here, you see that it refers to the 2004 movie *Spanglish,* which is not a relevant site for studying mixed languages. In fact, several of the sites in these search results do not appear to meet the criteria for being relevant, authoritative, accurate, objective, and current. The fifth site, however, is for a program on National Public Radio titled "Spanglish: A New American Language"; this site might be worth examining because it is a news story by a respected source.

Without a doubt, the Internet contains valuable information. However, when researching online, you have to take the time to do a focused key word search, sift through a variety of sources, and evaluate those sources carefully.

> *Doing research on the Web is like using a library assembled piecemeal by pack rats and vandalized nightly.*
>
> —Roger Ebert

Web Images Videos Maps News Shopping Gmail more ▼

# Google

Spanglish                                                                X   Search

About 9,080,000 results (0.36 seconds)                              Advanced search

**Everything**

📷 Images

🎬 Videos

📰 News

📚 Books

▼ More

**Chapel Hill, NC**
▼ Change location

**Any time**
Latest
Past 24 hours
▼ More search tools

Something different
ebonics
patois
broken english
franglais
50 first dates

▶ **Spanglish (2004) - IMDb** ☆
★★★★★ Rating: 6.7/10 - from 30,917 users
Directed by James L. Brooks. Starring Adam Sandler, Téa Leoni, Paz Vega. A woman and her
daughter emigrate from Mexico for a better life in America, where they start working for a
family where the patriarch is a ...
Full cast and crew - Plot Summary - Synopsis - Memorable quotes
www.imdb.com/title/tt0371246/ - Cached - Similar

**Spanglish - Wikipedia, the free encyclopedia** ☆
**Spanglish** refers to the code-switching of English and Spanish, in the speech of people who
speak parts of two languages, or whose normal language is ...
en.wikipedia.org/wiki/**Spanglish** - Cached - Similar

   **Spanglish (film) - Wikipedia, the free encyclopedia** ☆
   **Spanglish** is a 2004 American comedy-drama film written and directed by James L. Brooks,
   and starring Adam Sandler, Paz Vega, and Téa Leoni. ...
   Plot - Cast - Critical reception - Box office
   en.wikipedia.org/wiki/**Spanglish**_(film) - Cached - Similar

**Spanglish - Official Site** ☆
**Spanglish** - John Clasky (Adam Sandler) is a devoted dad whose skills as a chef have
afforded his family (T a Leoni, Cloris Leachman) a very upscale life, ...
www.sonypictures.com/homevideo/**spanglish**/ - Cached - Similar

**Spanglish, A New American Language ; NPR** ☆
Sep 23, 2003 ... A sign in Springfield, Mass. warns young Latinos: "No Hangear" -- don't hang
out on this corner. **Spanglish** -- a cross between Spanish and ...
www.npr.org/templates/story/story.php?storyId... - Similar - Add to iGoogle

**Spanglish: The Making of a New American Language - Google Books Result**
Ilan Stavans - 2004 - Foreign Language Study - 274 pages
An innovative resource, the first of its kind, documents the history and development of this
hybrid of Spanish and English in American cities; delves into its ...
books.google.com/books?isbn=0060087765...

**FIGURE 19.5** The first page of an Internet search in Google for "Spanglish," whose search results
include some 9,080,000 hits

## Online Periodicals and Newspapers

Most print magazines and newspapers have websites with content that
is free or available for a small fee. Often more people read the online version of the periodical than read the print version, and the online versions have the advantages of being frequently updated and easily
searched. Some periodicals, such as *Slate.com* and *Salon.com,* appear
only online. You need to carefully evaluate online periodicals as you do
other sources: examine the credentials of the authors, the affiliations of
the publishers, the amount of bias, and the sources for the published
information.

# Blogs

Blogs became popular in the late 1990s when individuals began to keep online diaries of their lives. In fact, the word *blog* is a contraction of "web log." Blogs typically contain writings, images, videos, links to other sites, and commentary by online readers. Most blogs are highly individualistic and personal, which makes them too unreliable to be used as serious sources. There are exceptions, however. Organizations such as the American Psychological Association and the National Council of Teachers of English publish blogs in which experts debate issues in the field. As with all sources, examine the credentials and credibility of blog writers.

# Wikis and Wikipedia

A wiki is a collaborative website of interlinked web pages that can be edited by more than one person. Most wikis are accessible only to a particular group of people. Businesses set up wikis for employees to post memos, reports, and other documents that multiple people can rewrite for everyone to see. Instructors create course wikis for class projects in which students exchange information and post documents to be revised.

The best known wiki is *Wikipedia*, an online encyclopedia launched in 2001 on which anyone can post and edit articles. In 2009, it had over 85,000 contributors who posted or edited more than 14 million articles in 260 different languages. Unlike other encyclopedias, there are no paid, credentialed editors hired to write entries, and as a result entries can contain omissions and faulty information. On the other hand, many entries are being constantly improved by volunteers, and readers can access discussions of the reliability of entries. If an entry lacks source information, it is usually flagged.

Like other encyclopedias, *Wikipedia* can be a useful way to begin researching your topic, but you should avoid directly referencing it in your writing. *Wikipedia* articles are best used for preliminary research or for gaining basic background knowledge. Rather that cite *Wikipedia* directly, go to the sources listed in the entries to access information written by more expert authors. If you see an inadequate entry in *Wikipedia*—such as this one on Spanglish—don't be afraid to use the knowledge you have about the topic to improve it yourself.

Most college English teachers discourage citing *Wikipedia* articles because of the ease with which entries can be made and revised. Check with your instructor if you have a question about using a *Wikipedia* entry.

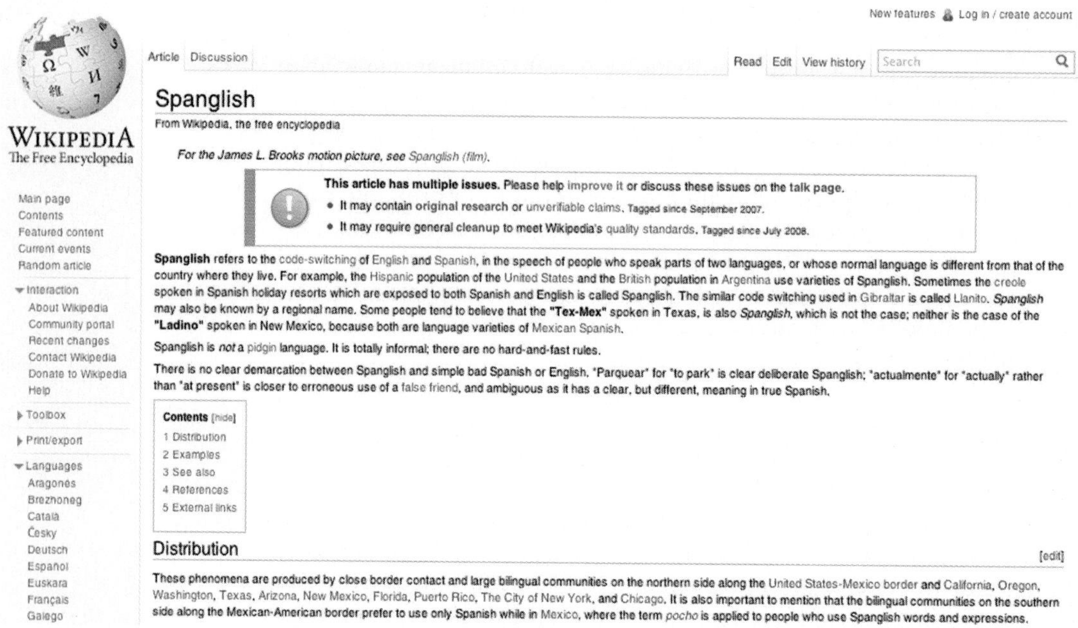

New features Log in / create account

Article Discussion Read Edit View history Search

WIKIPEDIA
The Free Encyclopedia

Main page
Contents
Featured content
Current events
Random article
Interaction
About Wikipedia
Community portal
Recent changes
Contact Wikipedia
Donate to Wikipedia
Help
Toolbox
Print/export
Languages
Aragonés
Brezhoneg
Català
Česky
Deutsch
Español
Euskara
Français
Galego

Spanglish

From Wikipedia, the free encyclopedia

*For the James L. Brooks motion picture, see Spanglish (film).*

**This article has multiple issues.** Please help improve it or discuss these issues on the talk page.

- It may contain original research or unverifiable claims. Tagged since September 2007.
- It may require general cleanup to meet Wikipedia's quality standards. Tagged since July 2008.

**Spanglish** refers to the code-switching of English and Spanish, in the speech of people who speak parts of two languages, or whose normal language is different from that of the country where they live. For example, the Hispanic population of the United States and the British population in Argentina use varieties of Spanglish. Sometimes the creole spoken in Spanish holiday resorts which are exposed to both Spanish and English is called Spanglish. The similar code switching used in Gibraltar is called Llanito. *Spanglish* may also be known by a regional name. Some people tend to believe that the **"Tex-Mex"** spoken in Texas, is also *Spanglish*, which is not the case; neither is the case of the **"Ladino"** spoken in New Mexico, because both are language varieties of Mexican Spanish.

Spanglish is *not* a pidgin language. It is totally informal; there are no hard-and-fast rules.

There is no clear demarcation between Spanglish and simple bad Spanish or English. "Parquear" for "to park" is clear deliberate Spanglish; "actualmente" for "actually" rather than "at present" is closer to erroneous use of a false friend, and ambiguous as it has a clear, but different, meaning in true Spanish.

**Contents** [hide]

1 Distribution
2 Examples
3 See also
4 References
5 External links

Distribution [edit]

These phenomena are produced by close border contact and large bilingual communities on the northern side along the United States-Mexico border and California, Oregon, Washington, Texas, Arizona, New Mexico, Florida, Puerto Rico, The City of New York, and Chicago. It is also important to mention that the bilingual communities on the southern side along the Mexican-American border prefer to use only Spanish while in Mexico, where the term *pocho* is applied to people who use Spanglish words and expressions.

**FIGURE 19.6** The entry for "Spanglish" in *Wikipedia*, which has been flagged as having "multiple issues" (note that readers are encouraged to talk about these issues and improve the article)

## Internet Research Checklist

- ☐ Internet research can be more time-consuming than library research.
- ☐ Use key words to sift through multiple Internet sites. Use Google Scholar or other specialized search engines to help narrow your search and locate information more appropriate to college papers.
- ☐ Evaluate Internet sources carefully for authority, accuracy, reliability and currency.
- ☐ Distinguish between print periodicals that have online versions and true online periodicals.
- ☐ Avoid using personal blogs as sources unless written by people with particular credentials and expertise.
- ☐ Go to *Wikipedia* only at the beginning of your research for an overview of your topic.

# USING SOURCES IN YOUR WRITING

By using sources in your writing, you demonstrate that you are knowledgeable about the topic and are aware of current controversies and issues. Be careful, however, not to let your outside sources take over your text; it is important to speak in your own voice. Most important, avoid the cut-and-paste method of writing in which you simply add information without weaving it into your own words. Aside from the obvious danger of this practice inviting plagiarism, it also robs you of your own voice. Instead, paraphrase, summarize, or quote the relevant information and then explain the significance of the information and show in your own voice how it connects with your own ideas.

Quotations, paraphrases, or summaries from the work of others cannot stand alone. All outside sources must be set up with a signal phrase and an explanation of the importance of the information to your own larger point.

The first of these steps—the signal phrase—connects your text to that of the source you want to incorporate. It establishes a context for the ideas you find important in the passage you're citing. Secondly, it gives you an opportunity to indicate the name of the author of the source you're using. In the following examples, the signal phrase "David Crystal argues" signals to the reader that information from a source will appear and that it will try to persuade us of a certain interpretation.

### Beginning

David Crystal argues that "varieties of English are now found everywhere, with colorful nicknames attached—Franglais, Tex-Mex, Chinglish, Japlish, Singlish, Spanglish" (165).

### End

"Varieties of English are now found everywhere, with colorful nicknames attached—Franglais, Tex-Mex, Chinglish, Japlish, Singlish, Spanglish," argues David Crystal (165).

### Middle

"Varieties of English are now found everywhere," argues David Crystal, "with colorful nicknames attached—Franglais, Tex-Mex, Chinglish, Japlish, Singlish, Spanglish" (165).

In the following example, the author's name is not included, but the signal phrase still indicates that information from a source is coming and goes a step further by interpreting the quote ("Spanglish is hardly unique").

> Some linguists argue that Spanglish is hardly unique in that "varieties of English are now found everywhere, with colorful nicknames attached—Franglais, Tex-Mex, Chinglish, Japlish, Singlish, Spanglish" (Crystal 165).

When integrating sources into your writing, it is also important to explain the relationship between your source and your purpose. Sources can be used for many ways. They are often used to provide background for a topic or to summarize prior research on a topic. For example, you could trace the evolution of other languages to provide background for your claim that Spanglish is becoming a language. You may also use sources to provide examples or evidence for your argument. For example, you could draw on examples of widely used Spanglish phrases to support your claim that the usage of Spanglish is becoming more uniform as it expands. Finally, you can take issue with the claims made by a source, making your argument a conversation that refutes what the source is saying. For example, if one of your sources claims that Spanglish is a type of slang, you could incorporate this idea and then counterargue point by point, making concessions when necessary.

In a college essay, you should always incorporate sources to achieve a particular purpose in your paper, not just for the sake of including them. In the example below, a signal phrase prepares you for the quotation, which is immediately explained and connected to the writer's purpose.

> When David Crystal states that "varieties of English are now found everywhere, with colorful nicknames attached—Franglais, Tex-Mex, Chinglish, Japlish, Singlish, Spanglish" (165), he implies that mixed dialects are simply a symptom of our nascently global world; however, the references to both "Tex-Mex" and "Spanglish" (near synonyms) reveals the prominence of Spanglish as an emerging language.

## Quoting

When using the exact words of the original source, you need to place quotation marks around any exact words or phrases that you borrow from your source. Remember to quote outside sources sparingly. You should only quote to emphasize important points or include an idea that your source has expressed in a particularly memorable way. Unless the quotation says something important and says it really well, you should paraphrase or summarize the passage, instead of using a direct quote.

You may prefer to use the author's name in the running text. In this case, MLA style asks you to give only the page number following an exact quotation:

> Jaime Mejia has noted that "rhetorical situations and strategies often include a tactical mixture of both English and Spanish" (52).

Alternatively, you can include both the author's name and the page reference in the in-text citation:

> Scholars note that "rhetorical situations and strategies often include a tactical mixture of both English and Spanish" (Mejia 52).

Often, you may want to only quote a short phrase from your source.

> Jaime Mejia points out that Spanglish speakers often utilize a "tactical mixture" of the two languages as a rhetorical strategy (52).

On the other hand, you may want to quote a longer section of a source. If your desired quotation exceeds four typed lines, you should format it as a block quotation. Format a block quote by beginning on a new line; indent the entire passage and include the citation at the end *after* the final punctuation mark. You should not use quotation marks with block quotations.

> In 1968, in response to a critical letter to the editor to her article in *New York Magazine,* Micho Fernandez responds:

> > Research in Spanglish is very difficult because few studies have been made of it and because the language is dynamic. Spanglish is Spanish, and so in my opinion, words like *estuja,* which are archaic, have been dug out by Spanish New Yorkers because of the phonetic resemblance to English, though I have found it to be a dead term. Many old Spanish words have been brought back to life and given new meanings. (6)

> Already in 1968, scholars were calling for the further study of Spanglish as an emerging language. Interestingly, Fernandez points to a connection between archaic terms and the emerging language of Spanglish. This is often a route of development for creole languages.

When using quotations, you must include the source's wording and punctuation exactly as it appears in the original.

### Formatting Quotations

| Quotation Within a Quotation | *Use single quotes to indicate the inner quotation.* Alluding to Shakespeare, Smith notes, "The situation was dire but 'All is well that ends well'" (15). |
|---|---|
| Adding Information to a Quotation | *Include necessary additional information in brackets.* "I have found it [*estuja*] to be a dead term" (Fernandez 6). |
| Omitting Information from a Quotation | *Use ellipses (. . .) to indicate an omission. If your omission begins at the end of a sentence, include the period and the ellipses.* "Research in Spanglish is very difficult . . . because the language is dynamic" (Fernandez 6). "Research in Spanglish is very difficult because few studies have been made of it and because the language is dynamic . . . . Many old Spanish words have been brought back to life and given new meanings" (Fernandez 6). |
| Error in the Original | *Repeat the error and include "[sic]" immediately after it to indicate that the error is in the original—not yours.* "Translation is a skill the difficulty of which cannot be underestimeted [sic]; as even the most diligent and unbiased translators are forced to put their own imprint on the original's meaning at some point in the translation process" (Flanagan 180). |

Remember to always use quotations for a purpose, and to introduce them with signal phrases (see page 543).

## Paraphrasing

To paraphrase means to put the author's language into your own words. By paraphrasing you can include another scholar's ideas using your own style; often, paraphrasing works more smoothly than quoting because the sentences containing your ideas and those containing your source's ideas flow better together, having been written in the same style. When you paraphrase, your task is to rewrite the passage by changing the sentence structure and order of ideas. In addition, you want to find synonyms (other words meaning about the same thing) for the author's words. A paraphrase captures the sense and meaning of an author's ideas, but without using his or her exact words.

Because paraphrasing is an art, it is a good idea to get some practice. Below is the original source with an ineffective and then an effective paraphrase. The highlighted words indicate that the paraphrase is too close to the original and could therefore be seen as plagiarism.

*Original Source:* The language policies of higher education are affecting more students in U.S. colleges and universities than ever before.

[Smith, Anna. *Language Policy in Higher Education*. San Francisco: Highlights, 2003.]

*Ineffective Paraphrase:* The language policies of U.S. universities and colleges affect more students than ever before (Smith 89).

This paraphrase is inadequate because it maintains the basic sentence structure of the original source; also it copies several distinctive phrases (for example, "than ever before"). Below, two effective paraphrases express the idea of the original with proper MLA citation, but do so in their own voice.

*Effective Paraphrase:* An increased number of U.S. college students are impacted by their school's language policies (Smith 89).

*Effective Paraphrase:* Smith has noted that an increased number of U.S. college students are impacted by their school's language policies (89).

This next paraphrase is ineffective because it maintains the basic sentence structure of the original source. A student who submitted this paraphrase would risk being accused of plagiarism because it copies several distinctive phrases so closely. Furthermore, this paraphrase is incorrectly cited by chapter number instead of page number (see Chapter 20 for more on proper citation).

*Original Source:* The teacher needs to be aware that in using television for language learning, s/he is hijacking the medium with which today's learners are probably the most familiar. This has its advantages and disadvantages.

[Mishan, Freda. *Designing Authenticity into Language Learning Materials.* Intellect Ltd., 2004.]

*Ineffective Paraphrase:* The teacher should be aware that in using television for language learning, she is kidnapping the medium with which today's learners are usually the most familiar. This has advantages and disadvantages (Mishan Ch. 6.1).

Both of the following examples use correct parenthetical citation conventions to indicate the source. (For more information about parenthetical citations, see Chapter 20.)

*Effective Paraphrase:* When teachers use programs on television to aid students in learning a language, they take the risk of using the most familiar medium to students. This has an upside but it also has a downside (Mishan 132).

## LANGUAGES and CULTURES

If you read languages other than English, you may wish to cite sources written in that language. As a courtesy to your readers—especially if they do not read the other language—you should translate any quoted text from its original language into English. Note in the body of your paper that you are the translator. When translating a passage, perform the following steps:

- Read it several times to make sure you understand it well.
- Do a draft translation in which you convey the meaning of the text as closely as possible.
- Consider carefully the various meanings of words in order to use the best one.
- Revise and edit your translation to ensure that it is understandable to readers.

*Effective Paraphrase:* Teachers who choose to use television as an aid to students learning a language should be aware that the medium is very familiar to their students, which means the technique has both benefits and costs (Mishan 132).

## Summarizing

A summary is a shortened version of a text that contains the text's most important ideas. The length of a summary varies according to your audience and purpose; it can be as short as a couple of sentences or as long as several paragraphs. Typically, when you write a summary, you don't give your opinion of the ideas in the text or evaluate the text itself.

When summarizing, follow these guidelines:

- Be sure that you thoroughly understand the original text.
- Focus on the main ideas in the text by examining the thesis, the topic sentences of paragraphs, and the conclusion.
- Briefly recreate the main ideas in the passage and cite the source material.
- Use quotations sparingly, if at all.
- Introduce the summary in your first sentence by giving the title and author.

Below is an example of an effective summary.

**Original Source:**

The thing is I don't think people thought of it as plagiarism, though. Educational systems were not set up for individual thought or any open expression. Students were not encouraged to speak up, especially if the opinions differed from the teachers. This was my impression in comparison to my college experience in U.S. I am thinking Indian students accustomed to growing up with that culture may have a different outlook on that.

Kumar, Jennifer. "Price of Plagiarism." *Study Abroad Chronicle.* 22 Dec. 2007. Web. 26 May 2010.

**Effective Summary:**

In her blog "The Price of Plagiarism," Jennifer Kumar says that cultural practices vary widely. When she was a student abroad in India, she learned that individual contributions from students were frowned upon in a culture where an authority person was shown respect by being quoted almost word for word.

## Incorporating Sources Checklist

- ☐ Use outside sources to support and develop your ideas.
- ☐ Incorporate your sources; avoid simply "cutting and pasting" material into your writing.
- ☐ Don't let the outside sources take over your writing; readers expect to see your ideas written in your own voice.
- ☐ Use quotations only to emphasize important points or convey an idea expressed in a memorable way.
- ☐ Paraphrase your source material by thoroughly putting the material into your own words.
- ☐ Indicate the author and page number (if available) in quoted, paraphrased, and summarized material.
- ☐ Aim for as exact a translation as possible.
- ☐ Summarize material by writing a shortened version of a text containing the main ideas.

# WRITING ASSIGNMENT

In 2005 the Public Broadcasting Service (PBS) aired "Do You Speak American?" This series highlighted the variety of languages spoken in the United States. Access the website of this show at www.pbs.org/speak and read several of the articles. Select one of the articles to summarize in a paragraph, being sure to paraphrase and cite the original text. Share your summary with other students in your class.

mycomplab

For support in meeting this chapter's objectives, follow this path in MyCompLab: Resources ⇒ Research ⇒ The Research Assignment ⇒ Finding Source and Evaluating Sources. Review the Instruction and Multimedia resources about finding sources, using the library, and evaluating sources, then complete the Exercises and click on Gradebook to measure your progress.

# 20 Documentation Styles

**Learning Objectives**

In this chapter you will:

- Learn the importance of documenting sources.
- Study the MLA and APA documentation styles.

University Child D

- Campus-base
- Stimulates s
  emotional, i
  and physica
- Provides un
  students ex
  observing y
  in classroo
  settings

*Two of the most common documentation styles are MLA and APA.*

When you conduct research in the United States, cite your sources using a documentation style appropriate for your academic discipline. Documentation styles are standardized formats for citing sources, which you use to tell your readers where you found the information that you gathered through research. In this chapter you'll study the documentation styles of the Modern Language Association (MLA), used in the humanities, and the American Psychological Association (APA), used in the social sciences and education. These are two of the most common documentation styles in U.S. higher education.

## OVERVIEW OF DOCUMENTATION STYLES

Writers document their sources in order to follow the conventions of their academic discipline and to avoid plagiarism. If you complete an assignment for a course or in the workplace and fail to cite your sources, your credibility will be damaged (at the very least) and you may even be suspended, expelled, or fired. Another reason for documenting your sources is so that your readers can locate the sources for their own interest and learning. Unless you are keeping a personal journal, you're writing for others. When you produce a text in a classroom, an organization, or a workplace, you're part of a community of readers who will respond to your writing either directly or indirectly. Information about your sources— where a particularly striking quote came from, the name of a magazine which published an interesting article—helps your readers to expand their own knowledge. Rules for documentation, such as the correct information to include on your works cited or references page at the end of the paper, ensure that you provide sufficient data for your readers to find and read your sources. Formatting guidelines help writers indicate the discipline or area of study of the paper. They also help writers provide information in a standardized way, both in giving proper credit to sources in the body of the paper and documenting sources at the end of the paper.

## MLA DOCUMENTATION

The documentation system of the Modern Language Association (MLA) is a two-part system that requires you to indicate the sources of your researched material in the text of the paper (called *in-text citations*), in addition to listing them at the end (called a *Works Cited page*). In-text citations connect the information you cite in the body of the text with the works cited list of sources at the end.

# In-Text Citations

Also called parenthetical citations, in-text citations in MLA style begin with the last name of the author of the source and then give the number of the page where the information appeared. No punctuation or other identifier is used. In general, you should place the in-text citation as close to the information, quotation, paraphrase, or summary of the source as you can without being obtrusive; usually this means at the end of the sentence or at a natural pause in the sentence.

> Among the world's children, "around two-thirds grow up in bilingual settings" (Crystal 17).

Alternatively, you can make in-text citations more concise and less obtrusive by working them into the running text of the essay. Use the author's name in the sentence and cite the page number:

> Crystal notes that among the world's children, "around two-thirds grow up in bilingual settings" (17).

The last name of the author also begins the works cited entries at the end of the paper, thus connecting the in-text citations with the list of works cited.

> Crystal, David. *English as a Global Language.* 2nd ed. New York: Cambridge UP, 2003. Print.

Thus, to learn more about children who grow up in bilingual settings, a reader can get the book and find the specific page where this information is given.

If your source has two or three authors, include all authors' last names, separated by commas using *and* before the final last name. If your source has four or more authors, either include all author last names in the citation, or the first author's last name followed by *et al.* in the citation.

> It is becoming more difficult for schools to recruit teachers for ESL and bilingual classrooms (Rock, Gregg, Gable, and Zigmond 36).

> Throughout the United States, "school district personnel are struggling to attract and retain high-quality teachers who can meet the unique academic and behavioral needs of an increasingly diverse student population" (Rock et al. 36).

When citing a text with no author, a shortened version of the title should appear in parentheses.

> Bilingual education has been eliminated in several states ("Bilingual" 12).

If you include two or more texts by the same author, include the first meaningful word in the source's title to help readers distinguish which work you are talking about. Remember to italicize book titles and place article titles in quotation marks.

> Among the world's children, "around two-thirds grow up in bilingual settings" (Crystal, *English* 37).

> According to research, "a slip of the tongue is really a slip of the phonological part of the brain" (Crystal, *How* 98).

## Formats for Other In-Text Citation Needs

| | |
|---|---|
| **Corporate Author** | Abbreviate long organizational names if they are easily recognizable.<br>*(United Nations 34)* or *(UN 34)* |
| **Indirect Source** | Try to include the original author in your text.<br>*Smith says that bilingual education needs are growing (qtd. in Arroyo 314).* |
| **Authors with the Same Last Name** | Use the first initial to distinguish between authors.<br>*(D. Jenkins 87)*<br>*(E. Jenkins 64)* |
| **Multiple Sources in a Single Citation** | Separate sources with a semicolon.<br>*Differences in the ways people speak, especially differences in the ways men and women use language, can often be traced to who has power and who does not (Tannen 83–86; Tavris 297–301).* |
| **Literary Work** | Include information that will help readers find your source in any edition of the text.<br>*In Shakespeare's* Macbeth, *the witches end the opening scene of the play with: "Fair is foul, and foul is fair" (1.1).* |
| **Email, Personal Interview, or Personal Communication** | Direct readers to the information in your Works Cited list by including the author's last name in parentheses.<br>*Spanglish usage is frowned upon in the state university system (Chaves).* |

Be sure to include in-text citations for all specific information, quotations, paraphrases, and summaries that you include in your paper—in short, all information that you take from a source should have an in-text citation. These in-text citations should be carefully woven into your own sentences. For more information, see Chapter 19.

## The Works Cited List

The list of works cited appears at the end of the paper, on a new page that continues the pagination from the rest of the paper; if the last page of the paper is page seven, the Works Cited page begins on page eight. The Works Cited page should have 1-inch margins and a header with your last name and the page number placed just like on all the other pages of your paper. The title of the page (Works Cited) should be centered. The first line of each entry should not be indented, but all subsequent lines should be indented by five spaces (known as a *hanging indent*). Double-space all text on your Works Cited page.

Although the example citations that follow are separated by type of source, the entries on your Works Cited page should appear in alphabetical order, beginning with the last name of the author.

If a work has more than one author, the second and subsequent authors' names are not reversed:

Roberge, Mark, Meryl Siegal, and Linda Harklau.

When citing more than one work by the same author, give the name in the first entry only. In subsequent entries, type three hyphens, followed by a period and the title of the work.

Crystal, David. *English as a Global Language.* 2nd ed. New York: Cambridge UP, 2003. Print.

—. *How Language Works.* New York: Overlook, 2005. Print.

When citing a work whose authors are not identified, list it alphabetically under the first word of the title of the work, excluding "the" or "a."

### Citing Books and Other Nonperiodical Print Sources

1. One author  557
2. Two or three authors  557
3. Four or more authors  557
4. Corporate or organization author  557
5. Author unknown  557
6. Edited collection or anthology  557
7. Translation  557
8. Second or later edition  557
9. Foreword, introduction, preface, or afterword  558
10. Unpublished dissertation or thesis (print)  558
11. Government document (print)  558
12. Pamphlet or brochure (print)  558

**Citing Books and Other Nonperiodical Print Sources.** The following information is given in the works cited listings for books:

- Author(s) name (last name first, other names written out in full), followed by a period.
- Title of the work *italicized*, followed by a period.
- Place of publication, followed by a colon.
- Publisher, followed by a comma.
- Date of publication, followed by a period.
- Medium (in this case, Print), followed by a period.

> Last Name, First Name. *Title.* Place of Publication: Publisher, Year of Publication. Medium of Publication.

**1. One author**

> Foer, Franklin. *How Soccer Explains the World: An Unlikely Theory of Globalization.* New York: HarperCollins, 2005. Print.

**2. Two or three authors**

> Ghuari, Pervez, and Sarah Powell. *Globalization.* London: DK Publishing, 2008. Print.

**3. Four or more authors**

> Buchholz, Elke, et al. *Art: A World History.* New York: Abrams, 2007. Print.

**4. Corporate or organization author**

> The World Bank. *Global Economic Prospects: Economic Implications of Remittances and Migrations.* Washington: World Bank, 2006. Print.

**5. Author unknown**

> *War: The Definitive Visual Guide.* London: DK Publishing, 2009. Print.

**6. Edited collection or anthology**

> Robbins, Richard H., ed. *Talking Points on Global Issues.* Boston: Allyn & Bacon, 2003. Print.

**7. Translation**

> Osterhammel, Jurgen, and Niels P. Petersson. *Globalization: A Short History.* Trans. Dona Geyer. Princeton: Princeton UP, 2009. Print.

**8. Second or later edition**

> Friedman, Thomas. *The World is Flat.* 3rd ed. New York: Picador, 2007. Print.

### 9. Foreword, introduction, preface, or afterword

Robbins, Bruce. Afterword. *World Bank Literature.* Ed. Amitava
Kumar. Minneapolis: U Minnesota P, 2002. Print.

### 10. Unpublished dissertation or thesis (print)

Pennell, Michael. "English in the 'Hurricane Winds of Change':
Labor Market Intermediaries in Two Indiana Counties."
Diss. Purdue U, 2005. Print.

### 11. Government document (print)

United States. House Committee on Armed Services. *National
Industrial Security Program: Addressing the Implications of
Globalization and Foreign Ownership for the Defense
Industrial Base.* Washington: GPO, 2009. Print.

### 12. Pamphlet or brochure (print)

*Teen Safety: Tips for Teens.* Oklahoma City: Oklahoma Dept. of
Labor, 2003. Print.

**Citing Print Periodicals.** The following information is given in the works cited
listings for print periodicals (newspapers, magazines, scholarly journals):

- Author(s) name (last name first, other names written out in full),
followed by a period.
- Title of the article (in quotation marks), followed by a period.
- Name of the periodical (italicized).
- Volume number and issue number (for a scholarly journal); use a pe-
riod to separate volume and issue, if both are available.
- Date of publication (for a scholarly journal, the year; for other periodi-
cals, the day, month, and year) in parentheses, followed by a colon.
- Page numbers of the article, followed by a period.
- Medium of publication (Print) , followed by a period.

Author. "Article Title." *Periodical Title.* Volume Number.
Issue Number (Date): Pages. Medium.

### 13. Journal with volume and issue numbers

Sadykova, Gulnara, and Jennie Dautermann. "Crossing
Cultures and Borders in International Online Distance
Higher Education." *Journal of Asynchronous Learning
Networks* 13.2 (2009): 89–114. Print.

### 14. Journal with issue number only

Lee, Christopher. "Enacting the Asian Canadian." *Journal of
Canadian Literature* 199 (2008): 28–44. Print.

**15. Magazine article**

Mudd, Philip. "Containing Terror." *Newsweek* 17 May 2010: 31. Print.

**16. Newspaper article**

Markoff, John. "Chinese Supercomputer Is Ranked World's Second-Fastest, Challenging U.S. Dominance." *New York Times* 31 May 2010: B3. Print.

**17. Review**

Jacobs, Barbara. Rev. of *Global Dreams: Imperial Corporations and the New World Order,* by Richard I. Barnet and John Cavanagh. *Booklist* 15 Jan. 1994: 880. Print.

**18. Editorial**

Herbert, Bob. "Our Epic Foolishness." Editorial. *New York Times* 1 Jun. 2010: A27. Print.

**19. Letter to the editor**

Wetherbe, Rebecca. Letter. *Time* 10 May 2010: 17. Print.

**Citing Online Sources.** The following information is given in the works cited listings for online sources:

- Author(s) (last name first, other names written out in full), followed by a period.
- Title of article or page, in quotation marks, followed by a period.
- Name of website in *italics*, followed by a period.
- Institution or organization producing/associated with the website.
- Date website was posted/revised.
- Medium (Web), followed by a period.
- Date of access (the date the writer conducted research on this website) in day/month (abbreviations are acceptable) and year, followed by a period.
- *Note:* In MLA style, it is no longer necessary to include a URL for online sources, *unless* the source cannot be easily located by typing the author and title into a search engine. If your source cannot be easily located, include the URL in angle brackets after the "Date of Access." Note as well that some professors may continue to require the URL.

Author. "Article/Page Title." *Website Title.* Publisher, Date Posted. Medium of Publication. Date of Access. <URL, if applicable>

## 20. Website, corporate, or organization author

Doctors Without Borders. "Donor Retreat Widens HIV/AIDS
  Treatment Gap in Africa." *Médecins Sans Frontières*.
  MSF-USA Association, 27 May 2010. Web. 2 Jun. 2010.

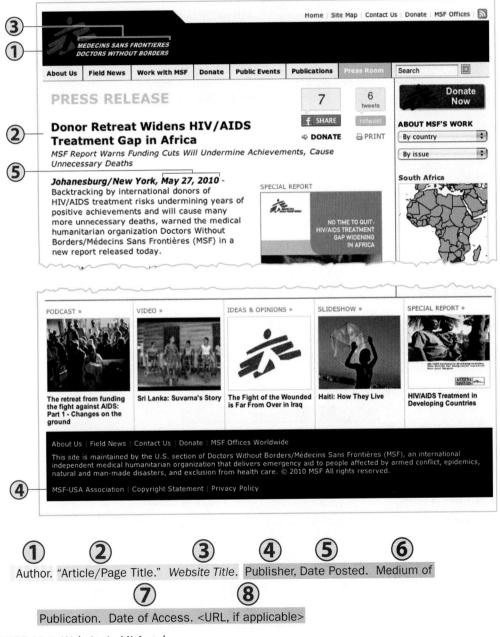

① Author. ② "Article/Page Title." ③ *Website Title*. ④ Publisher, ⑤ Date Posted. ⑥ Medium of
⑦ Publication. ⑧ Date of Access. <URL, if applicable>

**FIGURE 20.1**  Website in MLA style

### 21. Website, author unknown

"UK's First Water Desalination Plant Opens." *AFP*. Agence France-Presse, 2 Jun. 2010. Web. 2 Jun. 2010.

### 22. Article from an online periodical

Fonda, Daren. "Exporting: Selling in Tongues." *Time Magazine*. Time, 26 Nov. 2001. Web. 1 Jun. 2010.

### 23. Online book

Aesop. *The Aesop for Children*. Chicago: Rand McNally, 1919. Project Gutenberg, 2 Dec. 2006. Web. 2 June. 2010.

### 24. Article from an online journal

Cho, Hiromi, and Stephen Lacy. "International News Coverage in Local Japanese Newspapers." *The Web Journal of Mass Communication Research* 2.2 (Mar. 1999): n. pag. Web. 15 Aug. 2010.

### 25. Periodical article accessed through an online database

Fay, Jack R., Melvin L. Roush, and Sergey V. Shamenin. "Personal Income Tax Issues for International Students in the United States." *The CPA Journal* 80.3 (2010): 44+. *General OneFile*. Web. 3 Jun. 2010.

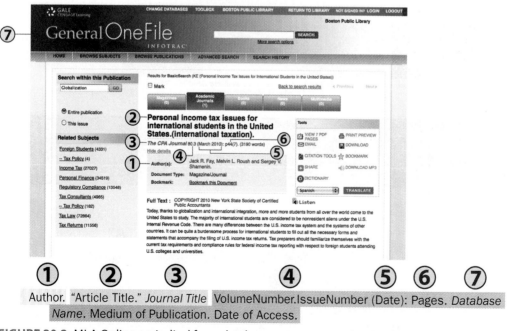

**FIGURE 20.2** MLA Online periodical from database

### 26. Blog posting

Gardner, Traci. "Grammar Myths for the ESL/ELL Classroom." *NCTE Inbox*. National Council of Teachers of English, 5 Mar. 2008. Web. 1 Jun. 2010.

### 27. Wiki entry

"Intercultural Communication." *Wikipedia*. Wikimedia Foundation, Inc., n.d. Web. 1 Jun. 2010.

### 28. YouTube or other video sharing

Pearson Education, prod. *Financial Times IPad Edition. YouTube.* YouTube, 17 May 2010. Web. 2 Jun. 2010.

### 29. Podcast

Kleffel, Ron. "The Art of Translation." Natl. Public Radio, 22 Nov. 2008. MP3.

**Citing Multimedia and Other Sources.** Include the following information for the works cited entries for multimedia sources:

- When discussing the contributions of a particular actor, director, musician, writer or so forth, begin the entry with that person's name (as is done for authors).
- Title of episode, segment, song, or scene (when relevant) in quotation marks, followed by a period.
- Title of program, series, album, artwork, or film in *italics*, followed by a period.
- Publication information, in this case the network call letters and city, broadcaster, or producer, followed by a comma.
- Broadcast or publication date, followed by a period.
- Medium (Television, Radio, CD or Audiotape, or Film).

Artist. "Title of Piece." *Larger Work Title.* Publisher, Date. Medium.

### 30. Film or video recording

*Wall Street: Money Never Sleeps*. Dir. Oliver Stone. Perf. Shia LaBoeuf, Michael Douglas, and Frank Langella. 20th Century Fox, 2010. Film.

**31. Television or radio program**

*Do You Speak American?* PBS. 5 Jan. 2010. Television.

**32. Song or audio recording**

Rihanna. "Disturbia." *Good Girl Gone Bad: Reloaded.* Def Jam, 2008. MP3.

**33. Commercial**

Target. Advertisement. ABC. 15 May 2010. Television.

**34. Advertisement (print)**

Papa John's Pizza. Advertisement. *People* 10 May 2009: 40. Print.

**35. Map**

*Arkansas.* Map. Comfort: Gousha, 1996. Print.

**36. Work of art**

O'Keefe, Georgia. *Sky above Clouds IV.* 1965. Oil on canvas. The Art Institute of Chicago, Illinois.

**37. Speech or lecture**

Kaplan, Robert, et al. "Understanding the Crisis in the Markets: A Panel of Harvard Experts." Harvard@Home. 25 Sept. 2008. Address.

**38. Personal interview**

Alee, David M., Architect. Telephone interview. 10 May 2010.

**39. Personal correspondence (letter or email)**

Jenkins, David. "New Policy for Use of 'Spanglish' in Written Assignments at AHS." Message to the author. 1 Jun. 2010. E-mail.

### One Student's MLA-Style Paper

Student Najwa Al-Tabaa wrote the following research paper for a literature course. Notice how she integrates the ideas and observations of other critics into her own argument, while using MLA style to correctly cite those sources both parenthetically and on a works cited page.

Najwa Al-Tabaa

May 13, 2009

English 5320

Dr. Jayasuriya

Speaking through Stories: Fairytale Monsters and
Their Stories

Both Salman Rushdie's *Shame* and Jean Rhys's *Wide Sargasso Sea* project fairytale-like stories as well as female protagonists (Sufiya Zinobia and Antoinette/Bertha Mason) who are imprisoned and silenced by their respective husbands. Ultimately, each character ends her story in a violent act. In considering Spivak's assertion that the subaltern female cannot speak, we must ask to what degree is violence for Sufiya Zinobia and Antoinette Cosway/Bertha Mason a move towards hegemony? By examining the parallels in the two women's lives, I will discuss how these characters are subaltern and question if they remain subaltern. Moreover, in considering Spivak's terms that the subaltern female cannot speak, I must also consider that perhaps one must re-interrogate the way "speak" is defined and mediated through the narrator(s) and ultimately reader(s) of these fictional texts and the ability of that form of speech to present agency to subaltern characters. Is it a true sense of agency since the character's speech is mediated through external speakers?

Since both Sufiya Zinobia and Antoinette Cosway/Bertha Mason are women in a privileged position their subalternity is perhaps not as "true." Spivak's example of a subaltern woman [Bhubaneswari Bhaduri] was also not a "true" subaltern. However, her gender as female, as with Sufiya Zinobia and Antoinette

1-inch margins at top,
bottom, and sides of
pages.

In-text citation for a
quote when the author
is not named in text.

Cosway/Bertha Mason, subscribes them to the role of the
subaltern: "both as object of colonialist historiography and as
subject of insurgency, the ideological construction of gender keeps
the male dominant. If, in the contest of colonial production, the
subaltern has no history and cannot speak, the subaltern as
female is even more deeply in shadow" (Spivak 804). The
ultimate removal from society of both Sufiya Zinobia and
Antoinette Cosway/Bertha Mason by dominating males in their
lives further emphasizes their subaltern status since they are not
only silenced, but also shadowed in the sense that their existence
and history are hidden from society.

Both Sufiya Zinobia and Antoinette Cosway/Bertha Mason are
imprisoned by their husbands (and father for Sufiya Zinobia),
chained in attics. The women are increasingly marginalized as they
can neither be "kill[ed] nor cure[d]" (Rushdie 250) which ultimately
results in establishing the sleeping beauty/beast paradigm. Since
her husband and father cannot bring themselves to kill Sufiya
Zinobia and there is no cure for her beast-like qualities, she is
locked and chained in the attic, and "twice in every twenty-four
hours, Omar Khayyam would go unobserved into that darkened
room . . . to administer the drugs that turned her from one fairytale into another, into sleeping-beauty instead of beauty-and-beast"
(Rushdie 250). Sufiya Zinobia's state of suspended animation
suggests that she is further doomed to straddle the fairytale
paradigm of sleeping beauty/beauty and beast; she is erased from
history and therefore cannot speak, as Spivak suggests.
Antoinette also succumbs to a similar disposition in that she also
is chained in the attic and begins to be described/envisioned by

Include a running head with your last name followed by the page number.

"Rochester" as transitioning from the similar sleeping beauty to beast paradigm. Albeit Rhys is not purposefully playing on the fairytale mythology as Rushdie does, however, she is rewriting a history that has similar fairytale-esque qualities. "Rochester" also struggles with the kill/cure conundrum that Raza Hyder and Omar Shakil struggle with, meaning that while "Rochester" sees/ assumes some inevitable state of sleeping beauty decay for Antoinette, as she becomes a madwoman, however, he is only able to metaphorically kill her rather than purposefully killing her: "Very soon she'll join the others who know the secret and will not tell it. Or cannot. Or try and fail because they do not know enough. . . . She's one of them. I too can wait—for the day when she is only a memory to be avoided, locked away, and like all memories a legend. Or a lie . . . " (Rhys 172). While "Rochester" cannot kill her in the literal sense (nor does he even attempt to cure her), he can formulate a conspiracy to do away with her history, her sense of self, and her agency, making her a subaltern despite her white Creole skin and higher social standing. His desire is to marginalize her so far that she becomes imaginary (a legend or a lie), suggesting the presence of a fairytale/myth aspect to Antoinette's story.

Through the loss or removal of their histories, both Sufiya Zinobia and Antoinette remain outside of culture, so far so that their connection to culture is mythologized by the dominating male presences. Justyna Deszcz discusses fairytales through the feminist lens and presents the concept that the discrepancy of the fairytale predicts that "Woman is doomed to remain outside culture, no matter whether she is perceived positive or negative. This in turn means she has no autonomy but can exist only as

In-text citation for a
source as quoted by
another source.

'male defined masks and costumes'" (qtd. in Gilbert and Gubar 19). For both characters, the male-defined masks and costumes are created by forcing them into the fairytale/mystified realm in which both the beauty/beast transformations and potentialities are locked away like all memories and encrypted in legends or lies. This display of male-dominating costuming of the female protagonists further infuses the struggle with existing as subalterns.

Another aspect of the road to subalternity that must be noted is the role of naming (and unnaming) in both novels. Where "Rochester" is quite purposefully and actively changes Antoinette's name to Bertha Mason, Omar Shakil recognizes that he should rename Sufiya Zinobia, but he cannot:

Block quotation
indented on the left.

> Can it be possible, he wondered, that human beings are capable of discovering their nobility in their savagery? Then he was angry with himself, remembering that she was no longer Sufiya Zinobia, that nothing was left in her which could be recognized as the daughter of Biliquis Hyder, that the Beast within had changed her for all time. 'I should stop calling her by her name,' he thought; but found that he could not. (Rushdie 270)

Omar Shakil's inability to rename his wife suggests that while he recognizes the role of male dominance as a tool for removing her agency, he cannot also help but recognize the humanity and the agency she gains through the legend she is accumulating. Nevertheless, one must also note the anger and desire he has to unname her as Sufiya Zinobia and rename her as the Beast he seems to recognize. In considering the case of Antoinette, however, "Rochester's" act of renaming her not only removes her

Al-Tabaa 5

agency, but eventually alienates her to the extent that she can no longer recognize her own history. "Rochester" imposes Antoinette's mother's name, identity, and madness on the daughter: "I hear him every night walking up and down the veranda. Up and down. When he passes my door he says, 'Goodnight, Bertha.' He never calls me Antoinette now. He has found out it was my mother's name" (Rhys 113). Antoinette's protests to the name change "Rochester" has given her suggests a further permeated construction of the fairytale mythology and the male-dominating masks and costumes Gilbert and Gubar refer to. Antoinette not only recognizes that names matter, but that with naming comes identity: "Names matter, like when he wouldn't call me Antoinette, and I saw Antoinette, drifting out of the window with her scents, her pretty clothes and her looking-glass" (Rhys 180). Antoinette has been pushed so far among the margins that she has lost her ability to recognize herself (she's drifting out the window) and furthermore has lost the ability to identify meaning in herself—she has become erased from history and therefore erased from meaning which furthers the unrecognizable quality she later gains: "But the nameless are never recognized by those exercising the act of naming; pushed to the margins of the discursive community, they are given no space and, consequently, no meaning" (Kimmey 121). While Sufiya Zinobia seems to retain a sense of agency through not being unnamed, she still similarly suffers a sense of lost meaning because while Omar Shakil cannot unname her, he also perpetuates her Beast identity as an additional act of naming.

Both the narratives of Sufiya Zinobia and Antoinette Cosway inhabit the fairytale spaces, imprisoned in the dungeon-like attics. In addition to the spatial aspect of the fairytale they inhabit, there

Al-Tabaa 6

is also a sense of timelessness for both characters. The space then, that Sufiya Zinobia (and to an extent Antoinette as well) inhabits is one that is outside of every boundary. Sufiya Zinobia is capable of existing in multi-locales and ephemeral spaces: "When her [Sufiya Zinobia] clandestine existence takes over completely and she overtly ravages the countryside spreading fear and terror. . . . Sufiya Zinobia represents the abjection that disturbs the prevailing order at all levels of the novel and she does not respect borders, positions and rules" (Strandburg 149). Sufiya Zinobia's lack of place/space allows for her to generate power through this ability to mitigate space and place. Moreover, Antoinette, while localized to the confines of Thornfield Hall, eventually is able to mentally and metaphorically move beyond the physical space of the building, empowering her to manipulate that stereotype in order to ultimately set herself free. "Whereas stereotypes' claim to absolute knowledge usually aim to discourage one from any further inquiry about the stereotyped category, the question of who is speaking to whom in the novel reveals and unsettles the process by which the stereotypes become loci of control and power" (Mardorossian 1084). The beauty/beast stereotype as well as the madwoman stereotype enables both women to gain control and power of their locations. However, this power control is not without acts of violence.

In considering the role of violence for both female protagonists, one must question whether violence enables a sense of agency and permits a voice to the subaltern. Fanon suggests that "at the level of individuals, violence is a cleansing force. It frees the native from his inferiority complex and from his despair and inaction; it makes him fearless and restores his self-respect" (98). Where violence for Fanon seems to enable agency, Aijaz

Al-Tabaa 7

In-text citation for a
summary when the
author is named in the
text.

Ahmad, on the other hand, suggests that while violence may not be

cleansing, it may however be powerful (147). And in considering

the role of the fairytale, this power seems to be intrinsic in

embracing the stereotypes that create the beauty/beast dichotomy

as well as the enigma of the madwoman.

The final question to consider then is—can violence enable

the subaltern female to speak? Spivak would argue, no. While the

subaltern female does engage in an act of power, she is

necessarily silenced and therefore can only gain a voice through

others: "All speaking, even seemingly the most immediate, entails

a distance decipherment by another" (Spivak 808). While the

subaltern women (Sufiya and Antoinette) are able to engage in an

act of agency, their ultimate role as subalterns still holds because

the speaking comes not from themselves but through mediated

narrative made by others—the reader is told about Sufiya Zinobia's

legend through the narrator of Shame, and Antoinette/Bertha

Mason's fate is bound between the pages of another text, *Jane

Eyre*, which is not even her own story.

However, the interceptions that Spivak mentions enable an

agency of these subaltern women ultimately expanding the

narrative to create a sense of solidarity between actor, reader, and

narrator: "Solidarity comes . . . from the deep recognition of our

most expansive self-interest. From the recognition that, like it or

not, our liberation is bound up with that of every other being on the

planet" (Levins Morales 125). Through the act of storytelling and

interception, both Sufiya Zinobia and Antoinette regain agency,

enabling them to have a voice, albeit a mediated voice unavoidably

attached to fairytale, myth, legend, and lies, but nonetheless a

voice which recreates a space and place in their own narrative

stories, as well as a larger narrative history.

Al-Tabaa 8

Works Cited

Ahmad, Aijaz. "Salman Rushdie's Shame: Postmodern Migrancy
and the Representations of Women." *In Theory*. London:
Verso, 1992: 123–58. Print.

Deszcz, Justyna. "Salman Rushdie's Attempt at a Feminist Fairytale
Reconfiguration in *Shame*." *Folklore* 115 (2004): 27–44.
*JSTOR*. Web. 4 Apr. 2009.

Fanon, Franz. "Concerning Violence." *On Violence: A Reader*. Ed.
Bruce B. Lawrence and Aisha Karim. Durham: Duke UP,
2007: 78–100. Print.

Gilbert, Sandra M., and Susan Gubar, ed. *Feminist Literary Theory
and Criticism: A Norton Reader*. New York: Norton, 2007. Print.

Kimmey, Deborah A. "Women, Fire, and Dangerous Things:
Metatextuality and the Politics of Reading in Jean Rhys's *Wide
Sargasso Sea*." *Women's Studies* 34: 113–31. Print.

Levins Morales, Aurora. *Medicine Stories: History, Culture and the
Politics of Integrity*. Cambridge: South End Press, 1998. Print.

Mardorossian, Carine M. "Shutting Up the Subaltern: Silences,
Stereotypes, and Double-Entendre in Jean Rhys's *Wide Sargasso
Sea*." *Callaloo* 22.4 (1999): 1071–90. *JSTOR*. Web. 4 Apr. 2009.

Rhys, Jean. *Wide Sargasso Sea*. New York: W. W. Norton, 1966.
Print.

Rushdie, Salman. *Shame*. New York: Random House, 2008. Print.

Spivak, Gayatri Chakravorty. "From Chapter 3: History (Can the
Subaltern Speak?)." *A Critique of Postcolonial Reason: Toward
a History of the Vanishing Present*. Cambridge: Harvard UP,
1999: 799–809. Print.

Strandburg, Lotta. "Images of Gender and the Negotiation of
Agency in Salman Rushdie's *Shame*." *NORA-Nordic Journal of
Feminist and Gender Research* 12.3 (2004): 143–52. Print.

# APA DOCUMENTATION

The American Psychological Association (APA) style is used by writers working in the social sciences and education. Authors writing on topics in the social sciences consult the current *Publication Manual of the American Psychological Association* (6th edition). A detailed description of these guidelines is offered below. In APA style, the list of sources at the end of the text is called a *References* page. As with the MLA style, writers must identify the sources of their researched material in the text of the paper. Without these in-text citations, readers would have no way of connecting information cited in the body of the text with the references list of sources at the end of the paper.

## In-Text Citations

APA formatted in-text citations are often referred to as the author-date style of citing references. Use the last name of the author and the publication year of the original source, adding a comma between the name and the year. If the passage cited refers to specific information (such as a quotation, paraphrase, or summary), give the specific page number, preceded by *p.* or *pp.* The passage cited here is a direct quotation.

> "The teacher needs to be aware that in using television for language learning, s/he is hijacking the medium with which today's learners are probably the most familiar" (Mishan, 2005, p. 132).

The last name of the author will also begin the "References" entry at the end of the paper, thus connecting the in-text citation with the list of references.

> Mishan, F. (2005). *Designing Authenticity into Language Learning*. Portland, OR: Intellect Books.

Thus, to learn more about integrating popular media into language learning settings, a reader can find the book and locate the specific page where this information is given.

You can also integrate the author's name into your text to make your in-text citations brief and inconspicuous.

> Mishan (2005) notes that language learners are aware of the universal conventions of television (p. 132).

When citing texts by two authors, include both authors' names separated by an ampersand (&) for every citation. When citing texts by three to five authors, include all authors' names, separated by commas, using the ampersand (&) before the final author, for the first citation. In any later citations, use the first author's last name followed by *et al.* and the date. For six or more authors, use the last name of the first author followed by *et al.* for every citation.

### First Citation

It is becoming more difficult for schools to recruit teachers for ESL and bilingual classrooms (Rock, Gregg, Gable, & Zigmond, 2009, p. 36).

### Second Citation

Throughout the United States, "school district personnel are struggling to attract and retain high-quality teachers who can meet the unique academic and behavioral needs of an increasingly diverse student population" (Rock et al., 2009, p. 36).

When citing a text with no author, a shortened version of the title should appear in parentheses.

Popular websites make cross-cultural language study easily accessible ("Parlo," 2010).

## Formats for Other In-Text Citation Needs

| | |
|---|---|
| **Corporate Author** | Always include the full name of the organization in your first citation. You can abbreviate in subsequent citations, if you provide the abbreviation in brackets in the first citation.<br>First Citation: *(United Nations [UN], 2001, p. 34)*<br>Second Citation: *(UN, 2001, p. 307)* |
| **Indirect Source** | Try to include the original author in your text.<br>*Smith says that bilingual education needs are growing (as cited in Arroyo, 2010, p. 314).* |
| **Multiple Sources in a Single Citation** | Separate sources with a semicolon.<br>*Differences in the ways people speak, especially differences in the ways men and women use language, can often be traced to who has power and who does not (Tannen, 2007, pp. 83–86; Tavris, 2001, pp. 297–301).* |
| **Email, Personal Interview, or Personal Communication** | References to personal communication go in your main text only and should not be included in the list of references at the end of the paper.<br>*Study abroad is appropriate for younger students (Robbins, personal communication, May 15, 2010).*<br>OR<br>*Robyn Robbins also suggested that study abroad was appropriate for younger students (personal communication, May 15, 2010).* |

Be sure to include in-text citations for all specific information, quotations, paraphrases, and summaries that you include in your paper—in short, all information that you take from a source should have an in-text citation. These in-text citations should be carefully woven into your own sentences. For more information, see Chapter 19.

## References List

The References page, listing every source cited in the paper, appears at the end of the paper. Place it on a separate page with a page number that continues the numbering of pages in the paper. The word "References" (no quotation marks) should be centered as the title of the page. The entries on the References page appear in alphabetical order beginning with the last name and *only* the initials of the first (and middle, if listed) names of the author.

In APA style, if a work has more than one author, the second author's name is also reversed:

Strunk, W., & White, E. B. (1979).

If more than one article or book by the same author(s) is cited (be sure authors are listed in exactly the same order on the title page of the text you are citing), list the references in order by the year of publication, starting with the earliest year. The entire citation, including the name or names of all authors, is repeated for each entry. List the entries in chronological order, with the earliest work first.

Olson, C. B. (1997). *Practical ideas for teaching writing as a process at the high school and college levels.* Sacramento: CDE Press.

Olson, C. B. (2002). *The reading/writing connection.* New York: Pearson.

If there are two entries in a single year, identify the earliest with an "a," followed by a "b" (2009a; 2009b), and so forth.

Kiliçkaya, F. (2007a). [Review of *WordChamp: Learn vocabulary faster,* produced by GlobaLinguist, Inc., 2007]. *Educational Technology & Society, 10*(4), 298–299. Retrieved from http://www.ifets.info/others

Kiliçkaya, F. (2007b). [Review of *Gerry's vocabulary teacher,* produced by CPR4ESL, 2007]. *Teaching English with Technology, 7*(2). Retrieved from http://iatefl.org

If no author is identified, the name of the article or website serves as the first word of the entry. Alphabetize all entries in one complete list using the hanging indent format (indent the second and all following lines of an entry by one-half inch).

When citing sources in APA style, you will need to look for a DOI, or "digital object identifier," a unique string of numbers and letters assigned by a registry service, the International DOI Foundation, that serves to identify the content and provide a link to an online location for books and articles in the social sciences. The publisher assigns a DOI when a work is electronically published. When DOIs are available they should be included in the reference for both print and electronic sources. All DOI numbers begin with a *10* and contain a prefix and a suffix separated by a slash. While DOIs can be assigned to books and other sources, you will most likely encounter them when working with periodical sources. When available, the DOI is typically located on the first page of the electronic journal article near the copyright notice.

### Citing Books and Other Nonperiodical Sources

### Citing Print Periodicals

**Citing Online Sources**

**Citing Multimedia and Other Sources**

**Citing Books and Other Nonperiodical Sources.** The following information is given in the References listings for books:

- Author(s) name, followed by a period.
- Year of publication, in parentheses, followed by a period.
- Title of the work, in *italics,* followed by a period.
- Place of publication (include city and state abbreviation) followed by a colon.
- Publisher (do not shorten or abbreviate words like *University* or *Press* but omit words like *Co., Inc.,* and *Publishers*), followed by a period.

Author. (Date) *Title.* City of Publication, State: Publisher.

**1. One author**

Timmerman, K. (2008). *Where am I wearing?: A global tour to the countries, factories, and people that make our clothes.* New York, NY: John Wiley & Sons.

**2. More than one author**

Mallor, J. A., Barnes, J. L., Bowers, T., & Langvardt, A. (2010). *Business law: The ethical, global, and e-commerce environment.* New York, NY: McGraw-Hill.

### 3. Eight or more authors

Damrosch, D., Pike, D., Alliston, A., Brown, M., duBois, P., Hafez, S., . . . Yu, P. (2004). *Teaching World Literature*. New York, NY: Longman.

### 4. Corporate or organization author

World Health Organization. (2009). *Global tuberculosis control: Epidemiology, strategy, financing.* Geneva, Switzerland: World Health Organization.

### 5. Unknown author

*100 events that shook our world*. (2003). New York, NY: Life.

### 6. Edited collection

Good, C. & Waldron, J. V. (Eds.). (2001). *The effects of the nation: Mexican art in an age of globalization.* Philadelphia, PA: Temple University Press.

### 7. Translation

Ludmer, J. (2002). *The gaucho genre: A treatise on the motherland* (M. Weigel, Trans.). Chapel Hill, NC: Duke University Press.

### 8. Second or later edition

Lee, W. M. L., Blando, J. A., Mizelle, N., & Orozco, G. (2007). *Introduction to multicultural counseling for helping professionals* (2nd ed.). Oxford, UK: Taylor & Francis.

### 9. Dissertation or thesis (unpublished)

Yamada, H. (1989). *American and Japanese topic management strategies in business conversations* (Unpublished doctoral dissertation). Georgetown University, Washington, DC.

### 10. Government document (print)

United States Census Bureau. (2010). *Statistical abstract of the United States*. Washington, DC: U.S. Government Printing Office.

### 11. Pamphlet or brochure (print)

> Division of Tuberculosis Elimination. (2009). *Tuberculosis—Get the facts!* [Pamphlet]. Washington, DC: Centers for Disease Control.

**Citing Print Periodicals.** The following information is given in the References listings for periodicals (newspapers, magazines, and scholarly journals):

- Author(s) (last name first, followed by the author's initials.), followed by a period.
- Date of publication (in parentheses), followed by a period.
- Title of the article (do not use quotation marks) with only the first word of the title, the first word of the subtitle, and any proper nouns in the title capitalized, followed by a period.
- Name of the journal (*italicized*) with the first word of the title and all nouns, verbs, and pronouns of the title capitalized, followed by a comma.
- Volume number (for a scholarly journal) *italicized*; if available, issue number in parentheses after the volume number, followed by a comma.
- Page numbers of the article, followed by a period.
- DOI (when available), lowercase followed by a colon (doi: . . .).

> Author. (Date). Article title. *Journal Title*. *Volume Number*(Issue Number), Pages. doi (if available)

### 12. Journal with continuous pagination

> Castagno, A. E. & McKinley B. J. B. (2008). Culturally responsive schooling for indigenous youth: A review of the literature. *Review of Educational Research*, *78*, 941–993. doi:10.3102/0034654308323036

### 13. Journal without continuous pagination

> Han, W. (2008). The academic trajectories of children of immigrants and their school environments. *Developmental Psychology*, *44*(6), 1572–1590. doi:10.1037/a0013886

### 14. Magazine

Swetala, C. (2010, May). On the border. *Gentlemen's Quarterly,* *80*(5), 76.

### 15. Newspaper

Ewing, J. (2010, June 2). Europe's debt crisis starts to weigh on manufacturing. *New York Times*, p. B8.

### 16. Article, author unknown

Two men who changed America. (2010, May). *Esquire,* 153(5), 32.

### 17. Review

Higgins, A. (2010, March 28). [Review of the book *For all the tea in China: How England stole the world's favorite drink and changed history*, by Sarah Rose]. *Washington Post*, p. B07.

### 18. Editorial

Europe's moves to ban veils hand ammo to extremists [Editorial]. (2010, May 27). *USA Today*, p. 10A.

### 19. Letter to the editor

Cohen, J. E. (2010, June 2). First aid for the economy [Letter to the editor]. *New York Times*, p. A24.

**Citing Online Sources.** The following information is given in the References for other sources:

- Author(s) (last name first, followed by first and middle initials).
- Date website was posted/revised (in parentheses).
- Name of specific page or article, followed by a period.
- Name of website in *italics*, followed by a period.
- Publication information (i.e., sponsoring organization).
- DOI (when provided), or URL address following the words "Retrieved from" (include date of access if the site is likely to change).

## 20. Website, corporate, or organization author

UNICEF. (2006, April 20). UNICEF's role in emergencies. *UNICEF.org.* Retrieved from http://www.unicef.org/emerg/index_33296.html

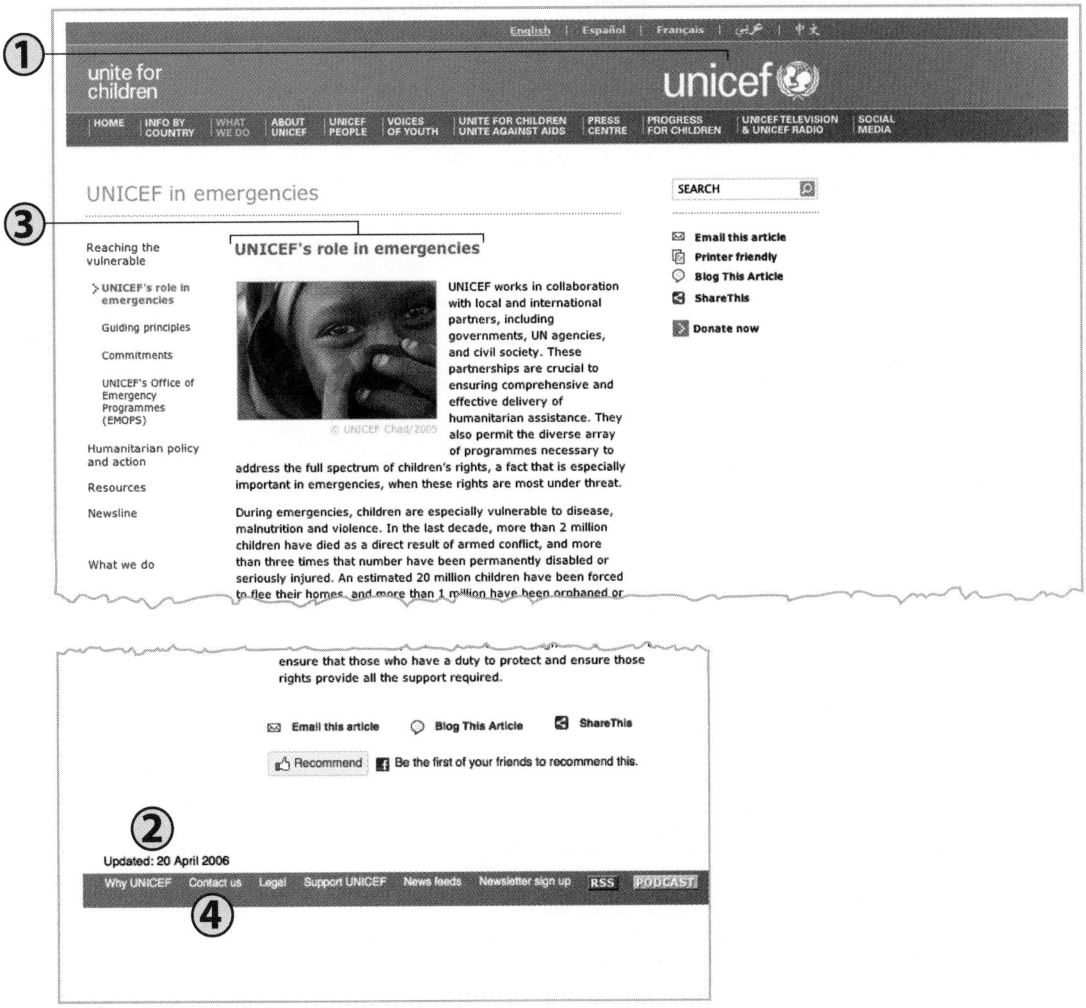

Author. (Date of Publication). Article Title. *Publication Information (website/sponsoring org).* Retrieved from URL

**FIGURE 20.3**   Website APA style

**21. Online scholarly journal article with digital object identifier (DOI)**

Noytim, U. (2010). Weblogs enhancing EFL students' English language learning. *Procedia: Social and Behavioral Sciences*, 2:2, 1127–1132. doi:10.1016/j.sbspro. 2010.03.159

Available online at www.sciencedirect.com

ELSEVIER

ScienceDirect — ⑤

Procedia Social and Behavioral Sciences 2 (2010) 1127–1132

⑥

Procedia — ④
Social and Behavioral Sciences

WCES-2010

③—Weblogs enhancing EFL students' English language learning

① — Usa Noytim[a] *

[a]Nakhon Pathom Rajabhat University, Nakhon Pathom 73000, Thailand

② Received October 9, 2009; revised December 18, 2009; accepted January 6, 2010

Abstract

This study investigated the potential value of Weblog use on English language learning in the context of a university in Thailand. It examined students' perceptions of and attitudes towards using Weblogs. A content analysis was used to analyse the data that derived from short questionnaires, interview questionnaires and student Blogs. The findings indicated that the students perceived Weblog as a tool for the development of their English, in terms of writing, reading, vocabulary, and recording their learning experience. The students also viewed Weblog as giving an opportunity and freedom for self-expression in English, writing for both a local and global audience, fostering creative, analytical and critical thinking skills, creating social interaction and good relationships between writer and reader, and supporting the learning community. Overall then, in spite of some minor limitations, they had positive attitudes towards Weblog use. These findings suggest that Weblogs can provide learning motivation and opportunities for authorship and readership, as well as the development of writing and learning strategies, including critical thinking.
© 2010 Elsevier Ltd. All rights reserved.

*Keywords:* Weblog; EFL; writing skill; reading skill; crticial thinking; social interaction.

1. Introduction

Weblog, asynchronous computer-mediated communication (CMC), offers another means of online communication (Murray & Hourigan, 2008). It is gaining popularity in the educational media and is extensively used in English language leaning contexts. A Weblog is a free user-friendly technology that is easily created, tailored, used, maintained, and frequently updated. The attractiveness of a Weblog is enhanced by its 'multimodality' (Kress, 2003) which includes texts (profile, reflections, and feedback), colors, images, audio and video files, and hyperlinks

* Usa Noytim. Tel.: +1166899148349; fax: +116634261066.
E-mail address: usanoytim@yahoo.com

⑦ — 1877-0428 © 2010 Published by Elsevier Ltd.
doi:10.1016/j.sbspro.2010.03.159

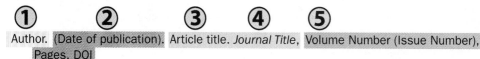

① ② ③ ④ ⑤

Author. (Date of publication). Article title. *Journal Title*, Volume Number (Issue Number), Pages. DOI

⑥ ⑦

**FIGURE 20.4** Online scholarly journal article with Digital Object Identifier (DOI)

### 22. Online scholarly journal article without DOI

Singleton, K. & Krause, E. M. S. (2009). Understanding cultural and linguistic barriers to health literacy. *The Online Journal of Issues in Nursing, 14*(3). Retrieved from http://www.nursingworld.com

### 23. Article from an online periodical

Lam, F. (2010, June 2). Fromage fort: The cheese that tried to kill me. *Salon*. Retrieved from http://www.salon.com

### 24. Online book

Duignan, P. (1998). *Bilingual education: A critique*. Retrieved from http://books.google.com/books

### 25. Blog posting

Kumar, J. (2007, December 22). Price of plagiarism [Web log comment]. Retrieved from http:// studyabroadchronicle.blogspot.com/2007/12/price-of-plagiarism.html

### 26. Wiki entry

Multiculturalism. (n.d.) *Wikipedia: The Free Encyclopedia*. Retrieved June 2, 2010, from http://en.wikipedia.org/wiki/multiculturalism

### 27. YouTube or other video sharing

United Nations. (2010). World environment day 2010: Many species, one planet, one future [Video]. *YouTube*. Retrieved from http://www.youtube.com/user/unitednations

### 28. Podcast

Bilingual teen torn between family duties, youth [Audio podcast]. (2007, July 24). *National Public Radio*. Retrieved from http://www.npr.org

**Citing Multimedia and Other Sources.** A large variety of media sources exist in today's world, including information gathered from television, radio, sound recordings, and motion pictures. The following information is given in the references listings for multimedia sources:

- Producer's name (last name first, initials), followed by "Producer" in parentheses [OR] Director's name (last name first initials), followed by

(Director) [OR] Songwriter's or artist's name (last name first, initials), [OR] Title of episode, segment, song, or scene (when relevant).

- Broadcast or publication date, in parentheses, followed by a period. (If you have both an "author" name and a segment name, the date follows immediately after "author" name.)
- Title of program, series, album, or film in *italics*, followed by media type in brackets followed by a period.
- Country of origin (film) or city where produced (television and sound recordings), followed by a colon and the producing company or distributor.

Artist. (Date). Segment [Item]. *Title of Larger Work*. City, State: Publisher.

### 29. Film or video recording

Boyle, D. (Director). (2008). *Slumdog millionaire* [Motion picture]. India: Fox Searchlight Pictures.

### 30. Television or radio program

Abrams, J. J., & Lindelof, D. (Producers). (2010). The End [Television episode]. In *Lost*. Oahu, HI: American Broadcasting.

### 31. Song or audio recording

Lady Gaga & Beyonce. (2009). Telephone. On *Fame Monster* [CD]. Los Angeles, CA: Interscope.

### 32. Personal correspondence or interview

This data was shared by P. Donoghue (email, December 11, 2009). (*Note:* personal communications are not included in the References in APA style.)

### One Student's APA-Style Paper

Student Randie Bossie combined her own observations of peer behavior with a scholarly interest in linguistics as she wrote the following research paper. Bossie follows the conventions of APA formatting as well as citation style.

Running Head: TEXTESE: THE EFFECTS OF TEXT MESSAGING

ON ENGLISH                                                  1

Supply an abbreviated title in all caps for the running head aligned left and the page number, aligned right. Include the words "Running Head."

Textese: The Effects of Text Messaging on English

and the Debate Surrounding It

Randi Bossie

University of Texas at El Paso

APA style includes a title page listing the title of the paper, the author's name, and the name of the university. Double-space all text on the title page and throughout the paper.

TEXTESE: THE EFFECTS OF TEXT MESSAGING ON ENGLISH          2

Abstract

Begin the abstract on a new page; call this page the "Abstract" (no quotation marks) centered. Do not indent the first line of the abstract.

This paper examines several studies and opinions about text messaging speak, to be referred to in the paper as "textese." Several sources, academic and nonacademic alike, are used in order to explore how textese affects the English language, how it influences English education, and surveys differing opinions about whether or not textese is a legitimate component of English. Some critics, such as John Sutherland (2002) argue that textese will be the downfall of the English language, while other critics, such as Lily Huang (2008), believe that textese stimulates creativity as well as literacy. Academic and official studies have been conducted as well, with different entities arriving at different results. This paper examines all of these sources in order to demonstrate the complex debate about this relatively simple language, textese.

An abstract is a concise summary (about 150–250 words in length) of the body of the paper.

TEXTESE: THE EFFECTS OF TEXT MESSAGING ON ENGLISH     3

Textese: The Effects of Text Messaging on English

and the Debate Surrounding It

    Text messaging is an international phenomenon that has had a
huge impact on various cultures, namely in the way that people
communicate with each other. In fact, it is estimated that a trillion text
messages are sent and received a year worldwide (Menand, 2008).
As the popularity of text messaging has increased, a new language
has arisen due to this technology. This new language is called by
many names, one example being "textese," and it has become very
controversial. While many studies have been launched to research
this linguistic phenomenon, columnists for periodicals such as *The
New Yorker* and *Newsweek* have been debating the legitimacy of this
new language. Although the debate has raged on, reaching a critical
point in the past few years, it seems as if textese is nothing more
than a harmless trend, despite the outcry that has been caused.

    Multiple factors have created textese. Very few characters
can be used when sending a text message. Additionally, most cell
phones have numeric keyboards, meaning that typing on a phone
is more complex than typing on a computer or typewriter. Since text
messaging is meant to be quick and efficient, textese reflects that.
Letters are substituted for words that sound phonetically similar,
such as "r" being substituted for "are." Because of this, textese
can be very confusing to those unfamiliar with it. Barasa and Mous
(2009) argue that textese uses the written language in a way that
is ground breaking and does not follow the rules people are used
to. Instead, textese uses shortcuts, which they argue create a
tight-knit community through a new, common language much like
any type of slang (Barasa & Mous, 2009).

    Additionally, text messaging has also introduced English as an
everyday language to many other countries and has encouraged

The title of the paper is centered on the first page of the main body, but is not in bold or italics.

In-text citation when the author is not named in the text.

*Italicize* newspaper, magazine, web page, book, and journal titles.

In-text citation when author is mentioned in the text.

Indent 1-inch on top, bottom, and side margins.

code switching, or alternating between two languages. In this sense, textese has truly become its own language. Louis Menand (2008) demonstrates the sovereignty of textese in his article "Thumbspeak." He writes that many languages, such as Czech and French, have adopted acronyms and contractions that are English in origin. One very common example of this is the acronym "LOL," which stands for "laughing out loud." Because many textese words are English in origin, other English words have become the standard as well. Menand (2008) writes that one such example of this is how French texters use "now" instead of *"maintenant"* since it is quicker.

Because of the revolutionary nature of textese, a debate about the legitimacy of it has arisen and some of the critics of textese are harsher than others. One such critic is John Sutherland (2002), a writer for *The Guardian*. In his controversial piece "Cn U Txt?" he argues that textese may possibly be the downfall of English. He makes his position clear by stating, "as a dialect, text ('textese'?) is thin and—compared, say, with Californian personalised licence plates—unimaginative. It is bleak, bald, sad shorthand. Drab shrinktalk". Sutherland (2002) continues to make his position clear by sardonically representing textese through a hypothetical conversation between characters he dubbed "Romeo" and "Juliet." Besides Sutherland's personal opinion and scathing commentary, the article lacks any substantial evidence, anecdotal or otherwise, against textese—ultimately, his thesis is that since textese is unsightly, it is illegitimate.

However, many other pundits argue that texting and textese are both very beneficial. In an article for *Newsweek*, Lily Huang (2008) writes that textese encourages creativity in its users. She compares the innovative vocabulary of textese to the many words

TEXTESE: THE EFFECTS OF TEXT MESSAGING ON ENGLISH          5

coined by Shakespeare. Furthermore, she points to an unnamed British study in which students were tested on vocabulary and reading, and it was found that students who texted often performed better and attained a higher score (Huang, 2008). Unfortunately, this evidence lacks credence since the study is unnamed and the scientific method behind it is not disclosed.

The argument goes beyond mainstream culture; many academic sources have picked up on this debate as well. In a paper presented at the 4th Symposium on Low-Educated Adult Second Language and Literacy Acquisition, Barasa and Mous (2009) presented their research involving Kenyan university students. They studied text messages from these students, all of whom were learning English as a second language. They found that textese can be helpful for Swahili speakers who are learning English as a second language:

> Our data corpus revealed the use of graphones in English messages where the words were not written with their original spelling but rather in the way that they would be pronounced. In extreme cases, the receiver is forced to pronounce the graphones loudly in order to understand the intended word and meaning. This feature seems to be integrated into English messages because of the syllabic nature of the Swahili language and its orthography that enables lexemes to be read and pronounced in the way that they are written. (Barasa & Mous, 2009, p. 237)

Barasa and Mous (2009) continue by saying that since textese helps Swahili speakers sound out English words, this helps them grasp conversational English better. As a result, they become better at pronouncing of English words (Barasa & Mous, 2009). Upon evaluating this study, it seems as if textese could actually be

TEXTESE: THE EFFECTS OF TEXT MESSAGING ON ENGLISH        6

beneficial in teaching some English language learners conversational English.

However, other studies have shown that textese may harm traditional English writing. A study reported by *Reuters* found that Irish students' writing skills are decreasing. According to the study, students are relying on shorter sentences, simpler syntax, and fewer vocabulary words because of texting ("Text messages harm," 2007). However, this study yielded very little information beyond this. It is unknown what the standards of this study were and how the students were tested.

The evidence against text messaging goes beyond official and academic studies. Many educators have stepped forward in order to provide their own anecdotal evidence. Jason Garner (2003), a teacher and graduate student, says that text messaging not only causes students to write essays in textese, it also causes students to lose concentration in class. He blames texting for making grading papers even more of a headache than it normally is. He advocates forcing students to write essays on a computer with the spellchecker on, but he had little else to say (Garner, 2003). Essentially, he simply seems discontent with the caliber of his students and blames text messaging for it, rightfully so or otherwise.

Naomi Baron (2009), a professor of linguistics, takes the middle road. She argues that English, like all languages, is ever changing and growing. She presents several changes that have occurred in English, such as the perplexing rule that one shall never end a sentence in a preposition that was invented only in the eighteenth century; additionally, she also alludes to the fact that English has changed a lot over hundreds of years, citing Chaucer as an example: "Chaucer would have written 'hath holpen' rather than 'has helped'" (Baron, 2009, p. 44). Both Huang (2008) and Menand (2008) echo this

TEXTESE: THE EFFECTS OF TEXT MESSAGING ON ENGLISH        7

sentiment; all three argue that textese is just the natural course of English. Baron (2009) ultimately argues that the issue of textese has been inflated by the media to be a much larger issue than it actually is and that while texting during class and textese can be obnoxious, they are not the downfall of the English language.

In his popular book *Texting: The Gr8 Deb8,* linguist David Crystal (2008) describes texting as a useful tool, and one which is not adversely affecting English. He compares text-speak to average slang, and says that despite common opinion, most students know when and when not to use text-speak. He writes, "not all young texters use the abbreviated form. And those who do use them do not use them very much—in as few as 6 percent of messages" (Crystal, 2008, p. 156). Through interviews he conducted as well as his own professional experience, Crystal (2008) demonstrates that texting is not used all the time by students as others, such as Sutherland (2002), would suggest. Ultimately, his argument is that textese is simply causing English to evolve in a new direction, and whether or not that is a good thing is subjective.

There is evidence both for and against textese, but ultimately it seems like textese does not appear as harmful as people say. Despite the argument from Sutherland (2002) and Garner (2003) that texting decreases literacy and ruins education, it seems that texting increases literacy and causes teenagers to write more often than they normally would. Ultimately, both Crystal (2008) and Baron (2009) make a salient point when they suggest that the debate about textese and the belief it is killing English is simply hyperbole. There is some evidence that textese is beneficial to students, but there is much less evidence that it is harmful. Really, it seems as if textese is a natural shift in the English language and that while it may be unsightly to some, it is innocent.

TEXTESE: THE EFFECTS OF TEXT MESSAGING ON ENGLISH          8

References

Barasa, S., & Mous, M. (2009). The oral and written interface in SMS: Technologically mediated communication in Kenya. In I. van de Craats & J. Kurvers (Eds.), *Proceedings of the 4th Symposium: Low-Educated Second Language and Literacy Acquisition*. Retrieved from http://lotos.library.uu.nl/publish/articles/000314/bookpart.pdf

Baron, N. S. (2009). Are digital media changing language? *Educational Leadership, 66* (6), 42–46.

Crystal, D. (2008). *Txting: The gr8 db8*. New York, NY: Oxford University Press.

Garner, J. (2003, September 19). Is this written in text or just bad spelling? *The Times Higher Education Supplement*. Retrieved from http://web.lexis-nexis.com/universe

Huang, L. (2008, August 2). The death of English (LOL). *Newsweek*. Retrieved from http://www.newsweek.com

Menand, L. (2008). Thumbspeak: Is texting here to stay? *The New Yorker*. Retrieved from http://www.newyorker.com

Sutherland, J. (2002, November 11). Cn u txt? *The Guardian*. Retrieved from http://www.guardian.co.uk

Text messages harm written language? (2007, April 25). *Reuters*. Retrieved from http://www.reuters.com

Begin the list of References on a new page. Center the title "References" (but do not put the word in quotation marks). Alphabetize all entries by the first word of the entry. Double-space all entries. First line of each entry is not indented, but all subsequent lines are (hanging indent).

For support in meeting this chapter's objectives, follow this path in MyCompLab: Resources ⇒ Research ⇒ Citing Sources ⇒ APA and MLA. Review the Instruction and Multimedia resources about citing sources, then complete the Exercises and click on Gradebook to measure your progress.

# PART 5

# Handbook

# 1

# Elements of English Sentences

This section of the handbook defines the terms of the basic elements of a sentence. Learning the names of these elements can help you to more easily identify errors in your writing. Although most first-year composition students have heard these terms before, many students need a review. Note the *Did You Know?* features throughout this section, which give more information to all students, particularly those whose native language is not English.

## 1. SENTENCE STRUCTURE

You can't write a paragraph, not to mention an essay, if you don't use sentences. Sentences are groups of words that contain a subject (what the sentence is about) and a predicate (what the subject is, does, or what is done to it). A sentence must have both a subject and a predicate to be complete, and each sentence must express a complete thought. Learning to recognize the parts of a sentence can help you create and revise your sentences more effectively.

## Subject

The subject of a sentence tells who or what is doing or being something. Usually, the subject is a noun (person, place, thing) or a pronoun (word that takes the place of a noun). Subjects can also be noun phrases or noun clauses (see this section, 5. Phrases and Clauses, for more information). In addition, a sentence can have more than one subject (a compound subject).

|  |  |
|---:|:---|
| Subject: | *Lucy* laughed. |
| Compound subject: | *Lucy and Andrea* laughed. |

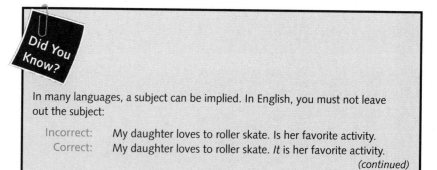

In many languages, a subject can be implied. In English, you must not leave out the subject:

|  |  |
|---:|:---|
| Incorrect: | My daughter loves to roller skate. Is her favorite activity. |
| Correct: | My daughter loves to roller skate. *It* is her favorite activity. |

*(continued)*

In some languages it is acceptable to place the pronoun that refers to the subject next to the noun that acts as the subject. In English, do not include such a pronoun.

Incorrect:    Eric he washed the car.
Correct:      Eric washed the car.

While English, and many other languages such as Spanish and Chinese, uses subject-verb-object (SVO) order, many languages do not. For instance, Japanese, Turkish, and Korean use subject-object-verb (SOV) order, and Arabic uses verb-subject-object (VSO) order:

English (Chinese, Spanish):    I study Japanese.
Japanese (Turkish, Korean):    I Japanese study.
                    Arabic:    Study I Japanese.

The issue of basic sentence structure is made even more difficult because many languages, including most Asian languages and Arabic, are written right-to-left instead of left-to-right.

## Verbs

A verb serves as part of the predicate of a sentence. It expresses the action or links the subject to the rest of the sentence. A verb can be one word (*drives*) or a verb phrase (*will have driven*). There are many facets of the verb: verbs have tense, voice, and mood, and they can be transitive or intransitive (see this section, 4. Verbs, for more information). Verbs might be action verbs, linking verbs, helping verbs, or compound verbs.

- Action verb: Eduardo *drives* race cars.
- Linking verbs (verb links the subject to the rest of the sentence. Common linking verbs: *am, are, is, was, were, be, been, being*): Sonia *is* graceful.
- Helping verbs (verb used with the main verb to form the complete verb of the sentence): Cho *was helping* his brother to clean the garage.
- Compound verbs (verb with more than one part): The dancing grizzly bear *amazed* and *amused* the audience.

## Modifiers

These add information to nouns, verbs, adjectives, and adverbs to better describe or limit that word. Modifiers can be a single word, a group of words, or a whole clause.

Modifier:    Corrine has a *dry* wit coupled with a *deadpan* delivery.

## Direct Objects

A direct object receives the action of a transitive verb (see page H-10) and answers some type of question (what? whom?) about the subject and predicate. Direct objects can be nouns, pronouns, noun phrases, or noun clauses.

> Eduardo drives *race cars*. ("Race cars" answers the question "what" in this sentence.)

## Indirect Objects

Instead of receiving the action of the sentence, an indirect object answers the question "to whom" or "for whom" about the subject and predicate. Indirect objects, like direct objects, can be nouns, pronouns, noun phrases, or noun clauses.

> His father gave *Eduardo* a race car. ("Eduardo" answers the question "to whom" in this sentence.)

## Subject Complement

A subject complement follows the verb in a sentence, usually a linking verb (often "to be"), and describes or renames the subject of the sentence.

> Kate is *charming*.

## Object Complement

An object complement also follows the verb in a sentence and describes or renames the object of the sentence.

> Dylan titled his poem *"Long Shot."*

## Conjunctions

Conjunctions link words or word groups together. Think of a junction on a highway: It links two roads together. A conjunction actually means to join together. There are several types of conjunctions: coordinating, subordinating, and correlative.

- ***Coordinating conjunctions*** join equal words or word groups (phrases, clauses). There are seven coordinating conjunctions in the English language (*for, and, nor, but, or, yet,* and *so*).

> Cheryl seemed pleased *but* didn't smile.
> Terri was on time for the interview *and* on top of her game.
> The sun was shining, *yet* the wind was cold.

- **Subordinating conjunctions** often join dependent clauses to independent clauses to form a complete thought. Some of the most frequently used subordinating conjunctions are *although, since, before, until,* and *because.*

  Please do not get up *until* it is time to go.
  *Because* he was very shy, he could not tell Nancy he liked her.

- **Correlative conjunctions** (*both . . . and, either . . . or, neither . . . nor*), like coordinating conjunctions, join equal parts of a sentence together.

  *Both* John *and* Ruth must attend the parent conference.
  *Neither* the aggrieved party *nor* the defendant could reach consensus on the settlement.
  *Either* we go to the movies *or* we go out to eat.

# 2. NOUNS AND PRONOUNS

## Nouns

As a person, you are a noun. So is your friend, your brother, your car, your house, your dog, and your iPod. People, animals, and things are nouns. So are ideas, like beauty, love, injustice. A noun can be proper and name a specific person, place, or brand, such as Justin Timberlake, Mexico City, or Chevrolet. Normally, proper nouns are capitalized. Nouns can also be common, such as movie star, city, or car. Normally, common nouns are not capitalized (unless they are the first word in a sentence).

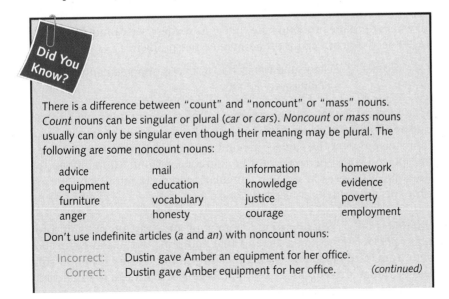

**Did You Know?**

There is a difference between "count" and "noncount" or "mass" nouns. *Count* nouns can be singular or plural (*car* or *cars*). *Noncount* or *mass* nouns usually can only be singular even though their meaning may be plural. The following are some noncount nouns:

| | | | |
|---|---|---|---|
| advice | mail | information | homework |
| equipment | education | knowledge | evidence |
| furniture | vocabulary | justice | poverty |
| anger | honesty | courage | employment |

Don't use indefinite articles (*a* and *an*) with noncount nouns:

| | |
|---|---|
| Incorrect: | Dustin gave Amber an equipment for her office. |
| Correct: | Dustin gave Amber equipment for her office. *(continued)* |

> If you need to express a quantity for a noncount noun, use *some, any*, or *more*.
>
> Correct: Dustin gave Amber *some* equipment for her office.
> Correct: Amber needs to buy *more* equipment for her office.

## Pronouns

Pronouns take the place of nouns. They help our sentences flow. Try to think of a world without pronouns:

> John took John's book to John's house, where John proceeded to read John's book.

This sentence sounds much better with pronouns:

> John took his book to his house, where he proceeded to read it.

Notice in the above sentence that as readers we are never confused as to whom the pronoun "he" or "his" refers (John). We also are clear about "it" (the book). As a writer, you want to make sure that when you use pronouns, you are clear on reference and agreement, and also that you do not shift person in the middle of your writing.

**Pronoun Reference.** The referent or antecedent of a pronoun (that is the noun to which the pronoun refers) must always be clear to your readers. Look at this pronoun problem:

> Incorrect: Elaine and Nancy had a serious disagreement, and now *she* is very angry.

To whom does the pronoun "she" refer? As readers, we cannot know. The writer needs to correct this pronoun reference problem:

> Correct: Elaine and Nancy had a serious disagreement, and now Elaine is very angry.

**Pronoun Agreement.** Pronouns must also agree in number, gender, and person (first, second, or third person). In the previous sentence about John, the pronoun "his" agrees in number (singular), gender (masculine), and person (third person) with the antecedent "John." In addition, the pronoun "it" agrees in number (singular), gender (neutral), and person (third person) with its antecedent "book."

**Pronoun Shift.** When writing a paragraph or essay, do not shift pronoun person unless logic dictates that you must. For instance, do not shift from third person to second person without reason. Pronoun shift can be difficult to edit because when we speak to others, we often shift person without any concern. Look at the following example and try to find where the shift in pronoun person occurs:

Incorrect:  Students should be careful to replace slang and jargon while editing. One thing you can do to catch slang and jargon is to read your essay out loud.

"Students" is in third person. Often writing instructors ask students to write their work in third person. However, in the above sentence, the writer changes to second person (*you*) without a logical reason to do so.

Correct:  Students should be careful to replace slang and jargon while editing. One thing *students* can do to catch slang and jargon is to read *their essays* out loud.

**Types of Pronouns.** There are many types of pronouns. Learning these terms and definitions can help you to see the big picture of pronoun use.

- **Personal pronouns** refer to people or things (*I, me, mine, we, us, our, ours, you, yours, she, her, hers, he, him, his, it, its, they, them, theirs*).
  *She* left *it* under the mat for *them*.

- **Indefinite pronouns** refer to "nonspecific" persons or things (*all, anyone, another, anybody, both, each, few, most, some, several, none, someone, no one, something,* etc.)
  All *anyone* can do is hope for the best.

- **Demonstrative pronouns** refer to a stated antecedent (*this, that, these, those*).
  Megan was aghast at Owen's rudeness. *That* was the last straw.

- **Relative pronouns** introduce relative clauses (*that, who, whom, which, what, whose, whoever*).
  The dish *that* Sylvia brought was delicious.
  Jeremy wanted to know *who* had opened the back door.

- **Reflexive and intensive pronouns** refer back to a referent or antecedent, or they stress a referent or antecedent (*myself, yourself, herself, ourselves,* etc.).
  Ken said that he *himself* had personally supervised the installation.
  Lucy had done all of the work *herself*.

- **Interrogative pronouns** introduce a question (*who, whose, what, which, whom*).
  *Whose* raincoat is the blue one?

# 3. ADJECTIVES AND ADVERBS

Adjectives and adverbs describe and thus give more information about other words. These parts of speech are called modifiers (because they act to modify or further define the meaning of words).

## Adjectives

Adjectives describe or modify nouns. They answer questions about the nouns, such as:

| | |
|---|---|
| ▪ Which ones? | *those* books |
| ▪ Whose? | *Jose's* books |
| ▪ What kind? | *science* books |
| ▪ How many? | *two* books |
| ▪ What condition? | *torn* books |
| ▪ What color? | *brown* books |
| ▪ What size? | *large* books |

**Did You Know?**

There are only three articles in the English language: *a, an,* and *the.*

- Articles are a special type of adjective. *The* is called a definite article because it refers to a specific noun. It can modify singular or plural nouns. *A* and *an* are indefinite articles, because they refer to a general class of noun, not a specific one. In addition, *a* and *an* are always singular.

  Kelly loves *a* sunny day. (Kelly loves sunny days in general.)
  Eryn loved *the* sunny day she spent at the beach. (Eryn loved a specific sunny day.)
  Dylan loved all *the* sunny days he'd spent in California. (Dylan loved a number of sunny days.)

- *A* comes before words that begin with consonants (any letter that is not a vowel). *A* is also used before words that begin with the vowel *u* if the *u* is pronounced.

  a uniform    a unicorn

- *An* comes before words that begin with vowel sounds (*a, e, i, o, u*). This makes them easier to pronounce.

  an aria    an eagle    an iPod    an owl    an uncle          *(continued)*

- Even though the letter *h* is a consonant, *an* is used before many words that begin with *h*, if the *h* is silent.

  an hour    an honor

- A and *an* modify singular nouns that can be counted (car, dog, umbrella). *The*, however, modifies both singular and plural nouns that can be counted, as well as nouns that name things that cannot be counted (equipment, information, homework, advice).

## Adverbs

While adjectives describe or modify nouns, adverbs describe or modify verbs, adjectives, and other adverbs. They answer questions such as the following:

| | |
|---|---|
| Where? | He put the book *there* on the table. |
| How? | He put the book down *softly*. |
| How often? | He read the Bible *frequently*. |
| When? | He returned the book *late*. |
| To what degree? | He returned the book *very* late. |

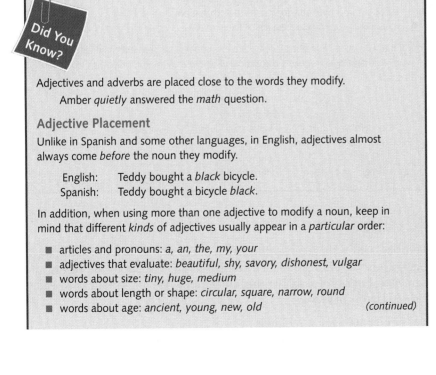

**Did You Know?**

Adjectives and adverbs are placed close to the words they modify.

Amber *quietly* answered the *math* question.

**Adjective Placement**

Unlike in Spanish and some other languages, in English, adjectives almost always come *before* the noun they modify.

English:    Teddy bought a *black* bicycle.
Spanish:    Teddy bought a bicycle *black*.

In addition, when using more than one adjective to modify a noun, keep in mind that different *kinds* of adjectives usually appear in a *particular* order:

- articles and pronouns: *a, an, the, my, your*
- adjectives that evaluate: *beautiful, shy, savory, dishonest, vulgar*
- words about size: *tiny, huge, medium*
- words about length or shape: *circular, square, narrow, round*
- words about age: *ancient, young, new, old*                    (continued)

- words about color: *magenta, turquoise, blue, green, red*
- words about nationality: *Belgian, Mexican, Japanese, Scottish, French*
- words about religion: *Buddhist, Catholic, Muslim, Jewish, Hindu, Presbyterian*
- words about the materials of the noun: *metal, wooden, glass, adobe, brick*
- nouns used as adjectives: *bathroom* floor, *track* team

  *His old, Belgian grandfather died suddenly.*
  *My inviting, oval, turquoise swimming pool is filled with warm water.*
  *The ancient, Hindu, silk rug needs to be cleaned.*

Finally, it's important to know whether to put a comma between two or more adjectives. If you can place "and" between the adjectives and the sentence still makes sense, then you need a comma.

- His *old* and *Belgian* grandfather died suddenly (the "and" between *old* and *Belgian* makes sense, so a comma should be placed between them).
- His old and Belgian and grandfather died suddenly (the "and" between *Belgian* and *grandfather* does *not* make sense, so no comma should be placed between these two words).

### Adverb Placement

Adverbs that modify verbs can appear at the beginning or end of a sentence, either before or after the verb, or between a helping verb and the main verb. The adverb should appear as closely as possible to the verb.

*Furiously*, Jon honked his horn at the drunken driver.
Jody's pet parrot *spasmodically* pecked at her food.
Bobbi *happily* filled the aquarium with guppies.
Cassie *swiftly* ran the length of the street.

In English, you should *not* place an adverb between a verb and its direct object since a direct object receives the action of the verb. However, Spanish inverts this order.

| | |
|---|---|
| Incorrect in English: | Hayley put quickly her toys away. (correct in Spanish) |
| Correct in English: | Hayley quickly put her toys away. |
| Incorrect in English: | Brian iced professionally the cake. (correct in Spanish) |
| Correct in English: | Brian professionally iced the cake. |

# 4. VERBS

Verbs are words that convey the action of the subject or express a state of being (*am, is, are*). Essentially, verbs link the subject to the rest of the sentence. For purposes of writing and editing, it is important to consider several factors of verbs:

- number (singular or plural)
- person (first, second, third)

- part (infinitive/simple form, past, past participle of regular and irregular verbs)
- tense (past, present, future, and variations on these tenses)
- mood (indicative, subjunctive, imperative)
- voice (active, passive)
- agreement with subject

In addition, writers should consider the type of verb, such as the following:

- linking verbs
- auxiliary (helping) verbs
- transitive/intransitive

These lists may seem intimidating, especially to those of you for whom English is a second language. However, most verbs are regular verbs, and once you understand how verbs work, a dictionary can quickly tell you if a verb is irregular or not and give you the information you need.

## Number and Person

Since verbs will often change spelling depending on whether the subject is singular or plural, and also depending on whether the subject is first, second, or third person, it is important to understand how these two factors work together.

| Person | Singular | Plural |
|---|---|---|
| Regular verb: *to walk* | | |
| First person | I walk. | We walk. |
| Second person | You walk. | You walk. |
| Third person | He (she, it) walks. | They walk. |
| Irregular verb: *to be* | | |
| First person | I am. | We are. |
| Second person | You are. | You are. |
| Third person | He (she, it) is. | They are. |

## Part

Verbs have three principal parts (simple form, past tense, and past participle). You form the past tense of regular verbs by adding *-ed* or *-d* to the simple (infinitive) form.

| Simple (Infinitive) Form | Past Tense | Past Participle |
|---|---|---|
| walk (to walk) | walked | walked |
| study (to study) | studied | studied |

Irregular verbs present more problems. Often, the past tense and past participle of irregular verbs do not end in -*ed*. As a result, if you are uncertain about how to form the past tense or past participle of a verb, it is important to check the verb in the dictionary.

| Simple (Infinitive) Form | Past Tense | Past Participle |
|---|---|---|
| be (to be) | was, were | been |
| go (to go) | went | gone |
| see (to see) | seen | saw |
| eat (to eat) | ate | eaten |
| choose (to choose) | chose | chosen |
| sing (to sing) | sang | sung |
| drive (to drive) | drove | driven |

## Tense

The form of a verb will change to reflect differences in time or tense. There are four forms for verbs: simple, progressive, emphatic, and modal. In addition to form, there are several possible tenses.

**Simple Form.** The simple form of the verb is also the infinitive form. There are five possible tenses in simple form, shown in the following examples for the regular verb "to love" and the irregular verb "to drive":

| | |
|---|---|
| Simple past | She *loved* the concert. They *drove* the entire distance in one night. |
| Simple future | She *will love* the concert. They *will drive* the entire distance in one night. |
| Present perfect | She *has loved* the concert. They *have driven* the entire distance in one night. |
| Past perfect | She *had loved* the concert. They *had driven* the entire distance in one night. |
| Future perfect | She *will have loved* the concert. They *will have driven* the entire distance in one night. |

**Progressive Form.** In addition to simple form, each tense also has a form, called progressive, which shows actions that are in the process of happening. There are six possible tenses in progressive form. Notice that in the progressive form -*ing* is added to the simple form of the verb.

| | |
|---|---|
| Present Progressive | Teddy *is cooking* the spaghetti. |
| Past Progressive | Teddy *was cooking* the spaghetti. |
| Future Progressive | Teddy *will be cooking* the spaghetti. |

| | |
|---|---|
| Present Perfect Progressive | Teddy *has been cooking* the spaghetti. |
| Past Perfect Progressive | Teddy *had been cooking* the spaghetti. |
| Future Perfect Progressive | Teddy *will have been cooking* the spaghetti. |

**Emphatic Form.** Not all verbs have an emphatic form. You form the emphatic form by combining the present (simple) form of a verb with the auxiliary verb "to do." We use the emphatic form to stress an action, to ask questions, and for negating an idea.

> I *do* the dishes. I *did do* the dishes.
>
> *Did* you *do* the dishes?
>
> Owen *did* not *do* the dishes.

**Modal Form.** There are several helping verbs, called "modals," that are used to complete verbs to express specific attitudes:

> will, would     shall, should     can, could     may, might, must

> She *would* go to the concert if she *could* drive.
>
> He *might* take her to the concert.
>
> They *should* allow the use of their facility, but they *might* not.

# Mood

Just as people have moods they convey to others by means of behavior or speech, verbs also have moods that writers use to indicate their attitude toward the subject. Verbs have three basic moods.

> *Indicative mood* is by far the most common and is used both to make statements and to ask questions:
>
> Susan *types* well. (statement)
>
> Why *does* Larry *wash* her laundry? (question)

> *Imperative mood* serves to give a direction or a command:
>
> *Listen* carefully to the teacher.
> *Pick* me *up* on time tonight.

> *Subjunctive mood* expresses a wish or suggests a situation contrary to the facts:
>
> If only he *were* a prince. (wish)
>
> If Ben *were* to agree to speak at our conference, he would not be able to go to Colorado for his family reunion. (situation contrary to fact)

## Agreement with Subject

Verbs must agree in number with the subject of the sentence. A singular subject needs a singular verb, and a plural subject needs a plural verb. If your instructor is marking "subject-verb agreement" errors on your drafts, please see Section 3: Punctuation, Spelling, and Mechanics to learn how to correct these mistakes.

## Linking Verbs

Linking verbs serve to link the subject and verb of a sentence together so that the complete verb describes or renames the subject in some way. A linking verb creates a subject complement (see this section, 1. Sentence Structure for more information on subject complements):

> Brian is the head of the group. (In this sentence, "Brian" is the subject, "is" is the verb, and "head of the group" is the subject complement. In other words, the subject "Brian" is further described by the subject complement.)

## Auxiliary (Helping) Verbs

Auxiliary means "helping." In the case of verbs, auxiliary verbs help to complete the verb by combining with the main verb to fill in the picture that the verb is trying to convey.

> Lucy *is* hailing a taxi.
>
> The Red Hats Club *did* take the train to the symphony performance.
>
> Vicki *had* left the diner before George received the message.

In this section, under Verb Tense, note that a helping verb is used to form each type of progressive tense. Common helping verbs are *to be, to do, to have.*

## Transitive/Intransitive

*Transitive verbs* take objects. In the following sentence, "sent" is a transitive verb and "angry letter" is the direct object.

> Wanda *sent* an angry letter.

Sometimes transitive verbs take both an indirect object and a direct object:

> Wanda *sent* the day care center (*indirect object*) an angry letter (*direct object*).

*Intransitive verbs* do not take objects.

> April *wept* copiously. (In this sentence, "copiously" is an adverb describing how April wept. It is not a direct object.)

Many English verbs can be either transitive or intransitive. For instance, when we change the wording on the above sentence, note how the verb becomes transitive, taking a direct object:

> April copiously *wept* tears of joy (direct object).

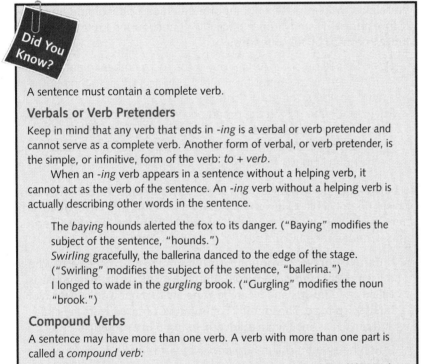

A sentence must contain a complete verb.

**Verbals or Verb Pretenders**

Keep in mind that any verb that ends in *-ing* is a verbal or verb pretender and cannot serve as a complete verb. Another form of verbal, or verb pretender, is the simple, or infinitive, form of the verb: *to + verb*.

When an *-ing* verb appears in a sentence without a helping verb, it cannot act as the verb of the sentence. An *-ing* verb without a helping verb is actually describing other words in the sentence.

> The *baying* hounds alerted the fox to its danger. ("Baying" modifies the subject of the sentence, "hounds.")
> *Swirling* gracefully, the ballerina danced to the edge of the stage. ("Swirling" modifies the subject of the sentence, "ballerina.")
> I longed to wade in the *gurgling* brook. ("Gurgling" modifies the noun "brook.")

**Compound Verbs**

A sentence may have more than one verb. A verb with more than one part is called a *compound verb:*

> The injured accident victim *stumbled* and *swayed* to the side of the road.

# 5. PHRASES AND CLAUSES

## Phrases

Learning about phrases is an important step in learning about how sentences work. A phrase is simply a group of words that does not contain a complete subject and a complete verb. There are four kinds of phrases: prepositional phrase, appositive phrase, verbal (participial, gerund, and infinitive) phrase, and absolute phrase.

**Prepositional Phrase.** A prepositional phrase begins with a preposition and takes an object in the form of a noun, pronoun, or group of words acting as a noun. This phrase serves to modify other words within the sentence.

> The line of ants crawled *over the hill*. ("Over" is the preposition; "hill" is the object of the prepositional phrase.)

**Appositive Phrase.** An appositive phrase provides additional information about a noun or pronoun in the sentence. Normally, the appositive phrase directly follows the noun or pronoun it describes. Sometimes "appositive phrase" is a misnomer since it isn't uncommon for the appositive phrase to consist of only one word.

> Dylan helped his sister *Amber* down the rocky embankment. ("Amber" is the appositive in this sentence, offering more information about the noun "sister.")
>
> They decided to hike in the desert around Hueco Tanks, *an area notorious for rattlesnakes*. ("An area notorious for rattlesnakes" serves as the appositive phrase in this sentence, further describing the noun "Hueco Tanks.")

**Verbal Phrase.** As discussed, a verbal is not a complete verb. Thus, verbal phrases do not serve as a verb but rather as a noun, adjective, or adverb. There are three types of verbal phrases: infinitive phrases, gerund phrases, and participial phrases.

- **Infinitive Phrase**: The infinitive is the simple form of the verb. When the word "to" comes before the simple form of a verb, that phrase is called an infinitive, and it can be joined with other words to form an infinitive phrase. The infinitive or infinitive phrase is very versatile and can act as an adjective, adverb, or noun in a sentence.

  > Dustin helped the children *to understand the difficult chapter*. (adverb phrase)
  >
  > *To bake the prizewinning cake* was Carol's goal in the contest. (noun phrase)

- **Gerund Phrase**: A gerund is the simple form of a verb + *-ing* and it serves as a noun in a sentence. A gerund phrase consists of a gerund and other words and acts as a subject, direct object, or the object of a prepositional phrase.

  > *Charging into the breach* saved the day. (subject)
  >
  > Ben loves *singing at the top of his lungs*. (direct object)
  >
  > Bonnie was furious *about losing her purse*. (object of prepositional phrase)

- **Participial Phrase**: Unlike gerund phrases, which act as nouns, participial phrases act as adjectives and therefore modify nouns or pronouns. As previously discussed, a present participle is formed by adding -*ing* to the simple form of a verb, whereas a past participle adds -*ed* to the simple form of regular verbs. Keep in mind that irregular verbs may not have the -*ed* ending.

> Rebecca watched her children *racing across the park*. ("Racing across the park" modifies the noun "children.")
> Many students, *saddened by the death of their teacher*, wept openly. ("Saddened by the death of their teacher" modifies the noun "students.")
> *Shrieking wildly*, the toddler kicked his brother. ("Shrieking wildly" modifies the noun "toddler.")

**Absolute Phrase.** An absolute phrase consists of a noun or pronoun, followed by a participle. It is called "absolute" because instead of acting as a modifier to a particular noun, verb, adjective, or adverb, it modifies the entire clause or sentence.

> *His body dripping oily sweat*, the plumber yanked the pipe out of the wall.
> The church choir belted out Handel's "Hallelujah Chorus," *the sopranos singing at top volume*.

# Clauses

Learning about clauses helps you to distinguish between sentence fragments and complete sentences. All clauses contain a complete subject and a complete verb, but that doesn't mean that all clauses are complete sentences. Independent (main) clauses are complete sentences, but dependent clauses are not, which means they need an independent (main) clause to complete the thought expressed.

**Independent (Main) Clause.** An independent clause has a complete subject, a complete verb, and expresses a complete thought.

> The baby cried.
> We went to the store.

**Dependent Clause.** A dependent clause has a subject and a verb, but it does not express a complete thought, and it needs another clause to complete it. There are two types of dependent clauses: subordinate clauses and relative clauses.

- **Subordinate clauses** (also called adverb clauses) begin with a subordinating conjunction. Common subordinating conjunctions are *after, although, as, because, before, if, since, that, though, unless, until, when, where, while.*

  *When the baby cried,* her mother picked her up. (The adverb clause modifies the verb "picked.")

  The dependent clause "When the baby cried" needs an independent clause in order to complete the thought. "Her mother picked her up" is an independent clause because it can stand on its own. It, therefore, is the main clause, or main idea, of the sentence.

- **Relative clauses** (also called adjective clauses) begin with relative pronouns (*who, whoever, whom, whomever, whose, that, what, whatever, which, whichever*). A relative clause can also begin with *when, where, why*:

  The boy *who is wearing the red shirt* bought a soda instead of milk. (The relative clause modifies the noun "boy.")

  In this above instance, the relative clause "who is wearing the red shirt" helps to identify which boy bought a soda instead of milk.

  Hiking in the high Rockies *when you are not dressed for it* can cause hypothermia.

  In the above sentence, the relative clause "when you are not dressed for it" serves as an adjective modifying the noun "hiking."

# 6. PREPOSITIONS, INTERJECTIONS

## Prepositional Phrases

Prepositional phrases consist of a preposition and its object. The object is a noun or pronoun, along with any words that modify or refer in some way to the object. Common prepositions include *about, above, across, after, among, behind, between, by, from, in, into, of, on, toward, up, with, within.*

The baby toddled *into* the room. [into + the room]
The meatloaf consisted mainly *of* onions. [of + onions]
The ball rolled *under* the sofa, *between* the back legs. [under + the sofa; between + the back legs]

The subject of a sentence can never be the object of a prepositional phrase. When trying to locate the subject, you can cross out all prepositional phrases. Next locate the noun or pronoun that is doing something or being something.

In English, the use of many prepositions is considered idiomatic; that is, there are few clear rules for when and how to use them. If you are learning English, pay attention to how prepositions are used when you are reading books, magazines, and newspapers. Also, pay attention to how people use them while speaking. It's also a good idea to keep a list of prepositional expressions so that you can refer to it when writing.

Even though the use of many prepositions is not governed by rules, there are some rules for using the most common prepositions, as well as prepositions that indicate time. In English, the most common prepositions are *in, on,* and *at.*

- *In* indicates some kind of enclosed area or a geographical area such as a city, state, or country:

  *in* the kitchen   *in* a coffin   *in* France   *in* San Francisco   *in* Chihuahua

- *In* can also indicate a period of time, such as a month, year, season, or part of a day:

  *in* the afternoon   *in* springtime   *in* 2001   *in* autumn   *in* the 1860s

- *On* indicates the top of something, such as a street, table, or counter, a day of the week, or a specific date:

  I left my coffee cup *on* the table.
  Lucy and Andrea are going out to eat *on* Friday.
  I start my vacation *on* September 1.

- *At* indicates a specific place, address, or location or a specific time:

  He lives *at* the corner of Mills and Main.
  The best buys are always found *at* the flea market.
  Let's meet *at* Chile's Restaurant *at* 5:00 p.m.

In addition to the prepositions *in, on,* and *at,* the most common prepositions for showing time are *for, during,* and *since.*

- *For* refers to an exact period of time that something lasts, a period that has a beginning and an end:

  He's been lifting weights *for* six months.
  I've been stranded at the airport *for* three hours.

- *During* refers to an indefinite period of time in which something happens:

  Kelly plans to visit her grandmother sometime *during* the Christmas
    holidays.
  Twice *during* her speech she forgot what she was going to say.   *(continued)*

- *Since* refers to a period of time that has passed between an earlier time and the present:

  *Since* his graduation from college, Alan has been working at the State Department.

  Trish has been much happier *since* she gave up dieting.

**Common Prepositional Transfer Errors**

Since it is difficult to directly translate prepositions from another language into English, it is easy to make errors. The following are some common prepositional errors:

Incorrect: He arrived *to* the test on time.
Correct: He arrived *at* the test on time.
Incorrect: Melissa waited to check out *on* the line.
Correct: Melissa waited to check out *in* line.

Whenever you are unsure about using the correct preposition, ask for help. Eventually, you will learn the most common prepositional idioms.

## Interjections

Interjections are words that express force and often emotion. Often, interjections are followed by exclamation marks. Almost always, when an interjection is part of a sentence, it can be removed without changing the meaning of the sentence. Common interjections are *hey, oh, ouch, yea, yippee, damn.*

*Hey!* You're sitting in my place.  *Wow!* You look great.
*Oh*, I forgot to get ice cream.  *Ouch!* That hurt.

## 7. TYPES OF SENTENCES

Sentences can be classified by the kinds and by the number of clauses they contain. There are four different types of sentences: simple, compound, complex, and compound-complex. (Red = independent clause; blue = dependent clause.)

**Simple Sentence.** This type of sentence is comprised of one independent clause. The clause may be short or long, and it may contain many different phrases, a compound subject and/or a compound verb, but it only has *one* independent clause.

Jose and Sonia went to the long-anticipated concert without a care in the world.

**Compound Sentence.** This type of sentence consists of two independent clauses linked by a comma and coordinating conjunction, or by a semicolon.

> Jose went to the concert, but Sonia stayed home.
> Jose was disappointed; Sonia was happy she didn't go.

**Complex Sentence.** This type of sentence has one independent clause and one (or more) subordinate (dependent) clauses.

> Jose went to the concert while Sonia stayed home.
> When Jose decided to go to the concert, Sonia was upset.

**Compound-Complex Sentence.** This type of sentence contains at least one dependent (subordinate) clause and two or more independent clauses joined by a comma and coordinating conjunction, or by a semicolon.

> Jose decided to go to the concert even though Sonia was sick, so she was upset.

# Correcting Sentence Errors

Note the *Did You Know?* boxes throughout this section that give more information to all students, particularly those whose native language is not English.

## 1. FRAGMENTS

A fragment is an incomplete sentence. Occasionally, writers use fragments for emphasis. However, fragments can be problematic in academic writing and you should strive to eliminate them from final drafts.

Usually, a fragment is one of two types:

- a phrase that lacks either a subject, a verb, or both
- a subordinate clause that has a subject and verb but begins with either a subordinating conjunction or a relative pronoun

### How to Check for Fragments in Your Writing

Imagine someone coming up to you and saying, "When you go to the store." You would hear the fragment and say, "What? What should I do when I go to the store?" An effective way to find fragments during the editing process is to read your essay aloud *backwards*, sentence by sentence. You can "hear" a fragment. After all, no one speaks in fragments! When you read your essay backwards, you will not gloss over the end punctuation; you will be forced to read each sentence just the way you've punctuated it.

### How to Correct Fragments

1. Check for verbals, which are not complete verbs. Note that they often end in *-ing*.

| | |
|---|---|
| Fragment: | The dogs ran back and forth, barking loudly. Their fur bristling. |
| Correct: | The dogs ran back and forth, barking loudly. Their fur bristled. |

2. If a fragment has both a subject and a verb, remove the subordinating conjunction or relative pronoun that has created the fragment.

Fragment:   After the girls hugged each other, crying and laughing at the same time.

Correct:   The girls hugged each other, crying and laughing at the same time.

Fragment:   The homecoming king was Joe. Who was not happy about being chosen.

Correct:   The homecoming king was Joe, who was not happy about being chosen.

3. Often, a fragment needs only to be joined to the preceding or following sentence to be corrected.

Fragment:   The girls hugged each other. Crying and laughing at the same time.

Correct:   The girls hugged each other, crying and laughing at the same time.

# 2. RUN-ON (FUSED) SENTENCES AND COMMA SPLICES

Each sentence needs its own end punctuation. When you fail to provide any punctuation between sentences, you create a run-on sentence, also called a fused sentence. **Run-on sentences** are confusing to your readers, which means your readers have to put more effort than necessary into understanding what you have written.

One type of run-on sentence is called a comma splice. When you place a comma between two independent clauses, you have committed *a comma splice.*

Run-on:   Tracy went to the apartment she didn't have the key.

Comma splice:   Tracy went to the apartment, she didn't have the key.

Note that in the first example, the two sentences are joined between *apartment* and *she*. In the second example, a comma appears between *apartment* and *she*. However, a comma is too weak a form of punctuation to separate two sentences alone; therefore, this is a comma splice.

There are four main ways to correct run-on sentences and comma splices.

- **First:** Place a period between the two sentences. This method requires you to capitalize the first word of the second sentence.

  Tracy went to the apartment. She didn't have the key.

- **Second:** Place a semicolon between the two sentences.

  Tracy went to the apartment; she didn't have the key.

- **Third:** Place a comma + a coordinating conjunction between the two sentences. Note that while there are seven coordinating conjunctions (*for, and, nor, but, or, yet, so*) in English, these words are not interchangeable: You need to select the conjunction that best conveys the relationship between these two independent clauses.

  | Conjunction | Definition |
  | --- | --- |
  | for | because |
  | and | in addition, also |
  | nor | not, neither |
  | but | however, unless |
  | or | as another possibility |
  | yet | however, unless |
  | so | as a result |

  Incorrect: Tracy went to the apartment, *so* she didn't have the key. (This sentence doesn't make any sense.)

  Correct: Tracy went to the apartment, *but* she didn't have the key.

- **Fourth:** Join the two sentences together with a subordinating conjunction or a relative pronoun.

  *Although* Tracy went to the apartment, she didn't have the key.
  Tracy, *who* went to the apartment, didn't have the key.

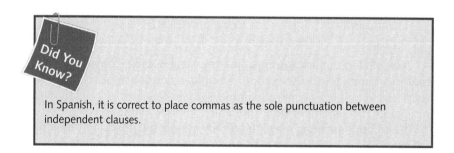

Did You Know?

In Spanish, it is correct to place commas as the sole punctuation between independent clauses.

# 3. MIXED STRUCTURE AND MISMATCHED PREDICATES

## Mixed Sentence Structure

A mixed sentence structure is exactly what it sounds like—you start with one structure and then change, in the middle of the sentence, to another structure. This is a common error in rough drafts.

| | |
|---|---|
| Mixed: | By going to the doctor at the first sign of a cold is a waste of money. |
| Correct: | Going to the doctor at the first sign of a cold is a waste of money. |
| Correct: | By going to the doctor at the first sign of a cold, a patient will waste money. |
| Mixed: | Because my boyfriend was always flirting with Amy is why I broke up with him. |
| Correct: | The reason I broke up with my boyfriend is because he was always flirting with Amy. |
| Correct: | Because my boyfriend was always flirting with Amy is the reason I broke up with him. |

## Mismatched Predicates

Mismatched predicates, also called faulty predication, occur when the predicate does not fit the subject in a logical manner.

| | |
|---|---|
| Mismatched predicate: | Immoral behavior is where you do something unethical. |

Note: Immoral behavior is an abstract concept, not a place ("where"). Thus, the subject cannot logically act in the manner the predicate indicates.

| | |
|---|---|
| Correct: | Immoral behavior is unethical. |
| Correct: | Immoral behavior results from unethical thinking. |

# 4. MISPLACED AND DANGLING MODIFIERS

A **misplaced modifier** is a modifier that is separated from the word or words it modifies, often resulting in a confusing or unintentionally funny sentence. To correct a misplaced modifier, move the modifier as close as possible to the word it is modifying.

| | |
|---|---|
| Misplaced modifier: | The server brought the steak to the man *covered with onions*. (Is the man covered with onions?) |
| Correct: | The server brought the steak *covered with onions* to the man. |
| Misplaced modifier: | Sheila strolled over to look at the birds *wearing her bathing suit*. (Are the birds wearing Sheila's bathing suit?) |
| Correct: | Sheila, *wearing her bathing suit*, strolled over to look at the birds. |

A **dangling modifier** modifies a word that is not actually in the sentence. The writer often believes the word has been stated, but that is not the case. To fix a dangling modifier, you must rewrite the sentence by adding in the word that the modifier is describing. To avoid a misplaced modifier, be certain to place the word correctly.

| | |
|---|---|
| Dangling modifier: | Looking for a new way to treat heart disease, medical advances were made. (Who is the person or people looking for a new way to treat heart disease?) |
| Correct: | Looking for a new way to treat heart disease, *researchers* made medical advances. |
| Dangling modifier: | After reading the book, the movie was disappointing. (Is the movie disappointed?) |
| Correct: | After reading the book, Hannah found the movie disappointing. |

# 5. ACTIVE AND PASSIVE VOICE

Verbs have both **passive** and **active** voice. Most readers prefer active rather than passive voice because active voice is more direct and makes clear who or what is acting. Passive voice, on the other hand, suggests that the subject is being acted upon. Sentences written in passive voice often use a form of the helping verb *to be* plus a past participle (see Section 1 on auxiliary verbs and participles).

Active voice: The traffic cop gave Lola a ticket.
Passive voice: Lola was given a ticket by the traffic cop.

While active voice is stressed in good writing, there is a reason why writers sometimes use passive voice. For instance, when you are describing an action that caused you to have an accident, using passive voice might help to distance you from your own actions:

Passive voice: The accident was caused because I didn't see the stop sign.

Another reason writers use passive voice is because the doer isn't known or isn't important to the point of the sentence:

Passive voice: The mixture is folded into the sauce.

# 6. SUBJECT-VERB AGREEMENT

Subjects and verbs must agree in number. Interestingly, a noun (subject) becomes plural when you add "s" to it; however, a verb that ends in "s" is singular:

The *girl plays* with the soccer ball.
The *girls play* with the soccer ball.

■ Most subject-verb agreement problems occur when words come between the subject and the verb; therefore, it is important to recognize the subject of the sentence. In order to do so, sometimes you must cross out prepositional phrases since the object of the prepositional phrase is sometimes mistaken for the subject of the sentence:

Incorrect: The *gifts* on the credenza *belongs* to me.
Correct: The *gifts* on the credenza *belong* to me.

■ A compound subject needs a plural verb:

Incorrect: My aunt and my niece *is* going to the movies.
Correct: My aunt and my niece *are* going to the movies.

■ Collective nouns (*family, group, audience, crowd, navy, faculty*) usually take a singular verb because such a group functions as a single unit.

Incorrect: The *family are* angry at the negative press coverage.
Correct: The *family is* angry at the negative press coverage.

■ Indefinite pronouns (*one, everyone, anyone, anything, each, every-body, nobody, nothing, no one, none, neither, either, somebody, some-one, something*) usually take a singular verb:

Incorrect:    *Everybody* in the school *are* going home now.
Correct:    *Everybody* in the school *is* going home now.

■ When the normal order of subject-verb is reversed, the verb must still agree with the actual subject:

Incorrect:    There *is* far too many *miles* to cover to go on foot.
Correct:    There *are* far too many *miles* to cover to go on foot.
Incorrect:    Where *is* my *purse and keys*?
Correct:    Where *are* my *purse and keys*?
Incorrect:    Through the mountains *are* the *pass* to the north.
Correct:    Through the mountains *is* the *pass* to the north.

# 7. VERB TENSE

Mistakes in verb usage involve more than subject-verb agreement errors:

**Tense Shift.** Often students change tense from past to present without any logical reason. This shift in verb tense is an error you can easily catch before turning in a final product.

Incorrect:    After Kathleen and Sandra *went* to the movies, they *are* ready to have a good lunch.
Correct:    After Kathleen and Sandra *went* to the movies, they *were* ready to have a good lunch.
Incorrect:    Ken *cleaned* the basement before Dylan *had said* he would clean it.
Correct:    Ken cleaned the basement before Dylan *said* he would clean it.

**Historical Present Tense.** When discussing literature, film, art, or histori-cal documents, use the present tense. Works of art, whether visual, writ-ten, historical, or musical, always exist in the present.

Incorrect:    In Shakespeare's *Hamlet*, the Prince of Denmark *was* caught up in an existential dilemma about whether life is worth living.
Correct:    In Shakespeare's *Hamlet*, the Prince of Denmark *is* caught up in an existential dilemma about whether life is worth living.

**Modals.** Modals are verbs used only as helping verbs (*can, might, should, could, must, will, may, shall, would*). The modal is joined to the simple form of the main verb. Also, unlike other helping verbs, modals do not change form to agree in number with the subject; neither does the main verb that follows:

> Sharon *might* drive to Montana tomorrow. *might* + drive
> Robin *would* dance if she knew how. *would* + dance
> Donna *shall* go to the memorial service. *shall* + go

The *exception* to this rule occurs when the modal is followed by another helping verb:

> Owen *could* have gotten his Ph.D. if he had continued his education. *could* + have + gotten

Another problem with modals is the confusion of the preposition "of" with the helping verb "have." These two words sound alike in English, but it is important not to confuse the two words:

> Incorrect: Dan should *of* picked up the speaker for the conference.
> Correct: Dan should *have* picked up the speaker for the conference.
> Incorrect: Lea Ann might *of* gone with us.
> Correct: Lea Ann might *have* gone with us.

**Two-Part Verbs.** Several verbs consist of two words. It is important when using these verbs to include both words as the verb in the sentence.

Common two-part verbs:

| | | | | |
|---|---|---|---|---|
| ask out | break down | call up | clean up | drop in |
| get along | give up | help out | keep up | leave out |
| make up | pick up | play around | put together | shut up |

> Incorrect: Judith decided to *drop* on Renee.
> Correct: Judith decided to *drop in* on Renee.
> Incorrect: Steve said, "*Keep* the good work!"
> Correct: Steve said, "*Keep up* the good work!"

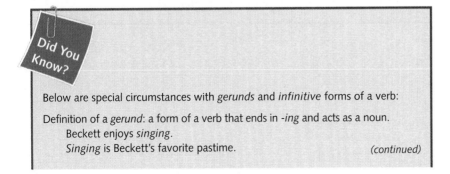

**Did You Know?**

Below are special circumstances with *gerunds* and *infinitive* forms of a verb:

Definition of a *gerund*: a form of a verb that ends in *-ing* and acts as a noun.
  Beckett enjoys *singing*.
  *Singing* is Beckett's favorite pastime.

*(continued)*

Definition of an *infinitive*: the word *to* + the simple form of a verb

Bob decided *to park* his SUV.

- The following verbs can be followed by either a *gerund* or an *infinitive* without changing the meaning when used in a sentence:

  begin    like    stand    love    continue    start    hate

  I began *to love* the concert when Richard came on stage.
  I began *loving* the concert when Richard came on stage.

- However, with other verbs, the meaning of a sentence changes depending on whether the verb is followed by a gerund or an infinitive:

  Jamye stopped *eating* chocolates. = Jamye cut chocolate out of her diet.
  Jamye stopped *to eat* a chocolate. = Jamye stopped to take a bite of chocolate.

- Some verbs may be followed by a gerund *but not* by an infinitive:

  | | | |
  |---|---|---|
  | admit | escape | quit |
  | appreciate | finish | recall |
  | avoid | imagine | resist |
  | deny | miss | risk |
  | discuss | practice | suggest |
  | enjoy | put off | tolerate |

  Correct:    Ashley admitted snitching the watermelon.
  Incorrect:    Ashley admitted to snitch the watermelon.
  Correct:    Bobbi stopped inviting the couple to dinner.
  Incorrect:    Bobbi stopped to invite the couple to dinner.

- Other verbs may be followed by an infinitive *but not* by a gerund:

  | | | |
  |---|---|---|
  | agree | hope | plan |
  | ask | manage | promise |
  | beg | mean | wait |
  | decide | need | want |
  | expect | offer | wish |
  | have | | |

  Correct:    Alan asked to leave early.
  Incorrect:    Alan asked leaving early.
  Correct:    Lydia hoped to marry her new boyfriend.
  Incorrect:    Lydia hoped marrying her new boyfriend.

# 8. NOMINALS AND THE VERB *TO BE*

Nominals are nouns created from verbs. Using nominals (also called nominalizations) tends to create a less dynamic piece of writing and can make writing sound stilted and bureaucratic. They not only create dull and leaden sentences but also rely too heavily on the verb *to be* and on a series of prepositional phrases. Avoiding nominals is a way to make your writing more lively and energetic.

Since nominals are nouns created from verbs, often nominals contain a form of the verb:

description (describe)

expectation (expect)

expression (express)

installation (install)

production (produce)

promotion (promote)

solution (solve)

Try to revise sentences that contain nominals, using the active verb instead of the nominalization:

| | |
|---|---|
| Nominalized: | Cheryl's expectation of receiving the promotion caused her to consider all of the ramifications. |
| Revised: | Since Cheryl expected to be promoted, she considered the ramifications. |
| Nominalized: | The magazine contained a description of the installation process for the thermostat. |
| Revised: | The magazine described how to install the thermostat. |
| Nominalized: | The objection of the Board chair was to the stultification of the language. |
| Revised: | The Board chair objected to the stultified language. |

# 9. PRONOUN AGREEMENT AND PRONOUN REFERENCE

## Pronoun Agreement

Pronouns are wonderful words that prevent writers from having to constantly restate nouns; however, when using pronouns you must make sure they agree in number with the nouns to which they refer. A singular pronoun refers to a singular noun; a plural noun requires a plural pronoun:

| | |
|---|---|
| Incorrect: | *One* of the students lost *their* book. |
| Correct: | *One* of the students lost *his* book. |
| Incorrect: | *Everyone* in the class was worried about *their* test score. |
| Correct: | *Everyone* in the class was worried about *his or her* test score. |
| Correct: | The *students* worried about *their* test scores. |

## Pronoun Reference

**Vague Pronoun Reference.** Not only should pronouns agree with nouns in number but they must also provide a very clear reference to the noun in question. This noun is called the pronoun referent or the pronoun antecedent. If your readers can't tell to what noun the pronoun is referring, you have committed a pronoun reference error.

| | |
|---|---|
| Vague: | In France, some of them are very cool to Americans. (To whom does "them" refer?) |
| Clear: | Some French citizens are very cool to Americans. |
| Vague: | In the article, they urged all students should get a swine flu shot. (To whom does "they" refer?) |
| Clear: | In the article, the immunologists urged all students to get a swine flu shot. |
| Vague: | Janice told Vicki that she would need new sheet music. (To whom does "she" refer?) |
| Clear: | Janice said, "Vicki, I need new sheet music." |
| Clear: | Janice told Vicki that she, Janice, would need new sheet music. |
| Vague: | If mothers neglect their children, we should turn them in to Child Protective Services. (To whom does "them" refer?) |
| Clear: | If mothers neglect their children, we should turn the mothers in to Child Protective Services. |

**Broad Pronoun Reference.** Broad pronoun reference happens when a pronoun stands for a whole group of words or ideas rather than a single, definable noun. Whenever you use pronouns such as *this, that,* or *it,* be careful that these pronouns refer back to a clear antecedent.

| | |
|---|---|
| Broad: | There are several factors to consider when deciding whether or not the day care facility should be granted a lease. *This* is what the committee needs to discuss. |
| Clear: | There are several factors to consider when deciding whether or not the day care facility should be granted a lease. *These factors* are what the committee needs to discuss. |

# 10. FAULTY PARALLELISM

When two or more words or groups of words in a sentence are parts of a pair or a series, these words or groups of words should be in parallel grammatical structures. Any repeated sentence elements (see Section 2) should be written in parallel form.

Faulty:    Susan sings, dances, and knows how to act.
Parallel:    Susan *sings, dances*, and *acts*. (parallel verbs)
Faulty:    Dylan likes to listen to music and playing drums.
Parallel:    Dylan likes *to listen to music* and *to play drums*. (parallel infinitive phrases)
Parallel:    Dylan likes *listening to music* and *playing the drums*. (parallel gerund phrases)
Faulty:    Her lectures are boring because she talks in a monotone, she doesn't use visual aids, and there's no questions allowed.
Parallel:    Her lectures are boring because she talks in a monotone, she doesn't use visual aids, and she doesn't allow questions. (parallel clauses)

In addition to making certain that repeated sentence elements are in parallel structure, certain words (such as articles, prepositions, and conjunctions) should also be in parallel form when used in a pair or a series.

Faulty:    The driver's education instructor told the students *that* they must have their driver's permits and they must have signed parental permission slips.
Parallel:    The driver's education instructor told the students *that* they must have their driver's permits and *that* they must have signed parental permission slips.
Faulty:    The instructors also cautioned students not *to* chew gum, eat snacks, or drink colas in the training cars.
Parallel:    The instructors also cautioned students not *to* chew gum, *to* eat snacks, or *to* drink colas in the training cars.

Relative subordinate clauses (clauses beginning with *which, that, who,* or *whom*) are preceded by a relative clause beginning with *which, that, who,* or *whom*.

Faulty:    Wayne is the person *who* not only loves Julia but has stood by her during bad times.
Parallel:    Wayne is the person *who* not only loves Julia but *who* has stood by her in bad times.

# SECTION 3
# Punctuation, Spelling, and Mechanics

Many students are surprised to learn that the rules of punctuation have not always been standardized. In fact, it was not until the mass printing of the Christian Bible that modern punctuation marks in English and most European languages began to be widely used. Some languages, such as Chinese, Japanese, and Korean, did not use any punctuation marks at all until very recently. However, without punctuation, many sentences would be confusing or ambivalent. For instance, consider the following: **Woman, without her man, is nothing.** Note how the meaning changes when the punctuation changes: **Woman: without her, man is nothing.** While punctuation (as other aspects of language) will continue to evolve, the rules of punctuation listed in this section are standard at this time.

## 1. COMMAS

Commas, as well as other forms of punctuation, are used to help the reader understand a piece of writing without a great deal of effort on the reader's part. Many writers are confused about when to use commas and when not to. Some writers seem to just close their eyes and use a "comma shaker," letting commas fall wherever they may! However, there are clear rules that dictate when commas must be used. It's not hard to learn these rules.

- Use commas with introductory elements (words, phrases, clauses). After an introductory element, place a comma to separate that element from the main clause of the sentence:

  *Finally*, we were allowed to leave the crime scene. (introductory word)

  After photographing the mess, we were allowed to leave the crime scene. (introductory phrase)

  Before the detectives started to interview the suspect, we were allowed to leave the crime scene. (introductory clause)

- Use commas to separate items in a series: these items can be words, phrases, or clauses. Don't use a comma before the first item in the series or after the last item.

  Dillon collected *guppies, goldfish,* and *angelfish*.

  When Lara came to work, she *turned off the alarm, made the coffee,* and *watered the begonia*.

**H-34**

*Sarah didn't read the assignment, she didn't complete the home-work,* and *she didn't study for the test.*

▪ Use commas to separate two independent clauses joined with a conjunction:

Mike wanted to go to the race, *but* he also needed to mow the lawn.
Mike could choose to please himself, *or* he could choose to please his mother.
The race was a once-in-a-lifetime chance to see his favorite NASCAR driver, *so* Mike decided to put off mowing the lawn.

▪ Use commas before and after elements that interrupt a sentence. If a word, phrase, or clause interrupts the flow of a sentence *and if* it could be removed from the sentence without changing the meaning, use commas before and after that element. If the element comes at the end of the sentence, use a comma before it.

Betty's first dinner party, *happily,* was a big success.
Marvin, *who fixed her plumbing,* was not able to come.
The dinner party, *held during the boxing championship,* was one of the biggest events of the Memorial Day weekend.
Marvin liked boxing more than social events, *especially dinner parties.*

▪ Use commas to set off transitional elements from the sentence.

Brian didn't want to see a romance movie, *however,* so Rebecca agreed to his favorite action movie.
*On the other hand,* Rebecca disliked horror movies.
She once had gotten nauseated, *for instance,* while watching a zombie flick.
*Therefore,* Brian avoided taking her to scary movies.

▪ Use commas in dates to separate the day of the month from the year. If the year is in the middle of the sentence, use a comma after the year.

Angel's birthday is *January 23, 2002*.
Oni was born on *September 8, 2003,* and was the first girl in the family.
The family was complete after Shane was born on *January 31, 2008*.

▪ Use commas in addresses. Separate the various parts of an address (such as the street, city, county, state or province, country) with commas. If an address appears in the middle of a sentence, place a comma after it.

Mary Lou has lived at *1304 Emeritus Drive, Kansas City, Missouri,* since she retired.

All U.S. presidents reside at *1600 Pennsylvania Avenue, Washington, DC.*

The farmer had spent his entire life in *Bernalillo County, New Mexico.*

■ Use commas in direct quotations of speech.

"Whenever we go out to eat," Martha complained, "you always choose the restaurant."

"That's not true," Dave replied.

According to Miles Martin, "The U.S. Postal Service delivers minor miracles every day."

■ When *not* to use commas:

1. Do not put a comma between a subject and a verb:

Incorrect:   The most wonderful day of our *vacation, was* the day we toured the Washington Mall.

Correct:   The most wonderful day of our *vacation was* the day we toured the Washington Mall.

2. Do not put a comma between compound subjects or compound verbs:

Incorrect:   *The winner of the pageant, and the Master of Ceremonies* posed for photos.

Correct:   *The winner of the pageant and the Master of Ceremonies* posed for photos.

Incorrect:   Although Margaret was chosen as 1st Runner-Up, *she decided to stay in the background, and to sit on the couch.*

Correct:   Although Margaret was chosen as 1st Runner-Up, *she decided to stay in the background and to sit on the couch.*

## 2. SEMICOLONS

Semicolons are a stronger form of punctuation than commas; you can use semicolons for several purposes.

■ Use a semicolon to separate two independent clauses that are closely related.

Sue enjoyed autumn more than any other *season; she* always planned a fall trip to see the leaves turn color.

■ Use a semicolon to separate items in a series that already includes commas.

Three young women were chosen to intern at the State Department: Lila, who had extensive experience in eastern European *languages;*

*Ann*, who was the daughter of a former *diplomat; and* Kelsey, whose stellar academic performance and leadership skills made her a strong choice.

■ Use a semicolon to link two independent clauses that are joined by a transitional word:

Most people say they don't believe in ghosts*; nevertheless,* almost everyone enjoys a good ghost story.

My cousin Kay believes in ghosts because of some experiences*; for example,* she once came face-to-face with the ghost of a Union soldier on the memorial of the Bull Run battlefield.

I wanted to visit the battlefield with Kay*; however,* she refused to return with me.

■ Do *not* use semicolons to separate independent and dependent clauses:

Incorrect:  Because Kelsey had stellar grades and strong leadership *qualities; she* was chosen to be an intern at the State Department.

## 3. COLONS

Colons are used to make meaning clear.

■ Use a colon to introduce a list. However, use the colon only when it will follow an independent clause. Never use a colon after a verb or after expressions like *such as* or *for example*:

Incorrect:  Connie needed several items from the store *such as:* milk, bread, butter, and eggs.

Incorrect:  Connie *needed:* milk, bread, butter, and eggs.

Correct:  Connie needed several items from the *store:* milk, bread, butter, and eggs.

■ Use a colon to introduce an explanation:

Connie agreed to something she had never allowed *before:* Her 12-year-old son could ride to the store on his bike.

The principal finally came to a *decision:* no tank tops in the gym.

# 4. END PUNCTUATION

End punctuation includes periods, question marks, and exclamation points.

## Periods

Periods are considered end punctuation marks; use them at the end of sentences, including indirect questions (remember that questions require a question mark at the end of the sentence):

| | |
|---|---|
| Sentence: | The colorful leaves fluttered to the grass. |
| Indirect Question: | Sue asked me when I expected the leaves to fall. |

## Question Marks

Use question marks after direct questions. Do not combine question marks with commas or periods.

| | |
|---|---|
| Incorrect: | She asked, "When do you think the leaves will fall?." |
| Incorrect: | "When do you think the leaves will fall?," she asked. |
| Correct: | She asked, "When do you think the leaves will fall?" |

## Exclamation Points

You might have noticed that some writers use exclamation points after every other sentence. However, exclamation points should be used very sparingly, such as when you are writing a sentence that needs emphasis or shows great emotion. Using them frequently would be like talking to someone who shouts each sentence: Most people would find that annoying or disturbing.

> Hannah went to the mall to shop for clothes because she needed a dress for her recital. She tried on dresses at five different stores, and nothing matched the picture she had formed in her mind of an elegant black dress with a ruffled neckline. She became tired and discouraged, and finally despaired of ever finding what she wanted. On her way through the north part of the mall to the parking lot, she glanced up at the window of a boutique she had overlooked, and there it was—*the perfect dress*!

# **5.** APOSTROPHES

An apostrophe is used to show possession, to form contractions, and to form some plurals.

## Possession

- Use an apostrophe to show that something belongs to someone or something. If the item belongs to one person, use *'s* after the noun that refers to the person, even if the noun already ends in *-s*.

  *Jackie's* violin is almost new.
  *Brooks's* violin, on the other hand, is over two hundred years old.

- If the thing belongs to more than one person and the noun that refers to these persons ends in *-s*, use only an apostrophe after the *-s*. If the plural noun doesn't end in *-s*, use *'s* after it.

  Most of the *students'* violins were rented.
  The *women's* contributions to the symphony were acknowledged.

- If the thing belongs to a person represented by a compound word, add *'s* to the last word in the compound word.

  Her father-in-*law's* long career spanned five decades.

- Do *not* use *'s* with the possessive form of personal pronouns (*yours, his, hers, ours, theirs, its, whose*):

  The pie plate is *hers*.
  The cat licks *its* fur.
  *Yours* is the fastest car in the race.

## Contractions

- Use an apostrophe to form a contraction, which is the combining of two words into one by omitting one or more letters. The *'s* indicates the omitted letters.

  There's (there is) only one life jacket in the boat.
  Since Harry's (Harry is) a strong swimmer, Betty will use the life jacket.
  However, Betty doesn't (does not) want to wear it.
  I'm (I am) going to insist that she put it on.

## Plurals

- Use an apostrophe to form the plural of letters or numbers used as words. *Exception:* With decades, simply add an *-s* (1960s).

  The judges gave me all 10's at the gymnastic meet.
  Please dot your *i*'s and cross your *t*'s; also, don't use so many
    therefores in your essay.

- Do *not* use apostrophes to form the plural of numbers, whether written in words or numerals.

  She scored somewhere in the nineties.
  She scored somewhere in the 90s.

- Do *not* use apostrophes when forming the plural of an abbreviation.

  Joshua lost all of my *Touched by an Angel* DVDs.

- Do *not* use apostrophes with decades; simply add an -*s* (1960s).

  The 1960s were years of social upheaval and changing norms.

- Do *not* use apostrophes to form simple plurals.

  The *cars* on the track belong to Jeff Gordon; however, the *fire-suits* belong to the team's sponsor.

Did You Know?

Originally, the apostrophe always represented omitted letters. When forming possession in older English, the convention was to say, "He borrowed John his book." In other words, the possessive pronoun directly followed its own antecedent, which was awkward and difficult to enunciate. As people spoke, their tongues would slide over the "h + i" in "his," and eventually the letters also disappeared from the written form of the language. "He borrowed John's book."

# 6. HYPHENS AND DASHES

## Hyphens

Use hyphens for compound nouns, compound adjectives, some prefixes, and some numbers. Since hyphen usage can be idiomatic (without rules), check a good dictionary when in doubt.

| | |
|---|---|
| compound nouns | president-elect |
| compound adjectives | blue-eyed girl; thirty-year-old Muslim; tried-and-true method |
| prefixes | ex-wife; self-preservation |
| numbers | eighty-six; one-tenth |

# Dashes

Dashes are often used in more informal writing to give special emphasis to the word or words that are set off. (A dash is formed by typing two hyphens—leave no space before, after, or between the hyphens.)

> Aunt Susan brought the brisket—as well as the side dishes and dessert—to the church hall.

> Irritation, embarrassment, and humiliation—that's what Stacey's two little brothers always seemed to cause her in public.

# 7. CAPITALS AND NUMBERS

## Capitals

Today, writers tend to use fewer capitals when the use of capitals is optional. Whenever these optional situations arise, be consistent with your use of capitals. The rules for capitals follow.

- Capitalize the personal pronoun *I*.

  Although I'm tired, I don't want to go home yet.

- Capitalize the first letter of the first word in every sentence.

  Let's go now. The first showing has shorter lines.

- Capitalize proper nouns (nouns that refer to a specific person, place, event, or thing). Do not capitalize common nouns (nouns that refer to a general category of persons, places, events, or things).

| Proper Noun | Common Noun |
|---|---|
| Providence College | the college |
| Mexico | a country |
| Sunday | a day |
| Mother (used as a name) | my mother |
| Senator Kennedy | a senator |
| God | a god |
| the South | south of the lake |
| The Declaration of Independence | a declaration |
| Chemistry 3302 | a chemistry class |
| the Civil War | a war |
| the Great Depression | an economic depression |
| Halloween, Christmas | autumn, winter |

■ Capitalize the names of organizations, institutions, and trademarks, as well as abbreviations of such.

My grandfather was a lifelong *Democrat*.
I hope to buy a *Thomasville* dining room set.
My friend and his family are members of the *NAACP*.
He received a basketball scholarship from the *University of Texas at El Paso*.
His sister also planned to attend *UTEP*.

■ Capitalize all words in titles except articles (*a, an, the*), coordinating conjunctions (*for, and, nor, but, or, yet, so*), and prepositions (such as *of, on, in, at, with, for*) unless they are the first or last word in the title.

*The Catcher in the Rye*
*The Last Temptation of Christ*
the *New York Times* (do not capitalize *the* before names of newspapers)

■ Capitalize the first word of quotations, but do not capitalize the first word in the second half of a quotation interrupted by an attributive tag.

Dale whispered, "I beg you to not cause a scene."
"I beg you," Dale whispered, "to not cause a scene."

## Numbers

It can be confusing to know when to spell out numbers and when to use numerals. In the fields of science, mathematics, and technology, writers often use numerals for all numbers. Check with your instructors in such courses about the conventions they want you to use in lab reports and essays. Otherwise:

■ Spell out numbers instead of using numerals from one through ninety-nine, as well as single-word numbers:

seven geese; a hundred bottle caps

■ Spell out numbers instead of using numerals when using two-word numbers (except possibly for science, mathematics, or business reports—check with your instructor).

thirty-nine plates

■ Spell out numbers instead of using numerals when using common fractions:

half of the donut; one-tenth of the total amount

■ Spell out numbers instead of using numerals when the number is expressed in two words:

two hundred students; three thousand protestors

- Spell out numbers instead of using numerals when the number begins the sentence:

  One hundred thirty-five band uniforms were donated by the corporation.

- Use numerals instead of spelling out words for all other numbers, including decimals, percentages, years, times of day, addresses, amounts of money that include cents, game scores, and when referring to chapters, pages, or lines of a text.

|  |  |
|---|---|
| Decimals: | His share of the profit was calculated at *21.27*. |
| Percentages: | Two of the students were awarded *30%* of the points. |
| Years: | He was born in *1991*. |
| Times of day: | Darkness now falls at *5:30* p.m. |
| Addresses: | They live at *1600* Pennsylvania Ave., Washington, DC. |
| Money that includes cents: | She received a refund of *$11.37*. |
| Game scores: | The Giants beat the Mets *12* to *9*. |
| Chapters, pages, and lines of text: | Please turn to Chapter *10*, page *247*, line *21*. |

# 8. QUOTATION MARKS AND ELLIPSIS POINTS

## Quotation Marks

Quotation marks are used to enclose the exact words of a writer or speaker, as well as the titles of short works such as articles, essays, poems, and songs.

- Use quotation marks to set off a writer's or speaker's **exact** words:

  According to Louis Brennan, the author of *Text-Speak Must Go*, "Those who limit most of their communication to text messages are damaging the complexity and texture of the languages they are abbreviating."
  "Don't be rude!" Robert exclaimed.

- Use quotation marks for titles of short works, such as articles in a magazine or newspaper, essays, poems, and songs.

  My favorite song is "Scarlet Tide" from the movie soundtrack *Cold Mountain*.
  Robert Frost's poem "Two Roads Diverged in a Yellow Wood" is one that almost every American high school student is required to read.
  "Civil Disobedience," an essay by Henry David Thoreau, is thought to have contributed to Ghandi's vision of nonviolent protest.

- Use quotation marks to set off words used ironically or needing special emphasis (limit this usage, which is termed "scare quotes," to the absolutely necessary):

  Chad denied that Cherie was his "significant other."

  Since Dad said that cleaning was "kid's play," Mom decided to let him clean the house by himself.

- When formatting block quotations, do *not* use quotation marks. Block quotes are quotations that are four typed lines or longer. These long quotes are set off, or blocked off, from the paper by indenting the quote ten spaces from the left margin. Block quotes must be introduced by a complete sentence followed by a colon. Note that the parenthetical citation in this case is placed outside of the last period of the quote.

  The author asserts how important it is for health care professionals to understand the needs of the family of the dying:

  > The most meaningful help that we can give any relative . . . is to share his feelings before the event of death and to allow him to work through his feelings. . . . If we tolerate their [relatives'] anger, whether it is directed at us, at the deceased, or at God, we are helping them take a great step towards acceptance without guilt. (Kubler-Ross 180)

- Conventions in quotations:

  1. Everything inside of quotation marks must be taken **exactly** from the text or the words of your source. You cannot change punctuation, vocabulary, sentence structure, or even misspellings or other errors (see information on the use of brackets for how to handle such errors inside a quotation).

  2. When quoting, you should always include an *attributive tag*, which indicates who wrote or spoke the content of the quotation. Attributive tags must be punctuated correctly:

     *Bette Davis quipped,* "Old age ain't for sissies!"

     "Old age," *Bette Davis quipped*, "ain't for sissies!"

     "Old age ain't for sissies!" *Bette Davis quipped*.

  3. However, when you place a quotation into a sentence you construct, you need not set off the quotation with punctuation, nor should you capitalize the first letter of the quoted material:

     Bette Davis quipped that "old age ain't for sissies!"

  4. When punctuating the end of a quotation, place commas and periods **inside** the end quotation mark:

     The librarian told us to "please be silent."

The librarian told us to "please be silent," and she lifted her finger to her lips.

5. Place semicolons and colons **outside** the end quotation mark:

The librarian told us to "please be silent"; then she lifted her finger to her lips.

The librarian commanded us to follow her "wishes": to be silent and still.

6. Use a single quotation mark (indicated by an apostrophe) to enclose a quotation that occurs within a quotation:

"Every single time it's Heidi's turn to cook," Karl complained, "she always says, 'I'm too tired; let's go out to eat.'"

7. When citing sources in your paper, some formats place citations inside parentheses at the end of the quotation. When following this type of citation format, place the comma or period after the parenthetical citation, **not** after the end of the quote:

Psychiatrist Elizabeth Kubler-Ross, in her ground-breaking book *On Death and Dying*, writes that "the more we are making advancements in science, the more we seem to fear and deny the reality of death" (7).

8. Place question marks and exclamation points within the end quotation mark if they are part of the quotation. Place them outside the end quotation mark if they belong to you.

Emily, who loved to dress up, was thrilled to find out that the restaurant stipulated "no tank tops allowed"!

Mark stared glumly at the stairway sign that said, "Race to the top!"

## Ellipsis Points

Ellipsis points are indicated with three spaced period marks and signify that words within a quotation have been omitted. When using ellipsis points, you must make certain that the quotation remains grammatically intact. When the omission occurs at the end of a sentence, a period mark is placed before the three ellipsis points to mark the end of the sentence.

The most meaningful help that we can give any relative . . . is to share his feelings before the event of death and to allow him to work through his feelings. . . . If we tolerate their [relatives'] anger, whether it is directed at us, at the deceased, or at God, we are helping them. . ." states Kubler-Ross (180).

Note that the first use of ellipsis points indicates omitted words within the sentence. The second use indicates that words were omitted at the end of the sentence, which requires an additional period mark. The third use of ellipsis points comes at the end of the quote itself, so the period mark goes after the parenthetical citation.

# 9. PARENTHESES AND BRACKETS

## Parentheses ( )

Sentences with parentheses are punctuated outside the parenthesis marks exactly as if there were no parenthetical expression. The parenthetical expression itself is also punctuated as though it stood on its own (except that you omit the final punctuation mark unless that punctuation mark is an exclamation point or a question mark).

- Use parentheses to set off additional, related comments or explanations:

    Jonathan couldn't bear for the elderly people (George and Martha Stillman, Shirley Owens, and Mariah Little) to have to stand throughout the entire ceremony.
    Lester insists (and I believe him!) that he did not perjure himself in court.

- Use parentheses to list numbers in a series that are part of a running text:

    In order to succeed in college, freshmen students need to achieve certain goals: (1) go to every class, (2) complete all reading and homework on time, (3) organize their priorities, and (4) get extra help with difficult subjects.

- Use parentheses to enclose citations in formats that require parenthetical documentation:

    According to Daniel Pool in his book *What Jane Austen Ate and Charles Dickens Knew*, "Death—early death—was no stranger to the nineteenth-century English family, and perhaps that is why they loved to weep over the lingering demises of Dickens's small heroes and heroines" (252).

## Brackets [ ]

Brackets are used to set off explanatory material that you insert into a quotation in order to clarify something readers might find confusing (since they are reading the quotation out of its context).

- This is often the case when the quote includes a pronoun but not the preceding antecedent or referent:

  "If we tolerate their [relatives'] anger, whether it is directed at us, at the deceased, at God, we are helping them take a great step towards acceptance without guilt," states Kubler-Ross (180).

- Brackets are also used to indicate that an error in the quoted text is in the original material and is not your error. In this case, you insert the Latin word *sic* (meaning "thus it is") right after the error:

  Judge Marchel commented, "After we hear the testamony [*sic*] of the defendant, we'll adjourn for the day."

- In addition, you can use brackets when you need to change something in the quotation to make it grammatically correct in the context of your sentence:

  Original source: "I believe prayer to be a force of reconciliation to reality rather than a wish-list of the way things should be," declared Rev. Lanham.
  Brackets: Rev. Lanham believes that "prayer [is] a force of reconciliation to reality rather than a wish-list of the way things should be."

## 10. ITALICS AND UNDERLINES

Italicize (or underline in handwritten or non-word-processed typewritten copy) the titles of books, magazines, long (book-length) poems, movies, television shows, newspapers, journals, computer software, and long musical scores (such as the title of a CD, opera, musical, etc.). When italicizing or underlining titles, include the articles *a, an*, and *the* only if they are part of the title. For instance, never italicize or underline *the* before the title of a newspaper.

- Italicize or underline titles:

  Ginny read *Wuthering Heights* in high school, and it unfortunately formed the ideal of what she believed true love to be.
  Albert got his material from <u>Newsday</u> magazine, as well as the <u>Encyclopedia Britannica.</u>
  Lydia chose to use the *New York Times*, the *Washington Post*, and the *San Francisco Chronicle* as her sources.
  We're going to see an exceptional production of *Grease*!
  Ken never missed an episode of *Ghost Whisperer*.
  When I bought my new laptop, I was given a free copy of *Windows 7*.

*Abbey Road* is Lisa's favorite Beatles' album.

Our choir has decided to tackle Handel's <u>Messiah</u>, despite our lack of strong sopranos.

■ Italicize or underline foreign words and phrases. However, any foreign words that have become integrated into the English language need not be italicized or underlined (if you are unsure whether a particular word should be italicized/underlined or not, consult a good dictionary):

*Carpe diem* is the best way to live your life!

"*Buenos dias, Senora!*" Jack called out to his Spanish teacher.

Betty and Frank decided to have burritos for lunch out on the back patio of the crumbling *hacienda*, despite the fact that coyotes had been spotted scavenging there recently. (The Spanish words burritos, patio, and coyotes have been integrated into English, thus italics are not needed. On the other hand, the Spanish word "hacienda" is not yet commonly spoken in English.)

# 11. ABBREVIATIONS

An abbreviation, a shortened version of word or phrase, can be used in formal papers in some instances.

■ Use standard abbreviations for titles and academic degrees before or after proper names:

Dr. David Carrasco
Ms. Joanne Waggoner
Kathy Taylor, M.D.
Alfred Nowell, Jr.

■ Use abbreviations for the names of organizations, corporations, agencies, or terms that are commonly known by their capitalized initials:

CBS    CIA    YWCA    DVD    CD-ROM

■ If you wish to abbreviate the title of something that is less well-known, spell it out the first time you use it, placing the abbreviation in parentheses directly after it. Your audience can be expected to know what the abbreviation stands for in every subsequent mention.

Duke University has done scientific studies on extrasensory perception (ESP) that the FBI is interested in employing. The Department of Homeland Security (DHS) is also interested in the research.

- Do not overuse the Latin abbreviation *etc.* (the abbreviation for *et cetera*, which means "and so forth"). Try not to use *etc.* in formal papers, but instead either use the English words "and so forth" or be more specific in your language.

  Poor:  Mindy and Jonas decided to pack all of their DVDs, CDs, books, papers, etc., even though they were going to be gone for only two months.

  Good:  Mindy and Jonas decided to pack all of their DVDs, CDs, books, and papers even though they were going to be gone for only two months.

  Good:  Mindy and Jonas decided to pack all of their DVDs, CDs, books, papers, and so forth, even though they were going to be gone for only two months.

- Do *not* use apostrophes when forming the plural of an abbreviation.

  Joshua lost all of my *Touched by an Angel* DVDs.

# 12. SPELLING AND HOMONYMS

Even with spell-checkers, spelling errors remain an issue in college composition, yet it takes very little effort to ensure that your paper is turned in free of these errors. Keep in mind that whether in school, the workplace, or in the personal arena, nothing reduces your *ethos* (your credibility) more than spelling errors. It is worth the time it takes to find and correct spelling errors before turning in final written products.

## Use a Spell-Checker

Spell-check programs are good, but they cannot ensure complete correctness, especially when the word you are attempting to spell is grossly misspelled. If you are unsure of how to spell the first few letters of a word, you probably need to do some dictionary work with alternate spellings in order to find the word you are looking for.

## Use a Dictionary

After looking up a word, find its meaning and see if that is the word you are looking for. Dictionaries first list the word, its syllabification (how you divide the word between lines), its pronunciation, its part of speech (including plural form), its meaning, and its origin (appears in brackets).

# Correct Homonym Errors

Spell-check programs rarely catch homonym errors (words that sound alike but which are spelled differently and which have different meanings). The most common homonym errors include the following:

**Its, It's.** *Its* is a possessive pronoun. Remember, possessive pronouns never contain an apostrophe. *It's* is a contraction of the words *it* and *is*.

> The cat licked *its* fur.
>
> *It's* going to be a difficult day.

*There, They're, Their.* *There* is an adverb, interjection, or a noun/pronoun that is often used as a "dummy subject." Keep in mind that the verb in such a sentence must agree with the actual subject, not the "dummy subject." *They're* is a contraction of the words *they* and *are*. *Their* is a possessive pronoun.

> Let's not go over *there*. *There*—do you see it? *There* is no excuse for turning in shoddy work.
>
> *They're* not going out to dinner tonight.
>
> *Their* house needs to be painted.

*To, Too, Two.* *To* (to the store) is both a preposition and a particle that helps to form the infinitive form of a verb (to go). *Too* is an adverb that means "also." *Two* is a number.

> I have *to* go *to* the store.
>
> She has to go to the store *too*.
>
> The *two* of us need to go to the store.

*Weather, Whether.* *Weather* is a noun that indicates climatic conditions. *Whether* is a conjunction that is used to introduce an indirect question that consists of multiple alternative possibilities and to indicate uncertainty between them.

> The *weather* outside is blustery and cold.
>
> *Whether* or not you want to go, you must.

*You're, Your.* *You're* is a contraction of the words *you* and *are*. *Your* is a possessive pronoun.

> *You're* in no condition to drive.
>
> *Your* car is parked down the street.

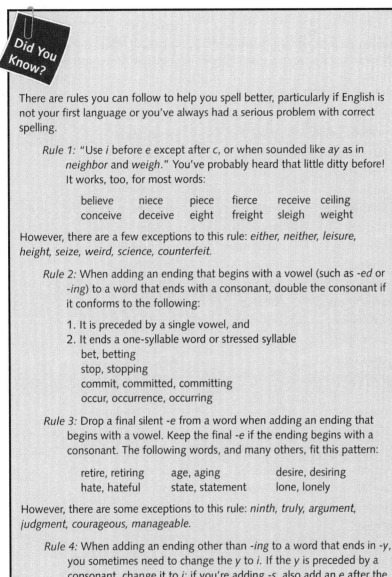

**Did You Know?**

There are rules you can follow to help you spell better, particularly if English is not your first language or you've always had a serious problem with correct spelling.

*Rule 1:* "Use *i* before *e* except after *c*, or when sounded like *ay* as in *neighbor* and *weigh*." You've probably heard that little ditty before! It works, too, for most words:

believe    niece    piece    fierce    receive    ceiling
conceive   deceive  eight    freight   sleigh     weight

However, there are a few exceptions to this rule: *either, neither, leisure, height, seize, weird, science, counterfeit.*

*Rule 2:* When adding an ending that begins with a vowel (such as *-ed* or *-ing*) to a word that ends with a consonant, double the consonant if it conforms to the following:

1. It is preceded by a single vowel, and
2. It ends a one-syllable word or stressed syllable
   bet, betting
   stop, stopping
   commit, committed, committing
   occur, occurrence, occurring

*Rule 3:* Drop a final silent *-e* from a word when adding an ending that begins with a vowel. Keep the final *-e* if the ending begins with a consonant. The following words, and many others, fit this pattern:

retire, retiring    age, aging        desire, desiring
hate, hateful       state, statement  lone, lonely

However, there are some exceptions to this rule: *ninth, truly, argument, judgment, courageous, manageable.*

*Rule 4:* When adding an ending other than *-ing* to a word that ends in *-y*, you sometimes need to change the *y* to *i*. If the *y* is preceded by a consonant, change it to *i*; if you're adding *-s*, also add an e after the *i*. If you're adding *-ing* or the *y* is preceded by a vowel, don't change it to *i*. Here are some common examples of this rule:

easy, easiest      duty, dutiful      reply, replies
marry, married     monkey, monkeys    play, played
apply, applying    dry, drying        stay, staying

## 100 Most Commonly Misspelled Words

If you have a lot of spelling errors, chances are a lot of the words you misspell are in the list below. Practice spelling these words correctly! You can make individual cards with the words that you misspell and work on memorizing the correct spelling.

| | | |
|---|---|---|
| absence | existence | maneuver |
| accommodate | fascinate | marriage |
| all right | February | meant |
| analyze | forty | minute |
| anoint | fulfill | misspelled |
| anonymous | government | necessary |
| benefit | grammar | ninth |
| boundary | guarantee | noticeable |
| business | guard | occurrence |
| category | height | often |
| committee | hoarse | optimistic |
| conscience | holiday | pamphlet |
| conscious | hygiene | parallel |
| corroborate | icicles | peculiar |
| counterfeit | imagine | persistent |
| dealt | indispensable | phenomenon |
| definitely | innocent | perseverance |
| despair | irresistible | principal |
| dilemma | jealousy | privilege |
| ecstasy | league | procedure |
| eighth | leisure | pursue |
| embarrass | license | receipt |
| exceed | losing | receive |
| recommend | sophomore | undoubtedly |
| repetition | subtle | until |
| rhythm | succeed | vacuum |
| ridiculous | supersede | vengeance |
| roommate | surgeon | vicious |
| schedule | tongue | warrant |
| seize | tragedy | weird |
| separate | truly | wholly |
| sergeant | tyranny | yacht |
| sheriff | | |

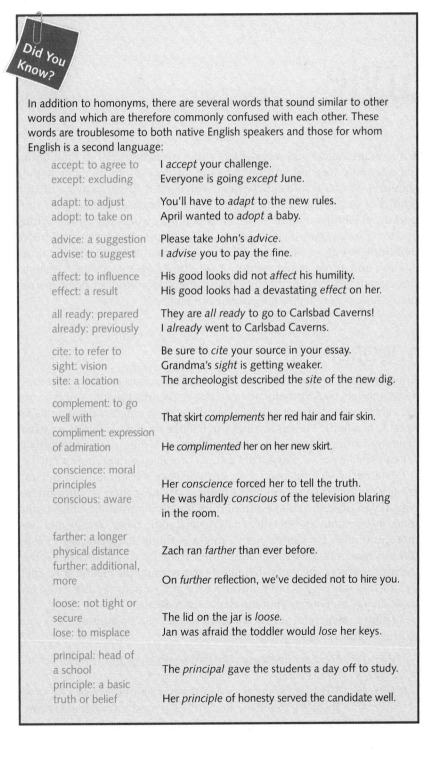

In addition to homonyms, there are several words that sound similar to other words and which are therefore commonly confused with each other. These words are troublesome to both native English speakers and those for whom English is a second language:

| | |
|---|---|
| accept: to agree to | I *accept* your challenge. |
| except: excluding | Everyone is going *except* June. |
| adapt: to adjust | You'll have to *adapt* to the new rules. |
| adopt: to take on | April wanted to *adopt* a baby. |
| advice: a suggestion | Please take John's *advice*. |
| advise: to suggest | I *advise* you to pay the fine. |
| affect: to influence | His good looks did not *affect* his humility. |
| effect: a result | His good looks had a devastating *effect* on her. |
| all ready: prepared | They are *all ready* to go to Carlsbad Caverns! |
| already: previously | I *already* went to Carlsbad Caverns. |
| cite: to refer to | Be sure to *cite* your source in your essay. |
| sight: vision | Grandma's *sight* is getting weaker. |
| site: a location | The archeologist described the *site* of the new dig. |
| complement: to go well with | That skirt *complements* her red hair and fair skin. |
| compliment: expression of admiration | He *complimented* her on her new skirt. |
| conscience: moral principles | Her *conscience* forced her to tell the truth. |
| conscious: aware | He was hardly *conscious* of the television blaring in the room. |
| farther: a longer physical distance | Zach ran *farther* than ever before. |
| further: additional, more | On *further* reflection, we've decided not to hire you. |
| loose: not tight or secure | The lid on the jar is *loose*. |
| lose: to misplace | Jan was afraid the toddler would *lose* her keys. |
| principal: head of a school | The *principal* gave the students a day off to study. |
| principle: a basic truth or belief | Her *principle* of honesty served the candidate well. |

# 4 Style

While grammatical and mechanical correctness is crucial in final drafts, there is more to good writing than the absence of errors. Your writing should show clarity and conciseness, with careful attention to the diction (choice of words) that will most effectively address your audience. It is important to eliminate unnecessary or repetitious words from your writing and to replace vague or abstract language with precise words. In addition, building a strong vocabulary will help you to communicate well in the academic and professional worlds. Note the *"Did You Know?"* sections throughout this chapter that give more information to all students, particularly those whose native language is not English.

## 1. WORDINESS

Good speakers and writers have one thing in common—they communicate concisely with virtually no unnecessary words. Haven't you felt your eyes glaze over when reading legal wording, governmental documents, or weighty academic tomes? Haven't you felt like dropping off to sleep when listening to the lecture of a wordy professor? Using too many words is called verbosity or verbiage. That sounds a lot like garbage, doesn't it?

Students trying to "pad" a paper to achieve a minimum word count are not fooling anyone and are certainly not doing their readers any favors. If you need to achieve a minimum length for a writing project, find more information and details, analyze your topic more clearly, and give more examples for clarity. Some students think that throwing in long phrases makes their writing sound impressive; however, the truth is that the more you cut the verbosity out of your writing, the clearer it is. Such writing not only better communicates what you want to say, but it also has more energy and brings your ideas into sharp focus.

Learn to search for words and phrases that can be omitted from your writing without changing the meaning:

Wordy: Most soldiers <u>generally</u> find <u>some kind of</u> an apartment to rent off-base.

Better: Most soldiers find an apartment to rent off-base.

Wordy: <u>There are</u> too many students <u>who</u> need second hand books.

Better: Too many students need second hand books.

Wordy:   <u>In today's modern society, a myriad of</u> parents are follow-
             ing someone else's rules of parenting rather than <u>learning</u>
             <u>to</u> rely <u>more</u> on their own sound instincts <u>and good sense.</u>

Better:   Many parents are following someone else's rules of parent-
             ing rather than relying on their own sound instincts.

Try reading the above sentences out loud. Notice how the meaning is quickly understood in the revised sentences, whereas in the wordy sentences the meaning gets lost in the verbiage. Asking your readers to slog through the mud of wordy writing is asking too much.

- ▪ *Eliminate repetition.* Avoid the following repetitious phrases:

| Repetitious | Replace with |
|---|---|
| past history | past *or* history |
| at this point in time | now, currently |
| consensus of opinion | consensus |
| end result | result |
| yellow color | yellow |
| in my opinion | (omit) |
| continue to remain | remain |
| connect together | connect |
| true fact | fact |
| 2 p.m. in the afternoon | 2 p.m. |
| truly believe | believe |
| cooperate with each other | cooperate |
| in today's modern society | today *or* omit |
| old adage | adage |

- ▪ *Eliminate unnecessary wordiness.* Avoid the following phrases:

due to the fact that
I think that
obviously
as you know
like I said
in my opinion
in this day and age
I have found that
in order to
to tell the truth

- ▪ *Combine short sentences.* Two or more short sentences that have the same subject or structure can be combined to eliminate many words. At the same time, combining short or choppy sentences can result in a more interesting sentence.

Wordy:   Our favorite tunes cause us to start moving to the beat. They
             help us to remember good times. They also lift our spirits.

Better:   Our favorite tunes help us move to the beat, remember
             good times, and lift our spirits.

## 2. COLLOQUIAL LANGUAGE AND SLANG

If communicating with an audience effectively calls for the use of collo-quial language or slang, by all means, use it! When writing expressively to your peers in an informal situation, colloquial (also known as conversa-tional) language and slang would probably make your writing vivid and authentic. Such language might include words and phrases such as *cool, neat, dude, chick,* and so on. Some slang words and phrases last for gener-ations while others pass out of the language quickly.

However, in formal writing situations, there is a danger in using collo-quial or slang expressions. Remember, we write to communicate with a particular audience. Whenever communication ceases to be effective, try a different strategy. In formal writing situations, especially in college or on the job, your audience is often not your peer group but is someone from a different generation who has expectations of your writing that colloqui-alisms and slang do not address. For most academic or professional writ-ing, standard English is your best choice.

## 3. JARGON AND PRETENTIOUS LANGUAGE

*Jargon* is the vocabulary common to a particular field, profession, or or-ganization. If your audience consists primarily of members of such a par-ticular group, it is fine to use the jargon, or technical language, of that group. The following example is from a text on learning MySQL by Ben Forta, whose audience consists of those familiar with database managing systems:

> As seen in Chapter 8, LIKE matches an entire column. If the text to be matched existed in the middle of a column value, LIKE would not find it and the row would not be returned (unless wildcard charac-ters were used). RECEXP, on the other hand, looks for matches within column values, and so if the text to be matched existed in the middle of a column value, RECEXP would find it and the row would be returned. (70)

> —Ben Forta. *MySQL Crash Course*. Indianapolis: SAMS Publishing, 2006.

This excerpt uses the technical jargon of this database managing system, and the intended audience would not find it difficult to understand.

However, the definition of jargon also encompasses the use of **pretentious language**, such as using multisyllabic or obscure words when simpler words would be clearer and more effective. Students might use pre-tentious language to impress an audience, but in writing, the bottom line is to communicate effectively, and pretentious language does not do that.

Imagine deciding to lend a friend a personal item:

"Okay, Judy, you can use my MP3 player tonight at the concert. I just want you to be careful with it because it cost me almost everything I earned at Pizza Hut last month, and I'm afraid to lose it."

Such a sentence is clear and direct. Judy gets the picture. You wouldn't say something like the following:

"Upon due consideration, Judith, I have made a decision that you will find fortuitous: you may, indeed, borrow my digital electronic device, which, as you undoubtedly recollect, I have in my possession due to such an overwhelming desire to own this previously referenced device that I was induced to purchase it with the recompense that I received for my month-long, albeit part-time labors at the Pizza Hut eating establishment. I pray that you will take great care of this personal artifact, for it is with some trepidation that I let it out of my sight."

The above paragraph is pretentious and sounds absurd. It is usually best to opt for clarity and simplicity when writing to a general audience.

# 4. DENOTATION, CONNOTATION

A word can carry a cultural, or emotional, weight along with its denotative meaning (**denotation** means dictionary definition). This cultural weight is called **connotation**. Words can have a positive, negative, or neutral connotation. For example, think of words that mean having little body fat: *scrawny, skinny, thin, slender.* Most women would rather be called *slender* than *skinny.* Why? Although both words mean essentially the same thing, *skinny* implies angular unattractiveness, whereas *slender* implies supple grace. However, most men would probably rather be called *thin* than *slender* since *slender* connotes a feminine quality rather than any masculine characteristic.

negative:  scrawny, skinny
neutral:  thin
positive:  slender

No one understands the connotative power of words better than the advertising industry. Analyze advertisements (whether print or electronic) that really appeal to you. You can be sure that the creators of the ad paid careful attention to the power of connotation.

For sale:  Run-down shack needs a lot of money to bring into shape. Cheap!

For sale:  Much lived-in home needs some TLC to make it a dream cottage. Be sure to grab this bargain while it lasts!

Both of the above advertisements convey the same information. Which ad would you answer?

You can choose words with a negative cultural weight when you wish to reinforce a negative impression of someone or something. On the other hand, words that have a positive connotation can help you create positive images.

# 5. SEXIST LANGUAGE

Have you ever heard the childhood rhyme "Sticks and stones may break my bones but words can never hurt me?" Not true, is it? Words can hurt far longer than any physical pain. The use of racist language is no longer tolerated in any public arena. Racist terms at the very least promote inaccurate, stereotypical thinking. In a similar fashion, language that promotes gender stereotypes lacks precision and can lead to sloppy analysis. For that reason, such language is no longer acceptable to professional or business audiences.

Historically, the masculine pronoun (*he, his, him*) and the word *man* could be used to refer to both men and women.

> A student should make certain to review his notes after each class.
> All men are equal in the sight of God.
> Mankind must protect the planet from ecological disaster.

However, linguists and psychologists have studied the subtle but damaging effects such biased language has on both genders, and the standard for English usage now embraces more inclusive language.

> Revised: Students should make certain to review their notes after each class. **or** A student should make certain to review his or her notes after each class.
> Revised: All people are equal in the sight of God.
> Revised: Humankind must protect the planet from ecological disaster.

In addition to making your language choices more inclusive, try to avoid making assumptions in your writing that are based on stereotypes. Don't assume all doctors and lawyers are men, or that all secretaries and nurses are female. Replace gender-biased terms with more accurate terms:

| Gender-biased Term | Accurate Term |
| --- | --- |
| chairman | chair *or* chairperson |
| fireman | firefighter |
| forefathers | ancestors |
| mailman | mail carrier, postal worker |

| | |
|---|---|
| policeman | police officer |
| salesman | sales representative |
| stewardess | flight attendant |
| waitress (or waiter) | server |

# 6. VAGUE, ABSTRACT WORDS AND CONCRETE LANGUAGE

You are probably aware that abstract words convey ideas, such as *love, truth, beauty, death, justice.* Concrete words, on the other hand, describe what can be touched, measured, or quantified, like *oak table, red silk scarf, chestnut-spotted basset hound.* Writing is usually made up of a mixture of abstract and concrete language.

■ For example, you might introduce an abstract concept for an informative or persuasive essay and use concrete examples to further your audience's comprehension.

For those students interested in the field of psychology, many different careers are possible, such as criminal psychology, the study of the criminal psyche as portrayed in the popular television drama *Criminal Minds*; clinical psychology, which is a field normally involving the care of people undergoing stressful life situations such as divorce, gender identity, post-traumatic stress syndrome, grief; and psychiatry, which is a field of medicine that treats everything from mild anxiety illnesses to severe mental illnesses with pharmaceuticals as well as clinical therapy.

■ Expressive or creative writing, especially poetry, is made more immediate and gripping with the use of concrete language and sensory images. Even so, a word can be concrete, like shoe, and still be vague and nondescriptive. For instance, what kind of shoe? What color? What material? What size?

All in black, she sashayed across the hall in four-inch patent leather stilettos.
The workman protected his feet with steel-tipped, brown suede boots in size 12 WW.

■ Avoid vague words by replacing them with specific details. For instance, words like *beautiful, lovely, ugly* evoke different images in different people. When you specify what **you** mean by "beautiful," you create the image you want your readers to see.

Vague:   The woman was *beautiful.*
Specific:  The thirty-three-year-old brunette had luminous amber eyes and generous, curvy lips that hinted at a smile.

- Also, nouns like *thing* or *something* can be replaced by more descriptive words:

  Vague:     He was worried about all the *things* he was supposed to do.
  Specific:  He was worried about being able to finish his calculus project, write his persuasive essay on eliminating the electoral college, and study for the minerals test in geology.

- Replace vague modifiers with more precise words:

  Vague:     She was a really *nice* girl with a lot of *nice* clothes.
  Specific:  She was kind and friendly, with a closet full of Chanel suits and Prada handbags.

The more concrete and specific your writing, whether it is academic, expressive, or creative, the more likely you are to capture the attention of your audience and to create memorable prose.

# 7. BUILDING VOCABULARY

To express yourself clearly, you need a good vocabulary. If you often feel you can't find the words you need to express yourself well when speaking or writing for class, consider taking intentional steps to improve your vocabulary. College presents opportunities to learn new words on a daily basis. If you take advantage of these opportunities, you will find yourself building a vocabulary of words that will serve you well in your academic and professional life.

## Ways to Improve Your Vocabulary

- ***Read.*** That may sound simple, but the most effective way to increase your vocabulary is to read often. In addition to your required reading, read magazines and books that interest and relax you. If you are interested in sports, read sports magazines and biographies. If fashion catches your eye, read fashion magazines. Mysteries are fun and relaxing. You can quickly learn new words while reading because, as you read, you can often determine a word's meaning from the **context** of the passage. For instance:

  Dad does not usually get angry, but today he was *livid* at my rudeness.

  From this sentence, you can determine that *livid* is a word that means angry. However, if you're not certain that you understand the meaning of a word from its context, look the word up. You can check the accuracy of your guess against the dictionary meaning. It is especially important to look up a word if it seems key to the meaning of a passage and/or if it is repeated several times.

■ *Ask.* If your instructor, friends, or classmates use a word you don't know, ask what it means and write down the word and definition. Most instructors are happy to define words they use in presentations.

■ *Play word games*. Word games, such as Scrabble or crossword puzzles (start with easy ones!), are a fun way to build vocabulary. You can also find web sites that will send you a new word to learn each day.

■ *Make vocabulary cards* . To intentionally build your vocabulary, you need to go about it in a systematic way. As you read:

> Circle words you don't know.
> Then, look up each word in a print or online dictionary.
> Write the word on one side of a 3- × 5-inch index card.
> On the other side, write the definition and compose a sentence using the word.
> Keep these cards in alphabetical order and practice them several times a week.
> Use each new word you learn in conversation or in writing at least once or twice.
> Add five words a week to your vocabulary.

■ *Learn roots, prefixes, and suffixes* . There are many common word roots, prefixes (letters that come before a word), and suffixes (letters that come after a word). When you learn the meanings, you can often accurately determine the word's meaning.

**English Word Roots**

| Root | Meaning | Examples |
|---|---|---|
| audi | to hear | audience, audio |
| bene | good | benefit, benevolence |
| geo | earth | geography, geometry |
| logo | word or thought | logic, biology, geology |
| manu | hand | manufacture, manual |
| photo | light | photography, telephoto |
| tele | far away | telepathy, telegraph |
| vid, vis | to see | visit, vision, video |

**English Prefixes**

| Prefix | Meaning | Examples |
|---|---|---|
| ante- | before | antebellum, antedate |
| anti- | against | antisocial, antibody |
| bi- | two | bilateral, bipolar |
| de- | from | declaw, desensitize |

| | | |
|---|---|---|
| hyper- | over, more | hypersensitive |
| mal- | bad | malpractice |
| post- | after | postwar, postscript |
| trans- | across | transport, transition |
| uni- | one | uniform, unicycle |

### English Suffixes

| Suffix | Meaning | Examples |
|---|---|---|
| -acy | state or quality | democracy, privacy |
| -dom | state of being | kingdom, freedom |
| -en | cause or become | cheapen, blacken |
| -ish | having the quality of | clownish |
| -less | lack of, without | childless, humorless |
| -ology | the study of | psychology |
| -ment | condition of | impediment, payment |
| -sion, -tion | state of being | confusion, transition |

Did You Know?

## Commonly Confused Words

Note that some of the words below can occasionally be used as different parts of speech.

| | | |
|---|---|---|
| accept, except | *Accept* (verb) means "to receive." The actor accepted the award. | *Except* (preposition) means "other than." They all want to go except Holly. |
| advise, advice | *Advise* (verb) means "to counsel." Mom advised me not to drive that night. | *Advice* (noun) means "counsel." I did not take her advice. |
| affect, effect | *Affect* (verb) means "to have an influence on." The economy has affected my job. | *Effect* (noun) means "result." Spending less money has been one effect of the economy. |
| among, between | *Among* (preposition) means "in the midst of" and is used for three or more people or things: We are all among friends. | *Between* (preposition) means "in or through the position or interval separating": You will find the irrigation pump between the two gates. |

*(continued)*

| | | |
|---|---|---|
| amount, number | *Amount* (noun) means an "indefinite sum": She saved a huge amount of money or her trip. | *Number* (noun) means a "countable sum": He has a number of fine paintings. |
| beside, besides | *Beside* (preposition) means "next to." She wants to stand beside her son. | *Besides* (preposition) means "moreover": Besides, next time is my treat. *or* "in addition to": She doesn't want anyone besides Nancy to come. |
| cite, site | *Cite* (verb) means "to quote": The professor cited Aristotle to define rhetoric. | *Site* (noun) means "location": The website did not provide enough data. |
| farther, further | *Farther* (adverb) is a comparative of "far" and refers to physical distance: Kelly can run farther than Sue. | *Further* (adverb) is also a comparative of "far" but refers to nonphysical advancement: Ben is further along in his studies than we thought. |
| fewer, less | *Fewer* (adjective) means "consisting of a small number" and refers to countable items: Fewer shoppers attended the grand opening of the mall than was hoped. | *Less* (adjective) is a comparative of "little" and is used to refer to mass items that are normally not countable: You need to use less sugar in those cookies. |
| lay, lie | *Lay* (transitive verb) means "to put" or "to place": Can you lay the book on my desk? | *Lie* (intransitive verb) means "to recline" or "to occupy": You may lie down on my bed. The fork lies next to the knife. |
| lose, loose | *Lose* (verb) means "to misplace": Don't lose your keys! | *Loose* (adjective) means "free" or "not fastened": The dogs got loose because the gate was loose. |

# 8. CLICHÉS

Clichés are expressions that have become worn with use, like old clothes that have been washed so much they have faded. No doubt the first time a cliché was used it was fresh and original, so much so that everyone started using it. When language becomes clichéd, it's time to find a fresh way to say it. Some common clichés are listed below:

better late than never

blind as a bat

busy as a bee

dead as a doornail

faster than a speeding bullet

fresh as a daisy

gentle as a lamb

last but not least

needle in a haystack

right as rain

sober as a judge

tough as shoe leather

Notice how many of these clichés are metaphors (or similes)—they compare one thing to something unlike it, for example: blind as a bat, busy as a bee, sober as a judge, tough as shoe leather, etc. At one time these comparisons were unique, but through overuse they have become hackneyed. Try not to use clichés in your writing because they will mark you as an unimaginative writer.

On the other hand, a good way to make your writing memorable is to create fresh metaphors instead of using clichés.

# 9. IDIOMS AND IDIOMATIC EXPRESSIONS

Idiomatic constructions are words or expressions that do not always conform to the rules of the language. For instance, to say that something is a "rule of thumb" in English, meaning that something is a rough measurement or standard, would make little sense to someone trying to directly translate the expression. What does a thumb have to do with measurement? Whose thumb? Many native English speakers do not know where the saying comes from although most would know what it means. This idiom is actually derived from an archaic English law, which stated that you couldn't beat your wife with anything wider than your thumb. The law is no longer in effect and is even offensive today, but it made perfect sense centuries ago. Another English expression, "mad as a hatter," means someone who is acting very strangely. This saying dates from more than a hundred years ago, when many people who made hats went insane because of their daily contact with mercury. Thus, in Lewis Carroll's *Alice in Wonderland*, the character of the Mad Hatter would have been easily understood by its nineteenth-century British audience.

In addition to idiomatic expressions, the use of prepositions can also be idiomatic (see Section 1, Elements of English Sentences, on prepositions, page H-18.) For instance, in England one stands "on line," whereas in America one stands "in line." To make matters even more confusing,

English has more prepositions than many other languages, including Spanish, so direct translation of prepositions is often impossible. Spanish also includes prepositional idioms that do not directly translate; for example, a simple and very common preposition such as the Spanish *en* can be translated not only as "in," the most common translation, but also as "to," "by," and "about," among others.

If you are unfamiliar with the correct use of prepositions in a paper you are writing or reading, or with a particular expression, it is best to seek help from a tutor since it takes time to learn the idioms of any language.

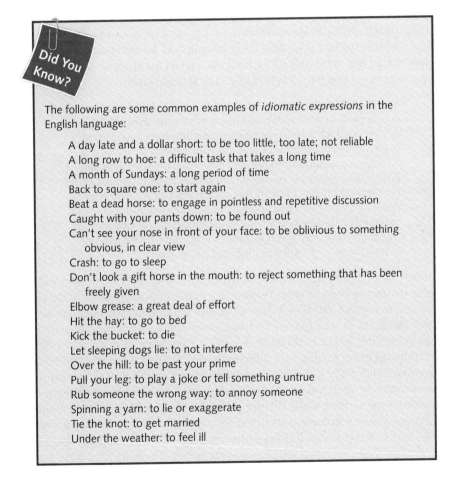

**Did You Know?**

The following are some common examples of *idiomatic expressions* in the English language:

A day late and a dollar short: to be too little, too late; not reliable
A long row to hoe: a difficult task that takes a long time
A month of Sundays: a long period of time
Back to square one: to start again
Beat a dead horse: to engage in pointless and repetitive discussion
Caught with your pants down: to be found out
Can't see your nose in front of your face: to be oblivious to something obvious, in clear view
Crash: to go to sleep
Don't look a gift horse in the mouth: to reject something that has been freely given
Elbow grease: a great deal of effort
Hit the hay: to go to bed
Kick the bucket: to die
Let sleeping dogs lie: to not interfere
Over the hill: to be past your prime
Pull your leg: to play a joke or tell something untrue
Rub someone the wrong way: to annoy someone
Spinning a yarn: to lie or exaggerate
Tie the knot: to get married
Under the weather: to feel ill

# Editing and Proofreading

## 1. THE IMPORTANCE OF EDITING AND PROOFREADING

If content is the racehorse of writing, editing is the farm horse. It's not fun to painstakingly check for mistakes in writing, and it can be even more difficult for the student who didn't pay attention to learning correct grammar, usage, and mechanics in school, as well as for students whose first language is not English. However, consider this scenario:

> You are applying for a dream job. You have excellent work habits and all of the background and knowledge needed to do an excellent job for your employers. However, since you are in a rush, you show up for your interview in cut-off jeans, a sweaty tee shirt, no socks, and flip-flops. Your hair sports grass and twigs from the lawn work you did just before your interview. How far do you think you would get in the interview process from the first impression you just gave your potential employer? Granted, appearance has little to do with how well you could do the job, but by demonstrating this lack of care for your appearance, the interviewer is going to make unfavorable assumptions about you. You will very likely not get the job.

In like manner, turning in a piece of writing that contains many errors tells your instructor, boss, or other readers that you don't care enough to check for and to correct mistakes. While ideas and content are the most important elements in any piece of writing, very few readers can get past a sloppy editing job to evaluate those ideas. Also, keep in mind that poor editing can make writing very difficult to read. It takes more effort to read poorly edited writing than to read well-written material. If you want to communicate effectively with your readership, you need to take the time to edit your writing well. On the other hand, don't begin the editing process before you have completed revising your writing so that it says what you want it to say. Editing is the last stage of the writing process, so spending time and effort editing an essay before it is in its final form is a waste of that time and effort.

## Samples of Poor Editing by Students

"\Discrimination is a serous offense, specially for women. Women are discriminated all the time, in jobs, in manageing, in schools, and in the home. Discrimination tells little girls they are not good enuf. They learn this in the home from there fathers and there mothers. They have to clean, there brothers don't. They have to cook, there brothers don't. They have to iron, there brothers don't. Then their told to be secretaries instead of doctors.

Scientist may no science, but scientist don't always now what is right and what is wrong. They want to learn all their is to know about the world, but many scientist don't consider how an invention could due more harm than good. Look at the atom bomb! But know we have to worry about stems cells and how that can cause unneccessary abortions just for science. In adition, when we make clones, will those clones become slaves and not have humane rights?

If you were to evaluate the above essay introductions, what kind of first impression do the errors give you about the quality of writing? Even though some of the ideas expressed are interesting, the first impression of these introductions is that the writing is substandard. Chances are, whatever your error patterns tend to be, you don't want to turn in a poorly edited piece of writing, either to your instructor or to your boss. You want to make a positive first impression that is carried through to the final sentence. Once you have completed the final revision of an essay's content and organization, proofread the essay carefully for mistakes before submitting it to the reader. Often, writers overlook errors in their own texts because they know what they meant to say, so they are blind to their mistakes when they read their own papers. To prevent this oversight of errors, you should proofread the text more than once, using one or more of the following techniques.

# 2. TIPS FOR PROOFREADING AND EDITING

1.  *Time Away:* If you try to proofread a text immediately after completing it, you will have difficulty noticing errors because the paper is so fresh in your mind. If you postpone proofreading it for a few hours or, better yet, a full day, you will discover that you are able to spot errors more easily.

2. *From Last to First:* One effective method for proofreading a text is starting with the last sentence and reading the text from the last sentence to the first. When you read a text in this reverse order, you are taking the sentences out of their natural order. By taking the sentences out of context in this manner, you will discover that errors become more apparent than when you read the sentences in natural order (from first sentence to last).

3. *Line by Line:* Checking each line for errors before moving to the next is also an effective technique for proofreading a text. You may proofread line-by-line by placing a ruler or a sheet of paper under the line that you are reading. When you are sure the line is free of errors, then move the ruler or sheet of paper to expose the next line for careful reading. This method is effective because it helps focus your attention.

4. *Read for Error Patterns:* Know the types of errors you have a tendency to make, and then proofread looking for those error patterns. Once you know your error patterns, you will be able to proofread for them. For example, if you know that you tend to write sentence fragments, read your essay through once looking specifically for sentence fragments. Then, if you know that comma splices are another error you often make, proofread your writing a second time for comma splices.

5. *Read Aloud:* Reading your text aloud or having someone else read your piece out loud to you is a good way to check for errors because often writers *hear* errors that they simply overlook when they read silently. Also, you can hear language that sounds awkward or stilted. When you read your own text, make sure that you read what you have actually written. Avoid the tendency to read what you meant to write rather than what appears on the page. One benefit of having someone else read your piece out loud to you is that the other person will tend to read what is actually written, errors and all.

6. *Use a Spell-checker:* Most word-processing programs have good spell-checker programs built in. Whenever your spell-checker program indicates a possible error, focus on the word and determine if you used the correct word and spelling. Unfortunately, most spell-checker programs cannot catch a type of spelling error called a homonym, which is a word that sounds like another word but that has a different spelling and meaning. The most common homonym errors in English involve confusing the following: *it's/its; their/they're/there; your/you're; bear/bare; here/hear; except/accept.*

You have invested a lot of time and energy writing, so you want to make sure that your piece communicates what you intended. You do not want errors to prevent the reader from fully understanding and appreciating your work. A few minutes spent carefully proofreading your text will help you avoid errors that detract from the value of your ideas and the quality of your writing.

# 3. FOR WRITERS WHO NEED EXTRA HELP WITH GRAMMAR AND USAGE

All of the above editing and proofreading strategies work well for all students, including those whose first language in not English; however, finding grammatical, usage, and punctuation errors is more difficult for nonnative English speakers. Some native speakers also have significant problems in recognizing and correcting these types of errors. The following strategies are useful if you have significant problems with English grammar, usage, and punctuation.

1. *Tutoring:* For each paper you are working on, schedule at least one tutoring session specifically for grammar, usage, and punctuation editing. Make certain that you schedule this session a few days before the final draft is due so that you have time to correct mistakes and to possibly schedule a second session, if necessary. Having a tutor fluent in English and well-versed in error patterns will help you to find errors and to correct them in a systematic way. In addition, getting help from a tutor can help you to correct idiomatic errors (that is, grammar and usage errors that are not governed by rules).

2. *Following Rules:* Throughout this Handbook are special notes ("Did You Know?") for any writer who needs or wants more information about the rules of grammar and punctuation. The Handbook Table of Contents lists these special sections. Even for students who don't have significant problems with grammar, usage, and punctuation, this information can serve as important reviews.

3. *Reading:* The more reading in any language you do, the better you will become at writing. Reading helps you to become familiar with the linguistic patterns and structures of a language and to learn its idioms and intricacies. Try to spend at least 30 minutes a day reading something you really enjoy. If you're interested in cars, read a magazine on cars and engines. If fashion is your area, there are many fashion magazines to choose from. Sports, music, art, mysteries, romance—there are books, journals, magazines, and websites for every type of interest, hobby, and passion.

## 4. EDITING SYMBOLS

When you are editing someone else's piece of writing, or when your instructor is marking your draft, it helps to know the universal symbols for errors, as listed below. Become familiar with these. Note that the page number in the Handbook referring to a fix for a particular error is listed next to the symbol.

| | |
|---|---|
| adj | adjective error (page H-8) |
| adv | adverb error (page H-9) |
| awk | awkward wording (page H-54) |
| cap | capital letter needed (page H-41) |
| case | shift in pronoun case (page H-6) |
| cs | comma splice (page H-23) |
| dm | dangling modifier (page H-26) |
| frag | sentence fragment (page H-22) |
| hom | homonym spelling error (page H-50) |
| lc | use lowercase (page H-41) |
| mm | misplaced modifier (page H-26) |
| pass | avoid passive voice (page H-26) |
| prep | preposition error (page H-18) |
| pr agr | pronoun agreement error (page H-31) |
| ref | error in pronoun reference (page H-31) |
| rep | repetitious (page H-55) |
| r-o | run-on sentence (page H-23) |
| -s | s needed at the end of the word (page H-27) |
| sp | spelling error (page H-60) |
| s-v | error in subject-verb agreement (page H-27) |
| trans | transition needed (page H-4) |
| v or vb | verb error (page H-10) |
| vt | verb tense error (page H-8) |
| w | too wordy (page H-54) |
| ? | meaning unclear (page H-59) |
| X | error marked or crossed out |

## 5. PROOFREADING MARKS

| | |
|---|---|
| insert comma | ⋀ |
| insert period | ⊙ |
| insert letter or word | ⋀ |
| insert quotation marks | ⋁ |
| omit space | ( ) |
| begin new paragraph | ¶ |

do not begin new paragraph
use lowercase letter
capitalize
omit
transpose letters (or words)

# 6. PROOFREADING CHECKLIST

As you proofread your paper, you may use the checklist below for errors. Sentence errors (fragments, run-ons, incoherence) are the most serious errors. You may need tutoring help to find and correct your errors; please keep in mind that if your surface errors are many, you may need to attend more than one tutoring session, so schedule your time accordingly.

**Sentence errors**
Fragments
Run-on sentences
Unclear sentences

**Verb errors**
Agreement
Verb tense
Past tense

**Word choice**
Correct word
Repetitive
Tone

**Pronouns**
Pronoun agreement
Pronoun reference
Unnecessary second person ("you")

**Punctuation**
Commas
Semicolons
Colons
Quotation marks
End punctuation (. ! ?)
Dashes

**Capitalization**

**Numbers**

**Italics/Underlines**

**Documentation**
In-text
Bibliography

**Spelling**
Homonyms

# Credits

## Text Credits

## Photo Credits

# Index

# How *The World of Writing* will help you achieve the Learning Outcomes Endorsed by the Council of Writing Program Administrators

| WPA Outcomes for First-Year Composition | Where *The World of Writing* addresses these outcomes |
|---|---|
| **Rhetorical Knowledge**<br>By the end of first year composition, students should<br><br>■ Focus on a purpose<br>■ Respond to the needs of different audiences<br>■ Respond appropriately to different kinds of rhetorical situations<br>■ Use conventions of format and structure appropriate to the rhetorical situation<br>■ Adopt appropriate voice, tone, and level of formality<br>■ Understand how genres shape reading and writing<br>■ Write in several genres | Part I, "Expanding Literacies," helps you write for different audiences and purposes. You learn to analyze your writing situation and develop strategies for selecting an appropriate format and overcoming obstacles. The focus is on writing in diverse linguistic and cultural settings: writing in the world.<br><br>Part II, "Expanding Influence," helps you to write in different genres, such as an academic essay, a grant proposal, and a brochure. |
| **Critical Thinking, Reading, and Writing**<br>By the end of first year composition, students should<br><br>■ Use writing and reading for inquiry, learning, thinking, and communicating<br>■ Understand a writing assignment as a series of tasks, including finding, evaluating, analyzing, and synthesizing appropriate primary and secondary sources<br>■ Integrate their own ideas with those of others<br>■ Understand the relationships among language, knowledge, and power | Part I, "Expanding Literacies," includes a chapter on how to read challenging academic texts.<br><br>Part II, "Expanding Influence," provides you with writing assignments that allow you to explore, observe, explain, investigate, argue, solve problems, and advocate for change. You'll also read a variety of texts on topics related to writing in the world.<br><br>Part IV, "Expanding Research," helps you use research to develop and support your points. |
| **Processes**<br>By the end of first year composition, students should<br><br>■ Be aware that it usually takes multiple drafts to create and complete a successful text<br>■ Develop flexible strategies for generating, revising, editing, and proofreading<br>■ Understand writing as an open process that permits writers to use later invention and rethinking to revise their work<br>■ Understand the collaborative and social aspects of writing processes<br>■ Learn to critique their own and others' works<br>■ Learn to balance the advantages of relying on others with the responsibility of doing their part<br>■ Use a variety of technologies to address a range of audiences | Part I, "Expanding Literacies," helps you develop a writing process that can be applied to different types of writing.<br><br>Part II, "Expanding Influence," shows you how to work with others to improve everyone's writing. You'll use different writing technologies to make your writing public.<br><br>Part III, "Expanding Writing Strategies," helps you to apply what you know about writing processes to composing documents used in the university and the workplace. |